THE NEW HANDBOOK OF
METHODS IN NONVERBAL
BEHAVIOR RESEARCH

Series in Affective Science

Series Editors
Richard J. Davidson
Paul Ekman
Klaus R. Scherer

THE NEW HANDBOOK OF METHODS IN NONVERBAL BEHAVIOR RESEARCH

Edited by

JINNI A. HARRIGAN
Department of Psychology, California State University, Fullerton, CA, USA

ROBERT ROSENTHAL
Department of Psychology, University of California, Riverside, CA, USA

KLAUS R. SCHERER
Department of Psychology, University of Geneva, Switzerland

OXFORD
UNIVERSITY PRESS

OXFORD

UNIVERSITY PRESS

Great Clarendon Street, Oxford OX2 6DP

Oxford University Press is a department of the University of Oxford.

It furthers the University's objective of excellence in research, scholarship,
and education by publishing worldwide in

Oxford New York

Auckland Cape Town Dar es Salaam Hong Kong Karachi
Kuala Lumpur Madrid Melbourne Mexico City Nairobi
New Delhi Shanghai Taipei Toronto

With offices in

Argentina Austria Brazil Chile Czech Republic France Greece
Guatemala Hungary Italy Japan Poland Portugal Singapore
South Korea Switzerland Thailand Turkey Ukraine Vietnam

Oxford is a registered trade mark of Oxford University Press
in the UK and in certain other countries

Published in the United States
by Oxford University Press Inc., New York

© Oxford University Press, 2005

British Library Cataloguing in Publication Data

Data available

Library of Congress Cataloguing in Publication Data

The new handbook of methods in nonverbal behavior research / edited
by Jinni A. Harrigan, Robert Rosenthal, Klaus R. Scherer.
p.; cm. – (Series in affective science)
Includes bibliographical references and index.
ISBN-13: 978-0-19-852961-3 (hardback : alk. paper)
ISBN-10: 0-19-852961-9 (hardback : alk. paper)
1. Body language–Research–Methodology. I. Harrigan, Jinni A.
II. Rosenthal, Robert, 1933- . III. Scherer, Klaus R. IV. Series.
[DNLM: 1. Nonverbal Communication–psychology. 2. Behavior
–physiology. 3. Research Design. BF 637.N66 N532 2005]
BF637.N66N49 2005
152.3'84–dc22

2005019362

Typeset by SPI Publisher Services, Pondicherry, India
Printed in Great Britain
on acid-free paper by
Biddles Ltd., King's Lynn

ISBN 0–19–852961–9 (Hbk.: alk.paper)   978–0–19–852961–3 (Hbk.)

10 9 8 7 6 5 4 3 2 1

CONTENTS

Supplementary materials

LIST OF CONTRIBUTORS

Elisha Babad School of Education, Hebrew University of Jerusalem, Jerusalem, ISRAEL

Frank J. Bernieri Department of Psychology, Oregon State University, 2550 SW Jefferson Way, Corvallis, OR 97331–5303, USA

Dana R. Carney Department of Psychology, Harvard University, 33 Kirkland Street, Cambridge, MA 02138, USA

Jeffrey F. Cohn Department of Psychology, University of Pittsburgh, 4327 Sennott Square, Pittsburgh, PA 15260, USA

Caroline Dillon Department of Psychiatry and Behavioral Sciences, Stanford University School of Medicine, 300 Pasteur Drive, Stanford, CA 94305, USA

Paul Ekman Department of Psychiatry, University of California, San Francisco, USA (retired)

Mark G. Frank Department of Communication, School of Informatics, The University of Buffalo (The State University of New York), Buffalo, NY14260, USA

Janine Giese–Davis Department of Psychiatry and Behavioral Sciences, Stanford University School of Medicine, 300 Pasteur Drive, Stanford, CA 94305, USA

John M. Gottman Department of Psychology, University of Washington, Box 351525, Seattle, WA 98195–1525, USA

Judith A. Hall Department of Psychology, Northeastern University, Boston, MA 02115, USA

Jinni A. Harrigan Department of Psychology, California State University, Fullerton, PO Box 6846, Fullerton, CA 92834–6846, USA

Patrik N. Juslin Department of Psychology, Uppsala University, Box 1225, SE – 751 42 Uppsala, SWEDEN

Ann Kring Department of Psychology, University of California, 3210 Tolman Hall #1650, Berkeley, CA 94720–1650, USA

Kelly O'Brien Relationship Research Institute, 4000 NE 41st Street, Building G, Seattle, WA 98195–1525, USA

Karen Altree Piemme Department of Psychiatry and Behavioral Sciences, Stanford University School of Medicine, 300 Pasteur Drive, Stanford, CA 94305, USA

Robert Rosenthal Department of Psychology, University of California, Olmsted Hall 1108, Riverside, CA 92521, USA

Klaus R. Scherer Department of Psychology, University of Geneva, 40 Boulevard du Pont d'Arve, CH – 1205 Geneva, SWITZERLAND

Alyson Shapiro Family & Child Nursing, University of Washington, Seattle, WA 98195–1525, USA

Barbara K. Stuart Department of Psychology, University of California, 3210 Tolman Hall #1650, Berkeley, CA 94720–1650, USA

Suzanne Twirbutt Department of Psychiatry and Behavioral Sciences, Stanford University School of Medicine, 300 Pasteur Drive, Stanford, CA 94305, USA

Dan K. Yoshimoto Relationship Research Institute, 4000 NE 41st Street, Building G, Seattle, WA 98195–1525, USA

FOREWORD

For many years the Handbook of Methods in Nonverbal Behavior Research (Scherer & Ekman, 1982) has served researchers looking for methods to study nonverbal behavior and the expression of affect. This new handbook, The New Handbook of Methods in Nonverbal Behavior Research (Harrigan, Rosenthal, & Scherer, 2005), is an updated volume with new material on coding and methodological issues for a variety of areas in nonverbal behavior: facial actions, vocal behavior, and body movement. Issues relevant to judgment studies, methodology, reliability, analyses, etc. have also been updated.

The topics in this volume are broad and include specific information about methodology and coding strategies in education, psychotherapy, deception, nonverbal sensitivity, and marital and group behavior. There is also a chapter detailing specific information on the technical aspects of recording the voice and face, and specifically in relation to deception studies. The material in this volume will be beneficial for both new researchers and those already working in the fields of nonverbal behavior, affect expression, and related topics. One of the outcomes of this volume will be to help in further refining research methods and coding strategies that permit comparison of results from various laboratories where research on nonverbal behavior is being conducted. This will advance research in the field and help to coordinate results so that a more comprehensive understanding of affect expression can be developed.

Acknowledgements

As there are far too many individuals that have facilitated the editing of the volume to be mentioned personally, the editors thank their collaborators and students whose efforts contributed to the development of this volume. They also express their gratitude to their families and friends for their kind support and interest.

CHAPTER 1

INTRODUCTION

JINNI A. HARRIGAN, ROBERT ROSENTHAL, AND
KLAUS R. SCHERER

The renaissance of theorizing and research on emotion in the last 30 years (after decades of neglect during the hegemony first of learning theory and then the excesses of the cognitive revolution) has been primarily due to the influential work on facial expression pioneered by Tomkins (1962, 1963) and vigorously pursued by Ekman (Ekman & Friesen 1975, 1978), Izard (1971, 1991), and their collaborators (Ekman *et al.* 1972, 1982, 1987; Ekman & Rosenberg 1997; Izard *et al.* 1980). Photos with the prototypical expressions of the basic emotions adorn most textbooks of psychology and remind students and researchers alike of the powerful role of nonverbal behavior during emotional episodes. Even though much of present-day emotion research is carried out with paper-and-pencil assessment of verbal reports of emotional experiences, the affective sciences are probably one of the areas that assign a privileged role to the study of the *non*verbal concomitants of emotional experiences. The chapters in this Handbook are intended to provide an overview of the methodology that is available for this purpose, along with examples from the use of these methods in current research on affective phenomena, focusing on particular channels or modalities of nonverbal expression or on important domains of application. In this introductory chapter, we discuss some of the basic issues inherent in any research activity that aims at the analysis of naturally occurring or experimentally induced behavior on the one hand or the inferences observers draw from such behavior on the other.

It has been 20 years since an earlier volume on research methods in nonverbal behavior research was published—*Handbook of methods in nonverbal behavior research* (Scherer & Ekman 1982). Since then, there have been almost 50 articles and books published each year featuring nonverbal behavior as a subject in its own right (i.e. facial expression, gaze, vocal quality, paralinguistic features, posture and body position, head nods, hand gestures, etc.) or as a measure of various attitudes, personality styles, diagnoses, or abilities. Online Psych Info indicates that 489 articles and books appeared between 1960 and 1981 in which nonverbal behavior was either the subject of study or used as a measure. The number has swelled to over 3000 articles and books since 1982, representing a six-fold increase. Examples include a broad range of research using nonverbal behavior (e.g. in relation to American Sign Language, as a measure of prejudice, as an aid in eyewitness memory, as an indicator of power and status, as reflecting communication difficulties for those suffering anorexia nervosa, as part of courtship signals, as reflecting emotional arousal in alexithymia, in judging personalities of strangers, and in detecting deception). There is hardly an area in the study of human behavior where nonverbal behavior is not involved.

There is a remarkable variety and number of research questions in many areas of psychology, anthropology, sociology, linguistics, psychotherapy, medicine, education, and the law where some form of nonverbal behavior has been used as an index. Consider, for example, studies of infant social development; expressions of attraction, persuasion, prejudice, compassion, compliance, affiliation, etc.; cultural differences in expressive behavior; clinical assessment and intervention; personality and attitude (e.g. extraversion, dominance, independence, defensiveness); legal testimony and jury selection; person perception; language acquisition; job interviews and evaluations; social cognition and information processing. In many of these areas, the assessment of nonverbal behavior serves as a measure of underlying affect. In consequence, the precise measurement of nonverbal behavior and the observer inferences based on it, are of central importance to the affective sciences.

The reasons for the relevance of this Handbook are several. One reason, indicated above, is that there has been a burgeoning of nonverbal behavior research since the earlier methodology volume was published. In addition, since nonverbal behavior is so readily used in research on human behavior (i.e. as a measure and as a subject in its own right), it is studied by researchers and theorists who come from the ranks of many diverse disciplines. A volume focused on research methodology specific to the nonverbal behavior area will enhance the efficiency, reliability, and comparability of the data collected within these diverse disciplines, and will help promote communication among disciplines. Data organized in such a fashion will spur the development of theories to better understand nonverbal behavior and its role in the many facets of human life.

The field of nonverbal behavior has graduated through the developmental stages of any new field, with well-formed subfields of behavior within the general domain of nonverbal behavior. These subfields include: facial actions, vocalizations, eye contact, body movement, and the perception of interpersonal space. Coding procedures have been developed, measures of reliability have been advanced, and specific techniques for data analysis have evolved.

For the new researcher coming into this vast field of inquiry, a methods text is invaluable, permitting the researcher to learn the various subsets of behavioral categorization, recording devices and techniques, appropriate reliability measures, and statistical analyses. Using well-established classification systems and methodological procedures allows researchers to concentrate on their specific questions and on the theoretical implications of their work, rather than having to create behavioral categories, coding strategies, reliability procedures, etc. This will lead to greater efficiency and reliability, and will permit comparability of data collected by different research labs and directed by different research questions. In time, such building on the work of pioneers in the field of nonverbal behavior and their followers, will allow for refinement of measurement techniques and analyses and, overall, will advance knowledge and theory in this rapidly growing field of inquiry.

For researchers from the diverse disciplines who study nonverbal behavior, the opportunity to select measures, coding and recording procedures, and analytic techniques, will allow comparison across research questions and theoretical orientations.

Finally, for the experienced nonverbal behavior researcher, this volume will provide updated material and information about the latest techniques available, presented by experts in the various subfields of nonverbal behavior.

This volume on nonverbal behavior methodology will inject a measure of organization in codification of nonverbal behaviors so that more standard and more reliable data are collected, and results from studies of divergent topics can be compared. To mention but a few examples of recommendations made in different chapters of this Handbook that are likely to greatly enhance the quality of the data and augment the comparability and cumulativeness of the results—recording techniques that ensure high quality of the research records for coding or judgment, observational and experimental designs that allow clear inferences from the behavioral data, objective and reliable measurement of standard sets of parameters in different domains, the use of standard measures of rater or judge reliability and validity, and the regular reporting of information such as confusion matrices and effect sizes.

There was no coherent theory to organize the study of nonverbal behavior in 1982, and today, 20 years later, there is still no articulated theory linking all the various categories of nonverbal behavior in a meaningful way. This state of affairs may be partially due to the different conceptual and categorization systems used to define and code nonverbal behavior. In addition, the amorphous nature, complexity, variety, and interactive quality of nonverbal behavior make it a difficult subject to unify. Describing all of a human being's behavior (save the verbal channel) is a daunting task. Complexities abound in the variety, fluidity, patterning, and environmental influence on single or combined nonverbal behaviors. However, a common theoretical foundation for nonverbal behavior has enormous potential for understanding human behavior. Theoretical progress is being made across the subfields of nonverbal behavior. For example, relationships have been found in the experience of emotion among physiology, facial action, and vocal signals. Associations have been revealed among personality characteristics, nonverbal displays, and medical and psychological conditions.

Technology (in the form, for example, of inexpensive, good-quality videography) has helped immensely in recording, preserving, analyzing, and comparing collected data. In addition to educating new researchers on these available technical methods, this volume will bring together research findings and knowledge from a variety of scattered journals and books.

Another value of this volume is the comprehensive overview of the field by leading researchers who provide informative, scholarly, and empirical as well as theoretical foundations for their work.

In the chapters of this book we will discover how the actions and patterns of the human subject in interactions with others can be studied across a diverse empirical framework. These writings will tell us where the field of nonverbal behavior has taken us in the last 20 years, what and how coding methodologies have been refined, and what is new in recording and data analysis. In summary, this volume will provide an up-to-date overview and hands-on information concerning the many methods and techniques that are available to code or rate affective behavior and emotional expression in different modalities.

The volume, apart from this introduction, is organized into three major sections: basic research methods and procedures, domains of application, and supplemental materials. The first section describes the basic research methods and procedures in the main subfields in nonverbal behavior: facial actions, vocalizations, and proxemics/kinesics/gaze. These chapters are devoted to discussions of relevant variables, coding strategies and instruments, methodology and research design considerations, and special analytic techniques. Probably the most widely recognized areas in nonverbal behavior are the face and the voice. Each of these chapters includes the most recent research on methods of studying the face (Chapter 2 by Jeffrey Cohn and Paul Ekman) and the voice (Chapter 3 by Patrik Juslin and Klaus Scherer) as signaling systems and offers critical comparisons of the procedures for distinguishing among facial movements and among vocal parameters, with assessment methods and instruments for each of these important subfields. Proxemics (use and perception of interpersonal space), kinesics (body/head movement), and gaze behavior are explored in Chapter 4 (by Jinni Harrigan). This chapter includes delineation of pertinent categories of head and body movement and position, and information on coding instruments and systems developed to describe the various actions of the body. Methods used for studying proxemics and eye contact are covered in this chapter, with attention to relevant variables for operationalizing gaze behavior and spatial parameters in social settings with respect to territoriality, intimacy, personal space, public behavior, and cultural differences. Chapter 5 (by Robert Rosenthal) describes research designs and methods for investigating the inferences observers draw from different nonverbal behaviors in judgment studies. It includes a systematic discussion of such matters as judge sampling and stimulus presentation, as well as various statistical analysis techniques.

The second section (domains of application) involves research investigations using composites of nonverbal behaviors and shows how these variables can be studied and understood in conjunction with one another. We begin with Chapter 6 in which Judy Hall, Frank Bernieri, and Dana Carney describe research methodology and analysis of data on interpersonal sensitivity with respect to the decoding or judging of others' affect and the encoding (i.e. exhibiting) of nonverbal behavior. In Chapter 7, Elisha Babad presents information regarding measurement issues of nonverbal behavior in the classroom from the perspective of the student and the teacher. Ann Kring and Barbara Stuart (Chapter 8) cover methodological issues with respect to psychopathology including both the therapists' and clients' nonverbal behavior, and important considerations for this special population. In Chapter 9, Mark Frank focuses on an area in the nonverbal behavior literature which has received a good deal of attention—deception. There are many important issues regarding the assessment of nonverbal behaviors which can reveal or conceal deceptive communication. Information on coding systems used in research on marital interaction is presented in Chapter 10 (by Dan Yoshimoto, Alyson Shapiro, Kelly O'Brien, and John Gottman). Their work discusses research design points, coding and reliability issues, and decisions for analyzing the intricate interplay of concomitant behaviors (i.e. facial actions, vocal tone, body movement, etc.). In Chapter 11 (by Janine Giese–Davis, Karen Altree Piemme, Caroline Dillon, and Susan Twirbutt), a detailed strategy is presented for coding and integrating variables composed of various nonverbal, vocal, and verbal behaviors that have been combined at a macrovariable level and representing conceptual domains such as emotion regulation, affect suppression, emotional self-efficacy, emotion restraint and repression.

Finally, the chapter in the supplemental materials section (Chapter 12 by Mark Frank, Patrik Juslin, and Jinni Harrigan) contains advice, including important technical information, which can serve as a guide for the acquisition of hardware and the design of the recording process. This section also contains the comprehensive introductory chapter from the first handbook, *Handbook of methods in nonverbal behavior research* (Scherer & Ekman 1982). This chapter is reproduced here, with extensive annotations and additional references, as many of the issues raised in that chapter remain relevant to the concerns of researchers today.

The reviews of the methodology for the measurement of nonverbal behavior in the affective sciences show that high-quality research in this area is complex, often straddling the disciplinary boundaries, costly, and time-consuming. However, the chapters in this Handbook also highlight the rewards, in particular the powerful insights into emotion processes and their role in social interaction gained through this type of research and the important potential for application in health, education, criminology, and organizational behavior. We hope that this volume can counteract the regrettable tendency in the study of affective phenomena to rely primarily on verbal report of felt affect. Feeling states are certainly a very important component of emotion, integrating many of the underlying component processes (Scherer 2004), but provides only one access to the phenomenon. In addition, given the many problems with verbal report, such as reliance on fallible memory, response, and self-presentation biases (Rosenthal & Rosnow 1969), asking people how they feel is hardly a royal road to understanding emotion or a gold standard for the 'true' state of the person (Scherer & Ceschi 2000).

Of course, nonverbal behavior is also subject to control or regulation in the interest of self-presentation or the manipulation of others. However, there is also 'leakage', in the form of markers for the use of display rules (e.g. pressing the lips together—Ceschi & Scherer 2003) or clues to deception (such as micromomentary facial movements—Ekman 2001; see also Chapter 9). Researchers can use such nonverbal cues to evaluate the total pattern of verbal and nonverbal behavior, much of which might be strategically controlled or strategically manipulated. Researchers focusing exclusively on verbal report, especially when it is obtained with standardized scales administered in an anonymous fashion via questionnaire or computer screen, lack this information and have to take the participant's verbal report at face value.

Just as researchers often place greater reliance on the interpretation of subtle non-verbal cues than on verbal statements, in everyday life, we all tend to scrutinize nonverbal facial, vocal, and gestural delivery as we interpret the verbal message. Thus, the inferences made from nonverbal cues constitute a topic of central importance to researchers in the affective sciences. Research has shown the incredible capacity of human beings to extract essential, and often valid, information from very small 'slices' from the stream of nonverbal behavior (Ambady & Rosenthal 1992). Such inferences are often at the root of our first, and often even more lasting impressions, of other people's personality, affect, competence, or behavioral intentions. Most of the processes described above, both with respect to the production of certain behaviors and of the rapid, automatic inferences, operate at an unconscious level and thus would not even be available for verbal report, even if the person concerned did not try to censor the information given or unwittingly bias the report. Thus, it is through the techniques described in this Handbook that researchers are able to access processes that are of central importance in understanding human affect, especially in sensitive contexts such as interpersonal relations, health, or deception.

References

Ambady, N. & Rosenthal, R. (1992). Thin slices of expressive behavior as predictors of interpersonal consequences—a meta-analysis. *Psychological Bulletin*, **111**, 256–74.

Ceschi, G. & Scherer, K.R. (2003). Children's ability to control the facial expression of laughter and smiling: knowledge and behavior. *Cognition and Emotion*, **17**, 385–411.

Ekman, P. (2001). Telling lies: clues to deceit in the marketplace, politics, and marriage (revised edn). New York: Norton.

Ekman, P. & Friesen, W.V. (1975). *Unmasking the face*. Englewood Cliffs, N.J.: Prentice–Hall.

Ekman, P. & Friesen, W.V. (1978). *Manual for the Facial Action Coding System*. Palo Alto, CA: Consulting Psychologists Press.

Ekman, P. & Rosenberg, E.L. (ed.) (1997). *What the face reveals: basic and applied studies of spontaneous expression using the Facial Action Coding System*. New York: Oxford.

Ekman, P., Friesen, W.V., & Ellsworth, P.C. (1972). *Emotion in the human face: guidelines for research and a review of findings*. New York: Pergamon Press.

Ekman, P., Friesen, W.V., & Ellsworth, P.C. (1982). Methodological decisions. In *Emotion in the human face* (2nd edn) (ed. P. Ekman), pp. 22–38. Cambridge, England: Cambridge University Press.

Ekman, P., Friesen, W.V., O'Sullivan, M., Chan, A., Diacoyanni–Tarlatzis, T., Heider, K., *et al.* (1987). Universals and cultural differences in the judgments of facial expressions of emotion. *Journal of Personality and Social Psychology*, **53**, 712–17.

Izard, C.E. (1971). *The face of emotion*. New York: Appleton–Century–Crofts.

Izard, C.E. (1991). *The psychology of emotions*. New York: Plenum.

Izard, C.E., Huebner, R.R., Risser, D., McGuinnes, G., & Dougherty, L. (1980). The young infant's ability to produce discrete emotion expressions. *Developmental Psychology*, **16**, 132–40.

Rosenthal, R. & Rosnow, R.L. (ed.). (1969). *Artifact in behavioral research*. NY: Academic.

Scherer, K.R. (2004). Feelings integrate the central representation of appraisal-driven response organization in emotion. In A.S.R. Manstead, N.H. Frijda, & A.H. Fischer (Eds.). *Feelings and Emotions: The Amsterdam Symposium* 136–157. Cambridge, Cambridge University Press.

Scherer, K.R. & Ceschi, G. (2000). Studying affective communication in the airport: the case of lost baggage claims. *Personality and Social Psychology Bulletin*, **26**, 327–39.

Scherer, K.R. & Ekman, P. (1982). *Handbook of methods in nonverbal behavior research*. Cambridge: Cambridge University Press.

Tomkins, S.S. (1962). *Affect, imagery, consciousness (Vol. 1)*. New York: Springer.

Tomkins, S.S. (1963). *Affect, imagery, consciousness (Vol. 2)*. New York: Springer.

BASIC RESEARCH
METHODS AND
PROCEDURES

CHAPTER 2

MEASURING FACIAL ACTION

JEFFREY F. COHN AND PAUL EKMAN

Introduction

Of all the nonverbal behaviors—body movements, posture, gaze, proxemics, voice—the face is probably the most commanding and complicated, and perhaps the most confusing. In part, the face is commanding because it is always visible, always providing some information. There is no facial equivalent to the concealment maneuver of putting one's hands in one's pockets. Whereas sounds and the body movements that illustrate speech are intermittent, the face, even in repose, may provide information about some emotion or mood state. Many nonverbal behaviors simply do not occur when a person is alone, or at least do so very rarely. For example, it would be unusual for someone to shrug or gesture hello when totally alone. Yet facial expressions of emotion may be quite intense even when a person is alone. They are occasioned not only by the presence of others. In fact, social situations can dampen facial expression of emotion (Ekman & Friesen 2003).

The face is commanding also because it is the location for the senses of smell, taste, sight, and hearing. It is the site of the intake organs for inputs of air, water, and food necessary to life. It is the output source for speech, and what we hear in part is determined by the lip movements we see with the speech (McGurk & MacDonald 1976). It commands attention because it is the symbol of the self. The faces of those we care about are hung on walls, displayed on desks, carried in wallets.

Multimessage, multisignal system

This commanding focus of attention is quite complex. The face can be considered as a multimessage, multisignal semiotic system (Ekman & Friesen 1978). It conveys not only the message of individual identity, but also messages about gender and race. Certain changes in the face reveal, more or less truthfully, age. There are standards for beautiful and ugly, smart and stupid, strong and weak faces. And apart from stereotypes, there have been claims for accurate information about personality traits, psychopathology, and intelligence from facial behavior (Bruce & Young 1998).

These different messages (identity, gender, beauty, traits, etc.) have, as their source, one of four types of facial signal systems: static, slow, artificial, and rapid. *Static* signs include the size, shape, and relative locations of the features and the contours produced by the underlying bony structure. These static signs are the likely vehicles for transmitting information about identity and beauty. Examples of *slow* sign vehicles would be the accumulation of wrinkles, pouches, and bags, which occur with and convey information about age. *Artificial* signs, such as cosmetics and plastic surgery, attempt to disguise these slow age signs. The *rapid* signs include the actions produced by the muscles (typically called expressions or displays), as well as changes in muscle tonus, blood flow, skin temperature, and coloring.

Most research on the face has focused just upon these rapid signs, in particular, the momentary movements of the face and the muscle tonus changes as sign vehicles for information about emotion and mood. Rapid signs may also be relevant sources for other messages, for correct or incorrect information about traits, attitudes, personality, and so on. Our focus in this chapter is upon methods for measuring momentary facial movement (expressions). We first distinguish between *sign vehicle* based and *judgment* based measurement, and then focus on three approaches to measuring sign vehicles of facial action: human observer based coding systems, facial electromyography, and automated measurement by computer vision (an emerging approach that shows promising concurrent validity with manual coding, increased efficiency, and powerful capabilities for analyzing the timing of facial action).

Sign-based versus judgment-based approaches

Ekman and Friesen (Ekman 1964, 1965; Ekman & Friesen 1969) distinguished two conceptual approaches for studying nonverbal behavior—namely, measuring judgments about one or another message and measuring the sign vehicles that convey the message.[1] Often either approach can be used to answer a question. Take, for example, the question whether facial expressions vary with psychopathology. Suppose a sample was available of facial behavior during interviews with patients who had a diagnosis of schizophrenia or depression, and with a control group who had no psychiatric problems. To utilize the *message judgment* approach, the facial movements in these interviews would be shown to a group of expert clinicians, who would be asked whether each person they viewed was normal, schizophrenic, or depressive. If the judgments were accurate, this would answer the question, showing that facial expressions do convey messages about psychopathology. To utilize the *measurement of sign vehicles* approach, some or all of the facial movements would be classified or counted in some fashion. If the findings showed, for example, that depressives raised the inner corners of their eyebrows more than the other two groups, whereas schizophrenics showed facial movements that very slowly faded off the face, this would also answer the question affirmatively.

---

[1] Over the years Ekman has proposed a number of different phrases to distinguish these two approaches. In previous discussions, the message judgment approach has been labeled the stimulus, communicative, or judgment approach, and the measurement of sign vehicles approach has been labeled the response, indicative, or components approach. It is to be hoped that the present terms, taken from semiotics, allow a more lucid differentiation of these two methods.

Although both approaches can answer the same or related questions, they yield different information. The message judgment approach would show that expert clinicians can tell from viewing a face whether a person is schizophrenic, depressive, or normal. That cannot be learned from the other approach, which does not determine whether observers can accurately judge this message. But by measuring the sign vehicles, it is possible to find out exactly what differs in the faces of the diagnostic groups. Is it the timing or the particular movements, or both, that show whether a person is depressive or schizophrenic? That cannot be learned from the first approach, which never determines exactly what the observers respond to when making their judgments.[2] Let us turn now to some of the other relationships between the outcomes of these two approaches. Consider these cases:

1. **Negative findings with message judgment and positive findings with sign vehicle measurement.** This suggests that people (at least those used in the study) do not know what to look for or cannot see the differences in facial behavior. Careful measurement of the facial sign vehicles might have revealed hitherto unknown differences. Once known, these clues to psychopathology might make it possible for observers to make judgments accurately. Or perhaps the clues are such that people will never be able to make this judgment accurately when viewing the behavior at real time—the differences in facial behavior might be too subtle to be seen without repeated or slowed viewing and precise measurement.

2. **Positive findings with message judgment and negative findings with sign vehicle measurement.** The positive results show that there must be some difference in the facial sign vehicles, for how else would the observers achieve accuracy in their judgment? This outcome shows that something must be faulty in the measurement of the sign vehicles. Either the measurement was not reliable or it was selective rather than comprehensive. The sign vehicles may have omitted movements or related cues, such as blushing, that may have differed between diagnostic groups and there was bad luck in selecting just those sign vehicles that did not differ.

3. **Negative findings with message judgment and negative findings with sign vehicle measurement.** This all-too-frequent outcome may occur because the face simply does not provide information about the topic being studied. Or something may have been faulty in the sampling. For example, there may not have been sufficient care in obtaining high agreement among experts about the diagnosis of the patients. Or perhaps the patients were receiving medications that suppressed some behavioral differences. Also, this outcome does not eliminate the possibility that there were differences in facial movement related to psychopathology that the observers did not know about or could not see (thus the message judgment approach failed), and that were missed by a faulty technique for measuring the facial sign vehicle. Was the

---

[2] The two approaches are complementary. One could use the sign vehicle approach to determine what facial expressions differ among diagnostic groups and the message judgment studies to determine which of those expressions influence message judgments about diagnosis. (Juslin and Scherer, in Chapter 3, discuss use of a modified Brunswikian lense model in this context. See also Hess *et al.* 1989.)

measurement of sign vehicles comprehensive rather than selective? If it was selective, the possibility always remains that movements unrelated to psychopathology were measured.

The difference between these two approaches—message judgment and the measurement of sign vehicle—has sometimes been confusing, because both may involve observers and many of the methodological issues, such as inter-observer agreement, are similar (see Chapter 5). It is what the observers do that matters. In message judgment, they make *inferences* about something underlying the behavior—emotion, mood, traits, attitudes, personality, and the like. For this reason, typically they are referred to as 'judges' or 'raters'. In measuring sign vehicles, the observers *describe* the surface of behavior—they count how many times the face moves, or how long a movement lasts, or whether it was a movement of the frontalis or corrugator muscle. As an example, upon seeing a smiling face, an observer with a judgment-based approach would make judgments such as 'happy', whereas an observer with a sign-based approach would code the face as having an upward, oblique movement of the lip corners.

Observers with a sign-based approach are supposed to function like machines, and often are referred to as 'coders'. In the final section of this chapter, we review the considerable progress that has been made, through research in computer vision, toward actually replacing human coders with machines and the prospects for automatic coding by computer facial image analysis.

Though message- and sign-based approaches can sometimes answer the same questions, they can also answer different questions, for they focus on different phenomena. Message judgment research is not typically focused on the face. The face is but an input, although there may be study of different types of faces, as in the psychopathology example. In message judgment studies, the focus is instead on the person observing the face and/or on the message obtained. Questions have to do with whether a difference is detectable or accurate; there are individual differences among observers, reflecting skill, gender, personality, etc. Messages obtained are best represented as dimensions or categories.

Facial sign vehicles are measured when the focus is upon unearthing something fairly specific about facial behavior itself, not about the perception of the face. It is the only method that can be used to answer such questions as:

1. **To what extent is the facial activity shown by newborns and infants systematic, not random, and which particular actions first show such systematic organization?** To answer this question, facial behavior shown during samples taken at different developmental points or in different situational contexts can be measured. Then the probabilities of particular co-occurrences and sequential patterns of facial actions can be evaluated (Cohn & Tronick 1983; Oster & Ekman 1978).

2. **Which particular facial actions are employed to signal emphasis in conversation?** Facial actions that co-occur with verbal or vocal emphasis must be measured to determine whether there are any actions that consistently accompany any emphasis (Ekman 1980).

3. **Is there a difference in the smile during enjoyment as compared to a discomfort smile?** The particular facial actions evident in smiling movements must be measured

when persons are known, by means other than the face, to be experiencing positive and negative affect (Ekman *et al.* 1980; Frank *et al.* 1993).

4. **Are there differences in heart rate that accompany nose wrinkling and upper lip raising versus opening the eyes and raising the brows?** Facial behavior must be measured to identify the moments when these particular facial configurations occur in order to examine coincident heart rate activity (Levenson *et al.* 1990).

These examples are not intended to convey the full range of issues that can be addressed only by measuring facial sign vehicles. They should, however, serve to illustrate the variety of questions requiring this approach. One might expect the measurement of sign vehicles approach to have been followed often, as it is required for study of many different problems. But there have been only a few such studies compared to the many that have measured the messages judged when viewing the face. It is much easier to perform the latter sort of study. The investigator need not tamper with the face itself, other than by picking some sample to show. Data are obtained quickly: one can measure observers' judgments much more quickly than one can describe reliably the flow and variety of facial movement.

Until recently, an important obstacle to research measuring sign vehicles has been the lack of any accepted, standard, ready-for-use technique for measuring facial movement. Each investigator who has measured facial movement has invented their technique, to a great degree, *de novo*, rarely making use of the work of their predecessors. Some have seemed to be uninformed by the previous literature. Even the more scholarly have found it difficult to build upon the methods previously reported, because descriptions of facial activity are often less clear than they appear upon first reading. A facial action may seem to be described in sufficient detail and exactness until an attempt is made to apply that description to the flow of facial behavior. For instance, descriptions of brow motion that omit specific appearance changes in facial lines and furrows and in the appearance of the upper eyelid omit information that may be needed to discriminate among related but different facial actions.

Three types of method for measuring facial sign vehicles

Three types of method for measuring facial sign vehicles are manual coding, facial electromyography (EMG), and automatic facial image analysis. Manual coding has been used the longest and is the most frequent approach for theoretical and applied research in facial expression. It has been especially informative to the development of automatic facial image analysis by computer vision (Cohn *et al.* 1990). Manual coding is unobtrusive and can be used both for live observation and for analysis of pre-recorded analogue or digital images. Facial EMG requires the use of surface or needle electrodes attached to the face and is typically the method of choice in laboratory studies of psychophysiology. Automatic facial image analysis by computer vision is an emerging methodology. Computer vision has been an active area of research for some 30 years (Duda & Hart 1973). Early work included attempts at automatic recognition of faces (Kanade 1973). Within the past decade, there has been increasing effort in automatic recognition of facial expression. We review techniques for measurement of facial sign vehicles by each of these approaches, as well as some of the initial applications of these techniques to theory and research in facial expression.

Manual coding techniques

The 14 techniques for measuring facial actions reviewed in this chapter cover a span of 78 years, from the 1924 report by Landis to the work of Ekman, Friesen, and Hager in 2002. Five were not presented by the authors as methods that could be used by others, but were reported in the course of describing substantive results. They have been included for various reasons. Landis is included because he was among the first to build a measurement system based on the anatomy of muscle action, and his negative findings were influential for the next 40 years. Frois–Wittmann (1930) and Fulcher (1942) were both innovative for their times, but their methods and findings have been largely forgotten by the current generation of researchers. McGrew's (1972) behavioral checklist has influenced those studying children from an ethological viewpoint. Nystrom (1974) has been included because there is much interest today in measuring facial action in infants. The other nine techniques reviewed represent all of the systems for measuring facial movement that have been proposed, some of which have attracted considerable interest and research activity.

A few reports describing facial actions in detail have been omitted. Discussions of facial behavior that did not report a procedure for measurement—such as Hjorstjo (1970) and Lightoller (1925), both of which provided enlightening discussions of the anatomical basis of facial movement—are not included. Depictions of facial expressions primarily designed to train observers to recognize emotion rather than measure facial movement (Ekman & Friesen 2003) are excluded, even though some investigators have used them to measure facial expression. Izard's Affex (1983), previously called FESM (1979a), has also been excluded because observers are required to judge emotion rather than describe the appearance of facial movement, which would fall under the judgment-based approach. Unlike most message judgment approaches to the measurement of the face, Izard's Affex provides the observers with training about the various clues believed to signal each emotion. There is no way to know, of course, what clues the observers actually rely upon when they make their emotion judgments, because all the investigator obtains is the end point in the observers' inferences. Though the aim of Affex is to provide quick data about emotions, it cannot allow investigation of what indeed are the facial clues to each emotion. Other techniques designed to provide economical measures of emotion—EMFACS (Ekman & Friesen 1982) and MAX (Izard 1983)—are considered in this chapter because they involve describing facial appearance rather than making direct inferences about underlying states. Reports that used but did not add new methodological features to one of the techniques reviewed here are excluded.

The measurement techniques that are reviewed share the features of being unobtrusive; of requiring a permanent visual record (still image or video) that allows slowed or multiple viewing, rather than being applicable to behavior as it occurs; and of relying upon an observer who scores or codes behavior according to a set of predetermined categories or items.

This chapter cannot teach the reader how to measure facial actions. Nor does it fully describe most of the measurement techniques, many of which would require a whole chapter, and some an entire book. Exceptions are the techniques of Birdwhistell (1952), Landis (1924), and Nystrom (1974), each of whom provided a little more detail than what is reported here. Instead, the emphasis of this chapter is upon the criteria to be considered in evaluating any measurement technique, either one of those available or one that the reader might devise. These criteria are:

1. the basis for deriving facial behavior units;
2. comprehensiveness;
3. separation of inference from description;
4. types of image records and persons with which the technique has been or may be used;
5. reliability;
6. validity;
7. individual differences;
8. cost.

The strengths and weaknesses of each technique will be made evident so that the reader is better able to choose which might be best for a particular research problem. Tables 2.1–2.3 and the appendix at the end of the chapter summarize the comparisons and provide examples. The techniques are organized in terms of their basis for deriving units of facial behavior: linguistic, ethological, theoretical, and anatomic.

The basis for deriving units

Each of the 14 human observer based measurement techniques contains a list of facial actions such as a brow raise, nose wrinkle, lip corners down, and so on. Measurement includes noting whether any action (or, with some techniques, combination of actions) is present. Later, we will consider how each technique describes actions and differentiates one action from another, but here we are concerned with the question of how the author decided upon his or her particular list. The lists vary in the number of items from a low of 22 to a high of 77. Some actions appear in all techniques, other actions in only some techniques, and still others in just one technique. Sometimes behavior that is treated as a single action by one technique appears subdivided as two distinct actions by others. For example, raising the eyebrows is treated as one behavioral unit by some techniques, but appears as three separate units—inner brow raise, outer brow raise, and the combination of inner and outer brow raise—in other techniques. Most authors did not explain what they considered when they included or excluded a facial action, what basis they had for subdividing that which another researcher had treated as a single action, or why they found it wise to collapse a distinction drawn by another investigator. In fact, most did not acknowledge the work of their predecessors, but instead acted as if they had invented their system and had no knowledge of differences between it and the systems of their earlier or contemporary colleagues.[3]

---

[3] Izard (1979b) said that, as part of an attempt to establish independent discovery, he deliberately did not examine Ekman and Friesen's Facial Action Coding System, even though it had already been published at the time when he was developing his measurement techniques.

Investigators—often failing to specify the sample, setting, or persons viewed—usually said only that they looked at behavior and that their list of facial actions was simply the product of what they saw. Something more is needed, however, to account for the differences among these techniques, even allowing for the fact that each investigator observed a different behavior sample. What stood out, which attributes were noticed when an action occurred, and how the flow of behavior was segmented by the investigator probably depended upon theoretical commitments. Only a few were explicit.

Birdwhistell (1952) tried to organize units and select behavior to construct a system to parallel linguistic units. Grant (1969) advocated the selection and organization of measurement units according to function. Brow raising, for instance, was chosen by Grant because it was said to serve an attention-getting function. This puts the cart before the horse, because the measurement technique so constructed was to be used to discover the function of those very behaviors. Among ethologists, Blurton Jones (1971) was most explicit in considering the anatomical basis for facial actions. In the case of brow raising, contraction of the frontalis was believed responsible. Blurton Jones did not say that anatomic basis of facial actions was the final or even the major basis for his decisions about what to include, and he did not specify how he arrived at his list of minimal units of behavior.

Ekman, Friesen, and Tomkins (1971), in contrast to the aforementioned investigators, derived their list of facial actions from explicit theory about the facial actions relevant to emotion, rather than from observation of some sample of behavior. The 'cart before the horse' criticism applies to them also. Although they could learn whether the actions proposed for an emotion accurately reflect that emotion, they could not discover signals for the emotion that they did not know about in advance. Izard, eight years later, also used theory about emotion signals as the basis for selecting actions to score in his measurement technique, MAX. His decisions were based on inspection of still photographs of posed emotions that had yielded high agreement among observers who made global judgments about emotion.

The anatomical basis of facial action provided another basis for deriving units of behavior. The measurement units were presumably based on what the muscles allow the face to do. Because we all have the same muscles (for all practical purposes), this approach might be expected to have led the investigators who followed it to arrive at the same listings of facial actions. This is not the case. For example, Landis (1924) had 22 actions and Frois-Wittmann (1930) 28, and yet they both claimed to have based their measurement units on the anatomy of facial action. In part, the discrepancies occurred because of explicit decisions to select only certain actions. Most standard anatomy texts list many, usually not all, facial muscles with rather simple, only partially correct, and usually quite incomplete accounts of how each muscle changes appearance. Most investigators who based their technique on anatomy selected only some muscles and usually did not explain the basis for their selection. Ekman and Friesen (1978; Ekman *et al.* 2002) and Ermiane and Gergerian (1978) were exceptions, each attempting to determine all the actions the anatomy allows by systematically exploring the activity of each single muscle. Ekman and Friesen also resurrected Duchenne's (1862) technique of determining how muscles change appearance by inserting a needle into and electrically stimulating muscles.

The discrepancies between the techniques of Ekman and Friesen (1978; Ekman *et al.* 2002), Ermiane and Gergerian (1978), and Izard (1983) are due to differences in purpose and in procedure for obtaining reliability. Both Ekman and Friesen and Ermiane and Gergerian attempted to include in their lists changes in appearance that are independent of each other. If a muscle contraction would produce two or three changes in appearance, these were gathered together as multiple indexes of the activity of one unit or muscle. For example, when the entire fontalis muscle acts, it will:

1. raise the eyebrows;
2. produce horizontal furrows running across the forehead (except in infants, who have a fatty pad in the forehead blocking such wrinkles);
3. expose more of the eye cover fold (the skin between the upper eyelid and the eyebrow).

Both Ekman and Friesen and Ermiane and Gergerian listed these multiple signs together as different ways of recognizing that this one action had occurred. Izard, however, treated signs (1) and (2) of frontalis muscle activity as separate measurement units, giving each equal, independent, separate status, failing to recognize that they are signs of the same action. He ignored sign (3). Alternatively, Izard failed to distinguish among facial actions that have different anatomic bases. As an example, pulling the lip corners down and raising or pulling up the lower lip are assigned the same MAX code even though they are produced by contraction of different facial muscles (Oster *et al.* 1992). These actions are coded separately in FACS (AU 15 and AU 17, respectively).

Izard (1983) also differed from the others in selecting only movements that he judged relevant to emotion. Any movements that did not figure in MAX formulas for proto-typic emotions were excluded (Oster *et al.* 1992). Ekman and Friesen (1978; Ekman *et al.* 2002) and Ermiane and Gergerian (1978) aimed to include all the possible appearance changes that the muscles can produce. This sometimes meant creating more than one measurement unit, if use of different strands of a single muscle or different portions of that muscle was found to produce visible different changes in appearance. For example, they distinguished a number of different facial action units that are based on various uses of what anatomists have termed one muscle—the *orbicularis oris*, which circles the lips. Izard included only some of these separate appearance changes.[4]

The Ekman and Friesen technique differed from the others in another important respect. Anatomy was only part of their basis for the derivation of measurable units. They also determined whether observers could reliably distinguish all of the appearance changes resulting from the various muscles. If two appearance changes could not be reliably distinguished, they were combined, even if different muscles were involved. If

----

[4] Strangely, Izard excluded specific actions that are said by many theorists to signal emotions and that are shown by Ekman and Friesen's data to be emotion signals. Izard and Dougherty (1981) say that actions were dropped that were not efficient, but inspection of that article and of earlier versions of Izard's scoring technique (FMCS) (Izard 1979*a*) suggests, instead, that Izard never considered a number of facial actions important to differentiating among emotions, especially in infants (Oster *et al.* 1992).

Ekman and Friesen erred, it was on the side of caution, by excluding distinctions that observers with considerable training might perhaps be unable to distinguish. The opposite error may have been made by Ermiane and Gergerian and by Izard (1983). They included distinctions in absence of evidence that each and every distinction could reliably be made by those who learn their system (see section below on reliability).

Comprehensiveness or selectivity

Three aspects of facial movement can be measured either selectively or comprehensively. *Type* refers to whether the facial action was a brow raise, inner brow raise, brow lower, or some other action. *Intensity* refers to the magnitude of the appearance change resulting from any single facial action. *Timing* refers to the duration of the movement, whether it was abrupt or gradual in onset, and so on. Most investigators have considered how to measure only the type of action, not its intensity or its timing. Type of action, intensity, and timing are discussed here and summarized in Table 2.1.

Type of action
A technique for measuring the type of facial action can be selective, measuring only some of the actions that can occur, or it may claim to be comprehensive, providing a means of measuring all visible facial action. There are advantages and disadvantages in each case. If the technique is selective, it is important to know what has been excluded; and if it claims to be comprehensive, there must be some evidence to establish that this is indeed the case.

The great advantage of a selective technique is economy. Because only some of the mass of facial actions must be attended to, the work can be done more quickly. Suppose an investigator wants to measure whether fear is reduced by exposure to one set of instructions versus another. A measurement technique that allows measurement of just the occurrence of three or four signals of fear would be ideal, because it will not matter if the occurrence of anger, disgust, distress, or some other emotion signal is missed. Even if the technique does not include *all* of the fear facial expressions (and at this time there is no conclusive or even definitive evidence about all the facial actions for *any* emotion), a selective technique could be useful. It might not matter that some or even most fear expressions were not scored, nor that blends of fear with other emotions were not scored; enough might be measured to show the effect. If the findings were negative, however, the investigator would not know whether the cause was an inadequate experimental treatment (in this example, the instructions might not have differed sufficiently) or failure to measure all of the fear expressions. In such an instance, the investigator might want to turn to a comprehensive technique.

Some questions require a comprehensive technique and cannot be answered with a selective one. Suppose the investigator wishes to discover which facial actions signal fear, anger, sadness, and so on, or to discover whether different actions are employed to serve a linguistic rather than an emotive function, or to learn what people show on their faces when their heart rate shows a sharp acceleration, or whether there are cultural or social class differences in facial actions during a greeting—a comprehensive technique would have to be employed. Once there was reasonably conclusive evidence on any of

Table 2.1 Summary of human observer based methods for measuring facial behavior for units and comprehensiveness

	Basis for deriving units	Comprehensiveness		
		Type of action	Intensity of action	Timing of action
Linguistically based				
Birdwhistell (1952)	Observation of inter-personal behavior; parallel linguistic units	Not claimed to be comprehensive; 53 actions	No provision	No provision
Ethologically based				
Blurton Jones (1971)	Observation of 500 still photographs of 2–5-year-old children	Measures any child's facial expressions; 52 actions	6 degrees of eye openness; 4 degrees of lip separation; 2 degrees of frowns	No provision
Brannigan & Humphries (1972)	Observation of children and adults	Not claimed to be comprehensive; 70 actions	No provision	No provision
Grant (1969)	Observation of children and adults	Not claimed to be comprehensive; 53 actions	No provision	No provision
McGrew (1972)	Observation of 3–4-year old children	Not claimed to be comprehensive; 31 actions	No provision	No provision
Nystrom (1974)	Observation of 1-month-old infants	Not claimed to be comprehensive; 35 descriptors	No provision	No provision
Young & Decarie (1977)	Observation of 36 infants	Measures 42 facial configurations; selected only to be relevant to emotion in the last quarter of first year in 6 test situations	No provision	No provision
Theoretically based				
Ekman *et al.* (1971)	Theory about emotion expression	Measures signs of just 6 emotions; 77 descriptors	No provision	Start-stop
Izard (1983)	Theory about emotion signals; data from posed still photographs	Measures just actions needed to identify emotion in infants; 29 descriptors	No provision	Start-stop

Continued

Table 2.1 Continued

	Basis for deriving units	Comprehensiveness		
		Type of action	Intensity of action	Timing of action
Anatomically based				
Ekman & Friesen (1978); Ekman et al. (2002)	Muscular	Measures all visible movements; 44 action units that singly or in combination can score any observed action	3-point intensity scale for 4 action units in 1978 version increased to 5-point intensity scale for all action units in 2002 version	Start–stop and onset–apex–offset
Frois–Wittmann (1930)	Muscular	Not claimed to be comprehensive; 28 descriptors	No provision	No provision
Fulcher (1942)	Muscular	Not claimed to be comprehensive; absence/presence of 16 muscular actions	Amount of movement in each of 3 facial areas related	No provision
Ermiane & Gergerian (1978)	Muscular	Measures all visible movements; 27 muscle actions	Each action rated only on 3-point intensity scale	No provision
Landis (1924)	Muscular	Not claimed to be comprehensive; 22 descriptors	Each action rated on 4-point intensity scale	No provision

these issues, then such evidence could provide the basis for selective use of portions of a comprehensive system. For example, Ekman and Friesen (1978); Ekman *et al.* (2002) and Ekman, Friesen, and Simons (1985), building upon the earlier research of Landis and Hunt (1939), have strong evidence about the particular combination of facial actions and the timing of those actions that index the startle reaction.[5] Once that has been replicated by other laboratories, those interested in the startle, in particular, could utilize just that portion of Ekman and Friesen's comprehensive scoring technique.

Only a comprehensive technique allows for discovery of actions that the investigator did not know about in advance and permits a complete test of an *a priori* theory about facial sign vehicles. Another advantage of a comprehensive technique is that it provides a common nomenclature for descriptions of facial behavior. If many investigators were to use the same comprehensive technique, comparison of findings would be facilitated because investigators, even those who used it selectively, would key their units to a single list of facial actions. Investigators considering selective scoring might well want first to study a comprehensive technique, in order to become acquainted with the entire array of facial actions, so that they could be explicit about what it is they are choosing not to measure.

Wedded to these advantages of comprehensive facial scoring is the disadvantage of cost. It takes more time to learn a comprehensive technique, and it takes more time to apply it, for nothing (presumably) is left out.

It is no accident that the only techniques that claim to be comprehensive—Ekman and Friesen (1978) and Ermiane and Gergerian (1978)—were anatomically based. An inductive approach would be too costly if comprehensiveness was the goal. Too large a sample of diversified behavior would have to be observed to have a reasonable likelihood of achieving completeness. By contrast, it should be possible to achieve comprehensiveness by exploring how each muscle works, because the muscles produce the actions observed. This is not as simple as it might first seem, because muscles can act in concert, not just singly. Facial expressions are rarely the consequence of the activity of a single muscle. Even the smile, which is principally the work of the single zygomatic major muscle, typically involves two or three other muscles as well, and not every smile involves the same other muscles. Moreover, what happens to appearance when muscles act in concert is not always the sum of the changes associated with each of the components. Analogous to co-articulation effects in speech, contraction of one muscle can modify the appearance change of another. The activity of one muscle also may obscure the presence of another. It is important, therefore, that a comprehensive technique lists not simply the ways of recognizing how each single facial action appears, but also the ways of scoring the occurrence of these units of facial action when they combine in simultaneous or overlapping time. Only the Ekman and Friesen technique has done so.

....

[5] In part because of its very uniformity, Ekman and Friesen consider the startle reaction to be not an emotion but instead a reflex. Some writers about emotion (Tomkins 1962) disagree and classify startle with the emotion of surprise. For further discussion and data on this issue, see Ekman *et al.* 1985.

A last issue regarding how comprehensively a technique measures the *type* of facial action is what evidence is provided to demonstrate that the system is what it claims to be. One wants to know whether the universe of facial movement can be described by the technique, or at least what part of the universe has been omitted. If there is uncertainty about comprehensiveness, it should be clear whether it is about just some or all actions. An empirical answer would be possible if either of the techniques claiming comprehensiveness (Ekman and Friesen and Ermiane and Gergerian) had scored large samples of facial actions of males and females of diverse ages, from various cultural, ethnic, and class backgrounds, in a wide variety of social and individual settings. The system of Ekman and Friesen has been used extensively in cross-cultural, developmental, and medical populations, and evidence for comprehensiveness, so far, is strong. A sample of this literature can be found in Ekman (1997).

Alternatively, comprehensiveness could be determined by experimentally generating all possible permutations of facial actions. Ekman and Friesen explored the comprehensiveness of their technique by producing voluntarily, on their own faces, more than 7000 different combinations of facial muscular actions. These included all permutations of the actions in the forehead area and, for the lower face, all of the possible combinations of two muscles and of three muscles. Although they believe their system is relatively comprehensive[6], only time and application to diverse samples of facial behavior will establish it to be so. Ermiane and Gergerian provided no evidence of comprehensiveness. They determined only that their system would describe the actions of single muscles and a few of the combined actions of two or three muscles.

Intensity of action

Actions vary not only in type (inner corner brow raise versus raise of the entire brow) but also in intensity. A brow raise may be weak or strong; the lift of the brow, the extent of exposure of the eye cover fold and gathering of skin on the forehead may be very slight or great. The intensity of a facial action may be of interest for a variety of reasons. For example, Ekman *et al.* (1980) found that the intensity of zygomatic major muscle action was correlated with retrospective self-reports about the intensity of happiness experienced.

Ermiane and Gergerian was the only one of the 13 other techniques to provide for comprehensive measurement of intensity. Nine of the techniques treated facial action as an all-or-nothing phenomenon, or as if there were evidence that variations in intensity are without significance. One (Grant) even confused intensity with type of action, listing as different action types appearance changes that are due only to variations in intensity. A few made provision for scoring the intensity of four or five actions (see Table 2.1). Good reliability and precision have been found for intensity scoring using FACS (Sayette *et al.* 2001). Ekman *et al.* (2002) found that the logic provided in the original version of FACS for measuring the intensity of four actions could be extended

---

[6] They acknowledge that for certain actions (for example, the movements of the tongue), their technique is not complete.

to the other facial actions, but evidence has not yet been provided that such extensions can be made reliably for all the actions in their technique.

Timing of action

A facial action has a starting and a stopping point. It is often more difficult to ascertain the exact determination of these points than to decide which action occurred. From start to stop, other aspects of timing may be distinguished:

1. *Onset time*: the length of time from the start until the movement reaches a plateau where no further increase in muscular action can be observed.
2. *Apex time*: the duration of that plateau.
3. *Offset time*: the length of time from the end of the apex to the point where the muscle is no longer acting.

Onsets and offsets may vary not only in duration but in smoothness. For example, an onset may increase at a steady rate or steps may be apparent (Schmidt *et al.* 2003*a*). Similarly, an apex may be steady or there may be noticeable fluctuations in intensity before the offset begins. When examined closely, the separate actions that compose a facial expression do not start, reach an apex, and stop simultaneously. In even a common expression, such as surprise, the raising of the eyebrows may reach an apex while the dropping of the jaw is still in onset.

For some questions, it is possible that simple counts of the occurrence of particular actions may be sufficient, without measurements of onset, apex, and offset. The investigator may want to know only how often or for how long a person raised the brow, wrinkled the nose, or depressed the lip corners. Even when interest is limited to simple summary measures of the occurrence of single actions, there is no rationale for using frequency rather than duration measures (which require stop-start determination) other than economy. A frequency count will under-represent those actions that go on for long periods of time and over-represent frequent brief actions.

Limiting measurement to single actions is hazardous, regardless of whether frequency or duration is measured. Nose wrinkling, for example, may signify one thing when it occurs in overlapping time with a lower lip depression (disgust) and something quite different when it flashes momentarily while the lip corners are pulled upwards (an action that Ekman and Friesen suggest functions like a wink to accentuate a smile). A pulling down of the lip corners may signify sadness when it accompanies raised inner corners of the brows with drooping upper eyelids. When this same action occurs with the entire brow raised and the lower lip pushed up it may be a disbelief gesture. These interpretations, which have not all been tested, cannot be tested unless the timing of actions is measured. What evidence does exist (Ekman & Friesen 1978) suggests that it is unwise to measure the face as if each action can be counted separately, as if each action has an invariant meaning apart from other actions that overlap in time.

Measurement of combinations of facial actions (what is usually meant by an expression) requires at least a determination that actions overlap, if not precise determination of the stopping and starting points of each action. Ekman and Friesen (1978) further suggest that it is overlap in the apex that is crucial to determining whether actions that co-occur are organized as part of the same event, signal, or expression. Their reasoning is that when one action begins (onset) while another action is fading (offset), it is not likely that they have been centrally directed as part of the same signal. Suppose, for example, that there has been an overlap in the apex of brow lowering, tightening and pressing together of the red parts of the lips, and raising the upper eyelid. Ekman and Friesen have hypothesized that these elements compose one of the anger expressions. Overlap in the apex of these actions would support their notion that an anger signal had occurred and that these actions should be so counted, and not tallied separately. Let us suppose that there was also a nose wrinkle, with an apex overlapping these anger actions. Ekman and Friesen suggest that this would be a blend of disgust with anger. If the nose wrinkling reached its apex as these anger actions were in offset, they suggest that it be characterized as a sequence of anger followed by disgust. Testing of these hypotheses requires precise measurement of onset, apex, and offset.

A number of other research questions also require comprehensive measurement of the timing of facial actions. For example, does a brow raise and upper eyelid raise occur before or during an increase in loudness in speech or a deceleration in heart rate? Ekman *et al.* (1985) found that onset time is crucial in isolating from idiosyncratic facial actions those muscular actions that always occur in unanticipated startle reactions. Only actions that began within 0.1 second were evident in all unanticipated startles; offset time did not distinguish the idiosyncratic from uniform facial actions. In another situation, offset time, rather than onset, may be crucial. For example, Ekman and Friesen (2003) hypothesized that stepped offsets occur more often in deceptive than in felt emotional expressions.

Most of the 14 techniques do not describe procedures for measuring starting and stopping points and ignore onset, offset, and apex measurement. The data reported usually consists only of frequency counts. While other features could be coded, no criteria are provided for how to do so. Ekman and Friesen's technique is the only one to describe how to measure these different aspects of timing.

Depicting facial measurement units

It is not as easy as it may at first seem to depict clearly what is referred to by a facial measurement unit. Some authors did not bother because they did not expect others to try to use their methods. Regrettably, this lack of clarity also has caused some uncertainty about their substantive results. Take the example 'down corners mouth', which is found in the measurement techniques of Birdwhistell (1952), Brannigan and Humphries (1972), Grant (1969), and Nystrom (1974). Does this phrase describe instances in which the mouth corners have been pulled down? Or those in which the mouth corners are down because the chin and lower lip have been pushed up in the middle? Or does it refer just to expressions in which the mouth corners are down because the center of the upper lip has been raised? Or is it all of them?

The first column in Table 2.2 describes how measurements were depicted in each of the 14 techniques. The chapter appendix lists how a particular facial action (brow raise) was depicted by each technique.

Table 2.2 Summary of human observer based methods for measuring facial behavior: unit depiction, inference/description, and application

	Way in which each unit is depicted	Use of inference or description	Types of records and persons to which measurement has been applied
Linguistically based			
Birdwhistell (1952)	Two or three words	Mixed (e.g. pout, smile, sneer)	Not known
Ethologically based			
Blurton Jones (1971)	Verbal description of changed appearance of features, a few drawings and illustrative photos	Mostly description but a few inferential terms (e.g. frown, pout)	Infants and children
Brannigan & Humphries (1972)	Verbal description	Mixed (e.g. wry smile, angry frown, sad frown, threat)	Children and adults
Grant (1969)	Primarily verbal description, some photos	Mixed (e.g. sad frown, aggressive frown, smile, sneer)	Children and adults
McGrew (1972)	Verbal description; compared to Grant, Blurton Jones	Mostly description but a few inferential terms (e.g. pout, frown, grin)	Children
Nystrom (1974)	Verbal description	Description	Neonates
Young & Decarie (1977)	Verbal description	Mixed (e.g. fear face, sad face, shy smile)	Infants in last quarter of first year
Theoretically based			
Ekman *et al.* (1971)	Photographs of descriptor	Description	Video and still photos of adults' posed and spontaneous expressions
Izard (1983)	Verbal description, photos, drawings, and video	Description	Video of infants
Anatomically based			
Ekman & Friesen (1978); Ekman *et al.* (2002)	Verbal description, still photos, and video examples of each action and certain combinations of actions	Description	Spontaneous, deliberate, and posed video and photos of neonates, children, adults, deaf stutterers, mental patients
Frois–Wittmann (1930)	Verbal description; very brief	Only one inferential term: frown	Still photos of poses by one adult
Fulcher (1942)	Verbal description; very brief	Description	Films of poses by blind and sighted children
Ermiane & Gergerian (1978)	Verbal description, still photos	Description	Adult poses and patients' spontaneous photographs
Landis (1924)	Verbal description	Description	Neonates

Most techniques used but a few words to describe each measurement unit. Some supplemented this description with a few still photographs. Only three techniques went beyond this step to provide more thorough illustration of each unit. Ekman and Friesen, Ermiane and Gergerian, and Izard's MAX technique all provided visual illustrations of every measurement unit. All provided some explanations of the anatomical basis of each action—Ekman and Friesen and Ermiane and Gergerian more thoroughly than Izard. Ermiane and Gergerian provided still photographs of each action and combination considered; Izard provided videos, photographs, and drawings; and Ekman and Friesen provided still photographs and video illustrations.

Separating inference from description

Although many investigators have been interested in inferring something about the signal value or function of facial actions, not all have recognized that such inferences should not be intermixed with descriptions in their measurement techniques. The measurement must be made in non-inferential terms that describe the behavior so that inferences about underlying states, antecedent events, or consequent actions can be tested by empirical evidence.

Mixing inference with description may also make the measurements quite misleading. Few single-muscle actions have an invariant meaning. Take the example of the so-called frown (lowering and drawing the brows together). This action is not always a sign of negative affect; depending upon the timing of the action, what other actions co-occur with it, and the situational context, it may signify quite different matters (Scherer 1992). It would be misleading to identify the occurrence of a frown when the brow lowering is signaling concentration or conversational emphasis.

Because humans make the measurement, inferences cannot be eliminated, but they need not be encouraged or required. If the person scoring a face identifies the brows being lowered and/or drawn together, the scorer may still make the inference that he or she is describing a frown. But Ekman and Friesen (1978) reported that when people use a measurement technique that is solely descriptive, as time passes the scorer increasingly focuses on the behavioral discriminations and is rarely aware of the possible meaning of the behavior. Although there can be no guarantee that inferences are not being drawn, a measurement technique should neither encourage nor require inferences about meaning by the terminology or descriptions it employs.

Both Ekman and Friesen and Izard separated their hypotheses about the signal value of facial actions from the descriptive materials to be used in training a person to measure facial behavior. Ermiane and Gergerian intermixed inferences about the meaning of behavior with the information necessary to learn their descriptive system. Theirs is the only technique to contain inferences about how given facial actions are indicative of specific personality processes and types of psychopathology. Birdwhistell (1952), Blurton Jones (1971), Brannigan and Humphries (1972), Grant (1969), McGrew (1972), Young and Decarie (1977), and Frois–Wittmann (1930) all mixed some inferential or emotional terms (e.g. frown, smile, sneer, angry frown) in with descriptive terms. (This is not always evident from the chapter appendix, because not all who mixed inference with description did so for the brow raise.)

Both Ekman and Friesen and Izard listed hypotheses about the emotion signaled by particular facial actions. Ekman and Friesen were explicit about the particular combinations of units they considered as emotion signals. Izard's MAX contains only those facial actions which, he claims, distinguish among the emotions. Ekman and Friesen have evidence that Izard is wrong, that he has excluded a number of actions relevant to emotions. For example, Izard does not include levator labii superioris caput infraorbitalis, which is relevant to both disgust and anger, except when this muscle acts unilaterally. Ekman *et al.* (1980) found that bilateral evidence of this muscle correlated with the subjective report of disgust. Ekman, Friesen & Ancoli (1980) also found that when this action is accompanied by the narrowing of the red margins of the lips (another action ignored by Izard), the signal changes from disgust to anger.[7] As another example, MAX omits reference to the buccinator, unilateral action of which is associated with contempt (Darwin 1872/1998; Ekman & Heider 1988).

Types of records and persons to which the measurement has been applied

Still or motion records

Although a number of techniques claim that they can be used with motion records, most have not dealt with the complexities in the timing of facial action that a motion record reveals. These investigators may never have been confronted with the complexity of the temporal organization of facial actions because of either the type of behavior or the type of record they examined. If only posed expressions were measured (as in the case of Ermiane and Gergerian), variations in timing might not be apparent. Posers generally try to perform all the required movements at once, in overlapping time, with similar very short onsets, long-held apexes, and abrupt short offsets. Preliminary data suggest that the relationship between intensity and duration of smile onsets varies, as well, between posed and spontaneous smiles. In the former, these parameters are uncorrelated, whereas in the latter they are highly correlated and consistent with automatic movement (Cohn & Schmidt 2004). An investigator who used his or her method only to score still photographs might not know of these complexities in timing because the camera shutter freezes all action. Though Izard (1983) has scored some motion records, he pre-selected only certain brief segments of videotape to score, segments in which the infants seemed to be emitting expressions that looked like those in posed photographs of adults. Thus he has not dealt with the complexities that a motion record reveals. Other investigators may have failed to consider the timing of facial movement because they tried to apply their systems in real time, as the behavior occurred, and even if they had videotape or film, they may not have examined the records in slowed or repeated replay.

It will be most important for investigators to make use of motion, measuring the timing of facial actions, whenever they want to study spontaneous behavior, taking a strictly descriptive approach; or to interrelate facial activity and some other simultaneous behavior (speech, respiration, body movement, etc.); or to distinguish configurations in which the temporary organization of multiple facial actions suggests that they be

----

[7] These errors are the product of limited sampling: Izard chose his actions on the basis of what he observed in a set of photographs of posed emotions.

considered parts of the same signal or expression. (See the discussion below of the research questions that require measurement of timing.)

Modifications for varying age levels

Ideally, a facial measurement system should be applicable to the study of individuals of any age by making provision for any modifications needed to measure infants or the aged. The appearance of certain facial actions is quite different in neonates and infants from what it is in young children and adults. Oster (1978), who worked with Ekman and Friesen during the final stages in the development of their measurement system, has studied the neuro-anatomical basis for these differences. She has provided (Oster & Rosenstein undated) a set of transformations for utilizing the Ekman and Friesen system with neonates and infants. Izard's MAX technique was specifically designed to measure infant facial expression. He provides only a few overly general descriptions of potentially confusing infant–adult differences. For investigators wishing to use MAX to code facial actions in adults (e.g. Sayette et al. 1992), it becomes important to know about how criteria may change with development. No other investigator has attended to the problem of how coding criteria may change with development.

Parallel problems may occur in measuring facial activity in quite elderly people, because age signs may necessitate some modifications in scoring rules to avoid mistakes in identifying certain actions. No one has considered this.

Reliability

The need for reliability is obvious to psychologists. To some anthropologists and sociologists, the quest for reliability has seemed a peculiar madness that deflects psychologists from the real problem at hand. For example, Margaret Mead, in the last years of her life, wrote 'Psychologists . . . are more interested in validity and reliability than in what they are actually studying' (Mead 1973). Yet if a measurement system cannot be shown to be reliable, there is no way of knowing whether even the investigator who invented the system recognizes the same facial action when it twice occurs. The need to demonstrate reliability seems especially important with facial behavior. For here, there is an enormous variety of behaviors that can occur, with no names for most. And those who have observed facial actions have produced very different catalogs.

Some ethologists (Young & Decarie 1977) have argued that if the same finding is obtained in two independent studies, there is no need to demonstrate that the measurement technique was reliable. This reasoning should not be applied to the area of facial measurement, where there have been completely contradictory reports by different investigators (e.g. the argument about universality between Birdwhistell and Ekman). If we knew that Birdwhistell and Ekman had each used a reliable measurement technique (preferably the same one), at least we could be certain about what was seen, and search for differences in sampling, situation, or interpretation as sources of their disagreement. When a measurement technique is intended to be usable by other investigators, it is especially important for its originator to demonstrate that he or she, as well as others, can use it reliably. (See also the first section of Chapter 1 in which reliability was discussed in the context of the relationship between the outcomes of message judgment studies and measurement of sign vehicle studies.)

Let us now consider various aspects of reliability, for it is not a simple matter to establish. A number of requirements can be enumerated:

1. The researcher, rather than just giving an overall index of agreement, should provide data to show that high agreement can be reached about the scoring of specific facial actions. Typically, some actions are easier to recognize than others. Unless reliability data are reported for the scoring of each facial unit, it is not possible to evaluate which discriminations may be less reliable.

2. Data on reliability should be reported from the measurement of spontaneous, not just posed, behavior, and from the flow of behavior as revealed in a motion record, not just from still photographs or slices abstracted from video, which may yield higher agreement.

3. Reliability data should be provided for (a) infants, (b) children, (c) adults, and (d) aged populations, because reliability for just one group does not guarantee reliability for the others.

4. The most common source of unreliability in behavioral measurement, whether it be of face or of body, is the failure of one person to see what another scores. Usually this occurs when an action is small in size. This source of disagreement can be attenuated if the technique specifies a threshold that must be surpassed for the action to be scored. Specifying minimum thresholds alerts the persons doing the scoring to subtle signs and provides explicit bases for decisions about when a change in appearance is likely to be ambiguous. A technique that provides such threshold definitions should therefore yield higher agreement.

5. Reliability should be reported not only for the person(s) who developed the technique, but also for learners who did not previously have experience with facial measurement. Data about the range of reliabilities achieved by new learners should be provided and compared to those for experienced or expert scorers. A technique will be more generally useful if it can be learned independently, without direct instruction from the developer. This usually requires a self-instructional set of materials, practice materials with correct answers, and a final test for the learner to take.

6. Reliability should be reported for the scoring of not just the type of action, but also of the intensity and timing of actions.

Of the 14 measurement techniques, five did not report data on any aspect of reliability. Others provided fairly sparse data on reliability—with the exception of Ekman and Friesen and Izard. Even these techniques did not meet all the requirements just listed. Table 2.3 lists the specific reliability requirements met by each technique.

Validity

Descriptive validity

The validity of a technique designed to measure facial movement entails questions on a number of levels. Most specifically (and concretely), validity requires evidence that the technique actually measures the behavior it claims to measure. When a technique

Table 2.3 Summary of human observer based methods for measuring facial behavior: reliability and validity

	Reliability	Validity			
		Descriptive	Emotional	Conversational	Other
Linguistically based					
Birdwhistell (1952)	Not reported	None	None	None	None
Ethologically based					
Blurton Jones (1971)	Data reported on requirements 1, 2, 3b, 6a	None	None	None	None
Brannigan & Humphries (1972)	Not reported	None	None	None	None
Grant (1969)	Not reported	None	None	None	Predicts severity of mental illness, but no data reported
McGrew (1972)	Data reported on requirements 1, 2, 3b, 6a	None	Spontaneous	None	Predicts gender differences and relation to agonistic interaction
Nystrom (1974)	Data reported on requirements 1, 2, 3b, 6a	None	None	None	None
Young & Decarie (1977)	Not determined by authors	None	Spontaneous, but no data reported	None	Said to differentiate infants' response when mother departs and when she frustrates, but no data reported
Theoretically based					
Ekman et al. (1971)	Data reported on requirements 2 and 3c	None	Posed and spontaneous: positive vs. negative, stressful vs. neutral film conditions; differentiates patterns of heart rate	None	Predicts attribution of emotion

Izard's MAX (1983)	Data reported on requirements 2, 3a-b, 5 and 6a	None	Posed	None	Provides preliminary data on relations to vocalization and body movement in infants

Anatomically based

Ekman & Friesen (1978); Ekman *et al.* (2002)	Data reported on requirements 1, 2, 3a-c, 4, 5, 6a & c	Meets performed actions and EMG criteria	Posed and spontaneous; measures intensity and type of emotion; differentiates startle reaction; differentiates certain deliberate from spontaneous expression	Measures syntactic and emphasis signals	None
Frois–Wittmann (1930)	Not reported	None	Posed	None	Predicts developmental changes; compares blind and sighted
Fulcher (1942)	Data reported on requirements 1, 2, 3b, 6a	None	Posed	None	None
Ermiane & Gergerian (1978)	Data reported only on scoring photos of poses and on requirement 3c	None	Posed	None	None
Landis (1924)	Not reported	None	None	None	Predicts individual differences

claims to measure brow raise, are the brows actually raised, or is it just the inner corners that are raised? If the technique claims to measure the intensity of an action, such as whether the brow raise is slight, moderate, or extreme, do such measurements correspond to known differences in the intensity of such an action? The problem, of course, is how to know what facial action occurs, what criterion to utilize independently of the facial measurement technique itself. Two approaches have been taken:

1. **Performed action criterion**: Ekman and Friesen trained people to be able to perform various actions on request. Records of such performances were scored without knowledge of the performances requested. Ekman and Friesen's Facial Action Coding System (FACS) accurately distinguished the actions the performers had been instructed to make.
2. **Electrical activity criterion**: Ekman and Friesen, in collaboration with Schwartz (Ekman *et al.* 1978) placed surface EMG leads on the faces of performers while the performers produced actions on request. Utilizing the extent of electrical activity observed from the EMG placements as the validity criterion, they found that FACS scoring of facial movement accurately distinguished the type and the intensity of the action. (This study is described in more detail in the section on EMG below.)

Utility or validity

Some measurement techniques contain hypotheses about the particular facial actions that signal particular emotions (Ekman and Friesen; Ekman, Friesen, and Tomkins; Ermiane and Gergerian; Izard). For these techniques, it is appropriate to ask whether the hypotheses are correct, but the answer does not pertain to the validity of the techniques, only to that of the hypotheses. Suppose the facial behaviors found to signal emotion were exactly the opposite of what had been hypothesized by the developer of the technique. Such evidence would not show that the technique was invalid, only that the hypotheses were wrong. In fact, the discovery that the hypotheses were wrong would itself require that the technique measure facial movement accurately. Suppose a study not only failed to support the investigator's hypotheses about the actions that signal emotions but found that there were no facial actions related to emotion. If one could discount the possibility that the sample did not include emotional behavior, this might suggest that the facial measurement technique was not relevant to emotion. It might have measured just those facial behaviors that are unrelated to emotion. Another technique applied to the same sample of facial behavior might uncover the actions related to emotion.

Two techniques (Ekman and Friesen and Ermiane and Gergerian) claim not to be specific to the measurement of any one type of message such as emotion, but to be of general utility, suitable for the study of any question for which facial movement must be measured. Such a claim can be evaluated by evidence that the technique has obtained results when studying a number of different matters.

Posed expressions

Many techniques can differentiate poses of emotion or judgments of emotion poses: Ekman and Friesen; Ekman, Friesen, and Tomkins; Ermiane and Gergerian; Frois–Wittman; Fulcher; Izard. In the studies that used a selective technique, it is not possible to know whether there might have been other facial actions, not included in the scoring technique, that might have predicted the emotion poses or judgments just as well or better. The two comprehensive techniques—Ekman and Friesen and Ermiane and Gergerian—provided that information. They were able to show that it was the movements they specified as emotion-relevant, not other movements, that were signs of particular emotions. Ekman and Friesen's FACS also predicted not only *which* emotion was posed or judged, but the *intensity* of emotion as well.

However, poses are, by definition, artificial. Although they may resemble spontaneous facial expressions in some respects (Ekman & Friesen 1982), one difference is that they are likely to be easier to score. The onset may be more coordinated and abrupt, the apex frozen, and the scope very intense or exaggerated. The velocity of smile onsets in relation to intensity also appears to differ markedly between posed and spontaneous smiles (Cohn & Schmidt 2004). Evidence that a technique is a valid measure of emotion cannot rest just upon measurement of poses; it is necessary to determine that the measurement will be valid when it measures spontaneous emotional expression.

Spontaneous expressions

A number of studies have shown the validity of Ekman and Friesen's FACS in measuring the occurrence of spontaneous emotional expressions. Ancoli (1979) studied autonomic nervous system (ANS) responses when subjects watched a pleasant or stress-inducing film. A different pattern of ANS response during the two films was found only during the times in each film-viewing period when the face registered maximal emotional response. In another study of that data, Ekman *et al.* (1980) found that FACS accurately predicted the subjects' retrospective reports of their emotional experience while watching the films: the intensity of happy feelings, the intensity of negative feelings, and, specifically, the intensity of the emotion of disgust. Ekman *et al.* (1985) differentiated the specific facial actions that signify a startle reaction from the emotional reactions subsequent to being startled. Both the type of actions and the onset time were crucial to this distinction. They also were able to differentiate a genuine from a simulated startle accurately. Ekman *et al.* (1981) and Hager & Ekman (1985) examined the differences between deliberate facial movements and spontaneous emotional expressions. Scoring the intensity of each specific facial action on each side of the face, they found that requested facial movements were asymmetrical more often than spontaneous emotional expressions: usually, the actions were more intense on the left side of the face for the deliberate, but not for the spontaneous, emotional expressions. Krause (1978) utilized FACS to measure facial actions during conversations among stutterers and non-stutterers. As he predicted, the facial actions specified in FACS as relevant to anger occurred more often among the stutterers. There is little or no comparable evidence that the other facial measurement techniques listed in Table 2.3 can be used to measure spontaneous emotional expressions.

The only exception is Izard's use of his MAX technique to study infants. He found that observers scoring brief segments of videotape showing infant expressions *selected* to correspond to adult posed expressions could reliably identify the actions making up those expressions. This shows that his technique can be used to identify at least those particular expressions when they occur in spontaneous behavior. At this point, however, there is no evidence to support Izard's claim that an infant producing a particular expression is experiencing a particular emotion or blend of emotions (Oster *et al.* 1992). The evidence suggests that emotion-specified expressions in infants may commonly occur in the absence of the hypothesized emotion (Camras 1992; Camras *et al.* 1996), and hypothesized emotions may occur in the absence of expression-specified expressions (Scherer *et al.* 2004). Infant expression also appears to be less differentiated than claimed by Izard (Matias & Cohn 1993). Because Izard has not described infants' facial behavior comprehensively, he cannot even specify how representative the selected expressions are in the behavior of infants of a given age and in a variety of situations.

Oster (1978; Oster & Ekman 1978) has provided more complete information about the range of facial muscle activity observed in infants and the infant's capacity for coordinated facial movement. Unlike Izard, she began not by looking for adult posed expressions but by analyzing the configurations and sequences of facial actions actually produced by infants in a variety of situations. Oster found that almost all of the single facial actions included in FACS are apparent early in life. Though certain combinations of facial actions common in adult facial expression can be observed in the newborn period, others have not been observed in infants. Oster (1978) has argued that the only way to determine the affective meaning and signal function of infants' facial expressions is by a detailed description of the expressions themselves—including their timing and sequencing—combined with a thorough functional analysis of their behavioral correlates and stimulus context. Though far from complete, Oster's work has provided evidence that complex, spontaneous facial actions observed in infants (e.g. smiling, brow knitting, pouting) are not random but represent organized patterns and sequences of facial muscle activity that are reliably related to other aspects of the infants' behavior (e.g. looking at or away from the caregiver, motor quieting or restlessness, crying). Such relationships can provide insights into the infant's affective state and cognitive processes.

Stable individual differences

Several studies have found moderate stability in FACS action units and predictive validity for a wide range of personality and clinical outcomes. Cohn *et al.* (2002) found moderate to strong stability in FACS action units over a 4-month interval; stability was sufficiently robust as to suggest that facial behavior could function as a biometric. Person recognition from FACS action units was comparable to that of a leading face recognition algorithm. Harker and Keltner (2001) found that FACS action units predicted adjustment to bereavement, teacher ratings of problem behaviors, and marital adjustment over periods as long as 30 years. Malatesta *et al.* (1989) found low to moderate stability in infant facial behavior over several months using MAX. There is no comparable evidence of stability or predictive validity for personality-related measures for the other measurement techniques.

Costs

This last criterion for evaluating measurement techniques was not included in Table 2.3 because Ekman and Friesen was the only study to provide information about time costs for learning to measure and for scoring a specified sample of behavior. It takes approximately 100 hours to learn FACS. More than half of the time is spent scoring practice materials (still photographs and video) included in FACS at the end of each chapter in the instructional manual. Ekman and Friesen do not know whether people will still achieve high reliability if they skip such practice; they do know that high reliability was achieved when all the instructional steps were followed.

The costs for using a measurement technique once it is learned are much more difficult to estimate. For FACS, and probably any other technique, the costs depend upon how densely the facial behaviors are packed in the time sample to be scored. Consider, first, comprehensive scoring in which FACS is used to measure *all* visible facial activity in a 15-second period. This could take as little as one minute if only one or two easily distinguished actions occurred and the investigator wanted only to locate start-stop points for each action. It could take as long as 10 hours, however, if the behavior was as densely packed as it is in the facial activity of deaf persons signing, and if onset–apex–offset was scored for every action. Ekman and Friesen have not observed any other instances in which facial behavior is so densely packed over so many seconds.

If selective rather than comprehensive scoring is done, the costs are lower. Presume that the investigator wants to score only actions that are said to be indicative of disgust, and they select the actions listed in the *Investigator's Guide to FACS* (Ekman & Friesen 1978; Ekman *et al.* 2002) that are predicted to be prototypic for that emotion. A 2:1 ratio, 30 seconds of scoring time for every 15 seconds of live action, is probably a reasonable estimate. Ekman and Friesen developed a more economical system for measuring the occurrence of single emotions, based on FACS. Occurrences of actions considered to be the most common signs of anger, fear, distress and/or sadness, disgust and/or contempt, surprise, and happiness are noted. In what they call EMFACS (Ekman & Friesen 1982) (EM standing for emotion), time is saved in three ways:

1. Scoring does not extend to the particular action, but only to whether a member of a group of specified actions occurred. For example, there are seven signs grouped together that Ekman and Friesen consider relevant to disgust. EMFACS does not differentiate among nose wrinkling, nose plus upper lip raising plus lower lip depression, nose wrinkling plus lower lip elevation, and so on. If any of these is seen, a check is made for that grouping. All actions not in one of the groupings are ignored.
2. Intensity of action is not scored, although intensity is included in the requirements for particular actions within a grouping. For example, a slight depression of the lip corners with slight pushing up of the lower lip is included in the sad grouping, but when those two actions are moderate or strong they are not included.
3. The timing of actions is not measured; only a frequency count is taken. EMFACS takes one-fifth the time of FACS, but of course it suffers from all of the problems already discussed in detail for selective as compared to comprehensive measurement techniques.

For a similar method of identifying action unit composites in infants, see Camras *et al.* (1992).

Izard's MAX technique is similar to Ekman and Friesen's EMFACS. It, too, combines actions presumed to be relevant to the same emotion, and makes no provision for scoring the timing or the intensity of action. Unlike FACS, it requires the scorer to examine different regions of the face separately and, admittedly, it includes in some regions changes in appearance that are due to actions in another region. By contrast, FACS and EMFACS alert the scorer to all the appearance changes resulting from particular muscles. Rather than inspecting an arbitrary division of the face in three regions, the scorer learns where to look in the face for those changes. Izard's MAX technique was developed by collapsing some of the distinctions he had made in his earlier FMCS technique, but FMCS was itself selective, not comprehensive. A benefit of EMFACS and the approach of Camras *et al.* in defining composites of action, in comparison to Izard's MAX and other selective techniques, is that what has been excluded is exactly specified.

Facial electromyography

Facial electromyography (EMG) measures the electrical activity of motor units in the striated muscles of the face. The force and velocity of movement are controlled by the number of motor units and their rate of firing. The size and shape of the waveform represents the movement, which may be visible to the eye or occult depending on the degree of activity and characteristics of the overlying tissue. The signal is recorded using surface electrodes attached to the skin, which is first prepared by a slight scraping and application of paste or solution to enhance electrical contact. Alternatively, fine wire needles are inserted into the muscle, which increases specificity. Thin cables or leads are run from the electrodes to a bio-amplifier.

The electrophysiology of EMG and its acquisition and processing are described in several sources (Cacioppo *et al.* 1990; Fridlund & Cacioppo 1986; Soderberg 1992). We discuss here the comprehensiveness, reliability, validity, and utility of facial EMG for measurement of facial motion. Unless otherwise noted, the material presented here refers to surface facial EMG.

Comprehensiveness or selectivity

Facial EMG has relatively low specificity but high spatial and temporal resolution. Because there is more than one muscle in most facial areas, and their fibers interweave or lie on top of each other (Fig. 2.1), placing leads on the surface of the face often has the consequence of picking up activity in more than just the muscle targeted by the investigator. Although investigators using surface EMG have usually been careful to talk about a *region* rather than a muscle, their reasoning and much of their interpretation assumes success in isolating the activity of specific muscles. Ekman and Friesen, in a joint study with Schwartz (1978), found that in the corrugator region, the activity of many muscles other than the corrugator itself was recorded by the electrode placed in this region: orbicularis oculi; levator labii superioris alaeque nasi; frontalis, pars medialis. The activity of these other muscles could be distinguished from that of corrugator and from each other, but these distinctions require more electrodes, some

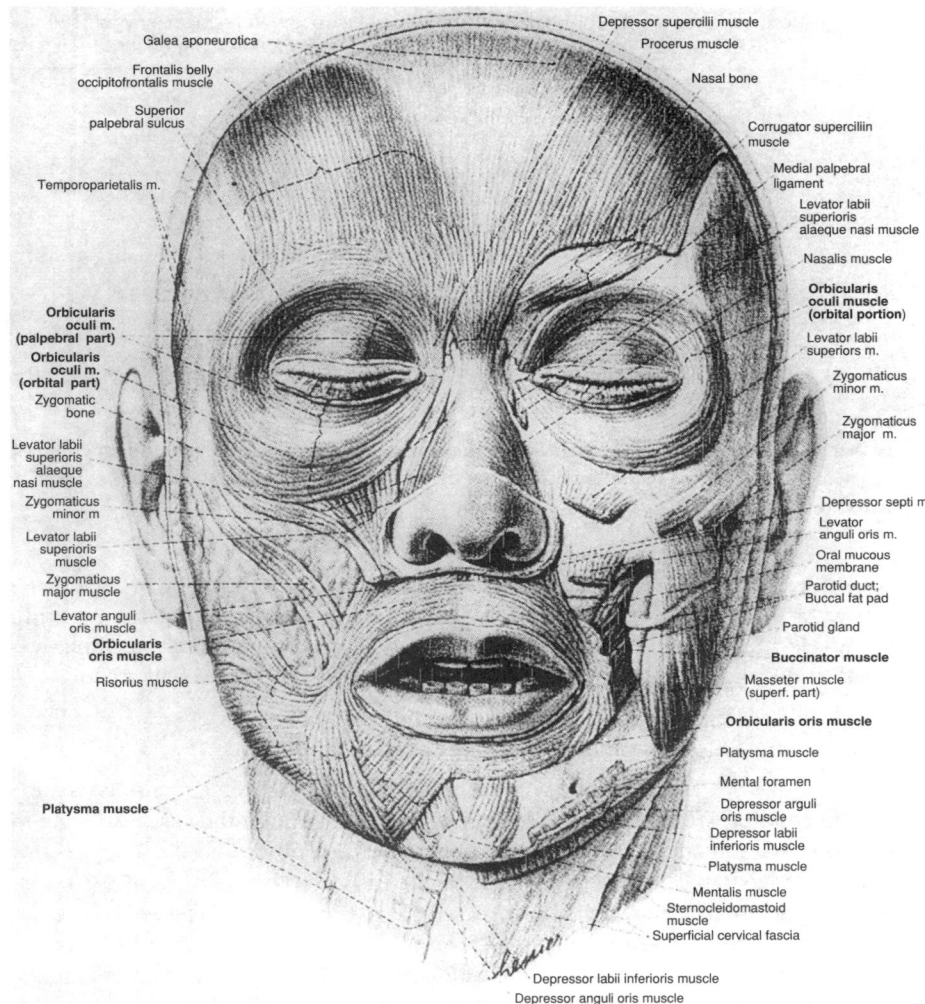

Figure 2.1 Muscles of the face (Clemente 1997).

of which must be placed in adjacent facial regions. Another way to obtain measurement of specific muscles, as noted above, is to insert fine wires into a muscle—a procedure that, though not as painful as it sounds, requires medical training and certification and is not practicable for many studies.

An advantage of facial EMG is its high temporal resolution, which makes it well suited for measuring emotions, which have rapid onset and short duration. An example of the temporal resolution of facial EMG is shown in Fig. 2.2 from Dimberg *et al.* (2002). Subjects were asked to contract their zygomatic major or corrugator supercilli muscles (AU 12 in FACS) in response to a picture of a happy or an angry face.

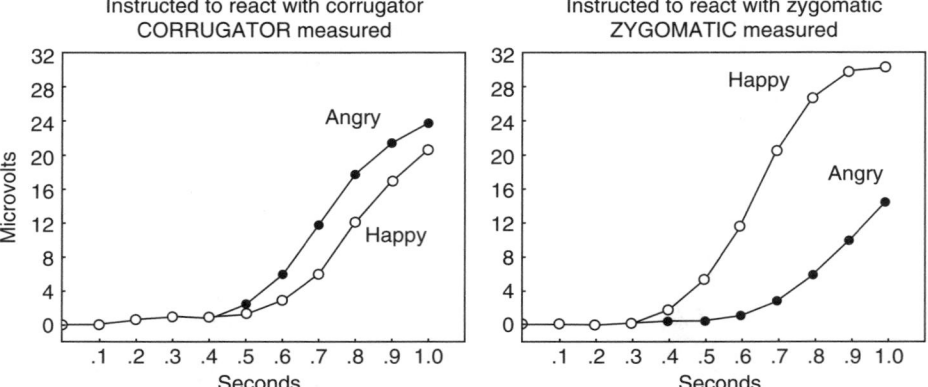

Figure 2.2 The mean facial EMG response for the zygomatic major and corrugator supercilii muscles plotted in intervals of 100ms during the first second of exposure when subjects were instructed to react as quickly as possible to a happy or an angry face (Dimberg *et al.* 2002).

Consistent with hypotheses that emphasize automaticity, contraction of zygomatic major was facilitated by the happy face, while contraction of the corrugator supercilii muscle was facilitated by the angry face. The temporal resolution of the recordings was sufficient to discriminate differences in response time within about a half second.

Types of persons to which the measurement has been applied

With few exceptions, use of facial EMG is limited to older children and adults. Infants and young children are difficult to test with facial EMG because they are less likely to tolerate electrodes attached to their faces. When the method has been used with this population, it has typically been restricted to the orbicularis occuli region for measurement of potentiated startle (Balaban *et al.* 1989; Schmidt & Fox 1998). In older children, use of EMG presents no special problems. We routinely record EMG in the zygotmatic major, corrugator supercilii, levator labii, and orbicularis occuli regions in children age 13 years and older, without event (Forbes *et al.* submitted).

Reliability

In the past, a problem with facial EMG was the lack of a standard system for specifying exactly where to place an EMG electrode in order to detect activity in a particular facial region. The efforts of Fridlund and Cacioppo (1986) to introduce guidelines for EMG placement have led to increasing standardization, which has largely overcome this problem. Method variance due to unknown variation in electrode placement has been reduced with increased adoption of these standards.

Nevertheless, some variation in placement is inherent in the use of electrodes on the face. Consider the use of surface EMG to measure whether there is more or less activity in the zygomatic major region on the two sides of the face. Any differences obtained might

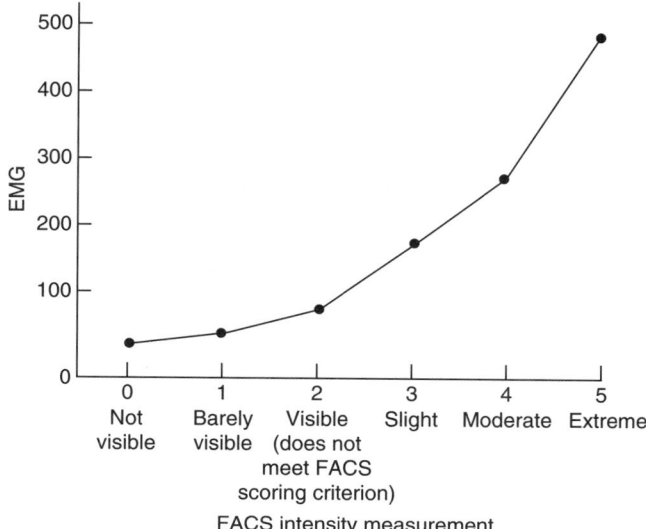

Figure 2.3 Plot of relationship between FACS and EMG measurement of performances of action unit 1 (frontalis, pars medialis).

not be due to the greater involvement of the right or left hemisphere but might, to an unknown extent, reflect differences in placement of the EMG electrode in relation to the muscle mass on the two sides of the face or to asymmetry in facial structure or tissue (Liu *et al.* 2003). Between-subjects designs, in which, for example, a measure of zygomatic major was correlated with a personality test score, would also be vulnerable to error owing to electrode placement. These problems can be circumvented by utilizing research designs in which EMG activity is compared in two or more conditions for each subject.

When EMG is used to measure change over time, and the leads must be placed on the face more than once, variations in placement of the leads on each occasion can introduce errors. Miller (1981/2) addressed this problem by devising a template that can be attached to a subject repeatedly, to ensure that electrode placement is identical on different occasions.

Reliability for EMG intensity has been shown by comparing EMG and FACS intensity scoring. Persons highly skilled in activating specific muscles (Ekman and Oster) contracted them on command at different intended intensity levels while a video record was made and surface EMG was recorded. FACS scoring was later found to be highly correlated with the EMG readings (Pearson $r = 0.85$) (Ekman *et al.* 1978). Figure 2.3 shows an example from this data—a plot of the relationship between EMG measures of electrical activity and FACS scoring of the intensity of action for a specific muscle.

Validity

A number of studies have used surface EMG to measure muscle activity in relation to emotion and found evidence of good concurrent and predictive correlation with self- and observer-reported emotion (Cacioppo *et al.* 1988, 1992; Cohn *et al.* 2002; Dimberg *et al.* 2002; Fridlund *et al.* 1990; Tassinary & Cacioppo 1992). Most of this literature has used facial EMG to discriminate between positive and negative emotion (Cacioppo *et al.* 1986).

An issue is whether EMG can provide measurement of more than just one or two emotional states. Most emotions cannot be identified by the activity of a single muscle. Happiness may be the only exception, but even here, evidence (Ekman *et al.* 1990; Frank *et al.* 1993) suggests that the differentiation of felt from simulated happiness, of controlled from uncontrolled happiness, and of slight from extreme happiness requires measurement of more than one muscle. Disgust might be measured by the activity of two muscles, and surprise by the activity of three. To measure anger, fear, or sadness, many muscles need to be measured. There are limits, however, to the number of leads that can be placed on a person's face without unduly interfering with the behavior under study. Nevertheless, there have been some successful efforts in discriminating among three or more emotions using facial EMG (Fridlund *et al.* 1984; Vrana 1993).

Utility

Facial EMG has had an important role in certain methodological studies of facial behavior. Mention was made earlier of Ekman and Friesen's use of fine-wire EMG to stimulate and record facial movement in order to discover how the muscles work to change appearance. Facial EMG could be used to help teach people how the muscles work as part of the process of teaching them a visual measurement procedure such as FACS or as part of physical rehabilitation in the case of facial neuromuscular disorders. Facial EMG can be used to calibrate and investigate measurement of visible facial behavior.

Another important use for facial EMG is to measure phenomena that are difficult or impossible to measure with techniques based on visible movements (Tassinary & Cacioppo 1992). Ekman *et al.* (1978) found that there are reliable electrical changes associated with muscle tonus changes that are not visible. For two muscles studied systematically (corrugator and frontalis, pars medialis), there were significant changes in EMG without any visible sign of activity when the performer was instructed just to think about each muscle. This study also showed that there are visible clues to muscle tension, measurable by EMG, when there is no movement. The persons measuring the faces with FACS guessed which muscle had been tensed when they could not see any movement. Sometimes the person guessing felt that there was no basis for the guess. At other times, there seemed to be evidence of very slight tightening or bulging of skin. Analyses showed that when these guesses were correct—when the scorer predicted which muscle the performer was tensing, even though no movement was visible—there was a greater increase in EMG than when the guesses were incorrect.

For measuring visible changes in the face, work reported in the next section suggests that facial EMG has high concurrent validity with visible intensity changes in onset phase of zygomatic major, with average correlation above 0.90.

Stable individual differences

Facial EMG shows moderate test–retest stability over relatively long intervals, comparable to that for self-reported emotion. As one example, in a longitudinal study of emotion regulation, 66 adults viewed short film clips on two occasions, 12 months or more apart. On both occasions, EMG was measured in four facial regions. After viewing each film, subjects rated their degree of enjoyment on Likert-type scales. EMG in the zygomatic major region was analyzed for the film intended to elicit enjoyment. Stability coefficients for facial EMG and self-reported emotion were nearly identical, 0.58 and 0.56 respectively (Cohn *et al.* 2002).

Costs

EMG requires specialized equipment and staff trained in psychophysiology, which entails significant laboratory and personnel costs. Data processing is efficient, however, and significantly less time-intensive than manual coding. The need to attach electrodes to the face, on the other hand, is mildly intrusive and is a limiting factor in use of EMG. Cabling from the electrodes to an acquisition device effectively confines the wearer's activity to a relatively small area, making use in naturalistic settings difficult. Telemetric recording, which dispenses with cabling, could be helpful in this regard (Gerleman & Cook 1992). Another limitation is that facial EMG may inhibit facial activity. Large or sudden head or facial motion can loosen the electrodes. To prevent these problems, subjects usually have been studied in isolation. Even when subjects have been studied in a social context (Fridlund 1991), social interaction among subjects tends to be avoided. Subjects typically have been measured when trying to pose, imagine, remember, or create for themselves an emotional experience. Even in these situations, if a subject makes a large expression, they will feel the tape that holds the electrode in place pull or tear, which could inhibit large expressions, even if the experimenter does not explicitly discourage large expressions by instruction, limit choice of task for the subject to perform, or impose restrictions on context, such as limiting social interaction. The seriousness of these concerns is difficult to evaluate since comparisons between manual coding and facial EMG have been few (Cohn & Schmidt 2004).

In summary, EMG may be the only method for measuring non-visible changes in muscular tension and for measuring changes that, while barely visible, involve not movement but bulging of the skin and would be hard to measure with any of the techniques described in Table 2.1. It also may be useful as a method for automatically measuring quantitative change in facial muscles related to emotion-eliciting stimuli. The need to attach electrodes to the face limits applications to those for which intrusive methods are feasible. To automatically measure quantitative change in facial muscles non-intrusively, other methods are needed.

Automatic facial image analysis

Within the past 5–10 years, there has been considerable effort toward automatic measurement and recognition of facial expression by computer vision, which is the science of extracting and representing feature information from digitized images and recognizing perceptually meaningful patterns. Early work used markers to enhance facial features (Kaiser & Wehrle 1992; Terzopoulos & Waters 1990), and markers are used still in some applications (Wachtman *et al.* 2001). What are referred to as motion capture techniques use reflective markers attached to the skin to facilitate feature extraction. Commercially available systems include those from Vicom℠ and Peak Performance℠. As with facial EMG, motion capture approaches are expensive and require specialized training and expertise to use; and reflectors attached to the skin may, as with electrodes, inhibit facial expression. Most current research in automatic facial image analysis requires no markers or other enhancement of facial features. We review progress here in the development of markerless systems for measurement of facial actions.

Most of the work in automatic facial expression recognition has focused on emotion-specified expressions, such as joy and anger (Black & Yacoob 1994; Essa & Pentland 1997; Lyons *et al.* 1998; Padgett & Cottrell 1998; Yacoob & Davis 1997). Within the last five years, the more challenging task of recognizing facial sign vehicles has received increasing attention. At least four research groups (see Table 2.4) have reported results for automatic recognition of facial sign vehicles in digitized video without aid of facial markers. All used FACS to define facial sign vehicles, due in large part to its descriptive power in modeling facial action.

Each of these four research groups has automatically recognized FACS action units without relying on artificial enhancement of facial features. Comprehensive reviews of the literature in automatic facial expression analysis and recognition can be found in Fasel & Luettin 2003; Pantic & Rothkrantz 2000*a*, 2003; and Tian *et al.* in press.

Automatic recognition of facial actions must solve four tasks: extraction of facial features, image alignment, action unit recognition, and system integration. We review each of these in turn and then evaluate the current state of the art in automatic action unit recognition. Before doing so, we first consider the type of video records required for analysis.

Table 2.4 Automatic recognition of facial action units

Research group	Key publications
Carnegie Mellon University / University of Pittsburgh	Cohn *et al.* 1999
	Lien *et al.* 2000
	Tian *et al.* 2001, 2002
	Cohn *et al.* 2004*a*
Delft University of Technology	Pantic & Rothkrantz 2000*b*, 2003, 2004
	Valstar *et al.* 2004
Institut Dalle Molle d'Intelligence Artificielle	Fasel & Luettin 2000
University of California San Diego	Bartlett *et al.* 1999
	Donato *et al.* 1999
	Littlewort *et al.* 2001
	Bartlett *et al.* 2004

Types of records and persons to which the measurement has been applied

Still or motion records

While image data may consist of either static images (e.g. photographs) or image sequences (video), analysis of the latter is much further advanced, and many of the methods (e.g. optical flow for feature extraction and head tracking for recovery of head orientation) require video input[8]. Video may be recorded using either analog or digital recordings. If recorded using analog tape, digitizing prior to analysis will be needed. Digitizing, until recently, required specialized equipment and training and was costly. As digital video becomes more common, the expense and expertise required in acquiring digital video or converting from analog video is greatly reduced.

Modifications for varying age levels

Most approaches to automatic facial image analysis have been applied only to adults. Analysis of infant facial actions is challenging because infant faces have relatively little texture and head movements are often sudden and large. Facial texture is important to feature extraction methods such as optical flow (described below), and sudden and large head motion is more difficult to track. Large variation in pose across an image sequence is challenging as well. We have some experience with automatic infant facial image analysis, and efforts are continuing (Cohn *et al.* 2000; Messinger *et al.* 2004). Other individual differences such as skin color, racial background, and gender have been examined. Action unit recognition appears to be unaffected by these factors (Cohn *et al.* 1999, 2003; Moriyama *et al.* 2004; Tian *et al.* 2001).

Tasks in automatic facial image analysis

Feature extraction

A number of approaches have been used to extract feature information from face images. These include difference imaging, principal components analysis (PCA), optical flow, and edge detection. A given system may use one or more of these in combination.

Difference imaging

In a digitized grayscale image, each pixel has an intensity value that varies between 0 and 255. Digitized color images have a larger range of intensity variation. Change from one image to the next may be computed by subtracting one image from another. Figure 2.4a shows an example of an infant with a relaxed facial expression and partially opened

---

[8]   In contrast, until recently almost all research in the related field of automatic face recognition has used static images. This is in part because applications in this area are driven by large databases, numbering millions of images, that already exist and the belief that face and head motion contribute little to person recognition. Evidence for the importance of face motion and video input and a broadening application base contribute to increasing interest in video for automatic face recognition (e.g. 1st IEEE Workshop on Face Processing in Video, 2004, Washington DC).

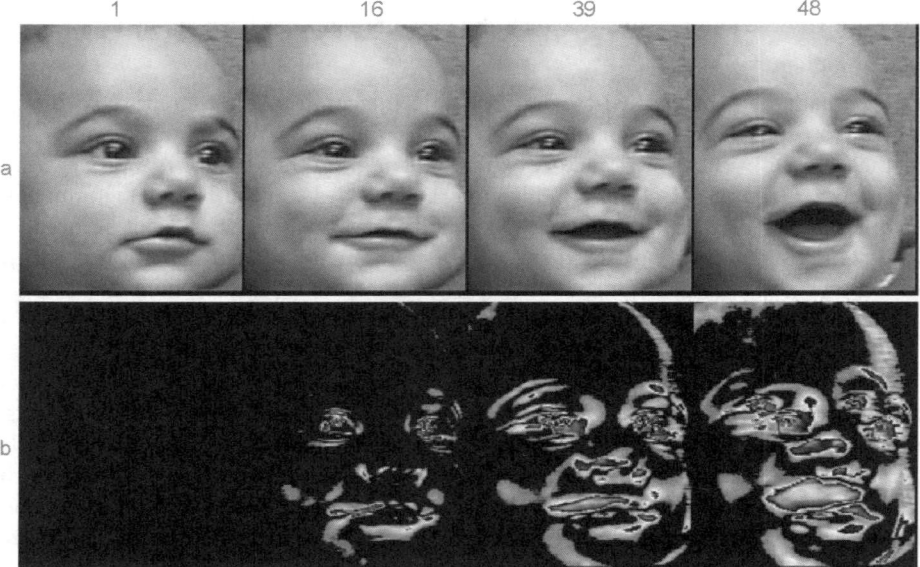

Figure 2.4 Example of difference images. Row (a) shows infant's facial expression changing from neutral to a Duchenne smile (AU 6+12). Row (b) shows the difference between the first and each subsequent image in row (a). Areas of white indicate motion caused by change in facial expression and/or head motion (Lien *et al.* 2000).

lips (AU 25 in FACS). Subsequent images in this row show the same infant beginning to smile (AU 6+12). The corresponding difference images appear in the next row (Fig. 2.4b). Pixels that change from one image to the next appear as white in the difference image. While this method is relatively efficient in identifying areas of motion, it fails to capture pixel-wise correspondence between face images. Different facial actions might produce identical patterns of intensity differences. Also, difference images are easily confounded by head motion, which can be seen in the example.

Principal components analysis (PCA)

Principal components analysis of digitized face images is another approach, initially developed for face recognition. High dimensional face images (e.g. 640 × 480 grayscale pixel arrays) can be reduced to a lower dimensional set of eigenvectors (or 'eigenfaces') (Turk & Pentland 1991). Under controlled conditions, eigenvectors can capture differences between action units. A generalization of PCA, referred to as independent components analysis (ICA), appears useful when covariation among pixels includes nonlinear relations. Like other approaches, PCA and ICA perform best when face images are viewed from the front and any head motion is small and remains parallel to the image plane of the camera. When these conditions are not met, image alignment, as discussed below, becomes a critical issue.

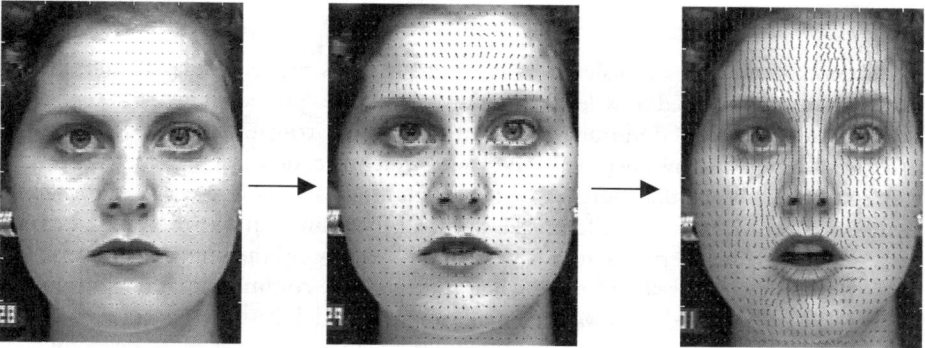

Figure 2.5 Example of dense flow extraction using the method of Wu *et al.* (2000). (From Lien *et al.* 2000)

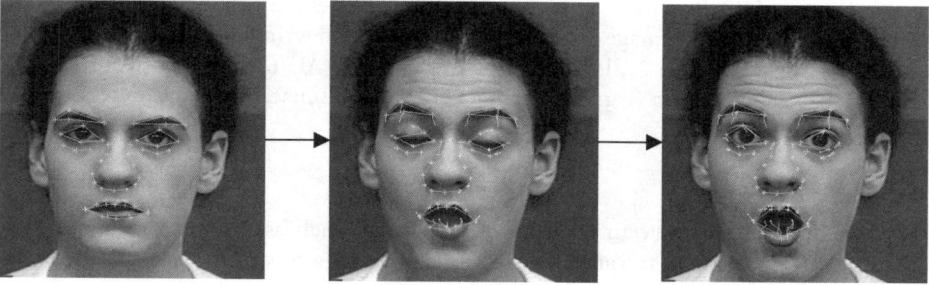

Figure 2.6 Example of feature-point tracking (Cohn *et al.* 1999).

Optical flow

In FACS, each action unit is anatomically related to contraction of a specific facial muscle. AU 12 (oblique raising of the lip corners), for instance, results from contraction of the zygomatic major muscle; AU 20 (lip stretch) from contraction of the risorius muscle; and AU 15 (oblique lowering of the lip corners) from contraction of the depressor anguli muscle. Muscle contractions produce motion in the overlying tissue. Algorithms for optical flow quantify the magnitude and direction of this motion. When optical flow is computed for the entire face image, it is referred to as **dense flow**. Figure 2.5 shows an example of dense flow extraction. In the initial image, each point represents a selected pixel whose motion will be represented by motion vectors across the image sequence. As the jaw drops, the eyes widen and the brows are raised. Dense flow systematically captures these facial actions.

Obtaining dense flow for the whole face image is computationally intensive. In our experience, it is more efficient to compute feature motion for a small set of localized facial features. Tracking specific 'feature points' in these regions yields motion that is highly consistent with that obtained from dense flow (Fig. 2.6). For action unit recognition, Lien *et al.* (2000) found that the two approaches to optical flow computation achieved similarly high accuracy for action unit recognition.

Edge detection

Facial motion produces transient wrinkles and furrows perpendicular to the motion direction of the activated muscle. These transient features provide information relevant to the recognition of action units. Contraction of the corrugator muscle, for instance, produces vertical furrows between the brows, which is coded in FACS as AU 4, while contraction of the medial portion of the frontalis muscle (AU 1) causes horizontal wrinkling in the center of the forehead. Some of these lines and furrows may become permanent with age. Permanent crows' feet wrinkles around the outside corners of the eyes, which is characteristic of AU 6 when transient, are common in adults but not in infants. When lines and furrows become permanent facial features, contraction of the corresponding muscles produces changes in their appearance, such as deepening or lengthening. The presence or absence of these lines and furrows in a face image can be found by edge feature analysis or by the use of spatial and frequency filters (Bartlett *et al.* 1999; Tian *et al.* 2000, 2002). Wrinkles and furrows present at rest may be 'removed' by thresholding the edge image. In our work, we detect wrinkles and furrows in the forehead (e.g. AU 1 and 2), lateral to the eye corners (AU 6), the nasal root (AU 4), and the nasolabial region (e.g. AU 10 and 12) by a combination of edge detection and spatio-frequency filters.

Image alignment

Facial actions often co-occur with head movement, such as when people raise their head in surprise or turn toward a friend while beginning to smile (Camras *et al.* 1996; Kraut & Johnson 1979). Expression may also vary as a result of individual differences in facial proportions (Farkas & Munro 1994; Schmidt *et al.* 2003*b*). Head motion, individual differences in facial proportions, and camera orientation are all potential confounds in extracting feature information from digitized face images (Kanade *et al.* 2000). Camera orientation may be frontal (that is, parallel to the image plane of the face) or to the side, which changes the appearance of face images. While variation due to pose and motion may be eliminated by securing the head in a clamp, as is typically done in neuro-imaging studies, or by wearing a head-mounted camera (Pantic & Rothkrantz 2004), these solutions are not without limitations. We seek accurate and efficient image alignment, which is critical for valid feature extraction, without imposing any constraints on subjects' activity.

When out-of-plane rotation of the head is small, either an affine or a perspective transformation of images can align images so that face position, size, and orientation are kept relatively constant across subjects, and these factors do not interfere significantly with feature extraction. The affine transformation is computationally faster, but the perspective transformation gives more accurate warping for a higher degree of out-of-plane rotation (Lien *et al.* 2000). For larger out-of-plane motion, it is necessary to model the head as a 3D object. Xiao *et al.* (2003) developed a 3D head tracker using a cylindrical head model. The tracker estimates, resonably precisely, the six degrees of freedom of head motion: movement in the horizontal and vertical planes, movement toward and away from the camera (i.e. scale), rotation, pitch, and yaw. Once these parameters are estimated, the face image is stabilized by warping each frame to a common orientation and size. In this way, motion due to expression is not confounded by rigid head motion. Figure 2.7 shows an example of automatic head tracking, image alignment, and feature localization.

An alternative to a cylindrical head model is to use either a generic face or person-specific face model. The UCSD group (Bartlett *et al.* 2001) used a generic face model to estimate 3D head position and warp face images to a common view. To date, this model requires manual initialization of each frame and so is not yet functional for automatic processing. The CMU/Pittsburgh group has developed a person-specific face model that automatically initializes and recovers full six degrees of freedom of head motion as well as tracks facial expression and direction of gaze (Xiao *et al.* 2004). Before the person-specific head model may be used, some training is required. Typically, 15–20 images are hand labeled prior to use. Like the cylindrical head model, the person-specific head model is robust to occlusion and runs at frame rate (30 frames per second) or faster (Gross *et al.* 2004; Xiao *et al.* 2004)

Action unit recognition

Once quantitative information is extracted from an image sequence, the measurements can be used to recognize facial actions. The data first are divided into a 'training' set and a 'testing' set. One is used for training a classifier; the other is used to test its validity and utility in an independent sample. A number of classifiers have been used. The most

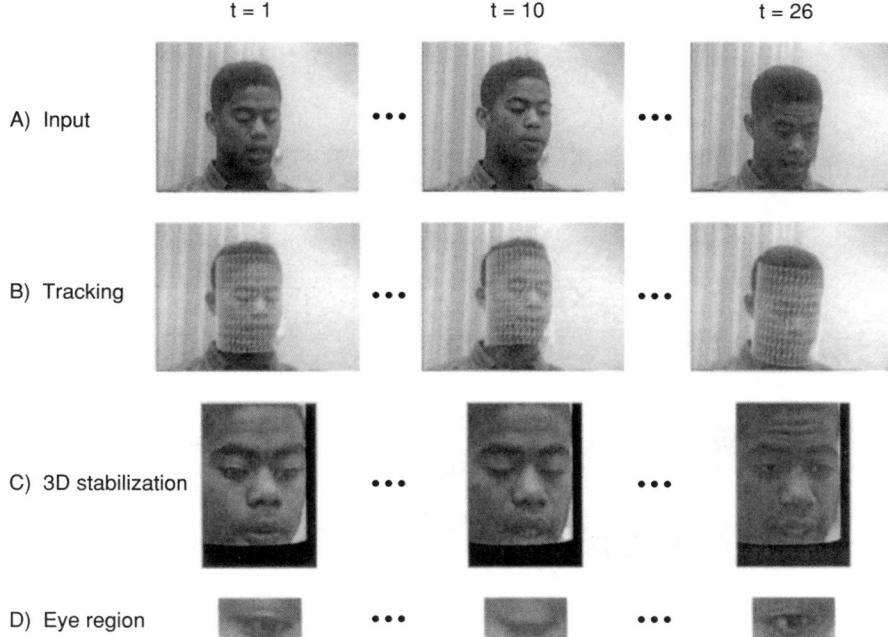

Figure 2.7 3D head tracking and image alignment (Cohn *et al.* 2003).

common are artificial neural networks (NN) and hidden Markov models (HMM). HMMs use temporal information, whereas NN algorithms, with few exceptions, do not. Lien *et al.* (2000) found that HMM and discriminant analysis produced highly similar results for their data. Bartlett *et al.* have been especially active in comparing the strengths and weaknesses of various classifiers (Bartlett *et al.* 2001, 2004). Their findings suggest that system performance may be optimized by careful selection. Whatever classifier is used, to ensure generalizability, it is important that training and testing images be independent, preferably with no subjects included in both training and testing image sequences, and that the number of image sequences and samples of target action units in each set be sufficiently large. While some investigators have used upwards of 500 or more sequences from 100 subjects with a minimum of 25 action units of each type (Cohn *et al.* 1999), others have used much smaller samples of action units and subjects, for which results may generalize poorly to new situations. Fasel and Luettin (2000), for instance, used image data from a single subject for training and testing their method of automatic action unit recognition.

System integration

For research purposes, the various components of an automated system need not be integrated. To be useful for theoretical and applied research in behavioral science, ease of use is an important feature. The CMU/Pitt automated facial analysis (AFA) system affords an example of how components may be integrated. Shown in Fig. 2.8 is an overview of version 3 of their system (Cohn & Kanade, in press; Cohn *et al.* 2004*a*).

Given an image sequence, the face and approximate location of individual face features are detected automatically in the initial frame. Then, the contours of the face

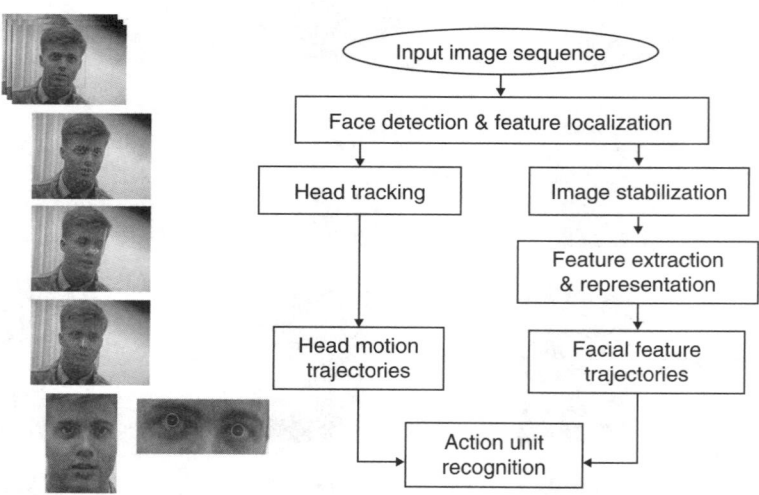

Figure 2.8 System diagram for CMU/Pittsburgh Automated Facial Image Analysis (AFA), version 3 (Cohn *et al.* 2004*a*).

features and components are adjusted manually, as needed in the initial frame, and the image sequence is processed. A cylinder-based 3D head model is used to estimate the six degrees of freedom of head orientation and to stabilize the face image across the image sequence. Stabilization entails warping each face image to a common frontal view. Both permanent (e.g. brows, eyes, lips) and transient (lines and furrows) face feature changes are tracked in the image sequence using a combination of optical flow, color, and edge detection (Tian *et al.* 2000, 2002). Facial feature parameters are fed to a neural network-based classifier for action unit recognition. Output from all processing steps is automatically stored in linked database files for export to statistical packages. The feature trajectories may be used to model the timing of facial actions as well as for action unit recognition (Cohn *et al.* 2004*b*; Schmidt *et al.* 2003*a*).

The system uses multiple types of image features (e.g. optical flow and edge information). For some action units, only one or another type of feature may provide useful information. For instance, with AU 14, which causes dimpling lateral to the lip corners, texture information rather than motion is needed. For most action units, the use of multiple features provides convergent information (as when smiling, or AU 12, is indicated by oblique motion of the lip corners and deepening and change in orientation of the nasolabial furrows), which increases precision of measurement and accuracy of action unit recognition (see also Bartlett *et al.* 1999).

Reliability

Approaches to automatic facial image analysis often entail some manual preprocessing, such as manually marking permanent facial features (e.g. eyes) in the initial image. To evaluate reliability of manual feature marking, Cohn and colleagues (1999) compared the results of pairs of coders for manual feature marking of 33 feature points. Mean inter-observer error was 2.29 and 2.01 pixels in the horizontal and vertical dimensions, respectively. Mean inter-observer reliability, quantified with Pearson correlation coefficients, was 0.97 and 0.93 in the horizontal and vertical dimensions, respectively. Most important, agreement on FACS coding between automated facial image analysis and manual FACS coding in several studies was comparable to that of manual FACS coding (Cohn *et al.* 1999, 2003; Tian *et al.*, 2001, 2002). This finding suggests that any error in feature labeling is unrelated to the accuracy of system performance. As techniques change, however, it will be important to continue to assess the reliability of any human preprocessing.

Validity

Concurrent validity for action unit recognition has been evaluated by comparing automatic and manual FACS coding of both directed facial action tasks and spontaneous facial behavior. Concurrent validity for intensity has been evaluated by comparing automatic facial image analysis and both facial EMG and q-sorts by human judges of spontaneous facial behavior. Spontaneous facial behavior included non-frontal orientation to the camera, small to moderate out-of-plane head motion, and occlusion by glasses.

Concurrent validity with manual FACS coding

Directed facial action tasks

Fasel and Luettin (2000) analyzed facial action in a subject who was an expert in FACS. For nine action units and seven action unit combinations, they achieved 74% accuracy. Pantic (2000*b*; Valstar *et al.* 2004) achieved moderate to high accuracy for 29 action units. This result was attained using dual views (frontal and profile), and facial actions were recorded using a head-mounted camera, which effectively eliminated head motion and pose variation. Others have used a single, tripod-mounted camera.

The most extensive studies of directed facial action tasks have been conducted by the CMU/Pittsburgh, UCSD, and Delft groups. The CMU/Pittsburgh group achieved 81–96% accuracy for 19 action units: six in the upper face (AU 1, 2, 4, 5, 6, 7) and 13 in the lower face (AU 9, 10, 12, 15, 17, 20, 25, 26, 27, 23, 41, 42, 45) (Tian *et al.* 2001, 2002). The action units recognized were ones most common in emotion expression and social behavior and represent 19 of 31 action units that have a known anatomical basis (Kanade *et al.* 2000). Moreover, action units were recognized whether or not they occurred in combinations, many of which involved co-articulation effects, which suggests that the system is capable of making the kinds of complex perceptual discriminations made by human observers. This capability is important because the number of possible action unit combinations numbers in the thousands. If the system had to learn each combination separately, the task would become intractable. These findings suggest that these systems are on course toward achieving the comprehensiveness of manual FACS coding.

Spontaneous facial behavior

Spontaneous facial behavior presents greater challenges to automatic facial image analysis than do directed facial action tasks. Orientation to the camera typically is non-frontal, moderate to large head motion is common, and facial occlusion by glasses, facial jewelry, and hand gesture occurs. In initial tests, we (Cohn *et al.* 2003) analyzed image data from Frank and Ekman (1997) in which subjects were interviewed about a mock theft as part of a study of deception. Image data from 10 subjects were analyzed. The subjects were ethnically heterogeneous, two wore glasses, and small to moderate out-of-plane head motion was common. All instances of AU 45 (blinking) during one minute of each interview were analyzed. Automatic facial image analysis (AFA) and manual FACS coding agreed in 98% of cases. In related work using the same image database of spontaneous facial behavior, AFA achieved 76% agreement between manual FACS coding of action units in the brow region and automatic recognition (Cohn *et al.* 2004*a*). These initial findings suggest concurrent validity of AFA with manual FACS coding of AU 1+2, 4, and 45 in spontaneous facial behavior with variable pose, moderate out-of-plane head rotation, and occlusion.

Concurrent validity with facial EMG for action unit intensity in spontaneous facial behavior

To evaluate concurrent validity for degree of eye closure (AU 45) in the Frank and Ekman image data described above, luminance intensity of the upper eye region, as determined automatically, was normalized over the range of 0 to 1. Luminance was darkest when the eye was open (normalized luminance = 1) and brightest (luminance = 0) when the eye was closed. Then, the digitized images were randomly sorted. Two researchers, blind to the results of automatic processing, manually sorted (i.e. q-sort) each sequence from eye open to closed to open. They next estimated the degree of eye closure on a scale from 0 (eye closed) to 1 (eye open). A representative example is shown in Fig. 2.6. In each of 10 sequences examined, automatic analysis and human judgment were highly consistent. An example is shown in Fig. 2.9.

To evaluate concurrent validity for contraction of zygomatic major (AU 12), Cohn *et al.* (2002) collected image and EMG data from subjects while they watched a film clip intended to elicit enjoyment. Contraction of the zygomatic major was determined by EMG. When visible smiling was observed, it was confirmed by manual FACS coding. Feature vectors from the lip corner were highly consistent with onset EMG recorded from the zygomatic major region. In 72% of cases with a distinct EMG and visible smile onset, feature point tracking by optical flow and facial EMG were highly correlated, with an average time lag of 0.23 seconds. An example is shown in Fig. 2.10.

Utility

AFA has been used to investigate theoretical and applied issues involving facial action. Some of the applications include assessment of facial neuromuscular disorders (Wachtman *et al.* 2001), facial asymmetry in biometrics (Liu *et al.* 2003), the timing of

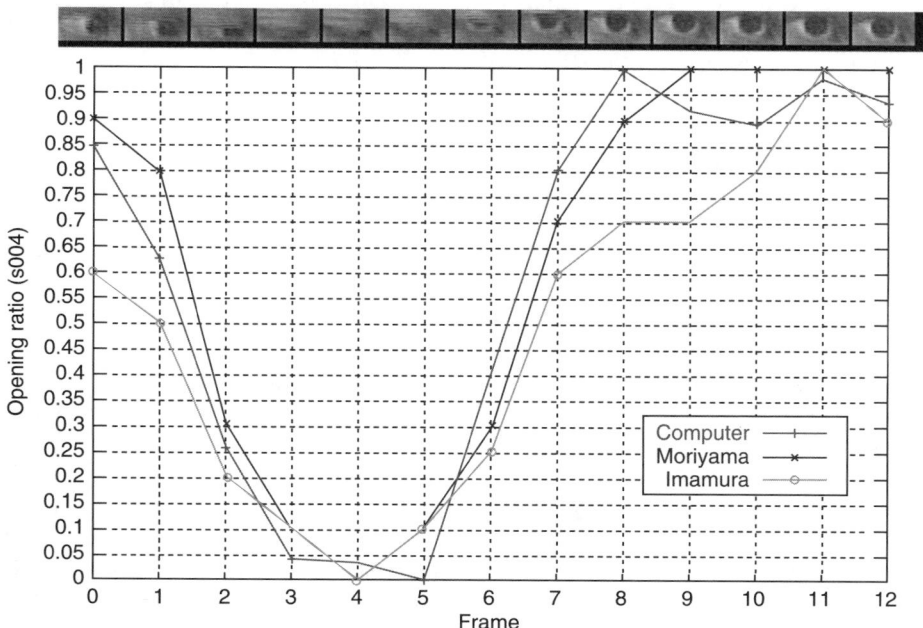

Figure 2.9 Comparison of manual and automatic ordering of blink sequence (Cohn *et al.* 2003).

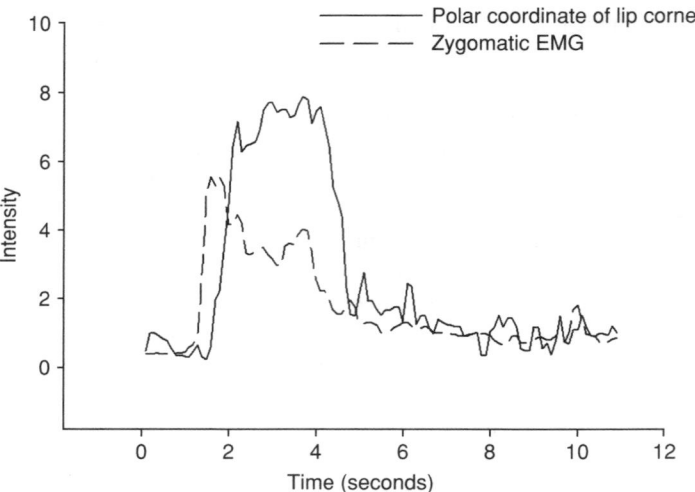

Figure 2.10 Example of the relation between zygomatic major EMG and displacement of the lip corner as determined by AGA (Cohn & Schmidt 2004).

spontaneous and deliberate smiles (Cohn & Schmidt 2004; Schmidt *et al.* 2003*a*), the relation between head motion, smiling, and direction of gaze (Cohn *et al.* 2004*b*), brow raising and lowering (Cohn *et al.* 2004*a*), and facial expression in infants (Cohn *et al.* 2000; Messinger *et al.* 2004). The scope of applications in theoretical and applied research can be expected to increase further as development efforts continue and the system becomes available to other investigators.

Remaining challenges

Before AFA and related systems are ready for release, several challenges must be addressed. These include how to parse the stream of behavior, prevent error accumulation, and increase automation. AFA and other systems have assumed that facial actions begin and end from a neutral face. In actuality, facial expression is more complex. Transitions among action units may involve no intervening neutral state. For AFA, parsing the stream of facial action units under these circumstances is a challenge. Human FACS coders meet this task, in part, by having a mental representation of a neutral face. For AFA, parsing will likely involve greater higher-order pattern recognition than has been considered to date.

Many of the methods used in AFA so far involve dynamic templates for which estimates are continually updated. With dynamic templates, error tends to propagate and accumulate across an image sequence. So far, most AFA applications have involved relatively short image sequences up to 10 seconds or so, for which error accumulation is not a significant problem. For longer sequences, an appropriate measure is required. The head tracking module in AFA overcomes this problem through a combined use of robust regression and reference images. Robust regression identifies and discounts the effects of outliers, and reference images provide a way to reinitialize estimates so as to reduce error accumulation. For head tracking, this approach has been highly successful. The cylinder model head tracker has performed well for image sequences as long as 20 minutes. Similar capability will be needed for action unit recognition.

Almost all current methods entail some manual initialization, such as labeling permanent facial features (e.g. eyes or mouth) with a computer mouse in one or more face images. This is especially the case when person-specific face models are used. These models may require hand labeling of 20 to 30 images. Once this is completed, these models are relatively robust to error accumulation and operate automatically on long sequences. While a fully automated system is not always necessary for all applications, increased automation will reduce the personnel costs of using the system and increase the kinds of applications for which it may be used.

Conclusions

This chapter has reviewed measurement techniques for only one type of signal—rapid, not slow or static. Among these, only one kind of rapid signal—visible movement—has been considered. Most of the studies that have used one or another technique to measure visible movement were concerned with only one of the many messages rapid signs may convey—information about emotion. Presumably, future research will expand to consider other messages and to develop methods for measuring rapid signals other than movement, as well as the variety of slow and static signals.

A few manual coding techniques have become widely used, especially that of Ekman and Friesen and, to a lesser extent, Izard. The former was designed to be applicable to the study of any message, not just emotion. Wedding studies of facial sign vehicles to studies using the more traditional message judgment approach should allow discovery of the particular actions that form the basis for correct and incorrect inferences when people judge facial expression (see Chapter 3; Oster *et al.* 1992). These techniques may also allow discovery of particular facial actions that are not customarily known or even knowable by the usual observer, movements that are too subtle and/or complex to notice or interpret when seen once, at real time.

As further research is generated by the facial measurement techniques reviewed here, the techniques themselves may undergo further development or be replaced by other measurement approaches. This development may be seen in the system of Ekman and Friesen, which exists now in three versions: the initial version (FACS 1978), FACS 1992 (update document based), and FACS 2002, which includes significant improvements in scoring criteria and in didactic materials, including extensive use of hyperlinked cross-referenced text and embedded video links in the CD version. With the release of new versions, such as that of FACS 2002, it becomes critical that those who publish findings using one or the other version identify which version they have used. Even better would be for investigators to use the most current version of a system, as is done routinely in fields such as intelligence testing and clinical diagnosis in which new versions of assessment instruments are common.

In part because of its descriptive power, the technique of Ekman and Friesen has encouraged a wide range of research on facial movement (Ekman & Rosenberg, in press) as well as become influential in the fields of computer animation (e.g. Parke & Waters 1996) and automated facial expression recognition, in which fine-grained description of motion parameters is needed.

The development of automated methods of facial expression analysis, in particular, is exciting. Automated analysis using computer vision produces both action unit recognition and quantitative measures of feature trajectories (e.g. Schmidt *et al.* 2003*a*). Initial work suggests that AFA has high concurrent validity for both action unit recognition and intensity variation, as assessed by trained observers and facial EMG. Automatic analysis has several potential advantages. By computing quantitative measures of facial action over time, powerful statistical techniques may be used to asses individual facial behavior and dyadic behavior, such as synchrony and dominance (Boker *et al.* 2002; Cohn & Tronick 1988). From an information processing perspective, comparisons between automated and human observer based facial expression analysis would afford a new means of studying social perception. In addition, a system that operates in real time could provide continuous monitoring and feedback for research and clinical applications. While work in this area is still in the early stages, initial applications to theoretical and clinical issues are encouraging.

Author notes

An earlier version of this chapter appeared in K.R. Scherer and P. Ekman (ed.) (1982) *Handbook of methods in nonverbal behavior research,* pp. 45–90. New York: Cambridge University Press. Portions reprinted with permission.

Preparation of this chapter was supported in part by NIMH grants MH 11976 and MH 06092 to Paul Ekman and NIMH grant MH 51435 to Jeffrey Cohn.

References

Ancoli, S. (1979). *Psychophysiological response patterns of emotion.* University of California San Francisco, San Francisco, California.

Balaban, M.T., Anthony, B.J., & Graham, F.K. (1989). Prestimulation effects on blink and cardiac responses of 15-month-old infants: reactions to facial expressions of emotion. *Developmental Psychobiology,* **22**, 115–27.

Bartlett, M.S., Braathen, B., Littlewort, G., Sejnowski, T.J., & Movellan, J.R. (2001). *A comparative study of alternative FACS coding algorithms. MPLAB-TR-2001–06.* San Diego, California: Institute for Neural Computation, University of California, San Diego.

Bartlett, M.S., Ekman, P., Hager, J.C., & Sejnowski, T.J. (1999). Measuring facial expressions by computer image analysis. *Psychophysiology,* **36**, 253–63.

Bartlett, M.S., Littlewort, G., & Movellan, J.R. (2004). Machine learning methods for fully automatic recognition of facial expressions and facial actions. *IEEE Conference on Systems, Man, and Cybernetics,* The Hague, The Netherlands.

Birdwhistell, R. (1952). *Introduction to kinesics.* Louisville, KY: University of Louisville Press.

Black, M.J. & Yacoob, Y. (1994). Recognizing facial expressions under rigid and non-rigid facial motions. *International Workshop on Automatic Face and Gesture Recognition*, Zurich, pp. 12–17.

Blurton Jones, N.G. (1971). Criteria for use in describing facial expression in children. *Human Biology*, **41**, 365–413.

Boker, S.M., Xu, M., Rotondo, J.L., & King, K. (2002). Windowed cross–correlation and peak picking for the analysis of variability in the association between behavioral time series. *Psychological Methods*, **7**, 338–55.

Brannigan, C.R. & Humphries, D.A. (1972). Human nonverbal behavior: a means of communication. In *Ethological studies of child behavior* (ed. N.G. Blurton Jones). Cambridge: Cambridge University Press.

Bruce, V. & Young, A. (1998). *In the eye of the beholder: the science of face perception.* New York: Oxford University Press.

Cacioppo, J.T., Martzke, J.S., Petty, R.E., & Tassinary, L.G. (1988). Specific forms of facial EMG response index emotions during an interview: from Darwin to the continuous flow hypothesis of affect-laden information processing. *Journal of Personality and Social Psychology*, **54**, 592–604.

Cacioppo, J.T., Petty, R.E., Losch, M.E., & Kim, H.–S. (1986). Electromyographic activity over facial muscle regions can differentiate the valence and intensity of affective reactions. *Journal of Personality and Social Psychology*, **50**, 260–8.

Cacioppo, J.T., Tassinary, L.G., & Fridlund, A.J. (1990). The skeletomotor system. In *Principles of psychophysiology: physical, social, and inferential elements* (ed. J.T. Cacioppo & L.G. Tassinary). New York: Cambridge University Press.

Cacioppo, J.T., Uchino, B.N., Crites, S.L., Snydersmith, M.A., Smith, G., Berntson, G.G., *et al.* (1992). Relationship between facial expressiveness and sympathetic activation in emotion: a critical review, with emphasis on modeling underlying mechanisms and individual differences. *Journal of Personality and Social Psychology*, **62**, 110–28.

Camras, L.A. (1992). Expressive development and basic emotions. *Cognition and Emotion*, **6**, 269–83.

Camras, L.A., Lambrecht, L., & Michel, G.F. (1996). Infant 'surprise' expressions as coordinative motor structures. *Journal of Nonverbal Behavior*, **20**, 183–95.

Camras, L.A., Oster, H., Campos, J.J., Miyake, K., & Bradshaw, D. (1992). Japanese and American infants' responses to arm restraint. *Developmental Psychology*, **28**, 578–83.

Clemente, C.D. (1997). *Anatomy: a regional atlas of the human body* (4th edn). Williams & Wilkins.

Cohn, J.F. & Kanade, T. (in press). Use of automated facial image analysis for measurement of emotion expression. In *The handbook of emotion elicitation and assessment* (ed. J.A. Coan & J.B. Allen). New York: Oxford University Press.

Cohn, J.F. & Schmidt, K.L. (2004). The timing of facial motion in posed and spontaneous smiles. *International Journal of Wavelets, Multiresolution and Information Processing*, **2**, 1–12.

Cohn, J.F. & Tronick, E.Z. (1983). Three month old infants' reaction to simulated maternal depression. *Child Development*, **54**, 185–93.

Cohn, J.F. & Tronick, E.Z. (1988). Mother–infant face-to-face interaction: influence is bidirectional and unrelated to periodic cycles in either partner's behavior. *Developmental Psychology*, **34**, 386–92.

Cohn, J.F., Campbell, S.B., Matias, R., & Hopkins, J. (1990). Mother–infant face-to-face interactions of postpartum depressed and non-depressed mothers. *Developmental Psychology*, 26, 15–23.

Cohn, J.F., Reed, L.I., Ambadar, Z., Xiao, J., & Moriyama, T. (2004a). Automatic analysis and recognition of facial actions and out-of-plane head motion in spontaneous facial behavior. *IEEE Conference on Systems, Man, and Cybernetics*, The Hague, The Netherlands.

Cohn, J.F., Reed, L.I., Moriyama, T., Xiao, J., Schmidt, K.L., & Ambadar, Z. (2004b). Multimodal coordination of facial action, head rotation, and eye motion. *Sixth IEEE International Conference on Automatic Face and Gesture Recognition*, Seoul, Korea, pp. 645–50.

Cohn, J.F., Schmidt, K.L., Gross, R., & Ekman, P. (2002). Individual differences in facial expression: stability over time, relation to self-reported emotion, and ability to inform person identification. *International Conference on Multimodal User Interfaces*, Pittsburgh, PA, pp. 491–6.

Cohn, J.F., Xiao, J., Moriyama, T., Ambadar, Z., & Kanade, T. (2003). Automatic recognition of eye blinking in spontaneous facial behavior. *Behavior Research Methods, Instruments, and Computers*, 35, 420–8.

Cohn, J.F., Zlochower, A.J., Lien, J.J.J., Hua, W., & Kanade, T. (2000). Automated face analysis. In *Progress in infancy research (Vol. 1)* (ed. C. Rovee–Collier & L. Lipsitt), pp. 155–82. Hillsdale, NJ: Erlbaum.

Cohn, J.F., Zlochower, A.J., Lien, J.J.J., & Kanade, T. (1999). Automated face analysis by feature point tracking has high concurrent validity with manual FACS coding. *Psychophysiology*, 36, 35–43.

Darwin, C. (1872/1998). *The expression of the emotions in man and animals* (3rd edn). New York: Oxford University Press.

Dimberg, U., Thunberg, M., & Grunedal, S. (2002). Facial reactions to emotional stimuli: automatically controlled emotional responses. *Cognition and Emotion*, 16, 449–71.

Donato, G.L., Bartlett, M.S., Hager, J.C., Ekman, P., & Sejnowski, T. (1999). Classifying facial actions. *IEEE Transactions on Pattern Analysis and Machine Intelligence*, 21, 974–89.

Duchenne, B. (1862). Mechanisme de la physionomie humaine; ou, analyse electrophysiologique de l'expression des passions. Paris: Baillière.

Duda, R.O. & Hart, P.E. (1973). *Pattern classification and analysis*. New York: Wiley.

Ekman, P. (1964). Body position, facial expression and verbal behavior during interviews. *Journal of Abnormal and Social Psychology*, 68, 295–301.

Ekman, P. (1965). Differential communication of affect by head and body cues. *Journal of Personality and Social Psychology*, 2, 725–35.

Ekman, P. (1980). Facial asymmetry. *Science*, 209, 833–4.

Ekman, P. (1997). Lying and deception. In *Memory for everyday and emotional events* (ed. N.L. Stein, P.A. Ornstein, B. Tversky, & C. Brainerd). Mahwah, NJ: Lawrence Erlbaum Associates.

Ekman, P. & Friesen, W.V. (1969). The repertoire of nonverbal behavior. *Semiotica*, 1, 49–98.

Ekman, P. & Friesen, W.V. (1978). *Facial action coding system*. Palo Alto, CA: Consulting Psychologists Press.

Ekman, P. & Friesen, W.V. (1982). *Rationale and reliability for EMFACS*. Human Interaction Laboratory, University of California, San Francisco (unpublished manuscript).

Ekman, P. & Friesen, W.V. (2003). *Unmasking the face: a guide to recognizing emotions from facial cues*. Cambridge, Massachusetts: Malor Books.

Ekman, P. & Heider, K.G. (1988). The universality of a contempt expression: a replication. *Motivation and Emotion*, **12**, 303–8.

Ekman, P. & Rosenberg, E. (ed.) (in press). *What the face reveals* (2nd edn). New York, NY: Oxford University Press.

Ekman, P., Davidson, R.J., & Friesen, W.V. (1990). The Duchenne smile: emotional expression and brain psychology II. *Journal of Personality and Social Psychology*, **58**, 342–53.

Ekman, P., Friesen, W.V., & Ancoli, S. (1980). Facial signs of emotional experience. *Journal of Personality and Social Psychology*, **39**, 1125–34.

Ekman, P., Friesen, W.V., & Hager, J.C. (ed.) (2002). *Facial action coding system*. Research Nexus, Network Research Information, Salt Lake City, UT.

Ekman, P., Friesen, W.V., & Simons, R. (1985). Is the startle reaction an emotion? *Journal of Personality and Social Psychology*, **49**, 1416–26.

Ekman, P., Friesen, W.V., & Tomkins, S.S. (1971). Facial affect scoring technique: a first validation study. *Semiotica*, **3**, 37–58.

Ekman, P., Hagar, J.C., & Friesen, W.V. (1981). The symmetry of emotional and deliberate facial actions. *Psychophysiology*, **18**, 101–6.

Ekman, P., Schwartz, G., & Friesen, W.V. (1978). *Electrical and visible signs of facial action*. San Francisco, California: Human Interaction Laboratory, University of California San Francisco.

Ermiane, R. & Gergerian, E. (1978). *Atlas of facial expressions (Album des expressions du visage)*. Paris: La Pensee Universelle.

Essa, I. & Pentland, A. (1997). Coding, analysis, interpretation and recognition of facial expressions. *IEEE Transactions on Pattern Analysis and Machine Intelligence*, **7**, 757–63.

Farkas, L.G. & Munro, I.R. (1994). *Anthropometry of the face and head*. New York: Raven Press.

Fasel, B. & Luettin, J. (2000). Recognition of asymmetric facial action units and intensities. *International Conference on Pattern Recognition*, Barcelona, Spain.

Fasel, B. & Luettin, J. (2003). Automatic facial expression analysis: a survey. *Pattern Recognition*, **36**, 259–75.

Forbes, E.E., Fox, N.A., Cohn, J.F., Galles, S.J., & Kovacs, M. (submitted) Children's affect regulation during a disappointment: psychophysiological characteristics, risk for depression, and behavior problems.

Frank, M.G. & Ekman, P. (1997). The ability to detect deceit generalizes across different types of high-stakes lies. *Journal of Personality and Social Psychology*, **72**, 1429–39.

Frank, M.G., Ekman, P., & Friesen, W.V. (1993). Behavioral markers and recognizability of the smile of enjoyment. *Journal of Personality and Social Psychology*, **64**, 83–93.

Fridlund, A.J. (1991). Sociality of solitary smiling: potentiation by an implicit audience. *Journal of Personality and Social Psychology*, **60**, 229–240.

Fridlund, A.J. & Cacioppo, J.T. (1986). Guidelines for human electromyographic research. *Psychophysiology*, **23**, 567–89.

Fridlund, A.J., Sabini, J.P., Hedlund, L.E., Schaut, J.A., Shenker, J.J., & Knauer, M.J. (1990). Audience effects on solitary faces during imagery: displaying to the people in your head. *Journal of Nonverbal Behavior*, **14**, 113–37.

Fridlund, A.J., Schwartz, G.E., & Fowler, S.C. (1984). Pattern recognition of self-reported emotional state from multiple-site facial EMG activity during affective imagery. *Psychophysiology*, 21, 622–37.

Frois–Wittmann, J. (1930). The judgment of facial expression. *Journal of Experimental Psychology*, 13, 113–51.

Fulcher, J.S. (1942). 'Voluntary' facial expression in blind and seeing children. *Archives of Psychology*, 38, 1–49.

Gerleman, D.G. & Cook, T.M. (1992). Instrumentation. In *Selected topics in surface electromyography for use in the occupational setting: expert perspectives* (ed. G.L. Soderberg), pp. 44–69). Washington, DC: U.S. Department of Health and Human Services.

Grant, N.B. (1969). Human facial expression. *Man*, 4, 525–36.

Gross, R., Matthews, I., & Baker, S. (2004). Generic vs. person specific AAMs. *British Machine Vision Conference*.

Hager, J.C. & Ekman, P. (1985). The asymmetry of facial actions is inconsistent with models of hemispheric specialization. *Psychophysiology*, 22, 307–18.

Harker, L. & Keltner, D. (2001). Expressions of positive emotion in women's college yearbook pictures and their relationship to personality and life outcomes across adulthood. *Journal of Personality and Social Psychology*, 80, 112–24.

Hess, U., Kappas, A., McHugo, G.J., Kleck, R.E., & Lanzetta, J.T. (1989). An analysis of the encoding and decoding of spontaneous and posed smiles: the use of facial electromyography. *Journal of Nonverbal Behavior*, 13, 121–35.

Hjorstjo, C.H. (1970). *Man's face and mimic language*. Lund: Studentlitterature.

Izard, C.E. (1979a). *Facial expression scoring manual (FESM)*. Newark, Delaware: University of Delaware.

Izard, C.E. (1979b). Personal communication.

Izard, C.E. (1983). *Maximally discriminative facial movement coding system (MAX)*.Unpublished manuscript, University of Delaware, Newark, Delaware.

Izard, C.E., & Dougherty, L.M. (1982). Two complementary systems for measuring facial expressions in infants and children. In C.E. Izard (Ed.), *Measuring emotions in infants and children*, 1, 97–126. New York: Cambridge University Press.

Izard, C.E., Hembree, E.A., Dougherty, L.M., & Spizzirri, C.C. (1983). Changes in facial expressions of 2 to 19-month-old infants following acute pain. *Developmental Psychology*, 19, 418–26. Unpublished manuscript, Instructional Resources Center, University of Delaware, Newark, Delaware.

Kaiser, S. & Wehrle, T. (1992). Automated coding of facial behavior in human-computer interactions with FACs. *Journal of Nonverbal Behavior*, 16, 67–84.

Kanade, T. (1973). *Picture processing system by computer complex and recognition of human faces*. Doctoral dissertation, Department of Electrical Engineering, University of Kyoto, Kyoto.

Kanade, T., Cohn, J.F., & Tian, Y. (2000). Comprehensive database for facial expression analysis. *IEEE Conference on Automatic Face and Gesture Recognition*, Grenoble, France pp. 46–53.

Krause, R. (1978). Nonverbales interaktives Verhalten von Stotterern. *Schweizrische Zeitschrift fur Psychologie und ihre Anwendugen*, 3, 16–31.

Kraut, R.E. & Johnson, R. (1979). Social and emotional messages of smiling: an ethological approach. *Journal of Personality and Social Psychology*, 37, 1539–53.

Landis, C. (1924). Studies of emotional reactions: II. General behavior and facial expression. *Journal of Comparative Psychology*, **4**, 447–509.

Landis, C., & Hunt, W.A. (1939). *The startle pattern*. New York: Holt, Rinehart & Winston.

Levenson, R.W., Ekman, P., & Friesen, W.V. (1990). Voluntary facial action generates emotion-specific autonomic nervous system activity. *Psychophysiology*, **27**, 363–84.

Lien, J.J.J., Kanade, T., Cohn, J.F., & Li, C.C. (2000). Detection, tracking, and classification of subtle changes in facial expression. *Journal of Robotics and Autonomous Systems*, **31**, 131–46.

Lightoller, G.H.S. (1925). Facial muscles: the modiolus and muscles surrounding the rima oris with some remarks about the panniculus adiposus. *Journal of Anatomy*, **60**, 1–85.

Littlewort, G., Bartlett, M.S., & Movellan, J.R. (2001). Are your eyes smiling? Detecting genuine smiles with support vector machines and Gabor wavelets. *Joint Symposium on Neural Computation*, 1–13, http://www.its.caltech.edu/~jsnc/2001/proceedings/

Liu, Y., Schmidt, K.L., Cohn, J.F., & Mitra, S. (2003). Facial asymmetry quantification for expression invariant human identification. *Computer Vision and Image Understanding*, **91**, 138–59.

Lyons, M., Akamasku, S., Kamachi, M., & Gyoba, J. (1998). Coding facial expressions with Gabor wavelets. *International Conference on Face and Gesture Recognition*, Nara, Japan.

Malatesta, C.Z., Culver, C., Tesman, J.R., & Shephard, B. (1989). The development of emotion expression during the first two years of life. *Monographs of the Society for Research in Child Development*, **54**.

Matias, R. & Cohn, J.F. (1993). Are max-specified infant facial expressions during face-to-face interaction consistent with differential emotions theory? *Developmental Psychology*, **29**, 524–31.

McGrew, W.C. (1972). *An ethological study of children's behavior*. New York: Academic Press.

McGurk, H. & MacDonald, J. (1976). Hearing lips and seeing voices. *Nature*, **26**, 746–8.

Mead, M. (1973). Review of Darwin and facial expression. *Journal of Communication*, **25**, 209–13.

Messinger, D., Acosta, S., Cassel, T., Ambadar, Z., & Cohn, J.F. (2004). *Automated measurement of infant expressions: are the dynamics emotional or facial*. International Society for Research in Emotion, New York, NY.

Miller, A.J. (1981/2). Electomyography in analysis of neuromuscular function. In *Hemifacial microsomia and other related craniofacial anomalies* (ed. E. Harvold). Cleft Palate Journal Monograph.

Moriyama, T., Kanade, T., & Cohn, J.F. (2004). Meticulously detailed eye model and its application to analysis of facial image. *IEEE Conference on Systems, Man, and Cybernetics*, The Hague, The Netherlands.

Nystrom, M. (1974). Neonatal facial-postural patterning during sleep: I. Description and reliability of observation. *Psychological Research Bulletin*, **14**, 1–16.

Oster, H. (1978). Facial expression and affect development. In *Affect development* (ed. M. Lewis & L.A. Rosenblum). New York: Plenum.

Oster, H. & Ekman, P. (1978). Facial behavior in child development. In *Minnesota Symposium on Child Development (Vol. 11)* (ed. A. Collins). Hillsdale, New Jersey: Erlbaum.

Oster, H. & Rosenstein, D. (undated). *Baby FACS: analyzing facial movement in infants*. Unpublished manuscript, New York, New York University.

Oster, H., Hegley, D., & Nagel, L. (1992). Adult judgments and fine-grained analysis of infant facial expressions: testing the validity of a priori coding formulas. *Developmental Psychology,* **28**, 1115–31.

Padgett, C. & Cottrell, G.W. (1998). A simple neural network model's categorical perception. *Cognitive Science Conference,* Madison, Wisconsin.

Pantic, M. & Rothkrantz, M. (2000*a*). Automatic analysis of facial expressions: the state of the art. *IEEE Transactions on Pattern Analysis and Machine Intelligence,* **22**, 1424–45.

Pantic, M. & Rothkrantz, M. (2000*b*). Expert system for automatic analysis of facial expression. *Image and Vision Computing,* **18**, 881–905.

Pantic, M. & Rothkrantz, M. (2003). Toward an affect-sensitive multimodal human–computer interaction. *Proceedings of the IEEE,* **91**, 1371–90.

Pantic, M. & Rothkrantz, M. (2004). Facial action recognition for facial expression analysis from static face images. *IEEE Transactions on Systems, Man, and Cybernetics. Part B: Cybernetics,* 1449–61.

Parke, F.I. & Waters, K. (1996). *Computer facial animation.* Wellesley, MA: A.K. Peters.

Sayette, M.A., Cohn, J.F., Wertz, J.M., Perrott, M.A., & Parrott, D.J. (2001). A psychometric evaluation of the Facial Action Coding System for assessing spontaneous expression. *Journal of Nonverbal Behavior,* **25**, 167–86.

Sayette, M.A., Smith, D.W., Breiner, M.J., & Wilson, G.T. (1992). The effect of alcohol on emotional response to a social stressor. *Journal of Studies on Alcohol,* **53**, 541–5.

Scherer, K.R. (1992). What does facial expression express? In *International Review of Studies on Emotion (Vol. 2)* (ed. K.T. Strongman), pp. 138–65. John Wiley & Sons Ltd.

Scherer, K.R., Zentner, M.R., & Stern, D. (2004). Beyond surprise: the puzzle of infants' expressive reactions to expectancy violation. *Emotion,* **4**, 389–402.

Schmidt, L.A. & Fox, N.A. (1998). Fear-potentiated startle responses in temperamentally different human infants. *Developmental Psychobiology,* **32**, 113–20.

Schmidt, K.L., Cohn, J.F., & Tian, Y. (2003). Signal characteristics of spontaneous facial expressions: automatic movement in solitary and social smiles. *Biological Psychology,* **65**, 49–66.

Schmidt, K.L., Tian, Y., & Cohn, J.F. (2003). The role of structural facial asymmetry in symmetry of peak facial expressions. *European Conference on Facial Expression, Measurement, and Meaning,* Rimini, Italy.

Soderberg, G.L. (ed.) (1992). *Selected topics in surface electromyography for use in the occupational setting: expert perspectives.* Washington, DC: National Institute for Occupational Health and Safety.

Tassinary, L.G. & Cacioppo, J.T. (1992). Unobservable facial actions and emotion. *Psychological Science,* **3**, 28–33.

Terzopoulos, D. & Waters, K. (1990). Analysis of facial images using physical and anatomical models. *IEEE International Conference on Computer Vision,* pp. 727–32.

Tian, Y., Cohn, J.F., & Kanade, T. (in press). Facial expression analysis. In *Handbook of face recognition* (ed. S.Z. Li & A.K. Jain). New York: Springer.

Tian, Y., Kanade, T., & Cohn, J.F. (2000). Eye-state detection by local regional information. *Advances in Multimodal Interfaces—ICMI 2000. Third International Conference,* Beijing, China, pp. 143–50.

Tian, Y., Kanade, T., & Cohn, J.F. (2001). Recognizing action units for facial expression analysis. *IEEE Transactions on Pattern Analysis and Machine Intelligence,* **23**, 97–115.

Tian, Y., Kanade, T., & Cohn, J.F. (2002). Evaluation of Gabor-wavelet-based facial action unit recognition in image sequences of increasing complexity. *Proceedings of the IEEE Conference on Automatic Face and Gesture Recognition*, pp. 229–34.

Tomkins, S.S. (1962). *Affect, imagery, consciousness*. New York: Springer.

Turk, M.A. & Pentland, A.P. (1991). Eigenfaces for recognition. *Journal of Cognitive Neuroscience*, 3, 71–86.

Valstar, M.F., Pantic, M., & Patras, I. (2004). Motion history for facial action detection in video. *Proceedings of the IEEE Conference on Systems, Man, and Cybernetics*, The Hague, The Netherlands.

Vrana, S.R. (1993). The psychophysiology of disgust: differentiating negative emotional contexts with facial EMG. *Psychophysiology*, 30, 279–86.

Wachtman, G.S., Cohn, J.F., VanSwearingen, J.M., & Manders, E.K. (2001). Automated tracking of facial features in patients with facial neuromuscular dysfunction. *Plastic and Reconstructive Surgery*, 7, 1124–33.

Wu, Y.T., Kanade, T., Li, C.C., & Cohn, J.F. (2000). Image registration using wavelet-based motion model. *International Journal of Computer Vision*, 38, 129–52.

Xiao, J., Baker, S., Matthews, I., & Kanade, T. (2004). Real-time combined 2D+3D active appearance models. *Proceedings of the IEEE Conference on Computer Vision and Pattern Recognition*, Washington D.C., 535–542.

Xiao, J., Kanade, T., & Cohn, J.F. (2003). Robust full motion recovery of head by dynamic templates and re-registration techniques. *International Journal of Imaging Systems and Technology*, 13, 85–94.

Yacoob, Y. & Davis, L. (1997). Recognizing human facial expression from long image sequence using optical flow. *IEEE Transactions on Pattern Analysis and Machine Intelligence*, 18, 636–42.

Young, G. & Decarie, T.G. (1977). An ethology-based catalogue of facial/vocal behaviors in infancy. *Animal Behavior*, 25, 95–107.

Appendix: How the facial action, brow raise, is described in each of the 14 measurement techniques

Birdwhistell

Raised brows.

Blurton Jones

A very conspicuous movement of raising the eyebrows which can be rather difficult to judge on photographs because of the individual variations in the resting position of the brows. One or more of the following criteria could apply:

(a) The height of the brow above the eye corner appears to be equal or more than the width of the open eye (Blurton Jones 1971, Fig. 3a—measure B equal or greater than A).
(b) Horizontal lines visible across the forehead above the brows.
(c) There is an enlarged area between the brow and the eyelids which is often highlighted (very pale) in photographs.

(d) There is a less sharp fall from the brow into the eye socket (orbit) because the brow is raised beyond the edge of the orbit which it normally covers. Therefore, there is less shadow between brow and eye than usual.

(e) The shape of the eyebrows change, becoming more curved when they are raised (but they are not curved when the brows are slanted or oblique as well as raised).

Brow raising is presumably a result of contraction of the frontal belly of the occipto-frontalis, which can occur simultaneously with corrugator or orbicularis occuli contraction. Thus, many oblique brows were also scored as raised.

Brannigan & Humphries

One or both eyebrows are raised and are held, at least briefly, in the raised position. They are not drawn in towards the midline and are not tilted.

Grant

The eyebrows are raised and stop in the raised position for an appreciable time (see Grant 1969, Plate 10A).

Flash. A quick raising and lower of eyebrows.

These two elements are very similar in use. They seem to have an attractive function, drawing the attention of the other person to the face. They are concerned with regulation and timing of speech.

Nystrom

Horizontal wrinkles.

Elevated brows.

(*Note*: These are listed by Nystrom as separate scoring items in his technique.)

Young & Decarie

Brow raise stare—

Brow: the eyebrows are raised and held giving them a curved appearance and creating horizontal creases on the brow. There is no inward movement of the eyebrows and no vertical furrow. Eyes: the eyes may be held wide open but not sparkling, wrinkling at the corners and forming pouching under the eyes. Blinking may be decelerated, and the head is definitely held in its regular forward position. Visual fixation on a specific target is characteristic of this expression. Mouth: as in normal face.

Other: as in normal face.

(*Note*: Young & Decarie present this as a total face score. No provision is made for scoring if the brow raise action occurs without the eye action or with some other mouth action.)

Ekman, Friesen, and Tomkins

(*Note*: Two photographs depict this scoring item. The authors' Facial Affect Scoring Technique contains only visual, not verbal, descriptions.)

Izard: MAX (Maximally Discriminative Facial Movement Coding System)

Code 20: the brows are raised in their normal shape. The forehead shows some thickening and the tissue under the eyebrows some thinning out as a result of the eyebrows being raised. The thickening or massing of tissue in the forehead gives way to long transverse furrows with increasing age. The nasal root is narrowed. The skin directly below the eyebrows is stretched upward.

Code 21: one brow is lifted higher than the other.

Code 30: the eyes have a widened and roundish appearance. The furrow above the eyelashes of the upper lid may be visible. The widened, roundish appearance of the eyes is brought about mainly by the eyebrow raise of code 20 that lifts and stretches the tissue between the eyebrow and the eyelid. The upper eyelid is not raised. The artist's drawing for 20 also illustrates 30.

(*Note*: Izard furnishes video examples of this action in addition to the artist's drawing.)

Ekman, Friesen, and Hager: FACS (Facial Action Coding System, 2002 version)

Action unit (AU) combination 1+2

(*Note*: This section on brow raise from the FACS manual is preceded in the manual by separate sections on the two components of this action—AU 1 (inner brow raise) and AU 2 (outer brow raise). All sections include still and video examples not included in this Appendix.)

Appearance changes due to AU combination 1+2

The combination of these two action units raises the inner (AU 1) and the outer (AU 2) corners of the eyebrows, producing changes in appearance which are the product of their joint action.

1. Pulls the entire eyebrow (medial to lateral parts) upwards.
2. Produces an arched, curved appearance to the shape of the eyebrow.
3. Bunches the skin in the forehead so that horizontal wrinkles appear across the entire forehead. The wrinkles may not appear in infants, children, and a few adults.
4. Stretches the eye cover fold so that it is more apparent.
5. In some people (those with deeply set eyes), the stretching of the eye cover fold reveals their upper eyelid, which usually is concealed by the eye cover fold.

In the FACS manual, compare the image 1+2 with image 0; inspect the video of AUs 1+2.

How to do AU combination 1+2

(*Note*: FACS teaches learners how to perform each action so that they can utilize their own facial actions to understand the mechanics and appearance of the face.)

This behavior should be easy for you to do. Simply lift your eyebrows up, both ends as high as you can. Note the wrinkling in your forehead. In some people the wrinkling does not occur but the skin is still bunched up. In some people these wrinkles are permanently etched (see 0 and w0) but they deepen noticeably when 1+2 acts. Suppress any tendency you may also have to lift your upper eyelid (AU 5) when performing 1+2. Make sure you are not pulling your brows together (AU 4) when you lift them.

Intensity scoring for AU combination 1+2

The criteria for AU 1 and those for AU 2 are altered significantly in this combination from the criteria for each alone. Do not use Section C for AUs 1 and 2, you must use the criteria listed below for the total configuration 1+2. The criteria for intensity scoring are described for roughly equal intensities of AUs 1 and 2. Of course, any combination of intensities of AUs 1 and 2 can occur in action unit combination 1+2, and to score these intensities (e.g. 1B+2C), you must consider the relative contribution of the separate AUs in the combination you score against the criteria listed below. When considering whether AU 2 is present when the action of AU 1 is clearly evident, be sure that any lifting of the outer eyebrows is not due merely to the action of AU 1 alone, as can occur with stronger AU 1s.

AUs 1A+2A in AU combination 1+2
The appearance changes for AUs 1+2 are sufficiently present to indicate AU 1+2, but are insufficient to score 1B+2B (e.g. the entire brow is raised a *trace*).

AUs 1B+2B in AU combination 1+2

1. Entire brow raised *slightly*.

   If you did not see the brows move it must also meet the additional criteria:

2. *Slight* horizontal wrinkles or muscle bunching reaching across forehead. If horizontal wrinkles are evident in the neutral face, change from the neutral appearance must be *slight*. (If you are scoring the face of an infant or child who never shows forehead wrinkles with AUs 1+2 or 1+2+4, then the wrinkling criterion needs to be discounted, and you must rely on the other criteria.)

   and

3. *Slightly* more exposure of eye cover fold than in neutral.

   or

4. If there is no wrinkling or bunching in the brow, but the brow raise and exposure of the eye cover fold is *marked*, you can score 1+2.

   AU 1C+2C in AU combination 1+2
   Entire brow is raised at least *markedly*, but less than for level 1D+2D. Wrinkling and eye cover fold exposure should both be evident and at least one should be at least *marked*, but the evidence is less than the criteria for 1D+2D.

   AU 1D+2D in AU combination 1+2
   Entire brow is raised at least *severely*. Wrinkling and eye cover fold exposure should both be evident and at least one should be at least *severe*, but the evidence is less than the criteria for 1E+2E.

   AU 1E+2E in AU combination 1+2
   The entire brow is raised *maximally*.

Frois–Wittmann

Brows raised.

Fulcher

Frontalis—which raises the brows wrinkling the forehead transversely.

Ermiane & Gergerian

Frontalis: the eyebrow levator. Externalized emotionality.
  (Raises the eyebrows.)
  Letting himself go to an impression.
  (*Note*: A few photographic illustrations show this action.)

Landis

Frontalis: this is the vertical sheet muscle of the forehead, the contraction of which produces transverse wrinkles ('the wrinkled brow').

CHAPTER 3

VOCAL EXPRESSION OF AFFECT

PATRIK N. JUSLIN AND KLAUS R. SCHERER

Introduction

Imagine yourself sitting in a cafeteria. Suddenly, you can overhear another person's conversation without being able to see the person in question. Within a few seconds of hearing that person's voice, you are able to infer the person's gender (a female), age (a young woman), and perhaps even her origin (from the south), social status (upper class), and physical health (having a cold). All this you can tell from hearing her voice, even though you are unable to understand the verbal contents of her conversation. Perhaps most importantly, through an immediate and seemingly effortless process of inference, you can obtain a rather precise impression of the woman's affective state, for example, irritation, anxiety, or cheerfulness.

Inferences about affective states and intentions from voice cues are fallible, but they are valid often enough to make your social life easier. They help you to navigate the complex terrain of social interactions that pervade everyday life. Effective action in social relationships requires an understanding of the covert psychological processes that underlie people's overt behavior and the environmental circumstances to which they are responding. We want to understand what people are trying to do and why. Any means that help us to achieve this goal is valuable.

The human voice is a common and ecologically important sound structure of our auditory environment. People may spend more time listening to voices than to any other type of sound (Belin *et al.* 2002). Judging from the results of self-report studies, relying on voice cues (e.g. volume, speed of talking) could actually be the most common way in which people infer other people's emotions in everyday life (Planalp 1998). Cross-cultural research confirms that people express emotions by screaming, yelling, speaking with a trembling voice, or using a low, quiet, slow, and monotonous voice (e.g. Wallbott *et al.* 1986). Hence, the voice is sometimes referred to as 'the mirror to our soul' (Sundberg 1998, p. 121). However, it has long been recognized that people also may use their voice to *influence* others. For instance, they may want to change someone else's opinion, communicate emotion to obtain support, create a certain impression, deflect criticism, or reinforce social bonds (Planalp 1998; Scherer 1985; see also Darwin 1872/1998). Thus, besides being an interesting topic in its own right, perception of emotions from voice cues serves as an important mediating factor for many other social phenomena (Zebrowitz 1990).

Understanding how the voice can be used to express and communicate emotions, and how people make inferences about emotions based on voice cues, is a fascinating but surprisingly difficult endeavor that falls under the purview of the study of *vocal expression*. In this chapter, vocal expression refers to qualities of speech apart from the actual verbal content. These aspects are usually referred to as *paralinguistic* or *nonverbal*, and they are nicely captured by the well-known phrase, 'It's not *what* she said, it's *how* she said it'. Speech researchers still debate the extent to which verbal and nonverbal aspects can be neatly separated, though that there is some degree of independence is illustrated by the fact that people often perceive 'mixed messages' in speech utterances—that is, that the words convey one thing, but the nonverbal cues convey something quite different (e.g. Bugental 1974). Indeed, it is one of the characteristic features of vocal affect expression that an evolutionarily old nonverbal signal system, coded in an iconic and continuous fashion, carries and intermeshes with verbal messages that are coded in an arbitrary and categorical fashion (Scherer 1982; Scherer *et al.* 1984). This interrelatedness, while contributing to the power of speech as a communication system, has had the consequence that many nonverbal communication researchers have regarded vocal expression as determined mainly by the rules of the language code, whereas many linguists have tended to ban nonverbal characteristics from their study. One can easily get the impression that nonverbal communication is 'after all a residual topic and that once orthodox language has been subtracted all that is left is a rubbish heap of nudges, shrugs, pouts, sighs, winks, and glances' (Miller 1990, p. 115). Yet, it has been recognized by philosophers and linguists that speech acts convey considerable meaning over and above the literal meaning of verbal content (Caffi & Janney 1994).

Largely neglected by language researchers, vocal expression research has often been the poor cousin of facial expression research, perhaps because in many people's eyes, *emotional expression* is nearly synonymous with *facial expression* (Planalp 1998). Research on facial expression has been highly successful (see Chapter 2), and there is some evidence suggesting that in humans, visual information may be more effective than auditory information (e.g. Burns & Beier 1973; Levitt 1964; Zaidel & Mehrabian 1969). Hence, the vocal channel has been somewhat overshadowed by the facial channel. Yet, the two channels share a number of similarities: faces and voices are similar in that both are characterized by a constrained physical structure, around which inter- and intra-individual variations convey information about the person's identity and emotional state, as well as linguistic information (Belin *et al.* 2002, p. 25). Like the face, the voice may convey discrete emotions such as anger and sadness reliably to a perceiver (Juslin & Laukka 2003), and it may even convey some emotions with cross-cultural accuracy (Elfenbein & Ambady 2002; Scherer *et al.* 2001a; see also p. 108).

However, there are also some important differences between the face and the voice, which renders each channel unique. Firstly, each channel has its advantages as well as drawbacks. For example, vocal expression may be more effective than facial expression over large distances (it is less sensitive to obstacles) and in dim light, whereas facial expression may be more effective than vocal expression in crowds of people where visual signals are easier to locate (Marler 1977).

Secondly, whereas facial expression seems to involve an elaborate spatial coding of visual features, whose configurations can be grasped almost instantly (and that can be 'frozen' in time without losing all vital information), vocal expression may be relatively more time-dependent, featuring a set of relatively independent cues that contribute, in an additive fashion, to emotion judgments (see p. 84). The fact that different emotions can be inferred with differential accuracy from the voice and the face (Scherer 1999) also suggests important differences in the nature of the underlying coding systems. The idea that the face and the voice involve different types of coding could perhaps be evoked to defend the (otherwise) unfortunate, and somewhat artificial, separation of the two channels, which seem to affect real-life emotion judgments in a complementary and integrated fashion (de Gelder 2000).

Thirdly, some authors have argued that vocal affect expression is particularly effective in producing 'emotional contagion' in perceivers (Eibl–Eibesfeldt 1989, p. 691; Lewis 2000, p. 270). One explanation could be that hearing is the perceptual modality that develops first. In fact, because hearing is functional even prior to birth, some associations among acoustic patterns and affective states may reflect prenatal experiences (Mastropieri & Turkewitz 1999).

Finally, whereas the face is strongly related to the visual arts, the voice is strongly related to music (e.g. Darwin 1872/1998; Spencer 1857), rendering it feasible to import research methods from voice research to music research, and vice versa (Juslin & Laukka 2003; Juslin & Sloboda 2001; Scherer 1995).

In order to understand current research on vocal expression, it is useful to consider its origin. Nonverbal aspects of speech have been discussed throughout most of Western intellectual history as one aspect of rhetorical techniques (Kennedy 1972). Modern research on vocal expression has seen peaks and troughs since its beginnings in the late 19th century, when the first recording and analysis systems were being developed. Early interest in how the voice reveals affect was mainly motivated by psychiatrists' attempts to diagnose various emotional disturbances (Scripture 1921; Skinner 1935), although a number of early efforts were also made to develop novel methods of measuring the emotional states of astronauts on space travel based on speech samples (Williams & Stevens 1969). Studies of vocal expression peaked during German 'expression psychology' (Helfrich & Wallbott 1986), only to decrease during the heyday of behaviorism and the advent of cognitive psychology. Since then, the field has been relatively fragmented, reflecting both that researchers have lacked theoretical frameworks (but see Scherer 1986, for one attempt) and that vocal expression is a multidisciplinary research field with contributions coming from psychology, acoustics, speech science, linguistics, medicine, engineering, and computer science.

Unfortunately, studies in different disciplines are not always easily integrated. For instance, there are differences between psychological and linguistic approaches to affect in speech in terms of both definitions and focus. While linguists may argue that psychologists do not take language and interaction into consideration, psychologists may retort that linguists stay psychologically uninformed and focus too much on ill-defined concepts such as 'involvement' (Caffi & Janney 1994). Another difficult issue is the study of prosody and intonation, as a large number of highly intertwined cues (pitch, amplitude, pauses, rhythm, etc.) carry syntactic, semantic, and pragmatic information (including affect and relational discourse structure). Given the complexity of these issues, we cannot discuss them in this chapter (for overviews, see Bänziger & Scherer, in press; Scherer *et al.* 2003). Another issue we cannot discuss in the current chapter, which focuses mainly on voice rather than speech style, is the set of variables linked to speech delivery, in particular disfluencies such as silent and filled pauses, false starts, hesitations, repetitions, and self-repair. While such disfluencies can be produced as a consequence of affective arousal, many other factors may be involved. In consequence, these phenomena have not been consistently studied in the literature on emotional expression. Overviews can be found in Feldstein and Siegman (1987).

After a promising start, during which certain vocal correlates to emotional arousal were established (Davitz 1964), the domain has stagnated, unable to resolve the debate on whether different emotions have different vocal profiles or whether the voice only conveys information about the speaker's arousal. Part of the problem has been the lack of differentiation and clear definitions of affective phenomena (but see Box 3.1 for proposed working definitions of different affective phenomena), and a general tendency to concentrate on just a few emotion categories or dimensions (see Module A). Another problem is that the domain has lacked systematic, long-term research programs. Only recently, as the affective sciences have gained a stronger foothold (e.g. Davidson *et al.* 2003), has research on vocal expression surged once again (e.g. Cowie *et al.* 2000). The number of studies devoted to vocal expression of different emotions in the 1990s represented more than a three-fold increase compared with the number of similar studies in the 1980s (Juslin & Laukka 2003). Given this renewed interest, it seems useful to take stock of what previous research has generated in terms of improved methodology and new empirical findings, so as to set the stage for continued fruitful research on this topic. This brings us to the aims of the present chapter.

The aims of this chapter are manifold. First, it is intended as a general introduction to the field for the newcomer. Thus, the chapter offers hands-on information on how to conduct studies of vocal affect expression. Second, we hope to contribute to increased cumulativeness and comparability across studies, for instance with respect to definitions, classification categories, methods, and reporting. Third, we want to highlight new developments in the field that have occurred since a previous chapter on this subject was written (Scherer 1982). There has actually been reasonable progress on several issues, and it is crucial that future research proceeds from the current state of the art. Fourth, we hope to encourage using the voice as a tool in testing emotion theories. Fifth, we want to offer the reader examples of applications in various practical domains that involve vocal affect expression. Finally, and perhaps most importantly, the aim of the chapter is inspirational: throughout the text, we will try to convey the enthusiasm we have for this field of study.

In our attempt to achieve these aims, we have opted for a chapter structure of a somewhat unusual kind. The chapter consists of a main text, which is interspersed with *boxes* (background material) and *modules* (practical guidelines) on particular topics that we refer to in the main text. We hope this will make it easier for the reader to quickly locate relevant information. The first section offers theoretical foundations. The following two sections focus on voice cues to affect and affect inferences from voice cues. In attempting such a broad review, it is difficult to avoid simplifying many

Box 3.1:   Working definition for affective phenomena

In this chapter, we discuss methods to analyze vocal behavior as a marker of affective processes. Although many of the techniques discussed are rather general, and could be equally applied to examine the specific voice qualities of individual speakers to determine age (Hummert *et al.* 1999) or other speaker characteristics (Brown *et al.* 1975), the focus here will be on changes in the voice that occur as a concomitant of affect. Consequently, it seems useful to briefly define the different types of affective processes that may occur. This is all the more necessary since there is a strong tendency in the field to use terms such as affect, mood, emotion, and feeling as virtually synonymous. As a result, there is a great deal of confusion, and many debates in the field could simply reflect that protagonists are using the same terms to refer to different phenomena.

We suggest using *affect* as a general, umbrella term that subsumes a variety of phenomena such as emotion, stress, mood, interpersonal stance, and affective personality traits. All of these states, which we will differentially define below, share a special affective quality that sets them apart from 'neutral' states. The root of the word 'affect' contains the most important element defining the difference: during an affective state, the person is 'affected' by something (e.g. an event, a thought, a social relationship, or a long-term behavior disposition) which has a consistent influence on the person's motivation, thought processes, physiology, and behavior (in particular, motor expression). These influences make the affective episode stand out from neutral, baseline states, both in the subjective experience of the person and in the perception of this person by an observer. Moreover, there are medium or long-term predispositions to act in affectively valenced fashion. For example, one might adopt an interpersonal stance in interacting with another person (e.g. hostility) or have a certain affective personality trait (e.g. neuroticism).

As shown in Table 3.1, one could use seven dimensions to differentiate different kinds of affective state in what is called a design-feature approach (e.g. Scherer 2000). The first three dimensions describe the nature of the affective reaction—its *intensity* and *duration* as well as the degree of *synchronization*; that is, how much the individual organismic systems are deflected from their normal functioning and work in a more coordinated fashion to adapt to a new situation or an emergency. Other discriminating dimensions are concerned with the type of elicitors that can bring about the respective state. Thus, *event focus* refers to the likelihood of the affect state being triggered by a specific object, event, or situation, as opposed to a strategic decision of the individual or a permanently existing personality disposition. *Appraisal elicitation* refers to the degree to which the type of reaction is due to the subjective evaluation of the significance of the event to a person, given momentary motives and goals or more long-term values. Finally, *rapidity of change* refers to how quickly the state can change (onset, offset, and change in quality), whereas *behavior impact* refers to the strength of the impact of the respective affect state on physiological responses, motor expression, and action tendencies.

Continued

Box 3.1: Cont'd

The distinction in Table 3.1 suggests three broad classes of affective states:

1. emotions and stress
2. moods and interpersonal stances
3. preferences/attitudes and affect dispositions (e.g. personality).

Emotions and stress are quite short but intense reactions to specific events of high pertinence to the individual. They produce reactions that entail a high degree of synchronization of all the subsystems; that is, coordinated changes in cognition, physiological arousal, motor expression, and motivational urge. These reactions are generally powerful and have a strong impact on behavior. On the other hand, they are likely to change very rapidly (e.g. due to a re-appraisal of the situation). Most research on vocal affect expression has focused on these two classes of affect, in particular stress due to workload or time pressure (e.g. Hecker *et al.* 1968; Tolkmitt & Scherer 1987), and emotions such as anger, fear, sadness, happiness, and disgust (e.g. Juslin & Laukka 2001; Murray & Arnott 1995; Scherer *et al.* 1991; see Module A, Table 3.4).

Moods and interpersonal stances are rarely generated by specific events or objects, and are not usually based on appraisal. Moods may occur for many different reasons, often unknown to the individual, triggered by factors such as fatigue, hormonal influences, or even the weather. Interpersonal stance refers to the affective style in which a person interacts with someone else, for instance in a cold and distant as compared to a warm and friendly fashion. Such stances, which may be adopted quite intentionally or may reflect an unconscious interpersonal attitude, usually last throughout an interaction episode or characterize the relationship between two individuals. For both of these affect states, which may last for hours or days and change only slowly, intensity is low, organismic subsystems are not highly synchronized, and the impact on behavior varies from weak to average. While perhaps more frequent than emotions (Cowie & Cornelius 2003) and often occurring in public situations, these states are rarely investigated regarding voice cues. This is possibly due to the lower intensity and the absence of strong physiological arousal, which may seem less promising in discovering strong voice effects (see p. 81). However, there is increasing evidence that speech style, as part of a particular interpersonal stance adopted in a particular situation, could have a powerful effect on the voice. For instance, Scherer *et al.* (1984) found that voice qualities judged as specific to a 'polite' style of speech were more resistant than other affective states to various kinds of manipulation.

Finally, preferences/attitudes are long-term affective evaluations of objects or persons that have a low intensity and relatively little impact on behavior, because situational factors are often stronger determinants of behavior (Scherer 2000). Little is known about the vocal correlates of the expression of such attitudes. There is more evidence on vocal markers of long-term affective predispositions or personality traits (e.g. Scherer 1979; Scherer & Scherer 1981), which are characterized by very low affective intensity, very low synchronization, and a behavioral impact which is usually felt only in interaction with situational variables. There is also a lot of work on vocal indicators of affective disorders that reflect short- to medium-length

Continued

Table 3.1 Design feature delimitation of different affective states (adapted from Scherer 2000)

	Intensity	Duration	Synchronization	Event focus	Appraisal elicitation	Rapidity of change	Behavior impact
Emotions: angry, sad, joyful, fearful, ashamed, proud, elated, desperate	large	small	large	large	large	large	large
Stress: tense, stressed, strained	large	medium	large	medium	large	medium	medium
Moods: cheerful, gloomy, irritable, listless, depressed, buoyant	small	medium	medium	small	small	medium	medium
Interpersonal stances: distant, cold, warm, supportive, contemptuous	medium	medium	small	small	small	large	medium
Preferences/attitudes: liking, valueing, desiring	medium	large	small	small	small	medium	medium
Affect dispositions: neurotic, habitually anxious, reckless, morose, hostile	small	large	small	small	small	small	medium

Note: Small dot = absent to low; medium dot = low to medium; large dot = medium to high.

Box 3.1: Cont'd

---

personality changes, in particular depression (e.g. Darby 1981; Ellgring & Scherer 1996; Kuny & Stassen 1993).

Although we will mention many of the different types of affective state in this chapter, the emphasis will be on stress and emotions. While stress is usually measured as a one-dimensional construct (although one could argue that there is not one type of stress but that each emotion can occur in a stressed variant e.g. anger stress, fear stress; Scherer 1990), there is considerable disagreement about how emotion should be conceptualized. Proponents of the *discrete emotions* approach (Ekman 1999; Izard 1993) argue that one should distinguish among a limited number of 'basic emotions' (following Darwin 1872/1998 and Tomkins 1962). This approach, which assumes emotion-specific patterning for vocal as well as facial and physiological responding, has strongly influenced research on vocal expression, and most studies in the field have attempted to identify vocal profiles for a certain number of such basic emotions (Juslin & Laukka 2003). This is also true for recent research in speech technology (Cowie *et al.* 2001).

In recent studies, however, many researchers have instead adopted a *dimensional* approach (e.g. Bachorowski 1999; Laukka *et al.*, in press; Schröder *et al.* 2001) that defines affective states as points in a two-dimensional space formed by *valence* (pleasant/unpleasant) and *activation* (aroused/sleepy) dimensions (Russell 1980; Russell & Feldman Barrett 1999). This approach involves traditional expectations about how arousal might affect the voice, but there has been little effort to understand the underlying mechanisms.

A third approach has been suggested by Scherer (1984), who argues that bodily expression, including the voice, is driven by the nature of the cognitive appraisal. Thus, Scherer (1986), in his *component process theory*, proposed a set of detailed predictions of vocal (and acoustic) changes based on the physiological effects of particular appraisal outcomes. (Examples of each of these theoretical approaches are provided in pp. 88–92.)

---

complex issues and omitting certain aspects of the topics discussed. However, throughout the chapter, we will continually provide references for further reading.

Theoretical foundations of vocal affect expression

The paradigm outlined in this section is partly based on Egon Brunswik's (1956) theory of perception. Reading this section may offer a better understanding of the reasons why we tend to recommend some research designs rather than others in later sections. Indeed, one of the crucial insights of the Brunswikian paradigm is that research methods should not be considered separate from their subject matter. Brunswik proceeded from a consideration of *biological function* in a particular *environment* to a description of a *psychological process* that reflects and exploits that environment. Then, he developed a *methodology* that matched the specific characteristics of this environment–mechanism relationship (Gigerenzer 2001).

Brunswik's paradigm is highly suitable for the study of vocal expression for three reasons. First, it takes an evolutionary perspective on human behavior, which implies a focus on the relationship between the organism and its ecology. Because the voice could be the most phylogenetically continuous of all nonverbal channels, it is useful to try to understand vocal expression in terms of a 'solution' to a certain adaptive problem in a particular environment.[1] Secondly, Brunswik's theory is a so-called *cue theory*, according to which perceivers make 'unconscious inferences' about objects or states of affairs on the basis of a set of fallible cues in the environment. Because this scenario seems to apply to inferences from voice cues, Brunswik's theory offers important insights that can help us to explain some of the peculiar characteristics of the vocal channel. Finally, Brunswik's theory involves a methodology (the lens model, representative design) that, we argue, is particularly suited to the study of vocal expression, and that offers a promising avenue towards a better understanding of vocal expression of affect. Each of these three aspects will be considered in turn.

Evolutionary perspectives

There seems to be wide agreement among researchers about the pertinence of evolutionary approaches to an understanding of vocal affect expression (e.g. Juslin & Laukka 2003; Owren & Bachorowski 2001; Papoušek *et al.* 1992; Scherer 1985). Vocal expression may be construed as an evolved psychological mechanism that serves crucial functions in social interaction: expression of emotions allows individuals to communicate important information to others, which may influence their behavior; recognition of emotions allows individuals to make quick inferences about the probable intentions and behavior of others (e.g. Buck 1984, Chap. 2; Plutchik 1994; Chap. 10). Because speech is a relatively recent addition to the human repertoire of communication systems, it is highly likely that our speechless forefathers had to make do, for millennia, with the same nonverbal signaling systems used by most nonhuman species (Scherer 1982). Consequently, we may learn a lot about vocal expression by considering its origins.

Many animals use sounds as a means of communication (e.g. Busnel 1977; Scherer 1985; Snowdon 2003), and following Darwin's (1872/1998) seminal work, many researchers of vocal communication have assumed that there is phylogenetic continuity of vocal expression (e.g. Papoušek *et al.* 1992). Ploog (1992) described the morphological transformation of the larynx, from a pure respiratory organ (in lungfish) to a respiratory organ with a limited vocal capability (in amphibians, reptiles, and lower mammals), and, finally, to the sophisticated instrument that humans use to speak in an emotionally expressive manner. The function of an organism's vocal behavior reflects both *physical* and *ecological constraints*.

Physical constraints include the actual physiological mechanism producing the sounds. The range of sound emission organs found in animals is large, and such organs

---

[1] This is in accordance with Brunswik's (1956) principle of behavior-research isomorphy: *research should focus where behavior focuses*. That is, to understand an organism's behavior in a particular context, we must understand the ultimate goals of its behavior.

may be located on all different parts of the body. However, in many higher vertebrates, specialized vocalization organs are found, usually working by means of propelled or aspirated air in a more or less differentiated tube equipped with modulating membranes or slit systems (e.g. vocal cords). These mechanisms often have additional organs, *resonators*, that amplify certain sound frequencies (Busnel 1977). This basic principle of *sound source* and *filter* (or resonator) applies to human voice production as well (see Box 3.2). For many lower animals, the form of the acoustic signal is a close physical expression of the mechanical structure that produces the sound, but higher

---

Box 3.2: Voice production and speech acoustics

Audible speech consists of sound waves produced through the processes of respiration, phonation, and articulation. Advanced measurement of vocal affect expression requires basic knowledge about voice and speech production and speech acoustics to interpret the meaning of various acoustic parameters extracted from the sound waves. In this box, basic principles of voice production and speech acoustics are introduced. For a more detailed discussion of these topics, the reader is referred to classic textbooks in this field (e.g. Borden *et al.* 1994; Denes & Pinson 1993; Kent 1997; Ladefoged 1993; O'Shaughnessy 2000).

Basic acoustic phenomena and parameters

Simple wave forms: amplitude and frequency. The simplest case is the sinusoidal wave form shown in Fig. 3.1a, produced by a vibrating sound source such as a tuning fork, graphed here as the periodic variation of sound pressure amplitude (on the y axis) over time (x axis). Because amplitude (a correlate of the perceived loudness of the sound) is always one of the terms used in displaying properties of wave forms, this type of description is referred to as display in the *time domain*. Sinusoidal wave forms oscillate in a regular, periodic fashion, going through complete cycles. The number of cycles per second indicates the periodicity or *frequency* of the wave, as measured in Hertz (Hz). The wave form can also be displayed in the *frequency domain* by an amplitude-by-frequency plot—the *spectrum*—which shows the maximal amplitude of the wave form at its specific frequency in the frequency range (see Fig. 3.1 f). In the spectrum display, amplitude is usually plotted logarithmically in decibels (dB) relative to the threshold of hearing and is referred to as the *energy* of the wave at its respective frequency. Figures 3.1b and 3.1g show a sine wave that has a higher frequency and a lower amplitude than that in Fig. 3.1a.

Complex wave forms: spectral decomposition. Most sound waves are much more complex than the simple sinusoid in Fig. 3.1a, but as the French mathematician Fourier has shown, it is possible to decompose any complex wave into sinusoid components (via Fourier analysis; e.g. Morrison 1994). In the example shown in Fig. 3.1, the complex wave (c) consists of the sinusoidal components (a) and (b), which differ in frequency and amplitude. Consequently, the spectrum of the complex wave (h) shows the *relative energy* of the two sinusoidal components at their respective frequencies.

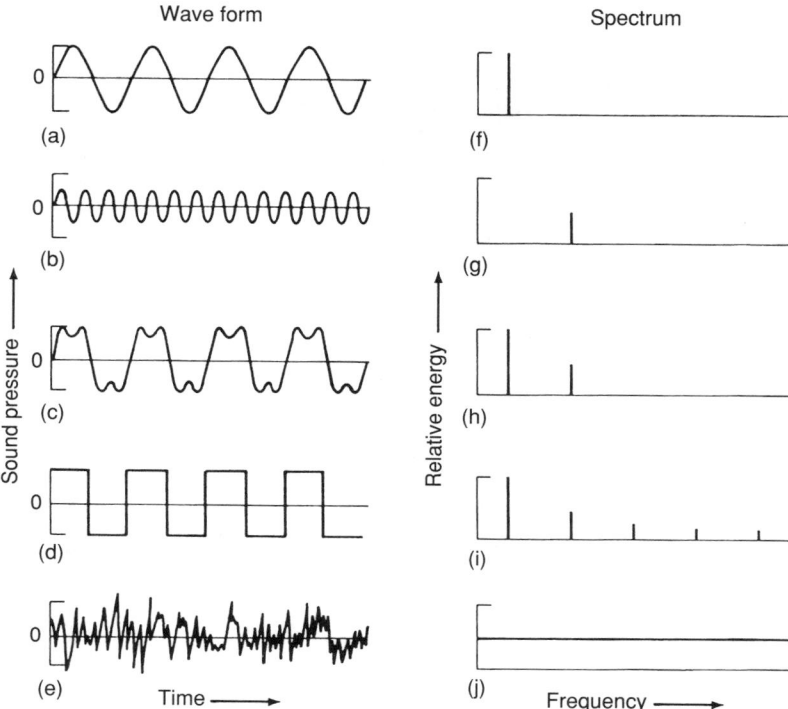

Figure 3.1 Wave forms and their spectra: (a, f) low-frequency sine wave; (b, g) high-frequency sine wave; (c, h) complex wave form–composite of (a, f) and (b, g); (d, i) square wave; (e, j) noise (see Box 3.2 for further explanation).

Fundamental frequency and harmonics. As shown in Fig. 3.1c, the periodicity of the complex wave form as a whole (the number of cycles per second) is determined by the sinusoidal component with the lowest frequency—the *fundamental frequency* (*F0*). This frequency roughly corresponds to what a listener perceives as the *pitch* of the sound. The higher-order components of complex waves are called *harmonics* (or overtones); they occur at frequencies that are integral multiples of the fundamental frequency. For example, a complex wave with F0 = 100 Hz can be decomposed into constituent sinusoids with frequencies of 200, 300, 400, and so on, representing energy concentrations in the frequency domain, as illustrated in the spectrum of the wave form in Fig. 3.1d. As the spectrum in Fig. 3.1i suggests, the relative energy of the higher harmonics decreases over the frequency range, and the slope of the harmonic spectrum is called *spectral tilt*.

Speech wave forms. Figure 3.2 shows a typical wave form (or time signal) for speech—the utterance 'she had been sad'. As the zoomed portion of the waveform (the word 'she') shows, the speech signal consists of a sequence of quasi-periodic and non-periodic portions. Quasi-periodic portions correspond to *voiced sounds* (based on vocal fold vibration); for example, vowels and consonants such as glides (i.e.

Continued

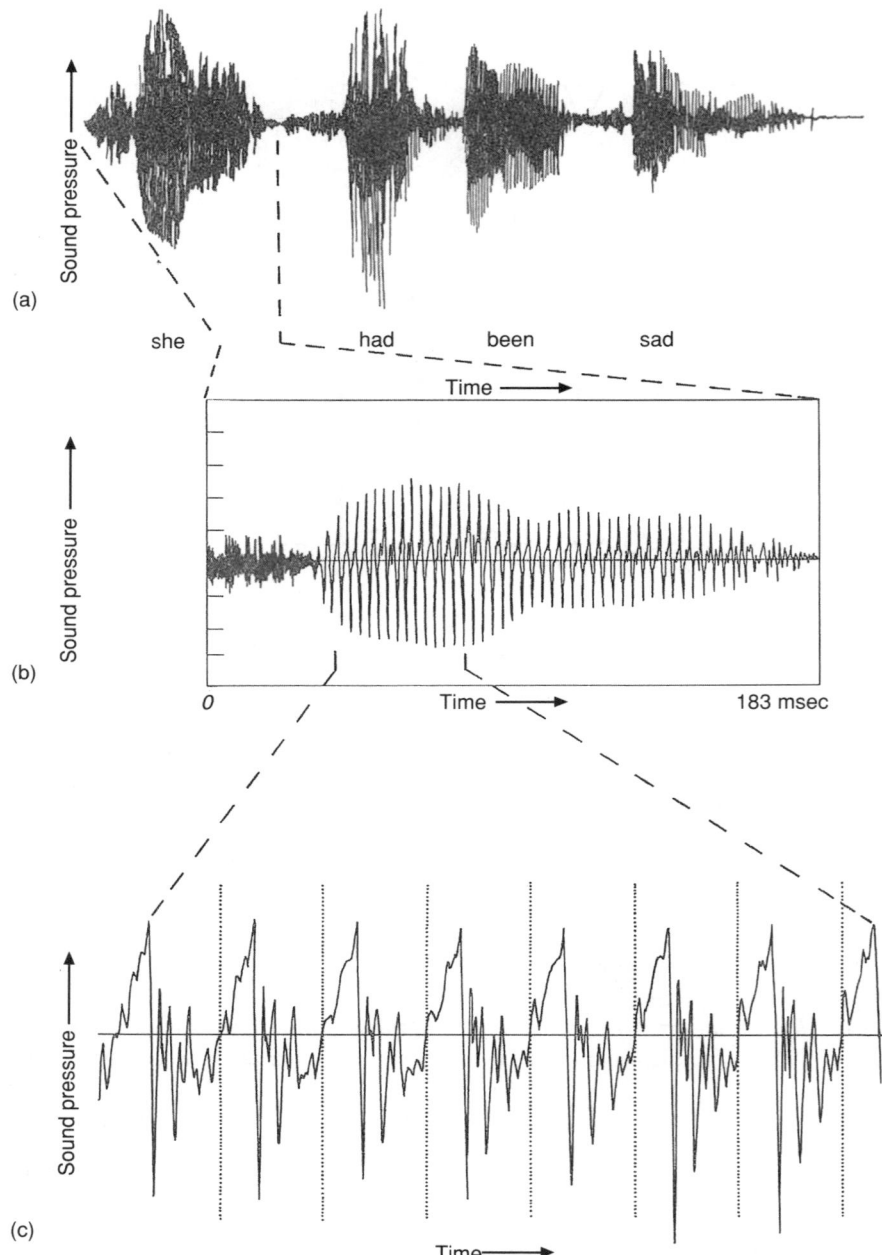

Figure 3.2 Illustration of a speech wave form with different degrees of temporal resolution. Time signal segments are given for: (a) the utterance 'she had been sad'; (b) the word 'she'; and (c) a segment from the vowel (i:) showing demarcation of individual periods.

Box 3.2:   Cont'd

vowel-like sounds that serve as consonants). Non-periodic portions correspond to *unvoiced sounds* (turbulent noise); for example, consonants such as *fricatives* (produced by air flowing through a narrow channel made by placing two articulating organs close together e.g. the tip of the tongue and the upper teeth, as in the pronunciation of English initial 'th' in 'thick') and *stops* (produced by obstructing airflow in the vocal tract by the lips or tongue). The spectra of the quasi-periodic speech sounds generally resemble the examples for periodic wave forms given in Fig. 3.1, but there are some specificities due to the fact that the vibrations produced at the voice source are filtered by the vocal tract (see 'Resonance' below).

The mechanism of voice and speech production

The basis of all sound making with the human vocal apparatus is air flow through the vocal tract powered by respiration. The type of sound produced depends on whether the air flow is set into vibration by rapid opening and closing of the glottis (so-called phonation), producing quasi-periodic voiced sounds, or whether it passes freely through the lower part of the vocal tract and is transformed into turbulent noise by friction at the mouth opening (non-periodic, unvoiced sounds). The quality of the sound is further determined by articulation and resonance. Figure 3.3 illustrates the major structures of the voice production mechanism as described below.

Respiration. The raw material for vocal behavior is air flow generated in the lungs through the joint action of the diaphragm and the thorax with the help of the respiratory muscles. The air column in the trachea below the glottis builds up pressure and thus serves as the power supply for phonation or frication.

Phonation. At the beginning of phonation, the vocal folds are set into a closed position by the muscular action of the laryngeal muscles. The continuous respiratory air flow compresses the air in the column below the glottis and builds-up *subglottal pressure.* When the pressure exceeds the closing force of the laryngeal muscles, the vocal cords open for a fraction of a second to release some of the pressure. The reclosing of the vocal cords is achieved by the elastic recoil of the folds themselves, and a so-called Bernoulli effect produced by the sudden drop of pressure in the glottis resulting in a sucking action. Both the overall tension and the adduction and abduction of the vocal folds are regulated by a large number of extra- and intralaryngeal muscles that act in combination to produce a *laryngeal setting* for voicing. The most important factors are the length, thickness, mass, and tension of the vocal folds. Thus, for example, the greater the length and the tension, and the smaller the mass and thickness of these ligaments, the faster they will open and close (which represents a higher rate of vibration and thus higher F0). Both F0 and *voice quality* (e.g. breathiness, roughness, sharpness) are strongly influenced by the timing of the glottal cycle (e.g. the relative duration of *closing, closed, opening,* and *open* phases). Figure 3.4 shows a graph of the glottal cycle that illustrates these variables. Depending on the slopes of opening and closing and the relative durations, the spectrum of a glottal wave form (i.e. *glottal spectrum*) will show different characteristics (e.g. with respect to spectral tilt).

Continued

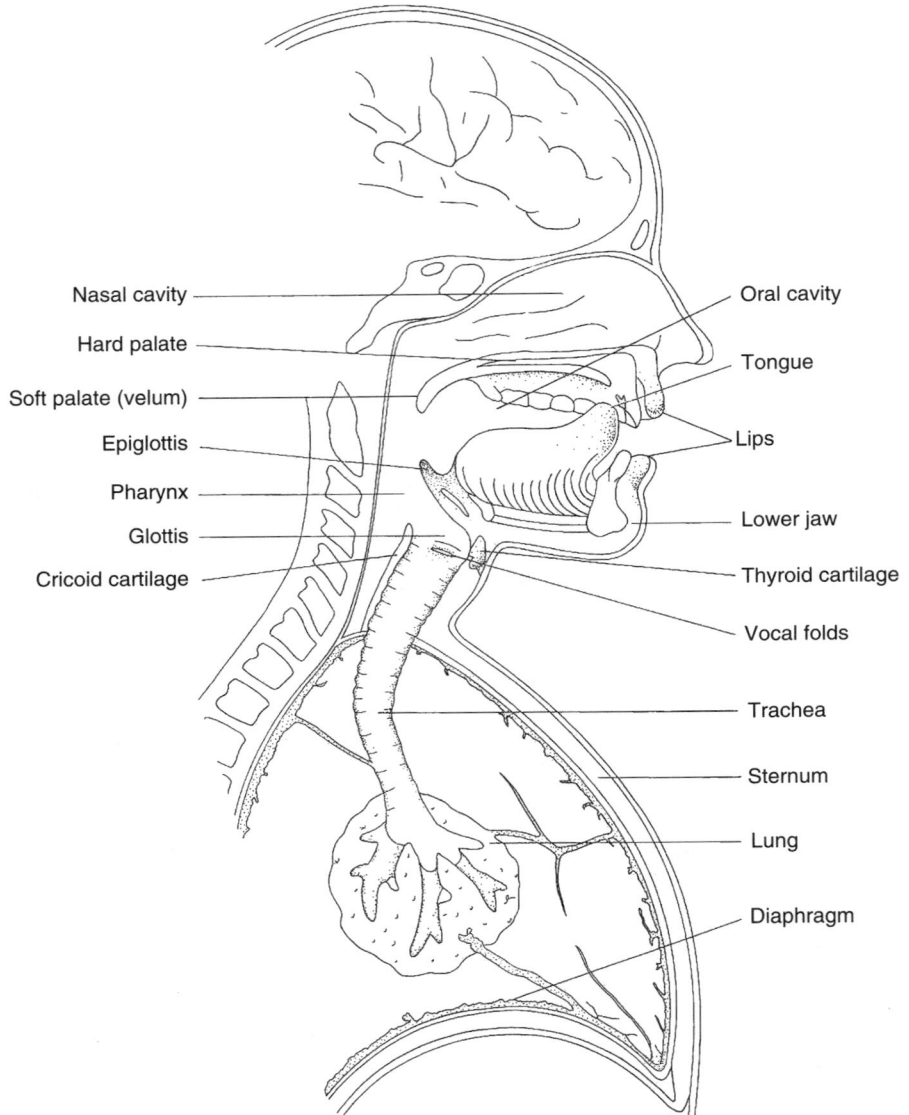

Figure 3.3 Schematic diagram of the human vocal mechanism.

Box 3.2:   Cont'd

While the details of the phonation process and the precise roles of the structures involved, especially of the different muscles, are not yet completely understood (but see Titze 1994 for a comprehensive overview), we do know that the nature of phonation is a powerful determinant of vocal features (and, consequently, of

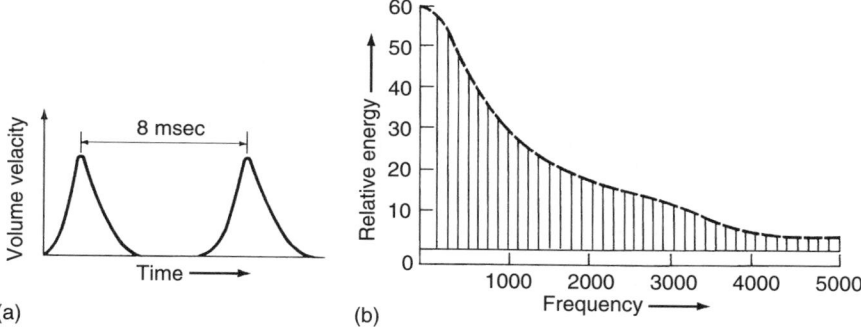

Figure 3.4 Wave form produced by the opening and closing of the vocal folds (glottal cycle) and the resulting spectrum: (a) time signal of wave form; (b) spectrum.

acoustic parameters). It is further important to note that the laryngeal setting in phonation is likely to be strongly affected by emotional arousal. The effects of psychological factors on the larynx are demonstrated by the quite frequent psycho-genic voice pathologies involving phonation problems (see Moses 1954; Perkins 1971; Stemple *et al.* 2000). Scherer (1986) has suggested that higher muscle tension during psychological arousal can produce shorter glottal pulses (higher F0) and more explo-sive opening and closing phases, with steeper onset and termination gradients in the glottal pulse wave form. The latter aspects will produce more relative energy in the higher frequencies, yielding a sharp, metallic-sounding voice quality. Conversely, in a state of high relaxation, the vocal folds may not close completely, or leave an anterior 'chink' open. This will influence the timing and shape of the glottal pulses in the opposite direction, yielding an auditory impression of 'breathiness' (Alku *et al.* 1997).

Articulation. Tongue, lips, teeth, hard and soft palate, and jaw all combine to produce specific configurations of the shape of the pharynx and the nasal and oral cavities in the service of producing language-specific speech sounds, either in the form of unvoiced sounds (mainly stops and fricative consonants) or voiced sounds (differ-ent vowels and voiced or semi-voiced consonants such as glides). Vowels are acous-tically distinguished by different formants in the vowel spectrum (explained below).

Resonance. The characteristics of a speech wave form (and of its spectrum) are determined by two quite different and largely independent factors: the glottal wave or pulse (determined by the subglottal pressure and the laryngeal setting) and the vocal tract resonance characteristics (transfer or filter function, mainly determined by the supralaryngeal articulatory setting). The glottal pulses pass through the *acoustical filter* of the vocal tract. This process is shown in Fig. 3.5, which illustrates the *source-filter theory* of speech production (Fant 1960) accepted by most speech scientists today. As a result of the glottal pulse's passage through the transfer function of the vocal tract, some of the harmonics in the spectrum of the pulse are amplified (producing local energy maxima called *formants*) and others are attenuated (*antiformants*). Both effects depend on the resonance characteristics of the exact articulatory setting in the vocal tract. Wave forms in Figs. 3.5a–c show the

Continued

Box 3.2:   Cont'd

> result of this filtering process in the time domain and wave forms in Figs. 3.5d–f, its
> equivalent in the frequency domain. It is this type of wave form, radiating at the
> mouth of the speaker, that serves as the basis for the objective measurement of
> acoustic parameters (see Module D).

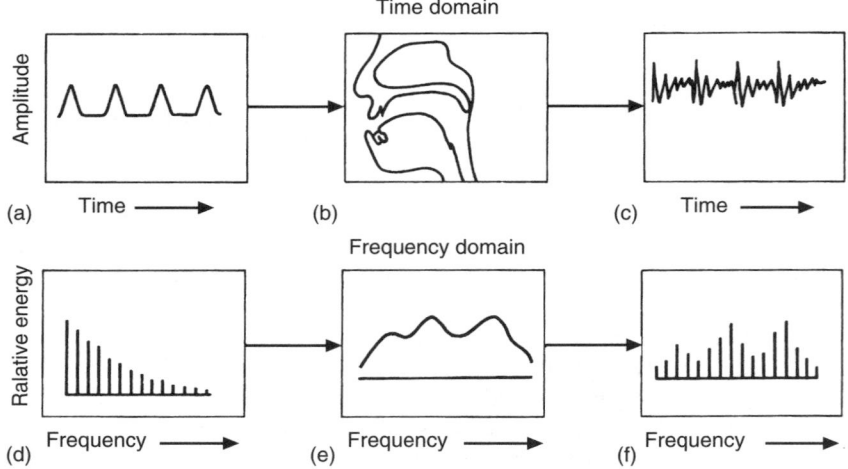

Figure 3.5 The source-filter theory of speech production: (a) glottal wave; (b) vocal tract shape;
(c) radiated sound wave; (d) glottal spectrum; (e) vocal tract transfer function; (f) acoustic
spectrum at mouth opening (adapted from Fant 1960).

animals have a more flexible physical structure, thanks to the possibility of varied use of
the same organ and a higher degree of brain control (Busnel 1977). The exact level of
differentiation in the sound-producing apparatus is reflected in the organism's vocal
behavior. Thus, for example, the primitive sound-producing apparatus in amphibians
(e.g. frogs) permits only a few calls, whereas the larynx of nonhuman primates makes
possible a great variety of vocal expressions (Ploog 1992).

Vocal behavior also depends on ecological constraints. In general, it appears that the
extent and richness of vocal behavior in an organism is correlated with its degree of
social cooperation. Thus, it may not be surprising to find that vocal expression seems
especially important in social mammals (e.g. MacLean 1993). It has been argued that
social grouping evolved as a means of cooperative defense, and that some kind of
nonverbal communication system had to develop to allow sharing of tasks, space, and
food (Boone & Buck 2003; Plutchik 1980). Vocal expression provides a means of social
coordination, and the need for efficient vocal communication may be particularly
pressing in humans, who display an unprecedented complexity of social interaction
(e.g. Buss & Kenrick 1998). Hence, one of the defining attributes of vocal expression

could be its social role: it provides 'markers' for the biological and social identity of individuals and their affective states (Scherer 1982).

Vocal expression seems to often occur in situations associated with basic survival problems that different organisms have in common (e.g. avoiding predators, finding food, competing for resources, and caring for offspring). Although biologists and ethologists have tended to shy away from using words such as affect or emotion in connection with animal behavior (Plutchik 1994, Chap. 10; Scherer 1985), a strong case could be made that most animal vocalizations (at least in social mammals) involve motivational states that are closely related to emotions (Hauser 2000; Marler 1977; Ploog 1986; Goodall 1986; Scherer 1985; Snowdon 2003). The affective states usually have to be inferred from the *situations* in which the vocalizations occurred. Comparative research has provided evidence of correspondences between the particular acoustic characteristics of an animal's vocalizations and particular emotional situations (Scherer 1985). One explanation of this finding may be that the expressive forms that such vocalizations take indirectly reflect the related situations or, more specifically, distinct physiological patterns that support the emotional behavior called forth by these urgent situations. Animal vocalizations often occur in tandem with autonomic arousal (e.g. Marler 1977), and physiological factors influence an organism's voice production in differentiated ways through their effects on the nature of phonation and resonance (see Box 3.2). Consequently, as a general principle, depending on the specific physiological state, one can expect to find specific acoustic features in the voice, even in humans (Scherer 1986; see also Spencer 1857).

However, although vocal affect expressions initially arose from physiological patterns, it is plausible that their precise form also reflects how they gradually became *ritualized* into formal signals shaped by ecological constraints. For example, vocal affect expression in animals seems to involve both categorical signals and graded signals, and the precise extent to which one or the other is used by a given animal seems to depend partly on its physical environment. As noted by Marler (1977, p. 56), accurate identification of an acoustic signal at a distance and under 'noisy' conditions, due to signal degradation (e.g. during hunting), should be easier with stereotyped and discrete signals than with highly variable signals. Because conditions such as these may apply to the human ecology also, we could expect to find at least some categorical effects in human vocal expression (Laukka 2004). On the other hand, even in discrete vocal expressions, fine variations may have informative value as well, indicating, for instance, the urgency of the situation.

Ecological constraints involve not only the physical environment but also the social, and although human vocal affect expression is based on phylogenetically old parts of the brain that are in many respects relatively similar to those of nonhuman primates, what is characteristic of humans is that they have much greater voluntary control over their vocalization (Jürgens 2002). Therefore, an important distinction must be made between so-called 'push' and 'pull' effects in the determinants of vocal expression (Scherer 1989). Push effects involve various physiological processes, such as respiration and muscle tension, which are 'naturally' influenced by emotional response; for instance, increased muscle tension produced by arousal of the sympathetic nervous system may influence breathing pattern, the shape of the vocal tract, and facial expression, all of which influence voice production. Pull effects, on the other hand, reflect external conditions that may lead to strategic posing of emotional expressions for manipulative purposes (e.g. Krebs & Dawkins 1984). This may involve social processes such as *self-presentation* (wanting to create certain impressions of oneself in the perceiver in terms of identity, ability, moral, and prestige) and *conventionalization* (stereotyping to enhance the clarity and shared meaning of signals; see Scherer 1985).

The evolutionary value of being able to simulate certain emotions (or intentions) is dependent on the initial existence of genuine expressions of emotions, wherefore the form of strategic signals should be based on genuine signals. Because vocal affect expression frequently involves a combination of push and pull effects, spontaneous and strategic vocal expression may be difficult to disentangle in real life.[2] Further research is clearly needed to better understand the relationship between push and pull effects.

Brunswik's lens model

So far, we have seen that vocal expression of affect can be regarded as an evolved mechanism that reflects both push (physiological reactions) and pull (strategic signaling) effects. The situation is further complicated by the fact that speakers may produce vocal effects in both an involuntary (automatic) and voluntary (controlled) fashion (Scherer 1994). Perceivers try to infer a covert variable—the underlying emotion or intention—on the basis of a set of overt voice cues. Unfortunately, individual voice cues are not wholly reliable indicators of the emotion. The uncertain nature of these cues reflects a number of variables including:

1. individual differences among speakers
2. interactions that involve the linguistic contents
3. degradation of acoustic signals in natural environments
4. interactions between push and pull effects

---

[2] The distinction between expression of genuinely felt affect and strategic signaling of affect that is not necessarily felt has, in fact, a long history in both philosophy and pragmatics (Caffi & Janney 1994). This is evident from many similar distinctions by authors in different disciplines: *cathartic* vs. *instigative* uses of speech (Aristotle 330 ca. BC/1932); *emotional* vs. *emotive* communication (Marty 1908); *ausdruck* vs. *appell* functions of language (Bühler 1934); and *spontaneous* vs. *symbolic* communication (Buck 1984). It is thus surprising that some emotion researchers have recently advocated strategic vocal signaling as a 'new' approach that should somehow replace the view that people express genuine emotions (e.g. Russell *et al.* 2003). There is no doubt that people spontaneously express emotions through the voice, and that they may even find it difficult to avoid doing so. In fact, it has been argued that the voice channel might be more susceptive to 'leakage' of emotion than other nonverbal channels (Ekman *et al.* 1976). On the other hand, it is equally clear that people often intentionally (whether consciously or not) pose emotions for strategic reasons. This dual aspect of vocal expression is something that one should take into consideration when designing studies of vocal expression (see Module B).

5. that a cue may be similarly associated with more than one emotion (e.g. fast speech rate may occur in both joy and anger signals, and thus speech rate is not a perfect indicator of either emotion).

The point is that the voice channel is *inherently* filled with noise. (*Noise* refers to that extraneous variability or information in the channel that is not part of the wanted signal or 'message'.) The implication is that researchers should expect to find much noise in data from studies of vocal expression, and in subsequent sections, we suggest ways of coping with noise in research designs. Understanding this aspect may be one of the keys to progress in the field (Juslin & Laukka 2003).

Studies of vocal affect expression have shown that individual voice cues are not perfectly correlated with the expressed affective states, and that there are intercorrelations between cues (Banse & Scherer 1996; Juslin & Laukka 2001) that partly reflect the voice production process (see Box 3.2). For instance, an increase in subglottal pressure increases not only the loudness, but also the fundamental frequency to some extent. These voice production constraints could help to explain some of the peculiar and often inconsistent results that have been obtained in studies of vocal expression. The characteristics of the vocal communication process may be quantitatively described using a variant of Brunswik's (1956) *lens model* (Scherer 1978, 1982). The lens model was originally intended as a model of visual perception, but it was later used mainly in judgment research (see Hammond & Stewart 2001). However, it has also been used by several researchers, including Brunswik himself, to study social perception (Brunswik 1956; Funder 1995; Scherer 1978), as well as music perception (Juslin 2000).

Figure 3.6 presents a modified version of Brunswik's lens model from Scherer *et al.* (2003). This model allows one to clearly distinguish between the *expression* (or encoding) of emotion on the sender side, *transmission* of the sound, and the *impression* (or decoding) on the receiver side, resulting in emotion inference. The model encourages voice researchers to measure the complete process including:

1. the emotional state expressed
2. the acoustically measured voice cues
3. the perceptual judgments of voice cues
4. the cognitive process that integrates all cues into a judgment of the encoded emotion.

The uncertain relationships between the various aspects can be modeled using correlational statistics (e.g. multiple regression, path analysis; see Module I). The transmission part is divided into acoustic voice cues and perceptual judgments of the same cues to highlight that the perceptual representation of cues may not correspond, in a one-to-one mapping, with their objectively measurable properties.[3] The subjective dimensions or categories used by naive listeners to differentiate voices and voice changes are referred to as *proximal cues* (see Module H). One further aspect of the transmission part that can be investigated involves the degradation of the acoustic

---

[3] Some versions of the lens model leave out subjective impressions of voice cues and index relationships between objectively measurable voice cues and judgments directly.

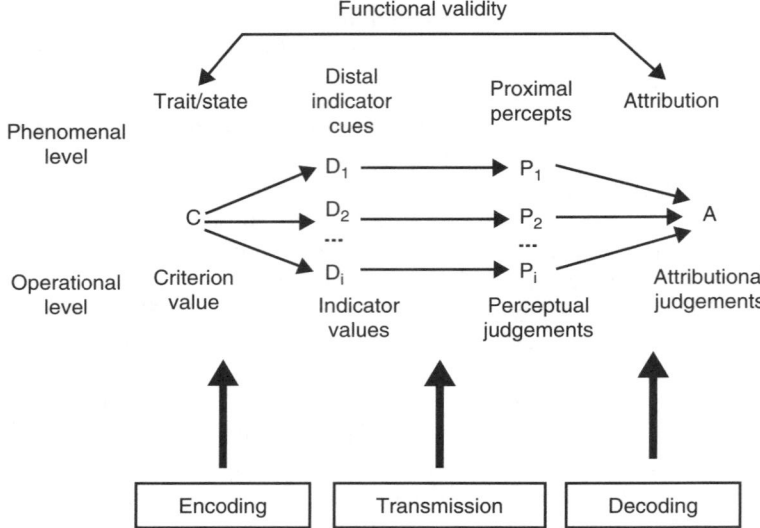

Figure 3.6 Modified form of the Brunswikian lens model applied to vocal expression of affect (from Scherer *et al.* 2003).

signals that will occur in natural environments due to factors such as attenuation, reverberation, and atmospheric turbulence (Wiley & Richards 1978).

Besides emphasizing the interdependent nature of the vocalization process, the lens model may illustrate how the process depends on voice cues that are *probabilistic* (uncertain indicators of the expressed emotion) though partly *redundant* (intercorrelated). As a consequence, decoders have to *combine* several different voice cues to achieve veridical perception. This is not a matter of pattern matching, however, since the voice cues contribute in an additive fashion to decoders' judgments—each cue is neither necessary nor sufficient, but the larger the number of cues used, the more reliable the communication. Brunswik's notion of *vicarious functioning* can be used to describe how decoders use the partly interchangeable cues in flexible ways, sometimes shifting from a cue that is unavailable to one that is available. The lens model captures the ways in which human perceivers have adopted perceptual strategies that reflect the structure of the environment: vicarious mediation of cues in the environment (i.e. multiple, fallible voice cues) is matched by vicarious functioning in the perceiver (i.e. flexible utilization of multiple, intercorrelated cues).[4]

---

[4] Note that the lens model can be applied equally well to the simple process of emotion *inference* based on vocal cues, and to the complete process of *communication* of emotion that includes both *sending intention* and *recognition*. Seyfarth and Cheney (2003) observed that a vocalization's potential to convey referential information is separate from the question of whether the vocalization is the result of affect or an intention or both. Similarly, in the classical rhetorical perspective, 'emotive activities are regarded as semiotic phenomena with communicative potential, regardless of whether they are 'sincere' or not' (Caffi & Janney 1994, p. 330).

The coding captured by the lens model has one particularly important implication—because the acoustic cues are intercorrelated to some degree, more than one way of using the cues might lead to a similarly high level of decoding accuracy (e.g. Dawes & Corrigan 1974; Juslin 2000). Further, different cues may substitute for one another (Slaney & McRoberts 2003, Appendix B). Brunswik's lens model might explain why there is accurate communication of emotions in vocal expression (see p. 108) despite considerable inconsistency in voice cues: multiple cues that are partly redundant yield a robust communicative system that is 'forgiving' toward deviation from optimal code usage. However, robustness comes with a price: the redundancy of the cues means that the same information is conveyed by many cues. This limits the information capacity of the channel (Shannon & Weaver 1949). A system of this kind involves 'compromise and a falling short of precision, but also the relative infrequency of drastic error' (Brunswik 1956, p. 145).

In this chapter, we propose an expanded lens model that also encompasses the processes of *cognitive appraisal* and *physiological response* (Fig. 3.7). In accordance with Scherer's (1986) theory, it is hypothesized that an emotion will reflect the cumulative outcome of appraisal of the specific event on a number of appraisal dimensions (see further discussion on p. 92). The outcomes of the separate appraisals are further assumed to have specific effects on physiological indices that influence voice production. Just as the cognitive appraisal will 'scatter its effects' in terms of a differentiated response to the particular conditions of the emotion-producing situation, the voice production process will 'scatter its effects' in terms of differentiated voice patterns that reflect the appraisal through its effects on physiology. This illustrates why perceiving emotions in other individuals is useful for one's own behavior orientation: quite possibly, the perceiver infers not simply the emotion as such, but also the speaker's cognitive appraisal of the actual situation (Ekman 1997; Scherer 1988). This hypothesis remains to be tested, although the present version of the lens model suggests that it can be profitable to directly manipulate appraisal dimensions in order to study their effects on physiological response patterns and voice cues (see Johnstone *et al.* 2001; see also p. 98). The extent to which the resulting voice patterns involve distinct emotion categories (as predicted by the discrete emotions approach) or an infinite number of different emotions (as predicted by the component process approach) is still uncertain, because most studies have not included a sufficiently large and well-differentiated set of emotion labels to be able to distinguish these approaches.

Implications for research

The characteristics captured by Brunswik's lens model have important consequences for how research on vocal expression should preferably be conducted. Specifically, the following four aspects need particular consideration. Firstly, the lens model implies that valid inferences about affect depend *equally* on the sender and the receiver. To understand vocal expression of affect, researchers need to study both sides of the lens model in combination. For example, the extent to which a speech sample features cues that reliably index affect will necessarily set the upper limit on the accuracy with which perceivers can infer the affect. Only an analysis of both aspects will allow a researcher to explain poor accuracy in terms of encoding or decoding.

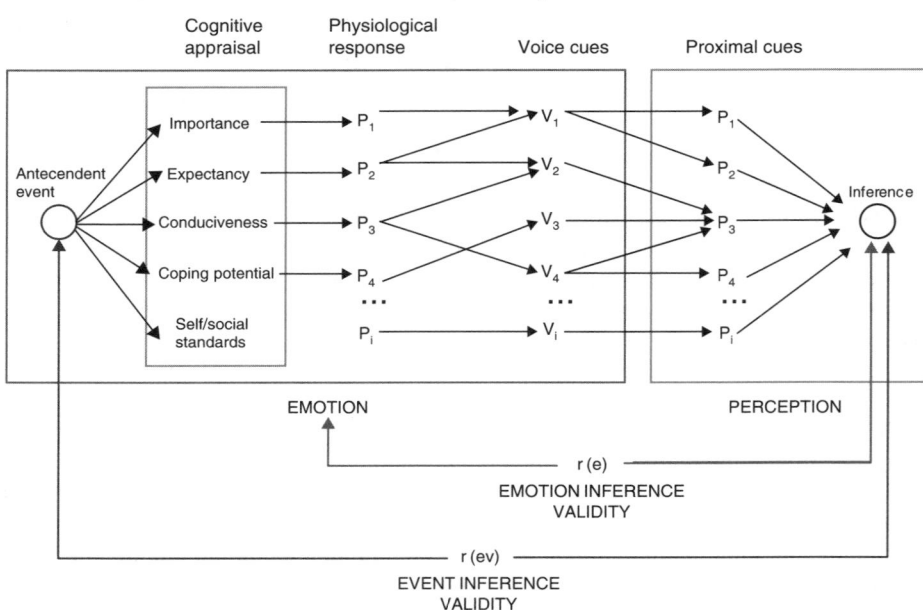

Figure 3.7 Extended lens model of vocal expression of emotion.

Secondly, and partly following from the previous point, researchers should strive to achieve *representative sampling* of both encoders and decoders (whereas most previous studies of social perception have followed a double standard, since they have only sampled decoders and not the social objects to be judged). Unless voice stimuli are sampled representatively, almost any level of decoding accuracy (or lack thereof) may be demonstrated in a given experiment. (Notably, several studies of vocal affect expression have relied on a single encoder; see Juslin & Laukka 2003, Table 2.)

Thirdly, because social perception focuses on 'distal' variables (i.e. the underlying emotion or intention) and not on proximal mediation (i.e. the cues themselves), researchers should expect to find stability at the distal level (i.e. decoding accuracy), albeit not on the mediation level (i.e. cue utilization). Researchers must adopt methods that can accommodate this aspect, allowing for variability at the mediation level, while still being able to demonstrate stability at the distal level. Traditional analysis of variance (which has been the method of choice in psychology) may not be the best way to capture this phenomenon. (See Module I for alternative analytic approaches.)

Fourthly, because each voice cue to affect is only probabilistic, researchers (like encoders and decoders, incidentally) need to consider *many* cues in order to capture the complete 'code' and thereby permit successful prediction of expressed as well as inferred emotions (see Module D). Any study that measures only a subset of voice cues runs the risk of leaving out significant aspects of the code involved in the process, which could lead to the invalid conclusion that voice cues do not discriminate among emotions. Analyzing many cues is also needed in order to permit encoders and decoders to display vicarious functioning of cues (e.g. cue substitution), which can help to explain stability at the distal level despite variability at the mediation level.

Voice cues to affect

Research questions

The basic assumption underlying most work on vocal affect expression is that there is a set of objectively measurable voice cues that reflect human affective states. While this assumption seems reasonable considering the origin and physiological basis of vocal expression (see p. 81), it has been called into question by some authors. Considerable effort has thus been invested to examine the relationships between voice and affect. Key questions include:

- Can voice cues be used to reliably measure underlying emotional states?
- Are different emotions expressed through different patterns of voice cues?
- To what extent are affective states other than emotions expressed by voice cues?
- Is it possible to detect lying on the basis of voice cues?
- Are emotions portrayed by actors different from emotions expressed spontaneously?
- Is there any theory that can account for the empirical findings?

Levels of description of vocal expression

Studies of vocal affect expression aimed at addressing the above questions could involve different levels of description of vocal behavior. Human vocalization is produced by the joint action of respiratory, phonatory, and articulatory processes (see Box 3.2). Consequently, each vocal expression can be characterized on:

1. the *physiological* level (e.g. describing nerve impulses or muscle innervation patterns that form the basis of the action of the structures involved in the voice production process)
2. the *phonatory-articulatory* level (e.g. describing the position or movement of the major structures involved, such as the vocal folds)
3. the *acoustic* level (e.g. describing characteristics of the speech wave form emanating from the mouth).

A number of different objective methods are available for investigating vocal expression on each of these levels (see Modules D and E). Although the various levels of description are not independent of one another (e.g. each articulatory setting of the vocal tract can, in principle, be reduced to the precise underlying physiological pattern of muscle innervation), it is crucial to keep these levels clearly differentiated. First, in many cases, we do not yet know the precise relationship between one level of description and another (e.g. the exact phonatory-articulatory setting responsible for a particular pattern of acoustic parameters). Secondly, in some cases, different processes on one level may lead to the same result on another level (e.g. several different phonation patterns may lead to the same acoustic parameter in the spectrum).

Many of the categorical systems that have been proposed for research on vocal expression (e.g. Crystal 1975; Crystal & Quirk 1964; Key 1977, pp. 92–100; Laver & Hutcheson 1972, pp. 11–14; Poyatos 1976; Trager 1958) do not differentiate between levels of description—a fact that makes it impossible to compare the various labels or categories (leaving aside the problems of reliable operationalization of the concepts). In many such systems, additional complications are created by the inclusion of various linguistic criteria such as *juncture*, sender intentions such as *manipulation attempts*, listener interpretations such as *complaining voice*, or cultural norms such as *over-high pitch*. Because of these shortcomings, and because most of the systems have rarely been used in empirical research, they will not be reviewed in this chapter. The primary concern here is the description of parameters that can be objectively assessed for each level of description or that seem useful for subjective measures of proximal cues in voice perception.

Summary of previous research

A large number of studies of vocal expression have attempted to specify what aspects of the voice are predictive of expressed or portrayed emotion. This endeavor, however, has proved to be more difficult than expected. This is due to both the numerous practical problems associated with studies of vocal expression (see Modules A–E and Chapter 12) and the complex nature of the voice production process itself (see Box 3.2). Hence, reviews of the literature on vocal expression commonly mention inconsistent results regarding voice cues to emotion (see Cowie *et al.* 2001; Frick 1985; Murray & Arnott 1993). Scherer (1986) thus pointed out an apparent paradox: whereas listeners seem to be accurate in decoding emotions from voice cues, scientists have been unable to identify a set of voice cues that reliably discriminate among emotions. Some researchers have thus argued that voice cues may reflect only the so-called activation dimension of emotions (Davitz 1964), or a combination of arousal and valence (e.g. Bachorowski 1999). However, these arguments could be premature, because recent research suggests that there is a great deal of acoustic differentiation of emotions in vocal expression. What seems needed to obtain such emotion differentiation is:

1. inclusion of a sufficient number of voice cues
2. precision in the labeling of the emotional states expressed
3. proper research designs (see Modules A–E).

In particular, it seems necessary to reach beyond single measures of the most common voice cues (e.g. fundamental frequency, rate, intensity), which may involve similar cue levels for different emotions, and to analyze other cues that differentiate among such emotions. There is actually a whole range of voice cues that can be used to index affective processes, but most previous studies have analyzed only a subset of these cues (see Table 3.5).

As explained in Box 3.1, different theories of emotion (discrete emotions, dimensions, and component processes) make different predictions about the results we should expect to obtain. Table 3.2 shows a set of empirically-derived predictions for patterns of voice cues for discrete emotions based on previous reviews of over a hundred studies of vocal expression of emotions (e.g. Juslin & Laukka 2003). Also included are the predicted changes in voice cues associated with emotional stress. As discussed earlier in p. 83, researchers should not expect to find that the data for any single speaker in a single study will rigidly conform to the predictions shown in Table 3.2. There are numerous sources of variability that may introduce noise into the vocal process (e.g. individual differences among speakers, interactions with the verbal material, push and pull effects, signal degradation). Across studies and speakers, however, one might expect results to converge around the patterns presented in Table 3.2, with scope for revisions, of course.

It should be noted that the predictions are more certain in regard to those emotions that have been more thoroughly studied (e.g. sadness) than for those investigated in only a few studies (e.g. love). In general, the results in Table 3.2 support both discrete emotion theories and component process theories in suggesting that there are emotion-specific patterns of cues in vocal affect expression that go beyond the simple affective dimensions of activation and arousal. However, there are several inconsistencies in the results reported so far that need to be resolved (see Juslin & Laukka 2003, Table 7).

Most studies of vocal affect expression have used emotion portrayals by professional actors, and an important question concerns the extent to which such portrayals differ from natural vocal expressions (see p. 96). The jury is still out—primarily because we have little data on natural expressions. However, a preliminary view of the available findings from studies that used natural speech samples or emotion induction, in comparison with those using emotion portrayals, is shown in Table 3.3. This comparison reveals, first of all, the urgent need for further studies using natural vocal expressions. However, it also indicates that the pattern of results is generally similar for the two types of speech samples. Hopefully, improved research methodology with regard to emotion induction methods and real-life recordings will allow researchers to make further comparisons of portrayals and natural expressions (see Module B).

In addition to discrete emotions, a number of studies have obtained preliminary results with regard to affect dimensions such as activation, valence, and potency. Activation is the dimension most studied, and the data are fairly consistent. High *activation* is associated with high mean F0, large F0 variability, fast speech rate, short pauses, increased voice intensity, and increased high-frequency energy (Apple *et al.* 1979; Breitenstein *et al.* 2001; Davitz 1964; Huttar 1968; Laukka *et al.*, in press; Levin & Lord 1975; Pereira 2000; Pittam *et al.* 1990; Scherer & Oshinsky 1977; Schröder *et al.* 2001; Uldall 1960). The results for valence are much more inconsistent. Some studies have found that positive *valence* is associated with low mean F0, large F0 variability, fast speech rate, shorter pauses, and low voice intensity (Laukka *et al.* in press; Scherer 1974; Scherer & Oshinsky 1977; Schröder *et al.* 2001; Uldall 1960). Other studies have failed to obtain a particular set of cues that convey different levels of valence (Apple *et al.* 1979; Davitz 1964; Pereira 2000).

The potency dimension has been less studied than activation and valence, and the results are inconsistent. High *potency* has been found to be associated with both high and low mean F0, and with both fast and slow speech rate; and further with low F0 floor, large F0 variability, high voice intensity, large voice intensity variability, and much high-frequency energy (Apple *et al.* 1979; Harrigan *et al.* 1989; Laukka *et al.*, in press;

Table 3.2 Empirically-based predictions for 15 voice cues associated with the most commonly investigated discrete emotions as well as stress/arousal

	Hot anger	Boredom	Disgust/contempt	Fear/anxiety	Happiness/joy	Love/tenderness	Sadness/grief	Surprise	Stress/arousal
F0 (M)	<	>	>	<	<	>	>	<	<
F0 (SD)	<	>	<	>	<	>	>	<	<
F0 contour	<	=	>	<	=	<>	>	<>	
Jitter	<	=	>	<	=	>	=	<	<
VoInt (M)	<	=	=	=	<	>	>	<	<
VoInt (SD)	<	>	<	<	<	>	>	<	<
F1 (M)	<	>	<	>	<	=	>	>	
F1 (bw)	>	<	>	<	>	=	<	<	
F1 Prec	<	>	<	>	<	>	>	>	
HF 500	<	>	<	<	=	>	>	>	<
SR	<	>	>	<	<	>	>	>	<
Pauses	>	=	<	=	>	=	<	<	<
Regularity	>	<	=	>	<	<	>	>	>
Attack	<	<	<	>	=	>	>	<	
Phonation	Shouted modal	Modal	'Chest' tone	Breathy falsetto	Modal	Modal	Breathy creaky	Breathy	

Note: ∧ = high; ∨ = low; == medium. (For details, see Juslin & Laukka 2003; Klasmeyer & Sendlmeier 2000; Scherer *et al.* 2003).

Table 3.3 Comparison of results from studies that used emotion portrayals with those that used natural or mood-induced vocal affect expressions (based on Juslin & Laukka 2003, Tables 2 and 7).

Voice cue	Method	Anger	Emotion Fear	Happiness	Sadness
Speech rate	Portrayal	Fast: 17	Fast: 18	Fast: 15	Fast: 1
		Medium: 3	Medium: 3	Medium: 2	Medium: 4
		Slow: 3	Slow: 1	Slow: 6	**Slow: 19**
	Natural	Fast: 6	Fast: 2	Fast: 3	Fast: 0
		Medium: 0	Medium: 0	Medium: 2	Medium: 1
		Slow: 1	Slow: 1	Slow: 0	**Slow: 6**
Voice intensity mean	Portrayal	**High: 24**	**High: 7**	**High: 16**	High: 0
		Medium: 1	Medium: 3	Medium: 4	Medium: 2
		Low: 0	Low: 6	Low: 0	**Low: 22**
	Natural	**High: 3**	**High: 3**	**High: 3**	High: 1
		Medium: 0	Medium: 0	Medium: 1	Medium: 0
		Low: 1	Low: 1	Low: 0	**Low: 4**
F0 mean	Portrayal	**High: 25**	**High: 19**	**High: 26**	High: 3
		Medium: 5	Medium: 8	Medium: 2	Medium: 0
		Low: 2	Low: 2	Low: 0	**Low: 28**
	Natural	**High: 6**	**High: 6**	**High: 7**	High: 1
		Medium: 0	Medium: 0	Medium: 0	Medium: 0
		Low: 2	Low: 1	Low: 1	**Low: 10**
F0 variability	Portrayal	**High: 21**	**High: 6**	**High: 24**	High: 1
		Medium: 4	Medium: 5	Medium: 1	Medium: 1
		Low: 3	**Low: 14**	Low: 1	**Low: 24**
	Natural	**High: 3**	**High: 2**	**High: 4**	High: 1
		Medium: 0	Medium: 0	Medium: 1	Medium: 0
		Low: 0	Low: 1	Low: 0	**Low: 3**
Voice quality (HF)	Portrayal	**High: 17**	**High: 5**	**High: 10**	High: 0
		Medium: 0	Medium: 2	Medium: 2	Medium: 0
		Low: 0	Low: 4	Low: 0	**Low: 15**
	Natural	**High: 2**	**High: 1**	**High: 2**	High: 0
		Medium: 0	Medium: 0	Medium: 0	Medium: 0
		Low: 0	Low: 1	Low: 0	**Low: 2**

Note: Values show the number of studies that obtained each result (bold text = most frequent).

Scherer 1974; Scherer & Oshinsky 1977; Schröder *et al.* 2001; Tusing & Dillard 2000; Uldall 1960). In sum, the findings support dimensional theories of vocal affect expression in that there seem to be some voice correlates of some affect dimensions, but, as in the case of discrete emotions, there are some inconsistent findings that need to be resolved. A dimensional approach may be especially suitable for studying affect states of a relatively weak intensity, such as moods (see Box 3.1).

Many more specific predictions can be made on the basis of appraisal theories (see Scherer *et al.* 2001*b* for a comprehensive review). Appraisal theorists generally assume that the efferent response patterns (e.g. physiological changes and facial/vocal expression) are produced by specific appraisal outcomes, and that they serve as adaptive responses to the need for information processing and action tendencies (see Scherer 1984 and Smith & Scott 1997 for discussions of this hypothetical patterning mechanism).

On the basis of his special brand of appraisal theory—the component process model—Scherer (1986) presented an extensive set of predictions concerning the physiological changes and the ensuing consequences for the voice production mechanism (componential patterning) that can be expected for appraisal results on specific dimensions. Briefly put, the model relies on the assumed functional consequence of a specific appraisal result to predict the pattern of peripheral physiological arousal that is likely to occur. Then, the effects of the respective physiological pattern on the voice production process are estimated and the acoustic concomitants are inferred. For instance, an event that is appraised as goal-obstructive by the individual may require strong action (e.g. fighting), which should lead to high sympathetic arousal with consequent changes for respiration and muscle tension, and thus changes in phonation (e.g. higher fundamental frequency, different glottal pulse shape producing energy changes in the spectrum; see Box 3.2). Similarly, it is predicted that an appraisal of high-coping potential (e.g. power to deal with an obstacle) will lead to facial changes evolutionarily linked to biting behavior. The configuration of the vocal tract produced by this setting will privilege certain filter characteristics of the vocal tract (see Kent 1997; Gobl & Ni Chasaide 2003), and will thus influence the energy distribution in the spectrum.

The evidence to date is consistent with many of Scherer's predictions, but also suggests important modifications (Banse & Scherer 1996; Juslin & Laukka 2001; Scherer *et al.* 2003). Johnstone *et al.* (2001) discuss a number of crucial issues that need to be taken into consideration when testing a theory of this kind. We foresee that novel developments with regard to obtaining speech samples (Module B) and measuring physiological changes (see Christie & Friedman 2004; Fahrenberg & Myrtek 1996; Herrald & Tomaka 2002) may lead to increased opportunities for tests and comparisons of different theories of vocal affect expression.

Conducting studies of voice cues to affect

Conducting a study of vocal affect expression involves a number of crucial steps including:

- choosing what affective states to investigate (Module A)
- obtaining speech samples (Module B)
- recording speech samples (see Chapter 12)
- segmenting speech samples (Module C)
- and measuring the voice at the acoustic (Module D) or physiological and phonatory-articulatory levels (Module E).

Further steps that are related to the study of affect inferences from voice cues are described in the section covering that topic (see p. 111). While few studies may encompass all of these aspects at once, a systematic research program devoted to vocal expression will probably involve most of these aspects in order to gain a deeper understanding of the topic.

Module A: Choosing affective states

Important questions for any study of vocal affect expression are what states to focus on and how they should be labeled. An overall recommendation is that the selection of labels is made in some systematic fashion (e.g. on a theoretical basis) rather than in a post-hoc fashion, though the procedure may obviously depend on the nature of the study to some extent. For instance, in some studies that use natural speech samples (see Module B), the affect expressed may have to be rated or coded after the recording, instead of being pre-determined by the researcher. Furthermore, the selection of affect labels might be different depending on its intended use. It seems important to make a distinction between *pragmatic* considerations and *scientific* considerations, which should not be confounded. Pragmatic considerations could concern questions about what would work in a practical application (e.g. how many emotions need to be distinguished in order for a particular emotion recognition device to be useful?). Scientific considerations, in contrast, concern the true nature of the phenomena in question (e.g. how many emotions are required to give a satisfactory account of vocal expression?) From a practical point of view, different theories of emotion may be equally useful, depending on the application. From a scientific perspective, however, it seems unlikely that all theories of emotion give an equally adequate account of vocal affect expression. Examples of how different theoretical approaches may be adopted in respect to vocal expression are provided on pp. 88–92. Below, we offer some more general recommendations regarding choice of affect labels.

First, it is paramount to distinguish between the different affective phenomena discussed in Box 3.1 (Table 3.1), such as emotions, moods, affective stances, and attitudes. In previous research, it has been quite common to intermingle affect labels that refer to different kinds of affect in the same speech sample. This may cause problems, since different kinds of affect may have different characteristics in terms of the time course, specificity, and strength of impact (Table 3.1). These differences may introduce noise into the statistical analyses (that are frequently conducted across different states; see Module I), which can obscure reliable effects. It seems preferable to analyze speech samples that consist of homogenous types of affective states. This implies that researchers must use precise procedures and instructions to be able to determine that a specific type of affect is expressed or portrayed.

Secondly, for a given type of affective phenomenon, say emotion, it is important to achieve sufficient precision in the labeling of the states so that all *genuinely* different states have different labels, whereas similar states are treated as such. There is currently no generally accepted system for classifying emotions, and the relationship between language and emotions is highly complex. There are many hundreds of words that refer to emotions in most Western languages, and studies of vocal affect expression could not possibly include all these labels. Thus, some reduction of the emotion labels is clearly necessary in order to make research feasible. Still, this reduction should not go too far. Table 3.4 shows the frequency with which 89 affect labels have been used in 104 studies of vocal expression. As may be seen, the default choice of labels has been a small set of emotions, roughly corresponding to the most commonly postulated basic emotions, such as joy,

Continued

Table 3.4 Frequency of occurrence of 89 affect terms in 104 studies of vocal affect expression (based on Juslin & Laukka 2003, Table 2)

Anger	85	Scornfulness	3	Desire	1
Fear	65	Shame	3	Disappointment	1
Sadness	65	Sorrow	3	Disdain	1
Happiness	44	Uncertainty	3	Dislike	1
Joy	31	Comfort	2	Dominance	1
Disgust	26	Confidence	2	Excitement	1
Surprise	24	Coquetry	2	Friendliness	1
Boredom	17	Disbelief	2	Fury	1
Contempt	15	Gladness	2	Grimness	1
Love	10	Hate	2	Hostility	1
Grief	9	Nervousness	2	Humor	1
Interest	7	Objectivity	2	Jealousy	1
Anxiety	6	Pleading	2	Indignation	1
Doubt	6	Pomposity	2	Insistence	1
Elation	5	Relief	2	Irritation	1
Satisfaction	5	Reproach	2	Kindness	1
Sympathy	5	Sarcasm	2	Lust	1
Admiration	4	Threat	2	Panic	1
Pain	4	Timidity	2	Pedantry	1
Tenderness	4	Accommodation	1	Pleasure	1
Affection	3	Aggression	1	Rage	1
Cheerfulness	3	Amusement	1	Relaxation	1
Contentment	3	Approval	1	Seductiveness	1
Determination	3	Astonishment	1	Shyness	1
Enthusiasm	3	Aversion	1	Solemnity	1
Impatience	3	Boldness	1	Startle	1
Irony	3	Calm	1	Tension	1
Laughter	3	Complaint	1	Terror	1
Longing	3	Defiance	1	Worry	1
Reverence	3	Delight	1		

Note: For consistency, all terms have been converted to nouns.

Module A: Cont'd

sadness, anger, fear, disgust, surprise, boredom, and contempt (the mean number of affect labels used in these studies was 5.89). However, it appears likely that vocal cues communicate a much larger variety of affective states as well as index subtle gradations within specific types of states. Consequently, apparent inconsistencies in data from previous studies might be partly explained by insufficient precision concerning the quality (Banse & Scherer 1996) as well as the quantity (Juslin & Laukka 2001) of affect.

Though the 'fuzziness' in the relationship between emotions and emotion words may never be fully resolved, it seems desirable to aim for more precision. To reduce emotion labels to a practically feasible number, without obscuring important differences between states, is a challenge for researchers of vocal affect expression. Table 3.4 clearly shows the need for replication in regard to affective labels that have been used in only a few studies. In addition, there is a need to examine the possibilities of expressing 'mixed' emotions in the voice (Carlson *et al.* 1993).

Module B: Obtaining speech samples

The question of how to obtain speech samples may seem to be just a technical problem of minor importance in comparison with the grander issues in the study of vocal affect expression. However, on the contrary, this aspect has important implications for a large number of theoretical issues in the field. Broadly speaking, there are three types of speech samples that have been used in studies of vocal affect expression, each with its own advantages as well as disadvantages:

1. emotion portrayals
2. natural vocal expressions
3. induced vocal expressions.

Precisely what kind of speech sample should be used in a given study obviously depends on the goal of the study, as well as on certain theoretical and practical considerations (discussed further below). For the field as a whole, however, the best probable procedure is to combine the different approaches to obtaining speech samples so as to mitigate the problems with each approach, thus making it possible to find converging data from different methods.

First, it may be useful to outline some general desiderata for a speech sample. One primary requirement is that the recording quality is as good as possible given the practical circumstances (see Chapter 12). Some voice measures are quite sensitive to poor recording quality, and could be distorted if the sound quality is deficient (see Module D); how serious this problem is depends on the study. Secondly, it is a crucial requirement that researchers can establish — beyond reasonable doubt — that a particular emotion is really expressed, or intentionally portrayed, in a given speech utterance, at least if the aim is to draw any conclusions about the 'sender' side of the process. In other words, researchers need some *independent criterion* of the expressed or portrayed emotion. Thirdly, it is important that the speech samples are natural-sounding or, more specifically, that they are truly representative of real-world vocal affect expressions (unless, of course, the goal is, for instance, to study how actors convey emotions in theater). Fourthly, if the aim of the study is to investigate voice cues of discrete emotions, the speech sample should consist of vocal affect expressions that are sufficiently intense to make it possible to obtain reliable differences between emotions.

Finally, in order for the results to be generalizable (if that is a goal), the speech sample must include utterances by many speakers. Notably, this is equally true regardless of whether the study is focusing on encoding or decoding; for instance, a listening test based on a single speaker may feature cues with a truncated range of levels as compared to the full range of levels that may occur in vocal expressions in general. The reason for this is that there are considerable individual differences among speakers, and if one relies on a single speaker (as, in fact, several studies have done in the past), there is a serious risk that obtained data (whether in terms of decoding accuracy or patterns of voice cues) are at least partly an artifact of the idiosyncratic features of the speaker.

Continued

Module B: Cont'd

Under normal circumstances, researchers are rarely able to meet all of the above requirements in one and the same study (hence, our recommendation for a 'multi-method' approach). Recently, it has been proposed that researchers should attempt to create more extensive and publicly available *databases* (instead of small *data sets*) to increase generalizability of results (Cowie & Cornelius 2003). This is important in ensuring that there is sufficient variability in the speech samples used with respect to speakers, languages, gender, emotions, cues, judges, and contexts. (For a review of 32 emotional speech databases, see Ververidis & Kotropoulos 2003.)

Emotion portrayals

The most common method of obtaining speech samples in previous studies is by recording *emotion portrayals* by professional actors (or, in some cases, lay persons) in a laboratory setting. Actors are usually asked to perform given verbal material (with standard content that remains the same throughout the session: numbers, letters of the alphabet, nonsense syllables, or regular speech material like words, sentences, or paragraphs) while portraying a set of discrete emotions, typically with high emotion intensity (van Bezooijen 1984).

Advantages of this method include experimental control and the production of strong effects on voice cues. (It is also easy to obtain the kind of balanced data set that is required for a number of voice manipulation techniques; see Module G.) One further advantage is that it is rather easy to achieve a good sound quality on the recordings.

One serious problem with this approach is the risk that emotion portrayals by actors in a laboratory may involve vocal affect expressions that differ in important ways from those that occur in real life. For instance, actors may overemphasize some voice cues, such as speech rate, at the expense of more subtle cues that are harder to control, such as jitter (see Table 3.5). Also, it seems likely that emotion portrayals involve more 'stereotypical' and conventional vocal affect signals than do 'natural' expressions. On the other hand, it may be argued that even in real life, people often enhance and modify their own expressions according to *display rules*, in ways that are not unlike acting (Banse & Scherer 1996; see also Chapter 2). A person who always displays emotion in an honest and uninhibited fashion may soon find him or herself in trouble!

There are ways to make emotion portrayals more similar to genuine vocal expressions, including actors' use of the Stanislavski technique (Stanislavski 1988), respiration-induced physiological effects (Bloch *et al.* 1987), or realistic scenarios (Banse & Scherer 1996), which can help them self-induce emotional states. Good emotion portrayals can be quite realistic, whereas poor portrayals can be very artificial. Thus, it is the responsibility of the researcher to assure that portrayals are of sufficient quality. This can be partly ascertained by conducting judgment studies of decoding accuracy and perceived naturalness (Banse & Scherer 1996).

Despite the problems associated with this type of speech sample, it is fair to say that most of what we know today about vocal affect expressions is thanks to the use of emotion portrayals. However, it is now vitally important to extend and modify the findings of this approach through the use of other types of speech samples.

Natural vocal expressions

The second most common method of obtaining speech samples is to record *natural vocal expressions* that may be assumed to express different emotions. Most early uses of this method involved recordings of conversation occurring prior to aviation accidents (e.g. Kuroda *et al.* 1976; Williams & Stevens 1969) or in psychotherapy (e.g. Eldred & Price 1958; Roessler & Lester 1976), with a consequent focus on affective states like fear, stress, and depression. More recently, researchers have recorded speech samples off the air (e.g. TV, radio), featuring journalists reporting from dramatic events or extracts from reality shows or games (see Douglas–Cowie *et al.* 2003; Greasley *et al.* 2000; Stibbard 2001). An unusual study by Brown (1980) used speech samples recorded in a very special situation — a child's birth.

The most crucial advantage of using natural vocal expressions is the increased likelihood that one can obtain 'ecologically valid' speech samples, particularly if the speaker is not aware that the speech is recorded. Also, naturally recorded speech may preserve more of the natural context of vocal expression than do laboratory samples (including the fact that speech is often part of an on-going dialogue).

The most serious problem with this method is the common difficulty of determining what state is felt or portrayed by the speaker in each utterance; the expressed (or portrayed) emotion usually has to be inferred from a close analysis of the situation in which the speech sample was obtained (as in animal research). However, there is no way of reliably determining the precise nature of the cognitive appraisal that might have induced the emotion, and different persons react differently to the same 'objective' situation. This is the most difficult problem of this approach and means that conclusions concerning vocal expression cannot be based on this method alone.

Another problem is that the sound quality is usually inferior in real-world recordings, which may prevent the analysis of certain voice cues. Unfortunately, and somewhat paradoxically, these may be some of the same cues that are most difficult to manipulate for actors and that, therefore, may be most likely to distinguish portrayed and natural vocal expressions of affect.

A number of systematic attempts to develop extensive databases featuring natural vocal expressions have been made in recent years (e.g. Douglas–Cowie *et al.* 2003). These provide an important complement to laboratory research. However, it would be a mistake to assume that all samples of natural vocal expressions represent genuinely felt emotions, 'uncontaminated' by acting or social conventions. As noted in our discussion of push and pull effects (see p. 81), natural speech often involves a combination of both effects. Further, previous attempts to rely on natural vocal expressions have been compromised by the fact that vocal expressions of full-blown emotions may occur relatively rarely in real life, and usually in intimate settings, whereas most recordings of natural expressions so far involve public situations.

Continued

Module B: Cont'd

To the extent that researchers want to capture strong emotions, they may have to dig deeper into the private life of people. Thus, for example, one possibility could be to use small, portable digital recorders that participants are asked to wear at all hours during the day, and that can be automatically activated by the voice of the speaker during conversation. These voice recordings may be augmented by information from electronic diaries (Bolger *et al.* 2003) and ambulatory physiological measures (Fahrenberg & Myrtek 1996) to help classify emotional states. This method could help to capture the rare moments of strong emotions in everyday life. On the other hand, it may also be important to understand milder affective states in speech such as moods and affective stances (especially for some computer applications; Cowie *et al.* 2001), in which case regular samples of natural vocal expression are useful.

Induced vocal expressions

A method which is used rather rarely, although it has considerable promise, is to actually *induce vocal affect expression* in the laboratory. Previous studies have used a variety of emotion-inducing techniques, such as mental imagery, emotion-inducing slides, the Velten technique (the speaker repeatedly reads highly emotional sentences in a highly expressive fashion), as well as experimenter-induced mood in the classic social-psychological tradition (for a review of mood-induction techniques, see, for example, Westerman *et al.* 1996). One of the more exotic (but perhaps methodologically and ethically questionable) procedures of induction used in vocal expression studies is hypnosis (Havrdová & Morávek 1979). Music has not been used thus far, despite its proven effectiveness as a mood induction method (Västfjäll 2002). Recent research has involved more sophisticated attempts to induce vocal expressions by means of computerized emotion induction batteries, direct manipulation of individual appraisal dimensions (Scherer *et al.* 2003), and computer games (Johnstone 2001; Kappas 1997). Other possibilities may be to manipulate facial expressions (Ekman *et al.* 1983) or to ask participants to retell emotional events from the past (Harrigan *et al.* 1991).

Advantages of the induction method include the combination of experimental control with the possibility of obtaining natural affect expressions. Thus, the researcher may obtain balanced data sets, while, at the same time, the expressions may not be as stereotyped as those in emotion portrayals. Also, it is feasible to investigate the complete chain of the expanded lens model (see Fig. 3.7). That is, one can manipulate dimensions of cognitive appraisal, thereby producing physiological changes (that can be indexed) that lead to certain voice changes (that are measured), which may be used in judgment studies (analyzing the judgments as well). Experimental induction could be especially efficient in studies of how stress affects the voice, for instance using demanding cognitive tasks of gradually increasing difficulty. In contrast, certain 'complex' emotions (e.g. remorse) may be difficult to induce in a laboratory.

One problem with this method is that the induced emotions are usually weak, which may render it difficult to establish reliable differences between discrete emotions. It is predicted by certain theories (e.g. the 'cone model' by Plutchik, 1994, Figure 4.3, p.102) that weaker versions of emotions will tend to be more similar to each other than stronger versions of the same emotions. In principle, it would probably be possible to induce stronger emotions as well, but not without violating ethical principles. Another problem is that, unless the researcher is able to manipulate the appraisals directly (which is rather uncommon so far), it is difficult to make sure that every participant has experienced the same emotion. This problem can perhaps be mitigated by using manipulation checks (e.g. emotion scales) or, preferably, by manipulating appraisals as such. However, one additional problem is then that the approach in this more sophisticated version is fairly demanding for the researcher, who must be able to achieve experimental manipulation of cognitive appraisal (itself quite a challenge; but see Herrald & Tomaka 2002), as well as obtain appropriate physiological and acoustical measures (Johnstone *et al.* 2001).

Module C: Segmenting speech samples

The expression 'flow of speech' nicely characterizes the continuity of spoken language, which, unlike written language, does not offer a ready-made hierarchy of units such as letters, words, sentences, and paragraphs. In speech, the only 'natural' demarcations are typically the beginnings and endings of utterances, which may be as short as a 'yes' or as long as a political speech. Generally, the stream of speech must be segmented for purposes of analysis, to allow the quantitative description of fairly homogeneous and thus comparable parts of an utterance. This is an important prerequisite for proper analysis conditions and adequate interpretation of acoustic analyses. Researchers can construct hierarchies of segments in which lower-level segments, such as words, constitute a higher-level segment, such as a sentence. The choice of segments and their demarcation depends both on the nature of the voice parameter to be assessed and on the specific research aims. There are two major types of segmentation: physical and perceptual.

Physical segmentation means that boundaries are determined exclusively on the basis of physical criteria — that is, patterns of events or sound energy distribution. This is often chosen if automatic processing of speech via electro-acoustic equipment is desired. The simplest type of physical segmentation is to cut up the speech signal into fixed-length time slots, for example, consecutive 300-millisecond periods. Their length can be the result of many factors: limitations of the analysis equipment, theoretical considerations, or constraints of the analysis conditions (e.g. temporal resolution depending on sampling rate in digital analysis).

One type of physical segmentation consists of the differentiation between sound periods and silent periods on the basis of presence or absence of sound energy (and often involves fixed-length time slots as lower-order segments). This approach is primarily used in *interaction chronography* — the automatic detection of sound–silence patterns in dyadic conversations (e.g. Chapple 1948; Feldstein & Welkowitz 1978; Jaffe & Feldstein 1970; Matarazzo *et al.* 1965). Physical segments can also be defined and automatically detected in terms of periodic and non-periodic portions of the speech wave form, resulting in voiced and unvoiced segments (see Box 3.2).

Continued

Module C: Cont'd

For voiced speech segments, the individual cycles of the wave form are sometimes used as even more molecular segments.

Given the explosion of speech technology and its manifold uses in speech recognition, there have been major advances in recent years in the techniques for automatic or semi-automatic (i.e. computer-aided) segmentation of the speech signal. The state of the art is documented in a special issue of the journal *Speech Communication* dedicated to 'Speech annotation and corpus tools' (Vol. 33, Nos. 1–2, 2001). *Annotation* goes beyond segmentation in that the issue is not only to segment the speech flow into meaningful units, but to also define and categorize these units by assigning specific meaning or functionality. However, segmentation is always a necessary component of annotation.

Perceptual segmentation requires that the human information-processing system demarcates segments on the basis of prior categorization. This may involve criteria similar to those used in physical segmentation. For example, rather than using automatic devices, one can use a human listener to determine sound and silence portions within an utterance. The results from these two types of segmentation do not always match, because the human listener is influenced by his or her expectations concerning the presence of short silent portions in articulated speech, and may therefore not detect or report these silences.

Most of the perceptual segments normally used to cut up speech are derived from phonology and linguistics. Obvious examples are *phonemes* (single speech sounds), *morphemes* (the minimal meaningful units of language), *clauses* (subdivisions of a sentence each containing a subject and a predicate), and *sentences* (combinations of words that are complete as expressing a thought, satisfy the grammatical rules of a language, and, in writing, are marked at the close by a period or full point). Though phonological and lexical units such as phonemes, *syllables* (combinations of phonemes), and morphemes are fairly easy to delimit and categorize, the classification is more difficult for the more molar units, such as clauses and sentences, because one rarely finds well-formed sentences (in the classic linguistic sense) in spoken language. One possible way of avoiding this problem is to segment phonemic clauses (Boomer 1978; Dittmann & Llewellyn 1967; Trager & Smith 1957). These units are defined by prosodic features of speech, such as the occurrence of a primary stress or a juncture pause in a portion of speech.

Other potential perceptual segments are defined by criteria involving speech content, such as the marking of speech acts (e.g. Gottschalk & Gleser 1969; Morley & Stephenson 1977; Wish *et al.* 1980). More formal molar perceptual segments are *turns* (i.e. periods of a conversation during which a speaker holds the floor) and conversations or monologues as a whole. Of course, many more types of perceptual segments involving categorizations by human listeners are possible. For example, a student of rhetoric may attempt to segment a monologue into different types of arguments. Sociolinguists try to distinguish segments of conversations in terms of particular topics. Anthropologists may attempt to segment verbal interactions according to the type of functions fulfilled: greetings, leave-takings, and the like. These examples show that there is virtually no limit to the perceptual segments that can be differentiated in verbal utterances on the basis of structural or functional criteria.

One major problem that is often overlooked in naive approaches to segmentation is that the human observer is a fallible segmenter, and so the reliability of the segmentation procedure must be assured. This is particularly important in cases where content or functional criteria are used for the segmentation, rather than more formal criteria that require less inference from the observer. In the general case, segments consist of several units of analysis. *Units of analysis* are those portions of the segments that form the basis for obtaining a value for some parameter; for example, pauses might be the units of analysis for the parameter *average length of silent pauses* per segment (e.g. an utterance). Similarly, 20-millisecond stretches of speech arbitrarily demarcated in the voiced portions of the speech signal might be the units of analysis for *average fundamental frequency.* One either computes means and variability measures for the values of the parameters assessed on the basis of these units, or plots these values across the segment (e.g. an *intonation contour* as a plot of F0 values across an utterance). For both of these types of measurement, reasonably large numbers of units per segment are needed in order to assure stability of average values or, in the case of sequential analysis, reliability of change patterns.

Module D: Measuring voice cues acoustically

Acoustic measurement of voice cues is probably the method that holds the greatest promise for researchers of nonverbal markers of affect. Acoustic parameters may be obtained objectively, economically, and unobtrusively from speech recordings, and reflect both voice production and physiological determinants (Scherer 1989). Acoustic analysis has been simplified by the recent development of some advanced software packages for digital speech analysis (discussed below). Paradoxically, however, with more advanced measurement systems, the researcher is faced with numerous choices and parameters that must be properly selected to get appropriate measures of voice cues. Consequently, basic knowledge about speech acoustics (see Box 3.2) is still required to make informed choices about appropriate measurements and analytic techniques. The National Center for Voice and Speech in the USA made several recommendations regarding procedures, methods, and technology that may be consulted by researchers interested in conducting acoustic voice measurements.

A major problem in any study of vocal expression aiming to describe acoustic correlates is to select what voice cues to analyze. There is actually a whole range of possible voice measures that can be taken, each with its own pros and cons. Voice cues can be broadly divided into those related to:

1. fundamental frequency (F0)
2. voice intensity
3. voice quality
4. temporal aspects of speech.

(For details on how these relate to voice production, see Box 3.2.) A number of different measures can be obtained for each of these four types of voice cues, and it

Continued

Module D: Cont'd

seems that a large number of cues may be required (see p. 88). Table 3.5 summarizes the most important cues in the study of vocal affect expression, including definitions of each cue.

Several considerations are relevant in selecting what cues to analyze. First, what voice cues to measure depends strongly on the goals of the study. For example, if the goal is to measure the overall level of affective arousal, no more than a handful of voice cues may be needed to make a reasonably accurate prediction. On the other hand, if the goal is to be able to distinguish discrete emotions based on voice cues, a considerably larger number of voice cues is clearly required (see Banse & Scherer 1996; Juslin & Laukka 2001). In Table 3.5 we suggest minimum standard sets of voice cues to measure in order to be able to index arousal and different emotions, respectively. These are only rough guidelines, however, because the suitability of specific cues may vary from one situation to another.

The possibilities of analyzing particular voice cues depend partly on the recording quality of the speech samples (see Chapter 12) and the software for analysis used (discussed below). Looking back on previous research, the amount of data available for a given voice cue is inversely related to the amount of difficulty involved in measuring and interpreting the cue. Most researchers have analyzed only the three 'classic' cues (speech rate, fundamental frequency, and voice intensity), whereas other cues (e.g. pauses, formants, glottal wave form, rhythm) have received little study (see Table 3.5). Rather than only relying on the measures used in previous studies, a researcher may also want to consider using novel measures that involve, for example, interactions among pairs of cues or 'higher-order variables' that reflect combinations of measures in ways that are more similar to how humans actually perceive the voice (see Module I for possible procedures for devising such higher-order variables). Thus, for example, the percept of 'vocal effort' may represent a combination of acoustic cues such as voice intensity and high-frequency energy.

Acoustic measurements are today usually conducted by means of some computer software dedicated specifically to this purpose. A range of programs are commercially available such as *Speech Viewers, Dr. Speech Science, Computerized Speech Laboratory, Cspeech,* and *Soundswell.* Different programs use different storage formats, although some programs handle many formats (e.g. WAV, NIST, and uncompressed AIFC). MP3 and Atrac formats should be avoided, because their sound compression seriously degrades the original sound quality. One of the most comprehensive commercial programs currently available is Kay's *Computerized Speech Laboratory* (CSL), a complete hardware and software system with high performance standards, although it is quite expensive. One of the more frequently used program packages is the *PRAAT* software, which was developed by Boersma and Weenink (1999). *PRAAT* is a flexible computer program for acoustic analysis of speech that can be freely downloaded at the following website: *http://www.fon.hum.uva.nl/praat/.* This program permits analysis of most voice cues of relevance to vocal expression of affect, including F0, voice intensity, frequency spectrum, formants, voice onset time, shimmer, and jitter. (A basic introduction to the PRAAT software can be found in van Lieshout 2003.)

Continued

Table 3.5 Definition and acoustic measurement of voice cues in vocal affect expression

Acoustic cues	Perceived correlate	Definition and measurement
Pitch		
Fundamental frequency (F0) (59)*	Pitch	F0 represents the rate at which the vocal folds open and close across the glottis. Acoustically, F0 is defined as the lowest periodic cycle component of the acoustic wave form, and is extracted by computerized tracking algorithms (Scherer 1982). *Various measures:* mean (M), standard deviation (SD), range (R), max, min, median, mode, and floor (i.e. the lower 5% of F0 values).
F0 contour (19)*	Pitch contour	Sequence of F0 values across an utterance. Besides changes in pitch, the F0 contour also contains temporal information. The F0 contour is hard to operationalize and most studies report only qualitative classifications (Cowie *et al.* 2001), the proportion of rising to falling F0 contours (Juslin & Laukka 2001), or the range and gradient of F0 fall at the end of the sentence (Scherer *et al.* 2003).
Jitter (13)*	Pitch perturbations	Small-scale perturbations in F0 related to rapid and random fluctuations of the time of the opening and closing of the vocal folds from one vocal cycle to the next. Extracted by various computerized tracking algorithms (Scherer 1989).
Intensity		
Intensity (39)*	Loudness of speech	Intensity is a measure of energy in the acoustic signal and it reflects the effort required to produce the speech. It is usually measured from the amplitude acoustic wave form. The standard unit used to quantify intensity is a logarithmic transform of the intensity called the decibel (dB) (Scherer 1982). *Various measures:* mean (M), standard deviation (SD), range (R), Max, Min, Median, Mode.
Attack (2)*	Rapidity of voice onsets	The attack refers to the rise-time or rate of rise of amplitude for voiced speech segments. Usually measured from the amplitude of the acoustic wave form (Scherer 1989).
Shimmer (–)*	Loudness perturbations	Refers to small regular or irregular variations of amplitude maxima in successive glottal cycles. Extracted by computerized tracking algorithms (Scherer 1989).
Temporal aspects		
Speech rate (41)*	Velocity of speech	The rate can be measured as overall duration or as units per duration (e.g. words per minute). It may include either complete utterances or only the voiced segments of speech (Scherer 1982). *Various measures:* syllables per second, relative duration of voiced versus unvoiced segments, syllable duration, duration of accented vowels, total duration of utterance with or without pauses.
Pauses (14)*	Amount of silence in speech	Refers to silent periods in an utterance and is usually measured in terms of absence of energy in the acoustic wave form (see Scherer 1982 for a discussion).

Continued

Table 3.5 Cont'd

Acoustic cues	Perceived correlate	Definition and measurement
Rhythm (5)*	Speech rhythm	*Various measures*: relative number (P_n) and duration (P_d) of pauses (longer than 200–300ms) within or between selected units of analysis. There is yet no standardized measure of speech rhythm, but it has been suggested that the degree of regularity versus irregularity of speech may distinguish among positive and negative emotions (Davitz 1964; Juslin & Laukka 2003, Table 7).
Voice quality		
High-frequency energy (24)*	Voice quality	Refers to the relative proportion of total acoustic energy above, versus below, a certain cut-off frequency (e.g. Scherer *et al.* 1991). As the amount of high-frequency energy in the spectrum increases, the voice sounds more 'sharp' and less 'soft' (von Bismarck 1974). Obtained by measuring the *long-term average spectrum* (LTAS), which is the distribution of energy over a range of frequencies, averaged over an extended time period. *Various measures*: HF 500, HF 1000, spectral slope (linear regression of energy distribution in the frequency band above 1000Hz).
Formant frequencies (10)*	Voice quality	Refers to frequency regions in which the amplitude of acoustic energy in the speech signal is high, reflecting natural resonances in the vocal tract. The first two formants largely determine vowel quality, whereas the higher formants may be speaker-dependent (Laver 1980). The mean frequency and the width of the spectral band containing significant formant energy are extracted from the acoustic wave form by computerized tracking algorithms (Scherer 1989). *Various measures*: mean (M) and bandwidth (bw) for F1, F2, F3, and F4.
Precision of articulation (8)*	Articulatory effort	The vowel quality tends to move towards the formant structure of the neutral schwa vowel (e.g. as in 'sofa') under strong emotional arousal (Tolkmitt & Scherer 1987). The precision of articulation can be measured as the deviation of the formant frequencies from the neutral formant frequencies, as reported in various sources. F1 (precision) is most commonly measured.
Glottal wave form (8)*	Voice quality	The glottal flow wave form represents the time air is flowing between the vocal folds (abduction and adduction), and the time the glottis is closed, for each vibrational cycle. The shape of the wave form helps to determine the loudness of the sound generated and also its timbre. A 'jagged' wave form represents sudden changes in airflow that produce more high frequencies than a 'soft' wave form. The glottal wave form can be inferred from the acoustical signal using inverse filtering (Laukkanen *et al.* 1996).

Note: Recommended minimum set of voice cues to index level of *affective arousal*: F0 (floor), F0 (SD), voice intensity (M), speech rate (syllables per minute), and HF 500. Recommended minimum set of voice cues to discriminate *different emotions*: F0 (floor), F0 (SD), F0 contour (up/down), jitter, voice intensity (M, SD), speech rate (syllables per minute), pauses (P_d), rhythmic regularity, HF 500, and F1 (M, precision).

* This value indicates the number of studies that provided data points for each basic parameter in 104 studies of vocal expression of emotions (Juslin & Laukka 2003) and can be used as a rough index of the relative frequency with which each parameter has been measured previously.

Module D: Cont'd

Speech samples can easily be imported to the *PRAAT* software by recording directly onto the computer hard disk using the built-in sound card (in which case a number of adjustments must be made with regard to recording level, sample frequency, mono/ stereo recording) or by importing a speech sample from a digital recorder (see Chapter 12). One can then segment voiced and unvoiced sounds, words, and syllables in the speech signal of each speech sample by using the 'label and segment' function in PRAAT. This segmentation makes it possible to extract each segment either individually or simultaneously for further analyses. Thus, for example, one can select a sustained vowel production of interest and then use the 'edit' function of *PRAAT* to play, visualize, as well as extract information regarding the local F0, intensity, high-frequency energy, formant frequencies, jitter, and shimmer. It should be noted that because F0 is directly proportional to the length of the vocal cords (see Box 3.2), males, females, and children have different modal F0s (males 128Hz and females 260Hz). The cursor of the *PRAAT* display allows for measurement of different durations (voiced and non-voiced parts of speech sounds, pauses, voice onset time). A very useful feature of *PRAAT* is the 'formant report' option, which provides a report on all formant values obtained for the analyzed segment. Note that only formant values that are directly comparable (of the same vowel) should be averaged. Though many of the algorithms for extraction of voice cues are fairly reliable, we nevertheless recommend that automatic measures are checked manually, for example by visually comparing obtained formant data with spectrograms. A wideband spectrogram with a bandpass filter of about 300Hz allows for comparison of obtained formants with typical formant values for different vowels of men, women, and children (see, for example, Malecot 1974; Minifie 1973; Peterson & Barney 1952; Kent 1997). The results from acoustic measurements should preferably be analyzed using multivariate statistical techniques (see Module I).

Module E: Measuring voice cues at the physiological and phonatory-articulatory levels

Most of the methods available for the description of speech (or vocal expression generally) at the *physiological* level are highly technical, and require that the researcher has a high level of expertise. Among the methods adopted by physiologists are the assessment of breathing patterns with the help of various devices (e.g. thermistors to measure temperature differences between inhaled and exhaled air, or strain gauges to measure chest movement) or *electromyographic* (EMG) measurement of muscle activity (using surface or needle electrodes). Because the use of such objective measurement devices is too costly, complicated, and obtrusive for most research on nonverbal behavior, researchers have tried to measure variables on the physiological level by using simpler procedures.

In those cases where physiological processes or correlates thereof are visible, observational methods or coding procedures can be used. For example, changes in

Continued

Module E: Cont'd

some actions of the facial musculature, particularly around the mouth, could play an important role in assessing the effect of arousal on articulatory processes. It may thus be possible to score some of the muscle action changes using Ekman and Friesen's Facial Action Coding System (see Chapter 2). Unfortunately, most of the muscles that contribute to speech production are not visible and cannot be assessed in this way. This is the case, for instance, with the musculature that regulates phonation (intra- and extralaryngeal muscles). Breathing, on the other hand, may be amenable to observation — either its visible correlates (e.g. chest movement, mouth opening) or its auditory correlates (e.g. exhalation and inhalation noises) might be assessed. Unfortunately, the possibilities for such observation appear to be very limited, and the accuracy and validity of data obtained in such a manner have not been systematically evaluated.

Precise measurement of vocalizations at the *phonatory-articulatory* level of description is also restricted to experts with access to sophisticated apparatus. For example, high-speed video devices may be used to film the movement of the vocal folds, allowing exact determination of duration and shape of glottal openings. X-ray films of the movement of articulatory structures, displaying the speed of movement and the relationship of the major articulators to each other, can be produced. Moreover, electrodes may be placed on various surfaces within the vocal apparatus (e.g. the tongue and the hard palate), and computer-assessed plots of type and duration of contact among parts of the articulators can be obtained in this way (Kent 1997). But such methods may be of little use for nonverbal behavior researchers who want to obtain practicable measurements of vocal expression for a fairly large number of speakers.

One possible approach to measurement of phonatory-articulatory variables is to use auditory assessment techniques, in which experts try to infer the nature of the phonatory and articulatory processes that have produced a particular audible sound. Speech scientists and phoneticians are often able to infer many aspects of the nature of the production process on the basis of acoustic patterns, because during their training they will frequently have attempted to produce particular sound patterns, trying to control the phonation and articulation apparatus, and will have observed the resulting acoustic patterns. Furthermore, they have access to the accumulated knowledge about the relationship between particular phonation and articulation processes and the resulting acoustic patterns of sound waves.

Many coding schemes for paralinguistic phenomena involve auditory assessment of voice quality variables produced by phonatory or articulatory processes (Crystal 1969, 1975; Key 1977; Poyatos 1976). However, the diverse use of terms available for the description of phonation and articulation patterns has led to some confusion in the definition of particular concepts and the underlying processes. Consequently, voice quality concepts are used somewhat idiosyncratically, and assessment of reliability is rare.

Auditory assessment procedures are often used to diagnose vocal pathology associated with unusual voice quality (e.g. Greene 1972; Perkins 1971; Travis 1971). For example, a *breathy* voice is due to incomplete closure of the vocal folds during phonation, which allows excess air to escape into the superior vocal tract. A *harsh* voice, on the other hand, is the description used for phonation characterized by hypertense musculature, which results in irregular periods of vocal fold opening. Similarly, as far as articulation processes are concerned, terms such as 'slurred' or 'clipped' refer to movements of the articulators that do not result in the 'ideal' position for the production of certain sounds. Titze (1994) has proposed a categorization of voice qualities that combines perceptual categories and phonatory-articulatory processes that may be found at the following website: *http://www.ncvs.org/ncvs/tutorials/voiceprod/tutorial/quality.html.*

More systematic efforts have been made to develop protocols for the perceptual evaluation of pathological voice quality, including the GRBAS scale (Hirano 1981), the Hammarberg and Gauffin (1995) perceptual scales, the Wilson voice profile (Wilson 1971, 1972), and Laver's voice profile analysis (Laver 1980; Wirz & Beck 1995). However, the validity and reliability of many of these scales cannot be considered to be established yet (Kreiman *et al.* 1993; Kreiman & Gerratt 1996).

Affect inferences from voice cues

Research questions

Human inferences about emotion based on voice cues are extremely common and important in everyday life (see the introduction). For instance, imagine that a man at a call center receives a phone call from a customer. Within a few seconds, the man taking the call is able to infer that the caller is angry, and that the person, in fact, is getting increasingly angry during their conversation. Studies of affect inferences from voice cues aim to explain how such judgments come about. Key questions are:

- Can listeners (reliably) judge the affect expressed in nonverbal aspects of speech?
- Do listeners from different cultures make similar affect inferences?
- What voice cues are listeners utilizing to make such inferences?
- How are these cues integrated into judgments?
- Is it possible to create a computer program that can automatically recognize emotion from voice cues?
- Are vocal affect expressions perceived in terms of categories or dimensions?

Summary of previous research

A primary question is to what extent listeners really *are* able to infer emotions, felt or otherwise, based on voice samples. In the most extensive review to date (Juslin & Laukka 2003), 39 studies of vocal affect expression, featuring a total of 60 listening experiments, were included in a meta-analysis of decoding accuracy based on forced-choice judgments. The meta-analysis included both within-cultural and cross-cultural studies. The data were summarized in terms of Rosenthal and Rubin's (1989) effect size index for one-sample multiple-choice type data, *pi* (π), that allows researchers to transform decoding accuracy scores involving any number of response alternatives to a standard scale of dichotomous choice, on which 0.50 is always the null value and 1.00

corresponds to 100% correct decoding. The results indicated that overall decoding accuracy was high for both within-cultural and cross-cultural vocal affect expression (see Table 3.6). The accuracy for within-cultural vocal expression was equivalent to a 'raw' accuracy score of $p_c = 0.70$ in a forced-choice task with five response alternatives (Rosenthal & Rubin 1989, Table 1). However, overall decoding accuracy was nearly 7% higher for within-cultural ($\pi = 0.90$) than for cross-cultural vocal expression ($\pi = 0.84$). It should also be noted that decoding was accurate for both emotion portrayals and natural vocal expressions (see Module B), as well as regardless of whether the stimuli were pre-selected from a larger pool of speech samples, or not.

The patterns of accuracy estimates for individual emotions were similar across the sets of data. Specifically, sadness ($\pi > 0.91$, $M = 0.92$) and anger ($\pi > 0.88$, $M = 0.91$) portrayals were best decoded, followed by fear ($\pi > 0.82$, $M = 0.86$) and happiness portrayals ($\pi > 0.74$, $M = 0.82$). Worst decoded throughout was tenderness ($\pi > 0.71$, $M = 0.78$), but it should be noted that the estimates for this emotion were based on fewer data points. This pattern of results differs from the pattern found in studies of facial expression of emotion, where happiness is usually better decoded than other emotions (e.g. Elfenbein & Ambady 2002). The standard deviation of decoding accuracy across studies was generally small. This result was surprising, as one would expect the accuracy to vary a lot depending on the emotions studied, the encoders, the verbal material, the decoders, the procedure, and so forth. However, it is consistent with the Brunswikian lens model (see p. 86), which predicts stability at the distal level (decoding accuracy), albeit not on the mediation level (cue utilization).

Table 3.6 Summary of results from a meta-analysis of decoding accuracy for different emotions (adapted from Juslin & Laukka 2003)

	EMOTION					
	Anger	Fear	Happiness	Sadness	Tenderness	Overall
Vocal expression						
Mean (unweighted)	0.93	0.88	0.87	0.93	0.82	0.90
95% confidence interval	± 0.021	± 0.037	± 0.040	± 0.020	± 0.083	± 0.023
Mean (weighted)	0.91	0.88	0.83	0.93	0.83	0.90
Median	0.95	0.90	0.92	0.94	0.85	0.92
Standard deviation	0.059	0.095	0.111	0.056	0.079	0.072
Range	0.23	0.35	0.49	0.20	0.19	0.31
Number of studies	32	26	30	31	6	38
Number of speakers	278	273	253	225	49	473
Cross-cultural vocal expression						
Mean (unweighted)	0.91	0.82	0.74	0.91	0.71	0.84
95% confidence interval	± 0.017	± 0.062	± 0.040	± 0.018	–	± 0.024
Mean (weighted)	0.90	0.82	0.74	0.91	0.71	0.85
Median	0.90	0.88	0.73	0.91	–	0.84
Standard deviation	0.031	0.113	0.077	0.036	–	0.047
Range	0.10	0.38	0.29	0.15	–	0.16
Number of studies	6	5	6	7	1	7
Number of speakers	69	66	68	71	3	71

Thus, previous research indicates that vocal communication of emotions is quite accurate, even across cultures, at least for certain emotions. However, there are various limitations of this research. Only a few emotions have been thoroughly studied (see Module A). Further, the use of forced-choice formats has been criticized on the grounds that participants are provided with only a limited number of response alternatives to choose from (Russell 1994). It could be argued that listeners manage the task by forming exclusion rules or guessing, without thinking that any of the response alternatives are appropriate to describe the expression (Frick 1985). Those studies that have used free labeling of emotions, rather than forced-choice, suggest that communication is still possible, though the accuracy is lower (Johnson *et al.* 1986; Kaiser 1962; Greasley *et al.* 2000; see Module F for a discussion of different response formats).

Context cues are probably important in shaping our judgments of emotion based on voice cues in everyday life (Planalp 1998). This may include such things as knowing that the person had just received a letter or a phone call, was getting married, or had a school assignment due. Context cues provide background information, and thereby alert the observer to a possible, or even likely, emotion. However, context cues are usually missing in laboratory experiments. An exception is a unique study by Cauldwell (2000) that showed that people may interpret the same vocal expression differently depending on the context. Hence, although the slightly stereotypical emotion portrayals by actors and the response formats most commonly used (e.g. forced choice) may artificially inflate the estimates of decoding accuracy, the lack of context is likely to *deflate* accuracy artificially. It has also been argued that perceivers may be more involved in the task of forming impressions in real life, and that high involvement and accountability yields more active information seeking and more complex judgment strategies, and thus greater decoding accuracy (Zebrowitz 1990). All things considered, the reported estimates of decoding accuracy may not be too far off the mark.

How do listeners arrive at their emotion inferences? One implication of the Brunswikian lens model discussed above (see p. 83) is that expression of emotion in the voice is conceptually separate from the utilization of voice cues by listeners. Hence, although a specific voice cue may be correlated with felt emotion in a speaker, this does not necessarily say anything about whether a listener actually *uses* this cue in his or her judgments. Conversely, if a listening test reveals that a listener is using a certain voice cue to make inferences about emotions, this does not itself mean that this cue is a *reliable* indicator of the expressed emotion. Each of the these processes has to be investigated in its own right, although preferably in a combined fashion.

A number of studies have attempted to capture the nature of listeners' emotion inferences based on voice cues. Different methodological approaches have been used that may be broadly differentiated in terms of type of experimental design (e.g. *representative* vs. *factorial* design) and type of voice stimuli used (e.g. *speech sample, synthesis,* or *resynthesis*). One method is to use speech samples that express different emotions and to analyze the relations among listeners' ratings of these voice samples and measures of representative, or naturally occurring, variations in voice cues (e.g. Banse & Scherer 1996, Table 8; Juslin & Laukka 2001, Table 7). Another approach is to use speech synthesis in order to systematically manipulate individual voice cues independently in a factorial design (including all possible combinations of cues) and to measure the effects of these cue manipulations on judgments (Scherer & Oshinsky 1977). This approach is effective in unequivocally establishing that a given cue really has effects on listener inferences (because all intercorrelations are eliminated by the design), although it may present listeners with certain cue combinations that would not occur naturally. Thus, an alternative approach may be to manipulate synthesized voice cues in such a way that they recreate the formal characteristics of the natural environment (e.g. in terms of the distributions of cue levels and cue intercorrelations), something that Brunswik (1956) referred to as *formal situational sampling*.

One final approach is afforded by resynthesis (copy synthesis), where one copies selected acoustic characteristics from real vocal expressions, and then uses them to resynthesize new expressions. This method makes it possible to manipulate certain cues of a vocal affect expression, while at the same time leaving other cues intact (e.g. Ladd *et al.* 1985; Schröder 2001). This procedure offers a useful combination of experimental control and natural-sounding speech. Still, certain aspects of the resulting stimuli may sound artificial.

To summarize, then, the pros and cons of analysis and synthesis have to be weighted against each other, and although a researcher may be forced to select a particular strategy in a specific investigation, research programs as a whole require the combined use of analysis and synthesis to reach a good understanding of the roles of individual voice cues (see Module G for a discussion of synthesis and manipulation techniques).

Studies of emotion inferences from voice cues using analysis and synthesis have revealed strong and systematic relationships among emotion inferences and a number of different voice cues. However, an important goal for future research may be to reach beyond these correlations and to develop a model of the actual perceptual process: how, exactly, are voice cues integrated in emotion perception? Some initial progress has been made in recent attempts to develop tools for automatic recognition of affect (e.g. Oudeyer 2003; Petrushin 2002; Slaney & McRoberts 2003), although these efforts were mainly focused on creating a high-performance system rather than on developing authentic models of how humans recognize emotions in speech. For instance, a call center could feature an automatic dialogue system that is able to determine, on the basis of a customer's vocal expression of anger, when it is advisable to pass over to the human operator (Batliner *et al.* 2003). However, from a basic research perspective, it is important to model the manner in which *humans* integrate information from various voice cues into emotion judgments.

One crucial problem is how human perceivers manage to infer not only the emotion expressed, but also the *intensity* of the emotion. It would seem that a computational model of emotion decoding from vocal cues requires the dual features of emotion categorization and intensity grading. In fact, a two-stage system for automatic emotion recognition and intensity estimation based on Hidden Markow Models was presented by Song *et al.* (2004). However, it is unclear whether that system works similarly to how human perceivers handle this task. One hypothesis suggested in previous research (Juslin & Laukka 2001) is that the emotion category is indexed by the *pattern* of voice cues, whereas the emotion intensity is indexed by the *absolute* levels of a subset of these same cues.

Another important question is how vocal expressions of emotion are subjectively perceived: are they perceived as discrete emotional categories or as varying along a few underlying emotion dimensions? Which of these perspectives best describe the phenomenology of the perceiver? One line of research that could help to answer this question, and that exploits some of the methods we have reviewed (e.g. synthesis, speech sample manipulation) are studies of categorical perception (Harnad 1987). Categorical perception occurs when continuous sensory stimulation is sorted out by the brain into discrete categories. A discrete-emotions approach to vocal expression (see Box 3.1) would predict that emotions are perceived as discrete categories. Some preliminary evidence supporting this prediction has been obtained (de Gelder & Vroomen 1996; Laukka 2004), and these results are consistent with the results from studies of perception of facial expressions (see Chapter 2). However, on the basis of the present evidence, it cannot be ruled out that categorical responses are explicitly or implicitly influenced by the existence of discrete, verbal emotion concepts.

Conducting studies of affect inferences from voice cues

The primary step in studies of emotion inferences from voice cues involves conducting judgment studies (see also Chapter 5), in which participants are asked to rate or recognize the emotions expressed (or portrayed) in speech samples (Module F). Further steps include synthesizing and manipulating speech samples (Module G), measuring proximal voice cues (Module H), and analyzing data using various multivariate statistics (Module I). All these steps are critically dependent on previous steps (Modules A and B), because the outcome from the procedures outlined in Modules F–I will reflect the nature of the speech samples used.

Module F: Conducting judgment studies

Judgment studies are highly important in studies of vocal expression, and there are many reasons why a researcher would like to conduct such a study. A listening test is the only way to determine that a given vocal affect expression conveys a specific state in a way that is correctly recognized by perceivers. Hence, in attempting to specify what voice cues are used in emotion inferences, it is mandatory to first establish that a speech sample indeed conveys such emotions. Furthermore, if the goal is to model listeners' cue utilization, the researcher needs to obtain, for instance, listeners' ratings on the relevant emotion dimensions that can be correlated with voice cues that have been measured (see Module D) or manipulated (see Module G). There are several issues that must be considered when planning a judgment study; here we will only review some basic options. (For a more extensive overview, see Chapter 5.)

An important problem in planning a judgment study is to choose an appropriate response format. The *forced-choice* format (i.e. choosing one emotion label from a short list) is a simple technique, which makes it possible to compare the judgment data with previous results involving the same response format. However, the accuracy could be artificially inflated or deflated if there is a small number of response options simply because the participants are unable to choose other, potentially more applicable response options. Frank and Stennett (2001) suggested that the latter

---

Continued

Module F: Cont'd

problem may be partly alleviated by introducing an additional option ('other emotion') that the participant can choose if none of the provided alternatives appears appropriate.

One problem in comparing accuracy scores from different studies is that they use different numbers of response alternatives in the decoding task. Rosenthal and Rubin's (1989) effect size index for one-sample multiple-choice type data, *pi* (π), allows researchers to transform accuracy scores involving any number of response options to a standard scale (see p. 107). Ideally, an index of accuracy should also take into account the *response bias* in the decoder's judgments (e.g. Wagner 1993). However, this requires that results are presented in terms of a so-called *confusion matrix*, which relatively few studies have reported. Table 3.7 shows an example of a confusion matrix, which is arguably the best way to present forced-choice data, because it reveals the exact distribution of correct and incorrect responses. A variant of forced-choice is to use an *adjective checklist* (e.g. marking any number of suitable affect labels from a list). This format does not force the judge to choose just one affect label, regardless of what he or she perceives in the stimulus. On the other hand, adjective checklists do not offer a standard measure of decoding accuracy, and the results may thus be more complicated to analyze.

Quantitative ratings (i.e. rating the stimulus on selected adjective scales that range from, say, 1 to 7) provide more information than do forced-choice data, and also mitigate one of the problems with the forced-choice format by allowing subjects to rate portrayals equally high on several emotion scales. However, quantitative ratings (like adjective checklists) do not offer a standard measure of accuracy that is easily compared across studies. (However, see Resnicow *et al*. 2004 for a suggested measure.) Still, if a researcher intends to use various multivariate statistics (see Module I) to model listeners' cue utilization, quantitative ratings are preferable to forced-choice judgments because they provide data on a more nearly interval scale required for these techniques. However, this format may also lead to difficulties with statistical analyses due to the large number of zeros for dimensions not used by the judge.

Free description (i.e. describing the stimulus using any words that come to mind) may be regarded as a more unbiased estimate of decoding accuracy because the judge's response is not influenced by the available response alternatives. As may be expected, there is greater variability in judges' responses when they use free description than when they use either forced-choice or adjective ratings. However, the use of open-ended formats is not without problems. There are several different words for the same emotion, and it is hard to decide whether or not different judges are perceiving the same emotion (i.e. regardless of the particular verbal label used).

In any case, it is desirable to use a wider variety of response formats in future research on vocal expression (Greasley *et al*. 2000), perhaps combining forced-choice with free description (as proposed by Rosenthal 1982) or using computer tools for continuous measurement of emotion perception from voice cues (Cowie *et al*. 2000).

Table 3.7 Example of confusion matrix in terms of listeners' forced-choice judgments of emotion in vocal expressions (adapted from Juslin & Laukka 2001)

	Emotion judgments					
	Anger	Disgust	Fear	Happiness	Sadness	No expression
Emotions portrayed						
Anger	58	18	6	4	2	12
Disgust	31	40	4	4	4	17
Fear	0	2	60	3	27	8
Happiness	6	3	21	51	6	12
Sadness	1	2	24	1	63	8
No expression	4	4	4	5	11	72

Note: The percent of correctly judged portrayals are given on the main diagonal. The off-diagonal cells show the confusions. $N = 2640$.

Module G: Synthesizing and manipulating speech samples

Is it possible to create a computer system that can add emotional expressivity to synthesized speech? Indeed, recent research has suggested that researchers are able to synthesize vocal affect expressions that are decoded with accuracy similar to that obtained for human speech (cf. p. 108). Synthesis of emotional speech has received increasing interest, from the original attempts to synthesize speech-like sound sequences on Moog synthesizers (e.g. Scherer 1974; Scherer & Oshinsky 1977) to more recent uses of speech synthesizers (Murray & Arnott 1995). Synthesis of vocal affect expression is useful both for voice researchers who want to test predictions about relationships among voice cues and emotion inferences, and for engineers who develop practical applications (e.g. in robots, communication systems for motor- and vocally-impaired individuals, call centers, lie detection, computer games, airport security; for reviews, see, for example, Hudlicka 2003; McKenzie *et al.* 2003; Picard 1997).

Early interest in speech synthesis focused largely on making synthesized speech intelligible, although with the intelligibility of synthetic speech approaching that of human speech (Greene *et al.* 1986), focus has now shifted to increasing the naturalness. One of the primary aspects of the absence of naturalness in synthetic speech is appropriate emotional expressivity. Hence, recent years have seen considerable progress in the attempts to create computerized systems that reliably convey different emotions to listeners. These systems usually consist of two main parts that are partly independent:

1. A set of principles (e.g. *prosodic rules*) for how each of a set of different emotions should be conveyed (commonly expressed formally in terms of a stand-alone computer program with various input parameters).
2. An implementation of these principles in a system for speech synthesis, such as a speech synthesizer.

The expressive principles for each emotion are normally derived from literature reviews as well as from heuristic adjustments based on listening tests.

Continued

Module G: Cont'd

There are, broadly speaking, three different approaches to synthesis (Schröder 2001). The choice of method depends on the researcher's aims. The different approaches involve a trade-off between flexibility of acoustic modeling and perceived naturalness. The optimal balance between these vary from situation to situation. For the researcher wanting to test detailed predictions about the effects of a large number of voice cues, flexibility may be the primary requirement. However, for the engineer trying to develop a system that works in applied contexts, naturalness may have a higher priority.

Rule-based synthesis (formant synthesis) creates synthesized speech entirely based on rules for how acoustic correlates of speech sounds should vary in order to achieve desired effects. No recordings of human speech are used in the implementation of the rules in the speech synthesis. The resulting speech sounds relatively unnatural and robot-like compared to most concatenative systems (see below), though a large number of parameters related to both voice source and vocal tract can be varied quite freely. This is, of course, interesting for modeling emotional expression in speech, where it is essential that a sufficient number of parameters can be included and varied systematically. Examples of rule-based synthesis are Murray and Arnott's (1995) HAMLET and Cahn's (1990) Affect Editor (which both rely on the commercially available speech synthesizer *DECtalk*), as well as Burkhardt's (2001) *emoSyn* system. Table 3.8 summarizes a set of prosodic rule set-ups from various previous studies that used rule-based synthesis (from Schröder 2001).

Another approach to synthesis is *diphone concatenation*, where audio recordings of human speakers are concatenated in order to generate the synthetic speech. The use of *diphones*, that is, stretches of the speech signal from the middle of one speech sound (*phone*) to the middle of the next, is common. F0 contours are produced through signal processing techniques that generate a certain amount of distortion. Yet, the resulting speech quality is usually considered more natural-sounding than that of rule-based synthesis. Most diphone systems only allow control over F0 and duration (and, sometimes, voice intensity), whereas voice quality is usually impossible to control. Studies using concatenative synthesis have shown that emotions can be conveyed to some extent, despite the lack of voice quality variations (e.g. Murray *et al.* 2000; Schröder 1999). But unless voice quality manipulation can be added also, concatenative synthesis is not sufficient for testing comprehensive theories of vocal affect expression. Examples of concatenative synthesis may be found in Schröder (1999) and Vroomen *et al.* (1993).

A third approach to synthesis is *unit selection* (i.e. corpus-based, large-database synthesis). This technique is usually perceived as sounding most natural, and involves selecting speech units of variable size from a large database — units that approximate a desired target utterance defined by a set of selection parameters. The outcome of this method depends primarily on the quality of the database. If well-matched speech units are found, the method may produce highly natural results, even without further signal processing. On the other hand, if no appropriate units are found for a particular case, the result may be quite inferior. Examples of synthesis using unit selection can be found in Iida *et al.* (2003) and Campbell (2004).

Table 3.8 Examples of successful prosodic rules for synthesis of emotional speech from various studies (adapted from Schröder 2001, Table 1)

Emotion	Language	Rule settings
Anger	British English	F0 mean: + 10Hz F0 range: + 9 semitones Tempo: + 30 words per minute Loudness: + 6dB Voice quality: laryngealization +78%; F4 frequency −175Hz Other: increased pitch of stressed vowels (secondary, +10% of pitch range; primary, +20% of pitch range; empathic, +40% of total pitch)
Boredom	Dutch	F0 mean: end frequency 65Hz (male speech) F0 range: excursion size 4 semitones Tempo: duration relative to neutrality 150% Other: final intonation pattern 3C; avoid final patterns 5&A and 12
Fear	German	F0 mean: +150% F0 range: +20% Tempo: +30% Voice quality: falsetto
Joy	German	F0 range: +50% F0 range: +100% Tempo: +30% Voice quality: modal or tense; F1, F2 +10% Other: main stressed syllables are raised 100%, syllables in between are lowered −20%
Sadness	American English	F0 mean: 0, reference line −1, less final lowering −5 F0 range: −5, steeper accent shape +6 Tempo: −10, more fluent pauses +5, hesitation pauses +10 Loudness: −5 Voice quality: breathiness +10, brilliance −10 Other: stress frequency +1, precision of articulation −5

Note: For further information, see the original studies cited in Schröder's (2001) review.

Module G: Cont'd

Sound examples of synthesized vocal affect expressions based on different methods can be found by searching the web, where many of the leading speech research laboratories demonstrate their work. Speech synthesizers that allow manipulation of various aspects of speech rate, pitch contour, and voice quality are now commercially available. Thus, for instance, *DECtalk* converts standard text into highly intelligible speech using a computer sound card and offers a choice of nine 'voice personalities', intonation and speed control, and built-in phonetic, linguistic, and pronunciation rules. Similarly, *TripleTalk* (PCI) features eight predefined voices, 10 volume levels, 10 different speeds, 100 unique pitches, and is fully configurable.

Continued

Module G: Cont'd

Parameters such as tone and intonation are also adjustable. Although both these systems are highly flexible, they may require some expert knowledge in order to make full use of their features. For further information on speech synthesis, see Santen *et al.* (1997) and Tatham and Morton (2003).

In addition to the various possibilities for synthesis and resynthesis, there are also several *content-masking procedures* that can be used in a systematic fashion. As the term implies, these procedures were originally devised to mask the verbal contents of vocal affect expressions (e.g. Starkweather 1956). However, because the procedures also disrupt or degrade different aspects of the paralinguistic features, they may also be used to investigate the role of specific voice cues.

Low-pass filtering (letting the speech signal pass through a filter that attenuates all energy above, say, 400Hz; Rogers *et al.* 1971) preserves the F0 contour, albeit it reduces the spectral content and attenuates the perceived loudness. Crucial aspects of voice quality are lost when using this method.

Random splicing (Scherer 1971), in contrast, preserves spectral contents but disrupts the temporal organization and the F0 contour (although summary measures, such as F0 mean, are largely preserved). This method was developed by splicing speech samples into small pieces of tape, randomly rearranging the pieces, and splicing them back together again, having eliminated all pauses. In the age of digital signal processing, this process is performed by means of an automatic editing procedure, which features a smoothing algorithm for the boundary transitions. A number of temporal aspects of speech (e.g. pausing, continuity of F0 contour, and rhythm) are disrupted by this method.

Reiterant speech is produced by replacing the syllables of an utterance with 'nonsense syllables' that generate a similar F0 contour (Friend & Farrar 1994). This method preserves F0 level, range, and contour, and also temporal features and voice quality.

It is important to note that although a fair degree of decoding accuracy can be obtained even with content-masked procedures, all of these procedures 'bias' the decoding process (in different ways, depending on the emotion). Hence, no speech sample that has been content-masked can be said to yield valid estimates of decoding accuracy. If (for some reason) content masking must be used to mask the verbal content, reiterant speech is probably the best procedure to use, because it leaves as much as possible of the voice cues unaltered (Friend & Farrar 1994). However, the fact that each procedure degrades or disrupts some information while leaving other information intact, and also leads to biases in the decoding of separate emotions, can be used to systematically study how different voice cues are involved in the emotion inference process (e.g. Scherer *et al.* 1972). Continued research on the particular effects of different masking techniques is clearly needed (Lakshminarayanan *et al.* 2003; van Bezooijen & Boves 1986).

Module H: Measuring proximal voice cues

This chapter focuses on objective measurements of various parameters of vocal expression, achieved through digital acoustic analysis, physiological assessment, or observation (sometimes in the form of judgments by voice experts based on auditory impressions). However, the normal listener is not an expert on voice production and will probably perceive and evaluate the sounds that reach his or her ear in a different manner. If the researcher's interest is exclusively focused on diagnosing the state of the speaker by means of voice analysis (i.e. the encoding aspect in the Brunswikian lens model), listener perception is of little interest. However, in studies focusing on communication, or on perceivers' cue utilization in person perception and emotion attribution, it is important to consider the dimensions or categories that naive listeners are using to distinguish different voices and voice changes.

While a century of research on psychoacoustics has provided extensive knowledge on how the characteristics of the human hearing mechanism processes acoustic information — particularly with regard to the representation of F0 as pitch, the detection of pitch changes, and the frequency bands to which our ear is particularly sensitive (e.g. Zwicker, 1982) — the nature of the proximal representation of voice cues is not very well understood at present. To date, little research effort has been expended on this question. For example, we do not know whether the dimensions and categories that people use in processing the acoustic voice cues they hear are congruent with the concepts that phoneticians, acousticians, and voice therapists are using. There is some evidence that even voice professionals do not show very impressive agreement in ratings of voice disorders on clinically relevant voice quality dimensions (Kreiman *et al.* 1993). The rating procedure can be improved by providing anchors for each perceptual voice dimension and allowing the judges to place all stimuli on a continuum with respect to each other and the anchors, for instance using an interactive, computerized procedure (Bänziger 2004).

The obvious approach to inventory the dimensions of naive listeners' impressions of voice differences and vocal change is to use 'folk categories' — that is, the verbal labels that people use to refer to and converse about their voice impressions (e.g. a 'blaring' voice). This assumes that languages have developed categories that are somehow important to communicate about salient voice dimensions. Unfortunately, there are many open questions concerning the verbal codability of proximal percepts. For example, do the verbal labels that a language makes available for the description of voices and vocalizations determine the categories that the perceiver will eventually use in processing such stimuli? Or are those proximal percepts independent of verbal labels and categories, so that they must be translated into verbal terms if a need to communicate proximal percepts arises (as when researchers ask about them)?

One of the major problems in assessing proximal percepts of voice parameters via verbal labels is that many of the terms available (e.g. *strident, harsh*, and *shrill*) have rather strong implied valence connotations (i.e. good–bad, normal–pathological). These implications are quite obvious for voice labels such as gloomy, strong, nice, or clear. It is interesting that many works of fiction use voice descriptions instead of personality or mood characterizations — presumably because the authors assume

Continued

the existence of stereotypical links between specific types of voice descriptors and personality and mood categories. Research on voice and personality has indeed confirmed that stereotypical inference rules linking particular voice characteristics to personality traits are very strong (e.g. Kramer 1963; Scherer 1972).

In spite of the many problems in attempts to measure proximal percepts of vocal expression characteristics, it is necessary to make a concerted effort to study the nature of these percepts in order to understand the process of voice cue utilization (as specified in the lens model in p. 83). One of the first steps is to attempt to develop standardized rating scales that incorporate the verbal labels used in different languages to describe vocalization characteristics in everyday life. Based on preparatory work by a group of linguists, phoniatricians, communication scientists, and psychologists, Bänziger and Scherer (2004) have developed and tested such a rating scale. Table 3.9 presents the categories of the scale, as well as the respective reliabilities and correlations with voice cues and emotion attributions. While this rating scale has been profitably used in a study of emotion inferences from vocal portrayals based on the Brunswikian lens model (Bänziger 2004), further efforts are required to elaborate such rating scales and adapt them to different languages.

Module I: Analyzing data from vocal affect expression studies

Results obtained in measurements of voice cues may be analyzed in a number of different ways. One critical issue is how to interpret the data for different emotions. Should the data for individual emotions be compared to each other, or to some presumably 'neutral' expression, or both? According to a basic principle in pragmatics, the emotional coloring of speech should be interpreted as 'deviations' from some general norm for speech expected in a particular context (e.g. Caffi & Janney 1994). The problem is to find an appropriate 'baseline' against which to compare changes in cues associated with various emotions. Several studies have classified data in terms of 'increases' or 'decreases', which means that the data are measured against average levels across emotions. One problem with this approach is that the average is affected by what emotions were featured in the analysis. Studies that use different sets of emotions will therefore produce different baselines, which means that the findings from different studies are not directly comparable (Juslin & Laukka 2001).

One proposed solution has been to use supposedly neutral vocal expressions as the baseline. However, this approach has yielded mixed results (e.g. Scherer *et al.* 1991), perhaps because it is not clear to actors how a term like 'neutral' should actually be interpreted. It is further unclear whether normal speech is ever truly 'neutral'. A better alternative might be to compare the data against recordings of natural speech for each speaker, thus providing a separate baseline for each speaker. Such voice recordings could be made, for instance, during the recording procedure or during interviews. Still, even natural (and presumably neutral) speech is highly variable over time, since speech itself is a dynamic process (e.g. Murray *et al.* 1996).

All of this suggests that finding useful baselines is one of the most important problems for studies of vocal expression in order to improve comparability across

Continued

Table 3.9 Average reliabilities of assessed voice categories; correlations with selected acoustic cues and emotional intensity ratings (adapted from Bänziger 2004)

	Average reliability		Acoustic cues[3]						Emotion attributions[3]			
	R[1]	R[2]	Int. mean	Int. range	F0 min.	F0 range	Duration	Energy <1kHz	Fear	Joy	Sadness	Anger
Articulation	0.32	0.87	0.28	0.33	−0.09	0.04	−0.13	−0.20	**−0.28**	0.22	−0.47	0.29
Intonation	0.40	0.91	**0.71**	**0.54**	**0.43**	**0.63**	−0.24	**−0.56**	0.09	**0.50**	−0.35	**0.42**
Loudness	0.85	0.99	**0.92**	**0.55**	**0.46**	**0.60**	−0.27	**−0.74**	0.06	0.16	−0.32	**0.76**
Pitch	0.52	0.94	**0.68**	**0.46**	**0.57**	**0.61**	−0.17	**−0.46**	**0.31**	**0.47**	−0.09	**0.31**
Roughness	0.31	0.86	0.35	0.09	0.30	0.27	0.07	**−0.40**	0.09	**−0.33**	0.13	**0.47**
Speed	0.66	0.97	**0.70**	0.20	0.33	0.33	**−0.74**	**−0.60**	0.21	0.16	**−0.49**	**0.59**
Sharpness	0.59	0.95	**0.89**	**0.50**	**0.53**	**0.67**	−0.27	**−0.72**	0.15	0.24	−0.25	**0.69**
Unsteadiness	0.47	0.93	−0.11	0.18	0.38	0.07	0.39	0.14	**0.60**	−0.01	0.67	−0.29

[1] r = single measure intraclass correlation
[2] R = average measure intraclass correlation
[3] Pearson correlations, N =144, p<0.05 in bold

- 'Articulation' (bad ↔ good articulation) ['articulation', mal ↔ bien articulée]
- 'Intonation' (monotonous ↔ modulated) ['mélodie', monotone ↔ modulée]
- 'Loudness' (weak ↔ strong) ['volume', faible ↔ forte]
- 'Pitch' (low ↔ high) ['hauteur', grave ↔ aiguë]
- 'Roughness' (not rough ↔ rough) [qualité 'rauque']
- 'Speed' (slow ↔ fast) ['vitesse', lente ↔ rapide]
- 'Sharpness' (not sharp ↔ sharp) [qualité 'perçante']
- 'Instability' (steady ↔ shaky) ['stabilité', ferme ↔ tremblante]

Module I: Cont'd

studies and making possible rigorous testing of theoretical predictions. This problem can be mitigated to some extent if researchers report the data in a more comprehensive fashion, including raw data in addition to various transformations and correlation analyses. This will allow other researchers to re-analyze the data for the purpose of comparing them with other data sets in meta-analyses.

Because vocal affect expression involves a large number of (partly) redundant cues that are imperfectly related to expressed or portrayed emotions (see p. 83), correlational statistics may be especially useful in analyzing the data since correlational methods, by default, provide measures of strength of relationship (or *effect sizes*) and also take into consideration the intercorrelations among voice cues. Multivariate methods are preferable to univariate inferential statistics, which fail to take into account the complex relations between voice cues and emotions. The precise choice of multivariate technique depends, of course, on the goals of the analysis.

If the goal is to predict the amount of a single, metric dependent variable (e.g. arousal) on the basis of a set of metric predictors (e.g. a subset of voice cues), *multiple regression analysis* may be the most useful method (Cohen *et al.* 2003). For instance, Juslin and Laukka (2001) were able to account for 70% of the variance in listeners' judgments of emotion intensity in vocal affect expressions based on five voice cues: F0 (floor), F0 (SD), F1, HF 500, and voice attack (see Table 3.5 for a definition of each cue). Such an analysis may also explore the contributions of interactions among voice cues (Aiken & West 1991), as well as non-linear function forms (e.g. inverted U-shaped curves) between voice cues and judgments.

However, if the dependent variable is multichotomous (i.e. nonmetric and consisting of categories), while the predictors are still metric, *multiple discriminant analysis* is the method of choice. Using this method, one may predict which emotion, out of a set of emotion categories, is expressed by a set of voice cues. Banse and Scherer (1996) conducted discriminant analysis with voice cues as predictors, and found that vocal affect expressions could be correctly classified at a rate and with error patterns similar to those of human judges (see also van Bezooijen 1984).

Further, if the goal is to find clusters of entities that have similar characteristics on certain metric dimensions (e.g. speech utterances with similar patterns of acoustic characteristics) and that form mutually exclusive groups, one can use *cluster analysis*. This method could perhaps be used in a bottom-up approach to empirically find groups of discrete emotions in speech samples based on voice characteristics alone, as long as the speech samples are 'representative' of the range of voice characteristics that occur in the natural environment.

On the other hand, if the goal is to transform judgments of object similarity (e.g. among speech utterances) into distances represented in a multidimensional space (e.g. in terms of emotion dimensions such as activation and valence), then *multidimensional scaling* is the preferred method.

If the goal is to analyze the inter-relationships among a large number of variables (such as voice cues), and to explain these variables in terms of their common underlying dimensions (or factors), one might conduct a *factor analysis*. This method could be used to find 'higher-order variables' (e.g. based on physiological principles of voice production; see Box 3.2) that underlie the separately measured acoustic cues. It seems possible that some of the past problems in the field reflect the fact that researchers have not yet found the optimal voice measures.

Last, but not least, if the goal is to model the *complete* communicative or inferential process in vocal expression (as in the lens model), then *structural equation modeling* (i.e. path analysis) might be the most useful method. There are also some novel techniques, such as data mining by means of neural networks (Petrushin 2002), that may be useful in analyzing vocal expressions. (For further discussion of multivariate techniques, see, for example, Hair *et al.* 1998.) Some of the more advanced software systems for speech analysis (e.g. *PRAAT*) include modules for certain multivariate analyses.

Given the large individual differences among encoders (and to some extent decoders), we recommend that researchers consider using an *ideographic* statistical approach (see Brunswik 1956) to analysis, in which the vocal behavior of individuals are modeled before the results are aggregated. This has seldom been done in previous research, but it could be one important step towards a better understanding of the variability in data from studies of vocal affect expression. As noted earlier, Brunswik's lens model may allow us to explain many of the inconsistencies in earlier findings in terms of the nature of the communicative or inferential process (see p. 85). This is because it allows the inherent variability of conditions *into* the statistical analysis, thereby explaining how stable 'distal' inferences are achieved despite instable (or variable) relationships at the mediation level. In the lens model, correlation statistics can be used to model listeners' cue utilization in a fashion analogous to how a speaker's use of voice cues can be modeled. For more detailed examples of the use of correlational statistics and path analysis to model communication of emotions using the lens model, see Scherer (1978), Juslin (2000), and Bänziger (2004).

Concluding remarks

The vocal channel of expression of affect has received rather less research attention than the facial channel (see Chapter 2), mirroring the relative emphasis placed on these modalities by the pioneers in this area (e.g. Darwin 1872/1998; Tomkins 1962). As this chapter suggests, this situation is about to change. In particular, the methodological difficulties associated with the storage and analysis of sound (Scherer 1982) have been partially resolved by the rapid development and availability of new technology for the digital storage, editing, and analysis of vocal utterances. However, the most important impetus for the proliferation of studies on vocal affect expression has been the recent interest in large-scale application of speech technology in automatic speech and speaker recognition and speech synthesis. Speech scientists and engineers have been able to make much progress in the sophistication and quality of such systems over the last 20 years, and the hardware and software to recognize speech and speakers automatically, or to have computers speak, is now widely available. However, the expected breakthrough in the mass marketing of these devices has not yet occurred, in large part because of the long-term neglect of the important role of affect in speech. For instance, automatic speech and speaker recognition that achieves a remarkable level of accuracy under controlled laboratory conditions produces a lot of recognition errors in field tests. Often this is because stress and other affective factors change the voice and speech parameters to such an extent that normal recognition algorithms fail. Similarly, even though synthetic speech (due to the use of diphone concatenation methods; see Module G) currently produces synthetic utterances with impressive quality and intelligibility (Santen *et al.* 1997), most people still prefer other humans, rather than computers, speaking to them. Often, the reason given is that synthetic speech sounds monotonous and lacks essential affective quality.

Partly in response to this problem — but doubtlessly also because of intrinsic interest in the phenomenon — work on vocal affect expression by speech scientists such as phoneticians and by engineers has been mushrooming (see the special issue of the journal *Speech Communication*, Vol. 40, Issue 1–2, 2003). Much of this research is published in proceedings of meetings such as Eurospeech or the International Conference on Spoken Language Processing (ICSLP) and is thus difficult to access for researchers who are not members of the respective networks. Conversely, researchers at the engineering end of the field often find it difficult to follow the widely dispersed publications on vocal affect expression in other disciplines. However, we feel that progress in this complex and exciting domain of research requires intensive interdisciplinary approaches. As this chapter shows, theoretical background and methodological competencies from many disciplines are required to conduct state-of-the art research in this domain. Hopefully, then, the current trend toward such interdisciplinary collaboration will continue. In conclusion, we will enumerate some desiderata for the future.

Much of the research to date has been untheoretical and unconcerned with the mechanisms that underlie vocal affect expression. We feel that the field has now reached a stage where it is feasible to plan research on the basis of established theoretical positions and, most importantly, to critically compare different approaches. In this chapter, we have advocated the Brunswikian lens model as a meta-structure for studies in this area, especially because it alerts researchers to important design considerations in studies of vocal affect expression. We have also emphasized that vocal expression involves the joint operation of push and pull effects, and the interaction of psychobiological and sociocultural factors, both of which urgently need to be addressed in future studies. So far there is very little cross-language and cross-cultural research in this area, which is surprising because phonetic features of language may constrain the affect-signaling potential of voice cues (see Scherer *et al.* 2001a, and the discussion of tone languages in Scherer *et al.* 2003.) Finally, the cumulativeness of research would increase if voice researchers could converge on measuring a standardized and relatively complete set of acoustic or perceptual cues in order to allow replication, and to adhere to standard forms of analyzing and reporting the results (e.g. providing confusion matrices and effect sizes). Such convergence on research methodology would make it easier to perform future meta-analyses (Juslin & Laukka 2003).

Another hope for future research is that we will see much more in the line of multi-modal approaches. As has been noted above, vocal expression of affect is usually part and parcel of a larger set of expressive behaviors that include facial expressions, gesture, posture, and so forth. Unless these modalities are studied jointly, the mutual constraints and dependencies cannot be empirically explored. Apart from the need to understand interactions between modalities with respect to the underlying mechanisms, these also play an important role in many technological applications, such as multi-modal computer interfaces in production, sales, service, education, and entertainment (Hudlicka 2003; Lisetti & Nasoz 2002; Paiva 2000). Current concern with the development of believable autonomous or virtual agents, capable of producing appropriate affect expression and understanding human affect communication, should be a powerful motor for greater multimodal integration in future research on the expression of affect.

Acknowledgements

The authors gratefully acknowledge helpful comments and suggestions by Tanja Bänziger, Jinni Harrigan, and Robert Rosenthal. The writing of this chapter was supported by the Swedish Research Council, the Bank of Sweden Tercentenary Foundation, the Swiss National Research Fund, and the European Network of Excellence HUMAINE (Human-Machine Interaction Network on Emotion).

References

Aiken, L.S. & West, S.G. (1991). *Multiple regression: testing and interpreting interactions.* London: Sage.

Alku, P., Strik, H., & Vilkman, E. (1997). Parabolic spectral parameter: a new method for quantification of the glottal flow. *Speech Communication, 22,* 67–79.

Apple, W., Streeter, L.A., & Krauss, R.M. (1979). Effects of pitch and speech rate on personal attributions. *Journal of Personality and Social Psychology, 37,* 715–27.

Aristotle (1932). *The rhetoric of Aristotle* (trans. L. Cooper). New York: Appleton. (Original work published c. 330 BC.)

Bachorowski, J.A. (1999). Vocal expression and perception of emotion. *Current Directions in Psychological Science, 8,* 53–7.

Bänziger, T. (2004). *Communication vocale des émotions: perception de l'expression vocale et attributions émotionnelles.* Unpublished doctoral dissertation, University of Geneva, Switzerland.

Bänziger, T. & Scherer, K.R. (in press). The role of intonation in emotional expressions. *Speech Communication.*

Bänziger, T. & Scherer, K.R. (2004). *A Brunswikian lens approach to the study of vocal communication of emotion.* Manuscript submitted for publication.

Banse, R. & Scherer, K.R. (1996). Acoustic profiles in vocal emotion expression. *Journal of Personality and Social Psychology, 70,* 614–36.

Batliner, A., Fischer, K., Huber, R., Spilker, J., & Nöth, E. (2003). How to find trouble in communication. *Speech Communication*, 40, 117–43.

Belin, P., Zatorre, R.J., & Ahad, P. (2002). Human temporal-lobe responses to vocal sounds. *Cognitive Brain Research*, 13, 17–26.

Bloch, S., Orthous, P., & Santibañez, G. (1987). Effector patterns of basic emotions: a psycho-physiological method for training actors. *Journal of Social Biology and Structure*, 10, 1–19.

Boersma, P. & Weenink, D. (1999). *Praat 3.8.24*. Computer software, Institute of Phonetic Sciences, University of Amsterdam, The Netherlands.

Bolger, N., Davis, A., & Rafaeli, E. (2003). Diary methods: capturing life as it is lived. *Annual Review of Psychology*, 54, 579–616.

Boomer, D.S. (1978). The phonemic clause: speech unit in human communication. In *Nonverbal behavior and communication* (ed. A.W. Siegman & S. Feldstein), pp. 245–62. Hillsdale, NJ: Erlbaum.

Boone, R.T. & Buck, R. (2003). Emotional expressivity and trustworthyness: the role of nonverbal behavior in the evolution of cooperation. *Journal of Nonverbal Behavior*, 27, 163–82.

Borden, G.J., Harris, K.S., & Raphael, L.J. (1994). *Speech science primer: physiology, acoustics and perception of speech* (3rd edn). Baltimore, MD: Williams & Wilkins.

Breitenstein, C., van Lancker, D., & Daum, I. (2001). The contribution of speech rate and pitch variation to the perception of vocal emotions in a German and an American sample. *Cognition & Emotion*, 15, 57–79.

Brown, B.L. (1980). The detection of emotion in voice qualities. In *Language: social psychological perspectives* (ed. H.Giles, W.P. Robinson, & P.M. Smith), pp. 237–45. Oxford, UK: Pergamon Press.

Brown, B.L., Strong, W.J., & Rencher, A.C. (1975). Acoustic determinants of perceptions of personality from speech. *International Journal of the Sociology of Language*, 6, 11–32.

Brunswik, E. (1956). *Perception and the representative design of psychological experiments*. Berkeley, CA: University of California Press.

Buck, R. (1984). *The communication of emotion*. New York: Guilford Press.

Bugental, D.E. (1974). Interpretation of naturally occurring discrepancies between words and intonation: modes of inconsistency resolution. *Journal of Personality and Social Psychology*, 30, 125–33.

Bühler, K. (1934). *Sprachtheorie. Die Darstellungsfunktion de Sprache*. Jena: Fischer.

Burkhardt, F. (2001). *Simulation emotionaler Sprechweise mit Sprachsyntheseverfahren (Simulation of emotional speech by means of speech synthesis)*. Doctoral dissertation, Technische Universität Berlin, Germany.

Burns, K.L. & Beier, E.G. (1973). Significance of vocal and visual channels in the decoding of emotional meaning. *Journal of Communication*, 23, 118–30.

Busnel, R.G. (1977). Acoustic communication. In *How animals communicate* (ed. T.A. Sebeok), pp. 233–51. Bloomington, IN: Indiana University Press.

Buss, D.M. & Kenrick, D.T. (1998). Evolutionary social psychology. In *The handbook of social psychology, Vol. 2* (ed. D.T. Gilbert, S.T. Fiske, & G. Lindzey), pp. 982–1026. Boston: McGraw–Hill.

Caffi, C. & Janney, R.W. (1994). Toward a pragmatics of emotive communication. *Journal of Pragmatics*, 22, 325–73.

Cahn, J.E. (1990). The generation of affect in synthesized speech. *Journal of the American Voice I/O Society*, 8, 1–19.

Campbell, N. (2004). Specifying affect and emotion for expressive speech synthesis. *Lecture Notes in Computer Sciences*, 2945, 395–406.

Carlson, R., Granström, B., & Nord, L. (1993). Synthesis experiments with mixed emotions: a progress report. In *Fonetik–93: papers from the 7th Swedish Phonetics Conference* (ed. J.S. Pettersson), pp. 65–8. Uppsala, Sweden: Department of Linguistics, Uppsala University.

Cauldwell, R. (2000). Where did the anger go? The role of context in interpreting emotions in speech. In *Proceedings of the ISCA workshop on speech and emotion* (CD-ROM) (ed. R. Cowie, E. Douglas–Cowie, & M. Schröder). Belfast, UK: International Speech Communication Association.

Chapple, E.D. (1948). The interaction chronograph: its evolution and present application. *Personnel*, 25, 295–307.

Christie, I.C. & Friedman, B.H. (2004). Autonomic specificity of discrete emotions and dimensions of affective space: a multivariate approach. *International Journal of Psychophysiology*, 51, 143–53.

Cohen, J., Cohen, P., West, S.G., & Aiken, L.S. (2003). *Applied multiple regression/correlation analysis for the behavioral sciences* (3rd edn). Hillsdale, NJ: Erlbaum.

Cowie, R. & Cornelius, R.R. (2003). Describing the emotional states that are expressed in speech. *Speech Communication*, 40, 5–32.

Cowie, R., Douglas–Cowie, E., Savvidou, S., McMahon, E., Sawey, M., & Schröder, M. (2000). FEELTRACE: an instrument for recording perceived emotion in real time. In *Proceedings of the ISCA workshop on speech and emotion* (CD-ROM) (ed. R. Cowie, E. Douglas–Cowie, & M. Schröder). Belfast, UK: International Speech Communication Association.

Cowie, R., Douglas–Cowie, E., Tsapatsoulis, N., Votsis, G., Kollias, S., Fellenz, W., *et al.* (2001). Emotion recognition in human-computer interaction. *IEEE Signal Processing Magazine*, 18, 32–80.

Crystal, D. (1969). *Prosodic systems and intonation in English*. Cambridge, UK: Cambridge University Press.

Crystal, D. (1975). *The English tone of the voice*. London: Arnold.

Crystal, D. & Quirk, R. (1964). *Systems of prosodic and paralinguistic features in English*. The Hague: Mouton.

Darby, J.K. (ed.). (1981). *Speech evaluation in psychiatry*. New York: Grune and Stratton.

Darwin, C. (1998). *The expression of the emotions in man and animals* (3rd edn). London: Harper–Collins. (Original work published 1872.)

Davidson, R.J., Scherer, K.R., & Goldsmith, H.H. (ed.). (2003). *Handbook of affective sciences*. New York: Oxford University Press.

Davitz, J.R. (1964). Auditory correlates of vocal expression of emotional feeling. In *The communication of emotional meaning* (ed. J.R. Davitz), pp. 101–12. New York: McGraw–Hill.

Dawes, R.M. & Corrigan, B. (1974). Linear models in decision making. *Psychological Bulletin*, 81, 95–106.

de Gelder, B. (2000). Recognizing emotions by ear and by eye. In *Cognitive neuroscience of emotion* (ed. R.D. Lane & L. Nadel), pp. 84–105. New York: Oxford University Press.

de Gelder, B. & Vroomen, J. (1996). Categorical perception of emotional speech (abstract). *Journal of the Acoustical Society of America*, **100**, 2818.

Denes, P.B. & Pinson, E.N. (1993). *The speech chain: the physics and biology of spoken language* (2nd edn). New York: Freeman.

Dittman, A.T. & Llewellyn, L.G. (1967). The phonemic clause as a unit of speech decoding. *Journal of Personality and Social Psychology*, **6**, 341–9.

Douglas–Cowie, E., Campbell, N., Cowie, R., & Roach, P. (2003). Emotional speech: towards a new generation of data bases. *Speech Communication*, **40**, 33–60.

Eibl–Eibesfeldt, I. (1989). *Human ethology.* New York: Aldine.

Ekman, P. (1997). Should we call it expression or communication? *Innovations in Social Science Research*, **10**, 333–44.

Ekman, P. (1999). Basic emotions. In *Handbook of cognition and emotion* (ed. T. Dalgleish & M. Power), pp. 45–60. Sussex, UK: John Wiley & Sons.

Ekman, P., Friesen, W.V., & Scherer, K.R. (1976). Body movement and voice pitch in deceptive interaction. *Semiotica*, **16**, 23–7.

Ekman, P., Levenson, R.W., & Friesen, W.V. (1983). Autonomic nervous system activity distinguishes among emotions. *Science*, **221**, 1208–10.

Eldred, S.H. & Price, D.B. (1958). A linguistic evaluation of feeling states in psychotherapy. *Psychiatry*, **21**, 115–21.

Elfenbein, H.A. & Ambady, N. (2002). On the universality and cultural specificity of emotion recognition: a meta-analysis. *Psychological Bulletin*, **128**, 203–35.

Ellgring, H. & Scherer, K.R. (1996). Vocal indicators of mood change in depression. *Journal of Nonverbal Behavior*, **20**, 83–110.

Fahrenberg, J. & Myrtek, M. (ed.). (1996). *Ambulatory assessment: computer-assisted psychological and psychophysiological methods in monitoring and field studies.* Seattle: Hogrefe.

Fant, G. (1960). *Acoustic theory of speech production.* The Hague: Mouton.

Feldstein, S. & Siegman, A.W. (ed.) (1987). *Nonverbal behavior and communication* (2nd edn). Hillsdale, NJ: Erlbaum.

Feldstein, S. & Welkowitz, J. (1978). A chronography of conversation: in defense of an objective approach. In *Nonverbal behavior and communication* (ed. A.W. Siegman & S. Feldstein), pp. 329–78. Hillsdale, NJ: Erlbaum.

Frank, M.G. & Stennett, J. (2001). The forced-choice paradigm and the perception of facial expressions of emotion. *Journal of Personality and Social Psychology*, **80**, 75–85.

Frick, R.W. (1985). Communicating emotion: the role of prosodic features. *Psychological Bulletin*, **97**, 412–29.

Friend, M. & Farrar, M.J. (1994). A comparison of content-masking procedures for obtaining judgments of discrete affective states. *Journal of the Acoustical Society of America*, **96**, 1283–90.

Funder, D.C. (1995). On the accuracy of personality judgment: a realistic approach. *Psychological Review*, **102**, 652–70.

Gigerenzer, G. (2001). Ideas in exile: the struggles of an upright man. In *The essential Brunswik: beginnings, explications, applications* (ed. K.R. Hammond & T.R. Stewart), pp. 445–52. New York: Oxford University Press.

Gobl, C. & Ní Chasaide, A. (2003). The role of voice quality in communicating emotion, mood and attitude. *Speech Communication,* **40**, 189–212.

Goodall, J. (1986). *The chimpanzees of Gombe: patterns of behavior.* Cambridge, MA: Harvard University Press.

Gottschalk, L.A. & Gleser, G.C. (1969). *The measurement of psychological states through the content analysis of verbal behavior.* Berkeley, CA: University of California Press.

Greasley, P., Sherrard, C., & Waterman, M. (2000). Emotion in language and speech: methodological issues in naturalistic settings. *Language and Speech,* **43**, 355–75.

Greene, M.C.L. (1972). *The voice and its disorders* (2nd edn). New York: Pitman.

Greene, B.G., Logan, J.S., & Pisoni, D.B. (1986). Perception of synthetic speech produced automatically by rule: intelligibility of eight text-to-speech systems. *Behavior Research Methods, Instruments, and Computers,* **18**, 100–07.

Hair, J.F., Anderson, R.E., Tatham, R.L., & Black, W.C. (1998). *Multivariate data analysis* (5th edn). London: Prentice–Hall.

Hammarberg, B. & Gauffin, J. (1995). Perceptual and acoustic characteristics of quality differences in pathological voices as related to physiological aspects. In *Vocal fold physiology: voice quality control* (ed. O. Fujimura & M. Hirano), pp. 283–303. San Diego, CA: Singular Press.

Hammond, K.R. & Stewart, T.R. (ed.) (2001). *The essential Brunswik: beginnings, explications, applications.* New York: Oxford University Press.

Harnad, S. (ed.) (1987). *Categorical perception. The groundwork of cognition.* New York: Cambridge University Press.

Harrigan, J.A., Gramata, J.F., Lucic, K.S., & Margolis, C. (1989). It's how you say it: physicians' vocal behavior. *Social Science and Medicine,* **28**, 87–92.

Harrigan, J.A., Lucic, K.S., & Rosenthal, R. (1991). Retelling anxious events: effects on trait and state anxiety. *Personality and Individual Differences,* **12**, 917–27.

Hauser, M.D. (2000). The sound and the fury: primate vocalizations as reflections of emotion and thought. In *The origins of music* (ed. N.L. Wallin, B. Merker, & S. Brown), pp. 77–102. Cambridge, MA: MIT Press.

Havrdová, Z. & Morávek, M. (1979). Changes of the voice expression during suggestively influenced states of experiencing. *Activitas Nervosa Superior,* **21**, 33–5.

Hecker, M.H.L., Stevens, K.N., Bismarck, G.V., & Williams, C.E. (1968). Manifestations of task-induced stress in the acoustic speech signal. *Journal of the Acoustical Society of America,* **44**, 993–1001.

Helfrich, H. & Wallbott, H.G. (1986). Contributions of the German 'expression psychology' to nonverbal behavior research. Part IV: the voice. *Journal of Nonverbal Behavior,* **10**, 187–204.

Herrald, M.H. & Tomaka, J. (2002). Patterns of emotion-specific appraisal, coping, and cardiovascular reactivity during an on-going emotional episode. *Journal of Personality and Social Psychology,* **83**, 434–50.

Hirano, M. (1981). *Clinical examination of voice.* New York: Springer.

Hudlicka, E. (2003). To feel or not to feel: the role of affect in human-computer interaction. *International Journal of Human-Computer Studies, 59*, 1–32.

Hummert, M.L., Mazloff, D., & Henry, C. (1999). Vocal characteristics of older adults and stereotyping. *Journal of Nonverbal Behavior, 23*, 111–32.

Huttar, G.L. (1968). Relations between prosodic variables and emotions in normal American English utterances. *Journal of Speech and Hearing Research, 11*, 481–7.

Iida, A., Campbell, N., Higuchi, F., & Yasamura, M. (2003). A corpus-based speech synthesis system with emotion. *Speech Communication, 40*, 161–87.

Izard, C.E. (1993). Organizational and motivational functions of discrete emotions. In *Handbook of emotions* (ed. M. Lewis & J.M. Haviland), pp. 631–41. New York: Guilford Press.

Jaffe, J. & Feldstein, S. (1970). *Stochastic models of the time patterns of dialogue: rhythms of dialogue.* New York: Academic Press.

Johnson, W.F., Emde, R.N., Scherer, K.R., & Klinnert, M.D. (1986). Recognition of emotion from vocal cues. *Archives of General Psychiatry, 43*, 280–3.

Johnstone, T. (2001). *The communication of affect through modulation of non-verbal vocal parameters.* Unpublished doctoral dissertation, University of Western Australia, Nedlands, Western Australia.

Johnstone, T., Van Reekum, C.M., & Scherer, K.R. (2001). Vocal expression correlates of appraisal processes. In *Appraisal processes in emotion. Theory, methods, research* (ed. K.R. Scherer, A. Schorr, & T. Johnstone), pp. 271–84. New York: Oxford University Press.

Jürgens, U. (2002). Neural pathways underlying vocal control. *Neuroscience and Biobehavioral Reviews, 26*, 235–58.

Juslin, P.N. (2000). Cue utilization in communication of emotion in music performance: relating performance to perception. *Journal of Experimental Psychology: Human Perception and Performance, 26*, 1797–813.

Juslin, P.N. & Laukka, P. (2001). Impact of intended emotion intensity on cue utilization and decoding accuracy in vocal expression of emotion. *Emotion, 1*, 381–412.

Juslin, P.N. & Laukka, P. (2003). Communication of emotions in vocal expression and music performance: different channels, same code? *Psychological Bulletin, 129*, 770–814.

Juslin, P.N. & Sloboda, J.A. (ed.). (2001). *Music and emotion: theory and research.* New York: Oxford University Press.

Kaiser, L. (1962). Communication of affects by single vowels. *Synthese, 14*, 300–19.

Kappas, A. (1997). *His master's voice: acoustic analysis of spontaneous vocalizations in an on-going active coping task.* Paper presented at the 37th Annual Meeting of the Society for Psychophysiological Research, Cape Cod, MA.

Kennedy, G. (1972). *The art of rhetoric in the Roman world. 300 BC–AD 300.* Princeton, NJ: Princeton University Press.

Kent, R.D. (1997). *The speech sciences.* San Diego, CA: Singular Press.

Key, M.R. (1977). *Nonverbal communication: a research guide and bibliography.* Metuchen, NJ: Scarecrow Press.

Klasmeyer, G. & Sendlmeier, W.F. (2000). Voice and emotional states. In *Voice quality measurement* (ed. R.D. Kent & M.J. Ball), pp. 339–57. San Diego, CA: Singular Press.

Kramer, E. (1963). Judgment of personal characteristics and emotions from nonverbal properties. *Psychological Bulletin*, **60**, 408–20.

Krebs, J.R. & Dawkins, R. (1984). Animal signals: mind-reading and manipulation. In *Behavioural ecology: an evolutionary approach* (2nd edn) (ed. J.R. Krebs & N.B. Davies), pp. 380–40. Oxford: Blackwell.

Kreiman, J. & Gerratt, B.R. (1996). The perceptual structure of pathologic voice quality. *Journal of the Acoustical Society of America*, **100**, 1787–95.

Kreiman, J., Gerratt, B.R., Kempster, G.B., Erman, A., & Berke, G.S. (1993). Perceptual evaluation of voice quality: review, tutorial, and a framework for future research. *Journal of Speech and Hearing Research*, **36**, 21–40.

Kuny, S. & Stassen, H.H. (1993). Speaking behavior and voice sound characteristics in depressive patients during recovery. *Journal of Psychiatric Research*, **27**, 289–307.

Kuroda, I., Fujiwara, O., Okamura, N., & Utsuki, N. (1976). Method for determining pilot stress through analysis of voice communication. *Aviation, Space, and Environmental Medicine*, **47**, 528–33.

Ladd, D.R., Silverman, K.E.A., Tolkmitt, F., Bergmann, G., & Scherer, K.R. (1985). Evidence of independent function of intonation contour type, voice quality, and F_0 range in signaling speaker affect. *Journal of the Acoustical Society of America*, **78**, 435–44.

Ladefoged, P. (1993). *A course in phonetics* (3rd edn). New York: Harcourt, Brace, Jovanovich.

Lakshminarayanan, K., Shalom, D.B., van Wassenhove, V., Orbelo, D., Houde, J., & Poeppel, D. (2003). The effect of spectral manipulations on the identification of affective and linguistic prosody. *Brain and Language*, **84**, 250–63.

Laukka, P. (2004). Vocal expression of emotion: discrete-emotions and dimensional accounts. *Comprehensive Summaries of Uppsala Dissertations from the Faculty of Social Sciences 141.* Uppsala, Sweden: Uppsala University Library.

Laukka, P., Juslin, P.N., & Bresin, R. (in press). A dimensional approach to vocal expression of emotion. *Cognition & Emotion.*

Laukkanen, A.–M., Vilkman, E., Alku, P., & Oksanen, H. (1996). Physical variations related to stress and emotional state: a preliminary study. *Journal of Phonetics*, **24**, 313–35.

Laver, J. (1980). *The phonetic description of voice quality.* Cambridge, UK: Cambridge University Press.

Laver, J. & Hutcheson, S. (ed.) (1972). *Communication in face to face interaction.* Harmondsworth: Penguin.

Levin, H. & Lord, W. (1975). Speech pitch frequency as an emotional state indicator. *IEEE Transactions on Systems, Man, and Cybernetics*, **5**, 259–73.

Lewis, M. (2000). The emergence of human emotions. In *Handbook of emotions* (ed. M. Lewis & J.M. Haviland–Jones), pp. 265–80. New York. Guilford Press.

Levitt, E.A. (1964). The relationship between vocal and facial communication abilities. In *The communication of emotional meaning* (ed. J.R. Davitz), pp. 87–100. New York: McGraw–Hill.

Lisetti, C.L. & Nasoz, F. (2002). MAUI: a multimodal affective user interface. In *Proceedings of the 10th ACM International Conference on Multimedia*, pp. 161–70. New York: ACM Press.

MacLean, P. (1993). Celebral evolution of emotion. In *Handbook of emotions* (ed. M. Lewis & J.M. Haviland), pp. 67–83. New York: Guilford Press.

Malecot, A. (1974). Cross-language phonetics. In *Current trends in linguistics 12. Linguistics and adjacent arts and sciences, 4* (ed. T.A. Sebeok), pp. 2507–36. The Hague: Mouton.

Marler, P. (1977). The evolution of communication. In *How animals communicate* (ed. T.A. Sebeok), pp. 45–70. Bloomington, IN: Indiana University Press.

Marty, A. (1908). *Untersuchungen zur grundlegung der allgemeinen grammatik und sprachphilosophie.* Halle: Niemeyer.

Mastropieri, D. & Turkewitz, G. (1999). Prenatal experience and neonatal responsiveness to vocal expressions of emotion. *Developmental Psychobiology,* **35**, 204–14.

Matarazzo, J.D., Wiens, A.N., & Saslow, G. (1965). Studies in interview speech behavior. In *Research in behavior modification* (ed. L. Krasner & L.P. Ullmann), pp. 179–212. New York: Holt, Rinehart & Winston.

McKenzie, F., Scerbo, M., Catanzaro, J., & Phillips, M. (2003). Nonverbal indicators of malicious intent: affective components for interogative virtual reality training. *International Journal of Human Computer Studies,* **59**, 237–44.

Miller, J. (1990). Communication without words. In *Ways of communicating* (ed. D.H. Mellor), pp. 113–24. Cambridge, UK: Cambridge University Press.

Minifie, F.D. (1973). Speech acoustics. In *Normal aspects of speech, hearing, and language* (ed. F.D. Minifie, T.J. Hixon, & F. Williams), pp. 235–84. Englewood Cliffs, NJ: Prentice–Hall.

Morley, L. & Stephenson, G. (1977). *The social psychology of bargaining.* London: George Allen & Unwin.

Morrison, N. (1994). *Introduction to Fourier analysis.* New York: Wiley.

Moses, P. (1954). *The voice of neurosis.* New York: Grune & Stratton.

Murray, I.R. & Arnott, J.L. (1993). Toward the simulation of emotion in synthetic speech: a review of the literature on human vocal emotion. *Journal of the Acoustical Society of America,* **93**, 1097–108.

Murray, I.R. & Arnott, J.L. (1995). Implementation and testing of a system for producing emotion-by-rule in synthetic speech. *Speech Communication,* **16**, 369–90.

Murray, I.R., Baber, C., & South, A. (1996). Towards a definition and working model of stress and its effects on speech. *Speech Communication,* **20**, 3–12.

Murray, I.R., Edgington, M.D., Campion, D., & Lynn, J. (2000). Rule-based emotion synthesis using concatenated speech. In *Proceedings of the ISCA Workshop on Speech and Emotion* (CD-ROM) (ed. R. Cowie, E. Douglas–Cowie, & M. Schröder). Belfast, UK: International Speech Communication Association.

O'Shaughnessy, D. (2000). *Speech communication: human and machine* (2nd edn). New York: IEEE Press.

Oudeyer, P.Y. (2003). The production and recognition of emotions in speech: features and algorithms. *International Journal of Human-Computer Studies,* **59**, 157–83.

Owren, M.J. & Bachorowski, J.A. (2001). The evolution of emotional expression: a 'selfish-gene' account of smiling and laughter in early hominids and humans. In *Emotions: current issues and future directions* (ed. T.J. Mayne & G.A. Bonanno), pp. 152–91. New York: Guilford Press.

Paiva, A. (ed.) (2000). *Affective interactions: toward a new generation of affective interfaces.* New York: Springer

Papoušek, H., Jürgens, U., & Papoušek, M. (ed.) (1992). *Nonverbal vocal communication: comparative and developmental approaches.* Cambridge: Cambridge University Press.

Pereira, C. (2000). Dimensions of emotional meaning in speech. In *Proceedings of the ISCA Workshop on Speech and Emotion* (CD-ROM) (ed. R. Cowie, E. Douglas–Cowie, & M. Schröder). Belfast, UK: International Speech Communication Association.

Perkins, W.H. (1971). *Speech pathology.* St. Louis, MO: C.V. Mosby.

Peterson, G.E. & Barney, H.L. (1952). Control methods used in a study of the vowels. *Journal of the Acoustical Society of America,* **24**, 175–84.

Petrushin, V.A. (2002). Creating emotion recognition agents for speech signal. In *Socially intelligent agents* (ed. K. Dautenhahn *et al.*), pp. 77–84. Dordrecht, The Netherlands: Kluwer.

Picard, R.W. (1997). *Affective computing.* Cambridge, MA: MIT Press.

Pittam, J., Gallois, C., & Callan, V. (1990). The long-term spectrum and perceived emotion. *Speech Communication,* **9**, 177–87.

Planalp, S. (1998). Communicating emotion in everyday life: cues, channels, and processes. In *Handbook of communication and emotion* (ed. P.A. Andersen & L.K. Guerrero), pp. 29–48. New York: Academic Press.

Ploog, D. (1986). Biological foundations of the vocal expressions of emotions. In *Emotion. Theory, research, and experience. Volume 3: Biological foundations of emotion* (ed. R. Plutchik & H. Kellerman), pp. 173–97. New York: Academic Press.

Ploog, D. (1992). The evolution of vocal communication. In *Nonverbal vocal communication: comparative and developmental approaches* (ed. H. Papoušek, U. Jürgens, & M. Papoušek), pp. 6–30. Cambridge: Cambridge University Press.

Plutchik, R. (1980). A general psychoevolutionary theory of emotion. In *Emotion: theory, research, and experience. Vol. 1: Theories of emotion* (ed. R. Plutchik & H. Kellerman), pp. 3–33. New York: Academic Press.

Plutchik, R. (1994). *The psychology and biology of emotion.* New York: Harper–Collins.

Poyatos, F. (1976). *Man beyond words: theory and methodology of nonverbal communication.* New York: New York State English Council.

Resnicow, J.E., Salovey, P., & Repp, B.H. (2004). Is recognition of emotion in music performance an aspect of emotional intelligence? *Music Perception,* **22**, 145–58.

Roessler, R. & Lester, J.W. (1976). Voice predicts affect during psychotherapy. *Journal of Nervous and Mental Disease,* **163**, 166–76.

Rogers, P.L., Scherer, K.R., & Rosenthal, R. (1971). Content filtering human speech: a simple electronic system. *Behavioral Research Methods and Instruments,* **3**, 16–18.

Rosenthal, R. (1982). Judgment studies. In *Handbook of methods in nonverbal behavior research* (ed. K.R. Scherer & P. Ekman), pp. 287–361. Cambridge: Cambridge University Press.

Rosenthal, R. & Rubin, D.B. (1989). Effect size estimation for one-sample multiple-choice-type data: design, analysis, and meta-analysis. *Psychological Bulletin,* **106**, 332–37.

Russell, J.A. (1980). A circumplex model of affect. *Journal of Personality and Social Psychology,* **39**, 1161–78.

Russell, J.A. (1994). Is there universal recognition of emotion from facial expression? A review of the cross-cultural studies. *Psychological Bulletin,* **115**, 102–41.

Russell, J.A. & Feldman Barrett, L. (1999). Core affect, prototypical emotional episodes, and other things called emotion: dissecting the elephant. *Journal of Personality and Social Psychology,* **76,** 805–19.

Russell, J.A., Bachorowski, J.A., & Fernández–Dols, J.M. (2003). Facial and vocal expressions of emotion. *Annual Review of Psychology,* **54,** 329–49.

Santen, J.P.H., Sproat, R.W., Olive, J.P., & Hirschberg, J. (ed.) (1997). *Progress in speech synthesis.* New York: Springer.

Scherer, K.R. (1971). Randomized splicing: a note on a simple technique for masking speech content. *Journal of Experimental Research in Personality,* **5,** 155–9.

Scherer, K.R. (1972). Judging personality from voice: a cross-cultural approach to an old issue in interpersonal perception. *Journal of Personality,* **40,** 191–210.

Scherer, K.R. (1974). Acoustic concomitants of emotional dimensions: judging affect from synthesized tone sequences. In *Nonverbal communication* (ed. S. Weitz), pp. 105–11. New York: Oxford University Press.

Scherer, K.R. (1978). Personality inference from voice quality: the loud voice of extroversion. *European Journal of Social Psychology,* **8,** 467–87.

Scherer, K.R. (1979). Personality markers in speech. In *Social markers in speech* (ed. K.R. Scherer & H. Giles), pp. 147–209. Cambridge, UK: Cambridge University Press.

Scherer, K.R. (1982). Methods of research on vocal communication: paradigms and parameters. In *Handbook of methods in nonverbal behavior research* (ed. K.R. Scherer & P. Ekman), pp. 136–98. Cambridge, UK: Cambridge University Press.

Scherer, K.R. (1984). On the nature and function of emotion: a component process approach. In *Approaches to emotion* (ed. K.R. Scherer & P. Ekman), pp. 293–318. Hillsdale, NJ: Erlbaum.

Scherer, K.R. (1985). Vocal affect signalling: a comparative approach. In *Advances in the study of behavior, Vol. 15* (ed. J. Rosenblatt, C. Beer, M.–C. Busnel, & P.J.B. Slater), pp. 189–244. New York: Academic Press.

Scherer, K.R. (1986). Vocal affect expression: a review and a model for future research. *Psychological Bulletin,* **99,** 143–65.

Scherer, K.R. (1988). On the symbolic functions of vocal affect expression. *Journal of Language and Social Psychology,* **7,** 79–100.

Scherer, K.R. (1989). Vocal correlates of emotional arousal and affective disturbance. In *Handbook of social psychophysiology* (ed. H. Wagner & A. Manstead), pp. 165–97. New York: Wiley.

Scherer, K.R. (1990). Stress et coping: nouvelles approches. *Cahiers Psychiatriques Genevois,* **9,** 155–62.

Scherer, K.R. (1994). Affect bursts. In *Emotions: essays on emotion theory* (ed. S. van Goozen, N.E. van de Poll, & J.A. Sergeant), pp. 161–96. Hillsdale, NJ: Erlbaum.

Scherer, K.R. (1995). Expression of emotion in voice and music. *Journal of Voice,* **9,** 235–48.

Scherer, K.R. (1999). Universality of emotional expression. In *Encyclopedia of Human Emotions, Vol. 2* (ed. D. Levinson, J. Ponzetti, & P. Jorgenson), pp. 669–74. New York: Macmillan.

Scherer, K.R. (2000). Psychological models of emotion. In *The neuropsychology of emotion* (ed. J. Borod), pp. 137–62. New York: Oxford University Press.

Scherer, K.R. & Oshinsky, J.S. (1977). Cue utilisation in emotion attribution from auditory stimuli. *Motivation and Emotion,* **1,** 331–46.

Scherer, K.R. & Scherer, U. (1981). Speech behavior and personality. In *Speech evaluation in psychiatry* (ed. J. Darby), pp. 115–35. New York: Grune & Stratton.

Scherer, K.R., Banse, R., & Wallbott, H.G. (2001*a*). Emotion inferences from vocal expression correlate across languages and cultures. *Journal of Cross-Cultural Psychology*, 32, 76–92.

Scherer, K.R., Banse, R., Wallbott, H.G., & Goldbeck, T. (1991). Vocal cues in emotion encoding and decoding. *Motivation and Emotion*, 15, 123–48.

Scherer, K.R., Johnstone, T., & Klasmeyer, G. (2003). Vocal expression of emotion. In *Handbook of affective sciences* (ed. R.J. Davidson, K.R. Scherer, & H.H. Goldsmith), pp. 433–56. New York: Oxford University Press.

Scherer, K.R., Koivumaki, J., & Rosenthal, R. (1972). Minimal cues in the vocal communication of affect: judging emotions from content-masked speech. *Journal of Psycholinguistic Research*, 1, 269–85.

Scherer, K.R., Ladd, D.R., & Silverman, K.E.A. (1984). Vocal cues to speaker affect: testing two models. *Journal of the Acoustical Society of America*, 76, 1346–56.

Scherer, K.R., & Schorr, A., & Johnstone, T. (ed.) (2001*b*). *Appraisal processes in emotion: theory, methods, research*. New York: Oxford University Press.

Schröder, M. (1999). Can emotions be synthesized without controlling voice quality? *Phonus*, 4, 35–50.

Schröder, M. (2001). Emotional speech synthesis: a review. In *Proceedings of the 7th European Conference on Speech Communication and Technology, September 3–7, 2001: Vol. 1*, pp. 561–4. Aalborg, Denmark: International Speech Communication Association.

Schröder, M., Cowie, R., Douglas–Cowie, E., Westerdijk, M., & Gielen, S. (2001). Acoustic correlates of emotion dimensions in view of speech synthesis. In *Proceedings of Eurospeech 2001, Vol. 1*, pp. 87–90. Aalborg, Denmark: International Speech Communication Association.

Scripture, E.W. (1921). A study of emotions by speech transcription. *Vox*, 31, 179–83.

Seyfarth, R.M. & Cheney, D.L. (2003). Signalers and receivers in animal communication. *Annual Review of Psychology*, 54, 145–73.

Shannon, C.E. & Weaver, W. (1949). *The mathematical theory of communication*. Urbana: University of Illinois Press.

Skinner, E.R. (1935). A calibrated recording and analysis of the pitch, force and quality of vocal tones expressing happiness and sadness; and a determination of the pitch and force of the subjective concepts of ordinary, soft and loud tones. *Speech Monographs*, 2, 81–137.

Slaney, M. & McRoberts, G. (2003). Baby ears: a recognition system for affective vocalizations. *Speech Communication*, 39, 367–84.

Smith, C.A. & Scott, H.S. (1997). A componential approach to the meaning of facial expressions. In *The psychology of facial expressions: studies in emotion and social interaction* (ed. J.A. Russell & J.M. Fernández–Dols), pp. 229–54. Cambridge, UK: Cambridge University Press.

Snowdon, C.T. (2003). Expression of emotion in nonhuman animals. In *Handbook of affective sciences* (ed. R.J. Davidson, K.R. Scherer, & H.H. Goldsmith), pp. 457–80. New York: Oxford University Press.

Song, M., Chen, C., Bu, J., & You, M. (2004). Speech emotion recognition and intensity estimation. *Lecture Notes in Artifical Intelligence*, 3046, 406–13.

Spencer, H. (1857). The origin and function of music. *Fraser's Magazine*, 56, 396–408.

Stanislavski, C. (1988). *An actor prepares.* London: Methuen. (Original work published in 1937.)

Starkweather, J.A. (1956). The communication value of content-free speech. *American Journal of Psychology,* **69,** 121–3.

Stemple, J.C., Glaze, L.E., & Klaben, B.G. (2000). *Clinical voice pathology: theory and management.* San Diego, CA: Singular–Thomson Learning.

Stibbard, R.M. (2001). *Vocal expression of emotions in non-laboratory speech: an investigation of the Reading/Leeds Emotion in Speech Project annotation data.* Unpublished doctoral dissertation, University of Reading, Reading, England.

Sundberg, J. (1998). Expressivity in singing: a review of some recent investigations. *Logopedics Phoniatrics Vocology,* **23,** 121–7.

Tatham, M. & Morton, K. (2003). *Expression in speech: analysis and synthesis.* Oxford, UK: Oxford University Press.

Titze, I.R. (1994). *Principles of voice production.* Englewood Cliffs, NJ: Prentice–Hall.

Tolkmitt, F.J. & Scherer, K.R. (1987). Effect of experimentally induced stress on vocal parameters. *Journal of Experimental Psychology: Human Perception and Performance,* **12,** 302–13.

Tomkins, S. (1962). *Affect, imagery, and consciousness: Vol. 1. The positive affects.* New York: Springer.

Trager, G.L. (1958). Paralanguage: A first approximation. *Studies in Linguistics,* **13,** 1–12.

Trager, G.L. & Smith, H.L. Jr. (1957). *An outline of English structure* (2nd edn). Washington, DC: American Council of Learned Societies.

Travis, L.E. (ed.) (1971). *Handbook of speech pathology and audiology.* New York: Appleton–Century–Crofts.

Tusing, K.J. & Dillard, J.P. (2000). The sounds of dominance: Vocal precursors of perceived dominance during interpersonal influence. *Human Communication Research,* **26,** 148–71.

Uldall, E. (1960). Attitudinal meanings conveyed by intonation contours. *Language and Speech,* **3,** 223–34.

van Bezooijen, R. (1984). *Characteristics and recognizability of vocal expressions of emotion.* Dordrecht, The Netherlands: Foris.

van Bezooijen, R. & Boves, L. (1986). The effects of low-pass filtering and random splicing on the perception of speech. *Journal of Psycholinguistic Research,* **15,** 403–17.

van Lieshout, P. (2003). *PRAAT short tutorial: a basic introduction (V. 4.2.1).* University of Toronto, Graduate Department of Speech-Language Pathology, Faculty of Medicine, Oral Dynamics Lab.

Västfjäll, D. (2002). A review of the musical mood induction procedure. *Musicae Scientiae, Special Issue 2001–2002,* pp. 173–211.

Ververidis, D. & Kotropoulos, C. (2003). A state of the art review on emotional speech databases. In *Proceedings of the First International Workshop on Interactive Rich Media Content Production: Architectures, Technologies, Applications, Tools, October 2003,* pp. 109–19.

Von Bismarck, G. (1974). Sharpness as an attribute of the timbre of steady state sounds. *Acustica,* **30,** 146–59.

Vroomen, J., Collier, R., & Mozziconacci, S.J.L. (1993). Duration and intonation in emotional speech. *Proceedings of the Third European Conference on Speech, Communication and Technol-*

ogy: Eurospeech 93, Vol. 1, pp. 577–80. Berlin, Germany: International Speech Communication Association.

Wagner, H.L. (1993). On measuring performance in category judgment studies of nonverbal behavior. *Journal of Nonverbal Behavior*, **17**, 3–28.

Wallbott, H.G., Ricci–Bitti, P., & Bänninger–Huber, E. (1986). Non-verbal reactions to emotional experiences. In *Experiencing emotion: a cross-cultural study* (ed. K.R. Scherer, H.G. Wallbott, & A.B. Summerfield), pp. 98–116. Cambridge, UK: Cambridge University Press.

Westerman, R., Spies, K., Stahl, G., & Hesse, F.W. (1996). Relative effectiveness and validity of mood induction procedures: a meta analysis. *European Journal of Social Psychology*, **26**, 557–80.

Wiley, R.H. & Richards, D.G. (1978). Physical constraints on acoustic communication in the atmosphere: implications for the evolution of animal vocalizations. *Behavioral Ecology and Sociobiology*, **3**, 69–94.

Williams, C.E. & Stevens, K.N. (1969). On determining the emotional state of pilots during flight: an exploratory study. *Aerospace Medicine*, **40**, 1369–72.

Wilson, F.B. (1971). *Voice disorders*. (Training tape produced at The Jewish Hospital of St. Louis, St. Louis, MO.)

Wilson, F.B. (1972). The voice-disordered child: a descriptive approach. *Language, Speech, and Hearing Services in the Schools*, **4**, 14–22.

Wirz, S. & Beck, J.M. (1995). Assessment of voice quality: the vocal profiles analysis scheme. In *Perceptual approaches to communication disorders* (ed. S.L. Wirz), pp. 3955. London: Whurr publishers.

Wish, M., D'Andrade, R.G., & Goodnow, J.E. (1980). Dimensions of interpersonal communication: correspondence between structures for speech acts and bipolar scales. *Journal of Personality and Social Psychology*, **38**, 848–60.

Zaidel, S.F. & Mehrabian, A. (1969). The ability to communicate and infer positive and negative attitudes facially and vocally. *Journal of Experimental Research in Personality*, **3**, 233–341.

Zebrowitz, L.A. (1990). *Social perception*. Milton Keynes, UK: Open University Press.

Zwicker, E. (1982). *Psychoacoustics*. New York: Springer.

CHAPTER 4

PROXEMICS, KINESICS, AND GAZE

JINNI A. HARRIGAN

Introduction

Chapter orientation

This chapter focuses on the methodologies for coding behaviors in proxemics, kinesics (i.e. body and head movements), and gaze. Working definitions for these three domains are:

- Proxemics is the study of our perception and structuring of interpersonal and environmental space.
- Kinesics refers to actions and positions of the body, head, and limbs.
- Gaze involves movements and direction of the eyes in visual interaction.

(In this chapter, kinesics is synonymous with body/head movement.)

For proxemics and gaze, the basic methodological design and behavioral coding strategies seem to have changed little since the early 1980s, and will be detailed in this chapter. Following upon the heels of the preceding chapters for coding facial actions and vocal behavior, the lack of development in codes and strategies for recording body movement is readily apparent. Although systematic research on kinesics began in earnest more than a half century ago, investigations have been of a piecemeal nature with a range of foci and methodologies developed in a variety of laboratories and conducted by researchers from a sweep of disciplines (e.g. psychology, communication, sociolinguistics, psychoanalysis). This, unfortunately, has resulted in a lack of coordination and state of disjointedness with respect to the development of a set of defined behavioral units for coding, comparable research methodologies, and theoretical constructs as a framework for understanding body movement. The present discussion of methodological issues in body movement research is divided into two segments: body positions and body actions. Each of these subsections includes historical information on the research strategies that evolved which may help provide a perspective to understand the current state of methodological and theoretical development in coding body movement, proxemics, and gaze.

The chapter will begin with some general conceptual issues and factors affecting coding decisions, and points to consider in choosing a methodological strategy and behavioral units for coding movement. The methodologies for proxemics and kinesics will follow, and coding for gaze behavior closes the chapter.

Feasibility of coding body movement

Humans, whether in individual or interactive settings, display a rich mosaic of actions, gestures, and postures with their bodies. This fact becomes immediately apparent when one sets out to code body movement. The number of actions and positions, speed in change of actions, versatility and subtlety of movement, individual variability of actions and positions, and interactive quality of the actions and positions themselves could easily be intimidating and lead to coder despair at ever being able to 'get a grip' on describing, tallying, and analyzing body actions. Coding, however, is manageable because of some specifics about body movement. There are three key features that make coding body movement feasible given the varied number of moveable body parts and intricacies of combined movements.

Modest number of moveable body parts

An advantage in coding body movement, that helps reduce the intricacy of coding, is that the 'body tableau', while vast in the sheer number of millimeters (e.g. compared with the face), is comprised of only a few moveable parts. The legs, arms, and trunk are primarily involved in movements for positioning the body. The upper arms, forearms, thighs, or calves cannot be moved individually. The shoulders, elbows, and knees can be moved and such movements may be relevant to affect, but with the exception of shoulder shrugging, elbows and knees typically are moved as part of an arm or leg movement. All of these body parts may be of interest in studies of walking or approach, but generally it is the appendages of the limbs which garner attention in social encounters and settings where affect expression is likely. The two body parts that involve the most movement are the head and hands, and these have received the most attention in body movement research.

Behavioral repertoire limitations

Of the many possible actions and positions that can be performed by the body, anatomically speaking, some actions rarely, if ever, occur. For example, it would be very unusual for someone to converse with another interactant while leaning his/her trunk in an extreme backward position, or for a person to display nonstop hand gestures when listening. Social conventions—'display rules' (Ekman 1972)—guide our behavior by the exercise of culturally learned rules that govern 'when it is appropriate to express an emotion and to whom one can reveal one's feelings' (Ekman & Rosenberg 1997, p. 10). Behaviors that are exhibited outside the expected presentation of oneself usually are so atypical as to be diagnostic with respect to mental or emotional stability or level of intellectual functioning. Goffman (1959, 1963) wrote eloquently about his observations of acceptable nonverbal behavior in various public and private social encounters (e.g. staff meetings, sidewalk maneuvers, ceremonial gatherings, waiting areas).

Co-occurrence of behaviors

Another feature of body movement that mitigates the complexity of coding is that body movements often are displayed together. Movements can occur simultaneously (e.g. repositioning the trunk and legs) or in sequence (e.g. hand and head movements in speaker turn–exchange), and many complement facial behaviors (e.g. smiling and head nodding) and vocal behaviors (e.g. angry vocal tone and clenched hands). Movements which have a temporal relationship to one another allow for ease in coding because two movements are visually easier for a coder to observe than one behavior, thus reducing 'omission' errors (i.e. not coding a behavior that occurred). In addition, temporally occurring movements often provide information regarding functional aspects of movement patterns.

Comparisons of nonverbal and verbal behavior codes

Prior to setting out to code body movement, several points need be considered when deciding what movements to code and how to code them. These ideas were first detailed by Ekman and Friesen (1969*a*) in an early article on coding nonverbal behavior, and have been mentioned frequently by others when discussing nonverbal behavior coding (Knapp & Hall 1992; Rosenfeld 1987). Several of these issues deal with drawing parallels between nonverbal and verbal communication.

Correspondence between behavior and meaning

Body movements cannot be translated as directly as verbal behavior. A word has a specific, defined meaning that always, and for everyone who knows the word, represents that meaning, and by itself the word bears no relationship to its referent (see Appendix to this volume). Although several pop-psych books, written in the 1970s, continue to have wide audience appeal, the premise of these books does a disservice to the field of nonverbal behavior research. Books such as *Body Language* (Fast 1970), *How To Read A Person Like A Book* (Nierenberg & Calero 1971), *People Reading* (Beier & Valens 1975), and *The Body Language of Sex, Power, and Aggression* (Fast 1977) assume that various body actions and positions represent specific information when they are displayed (i.e. encoded) and that the meaning of these body actions are encoded and decoded (i.e. interpreted) unequivocally. Unlike certain facial expressions, there are few, if any, body movements that have invariant meaning within or across cultures. Some hand and head actions (e.g. shrugging, various insulting hand movements, head nodding) can be interpreted in a language-like fashion by individuals within a culture, and between cultures who are knowledgeable about each other's nonverbal behaviors, but even within a culture, body movements do not carry the same meaning each and every time they are displayed. For example, one could nod to signal 'Yes' to a question, or nod as one of several listener responses to a speaker; the latter does not indicate assent, but only that the listener is following the speaker's comments. Birdwhistell (1970), for one, mentioned several kinds of nods (e.g. 'understanding nod', 'control nod'); Giges (1975) referred to types of nodding by the 'rescue nodder', 'put-down nodder', etc. Further, a person might fold her arms across her chest when standing not to indicate a 'lack of approachability', but rather to increase body warmth in a cool environment (Raja & Nicol 1997) or because of having no place to put her hands (e.g. pockets).

Although one can indicate assent by nodding or halt another with certain hand gestures, these actions are not always encoded or decoded universally. Many of the actions of the hands and body are so idiosyncratic as to carry little specific meaning.

Intention and behavioral displays

The issue of encoding and decoding nonverbal behavior for the purpose of conveying information involves not just the 'code' (i.e. actions conveying messages), but also the notion of 'intention' (Dittman 1987; Ekman & Friesen 1969a). In verbal communication, there is a deliberate attempt to send a message to another. Although there are times when one blurts out or emits an unintended verbalization, most often the speaker consciously produces a verbal message for the purpose of exchanging information with another. This is not to suggest that verbalizations are always completely planned and thought out in advance, but, relatively speaking, that is usually the case, (i.e. one thinks about what one wants to say).

With nonverbal behavior, the notion of intention is less clear-cut. A person might nod to answer a question or put a vertical index finger to the lips to shush a child, and both actions are thought to be intentional, deliberate attempts to communicate with another. But consider the degree of 'intention' when a person gradually creates greater distance from an interlocutor by pulling back from a forward lean and turning slightly to the side while recrossing the legs away from the interlocutor. Similarly, there may be little or no 'intention' when a person inadvertently rubs his/her hands while being interviewed for a desired job, exhibits a hand gesture when speaking, scratches the chin when thinking about a problem, nods when listening to another, or rearranges hair or clothing when flirting. While these behaviors might provide information to an observer, none of these may have been performed 'intentionally'. Thus, the encoding of nonverbal behaviors may range from conscious, deliberate messages to actions performed more automatically, without awareness and with far less control (Dittman 1987).

Idiosyncratic and shared meanings

Ekman and Friesen (1969a) distinguished between the idiosyncratic and the shared meaning of behaviors, with the former referring to a behavior peculiar to a single individual, and the latter, a behavior whose meaning is common to a set of persons (Ekman & Friesen 1969a, p. 54). It is not the action itself that is idiosyncratic or shared, but the meaning attributed to it. These idiosyncratic and shared meanings can refer to encoders or decoders (e.g. idiosyncratic chin scratching versus a hand wave in greeting). These authors further note that nonverbal behavior can be 'informative' with shared decoded meaning among some set of observers, who may or may not be inaccurate in their decoding of meaning, and when the encoder may not have necessarily intended to convey a message via their nonverbal behavior. A behavior may be 'communicative'; in which case, it is consciously sent by an encoder to another person, although it may not be accurately conveyed or interpreted. Lastly, Ekman and Friesen (1969a) classified nonverbal behaviors as interactive where the encoder's behavior influences the interactive behavior of another, whether intended or not (p. 56). Thus, an informative act might be fidgeting when apprehensive or waving 'Hello'; a communicative act might be nodding to indicate 'Yes' or using a hand gesture to signal 'Come here' that is not understood by the decoder; and an interactive behavior could include nodding when listening to a speaker or restless posture shifts suggesting boredom when listening.

Avoiding behavioral terminology bias

A important point when deciding what movements to code is that just as with coding facial actions, the terminology for the measures selected for coding body actions and positions, as much as possible, needs to be descriptive rather than inferential. This is critical in preventing bias associated with inferred meaning based on terminology. For example, describing a leg posture as 'open' may carry the implied meaning that the person is receptive or accessible, rather than merely sitting with uncrossed legs. A hand movement labeled as a 'suppressed movement' may be characterized more descriptively as 'one hand placed on the other hand'. Referring to a nod as a 'positive nod' and a head shake as a 'negative nod' carries considerable inference about the behavior coded.

Key concepts in coding body movement

The body and affective content

While there are specific emotion universals for facial actions (see Chapter 2) and vocal behaviors (see Chapter 3), body movements alone do not convey specific emotion content. A clenched fist by itself does not necessarily convey anger, nor do insulting hand motions or a shaking head. Body actions can provide information regarding the intensity of the felt emotion (Dittman 1987; Ekman & Friesen 1974) and, together with facial actions and vocal cues, can accent or emphasize affect, but it is primarily the face and voice that carry specific affect. Body positioning offers information about attitude, status, interpersonal role, motives, and personality characteristics of the encoder, and reveals perceptions of decoders. To some extent, the body's positions and actions provide a backdrop for helping to interpret the meaning of more subtle facial and vocal affect.

Moderator variables

Since body movements tend to be more idiosyncratic and culture-bound, one caveat that may be more applicable in coding body movements than in coding facial or vocal behavior is the important moderating effects of gender and culture and, to a lesser degree, age, in the display and interpretation of many body actions and positions. Some examples are:

- the greater frequency of eye blinking by females compared with males;
- the hand gesture for 'Come here' in the United States compared with the gesture in Italy;
- the closer seating proximity for young children versus middle-aged adults.

Theoretical orientation

A important point to consider when deciding on a coding strategy for body movement parallels a dichotomy suggested between 'structural' studies (i.e. concerned with movement/vocal patterns within and between people) and 'external variable' studies (i.e. concerned with nonverbal behaviors in relation to other variables such as personality, role, other nonverbal behaviors) (Duncan 1969). As Ekman *et al.* (see Appendix to this book) have indicated, this distinction may be artificial and irrelevant because the choice of methodologies is driven by the type of data needed to support the answers to the researcher's questions. When examining body movement, the researcher can opt to quantify body positions, body actions, or both, and be selective or comprehensive in coding individual movements, or code at a micro versus macro level of analysis. But the research questions will determine whether one is to code movements at a micro level of analysis in a comprehensive fashion using a structural approach, to code movements at a macro level of analysis in a selective fashion using an external variable approach, or to code using some combination of approaches. The former would be highly appropriate for the study of body movement in relation to specific elements in speech (e.g. relating the placement of a hand gesture occurring concurrently with specific content in the speech stream). The latter might be more useful for a comparison of 'friendly' versus 'unfriendly' interviewer styles where data are collected on the frequencies of nodding, smiling, hand gestures, forward lean, etc. Finally, a researcher can decide to combine various nonverbal actions into conceptual categories together with verbal behavior (e.g. angry words, facial action units indicating anger, hands in fists, body tense, etc.) (see Chapters 10 and 11).

Each of the points described above need to be thoughtfully considered before the investigator chooses the research approach, level of analysis, comprehensiveness of coding, selection of and naming of nonverbal variables, and data analysis methods.

Proxemics

What is it and how is it measured?

In proxemic research, the focus of attention is on the perception, use, and structuring of space. Although an individual's behavior may be of interest with respect to spatial arrangements in the nonhuman environment, most often we study how spatial use affects and reflects relationships between and among individuals as a member of a dyad or larger group, and whether it is intentional (i.e. seeking interaction) or inadvertent (i.e. in public settings). Most research efforts and, therefore, methodologies, have been concerned with interactional settings. For example, we may want to know how people position themselves in a conversational setting with friends, intimates, or strangers. Perhaps we want to know something about the use of space in business, health, or educational settings to answer questions regarding employee engagement in task-focused groups, family members' orientations to one another in psychotherapy, physician–patient consultation styles, or effective teacher–student instruction.

The literature on proxemics and how it is described or measured, overwhelmingly indicates that the 'distance' between interactants was coded most often. While distance is an important variable in proxemics, it is a limited and unsophisticated measure of the factors that make up the invisible, yet precious, three-dimensional space that separates us from one another. Hall (1963, 1973), whose work will be detailed below, takes a comprehensive view of our spatial relationships to one another and to the nonhuman environment. His view reflects an interactive approach which emphasizes the distance-regulating features of our sensory equipment, as well as body orientation, to describe our interface with others. His coding variables are listed in Fig. 4.1 and can be summarized as including: distance, postural identifiers (e.g. sitting, standing), orientation of frontal body plane (i.e. degree one faces another), and input from the senses of touch, vision, audition, olfaction, and temperature (e.g. perceiving heat from another's body).

Research approaches

As the brief historical overview of research strategies which follows will reveal, there are two main techniques for conducting proxemic studies: projective strategies and laboratory or field studies. Projective strategies are the most common (Aiello 1987), representing approximately 40% of studies. There are several measures used in projective strategies, but all require that participants imagine the distance at which they would be comfortable with their choice of seating position in relation to another interactant or with another's approach toward them. Such techniques require marking placements on a form (Comfort Interpersonal Distance Scale; Duke & Nowinckis 1972), manipulating miniature figures, or choosing positions in photographs. Kuethe (1962) used felt figures and Pedersen (1973) adopted silhouette placements of figures to indicate seating, standing, and approach preferences. Hayduk (1983) and Aiello (1987) both have argued strongly against the use of projective techniques to measure personal space because of poor correlations between projective and real-life interactional studies, and the fact that the scaled down projective figures do not parallel life-size differences. These difficulties are particularly apparent in studies of approach, (i.e. effects of a person entering one's spatial comfort zone).

    The second type of proxemic study involves interactions in naturalistic field settings or laboratories. For Hall's (1974) qualitative observations, unobtrusive use of a camera was 'indispensable', permitting re-examination of behavior between interactants with respect to distance cues. Videotape recorders, with slow motion facilities and digital counters, permit greater accuracy in determining distance. Scherer (1974) developed a technique—photogrammetry—which involves a mathematical formula to remove errors in coding distance resulting from the angle of the participants with respect to the camera. Thus, this technique permits greater accuracy in coding distance from videotaped or filmed interactions. Edmonson and Han (1983) marked the floor tiles with tape, making a grid, which permitted precise measurement of videotaped participants engaged in various activities. Their camera was perched high above the participants for better alignment and so as not to interfere with the participants' interactions. Such ceiling positioned cameras suggest an important strategy for measuring distance accurately. In the future, perhaps such instruments as global positioning devices might be used to record distance as well as other proxemic variables.

Proxemic measures

The degree to which proxemics was the main focus of study determined which variables were included. These were few and, typically, distance, frontal body orientation, touch,

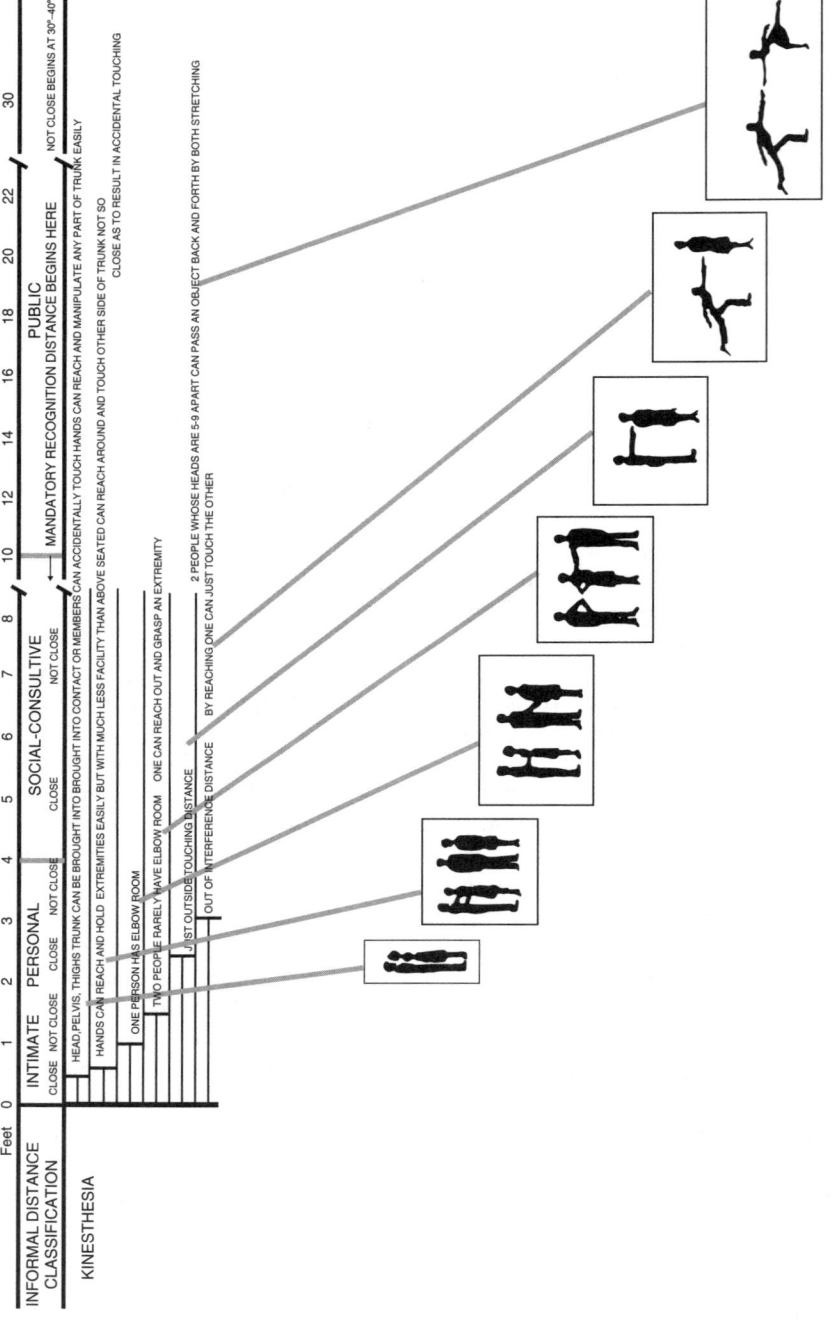

Figure 4.1 Functional implications of proxemic zones. The kinesthetic portion is illustrated with sketches to indicate visually how these distances are set. (Reproduced from Hall 1979, p. 307)

and gaze were measured. In studies where proxemics was less of a focal point, only distance and, more rarely, orientation, was ascertained. At first glance, distance appears to be a straightforward variable to measure, but a variety of different reference points have been used to represent the 'distance' between interactants: measured from their heads, noses, knees, torsos, feet, or chair edges. Sometimes the number of floor tiles between interactants was counted, and floor tile size also varied widely. Of course, these measures differ greatly depending on whether interactants were standing or sitting. Coders have been trained to estimate the distance rather than interrupt the interaction to measure. Often the actual method of measuring and instrumentation was unstated. The lack of uniformity and specificity of measurement makes it difficult to compare research findings across studies.

In some studies where the independent variable was another interactant's gender, age, culture, personality characteristic (e.g. friendliness, dominance, inconsistency), or some other feature (e.g. physical disability, criminality), distance was measured by the seat chosen by the participant or distance he/she approached another participant. For example, Weitz (1972) found that participant's chair placement reflected their attitude toward someone of a different race. In other studies, the participant's chair was positioned so that it could not be moved, and researchers manipulated the distance of a confederate (e.g. seated close or far) with respect to the participant.

A large body of work has been conducted in proxemic research on approach distance (considered below). For example, Mehrabian (1968) asked participants to approach a coat rack as if it were a person, stopping at the point where they felt comfortable interacting with that 'person'.

Research overview

A brief historical overview within the areas of proxemic research may help the reader understand the development of this field and measures used to study it.

Person to person

The appropriate starting point for proxemics is the work of the insightful anthropologist, Edward T. Hall, who first used the label 'proxemics'. Using naturalistic methods, and based on his extensive observations of humans' use of space, attention to cultural differences, and the evidence from animal behavior with specific reference to crowding and territorality, Hall (1963, 1973) developed a notation system of personal distance that has become the foundation of measurement in proxemics. Hall's ideas and theory were greatly influenced by the ethologist, Hediger (1961), whose work in zoology and animal behavior focused on the sensory worlds of the interactants in relation to personal distance.

Hall (1963) divided our spatial world into four social distances, each with a close and far phase, and each based on varying information available from vision, audition, olfaction, thermal reception, and kinesthesia (i.e. sensation of physical alignment of head/body). These four social distances (i.e. intimate, personal, social/consultive, and public) span zero to 30 feet, and vary according to type of interaction and the status of and affiliation between interactants. Although Hall did not ascribe precise quantitative values to the codes in his notation system, he described in intricate detail the various nonverbal and vocal cues available to our distance and immediate sensory receptors (see Fig. 4.1). For example, mothers and infants frequently inhabit the close phase of the intimate distance, zero to 18 inches, where they can easily touch, smell, feel body heat of, and hear faint sounds (e.g. grunts, coos) of their interactant, though such closeness limits vision to a blurred or distorted view of the other. More specifically, one of Hall's codes (1973) considered under 'kinesthesia' is body orientation, which ranges from sitting back to back, sitting side by side, and sitting at right angles to facing each other. Likewise, the body distance code ranges from two people leaning out of reach of one another, through 'two arms extended' toward each other, to 'maximum body contact'.

Hall (1966) acknowledged the approximate nature of these distance zones, commenting on variations resulting from the influence of personality or environmental factors. In their extensive review, Altman and Vinsel (1977) concluded that Hall's 'qualitative ideas' regarding distance zones to describe human spatial behavior were supported by research findings, although they acknowledged differences in these distance dimensions for standing and sitting.

Watson and Graves (1966) created a scoring system, with a range of scores, to operationalize seven of the eight dimension codes described by Hall (1963, 1973): frontal body orientation, distance, touch, visual clarity, thermal detection, olfaction, and vocal loudness. Postural identifiers (e.g. standing, sitting) were uniform. For example, touch was coded from 'holding and caressing' (0), through 'spot touching' (4), to no contact (6). Their results showed that, compared with American college students, Arab students interacted more closely on all dimensions, and the authors were able to pinpoint precisely these differences for all seven dimensions (Watson & Graves 1966). Other measures for coding the distance between interactants exist. Jones and Aiello's (1973) measure is based on the ability to reach out and touch another, and the measure contains adjustments for height differences as well. Sigelman and Adams (1990) used a scaled map in a naturalistic observational study to plot the distance between parents and their children.

Person in environment

In his writings, Hall (1966, 1974) also commented on how space is organized in a community and the effect these patterns have on communication. Spaces reflect environmental arrangements (e.g. furniture, architecture) that encourage or promote communication (i.e. sociopetal space) or provide for solitary actions (i.e. sociofugal space). Systematic studies of spatial arrangements in social interaction were investigated extensively by Sommer, who was interested in how people arranged themselves in 'semi-fixed' space with respect to concepts of leadership, status, productivity, and affiliation (Sommer 1959, 1961: Sommer & Becker 1969). He defined 'personal space' as 'an area with invisible boundaries surrounding a person's body into which intruders may not come' (Sommer 1969, p. 26). Sommer reported four distinct patterns for 'relational space' depending on the type of task: conversational, cooperative, competitive, or coacting. Others have supported Sommer's results, finding, for example, that those of higher status tend to occupy end positions at a rectangular table, where they participated more, were rated as more influential, and received more gaze from other participants (Strodtbeck and Hook 1961).

Approaching others

A popular focus in proxemic research has been approach distance, most often measured by the 'stop-distance procedure' in which a participant signals 'stop', to indicate their level of discomfort with respect to an approaching experimenter or confederate (Hayduk 1983). Aiello (1987) reports more than 100 studies using this procedure. Hayduk (1981*a*, *b*) altered the angle of approach, and Aiello and colleagues investigated seat preference with respect to distance from interactants (Aiello & Jones 1971; Aiello & Thompson 1980).

Responses to encroachment

Other phenomena are important in proxemic research, though these are not often fully operationalized or clearly measured: territoriality, defense, crowding, boundary markers, and similar topics involving maneuvering and maintaining personal space in public places. Goffman's (1963, 1971) elegant observations of people's behavior in public and the use of physical and social barriers to maintain some degree of psychological privacy in public settings ('civil inattention'), are eloquent and insightful, but are not precise or cue-specific in terms of measuring the phenomenon.

The concept of crowding is defined not entirely by population density, but also with respect to other relevant variables: time spent in the area, interaction expectancies, focus of attention on self or others (Zlutnick & Altman 1972), degree of social stimulation (Desor 1972), gender, and room size (Ross *et al.* 1973). Stokols (1972) defined 'social density' as the physical spacing between people that is related to the number of people, 'spatial density' as physical spacing related to the amount of space available to people, and 'crowding' as a negative psychological state related to dense spaces. Hayduk (1981*a*) conducted the most detailed study of 'permeability', or reaction to intrusions, concluding that the 'degree of discomfort was proportional to the extent of intrusion' (p. 284).

Altman has made significant contributions in his work on crowding, territoriality, and interpersonal relations (Altman 1975; Altman & Taylor 1973; Sundstrom and Altman 1976). He delineated three types of territories—primary, secondary, and public (Altman 1975)—and described various ways people maintain some degree of privacy through the use of physical barriers, place markers, and adjustments in verbal and nonverbal behavior to discourage interaction. Similarly, Lyman and Scott (1967) developed a classification system for various territories based on the degree of personal autonomy (i.e. body, home, interactional, and public), and outlined categories of territorial incursion (violation, invasion, and contamination). Applying the defining features of these territories to real-life settings has not proved to be straightforward, however. The lines defining interactional and public, and secondary and public territories often are fuzzy, with considerable overlap depending on critical variables such as density, use of boundary markers, status, degree of acquaintanceship, and other relevant factors. Sommer conducted a series of studies showing the effect of 'markers' to defend one's personal space in a public setting, to reduce incursion by others, and to maintain one's possession of personal space while the owner was absent (Sommer 1967, 1969; Sommer & Becker 1969). His studies include greater precision than others in defining markers, measuring distances between interactants, and categorizing the resulting behavior of the interactants.

Methodological issues

Hayduk (1983) and Aiello (1987) provide thoughtful and comprehensive reviews of proxemic research, covering measures and methodological issues, theoretical interpretations, problem areas, and detailed findings with respect to spatial behavior and relevant factors (i.e. age, gender, culture, personality, relationship, environment, and intrusion or invasion). Aiello notes that, like many subtopics in nonverbal behavior, researchers from many disciplines have studied personal space: Hall, Sommer, and others consider the use of space from a naturalistic, observational viewpoint; and, often, psychologists and sociologists analyze the effects of empirical manipulations of proxemic cues on participants or the effects of another manipulated variable on participants' proxemic behavior.

Aiello remedies a definitional problem, noted by others (Knowles 1980; Patterson 1975), by using the term 'interpersonal space', which focuses on the communicative function, rather than the often used term 'personal space', which stresses the protective function. Researchers seeking specific results with respect to certain proxemic variables and relevant factors will benefit from Hayduk (1983) and Aiello's (1987) reviews of more than 700 studies. For future researchers, Hayduk (1983) and Aiello (1987) recommend the continued development of methods and measurement techniques and research attention to gender and cultural differences in studies of spatial behavior.

Summary and coding recommendations

As the brief historical overview of research in proxemics shows, there have been few developments since Hall outlined his notation system (1963, 1973). A few coding suggestions can be culled from this literature. As in any other area of investigation, decisions about which proxemic variables to code depend on the research question(s). When proxemic patterns are of primary interest, it may be appropriate to use measures developed by Hall: postural identifiers, distance, orientation, touch, vision, audition, olfaction, and thermal detection. These variables permit a comprehensive and accurate assessment of spatial cues but, for each variable, scores need to be assigned to each cue within a category to operationalize the range of possible cues (see Watson & Graves 1966).When proxemic cues are secondary or tangential to the research question(s), distance, orientation, and touching may be sufficient to capture information regarding the spatial separation between interactants. For example, trained coders evaluated videotaped interactions at several intervals by choosing one of:

1. eight possible distances between interactants' heads and torsos;
2. seven possible orientations for interactants toward one another;
3. six possible types of touching (Remland *et al.* 1995).

In our research manual for interactions of two or more individuals, proxemic variables include: distance (based on floor tile markings), trunk lean and orientation, postural shifts, touch, and gaze (Harrigan & Carney 2005).

Although Hall's proxemic system contains codes for gaze, audition, and touch, researchers also frequently include these as individual categories in studies where proxemic cues are coded. For example, Grahe and Bernieri (1999) rated the degree of mutual eye contact, in addition to proximity and orientation. While some proxemic cues such as distance and orientation can be separated more easily in some studies, the Intimacy Equilibrium Model presented by Argyle and colleagues (Argyle & Dean 1965; Argyle & Cook 1976) demonstrates the strong relationship between proximity and eye contact. This model will be discussed in detail in the section on gaze in this chapter.

Finally, body positional cues are alluded to in Hall's system under the code for estimating body distance, but are not considered as separate categories of proxemics. Body positional cues include trunk lean and positions of the arms, legs, and head with respect to another interactant. These will be discussed in more detail in the following section on body position but, clearly, interactional space is greatly altered by these cues. For example, leaning toward another greatly reduces the distance between participants and makes one available for touching, mutual eye contact, olfaction, and thermal detection.

In summary, proxemic cues of importance for coding interactive behavior include: postural identification (i.e. sitting, standing), distance, frontal orientation, and body positioning. Depending on the research objectives, touch, eye contact, olfaction, and audition also may be coded. Considerable work needs to be accomplished in proxemic research to precisely define and operationalize scoring methods for proxemic cues. This will allow study results to be more easily compared and theoretical implications for these behaviors to be examined and understood.

Kinesics

Where the action is

The predominant loci of attention in body movement research (kinesics), has been on the hands and head, two areas with the greatest overall movement frequency. For body movements in general, and for the head and hands specifically, researchers' coding methods are varied, rarely well-defined, and, with few exceptions, are not often organized conceptually or theoretically. Although kinesic research remains relatively embryonic, classifications and coding strategies will be presented using a historical, developmental approach to describe the various advances in body movement research.

Actions and positions

The evolution of methodological strategies for coding body movement has been focused primarily on 'action' behaviors—that is, discrete units of body action which are not part of body positioning and which have relatively distinct 'onset' (i.e. beginning of action) and 'offset' (i.e. end of action) points, and which may or may not be intentional or interpretable by others. These body actions are displayed by the head, shoulders, hands, and feet, and involve activities such as nodding, shrugging, gesturing, scratching, and kicking. These action behaviors are supported by 'position' behaviors—that is, movements associated with positioning the body, and which are less subject to frequent change and can be more easily codified. Like action behaviors, position behaviors usually are described in relation to another interactant and typically include reference to: overall posture (i.e. sitting, standing, lying), trunk or frontal orientation (i.e. facing, turned away), trunk lean (i.e. forward, straight, backward, sideways), and arm and leg positions (e.g. folded arms, uncrossed legs) which includes the feet (e.g. flat on floor, under chair, on other knee).

Body actions often are considered expressive movements which may or may not be displayed, and usually have easily discernible beginning and end points. Body position, on the other hand, is always present and available for coding in the sense that a person's body is continually in a posture with torso, arms, and legs arranged in relation to one another. Body actions mainly involve the hand and head; their coding will be described following discussion of body positions.

With respect to all body movements, body positions are the largest units to code compared with body actions. Body positions involve the least variation from person to person, and change relatively infrequently. Because the individual body positions tend not to occur in isolation from one another, they often can be considered as a unit. For example, a shift in trunk lean or orientation usually affects the position of the arms and sometimes the legs. Similarly, a woman's folded arm position might be interpreted as indicating a 'lack of approachability' if she also turned her body and head away, but any one of these actions alone would not be sufficient to warrant that same interpretation (e.g. her folded arms could be an attempt to keep warm). The phenomenon of self-synchrony (described below) assumes the coordinated interaction of an individual's body positions and movements; likewise, interactional synchrony describes synchronous positions and movements between and among interactants.

In this chapter, the term 'body positions' is used to represent the alignment of the body and its appendages, and includes such specific categories as trunk lean, trunk orientation, arm and leg position, and postural shifts. These behaviors provide information regarding one's attention, interest, and attitude, and may convey inferential or stereotypic information about the encoder's personality characteristics. For the most part, body positions carry little information about specific affect compared with face and voice cues (Ekman & Friesen 1974). It is hard to imagine a positional cue that conveys a specific emotion on its own without the benefit of facial, head, or hand actions, but body position and alignment can provide information regarding the degree of tension an individual is experiencing and something of the intensity of an emotion (Ekman & Friesen 1969a).

Because body positioning deals with the placement of the body in space, it bridges the research areas of proxemics and body actions. Hall (1963) included many of the body position behaviors (e.g. frontal body orientation, postural identifiers, touching) in his coding system for describing the interpersonal space between interactants.

Early coding systems for body movement

A brief overview will help provide the reader with relevant information on research methodology that was developed prior to the earlier handbook (Scherer & Ekman 1982) and up to the present time. This historical overview is not intended to be comprehensive, but to aid researchers in understanding the theoretical perspectives in body movement research and the development of strategies to code behavior based on such theories. This section will be followed by methods and techniques for coding body positions and actions.

Several creative coding systems were developed during the 1950s for recording body positions and actions. Most of these are based on anatomical features and segmenting the body in relation to the skeletal system. Use of these strategies for coding nonverbal behavior generally has been abandoned because, while the notation systems are comprehensive, a variety of problems forestall their use.

Labanotation (Hutchinson 1961; Laban 1956) is a movement notation system designed specifically for dance (thus the great attention to specific foot actions) and based on a theory of movement in the expression of dance. It is modeled after a musical notation system, and permits the construction of a record of the actions of various body parts over time. Symbols are used to show the quantitative and qualitative features of movement including direction, duration, and intensity, but precise measurement of smaller nonverbal acts (e.g. of fingers) is not possible. Since the symbols represent the actions or positions of the body, no inferences are necessary on the part of the coder. However, there are several coding challenges:

- the large number of symbols to be learned;
- the use of arbitrary symbols that are not intuitive;
- locating symbols in the graph's frame is tedious;
- the system is very time-consuming;
- the isolation of body movements precludes the communicative value of considering behaviors organized as a unit (e.g. pursed lips, averted gaze, crossed arms, less direct frontal body orientation).

Another coding method is the Eshkol–Wachmann (EWMN) system (Eshkol & Wachmann 1958) detailed by Golani (1969). This notation system, also originally developed for dance, has been used for behavioral observations in human research and in animal studies. The system is based on a circle, and movements and postures are measured in units of 360 degrees, permitting coding of a range of nonverbal behaviors in relation to one another. Again, like Labanotation, using numerical values in the EWMN system does not require subjective inferences in the various coding units, but similar challenges are incurred.

Birdwhistell (1952, 1970), an anthropologist, was a pioneer in the study of body movement and known for originating the structural or descriptive approach to studying body movement. He believed strongly in not drawing a distinction between verbal and nonverbal behavior in the study of human communication, and designed a notation system for describing the structure of movement that was patterned after linguistic principles. A 'kineme' is similar to a phoneme (i.e. smallest meaningful sound

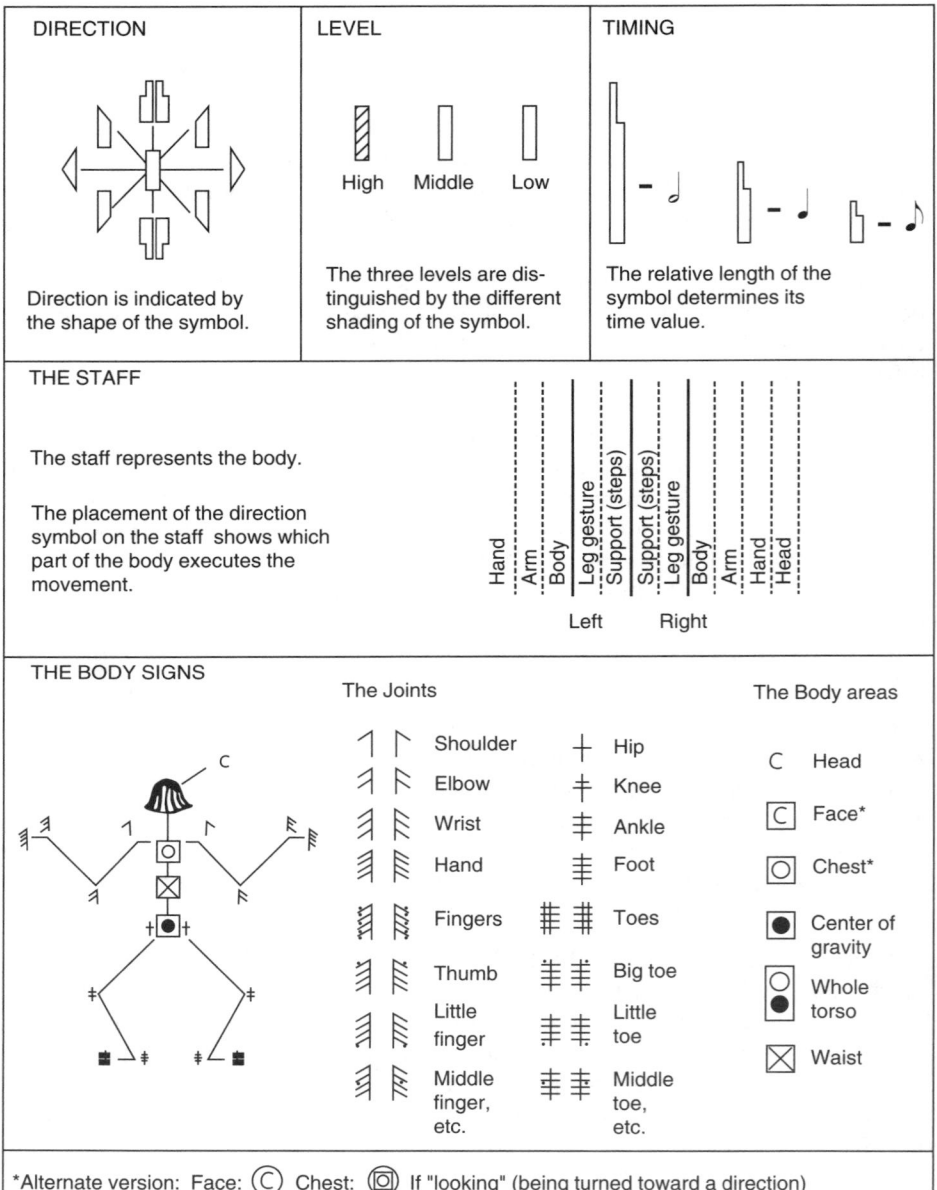

Figure 4.2 Some symbols used in Labanotation. (Reproduced from Hutchinson 1961, p. 263)

unit of speech), and represents the most elementary unit of behavior, while 'kine-morphs' (analogous to morphemes) are combinations of kinemes, and 'kinemorphic constructions' are still larger units of combined kinemorphs. For example, a kineme would be a lateral head sweep or a head tilt (Birdwhistell 1970). Each kineme is depicted by a specific symbol entered onto a precise and complete verbal transcription. For example, Birdwhistell's most famous analyzed film segment, 'The Cigarette Scene', is an in-depth description of the 18-second segment isolated into the minute movements (i.e. kinemes) of the face, head, and body for each interactant, together with the verbal stream. The analysis shows the relationship between the nonverbal and verbal behavior using Birdwhistell's (1970) descriptive linguistic model. A partial example of Bird-whistell's system for the arm is listed in Table 4.1.

Scheflen (1964, 1966), a psychiatrist, studied filmed therapist–client interviews and, like Birdwhistell, who greatly influenced him, described a hierarchy of behaviors within an interaction. 'Points' correspond to the smallest units of behavior (e.g. head cock, hand gesture, facial grimace), while 'positions' include speech utterances and actions that are linked as a configuration representing a theme (e.g. listening, defending, narrating). Lastly, 'presentation' denotes a sustained interaction (e.g. a conversation, a therapy session) (Scheflen 1966). Each of these three levels is marked by a change in movement or posture. For example, postural shifts often mark a change from one position to another and correspond to a change in interaction activities (e.g. from speaking to listening) (Scheflen 1972). Scheflen, like Birdwhistell, stressed the import-ance of 'context analysis' in understanding the subtle weaving of nonverbal and verbal behavior (Scheflen 1965). He used a courtship movement analogy to describe the functional aspects of body movement in establishing rapport in any social interaction. For example, 'courtship readiness' is displayed by 'high muscle tonus' and 'preening' actions, while the positioning phase of the interaction is represented by the alignment of each interactants' body to the other; and actions of 'appeal' appear throughout the interaction in gaze holding, 'presenting the palm', and head tilting.

The research approach taken by both Birdwhistell and Scheflen in the study of body movement was a holistic one, advocating 'context analysis', which stressed the import-ance of the context in understanding patterns of nonverbal behavior. This approach has

Table 4.1   Kinesic macrorecording (partial list for arm positions)

Notation symbol*	Symbol meaning
AA	Biarmed activity
RA	Right arm
XAA	Arms behind back
AXA	Arms folded across chest
AxA	Arms across body—hands touching below chest
AxbA	Arms across body—hands touching across belly
AxgA	Arms across body—hands touching across genitals
ATA	Arms hanging at sides
'ATA'	Arms swinging (as in walking)

* Birdwhistell 1970, p. 371

often been referred to as the 'natural history' method or structural approach to studying expressive behavior, and has been promoted by those in anthropology, linguistics, sociolinguistics, psychiatry, and other fields (Bateson 1971; Kendon 1970; Kendon & Ferber 1973; McQuown 1971).

The Bernese system for coding nonverbal behavior was designed by Frey, in his dissertation (1971), and further developed with von Cranach and with Pool. This system purports to cover all possible spontaneous movements that occur when participants are seated, and includes the head, trunk, arms, hands, legs, and feet. The Bernese system is based on the principle of position–time–series notation that assigns numerical codes to the various deviations of body parts from the base positions (e.g. a head tilt to the left and down is given a numerical value to represent the degree to which the head has deviated from the 'normal' position which is upright and facing straight ahead). The system permits detailed, comprehensive, and reliable transcription of videotaped behavior into 'high resolution data protocols'. The Bernese system codes position and movement every 16 seconds (originally based on the 16 frame per second movie film) so as to represent 'fluid movement' (Frey & Pool 1976). The described positions are made with reference to the three Cartesian axes (horizontal, vertical, and depth), and can represent concepts such as expansiveness, reaching out, concordance, imitation, and others (Frey & von Cranach 1973; Frey & Pool 1976). The Bernese spatiotemporal parameters cover all changes in movement from moment to moment and, since it avoids the use of psychological constructs labeled by the experimenter, it is considered less evaluative and subjective compared with other coding systems (Argyle 1975; Ekman & Friesen 1969a).

The descriptive accuracy of this system was demonstrated in a study requiring coders trained in the Bernese system to draw models' positions from data protocols which had been developed from descriptions of the models' original positions; 98% of the positional codes were identical to the original (Frey & Pool 1976). Bente and colleagues developed 3D animation programs based on transcriptions of head positions using the Bernese system (Bente 1989), and further, showed that observers' rated impressions of individuals in computer 3D animations and original videotaped interactions were nearly identical (Bente *et al.* 2001).

Context and kinesics

At about the time that Birdwhistell and Scheflen were describing their findings and developing structural theories to explain the relationships between semantic content, body movement, and the social interaction function of body movement, other researchers, conducting systematic studies, noted precise, systematic relationships between speech and movement.

Nonverbal and verbal congruence

Boomer (1963), and with Dittman (Boomer & Dittman 1964), investigated verbal–nonverbal congruence, determining units of speech and types of pauses, and the timing of body movements in relation to these. Boomer's (1965) work stimulated studies on speaker–listener turn exchange by focusing on the special relationships among certain body movements (e.g. of hand, head), vocal hesitations and pauses in speech (i.e. hesitation, juncture, filled), and the phonemic clause (i.e. unit of speech characterized by specific prosodic (intonation) patterns (Trager & Smith 1957). This work prompted a series of studies by Dittman and Llewellyn (1967, 1968) on the characteristics of speaker and listener behaviors in conversation. They reported on the precise placement of 'listener responses' (i.e. acknowledgment responses such as nods and 'M'hum') within speakers' utterances. Others corroborated these results (Duncan & Fiske 1977; Matarazzo & Wiens 1972; Rosenfeld 1966, 1978; Rosenfeld & Hancks 1980; Yngve 1970).

Dittman (1972) further elaborated speakers' frequent use of body actions ('fidgeti-ness') during non-fluent versus fluent speech. He posited a cognitive–speech relation-ship such that body movements facilitated speakers' utterance constructions, particularly during non-fluent hesitations, and suggested a possible neurological basis for this behavior. Dittman (1977) also described developmental patterns in conversa-tional behavior.

At approximately the same time as Boomer and Dittman's work, others investigated the movement–speech relationship of individuals, and between individuals. Condon and Ogston (1966, 1967) first described 'self-synchrony' as the correspondence between a person's body movements and his/her speech utterances at the phonemic, syllabic, and lexical levels. An example of self-synchrony is the display of a rhythmic hand gesture in tempo with the rhythm of one's speech. Condon and Ogston (1966, 1967) described 'interactional synchrony' as the coordination between listeners' movements and speakers' utterances. Using frame-by-frame microanalysis of filmed sequences, they found that listener movements were patterned on the speaker's speech stream. Small movements of the listener's head, eyes, wrist, mouth, and fingers occurred at phoneme changes in the speaker's talk.

Kendon (1970) reported similar results and suggested that, even when the listener could not observe the speaker, the listener's precision in synchronized actions suggested that the listener had anticipated the meaning of the speaker's utterance before the speaker finished talking. He further postulated that the listener's coordinated move-ments with the speaker's utterance reflected cognitive processes involved in processing speech, just as the synchronization between speaker's movements and speech reflected the speaker's cognitive processes in producing speech. This remarkable entrainment between speakers and listeners is present quite early in life, as Condon and Sander (1974) showed in two-week-old infants whose movements were coordinated with the adults' speech, but not with non-speech sounds. Condon (1980, 1982) described problems in displays of synchrony in children with various developmental and learning disorders. Some of the functions served by synchrony include:

- to regulate speaker turn exchange (Dittman & Llewellyn 1969; Duncan & Fiske 1977; Hadar *et al.* 1985);
- to reflect rapport (Scheflen 1964; Tickle–Degnen & Rosenthal 1987);
- to show attention and comprehension (Kendon 1970).

Studies on speaker–listener interaction require careful coordination of videotaped behaviors of each interactant and coding of each body movement at a micro level of analysis. This type of analysis requires meticulous inspection and coding, and precision in locating these movements in time and in relation to the other interactant.

While there has been criticism of Condon's method of measuring synchrony (McDowall 1979; Rosenfeld 1981), other researchers' work attests to the existence of the phenomenon (Davis 1982; Kendon 1972). A clever series of studies by Bernieri and colleagues avoided the earlier criticisms of the methodology of measuring synchrony by using judges' ratings of synchrony ('simultaneous movement, tempo similarity, coordination, and postural sharing') for mother–infant and teacher–student dyads, in adult conversations, and in full video versus mosaic segments (Bernieri 1988; Bernieri *et al.* 1994).

For a more thorough treatment of the theoretical, definitional, and methodological issues regarding synchrony, consult the work of Bernieri and colleagues (Bernieri *et al.* 1988, Bernieri & Rosenthal 1991).

A companion notion to synchrony is postural or interpersonal congruence. Mehrabian (1972) suggested that the angle of postural lean (i.e. lean of the trunk forward, sideways, back, or straight) was highly related to interpersonal attitude and status. Scheflen, too (1964, 1965), had noted that psychotherapy patients and therapists tended to match the alignment of their limb and trunk positioning, particularly when rapport was high. Trout and Rosenfeld (1980) showed that observers attributed 'greater rapport to the congruent-limb episodes' compared with noncongruent segments. 'Bookending' was used to refer to mirror image positions of individuals on either side of a person(s) sitting between them and suggests a close involvement of the individuals involved (Scheflen 1972).

Channel studies

A popular approach to studying body movement has been channel studies, in which information from various expression modalities (i.e. face, voice, body, verbal) is compared and contrasted (Bugental *et al.* 1970; Gallois & Callan 1986; O'Sullivan *et al.* 1985; Rosenthal *et al.* 1979). For example, Lessin and Jacob (1984) reported greater inconsistencies in verbal–nonverbal behavior patterns in interactions between parents and delinquent children compared with 'normal' families.

Body positions

This section will begin with a summary of research efforts to code and define body movements gleaned from investigations which include assessment of 'body movement'. To understand how investigators have coded body positions in research studies, a thorough perusal of the literature was conducted using PsycInfo of the SilverPlatter database computer search program. The terms used were body, trunk, or torso with posture, positioning, movement, lean, orientation, and postural shifts. A similar review was made for arm and for leg position, movement, posture, and shifts. Over 100 research reports (most since 1982) were revealed that specifically used the search terms. Unfortunately, few of these offered adequate descriptions of the coded behavior. A study's title or abstract might refer to 'trunk shifts' but, in the methodology, there was no indication whether these:

1. involved only the 'trunk' (i.e. torso) or also included (or were exclusively) arm or leg movement changes, or
2. involved trunk lean, orientation, or rotation changes.

As can be seen in the summary for body positions below, much work remains to be accomplished on specifically defining the body positions and how these can be coded.

Trunk lean

Trunk lean was the most popularly coded body position variable. Lean typically refers to the angle of the trunk with respect to a vertical line drawn from the midline of the head and chest, to the hips. Trunk lean is recorded as upright or erect (i.e. head and shoulders in a direct vertical line over the hips), forward lean (i.e. head and shoulders forward of upright relative to the hips), or backward lean (i.e. head and shoulders backward of upright relative to the hips) (Bente 1989; Bernieri, & Gillis 1995; Davis & Hadiks 1994; Mehrabian 1968). Most often, forward or backward lean were made with reference to another interactant; one study referenced lean with respect to the table between interactants. Sometimes this lean has been described further within a range of 5–45 degrees angle from upright (Cappella & Greene 1984; Fairbanks *et al.* 1982).

Several researchers also included sideways turn of the trunk to the left or right, and others referred to 'trunk swivel', 'trunk rotation', or 'trunk turn', where the shoulders are turned so that one shoulder is in front of the hips and one shoulder is behind the hips (Bente 1989; Davis & Hadiks 1994; Hall 1984; Vrij 1994).

Trunk lean was nearly always described with reference to a seated position, but there were also investigations which included 'upper body lean' when standing (Argyle & Dean 1965; Mehrabian 1968). Researchers sometimes recorded only the percentage of time spent in a forward or in a backward lean. There were also the more ambiguous codings of 'body lean change', 'body lean away', 'slouching', 'slumping', 'rocking', 'crouching', 'settling', and 'rigid torso'.

Trunk orientation

The trunk also can be described with reference to 'orientation' (i.e. degree to which an encoder's frontal body surface faces (vis-a-vis) another encoder. Orientation most often was coded within a range from zero to 90 degrees, depending on whether the encoder was directly facing (i.e. zero degrees) or facing away from (i.e. turned away at a right angle, 90 degrees) his/her interlocutor (Capella & Green 1984; Davis & Hadiks 1994; Gifford 1982; Honeycutt 1989, Mehrabian 1969; Street & Buller 1988). Sometimes orientation was described only as 'turned away' or 'immediate', and was not further delineated. In some instances, coding of orientation was based on the alignment of the encoder's shoulders with the plane of her/his seat edge or the plane of the interactant's shoulders (Bernieri & Gillis 1995).

The lack of definition for body variables often proved frustrating. For example, Berry and Hansen (2000) reported positive relationships between personality variables such as 'agreeableness' and 'extraversion' and body position characterized as 'open', which included ratings for both body orientation and body posture. While researchers may conjecture what 'open' might refer to in regard to body position, our conjectures may not be the same.

Arm, leg, and foot positions

With the exception of the numerous studies concerned with hand actions, attention to the arms, legs, and feet in body movement research has focused on frequencies of arm and/or leg 'movement' or 'shifts' of any kind, or noting arm and leg positions with regard to the degree of 'openness', 'symmetry', or 'relaxation' (terms which were rarely defined further). Sometimes researchers coded the presence of specific types of arm positions such as arms akimbo or 'folded' arms. Mabry (1989), for example, defined five arm-specific positions. Bente (1989) described arm movements with respect to horizontal, vertical, and forward or backward axes, while Kendon (1972) used the terms 'extension', 'retraction', and 'rotation' to characterize arm movements. In our research (Harrigan & Carney 2005), we code arm and leg positions with a code representing the actual configuration (e.g. arms folded, arms resting together in lap, legs crossed ankle on knee, lower legs and feet beneath the chair etc.).

Postural shifts

A majority of studies reported total frequency of 'postural shifts' or 'postural movements' (Buller & Aune 1987; Comadena 1982; Frances 1979; Vrij 1994), and sometimes body positions were described as 'rigid' or 'tense'. However, exactly what was meant by all these terms was again unclear. 'Postural shifts' were sometimes defined as any change in position or posture, but in at least one study, 'leg movements' was the sole variable in this category. In one example of how postural shifts were used, investigators reported the effect of a psychotropic medication on patients' nonverbal behaviors, including 'posture shifts'. Unfortunately, these again were not defined (Ranelli & Miller 1981). A few studies included specific, descriptive information with definitional details of the coded behavior for body position. An example is work by Hewes (1957) who studied and described, rather exhaustively, the world distribution of postures adopted for sitting and standing.

Body actions

Social psychologists studying nonverbal behavior complemented the work of investigators conducting structural and descriptive studies by focusing their attention on underlying states revealed by nonverbal behavior—the so-called 'external variable' approach. The best known work is that of Ekman and colleagues. Ekman and Friesen (1969a) outlined a coding system, including five categories of nonverbal behavior: emblems, illustrators, regulators, adaptors, and affect displays. (The latter refers primarily to the face and is more thoroughly discussed in Chapter 2.) Ekman and Friesen's categories for movements have been the most frequently used by researchers compared with any other coding strategy (e.g. Labanotation, Birdwhistell's kinesics). Indeed, Ekman and Friesen's categories are used so widely that in their methodological descriptions, researchers do not even define the variables but simply reference Ekman and

Friesen (1969a). Their work also provides a theoretical framework for understanding hand movements in particular. For these reasons, Ekman and Friesen's categories will be detailed extensively here.

This review will show the current stage of the research on hand movements—slowly evolving, but yet rudimentary and uncoordinated methodologically and theoretically. The review will be followed by suggestions for investigators interested in coding hand movements. As mentioned earlier, the great focus in body actions has been on the hands, and Ekman and Friesen's (1969a) coding system is not an exception.

Emblems

The term 'emblem' comes from the work of Efron (1941) who provided an impressive, descriptive study of gestures used by second generation Jews and Italians in New York City. Ekman and Friesen refined their definition of emblem to refer to symbolic actions which have a 'specific verbal translation known to most members of a subculture, and is typically intended to send a message' (Ekman & Friesen 1977, p. 38). Some examples include: nod, shoulder shrug, and 'OK' sign. Because these acts are so communicative, emblems are more intentional and less idiosyncratic than other types of movements, and, depending on the individual's emotional state, can result in 'emblematic slips' much like slips of the tongue (Ekman 1977).

Using an encoding–decoding procedure (i.e. back-translation) in which native speakers' displays of various emblems were judged by members of the same speech community, a list of emblems was compiled (Johnson *et al.* 1975). Decoding reliability in this study was quite high and indicated specific emblems that can be used for: making requests, conveying insults, indicating personal needs, providing replies, and giving greetings or goodbyes, within at least an American subculture (San Francisco Bay area). There are a number of studies on cultural differences in emblems (see Box 4.1).

Illustrators

A second category of nonverbal behavior described by Ekman and Friesen, illustrators are 'movements directly tied to speech, serving to illustrate what is being said verbally' (1969a, p. 68). These movements can accent or emphasize a word or phrase (baton), draw the shape of the referent (pictograph), sketch a path or direction of thought (ideograph), depict a bodily action (kinetograph), or be movements that point to an object (deictic) or depict a spatial (spatial) relationship (1969a, p. 68).

Box 4.1 Emblems in different cultures

Investigators have reported lists of emblems for a variety of other cultures (Barakat 1973; Creider 1977; Ekman 1976; Morris *et al.* 1979; Saitz & Cervenka 1972; Sparhawk 1978). Emblems are defined similarly by other researchers and are labelled: semiotic gestures (Barakat 1973), formal pantomimic gestures (Wiener *et al.* 1972), expressive gestures (Zinober & Martlew 1985), autonomous gestures (Kendon 1983), and symbolic gestures (Krauss *et al.* 1996; Ricci-Bitti & Poggi 1991).

While emblems are typically exhibited purposefully and tend to be culture-specific (although the latter is less so as culture-to-culture contact increases via media sources), the display of illustrators usually involves less direct awareness and intention, and these acts generally do not have meaning separate from the verbal speech stream; typically, listeners do not gesture, for example. Like emblems, illustrators are culturally learned and have an effect on observers' impressions of the encoder (Ekman & Friesen 1969*a*, p. 69).

Illustrators also have been labeled as: object-focused movements (Freedman & Hoffman 1967), hand illustrators (Cohen & Harrison 1973), gesticulations (Kendon 1980), illustrative gestures (Street & Buller 1987), representational gestures (McNeill 1992), and conversational gestures (Krauss *et al.* 1996). Several studies have been conducted on the functions of illustrators (see Box 4.2)

Adaptors

The third category in Ekman and Friesen's (1969*a*) classification system was originally labeled 'adaptors' and, of the three types (self, object, alter), self-adaptors have received the most attention in Ekman's and other researchers' investigations. This label was changed to 'self-manipulator' (Ekman & Friesen 1977) and then 'body manipulator' (Ekman 1977) because 'self-adaptor' was considered 'too theoretically laden' (Ekman 1977, p. 46). (See Ekman and Friesen 1969*a*,*b*, 1972, 1974 for more theoretical detail on adaptors.)

Although Ekman's newer terminology for these actions was intended to be more descriptive, the term 'self-adaptor' is most often used by those who study these hand movements (Grahe & Bernieri 1999; Heilveil & Muehleman 1981; Hill & Stephany 1990; Street & Buller 1988; Vrij 1995) and will be the term used here. These actions have been given a variety of names: 'embarrassed hands' (Ferenczi 1914), 'autistic' movements (Krout 1935), 'self-manipulators' (Rosenfeld 1966), 'body-focused' movements (Freedman 1972, 1977; Freedman & Hoffman 1967), 'self-touching gestures' (Kimura 1976), 'manipulative gestures' (Edelman & Hampson 1979), 'contact acts' (Bull & Connelly 1985), and 'self-touching' (Harrigan 1985; Harrigan *et al.* 1987; Shreve *et al.* 1988).

Self-adaptors involve one part of the body doing something to another body part such as scratching one's head, stoking the chin, hand-to-hand movements, lip licking, and hair grooming (Ekman 1977, p.47). These movements often are considered grooming or personal actions, best not displayed in polite society (Ekman 1977). Another type of adaptor—object manipulator—occurs in similar circumstances and involves such actions as playing with a pencil, twisting a book of matches, scratching the ear with a paper clip, and other actions involving handling an object or using an object for some type of body contact (p. 47). Either type of adaptor is usually displayed 'with little awareness, without the deliberate intent to communicate a message' (Ekman & Friesen 1977, p. 39). Such actions, however, seem to convey some diffuse information to observers regarding the encoder's emotional state, pathology, deceptiveness, and general personality traits (Ekman 1977; Ekman & Friesen 1974, 1977; Ekman *et al.* 1976).

Box 4.2   Functions of illustrators

The function of illustrators is complex, and research has focused on several perspectives. Illustrator frequency was related to psychopathology, deception, and ratings of the encoder's personality (Ekman & Friesen 1969a, 1977; Ranelli & Miller 1981). A common theme of hand gestures is function: to aid listeners' understanding of the speaker's remarks, to help speakers produce speech, or to assist both. Speakers displayed illustrators more often when a listener was present (Cohen & Harrison 1973; Mahl 1961), and while these actions seemed to aid listeners in understanding complex descriptions (Cohen 1977), this notion is far from clear (Feyereisen & deLannoy 1991; Kendon 1994; Krauss *et al.* 1995; Krauss & Hadar 2001; Rimé & Schiaratura 1991) as speakers also displayed a high frequency of gestures when listeners were not present (Cohen & Harrison 1973).

At the Columbia University CommLab, Krauss and colleagues have conducted extensive empirical research on 'conversational gestures' and distinguished two types: motor movements and lexical movements (Krauss *et al.* 1996). The former represent actions in which the 'hand shape remains fixed during the gesture, which may be repeated several times' (p. 393). These are similar to Ekman and Friesen's (1972) 'batons' and Kendon's (1983) 'beats'. Like Ekman and Friesen (1969a) and others (Kendon 1983), Krauss and associates define 'lexical movements' as actions that 'vary in length, are nonrepetitive, complex, and changing in form . . . and appear related to the semantic content' (Kraus *et al.* 1996, p. 393). Three criteria are used to show the relation of gestures to speech:

1. These acts do not occur without speech and are only made by speakers.
2. They are 'temporally coordinated with speech'.
3. They are 'related in form to the semantic content of the speech they accompany' (Kraus *et al.* 1996, p. 392).

Although the pervasive belief is in the 'gestures as communication' hypothesis (i.e. gestures help communicate information to listeners), supportive empirical evidence is minimal. Researchers have shown that listeners were better able to draw figures from descriptions by speakers who were permitted to gesture (Graham & Argyle 1975) or guess objects based on speakers' descriptions (Riseborough 1981), but success was marginal and limited. Krauss, too, demonstrated that judges were able to draw parallels between a gesture and it's 'lexical affiliate' (i.e. word/phrase associated with gesture), but only with gestures involving 'locations' or 'actions', compared with 'objects' and 'descriptions' (Krauss *et al.* 1991).

Based on their results, Krauss and colleagues contend that gestures convey a limited amount of information to listeners, but are useful for speakers (Hadar *et al.* 1998; Krauss & Hadar 2001). For example, speakers had more difficulty retrieving lexical items to describe what they had previously viewed if the speakers were prevented from gesturing, but lexical clarity and speed was considerably better when they were permitted to gesture (Krauss *et al.* 1996). Preventing speakers from displaying gestures either resulted in speech disfluencies (Rauscher *et al.* 1996; Rimé 1982) or had little effect on speech production (Graham & Heywood 1976). Not surprisingly,

Continued

Box 4.2: Cont'd

Krauss *et al.* (1991) found that gestures presented without speech resulted in less communication accuracy than when accompanied by speech. Interestingly, aphasics with word retrieval problems gestured more than normals or aphasics with conceptual problems (Hadar *et al.* 1998), and training aphasics to exhibit gestures helped their word retrieval (Hanlon *et al.* 1990). Dittman and Llewellyn (1969), like others (Christenfeld *et al.* 1991; Freedman & Hoffman 1967), observed a higher frequency of gestures when word retrieval failures occurred, and posited a tension reduction hypothesis in which gestures helped alleviate tension generated by word retrieval difficulties.

Finally, Krauss and colleagues' conjectures regarding the association between speech and gesture as a communication unit may be reflected in the spontaneous gestures congenitally blind individuals exhibit while speaking (Blass *et al.* 1974).

The research findings of both Freedman and Harrigan and colleagues, on body-focused movements or self-adaptors (see Box 4.3), suggest two critical distinctions regarding the display and interpretation of these hand actions. First, in most studies no distinction has been made with respect to the area where the action occurs; and second, the temporal length of the self-touching is not considered usually. There are exceptions, however. Friesen *et al.* (1979) focused on the classification of hand movements and coding reliabilities. They included 'brief' (i.e. less than 2 seconds) and 'long' (i.e. more than 2 seconds) manipulations (i.e. self-adaptors), and distinguished between face, hand, and other manipulations. One rationale for their temporal distinction was that a brief manipulator 'seems to accomplish something' (p. 107), whereas long manipulations appeared more like the fidgeting, unpattterned movements described by Freedman and colleagues. In addition, Friesen *et al.* (1979) noted that the region or area of the body that was manipulated was important, as was the type of self-adaptor (e.g. scratching, rubbing, picking). Buller and Aune (1987) also coded self-adaptors with respect to body area and temporal parameters, and Mintzlaff *et al.* (1999) found differences for type of self-adaptors and 'defensiveness'. Several studies have focused on the functions and descriptive characteristics of adaptors (self-touching) (see Box 4.3)

The point of this discussion is to direct researchers' attention to the possibility that it may be more productive or illuminating to distinguish between self-adaptors based on temporal length, body area, and type of action. In general, researchers have included only one inclusive category for coding self-adaptors, and the results of the few studies cited below suggest that significant information may be lost when all self-adaptors are lumped together as though they represent the same act.[1]

---

[1] The area of touch, in which one person touches another, will not be covered in this chapter because, in general, touching others does not often occur in most social interactions. Exceptions include: greetings and farewells, intimate encounters, providing comfort or service to another, aggressive confrontations, and the like. This omission of touch is not intended to indicate that touch is not worthy of study. On the contrary, it is an important and powerful

Box 4.3 Functions of adaptors (self-touching)

Generally, the most typical explanation for self-adaptors has been an affective one (i.e. these acts are attempts to cope with feelings and emotional states). Self-adaptors provide sensory stimulation and are performed to relieve self or bodily needs, to comfort or irritate, to release emotional arousal, or otherwise provide ministration to the self (Ekman & Friesen 1969*b*, 1974). Ekman and Friesen (1969*a*) hypothesized that self-adaptors represent unintended 'emotional leakage', betraying an individual's aroused affect. These actions have been associated with anxiety, guilt, hostility, suspiciousness, and stress (Dittman 1972; Ekman & Friesen 1974; Mahl 1968).

Despite these claims about the function of self-adaptors, there are few direct studies of self-adaptors. In the studies that do exist, the 'negative' impression of self-adaptors has not always been observed. For example, confederates who displayed self-adaptors were rated as more likeable, outgoing, honest, and easier to work with compared with those who did not display self-adaptors (Harrigan *et al.* 1987), and replicated results showed that doctors and patients who self-touched, compared with those who did not, were regarded as more expressive, warm, sincere, and natural, though slightly less calm (Harrigan *et al.* 1986*a,b*). Using contrast analyses, researchers showed that the encoders' role and type of self-adaptor significantly affected decoders' ratings of the individual. For instance, hand-to-hand rubbing by job interviewees and patients was judged as more appropriate than by friends or strangers, and nose rubbing was regarded as warm and expressive compared with hand or arm rubbing (Harrigan *et al.* 1991). These results reflect the fact that the type of self-adaptor was an important factor, as was the role of the self-toucher and the other behaviors displayed at the same time (e.g. nodding, leg recrossing).

The idea of different interpretations for different self-adaptors was revealed by Goldberg and Rosenthal (1986) who classified self-touching based on body area, and found interesting differences for gender, area, and formality of interview (e.g. more upper torso/neck self-touching was displayed by males in same sex dyads).

Freedman and colleagues have developed a compelling theoretical view of hand movements with regard to verbal representation. Accordingly, effective communication requires both the 'enactive kinesic system organized toward the representing of thought, and a supportive kinesic system organized toward the attaining of focal attention' (Freedman 1977, p. 111). The former system is represented by hand gestures, labeled as 'object-focused movements', while the latter are termed 'body-

Continued

action which is compelling and capable of affecting another in positive or negative ways. Display rules and conventions regarding touch are themselves a subject of sensitivity, sometimes causing confusion and misinterpretation. Thorough reviews can be found in Heller & Schiff (1991) and Jones (1994). Examples of touch studies include those concerned with: gender (Hall & Veccia 1990), cultural differences (Albert & Ha 2004; Nail *et al.* 2003), and medical or psychotherapeutic contact (McNeill & Fawn 2004; Stenzel & Rupert 2004; Wendler 2003). Perhaps some of the most profound results on the effects of touch are those by Tiffany Field, showing dramatic gains from the use of touch on premature infants with respect to weight gain and developmental advances (Field 2001).

Continued

focused movements' (i.e. self-touching). Rather than concentrating on the underlying states, motivations, or feelings of the encoder, or the role of these movements with respect to the speaking–listening roles, Freedman's efforts were to understand these movements in relation to the cognitive aspects of the speech process. 'When there is some strain between the image and symbol, the action creates a kinesic experience at the very point at which the arbitrary symbol must be articulated' (Freedman 1977, p. 113). Thus, the gesture helps 'buttress the clarity of the image', connecting the image and word.

Whereas object-focused movements are elicited by tasks in which participants need to put cognitive experiences into words, body-focused movements appear when there is interference in the focus of the speaker's attention or organization of thought (Freedman 1972, 1977). Such soothing, grooming, or rubbing actions regulate sensory input to help the speaker maintain attention and 'ward off intrusive cues'. Evidence for these ideas is provided by studies showing that:

1. Confrontations with cold interviewers resulted in more body-focused movements because interviewers' disinterest interfered with speakers' descriptions of personal events (Freedman *et al.* 1972).
2. Participants who displayed pervasive body-focused movements made fewer errors on the Stroop interference test (Barroso *et al.* 1978).

Freedman (1977) also described developmental trends with respect to the frequency and laterality of object and body-focused movements that are intriguing, although short on empirical data. In addition to the speaker's hand movements, the listener's participation in 'the process of information filtering and decoding' also may be inferred from body-focused movements (Freedman *et al.* 1978).

A descriptive study of self-adaptors showed that physicians and patients displayed self-touching differently depending on semantic content, temporal location, and area touched (Harrigan 1985). For example, self-adaptors rarely occurred during silence and were more frequent during interruptions or speech disfluencies; and physicians were more likely to exhibit a 'grooming' (e.g. readjust clothing/hair) self-adaptor as they began interacting with the patient, while patients self-touched more when answering the physicians' questions.

Finally, for Freedman and colleagues, an important distinction is made between brief (i.e. less than 3 seconds), 'discrete' body-focused movements that appear to have an instrumental function (e.g. scratching the nose) and those of a more 'continuous' (i.e. longer than 3 seconds), unpatterned nature (e.g. finger-to-hand, hand-to-body manipulations) (Freedman 1972; Freedman *et al.* 1973). For example, higher frequencies of the more continuous, unpatterned (i.e. repetitive and nondirected) body-focused movements were related to degree of clinical pathology in depression (Freedman 1972), schizophrenia (Grand *et al.* 1975), and isolation proneness and belligerence in chronic schizophrenia (Grand 1977). Similarly, patients' presentation of 'hidden agendas' (i.e. patient problem that was not the stated purpose of the appointment and was difficult to express, such as unwanted pregnancy, domestic violence, cancer fears) was associated with more body self-adaptors than hand self-adaptors (Shreve *et al.* 1988).

Regulators

Regulators represent another category of nonverbal behavior distinguished by Ekman and Friesen (1969*a*). These are 'actions which maintain and regulate the back-and-forth' flow of conversation between speakers and listeners (p. 82), and include nods, eye contact, postural shifts, eyebrow movements, and utterances such as 'mm-hmm'. Regulators contain no meaning by themselves but 'convey information necessary for the pacing of the conversation' (p. 82). These actions usually occur on the 'periphery of awareness' on the part of the encoder. They are not as intentional as emblems, illustrators, or adaptors, and are maintained in one's repertoire as 'highly over-learned habits' (p. 83).

Other researchers have studied these conversational exchange behaviors (Duncan 1972, 1983; Edelsky 1981; Erickson 1975; Harrigan 1985; Scheflen 1964). Duncan and Fiske (1977) detailed, with thoroughness, the use of body movements (head, hand, eye contact, postural shifts, vocal changes) in an elaborate rule system for the smooth exchange of speaking and listening roles in dyads. Similarly, other investigators have described turn-taking rules in group interactions (Dabbs & Ruback 1984; Harrigan 1985). The 'functional' purpose of 'interactive' gestures has been proposed by Bavelas (1994) who included 'delivery', 'citing', 'seeking', and 'turn' gestures. (See Feldstein and Welkowitz 1987 and Rosenfeld 1987 for a more complete discussion of definitional issues in 'turn-taking' research.) Hand movements coded in our research program (Harrigan & Carney 2005) involving social interactions in a conversational distance include: speech illustrative gestures, emblems (when these rare behaviors occur), self-touching delineated by duration and location, and object manipulations (e.g. fingering a pencil).

Head movements

The last category of body movements to consider is head movements. Not surprisingly, the most typical action counted when coding head movement is nodding, but other movements also are notable: shaking, tilting (i.e. head drawn toward shoulder; sometimes termed 'head cocks'), and movements associated with gaze such as turning the head or the slight movements which occur when speaking or listening (Condon & Ogston 1966, 1967; Kendon 1970). Still other references to head movement include: 'dipping' (i.e. downward movement), 'bobbing' and 'tossing' (i.e. drawing head up sharply), 'thrusting' (i.e. abrupt upward lift toward interactant), 'dropping' (i.e. abrupt downward movement), and 'postural shifts' (i.e. head turns). Frequently, 'head movements' were coded, referring to 'any' movement of the head.

There are more than 70 articles in which head movements were coded in humans, and of these, nearly 80% were on nodding. 'Nodding' is not a distinctly human activity; it is displayed by mice, dogs, rats, horses, birds, and insects in courtship displays, pathological states, and in human–animal contact. In addition to its expressive function, nodding in humans is one of several stereotypical movements often exhibited in pathological brain states (e.g. dementia, tissue damage, psychosis, mental retardation, aphasia, nystagmus (persistent, rapid, side-to-side eye movement)).

Research articles on coding of human expressive head movements were discovered searching PsycInfo with the terms 'head nod', 'head shake', 'head tilt', 'head cock', 'head dip', and 'head movements'. Additional references were collected from the computerized literature search described earlier for 'nonverbal behavior' which included nods and other actions of the head. Close perusal was made of 55 research articles/chapters on nodding, 14 on shaking, eight on tilting, and 25 involving 'any' head movement.

Researchers defined nodding with descriptions which incorporated the type as well as direction of movement: cyclical or continuous, up/downward or forward/backward motions on the vertical or sagittal plane. Sometimes these movements were only called 'affirmative' or 'positive' nods. Likewise, descriptions of head shaking included cyclical or continuous, side-to-side, left/right motions on the horizontal or traverse plane. These actions were also referred to as 'negative nods', 'normal movements in speech', 'shaking to emphasize speech', and 'horizontal nodding'. Head tilts were described as a sideways or lateral tilt of the head toward the shoulder. McGrew (1972) was by far the best at providing a technical definition of nodding: '... head is moved forward and backward on the condyles resting on the atlas vertebra, resulting in the face moving down and up' (p. 57). Generally, in most research reports, little description was given for the coded head actions.

There are very few studies of head shaking as a coded head behavior. Hill and Stephany (1990) found that clients reported feeling supported when listening therapists exhibited head shaking in addition to nodding. Shaking by the therapist was thought to convey sympathy with the client's plight. Comparison studies using nodding and head shaking showed that participants who were induced to nod (versus head shake) were more likely to agree with an editorial that they read (Wells & Petty 1980). Similarly, researchers demonstrated that head shaking (versus nodding) produced more prosocial feelings toward a videotaped individual who described a personal, negative situation (Tamir *et al.* 2004). Human faces are learned faster when accompanied by nodding or shaking compared with no movement (Lander & Bruce 2003), and both actions appear to operate as a mnemonic for positive and negative (respectively) thoughts and feelings (Förster & Strack 1996; Tom *et al.* 1992). Reminiscent of earlier work by Dittman and Llewellyn (1967, 1968), studies have shown that rhythmic head movements produced during speech improved speech perception (Munhall *et al.* 2004). Such head movements are thought to be linked to the production of suprasegmental features of speech like stress, amplitude, and pitch (Hadar *et al.* 1983, 1984).

While there are a few studies involving head tilting (Noller & Callan 1989; Noller & Gallois 1985; Troisi & Moles 1999), significant results were minimal: head tilts occurred more often in families with adolescent daughters and were displayed more by adolescents and wives (versus husbands) (Noller & Callan 1989; Noller & Gallois 1985). As indicated earlier, there are a great many studies on nodding (see Box 4.4).

In summary, although head movements commonly occur in social interactions, only nodding has received much attention. Like other areas of body movement, head actions have not been diligently defined. In our research (Harrigan & Carney 2005), head actions include nodding, shaking, and tilting, with a miscellaneous category for any movement that is not one of the former head actions; the latter are subtle and often occur when speaking or as listener responses. Head movements associated with direct-

---

Box 4.4   Research findings on nodding

Many and varied research questions have been addressed in which nods operated as an independent variable (e.g. signaling interest) or a dependent variable (e.g. nodding frequency when lying). A brief review of such studies will illustrate the range of research on nods.

As indicated earlier, nods are associated with listener feedback to the speaker, suggesting that the listener is following the speaker's comments (Duncan & Fiske 1977; Matarazzo & Wiens 1972; Rosenfeld 1978; Rosenfeld & Hancks 1980; Yngve 1970). Birdwhistell (1970) offered several forms of the nod to represent different conversation control functions. There is a substantial literature demonstrating the powerful reinforcing relationship between interviewer nodding and the amount and type of information provided by clients (Matarazzo *et al.* 1964; O'Brien & Holborn 1979; Pope & Siegman 1972). Nodding was reflected in positive impressions of counselors and other interactants (D'Augelli 1974; Förster & Strack 1996; Fretz 1966; Harrigan *et al.* 1991; Hill & Stephany 1990; Mehrabian 1969; Seay & Altekruse 1979), and was exhibited more by those with similar attitudes (Kleck 1970). Feldman (1985) reported striking differences in nodding as a listener response by White and Black Americans. Displays of nodding occurred often during settings of approval seeking (Mehrabian & Ksionzky 1972; Rosenfeld 1967), approval providing (Rosenthal & Jacobson 1968), and persuasion (Mehrabian & Williams 1969).

Nodding is seen as an emblem where the members of the culture displaying it regard it as an affirmative response (Ekman 1976; Jakobson 1972; Johnson *et al.*1971; Morris *et al.* 1979; Saitz & Cervenka 1972). Gender differences show that females consistently displayed more nods than males (Hall 1984; Jones *et al.* 1999). Nodding decreased during intrusions (Sundstrom 1975), conflict (Feeney *et al.* 1999), and social anxiety (Ayers 1989; Shibata 1990), but increased when interactants sat close (Kleck 1970). Like other expressive behaviors, nodding decreased during depression (Ekman & Friesen 1974) and increased during recovery from depression (Troisi *et al.* 1989), and greatly increased in psychotic states (LeJeune 1989). Nodding has been shown to both increase (Buller *et al.* 1989; O'Hair *et al.* 1981) and decrease (Comadena 1982; Mehrabian & Williams 1969) in deception.

---

ing and changing gaze are coded with reference to the specific gaze variable (e.g. gaze at interactant). Our definitional reference points for the three head actions are based on imaginary lines drawn horizontally across the tip of the nose (nod), and vertically from the top of the face to the chin, bisecting the nose (shake)—resulting in two axes and four quadrants. When the nose crosses either of the imaginary lines and enters both the lower and upper half (or section) of the vertical dimension (nod), or enters both the left and right halves of the horizontal section (shake), it is coded accordingly. Head tilts involve movements of the head being drawn toward either shoulder. Two other movements can be coded. A head dip involves drawing the chin toward the chest without an upward lift (as in a nod), and a head toss is an upward lift of the chin without a subsequent movement downward (like a nod); a head toss is often an abrupt action. The latter two actions occur very rarely. All of these actions vary in intensity, breadth, and frequency and range from fast, vigorous, long nods to slow, subtle, narrow head shakes.

Technology for coding head movements is minimal to nonexistent. Hadar *et al.* (1985) used a polarized light goniometer (instrument for measuring relationships of moving body parts to one another e.g. legs and trunk while walking) to systematically record the up/down and left/right cycles in nodding and shaking (respectively) to demonstrate their relationship to various conversational behaviors (e.g. listener responses, speaker-turn attempts, speech stress). Bente (1989) developed a computer program (see below) that is capable of generating scripts for graphic computer animations of head (and body) movement.

Other approaches to studying body movement

Behavioral rating studies

Behavioral rating studies are a less time-consuming method of determining the individual effects of specific body movements (e.g. hand gestures, nods, posture shifts). In these studies, body movements are not coded individually but rather, are rated. Thus data collection (i.e. ratings) is considerably more economical. Burgoon and others (Burgoon & Koper 1984; Burgoon *et al.* 1990; Guerrero 1997) asked observers to rate participants' behavior using bipolar adjectives reflecting:

1. global assessments of overall behavior (e.g. calm, composed, reticent, attentive);
2. specific combinations of participants' body movements such as 'random movement' (e.g. self-touching, rocking, twisting) and 'kinesic pleasantness' (e.g. nodding, smiling).

These indices of body movement and global measures of arousal were shown to be highly correlated in the psychotherapy context (Burgoon *et al.* 1992). A recent meta-analysis showed the important influence of communication channel (visual, vocal, or both) on ratings of participants' state anxiety and trait anxiety (Harrigan *et al.* 2004). Hall and Friedman (1999) combined both global ratings and measurement of discrete behaviors in a study on status, gender, and nonverbal behavior.

Instrumentation for coding body movement

Scherer and Wallbott (1985) presented an approach to studying nonverbal behavior that focused on distinguishing among variables derived from the Brunswikian lens model (Brunswik 1956) where:

1. motor cues might include EMG recordings of facial behavior or elaborate devices to position the head and measure gaze behavior with remarkable accuracy;
2. distal cues could include the study of acoustic wave forms (e.g. to capture amplitude, fundamental frequency, and intonation patterns) or light-emitting devices (LEDs) to acquire precise measurements of body movements;
3. proximal cues could involve codings of or impressions of behaviors by observers such as hand gestures, nods, and shoulder shrugs.

In line with this model was a coding technique developed by Frey and Pool (1976) where a cross-hair device was inserted into a videotape recording and used by coders to locate various head and body movements with reference to the vertical and horizontal lines. There are a few studies by one research group (Bente *et al.* 1998, 2001) in which the positions and movements of the head, trunk, and limbs were categorized using a computerized version of the Bernese system (see p. 153). Their work also permitted a computer simulation of positions and movements transformed from actual dyadic interactions which then could be modified or reconfigured to assess impressions of various lifelike body movements and positions (Bente *et al.* 1996). Transducers (small ultrasonic devices) can also be attached to various body parts and a microcomputer can then determine receiver–transducer distances and plot 3D positions of movement (Altofer *et al.* 2000).

Finally, Blascovich and colleagues (2002) and others (Biocca & Levy 1995; Guye–Vuilleme *et al.* 1999) have developed methods of studying nonverbal behavior using computer-generated 'immersive virtual environments' (IVEs). For example, Bailenson *et al.* (2003) showed that participants approached by a virtual human in a virtual room behaved in a manner that was similar to human-to-human approach (Hayduk 1983). These efforts offer considerable advantages to researchers interested in nonverbal behavior.

Training coders and determining reliability for coded body movement

The most common method of recording body movements is with the use of human observers. Typically, the researcher begins with clear definitions and parameters of each of the behaviors to be coded, and trains coders, often students, in recording the specific behaviors. Coders learn the various behaviors and their descriptions, view samples of the participants' behavior, and record the designated behaviors as frequency or duration tallies, or based on the specific time of occurrence, or in relation to some other feature of the interaction (e.g. speaking turn, greeting, response to interviewer). Most often, behavior is coded from videotaped interactions which permit the viewing and reviewing that is necessary to establish a high level of accuracy and confidence in the coded behaviors.

After the initial training and practice, the coders' data is checked for reliability and, if necessary, additional clarification of the variables and re-training is instituted to increase accuracy in future coding. Respectable reliabilities can be obtained for most body movements. When acceptable reliabilities are established, each coder then works independently, completing the coding of the behaviors in question. Continued reliability checks throughout the coding procedure help maintain a high level of accuracy in coding.

It goes without saying that whenever behaviors are coded and counted, the accuracy of the behavioral coding is paramount. The limited range of methods for defining and measuring coded body movements parallels a similar difficulty with regard to assessing reliability for coded body movement. Acceptable reliability thresholds are most often set at 0.80 or better (Baesler & Burgoon 1987; Becker–Stoll *et al.* 2001; Friesen *et al.* 1979). Although there are some studies in which two coders recorded all of the behaviors (Goldberg & Rosenthal 1986; Harrigan *et al.* 1985; Mehrabian & Friar 1969; Mintzlaff *et al.* 1999; Shreve *et al.* 1988), typically 10–25% of the total data collected has been coded by at least two coders (Duncan & Fiske 1977; Jurich & Jurich 1974; O'Leary & Gallois 1985).

There are several methods that have been used to ascertain interrater reliability: percent agreement, Cohen's *kappa,* Spearman's *rho,* Pearson's *r,* Ebel's or Winer's interrater analysis using intraclass correlation, and Rosenthal's (1987) application of the Spearman–Brown formula. It is not within the scope of this chapter to cover the important aspects of reliability with respect to coding body movement, as this is thoroughly discussed in Chapter 5. With regard to specific reliabilities for body movement, Baesler and Burgoon (1987) conducted the most thorough evaluation of reliability measures for nonverbal behavior. From their data of 40-plus studies, Baesler and Burgoon (1987) found very high (i.e. 0.81 or better) median reliabilities for all categories of body movement (e.g. hand gestures, arm and leg positions, trunk movements, self-touching, nodding, postural shifts).

Suggestions for coding body positions and actions

Several elements of the research study affect the choice of body movements one might include: the number of interactants, setting and relationship between interactants, and how the research question is reflected in body movement. Investigations in which body positions and actions are either measured or manipulated primarily involve dyadic interactions, although there are some studies involving members of a group (Altorfer *et al.* 1992; Harrigan 1980, 1985; Mabry 1989; Noller & Callan 1989). While one might display a nod, shrug, gesture, or the like when alone, these actions are very rare and often are associated with vigorous mental debate as one thinks through an issue or puzzles out a problem. Many body actions are expressive and, thus, more likely in interactive versus solitary settings. The paucity of studies of body movement in groups is likely related to the difficulty of coding behavior for more than two individuals such as a participant and confederate, interviewer and interviewee, mother and child, etc. Research settings for studies on body movement include: therapy interactions, employment interviews, conversations between friends or strangers, or encounters in a lab, educational, or public environment.

The research question is an important determinant of what body movements are chosen to be manipulated or coded. As indicated earlier, body movements do not provide direct information about affect, but can convey significant information about the strength of an affect (e.g. an angry face with a clenched fist and tense upper body, or a sad voice with drooping posture and curtailed hand and head actions). Whether intentional or not, many body actions are expressive and conducive to revealing personal attributes (e.g. warm, impulsive, argumentative, stable) and motivations such as attentiveness, interest, vitality, sociability, competitiveness, etc. Body positions may convey one's attitude, status, and degree of affiliation, based on how one positions her/himself in relation to another (e.g. sitting close, facing, and leaning slightly forward toward an interactant versus sitting turned and angled away with crossed legs between interactant and self). In some studies, one category of body movements may be more important than another. So, investigations of turn-taking will be focused on hand and head actions relevant to speaking and listening (e.g. speech-related gestures, nods), while those directed toward cultural similarity and diversity in hand actions will concentrate on emblems of the hands and head.

A guide for decisions regarding which of the many body positions and actions to include in a study may be suggested:

1. when the research questions are focused on the more enduring qualities of the interaction (e.g. status, attitude, affiliation), body positions may provide initial impressions;
2. for questions regarding characteristics which can change quickly and from moment to moment (e.g. warmth, animation, vigor), expressive hand and head actions may be most evocative.

Body positions are often tallied individually, but may contribute more information when treated together (e.g. change in trunk lean and orientation with repositioning the arms and legs). Both body positions and actions contribute different information about the encounter and often work together. For example, several coded behaviors were included in studies of those who were physicians, deceivers, embarrassed, courting couples: distance, trunk lean and orientation, arm and leg positions, head and hand actions, and smiling and gaze (Costa *et al.* 2001; Grammer *et al.* 2000; Harrigan *et al.* 1985).

Gaze

A literature review on 'gaze' (including eye contact, looking, glancing, visual attention) since the 1982 Handbook recovered over 1700 articles, but only a small portion (13%) was relevant to affect and nonverbal behavior. Few of these had clear descriptions of the methodology used in coding gaze. Exline and Fehr's (1982) stellar review of research methodologies in coding gaze in the 1982 Handbook, and Fehr and Exline's (1987) chapter review on research results in gaze research have not been eclipsed. The present brief review will focus on points made by these authors, with respect to research methodology for gaze, as well as those of other researchers.

Functions of gaze

One of the first to study gaze directly was Kendon (1967) who distinguished several functions of gaze:

1. Monitoring—'to gather information about how [an interactant] is behaving' (p. 53) (i.e. to seek feedback or a 'response' from a listener.
2. Regulatory—to signal one's intentions with respect to 'floor apportionment' (i.e. switching speaking turns; see below).
3. Expressive—to reveal feelings and attitudes (e.g. gaze avoidance at points of 'high emotion').

With respect to (3), the eyes play an important role in Ekman and Friesen's (1975) descriptions of the universal emotions (widened eyes in fear; tensed lower lids in anger;

see Chapter 2). Recent research results (Adams & Kleck 2003) showed that direct versus averted gaze significantly facilitated the processing of facial expressions of affect. Direct or averted gaze also influenced participants' speed in gender categorization of targets and rate of accessing semantic memory (Macrae *et al.* 2002).

Von Cranach (1971) considered gaze as part of a general 'orienting behavior'. Gaze is unique among nonverbal behaviors in that it is a sensory/perceptual organ for gathering information and also acts as a signal to others. For example, Cary (1978) suggested that following a glance of recognition at a stranger, gaze avoidance is typical, and that heightened gaze indicates a desire for communication. Goffman (1963) discussed the rule-governed nature of gaze, citing examples such as 'civil inattention' (i.e. not gazing at strangers in public settings) or 'cutting' (i.e. visually ignoring another). Because our gaze patterns provide information regarding our attention, interest, and possible motivations and intentions, gaze has been the subject of much research. More recently, gaze has been less frequently studied as an individual class of variables (e.g. mutual gaze, staring, glances) but, rather, studied with other nonverbal behaviors subsumed under larger constructs such as affiliation, intimacy, conversation, attention, and dominance.

Research considerations for gaze

Location

One of the first questions a researcher must decide is **where** the data will be collected—in a naturalistic environment or in the laboratory. The obvious distinction between these is in the degree of control over the participants' behavior and technical issues involving measurement precision, obtrusiveness, reliability, and validity. While there are public locations where people can be observed inconspicuously, the distance at which this must be accomplished may compromise the collection of reliable and valid data, and may limit the number of gaze variables that can be accurately recorded. For example, in La France and Mayo's (1976) study, observers were able to record, via stopwatches and tally sheets, the amount of time spent listening and looking at the face of another in an interacting dyad. Settings were public (e.g. cafeterias, hospital waiting rooms, fast-food outlets). Problems in such circumstances arise from distance from the observed, as well as positioning of observers, acuity, and reliability of measures. Many of these problems can be resolved by videotaping the interactions, but this results in other perplexing issues—narrowed scope of observation (due to video camera position), illumination, and obtrusiveness. Kendon and Ferber (1973) were able to position a camera inconspicuously at a distance from the observed, but detecting a person's visual target was impossible to specify unequivocally. While a zoom lens (Cary 1978) helps remedy this difficulty and provides higher resolution, problems remain with illumination, movement out of the camera range, and expense. In a laboratory, many of these challenging issues can be resolved.

The difficulties inherent in measuring gaze in the field have led many researchers to choose manipulation rather than measurement of gaze in such settings. The effects of confederate's gaze on the observed were studied with respect to staring (Ellsworth *et al.* 1972), aiding a victim (Ellsworth & Langer 1976), giving money (Kleinke 1977), and compliance (Snyder *et al.* 1974). In these studies, however, it was often difficult, to impossible, to judge whether or not participants had been aware of confederates' gaze. Assessing participants' awareness of another's gaze in the field (e.g. in a cafeteria, car, airport) is nearly infeasible compared with the lab, where technical equipment, one-way mirrors, and confederates' faces are readily apparent, and where questionnaires assessing confederate gaze can be easily administered to participants.

Number of participants

A second consideration in gaze research is the number of participants observed at any one time. While field studies can be used to record participants' gaze at others or at objects, the laboratory is essential for precise coding of visual behavior in social interaction. Deciding on the observational setting is necessarily based on the researcher's unit of analysis. Is the research question based on the effect of social stimuli (e.g. interviewer warmth) on a participant, or the relationship between two interactants (e.g. conversational roles)? In the former case, participants' gaze behavior can be measured while a confederate's gaze pattern is controlled (Aiello 1972; Exline *et al.* 1965); training and frequent checks of confederate's nonverbal behavior is essential. If the confederate's gaze also is allowed to vary, measurement of the confederate's gaze also is required for valid data. When data on both participants' gaze patterns are needed to answer research questions, technical challenges arise which necessitate equipment to record both parties and to integrate accurately the gaze behavior (e.g. split-screen).

Use of confederates

While permitting control over some features of visual interaction, use of a confederate also results in a loss of spontaneity. Confederates can be trained to look at the participant at specific times during the interaction (Fehr 1981; LeCompte & Rosenfeld 1971) or according to specified visual patterns (e.g. continuously, only while talking) (Argyle *et al.* 1974). Remarkable precision in controlling confederate gaze was obtained by administering slight cueing shocks to the confederate's hand without the participants' awareness (Ellyson *et al.* 1980).

Even if they are unaware of the research hypothesis, introducing a confederate also exposes the possibility that other confederate behaviors systematically bias (Rosenthal 1966) the results (e.g. behaving more 'warmly' to participants in no or low gaze conditions). Exline and Fehr (1982) reported that confederates experienced 'affective reactions' to altering their normal gaze patterns, and this affected other nonverbal behaviors (e.g. nods, gestures, posture).

An additional factor to consider is that confederates may not behave similarly to all participants. Assessing the effect of confederate's gaze on participant behaviors or attitudes requires attention to the possibility that such behaviors and impressions may be affected by the gaze patterns under investigation or by the confederate's discomfort with violating gaze norms, the attendant arousal associated with gaze at another (Ellsworth 1975), or receiving gaze from another (Exline 1972; Exline & Fehr 1982). Training can help reduce these affective reactions and standardize confederate behavior (Ellsworth & Ross 1975), but investigation of potential effects is warranted.

Selection of gaze variables

Like many other research considerations, choosing the gaze variables depends upon the research question. 'Gaze' refers to where an individual looks and 'eye contact' (i.e. mutual gaze) references direct eye to eye looking between individuals. Most often in a dyad, gaze variables include:

1. frequency—number of glances at partner;
2. total duration or total gaze—total number of seconds looking at partner;
3. proportion of time looking during a specified activity (e.g. listening, speaking);
4. average duration—mean duration of individual glances;
5. standard deviation of glances;
6. mutual gaze—number of seconds that partners look into each other's eyes simultaneously (Argyle & Ingham 1972; Exline & Fehr 1982).

Of these, (6) has been the most investigated. Many of these variables are intercorrelated (Duncan & Fiske 1977; Exline & Fehr 1982; Kendon & Cook 1969). Von Cranach (1971) has suggested 'face gaze' to denote glances toward another's face when eye contact cannot be determined precisely, and 'eye gaze' for reference to looking into another's eyes (Harper *et al.* 1978). Kirkland and Lewis (1976) distinguished other forms of eye movement—glance, look, gaze, leer, and stare—on the basis of duration.

Prevailing topics in gaze research

There are two areas in gaze research which have received considerable attention in studies of visual interaction with adults: the role of gaze in conversation as a mechanism for speaker switching, and the role of gaze in balancing the level of intimacy between interactants. Research on the function of gaze in the expression of affect has been rather limited. While the eyebrows and musculature surrounding the eyes play a prominent role in the Facial Affect Coding System developed by Ekman and Friesen (1978), a person's visual focus is relevant only for the expression of sadness (i.e. gaze down). Participants induced to feel depressed exhibited less gaze toward a confederate (Natale 1977), as did those reporting embarrassment (Edelmann & Hampson 1979) and anxiety (Jurich & Jurich 1974), and actresses expressing despair, rage, annoyance, or anxiety (Lalljee cited in Argyle & Cook 1976, pp.79–80; see also Lalljee 1978). The relationship between gaze patterns and emotional experiences clearly requires considerable clarification. It may be that gaze is germane for only a few emotions or that it may be relevant in showing emotional intensity. These and similar questions concerning gaze and emotion remain unanswered.

Gaze in conversational roles

One of the most often studied topics in gaze research is the relationship between gaze and speaking–listening roles in conversation. In dyads, listeners spend considerably more time gazing at their speakers than they do when speaking (Ellyson *et al.* 1980; Exline *et al.* 1965; Kendon 1967). Researchers have attributed this difference to the fact that speakers need to decrease external distraction in order to attend to the planning and delivery of speech, and to decrease sensory overload. Listeners presumably are providing feedback to speakers concerning their interest. Mutual gaze, although physiologically arousing (Argyle & Dean 1965; McBride *et al.* 1965), occurs frequently in social interaction, and is reported to be related to topic intimacy and distance (Argyle & Cook 1976; Fehr & Exline 1987).

Strongman and Champness (1968) proposed a probabilistic formula ('chance model') to predict the amount of mutual gaze from levels of individual gaze, and while researchers substantiated expected levels of mutual gaze in independent studies (Lazzerini *et al.* 1978; Rutter *et al.* 1977), Exline and Fehr (1982) point out that 'another human is a socially significant event that captures far more of our attention... than a truly chance model would predict' (p. 115). Very little research exists on gaze in conversations of more than two individuals; however, more speaker-to-listener gaze was reported in group interactions (i.e. three or more) (Exline 1963; Harrigan & Steffen 1983; Weisbrod 1956 (as reported in Argyle & Cook 1976)).

Gaze also plays an important role in speaker-turn exchange in conversations. Kendon (1967) described a distinctive pattern of gazing at speaker–listener transition points in which speakers gaze away when initiating an utterance and look toward their listener at the conclusion of a turn. This signaling effect of gaze has been confirmed for at least the terminal phase of turn-taking (Beattie 1981; Duncan & Fiske 1977; Rutter *et al.* 1978; Wiemann & Knapp 1975). Contradictory results may be related to durations of the 'switching phase', presence of hesitant speech, definitions of an utterance, and duration of gaze sampling (Fehr & Exline 1987; see also Goodwin 1981). Gaze patterns for speaker-turn switching may differ in dyads compared with group conversational cues. For example, Harrigan and Steffen (1983) found that speakers in a group conversation tended to gaze toward a listener when beginning a speaking turn; this was especially true for successful interruptions.

Intimacy equilibrium model

The Intimacy Equilibrium Model (Argyle & Dean 1965; revised Argyle & Cook 1976) suggests that there are approach-avoidance forces at work in eye contact with another person and that these forces are held in check by components of intimacy which can be changed to maintain equilibrium for either party. Thus, if one experiences too much intimacy with another, changes can be made in the degree of eye contact, physical distance, topic intimacy, smiling, etc.. This model has received considerable attention. Stephenson *et al.* (1973) conducted several studies of the effect of increased gaze associated with increased distance and determined that their results supported the equilibrium hypothesis. Cappella (1981) and others (Ellsworth 1978), however, reported some compensatory actions when intimacy increased, but also noted reciprocal actions. Finally, Patterson (1982) included social control together with intimacy as forces which result in compensatory and reciprocal actions.

Measurement issues in gaze research

Reliability

Finally, issues involving reliability and validity need to be considered. Coders have been shown to be quite reliable in discerning another's gaze under optimal conditions, with reliabilities ranging between 0.88 and 0.99 (Exline & Fehr 1982). Argyle and Cook (1976) provide detailed data on reliability of gaze observations. High reliability estimates are more likely to be obtained when coding is based on videotaped or filmed, rather than live, sequences because of the advantages of replay and slow motion viewing. Advanced new technologies can more accurately track eye movements; these are often used in studies of visual attention. Eizenman developed the instrumentation and software analyses and, together with colleagues (Eizenman *et al.* 2003), has demonstrated remarkable specificity in fixations and glance durations using the high-resolution eye tracker. This instrument could be placed behind a participant (A) who receives the gaze of another participant (B) to more definitively code the gaze from B to A.

Estimating another's gaze

Studies of participants' assessments of another's gaze have met with mixed results. Argyle and Williams (1969) determined that participants were generally unaware, while Ellsworth and Ross (1975) noted that the degree of gazing (high or low) had a direct bearing on participants' sensitivity. The meaning attributed to another's gaze can be assessed by ratings or questionnaires of the interacting confederates (Argyle *et al.* 1974) or videotaped others (Kleck & Nuessle 1968; Kleinke *et al.* 1974).

Validity

Validity in coding visual interaction is more problematic to ascertain. ' Humans are not as accurate as desired in determining when others look them *directly* [italics added] in the eye(s)' (Exline & Fehr 1982, p. 122). Validity levels for 'eye-directed' gaze are considerably worse than for 'face-directed' gaze. Participants' attempts to discriminate gazes into their eyes versus other parts of their face resulted in very low accuracy (10–35% accurate depending on distance) (Krüger & Hückstedt 1969; cited in Exline & Fehr 1982; see also Ellgring 1970). However, there seems to be a wide margin to the left and right of one's face ('off-the-face gazes') that is interpreted as gaze from another (Gibson & Pick 1963). Judgment errors increase as the head deviates from a straight-on position, as distance between interactants increases, or as gaze duration decreases (Argyle & Cook 1976; Exline & Fehr 1982).

Obtaining maximally valid data requires the use of restrictive and cumbersome techniques (e.g. chin rests, head sets) to control the sender's line of gaze, and may be superfluous in light of comments by Vine (1971) and others (Argyle 1970; Exline & Fehr 1982) who contend that in natural settings, interactants look at another's face or well away from each other. Goodwin (1981) noted that a change in gaze is nearly always accompanied by a change in head orientation. As Exline (1972) argued: 'where the receiver thinks the sender looks is more important than where the sender does precisely focus' (p. 204). Validity of observer measurement improves with training (von Cranach & Ellgring 1973). For more precise measurement of gaze, there are oculometers that permit moment-to-moment tracking of eye movement with minimally obtrusive head gear. Finally, in recorded interactions, the obtrusiveness of the camera resulted in decreased participants' gaze, more face self-touching, and more anxious feelings. Covert recording is often permitted by present-day research ethics, provided the benefits outweigh potential harm, and in such studies very few participants indicated concern or refusal (Exline & Fehr 1982).

Specific recommendations for coding gaze

Exline and Fehr (1982) listed the following recommendations for obtaining valid and reliable data for gaze:

1. Have dyad members face each other directly.
2. Place observers or TV cameras directly behind receivers.
3. Keep the sender–receiver distance as small as possible.
4. Test the visual acuity of observers.
5. Train the observers with feedback trials.
6. Have some eye-level lighting to reduce shadows in the eye socket.
7. Obtain reliability estimates from all observers.
8. Schedule fatigue breaks into coding sessions. Observers may relieve the eye strain associated with long-term focusing on the eyes of a sender by moving their heads while keeping their eyes focused on the target. The head movement changes the muscles used for focusing (p. 125).

The specific methods of recording gaze data are guided by expense, variables of interest, measurement context, and investigator's skill with complex technologies.

Conclusions regarding proxemics, body movement, and gaze coding

This overview of studies on body movement, proxemics, and gaze was intended to provide information on the methods of coding and the descriptions of coded behaviors that have been used previously by investigators. The extensive, though noncomprehensive, reviews of each section were offered to guide the researcher in determining appropriate variables for study. In summary, the coding strategies for body movement reveal the following:

1. *Proxemics* With respect to proxemic behavior, a reasonably well-defined system seems to have evolved (Watson & Graves 1966) using a variation of Hall's (1963) coding scheme. Subtle fine-tuning may be necessary to help establish more accurate distinctions for levels of a few of the proxemic codes (e.g. olfaction, visual clarity). Sommer (1969) and Hayduk (1981b) suggested some excellent ideas for studying spatial arrangements in 'semi-fixed' space, but considerable development is necessary to measure such variables as intrusion, boundary markers, and seat placement at meeting sites. Lastly, greater methodological development is necessary for reliably determining 'approach distance' (Aiello 1987; Hayduk 1983).

2. *Kinesics: trunk positions* Coding methods for body movement in general lag behind proxemic, gaze, facial, and vocal measures, and this is most apparent in strategies for recording body posture and realignment. A great majority of the studies coding posture, body position, or posture shifts were significantly lacking in definition and precise labeling of the behavior in question. 'Postural shifts' might refer to change in trunk position in one study and changes in arm/leg posture in another. Trunk position (e.g. forward lean) and trunk orientation (i.e. degree to which one faces interlocutor) both need to be coded when determining the angle of the trunk with respect to other interactants. Both represent different dimensions of the frontal body surface (i.e. torso front from neck to waist), and both relate to the distance between interactants. Measurement of trunk angle (i.e. degree of torso tilt from the hips) could benefit from greater precision with regard to the forward-backward and side-to-side angles. While codes representing the degree to which the frontal body surface (i.e. trunk orientation) is turned directly toward another lack a broader range of interval codes than the two or three gradations typically found in investigations (e.g. 0, 45, or 90 degrees), increased precision may not be warranted as, typically, people tend to face one another within a small scope of possible orientations. It may be more beneficial to determine how orientation, lean, distance, and gaze combine to show attention, interest, positive regard, etc.

3. *Kinesics: arm and leg positions* There is a lack of comprehensiveness in labeling and description of various alignments, but also, and more critically, when arm and leg positions are coded, they are commonly referenced with respect to the degree of 'openness' rather than a less biased labeling based on the degree to which the hands, arms, legs, or feet meet, intersect, or are intertwined. Appendages could be described based on whether or not they meet (e.g. hand on hand), are in a parallel or symmetrical position (e.g. arms on arm rests), or crossed (e.g. legs crossed, knee on knee). 'Open' positions might imply the notion of being unguarded or accessible, whereas 'closed' postures might imply protectiveness, reticence, and unrevealing obstruction. A hand-on-hand posture appears considerably different than arms folded across the chest, yet in some studies both are considered 'closed' postures. It may be more instructive to more fully describe the specific position (e.g. right arm bent at elbow with chin on palm, left arm on arm rest).

4. *Kinesics: hand actions* While there is considerable creative work being conducted on hand gestures (i.e. illustrators) with regard to function, meaning, and timing, other hand actions need further development with respect to coding. Information on the function, connotation, and implication of self-touching, for example, could benefit from more specificity in the type of action (e.g. scratching, rubbing, picking, arranging), area touched (e.g. nose, arm, hair, clothing), and duration of the self-touching. Similar information can be added with respect to objects manipulated in a non-task manner (e.g. fingering a paperclip or pencil). There is very little mention in coding body movement of the actions involving the feet. Shoulder shrugs are not often included in studies in which body movement is coded—the exception being studies on cultural emblems. Although shrugs, object manipulations, head cocks, and other movements (e.g. head dip or head toss) may be displayed less commonly compared with hand gestures, self-touching, or nods, such actions may contribute

to our understanding of human body movement when they are combined in patterns with other actions (e.g. shoulder shrug with head tilt and lip purse) or in assessments of total activity.

5. *Kinesics: head actions* Head movements also suffer from shortsightedness in definition clarity. Nods and shakes are assumed to be interpreted similarly by investigators, but as this review indicated, bringing the head downward, without then raising it, was counted as a nod, and head shakes have been defined as 'negative head nods'. There is little mention of head tilts or cocks, where the angle of the head and shoulder is reduced, nor is there much attention given to the various slight circular and left–right movements made by speakers and listeners, except in studies on synchrony.

6. *Gaze behavior* The methodology and design strategies for coding gaze behavior outlined by Exline and colleagues (Exline 1972; Exline & Fehr 1982; Fehr & Exline 1987) have often been adopted by others, or formed the basis of something similar. They represent the most valuable consideration of the relevant aspects of coding gaze.

As is readily apparent, significant methodological work remains for coding body movement. The following are a few areas requiring further development:

- precise definitions for and labeling of the coded behavior;
- greater uniformity in the methodology for and process of coding various behaviors to permit comparability of research results;
- elaboration of methods of training and re-training of coders;
- greater uniformity in establishing reliability (see below) of the coded behaviors.

Selecting measures of body movement—decisions

Several questions arise for the researcher who is interested in coding body movements for research purposes. The first decision concerns how body movement variables will be used:

1. as a dependent variable to reflect changes in some characteristic of the encoder such as emotional state, personality structure, social role, status, or attitudes or motives regarding others or about objects/concepts, or
2. as an independent variable where body movements are manipulated to observe the effect on participants.

For example, in deception studies, the dependent variables might be the frequency of selected body movements exhibited by deceivers and nondeceivers. Similarly, the precise location and duration of selected body movements might be determined for conversational participants to better understand speaker-turn exchange. As independent variables, certain body movements might be selected to represent different levels of encoder features such as empathy, friendliness, deception, arousal, dominance, in order to observe the effect on participants' behavior or ratings of encoders. A researcher may be interested in the types of listener behavior most likely to elicit specific information from the speaker, and so might compare and contrast the rate of nodding, the amount of gaze, or the frequency of hand gestures.

There are further decisions which must be made for either type of study where body movements are used as variables. For studies in which body movements are counted in order to compare some feature of the encoder or the situation, the movements selected to reflect the researcher's question must be determined with care.

The research hypotheses also drive the selection of the level of analysis of the body movements: microscopic or macroscopic. Microscopic measures typically include small, fine-grained movements of the head, fingers, gaze, or body and may be related to changes in the speaker's stream of speech, to interactive courtship signals, or to subtle changes in a psychotherapy setting. Macroscopic measures include large-scale, molar behaviors such as postural changes, hand gestures, and nods. An intermediate level could include macroscopic behaviors and some finer movements of the head and hands. The level of analysis needs to reflect the type of information to be gained by coding body movement.

Along with the level of analysis is another significant measurement issue—the time interval for the coded behavior. Researchers code behavior with respect to frequency counts or the duration of time that a behavior lasts. While both are highly correlated, each offers different information: how often a behavior occurs versus how long a behavior is present. Certainly it is far less time consuming to code the frequencies of various behaviors which can be tallied on paper or keyboard entries. It is more difficult to record duration (i.e. time from when a behavior begins until it ends), but durations also can produce frequencies, and often it makes sense to code durations rather than frequencies for those behaviors which are infrequent but enduring. For example, an individual may display one self-touching on the hand (e.g. scratching, rubbing) that lasts several tenths of a second, or continuously rub or stroke the hand for a significant portion of the total time. Likewise, a seated person may swing her/his knee-on-knee crossed leg continuously or several times briefly during the course of an interaction. In sum, the time interval chosen for coding behavior depends on the researcher's question, the number of behaviors included, and the resources available for coders.

Future work in body movement coding

As this chapter has shown, there is much work that needs to be accomplished on coding body movement, specifically kinesics; coding is less of a problem in the areas of proxemics and gaze. Development of coding methodologies and instrumentation is one obvious area of needed upgrade beyond our current state of investigation. Research results accrued across various labs can be more easily compared when variable definitions and labels, coding techniques, and estimates of reliability are similar. Such an integration also would be of great benefit to new researchers. In our lab, we have continually refined a coding system and process which incorporates aspects of several available systems. Our manual includes variable lists and definitions, methods for coding and training coders, and information on frequencies and durations and locating the behavior with respect to the speech stream or other movements (Harrigan & Carney 2005). Body positioning and actions, and proxemic and gaze measures are included.

In addition, the work of Blascovich, Bente, Frey, and others, using computer simulations, virtual environments, and robotics, offers a unique opportunity to examine

Table 4.2   Coding categories and measurements for proxemics and kinesics[1]

Proxemics
Physical distance—measured as distance between interactants using a marked floor grid or floor tiles.
Kinesics: body positions
Trunk lean[2]—measured in increments based on the angle of 90° between an erect spine and the legs (i.e. lap)
   when seated:
   1. Forward at 30°, 45°, or 60° from 90° upright toward other
   2. Erect at 90° upright posture of trunk
   3. Backward at 30°, 45°, or 60° from 90° upright away from other
   4. Sideways at 30°, 45° or 60° left or right
Trunk orientation[2]—measured in increments ranging from:
   1. 0° (facing other)
   2. 30° (turned slightly away from other)
   3. 45° (turned further away from other)
   4. 90° (sitting at right angles to other)
Arm positions—coded as one of nine possible arm alignments.
Leg positions—coded as one of five possible leg alignments.
   Leg movement—jiggling, wiggling, swinging
   Foot movement—tapping, bouncing, twitching, wiggling
Kinesics: body actions
Speech illustrative gestures—hand movements directly tied to speech; used to illustrate what is being
   verbalized.
Self-touching—any hand-to-body contact (includes head, face, limbs) not regarded as a speech illustrative
   gesture (e.g. indicating the self in speech by pointing to and touching the chest); also includes duration and
   location of self-touching.
Object adaptors—manipulations of objects that are not part of the self (e.g. jewelry, glasses) nor task-oriented
   (e.g. using a pencil) e.g. manipulating paper clips, book of matches, papers, etc.
Touch—touching other interactant not regarded as a speech illustrative gesture (e.g. indicating the other in
   speech by pointing to and touching other's chest).
Kinesics: head actions
Based on imaginary lines drawn horizontally across the tip of the nose and vertically from the top of the face
   to the chin bisecting the nose resulting in four quadrants of the face.
   1. Nod—head moved so nose crosses imaginary line separating the face into upper and lower sections
   2. Shake—head moved so nose crosses imaginary line separating the face into left and right sections
   3. Tilt—head moved toward shoulder
   4. Dip—chin drawn toward the chest without subsequent upward lift as a nod
   5. Toss—chin raised upward without subsequent dip downward like a shake; head toss is often an abrupt
   action
Miscellaneous—subtle, non-distinct movements not defined by the above head actions.

[1] Harrigan & Carney 2005
[2] These behaviors could be listed under proxemics using Hall's (1973) body position, but are included here so
   that all body movements can be grouped together.

movements of encoders, interactions of participants, and perceptions of decoders with greater consistency and presentation of stimulus materials. There are significant advances in technologies for the face and voice (e.g. voice and face recognition and simulation) which have built upon the precision of findings in these research areas. Computer digitalization of data could afford access for analyses of combinations of various movements, as well as offer the opportunity for comparisons across research labs.

Finally, a domain of body movement research that has been sadly neglected is the development of theoretical viewpoints on the function, patterning, and interaction of actions and positions. This oversight may have arisen because of the lack of specificity in coding various movements. Overall, there is ample opportunity for research work on methodology, instrumentation, and data storage and comparison, in addition to areas of specific interest with respect to kinesics, proxemics, and gaze.

References

Adams, R.B. & Kleck, R.E. (2003). Percieved gaze direction and the processing of facial displays of emotion. *Psychological Science,* **14**, 644–7.

Aiello, J.R. (1972). A test of equilibrium theory: visual interaction in relation to orientation distance and sex of interactants. *Psychonomic Science,* **26**, 335–6.

Aiello, J.R. (1987). Human spatial behavior. In *Handbook of environmental psychology, Vol. 1* (ed. D. Stokols & I. Altman), pp. 389–504. New York, NY: Wiley

Aiello, J.R. & Jones, S.E. (1971). Field study of the proxemic behavior of young children in three subcultural groups. *Journal of Personality and Social Psychology,* **19**, 351–6.

Aiello, J.R. & Thompson, D.E. (1980). When compensation fails: mediating effect on sex and locus of control as extended interaction distances. *Basic and Applied Social Psychology,* **1**, 65–82.

Albert, R.D. & Ha, I. (2004). Latino/Anglo-American differences in attributions to situations involving touch and silence. *International Journal of Intercultural Relations,* **28**, 253–80.

Altman, I. (1975). *The environment and social behavior.* Monterey, CA: Brooks/Cole.

Altman, I. & Taylor, D.A. (1973). *Social penetration: the development of interpersonal relationships.* New York, NY: Holt, Reinhart & Winston.

Altman, I. & Vinsel, A.M. (1977). Personal space: an analysis of E.T. Hall's proxemics framework. In *Human behavior and the environment: Vol. 2 Advances in theory and research* (ed. I. Altman & J.F. Wohlwill), pp. 181–259) New York, NY: Plenum.

Altofer, A., Goldstein, M.J., Miklowitz, D.J., & Nuechterlein, K.H. (1992). Stress-indicative patterns of non-verbal behaviour: their role in family interaction. *British Journal of Psychiatry,* **161**, 103–13.

Altofer, A., Jossen, S., Wurmle, O., Kasermann, M.L., Foppa, K., & Zimmerman, H. (2000). Measurement and meaning of head movements in everyday face-to-face communicative interaction. *Behavior Research Methods, Instruments, and Computers,* **32**, 17–32.

Argyle, M. (1970). Eye-contact and distance: a reply to Stephenson & Rutter. *British Journal of Psychology,* **61**, 395–6.

Argyle, M. (1975). *Bodily communication.* London: Methuen.

Argyle, M. & Cook, M. (1976). *Gaze and mutual gaze.* Cambridge, UK: Cambridge University Press.

Argyle, M. & Dean, J. (1965). Eye-contact, distance and affiliation. *Sociometry,* **28**, 289–304.

Argyle, M. & Ingham, R. (1972). Gaze, mutual gaze, and proximity. *Semiotica,* **6**, 32–49.

Argyle, M. & Williams, M. (1969). Observer or observed? A reversible perception in person perception. *Sociometry,* **32**, 396–412.

Argyle, M., Lefebre, L., & Cook, M. (1974). The meaning of five patterns of gaze. *European Journal of Social Psychology*, **4**, 125–36.

Ayers, J. (1989). The impact of communication apprehension and interaction structure on initial interactions. *Communication Monographs*, **56**, 75–88.

Baesler, E.J. & Burgoon, J.K. (1987). Measurement and reliability of nonverbal behavior. *Journal of Nonverbal Behavior*, **11**, 205–33.

Bailenson, J.N., Blascovich, J., Beall, A.C., & Loomis, J.M. (2003). Interpersonal distance in immersive virtual environments. *Personality and Social Psychology*, **29**, 819–33.

Barakat, R. (1973). Arabic gestures. *Journal of Popular Culture*, **6**, 749–92.

Barroso, F., Freedman, N., Grand, S. & van Meel, J. (1978). Evocation of two types of hand movements in information processing. *Journal of Experimental Psychology: Human Perception and Performance*, **4**, 321–9.

Bateson, G. (1971). In *The natural history of an interview* (microfilm collection of manuscripts on cultural anthropology, 15) (ed. N.A. McQuown, G. Bateson, R.L. Birdwhistell, H.W. Brosin, & C.F. Hockett). Chicago: University of Chicago.

Bavelas, J.B. (1994). Gestures as part of speech: methodological implications. *Research on Language and Social interaction*, **27**, 201–21.

Beattie, G.W. (1981). The regulation of speaker turns in face-to-face conversation. *Semiotica*, **34**, 55–70.

Becker–Stoll, F., Delius, A., & Scheitenberger, S. (2001). Adolescents' nonverbal emotional expressions during negotiation of a disagreement with the mothers: an attachment approach. *International Journal of Behavioral Development*, **25**, 344–53.

Beier, E.G. & Valens, E.G. (1975). *People reading*. New York, NY: Warner Books.

Bente, G. (1989). Facilities for the graphical computer simulation of head and body movements. *Behavior Research Methods, Instruments, and Computers*, **21**, 455–62.

Bente, G., Donaghy, W.C., & Suwelack, D.(1998). Sex differences in body movement and visual attention: an integrated analysis of movement and gaze in mixed sex dyads. *Journal of Nonverbal Behavior*, **22**, 31–58.

Bente, G., Feist, A., & Elder, S. (1996). Person perception effects of computer simulated male and female head movement. *Journal of Nonverbal Behavior*, **20**, 213–28.

Bente, G., Kramer, N.C., Petersen, A. & de Ruiter, J.P. (2001). Computer animated movement and person perception: methodological advances in nonverbal behavioral research. *Journal of Nonverbal Behavior*, **25**, 151–66.

Bernieri, F. (1988). Coordinated movement and rapport in teacher–student interactions. *Journal of Nonverbal Behavior*, **12**, 120–38.

Bernieri, F. & Gillis, J.S. (1995). The judgment of rapport: a cross-cultural comparison between Americans and Greeks. *Journal of Nonverbal Behavior*, **19**, 115–30.

Bernieri, F. & Rosenthal, R. (1991). Coordinated movement in human interaction. In *Fundamentals of nonverbal behavior* (ed. R. Feldman & B. Rime), pp. 401–31. New York, NY: Cambridge University.

Bernieri, F., Davis, M.J., Rosenthal, R., & Knee, C.R. (1994). Interactional synchrony and rapport: measuring synchrony in displays of sound and facial affect. *Personality and Social Psychology*, **20**, 303–11.

Bernieri, F., Resnick, J.S., & Rosenthal, R. (1988). Synchrony, pseudosynchrony, and dissynchrony: measuring of entrainment process in mother–infant interactions. *Journal of Personality and Social Psychology*, **54**, 243–53.

Berry, D.S. & Hansen, J.S. (2000). Personality, nonverbal behavior, and interaction quality in female dyads. *Personality and Social Psychology*, **26**, 278–92.

Biocca, F. & Levy, M. (1995). *Communication in the age of virtual reality*. Hillsdale, NJ: Lawrence Erlbaum.

Birdwhistell, R.L. (1952). *Introduction to kinesics*. Louisville, KY: University of Louisville.

Birdwhistell, R.L. (1970). *Kinesics and context*. Philadelphia: University of Pennsylvania.

Blascovich, J., Loomis, J., Beall, A., Swinth, K., Hoyt, C., & Bailenson, J.N. (2002). Immersion virtual environment technology as a methodological tool for social psychology. *Psychological Inquiry*, **13**, 103–24.

Blass, T., Freedman, N., & Steingart, I. (1974). Body movement and verbal encoding in the congenitally blind. *Perceptual and Motor Skills*, **39**, 279–93.

Boomer, D.S. (1963). Speech disturbance and body movement in interviews. *Journal of Nervous and Mental Disorders*, **136**, 263–6.

Boomer, D.S. (1965). Hesitation and grammatical encoding. *Language and Speech*, **8**, 148–58.

Boomer, D.S. & Dittman, A.T. (1964). Speech rate, filled pause, and body movement in interviews. *Journal of Nervous and Mental Disorders*, **139**, 324–7.

Bugental, D.E., Kaswan, J.W., & Love, L.R. (1970). Perception of contradictory meanings conveyed by verbal and nonverbal channels. *Journal of Personality and Social Psychology*, **16**, 647–50.

Brunswik, E. (1956). *Perception and the representative design of psychological experiments*. Berkeley & Los Angeles: University of California.

Bull, P. & Connelly, G. (1985). Body movement and emphasis in speech. *Journal of Nonverbal Behavior*, **9**, 169–87.

Buller, D.B. & Aune, R.K. (1987). Nonverbal cues to deception among intimates, friends, and strangers. *Journal of Nonverbal Behavior*, **11**, 269–90.

Buller, D.B., Comstock, J., & Aune, R.K. (1989). The effect of probing on deceivers and truthtellers. *Journal of Nonverbal Behavior*, **13**, 155–71.

Burgoon, J.K. & Koper, R.J. (1984). Nonverbal and relational communication associated with reticence. *Human Communication Research*, **10**, 601–26.

Burgoon, J.K., Birk, T., & Pfau, M. (1990). Nonverbal behaviors, persuasion, and credibility. *Human Communication Research*, **17**, 140–69.

Burgoon, J.K., Le Poire, B.A., Beutler, L.E., Bergan, J., & Engle, D. (1992). Nonverbal behaviors as indices of arousal: extension to the psychotherapy context. *Journal of Nonverbal Behavior*, **16**, 159–78.

Cappella, J.N. (1981). Mutual influence in expressive behavior: adult–adult and infant–adult dyadic interaction. *Psychological Bulletin*, **89**, 101–32.

Cappella, J.N. & Green, J.O. (1984). The effects of distance and individual differences in arousability on nonverbal involvement: a test of discrepancy-arousal theory. *Journal of Nonverbal Behavior*, **8**, 259–86.

Cary, M.S. (1978). Does civil inattention exist in pedestrian passing? *Journal of Personality and Social Psychology*, 36, 1185–93.

Christenfeld, N., Schacter, S., & Bilou, F. (1991). Filled pauses and gestures: it's not coincidence. *Journal of Psycholinguistic Research*, 20, 1–10.

Cohen, A.A. (1977). The communicative functions of hand illustrators. *Journal of Communication*, 27, 54–63.

Cohen, A.A. & Harrison, R.P. (1973). Intentionality in the use of hand illustrators in face-to-face communication situations. *Journal of Personality and Social Psychology*, 28, 276–9.

Comadena, M.E. (1982). *Nonverbal cues in the perception of deception*. Paper presented at the meeting of the Eastern Communication Association, Hartford, CT, May 1982.

Condon, W.S. (1980). Interactional synchrony and cognitive and emotional processes. In *The relationship of verbal and nonverbal communication* (ed. R. Feldman & B. Rime), pp. 49–65. The Hague: Mouton.

Condon, W.S. (1982). Cultural microrythms. In *Interaction rhythms* (ed. R. Feldman & B. Rime), pp. 53–77. New York, NY: Human Sciences Press.

Condon, W.S. & Ogston, W.D. (1966). Soundfilm analysis of normal and pathological behavior patterns. *Journal of Nervous and Mental Disease*, 143, 338–47.

Condon, W.S. & Ogston, W.D. (1967). A segmentation of behavior. *Journal of Psychiatric Research*, 5, 221–35.

Condon, W.S. & Sander, L.W. (1974). Synchrony demonstrated between movements of the neonate and adult speech. *Child Development*, 45, 456–62.

Costa, M., Dinsbach, W., Mansfield, A.S.R., & Bitti, P.E.R. (2001). Social presence, embarrassment, and nonverbal behavior. *Journal of Nonverbal Behavior*, 25, 225–40.

Creider, C. (1977). Toward a description of East African gestures. *Sign Language Studies*, 14, 1–20.

Dabbs, J.M., Jr., & Ruback, R.B. (1984). Vocal patterns in male and female groups. *Personality and Social Psychology Bulletin*, 10, 518–25.

D'Augelli, A.R. (1974). Nonverbal behavior of helpers in initial helping interactions. *Journal of Counseling Psychology*, 21, 360–3.

Davis, M. (ed.) (1982). *Interaction rhythms*. New York, NY: Human Sciences Press.

Davis, M. & Hadiks, D. (1994). Nonverbal aspects of therapist attunement. *Journal of Clinical Psychology*, 50, 393–405.

Desor, J.A. (1972). Toward a psychological theory of crowding. *Journal of Personality and Social Psychology*, 21, 79–83.

Dittman, A.T. (1972). The body movement–speech rhythm relationship as a cue to speechencoding. In *Studies in dyadic communication* (ed. A.W. Siegman & B. Pope), pp. 135–51. New York, NY: Pergamon.

Dittman, A.T. (1977). The development of conversational behavior. In *Communicative structures and psychic structures* (ed. N. Freedman and S. Grand), pp. 33–147. New York, NY: Plenum.

Dittman, A.T. (1987). The role of body movement in communication. In *Nonverbal behavior and communication* (2nd edn) (ed. A.W. Siegman & S. Feldstein), pp.37–64. Hillsdale, N.J.: Lawrence Erlbaum.

Dittman, A.T., & Llewellyn, L.G. (1967). The phonemic clause as a unit of speech decoding. *Journal of Personality and Social Psychology*, 6, 341–9.

Dittman, A.T. & Llewellyn, L.G. (1968). Relationship between vocalizations and headnods as listener responses. *Journal of Personality and Social Psychology*, **9**, 79–84.

Dittman, A.T. & Llewellyn, L.G. (1969). Body movement and speech rhythm in social conversation. *Journal of Personality and Social Psychology*, **11**, 98–106.

Duke, M.P. & Nowinckis, S. (1972). A new measure and social-learning model for interpersonal distance. *Journal of Experimental Research in Personality*, **6**, 119–32.

Duncan, S.D., Jr. (1969). Nonverbal communication. *Psychological Bulletin*, **72**, 118–37.

Duncan, S.D., Jr. (1972). Some signals and rules for taking speaking turns in conversation. *Journal of Personality and Social Psychology*, **23**, 283–92.

Duncan, S.D., Jr. (1983). Rules and strategy in conversation. *New directions for the methodology of social and behavioral science*, **15**, 23–39.

Duncan, S.D., Jr. & Fiske, D.W. (1977). *Face-to-face interaction: research, methods, and theory.* Hillsdale, NJ: Lawrence Erlbaum.

Edelman, R. & Hampson, S. (1979). Changes in non-verbal behavior during embarrassment. *British Journal of Social and Clinical Psychology*, **18**, 385–90.

Edelsky, C. (1981). Who's got the floor? *Language and Society*, **10**, 383–421.

Edmonson, B. & Han, S.S. (1983). Effects of socialization game on proximity and prosocial behavior of aggressive mentally retarded institutionalized women. *American Journal of Mental Deficiency*, **87**, 435–550.

Efron, D. (1941). *Gestures and environment.* New York: Kings Crown Press. (Republished as *Gesture, race and culture.* (1972). The Hague: Mouton.)

Eizenman, M., Yu, L.H., Grupp, L., Eizenman, E., Ellenbogen, M., Gemar, M., et al. (2003). A naturalistic visual scanning approach to assess selective attention in major depressive disorder. *Psychiatry Research*, **118**, 117–28.

Ekman, P. (1972). Universals and cultural differences in facial expressions of emotion. In *Nebraska Symposium of Motivation, Vol. 19* (ed. J.K. Cole), pp. 207–83. Lincoln: University of Nebraska.

Ekman, P. (1976). Movements with precise meanings. *Journal of Communication*, **26**, 14–26.

Ekman, P. (1977). Biological and cultural contributions to body and facial movement. In *The anthropology of the body* (ed. J. Blacking). London: Academic.

Ekman, P. & Friesen, W.V. (1969a). The repertoire of nonverbal behavior: categories, origins, usage, and coding. *Semiotica*, **1**, 49–98.

Ekman, P. & Friesen, W.V. (1969b). Nonverbal leakage and clues to deception. *Psychiatry*, **32**, 88–105.

Ekman, P. & Friesen, W.V. (1972). Hand movements. *Journal of Communication*, **22**, 353–74.

Ekman, P. & Friesen, W.V. (1974). Nonverbal behavior and psychopathology. In *The psychology of depression: contemporary theory and research* (ed. R.J. Friedman and M.M. Datz), pp. 203–32. Washington, D.C.: Winston & Sons.

Ekman, P. & Friesen, W.V. (1975). *Unmasking the face.* Englewood Cliffs, N.J.: Prentice–Hall.

Ekman, P. & Friesen, W.V. (1977). Nonverbal behavior. In *Communication and social interaction* (ed. P.F. Ostwald), pp. 37–45. New York, NY: Grune and Stratton.

Ekman, P. & Friesen, W.V. (1978). *Facial action coding system: a technique for the measurement of facial movement.* Palo Alto, CA: Consulting Psychologists Press.

Ekman, P. & Rosenberg, E.L. (ed.) (1997). *What the face reveals.* New York, NY: Oxford University Press.

Ekman, P., Friesen, W.V., & Scherer, K. (1976). Body movement and voice pitch in deceptive interaction. *Semiotica,* **16,** 23–7.

Ellgring, J.H. (1970). Judgment of glances directed at different points in the face. *Zeitschrift fuer Experimentelle und Angewandte Psychologie,* **17,** 600–7.

Ellsworth, P.C. (1975). Direct gaze as a social stimulus: the example of aggression. In *Nonverbal communication of aggression* (ed. P.Pliner, L. Krames., & T. Alloway). New York, NY: Plenum.

Ellsworth, P.C. (1978). The meaningful look. Review of Argyle & Cook, 1976. *Semiotica,* **24,** 341–51.

Ellsworth, P.C. & Langer, E.J. (1976). Staring and approach: an interpretation of the stare as a nonspecific activator. *Journal of Personality and Social Psychology,* **33,** 117–22.

Ellsworth, P.C. & Ross, L. (1975). Intimacy in response to direct gaze. *Journal of Experimental Social Psychology,* **11,** 592–613.

Ellsworth, P.C., Carlsmith, M., & Henson, A. (1972). The stare as a stimulus to flight in human subjects. *Journal of Personality and Social Psychology,* **19,** 302–11.

Ellyson, S.L., Dovido, J.F., Corson, R.L., & Vinicur, D.L. (1980). Visual dominance behavior in female dyads: situational and personality factors. *Social Psychology Quarterly,* **43,** 328–36.

Erickson, F. (1975). On the function of proxemic shifts in face-to-face interaction. In *Organization of behavior in face-to-face interaction* (ed. A. Kendon, R.M. Harris, & M.R. Key), pp. 175–87. The Hague: Mouton.

Eshkol, N. & Wachmann, A. (1958). *Movement notation.* London: Weidenfeld & Nicolson.

Exline, R.V. (1963). Explorations in the process of person perception: visual interaction in relation to competition, sex and need for affiliation. *Journal of Personality,* **31,** 1–20.

Exline, R.V. (1972). The glances of power and preference. In *Nebraska symposium on motivation,* Vol. 19 (ed. J.R. Cole), pp. 163–206. Lincoln: University of Nebraska Press.

Exline, R.V, & Fehr, B.J. (1982). The assessment of gaze. In Handbook of methods in nonverbal behavior research (ed. K.R. Scherer & P. Ekman), pp. 91–135. Cambridge: Cambridge University Press.

Exline, R.V., Gray, D., & Schuette, D. (1965). Visual behavior in a dyad as affected by interview content and sex of respondent. *Journal of Personality and Social Psychology,* **1,** 201–9.

Fairbanks, A.L., McGuire, T.M., & Harris, J.C. (1982). Nonverbal interaction of patients and therapists during psychiatric interviews. *Journal of Abnormal Psychology,* **91,** 109–19.

Fast, J. (1970). *Body language.* New York, NY: Pocket Books.

Fast, J. (1977). *The body language of sex, power, and aggression.* New York, NY: Lippincott.

Feeney, J.A., Noller, P., Sheehan, G., & Peterson, C. (1999). Conflict issues and conflict strategies as contexts for nonverbal behavior in close relationships. In *The social context of nonverbal behavior* (ed. P. Philippot, R.S. Feldman, & E.J. Coats), pp. 348–71. Cambridge, UK: Cambridge University Press.

Fehr, B.J. (1981). The communication of evaluation through the use of interpersonal gaze in same- and inter-racial female dyads. *Dissertation Abstracts International,* **41** (**05**), 11-B. UMI No. 4307.

Fehr, B.J. & Exline, R.V. (1987). Social visual interaction. In *Nonverbal behavior and communi-cation* (2nd edn) (ed. A.W. Siegman & S. Feldstein), pp. 225–326. Hillsdale, N.J.: Lawrence Erlbaum.

Feldman, R.S. (1985). Nonverbal behavior, race, and the classroom teacher. *Theory Into Practice*, **24**, 45–9.

Feldstein, S. & Welkowitz, J. (1987). A chronology of conversation: in defense of an objective approach. In *Nonverbal behavior and communication* (2nd edn) (ed. A.W. Siegman & S. Feldstein), pp. 435–99. Hillsdale, N.J.: Lawrence Erlbaum.

Ferenczi, S. (1914). Embarrassed hands. In *Further contributions to the technique and theory of psychoanalysis*, pp. 315–16). London: Hogarth Press (1926).

Feyereisen, P. & deLannoy, J.D. (1991). *Gesture and speech: psychological investigations.* Cambridge: Cambridge University Press.

Field, T. (2001). *Touch.* Cambridge, MA: MIT Press.

Förster, J. & Strack, F. (1996). Influence of overt head movements on memory for valenced words: a case of conceptual-motor compatibility. *Journal of Personality and Social Psychology*, **71**, 421–30.

Frances, S.J. (1979). Sex differences in nonverbal behavior. *Sex Roles*, **5**, 519–35.

Freedman, N. (1972). The analysis of movement behavior during the clinical interview. In *Studies in dyadic communication* (ed. A. Siegman & B. Pope), pp. 153–75). New York, NY: Pergamon.

Freedman, N. (1977). Hands, words, and mind: on the structuralization of body movements during discourse and the capacity for verbal representation. In *Communicative structures and psychic structures* (ed. N. Freedman and S. Grand), pp. 109–32. New York, NY: Plenum.

Freedman, N. & Hoffman, S.P. (1967). Kinetic behavior in altered clinical states: approach to objective interviews. *Perceptual and Motor Skills*, **24**, 527–39.

Freedman, N., Barroso, F., Bucci, W., & Grand, S. (1978). The bodily manifestations of listening. *Psychoanalysis and Contemporary Thought*, **1**, 15–194.

Freedman, N., Blass, T., Rifkin, A., & Quitkin, F. (1973). Body movements and the verbalencoding of aggressive affect. *Journal of Personality and Social Psychology*, **26**, 72–85.

Freedman, N., O'Hanlon, J., Oltman, P., & Witkin, H.A. (1972). The imprint of psychological differentiation on kinetic behavior in varying communicative contexts. *Journal of Abnormal Psychology*, **79**, 239–58.

Fretz, B.R. (1966). Postural movements in a counseling dyad. *Journal of Counseling Psychology*, **13**, 335–43.

Frey, S. (1971). *Eine methode zur quantitativen bestimmung der variabilitat des bewegungsverhal-tens.* Unpublished doctoral dissertation. University of Regensburg.

Frey, S. & Pool, J. (1976). *A new approach to the analysis of visible behavior.* Research reports from the Department of Psychology at the University of Berne.

Frey, S. & von Cranach, M. (1973). A method for the assessment of body movement variability. In *Social communication and movement* (ed. M. von Cranach & I. Vine), pp. 389–418). New York, NY: Academic.

Friesen, W.V., Ekman, P., & Wallbott, H.G. (1979). Measuring hand movements. *Journal of Nonverbal Behavior*, **1**, 97–112.

Gallois, C. & Callan, V.J. (1986). Decoding emotional messages: influence of ethnicity, sex, message type, and channel. *Journal of Personality and Social Psychology*, 51, 755–62.

Gibson, J.J. & Pick, R.B. (1963). Perception of another person's looking behavior. *American Journal of Psychology*, 76, 386–94.

Gifford, R. (1982). Projected interpersonal distance and orientation choices: Personality, sex, and social situation. *Social Psychology Quarterly*, 45, 145–52.

Giges, B. (1975). Using your head: notes on nodding. *Transactional Analysis Journal*, 5, 264–66.

Goffman, E. (1959). The presentation of self in everyday life. Garden City, NY: Doubleday Anchor Books.

Goffman, E. (1963). *Behavior in public places.* New York, NY: The Free Press.

Goffman, E. (1971). *Relations in public.* New York, NY: Harper Colophon Books.

Golani, I. (1969) *The golden jackal.* TelAviv: The Movement Notation Society.

Goldberg, S. & Rosenthal, R. (1986). Self-touching behavior in the job interview: antecedents and consequences. *Journal of Nonverbal Behavior*, 10, 65–80.

Goodwin, C. (1981). *Conversational organization: interactions between speaker and hearers.* New York, NY: Academic.

Graham, J.A. & Argyle, M. (1975). A cross-cultural study of the communication of extra-verbal meaning by gestures. *International Journal of Psychology*, 10, 57–67.

Graham, J.A. & Heywood, S. (1976). The effect of elimination of hand gestures and of verbal codability on speech performance. *European Journal of Social Psychology*, 5, 189–95.

Grahe, J.F. & Bernieri, F.J. (1999). The importance of nonverbal cues in judging rapport. *Journal of Nonverbal Behavior*, 23, 253–69.

Grammer, K., Kruck, K., Juette, A., & Fink, B. (2000). Nonverbal behavior as courtship signals: the role of control and choice in selecting partners. *Evolution and Human Behavior*, 21, 371–90.

Grand, S. (1977). On hand movements during speech: studies of the role of self-stimulation in communication under conditions of psychopathology, sensory deficit, and bilingualism. In *Communicative structures and psychic structures* (ed. N. Freedman and S. Grand), pp. 199–221) New York, NY: Plenum.

Grand, S., Freedman, N., Steingart, I., & Buchwald, C. (1975). Communicative behavior in schizophrenia. *Journal of Nervous and Mental Disease*, 161, 293–306.

Guerrero, L.K. (1997). Nonverbal involvement across interactions with same-sex friends, opposite-sex friends and romantic partners: consistency or change? *Journal of Social and Personal Relationships*, 14, 31–59.

Guye–Vuillieme, A., Capin, T.K., Pandzic, I.S., Thalmann, N.M., & Thalmann, D. (1999). Nonverbal communication interface for collaborative virtual environments. *Virtual Reality Journal*, 4, 49–59.

Hadar, U., Steiner, T.J., Grant, E.C., & Rose, F.C. (1983). Head movement correlates of juncture and stress at sentence level. *Language and Speech*, 26, 117–29.

Hadar, U., Steiner, T.J., Grant, E.C., & Rose, F.C. (1984). The timing of shifts in headposture during conversation. *Human Movement Science*, 3, 237–45.

Hadar, U., Steiner, T.J., & Rose, F.C. (1985). Head movements during listening turns in conversation. *Journal of Nonverbal Behavior*, 9, 214–28.

Hadar, U., Wenkert–Olenik, D., Krauss, R.M., & Soroker, N. (1998). Gesture and the processing of speech: neuropsychological evidence. *Brain and Language*, 62, 107–26.

Hall, E.T. (1963). A system for notation of proxemic behavior. *American Anthropologist*, 65, 1003–26.

Hall, E.T. (1966). *The hidden dimension*. New York, NY: Doubleday.

Hall, E.T. (1973). *Handbook for proxemic research*. Washington, D.C.: Society for the Anthropology of Visual Communication.

Hall, E.T. (1974). Proxemics. In *Nonverbal Communication* (ed. S. Weitz), pp. 205–29. New York, NY: Oxford University Press.

Hall, E.T. (1979). Proxemics. In S. Weitz (Ed.) *Nonverbal Communication: Readings with Commentary* (2nd ed.). New York, NY: Oxford University Press.

Hall. J.A. (1984). *Nonverbal sex differences*. Baltimore: Johns Hopkins University Press.

Hall. J.A. & Friedman, G.B. (1999). Status, gender, and nonverbal behavior: a study of structured interactions between employees of a company. *Personality and Social Psychology Bulletin*, 25, 1082–91.

Hall. J.A. & Veccia, E.M. (1990). More 'touching' observations: new insights on men, women, and interpersonal touch. *Journal of Personality and Social Psychology*, 59, 1155–62.

Hanlon, R.E., Brown, J.W., & Gertsman, L.J. (1990). Enhancement of naming in nonfluent aphasia through gesture. *Brain and Language*, 38, 298–314.

Harper, R.G., Wiens, A.N., & Matarazzo, J.D. (1978). *Nonverbal communication: the state of the art*. New York, NY: Wiley.

Harrigan, J.A. (1980). Methods of turn-taking in group interaction. In *Papers from the 16th Regional Meeting of the Chicago Linguistic Society*, pp. 102–12. Chicago: Chicago Linguistic Society.

Harrigan, J.A. (1985). Self-touching as an indicator of underlying affect and language processes. *Social Science and Medicine*, 20, 1161–8.

Harrigan, J.A. & Carney, D.R. (2005). *A coding method for body/head positions and actions*. Laboratory manual.

Harrigan, J.A. & Steffen, J.J. (1983). Gaze as a turn-exchange signal in group conversations. *British Journal of Social Psychology*, 22, 167–8.

Harrigan, J.A., Kues, J.R., Steffen, J.J., & Rosenthal, R. (1987). Self-touching and impressions of others. *Personality and Social Psychology Bulletin*, 13, 497–512.

Harrigan, J.A., Kues, J.R., & Weber, J.G. (1986a). Impressions of hand movements: self-touching and gestures. *Perceptual and Motor Skills*, 63, 503–16.

Harrigan, J.A., Lucic, K.S., Kay, D., McLaney, M.A., & Rosenthal, R. (1991). Effects of expresser role and body location of self-touching on observers' perceptions. *Journal of Applied Social Psychology*, 21, 585–609.

Harrigan, J.A., Oxman, T.E., & Rosenthal, R. (1985). Rapport expressed through nonverbal behavior. *Journal of Nonverbal Behavior*, 9, 95–110.

Harrigan, J.A., Weber, J.G., & Kues, J.R. (1986b). Attributions of self-touching performedin spontaneous and posed modes. *Journal of Clinical and Social Psychology*, 4, 433–446.

Harrigan, J.A., Wilson, K., & Rosenthal, R. (2004). Detecting state and trait anxiety from auditory and visual cues: a meta-analysis. *Personality and Social Psychology Bulletin*, 30, 56–66.

Hayduk, L.A. (1981*a*). The permeability of personal space. *Canadian Journal of Behavioral Science*, **13**, 274–87.

Hayduk, L.A. (1981*b*). The shape of personal space: an experimental investigation. *Canadian Journal of Behavioral Science*, **123**, 87–93.

Hayduk, L.A. (1983). Personal space: where we now stand. *Psychological Bulletin*, **94**, 293–335.

Hediger, H. (1961). The evolution of territorial behavior. In *Social life of early man* (ed. S.L. Washburn), pp. 34–57. New York, NY: Wenner–Gren Foundation for Anthropological Research or Viking Fund Publications in Anthropology no. 31.

Heilveil, I. & Muehleman, J.T. (1981). Nonverbal clues to deception in a psychotherapy analogue. *Psychotherapy: Theory, Research & Practice*, **18**, 329–35.

Heller, M.A. & Schiff, W. (ed.) (1991). *The psychology of touch*. Hillsdale, NJ: Lawrence Erlbaum.

Hewes, G.W. (1957). The anthropology of posture. *Scientific American*, **196**, 123–32.

Hill, C.E. & Stephany, A. (1990). Relation of nonverbal behavior to client reaction. *Journal of Counseling Psychology*, **37**, 22–6.

Honeycutt, J.M. (1989). Effects of preinteraction expectancies on interaction involvement and behavioral responses in initial interaction. *Journal of Nonverbal Behavior*, **13**, 25–36.

Hutchinson, A. (1961). *Labanotation*. New York, NY: New Directions.

Jakobson, R. (1972). Motor signs for 'Yes' and 'No'. *Language in Society*, **1**, 91–6.

Johnson, H.G., Ekman, P., & Friesen, W.V. (1975). Communicative body movements: American emblems. *Semiotica*, **15**, 335–53.

Jones, S.E. (1994). *The Right Touch: Understanding and Using the Language of Physical Contact*. Creskill, N.J.: Hampton Press, Inc.

Jones, S.E. & Aiello, J.R. (1973). Proxemic behavior of black and white first, third, and fifth-grade children. *Journal of Personality and Social Psychology*, **25**, 21–7.

Jones, E., Gallois, C., Callan, V., & Barker, M. (1999). Strategies of accommodation: development of a coding system for conversational interaction. *Journal of Language & Society*, **18**, 123–52.

Jurich, A.P. & Jurich, J.A. (1974). Correlations among nonverbal expressions of anxiety. *Psychological Reports*, **34**, 199–204.

Kendon, A. (1967). Some functions of gaze direction in social interaction. *Acta Psychologica*, **26**, 22–63.

Kendon, A. (1970). Movement coordination in social interaction: some examples described. *Acta Psychologica*, **32**, 1–25.

Kendon, A. (1972). Some relationships between body motion and speech: an analysis of an example. In *Studies in dyadic communication* (ed. A.W. Siegman & B. Pope), pp. 177–210. New York, NY: Pergamon.

Kendon, A. (1980). Gesticulation and speech: two aspects of the process of utterance. In Relationship of verbal and nonverbal communication (ed. M.R. Key), pp. 207–28. The Hague: Mouton.

Kendon, A. (1983). Gesture and speech: how they interact. In *Nonverbal Interaction* (ed. J.M. Wiemann & R.P. Harrison), pp. 13–45. Beverly Hills, CA: Sage.

Kendon, A. (1994). Do gestures communicate? A review. *Research on Language and Social Interaction*, **27**, 175–200.

Kendon, A. & Cook, M. (1969). The consistency of gaze patterns in social interaction. *British Journal of Psychology*, 60, 481–94.

Kendon, A. & Ferber, A. (1973). A description of some human greetings. In *Comparative ecology and behavior of primates* (ed. R.P. Michael & J.H. Croo), pp. 591–668. London: Academic.

Kimura, D. (1976). The neural basis of language qua gesture. In *Studies in neurolinguistics* (ed. H.Whitaker & H.A.Whitaker). New York, NY: Academic.

Kirkland, J. & Lewis, C. (1976). Glance, look, gaze, and stare: a vocabulary for eye-fixation research. *Perceptual and Motor Skills*, 43, 1278.

Kleck, R.E. (1970). Interaction distance and non-verbal agreeing responses, *British Journal of Social and Clinical Psychology*, 9, 180–2.

Kleck, R.E. & Neussle, W. (1968). Congruence between indicative and communicative functions of eye contact in interpersonal relations. *British Journal of Social and Clinical Psychology*, 7, 241–6.

Kleinke, C.L. (1977). Compliance to requests made by gazing and touching experimenter in field settings. *Journal of Experimental Social Psychology*, 13, 218–23.

Kleinke, C.L., Meeker, F.B., & La Fong, C. (1974). Effects of gaze, touch, and use of name on evaluation of 'engaged' couples. *Journal of Research in Personality*, 1, 368–73.

Knapp, M.L. & Hall, J.A. (1992). *Nonverbal communication in human interaction*. Fort Worth, TX: Holt Rinehart & Winston.

Knowles, E.S. (1980). An affiliative conflict theory of personal and group spatial behavior. In *Psychology of group influence* (ed. P.B. Paulus). Hillsdale, NJ: Erlbaum.

Krauss, R.M. & Hadar, U. (2001). The role of speech-relationed arm/hand gestures in word retrieval. In *Gesture, speech, and sign* (ed. R. Campbell & L. Messing), pp. 93–116. Oxford: Oxford University Press.

Krauss, R.M., Chen, Y., & Chawla, P. (1996). Nonverbal behavior and nonverbal communication. What do conversational hand gestures tell us? In *Advances in experimental social psychology*, *Vol. 28* (ed. M.P. Zanna), pp. 389–450. San Diego, CA: Academic Press.

Krauss, R.M., Dushay, R.A., Chen, Y., & Rauscher, F. (1995). The communicative value of conversational hand gestures. *Journal of Experimental Social Psychology*, 31, 533–52.

Krauss, R.M., Morrel–Samuels, P., & Colasante, C. (1991). Do conversational hand gestures communicate? *Journal of Personality and Social Psychology*, 61, 743–54.

Krout, M.H. (1935). Autistic gestures: an experimental study in symbolic movement. *Psychological Monographs*, 46, 119–20.

Krüger, K. & Hückstedt, B. (1969). Judgments of view direction. *Zeitschrift fuer Experimentelle und Angewandte Psychologie*, 16, 452–72.

Kuethe, J.L. (1962). Social schemas. *Journal of Abnormal and Social Psychology*, 64, 31–8.

Laban, R. (1956). *Principles of dance and movement notation*. London: MacDonald & Evans.

LaFrance, M. & Mayo, C. (1976). Racial differences in gaze behavior during conversation: two systematic observational studies. *Journal of Personality and Social Psychology*, 33, 547–52.

Lalljee, M. (1978). The role of gaze in the expression of emotion. *Australian Journal of Psychology*, 30, 59–67.

Lander, K. & Bruce, V. (2003). The role of motion in learning new faces. *Visual Cognition*, 10, 897–912.

Lazzerini, A.J., Stephenson, G.M., & Neave, H. (1978). Eye-contact in dyads: a test of the independence hypothesis. *British Journal of Social and Clinical Psychology*, **17**, 227–9.

LeCompte, W.F. & Rosenfeld, H.M. (1971). Effects of minimal eye contact in the instruction period on impressions of the experimenter. *Journal of Experimental Social Psychology*, **7**, 211–20.

LeJeune, J. (1989). Psychotic behaviour and folic acid medication: preliminary report on two cases. *Journal of Orthomolecular Medicine*, **3**, 11–12.

Lessin, S. & Jacob, T. (1984). Multichannel communication in normal and delinquent families. *Journal of Abnormal Child Psychology*, **12**, 369–84.

Lyman, S.M. & Scott, M.B. (1967). Territoriality: a neglected sociological dimension. *Social Problems*, **15**, 236–49.

Mabry, E.A. (1989). Developmental aspects of nonverbal behavior in small group settings. *Small Group Behavior*, **20**, 190–202.

Macrae, C.N., Hood, B.M., Milne, A.B., Rowe, A.C., & Mason, M.F. (2002). Are you looking at me? *Psychological Science*, **13**, 460–4.

Mahl, G.F. (1961). Measures of two expressive aspects of a patient speech in two psychotherapeutic interviews. In *Comparative psycholinguistic analysis of two psychotherapeutic interviews* (ed. L.A. Gottschalk), pp. 91–114. New York, NY: International Universities.

Mahl, G.F. (1968). Gestures and body movements in interviews. In *Research in psychotherapy* , *Vol. 3* (ed. J.M. Shlien), pp. 295–346. Washington, D.C.: American Psychological Association.

Matarazzo, J.D. & Wiens, A.N. (1972). *The interview.* Chicago: Aldine.

Matarazzo, J.D., Saslow, G., Wiens, A.N., Weitman, M., & Allen, B.V. (1964). Interviewer head nodding and interviewee speech durations. *Psychotherapy: Theory, Research, & Practice*, **1**, 54–63.

McBride, G., King, M.G., & James, J.W. (1965). Social proximity effects on galvanic skin responses in adult humans. *Journal of Psychology*, **61**, 153–7.

McDowall, J.J. (1979). Microanalysis of filmed movement: the reliability of boundary detection by observers. *Environmental Psychology and Nonverbal Behavior*, **3**, 77–88.

McGrew, W.C. (1972). *An ethological study of children's behavior.* New York, NY: Academic.

McNeill, D. (1992). *Hand and mind: what gestures reveal about thought.* Chicago: University of Chicago.

McNeill, H. & Fawn, M. (2004). Ethical considerations in the use of nonerotic touch in psychotherapy with children. *Ethics and Behavior*, **14**, 123–40.

McQuown, N.A. (ed.) (1971). *The natural history of an interview.* Microfilm Collection of Manuscripts on Cultural Anthropology, 15th Series. Chicago: University of Chicago Regenstein Library.

Mehrabian, A. (1968). Inference of attitudes from the posture, orientation, and distance of a communicator. *Journal of Consulting and Clinical Psychology*, **323**, 296–308.

Mehrabian, A. (1969). Significance of posture and position in the communication of attitude and status relationships. *Psychological Bulletin*, **71**, 359–72.

Mehrabian, A. (1972). *Nonverbal communication.* Chicago: Aldine–Atherton.

Mehrabian, A. & Friar, J.T. (1969). Encoding of attitude by a seated communicator viaposture and position cues. *Journal of Consulting and Clinical Psychology*, **33**, 330–6.

Mehrabian, A. & Ksionzky, S. (1972). Categories of social behavior. *Comparative Group Studies*, 3, 425–36.

Mehrabian, A. & Williams, M. (1969). Nonverbal concomitants of perceived and intended persuasiveness. *Journal of Personality and Social Psychology*, 13, 37–58.

Mintzlaff, V., Carney, D., & Harrigan, J.A. (1999). *The link between defensiveness and nonverbal behavior: the hands have it.* Paper presented at the meeting of the American Psychological Society, Denver, CO, June 1999.

Morris, D., Collett, P., Marsh, P., & O'Shaughnessy, M. (1979). *Gestures: their origins and distribution.* London: Jonathon Cape.

Munhall, K.G., Jones, J.A., Callan, D.E., Kuratate, T., & Vatikiotis–Bateson, E. (2004). Visual prosody and speech intelligibility. *Psychological Science*, 15, 133–7.

Nail, P.R., Harton, H.C., & Decker, B.P. (2003). Political orientation and modern versus aversive racism: tests of Dovido and Gaertner's (1998) integrated model. *Journal of Personality and Social Psychology*, 84, 754–70.

Natale, M. (1977). Induction of mood states and their effect on gaze behaviors. *Journal of Consulting and Clinical Psychology*, 45, 960.

Nierenberg, G.I. & Calero, H.H. (1971). *How to read a person like a book.* New York, NY: Pocket Books.

Noller, P. & Callan, V.J. (1989). Nonverbal behavior in families with adolescents. *Journal of Nonverbal Behavior*, 13, 47–64.

Noller, P. & Gallois, C. (1986). Sending emotional messages in marriage: non-verbal behaviour, sex, and communication clarity. *British Journal of Social Psychology*, 25, 287–97.

O'Brien, J.S. & Holborn, S.W. (1979). Verbal and nonverbal expressions as reinforcers in verbal conditioning of adult conversation. *Journal of Behavior Therapy & Experimental Psychiatry*, 10, 267–71.

O'Hair, H.D., Cody, M.J., & McLaughlin, M.L. (1981). Prepared lies, spontaneous lies, Machiavellianism, and nonverbal communication. *Human Communication Research*, 7, 325–39.

O'Leary, M.J. & Gallois, C. (1985). The last ten turns: behavior and sequencing in friends' and strangers' conversational findings. *Journal of Nonverbal Behavior*, 9, 8–27.

O'Sullivan, M., Ekman, P., Friesen, W., & Scherer, K. (1985). What you say and how you say it: the contribution of speech content and voice quality to judgments of others. *Journal of Personality and Social Psychology*, 48, 54–62.

Patterson, M.L. (1975). Personal space: time to burst the bubble? *Man-Environment Systems*, 5, 67.

Patterson, M.L. (1982). A sequential model of nonverbal exchange. *Psychological Review*, 89, 231–49.

Pedersen, D.M. (1973). Prediction of behavioral personal space from simulated personal space. *Perceptual and Motor Skills*, 37, 803–13.

Pope, B. & Siegman, A.W. (1972). Interviewer–interviewee relationship and verbal behavior of interviewee. *Psychotherapy*, 3, 819–25.

Raja, I.A. & Nicol, F. (1997). A technique for recording and analysis of postural changes associated with thermal comfort. *Applied Ergonomics*, 28, 221–5.

Ranelli, C. & Miller, R.E. (1981). Behavioral predictors of amitriptyline response in depression. *American Journal of Psychiatry*, **138**, 30–4.

Rauscher, F.B., Krauss, R.M., & Chen, Y. (1996). Conversational hand gestures, speech and lexical access: the role of lexical movements in speech production. *Psychological Science*, **7**, 226–31.

Remland, M.S., Jones, T.S., & Brinkman, H. (1995). Interpersonal distance, body orientation, and touch: Effects of culture, gender, and age. *The Journal of Social Psychology*, **135**, 281–297.

Ricci-Bitti, P.E. & Poggi, I. (1991). Symbolic nonverbal behavior: talking through gestures. In *Fundamentals of nonverbal behavior* (ed. R.S. Feldman & B. Rimé), pp. 433–57. New York/Cambridge: Cambridge University Press.

Rimé, B. (1982). The elimination of visible behaviour from social interactions: effects on verbal, nonverbal and interpersonal behavior. *European Journal of Social Psychology*, **12**, 113–29.

Rimé, B. & Schiaratura, L. (1991). Gesture and speech. In *Fundamentals of nonverbal behavior* (ed. R.S. Feldman & B. Rimé), pp. 239–84). New York/Cambridge: Cambridge University Press.

Riseborough, M.G. (1981). Physiographic gestures as decoding facilitators: three experiments exploring a neglected facet of communication. *Journal of Nonverbal Behavior*, **5**, 172–83.

Rosenfeld, H.M. (1966). Instrumental affiliative functions of facial and gestural expressions. *Journal of Personality and Social Psychology*, **4**, 65–72.

Rosenfeld, H.M. (1967). Nonverbal reciprocation of approval: an experimental analysis. *Journal of Experimental Social Psychology*, **3**, 102–11.

Rosenfeld, H.M. (1981). Whither interactional synchrony? In *Prospective issues in infancy research* (ed. K. Bloom), pp. 71–97. Hillsdale, NJ: Erlbaum.

Rosenfeld, H.M. (1987). Conversational control functions of nonverbal behavior. In *Nonverbal behavior and communication* (ed. A.W. Siegman & S. Feldstein), pp. 563–601. Hillsdale, NJ: Erlbaum.

Rosenfeld, H.M. & Hancks, M. (1980). The nonverbal context of verbal listener responses. In *The relationship of verbal and nonverbal communication* (ed. M.R. Key), pp. 193–206. The Hague: Mouton.

Rosenthal, R. (1966). *Experimenter effects in behavioral research*. New York, NY: Appleton–Century–Crofts.

Rosenthal, R. (1987). *Judgment studies: design, analysis, and meta-analysis*. Cambridge: Cambridge University Press.

Rosenthal, R. & Jacobson, L. (1968). *Pygmalion in the classroom*. New York, NY: Holt, Rinehart, & Winston.

Rosenthal, R., Hall, J.A., DiMatteo, M.R., Rogers, P.L., & Archer, D. (1979). *Sensitivity to nonverbal communication: the PONS test*. Baltimore: Johns Hopkins University Press.

Ross, M., Layton, B., Erickson, B., & Schopler, J. (1973). Affect, facial regard and reactions to crowding. *Journal of Personality and Social Psychology*, **28**, 69–76.

Rutter, D.R., Stephenson, G.M., Ayling, K., & White, P.A. (1978). The timing of looks in dyadic conversation. *British Journal of Social and Clinical Psychology*, **17**, 17–21.

Rutter, D.R., Stephenson, G.M., Lazzerini, A.J., Ayling, K., & White, P.A. (1977). Eye contact: a chance product of individual looking? *British Journal of Social and Clinical Psychology*, **16**, 191–2.

Saitz, R.L. & Cervenka, E.J. (1972). *Handbook of gestures: Colombia and the United States*. The Hague: Mouton.

Scheflen, A.E. (1964). The significance of posture in communication systems. *Psychiatry*, **27**, 316–31.

Scheflen, A.E. (1965). Quasi-courtship behavior in psychotherapy. *Psychiatry*, **28**, 245–57.

Scheflen, A.E. (1966). Natural history method in psychotherapy: communicational research. In *Methods of research in psychotherapy* (ed. L.A. Gottschalk & A.H. Auerbach). New York, NY: Appleton–Century–Crofts.

Scheflen, A.E. (1972). *Body language and social order*. Englewood Cliffs, NJ: Prentice–Hall.

Scherer, K.R. & Ekman, P. (ed.) (1982). *Handbook of methods in nonverbal behavior research*. Cambridge: Cambridge University Press.

Scherer, K.R. & Wallbott, H.G. (1985). Analysis of nonverbal behavior. In *Handbook of discourse analysis* (ed. T.A. van Dijk), pp.199–230. London: Academic Press.

Scherer, S.E. (1974). Proxemic behavior of primary school children as a function of their socio-economic class and subculture. *Journal of Personality and Social Psychology*, **29**, 800–5.

Seay, T.A. & Altekruse, M.K. (1979). Verbal and nonverbal behavior in judgments of facilitative conditions. *Journal of Counseling Psychology*, **26**, 108–19.

Shibata, T. (1990). Effects of body satisfaction on social anxiety and self-disclosing behavior in adolescence. *Japanese Journal of Psychology*, **61**, 123–6.

Shreve, E.G., Harrigan, J.A., Kues, J.R., & Kangas, D.K.(1988). Nonverbal expressions of anxiety in physician–patient interactions. *Psychiatry*, **51**, 378–84.

Sigelman, C.K. & Adams, R.M. (1990). Family interactions in public: parent–child distance and touching. *Journal of Nonverbal Behavior*, **14**, 63–75.

Snyder, M., Grethe, J., & Keller, K. (1974). String and compliance: a field experiment on hitchhiking. *Journal of Applied Social Psychology*, **4**, 165–70.

Sommer, R. (1959). Studies in personal space. *Sociometry*, **22**, 247–60.

Sommer, R. (1961). Leadership and group geography. *Sociometry*, **24**, 99–110.

Sommer, R. (1967). Sociofugal space. *American Journal of Sociology*, **72**, 654–60.

Sommer, R. (1969). *Personal space: the behavioral basis of design*. Englewood Cliffs, NJ: Prentice–Hall.

Sommer, R. & Becker, F.D. (1969). Territorial defense and the good neighbor. *Journal of Personality and Social Psychology*, **11**, 85–92.

Sparhawk, C.M. (1978). Contrastive identification features of Persian gesture. *Semiotica*, **24**, 49–86.

Stenzel, C.L. & Rupert, P.A. (2004). Psychologists' use of touch in individual psychotherapy. *Psychotherapy: Theory, Research, Practice, & Training*, **41**, 332–45.

Stephenson, G.M., Rutter, D.R., & Dore, S.R. (1973). Visual interaction and distance. *British Journal of Psychology*, **64**, 251–7.

Stokols, D. (1972). On the distinction between density and crowding. *Psychological Review*, **79**, 275–77.

Street, R.L. & Buller, D.B. (1987). Nonverbal response patterns in physician–patient interactions: a functional analysis. *Journal of Nonverbal Behavior*, **11**, 234–53.

Street, R.L. & Buller, D.B. (1988). Patients' characteristics affecting physician–patient nonverbal communication. *Human Communication Research,* 15, 60–90.

Strodbeck, F.L. & Hook, L.H. (1961). The social dimensions of a twelve man jury table. *Sociometry,* 24, 397–415.

Strongman, K.T. & Champness, B.G. (1968). Dominance hierarchies and conflict in eye contact. *Acta Psychologica,* 28, 376–86.

Sundstrom, E. (1975). An experimental study of crowding: effects of room size, intrusion, and goal blocking on nonverbal behavior, self-disclosure, and self-reported stress. *Journal of Personality and Social Psychology,* 32, 645–54.

Sundstrom, E. & Altman, I. (1976). Interpersonal relationships and personal space: research review and theoretical model. *Human Ecology,* 4, 47–67.

Tamir, M., Robinson, M.D., Clore, G.L., Martin, L.L., & Whitaker, D.J. (2004). Are we puppets on a string? The contextual meaning of unconscious expressive cues. *Personality and Social Psychological Bulletin,* 30, 237–49.

Tickel–Degnen, L. & Rosenthal, R. (1987). Group rapport and nonverbal behavior. *Review of Personality and Social Psychology,* 9, 113–36.

Tom, G., Petterson, P., Lau, T., & Burton, T. (1992). The role of overt head movement in the formation of affect. *Basic and Applied Social Psychology,* 12, 281–9.

Trager, G.L. & Smith, H.L. (1957). *An outline of English structure.* Washington, D.C.: American Council of Learned Societies.

Troisi, A. & Moles, A. (1999). Gender differences in depression: an ethological study of nonverbal behavior during interviews. *Journal of Psychiatric Research,* 33, 243–50.

Troisi, A., Pasini, A., Bersani, G., Guispini, A., & Ciani, N. (1989). Ethological predictors of amitriptyline response in depressed outpatients. *Journal of Affective Disorders,* 17, 129–36.

Trout, D.L. & Rosenfeld, H.M. (1980). The effect of postural lean and body congruence on the judgment of psychotherapeutic rapport. *Journal of Nonverbal Behavior,* 4, 176–90.

Vine, I. (1971). Judgment of direction of gaze: an interpretation of discrepant results. *British Journal of Social and Clinical Psychology,* 10, 320–31.

von Cranach, M. (1971). The role of orienting behavior in human interaction. In *Behavior and environment: the use of space by animals and man* (ed. A.H. Esser), pp. 217–37. New York, NY: Plenum.

von Cranach, M. & Ellgring, J.H.(1973). Problems in the recognition of gaze direction. In *Social communication and movement* (ed. M. von Cranach & I. Vine). New York, NY: Academic Press.

Vrij, A. (1994). The impact of information and setting on detection of deception by police officers. *Journal of Nonverbal Behavior,* 18, 117–37.

Vrij, A. (1995). Behavioral correlates of deception in a simulated police interview. *Journal of Psychology,* 129, 15–28.

Watson, O.M. & Graves, T.D. (1966). Quantitative research in proxemic behavior. *American Anthropologist,* 68, 971–85.

Weisbrod, R.M. (1956). *Looking behavior in a discussion group.* Unpublished manuscript, Cornell University, Ithaca, NY.

Weitz, S. (1972). Attitude, voice, and behavior: a repressed affect model of interracial interaction. *Journal of Personality and Social Psychology,* 24, 14–21.

Wells, G. & Petty, R. (1980). The effects of overt head movements on persuasion: compatibility and incompatibility of responses. *Basic and Applied Social Psychology*, 1, 219–30.

Wendler, M.C. (2003). Effects of Tellington touch in healthy adults awaiting venipuncture. *Research in Nursing and Health*, 26, 40–52.

Wiemann, J.M. & Knapp, M.L. (1975). Turn-taking in conversation. *Journal of Communication*, 25, 75–92.

Wiener, M., Devoe, S., Rubinow, S., & Geller, J. (1972). Nonverbal behavior and nonverbal communication. *Psychological Review*, 79, 185–214.

Yngve, V.H. (1970). *On getting a word in edgewise*. Papers from the sixth regional meeting of the Chicago Linguistic Society, pp. 567–77. Chicago: Chicago Linguistic Society.

Zinober, B. & Martlew, M. (1985). Developmental change in four types of gesture in relation to acts and vocalizations from 10 to 21 months. *British Journal of Developmental Psychology*, 3, 293–306.

Zlutnick, S. & Altman, I. (1972). Crowding and human behavior. In *Environment and the social sciences: perspectives and applications* (ed. J. Wohlwill and D. Carson.), pp. 44–60. Oxford, UK: American Psychological Association.

CHAPTER 5

CONDUCTING JUDGMENT STUDIES: SOME METHODOLOGICAL ISSUES

ROBERT ROSENTHAL

Although the focus of this chapter is on nonverbal behavior in the affective sciences, the basic principles described apply to any context in which judgment studies are conducted. The term 'judgment studies' refers most generally to those studies in which behaviors, persons, objects, or concepts are evaluated by one or more judges, raters, coders, or categorizers, referred to collectively as 'judges'. These judges may be general experts, specialist-experts, members of the general public, college students and the like; the judgments they are asked to make run the gamut from the degree of warmth shown by a psychotherapist to the affect or creativity shown in a work of art. In this chapter we consider some of the fundamental methodological issues that contemporary researchers will want to consider when they conduct judgment studies including issues of the nature of judgment studies, the reliability of judgments, the selection of judges, the formation of composite variables, and some related topics.

Introduction

Research in nonverbal communication very often requires the use of observers, coders, raters, decoders, or judges. Although distinctions among these classes of human (or at least animate) responders are possible, we shall not distinguish among them here but, rather, use these terms more or less interchangeably.

Judgment studies may focus on nonverbal behaviors considered as independent variables; for example, when the corners of the mouth rise, do judges rate subjects as being happier? Judgment studies may also focus on nonverbal behaviors considered as *dependent* variables; for example, when subjects are made happier, are the corners of their mouths judged as having risen more?

Judgment studies may employ a variety of metrics, from physical units of measurement to psychological units of measurement. For example, the movement of the corner of the mouth can be given in millimeters, while judges' ratings of happiness may be given on a scale (perhaps of seven points) ranging from 'not at all happy' to 'very happy'.

The judgments employed in a judgment study may vary dramatically in their reliability. Thus, judgments based on physical units of measurement are often more reliable than are judgments based on psychological units of measurement, although, for some purposes, the latter may be higher in validity despite their being lower in reliability (Rosenthal 1966). This may be due to the lower degree of social meaning

Table 5.1 Dimensions tending to distinguish various types of judgment studies

Dimensions	Examples
Type of variable	Dependent vs. independent variables
Measurement units	Physical vs. psychological units
Reliability	Lower vs. higher levels
Social meaning	Lower vs. higher levels

inherent in the more molecular physical units of measurement compared to the more molar psychological units of measurement. Table 5.1 shows some of the dimensions upon which it is possible to classify various judgment studies.

The judgment study model

The underlying model of a basic judgment study is shown in Fig. 5.1. One or more encoders characterized by one or more attributes (e.g. traits, states) (A) are observed by one or more decoders who make one or more judgments (C) about the encoders on the basis of selectively presented nonverbal behavior (B). The AB arrow refers to the relationship between the encoder's actual attribute (e.g. state) and the encoder's non-verbal behavior. The AB arrow reflects the primary interest of the investigator who wishes to employ the nonverbal behavior as the dependent variable. The BC arrow reflects the primary interest of the investigator who wishes to employ the nonverbal behavior as the independent variable. The AC arrow reflects the primary interest of the investigator interested in the relationship between the encoder's attribute and the decoders' judgment (e.g. the decoders' accuracy).

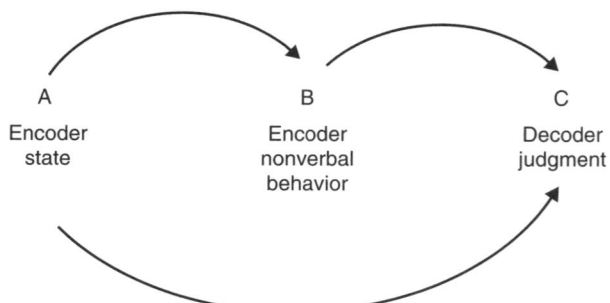

A	B	C
Encoder state	Encoder nonverbal behavior	Decoder judgment

Figure 5.1 A simple model of judgment studies

The nonverbal behavior (B) presented to the decoders tends to be highly selected as part of the research design. Investigators interested in facial expressions might present still photographs of the face (e.g. Ekman 1973; Ekman *et al.* 1987), while investigators interested in tone of voice might present speech that is content-standard (Davitz 1964), randomized-spliced (Scherer 1971), or content-filtered (Rogers *et al.* 1971). Investigators interested in comparing the relative efficiency of cues carried in various channels of nonverbal communication might provide access to different channels of nonverbal cues (e.g. face, body, tone of voice) (Rosenthal *et al.* 1979; Scherer *et al.* 1977).

To summarize the simple judgment model then, we have encoder attributes (e.g. states) (A), manifested behaviorally (B), and decoded by judges (C). The states then are antecedents of both the nonverbal behaviors and the decoders' judgments.

A more complex judgment study model based on Brunswik's (1956) lens model has been described by Scherer (1978).

The purposes of judgment studies

Judgment studies serve many purposes. In terms of our simple model of judgment studies (Fig. 5.1), the focus of a judgment study may be on the encoder state or other attribute (A), the encoder's nonverbal behavior (B), the decoder's judgment itself (C), the AB, AC, and BC arrows, or the ABC chain.

Encoder state

Suppose we wanted to develop a system for the diagnosis of anxiety in college students from various nonverbal cues (e.g. Harrigan *et al.* 1996). Suppose further that we had available film clips of 30 students being interviewed. Before we could correlate various nonverbal behaviors with the degree of anxiety of the students we would have to ascertain their 'actual' anxiety level. One way of defining this might be to show the 30 film clips to a sample of experienced clinical psychologists or other experts on anxiety, and obtain ratings of the degree of anxiety shown by each college student.[1] The mean rating of anxiety of each stimulus person (encoder) becomes the operational definition of the true state of the encoder. Note that our emphasis here is on defining the encoder state, *not* on specifying the cues that might have led the expert judges to decide on what ratings they would give. In addition, note that this particular judgment study, done for the purpose of estimating parameters (mean anxiety) rather than establishing relationships, was a kind of preliminary study to be followed up by a study linking the state of anxiety to the nonverbal concomitants (an AB arrow) (Rosenthal and Rosnow 1975*a*, 1991).

Encoder nonverbal behavior

Suppose we wanted to study the mediation of teacher expectancy effects (Rosenthal 1966, 1969, 1974, 1976, 1985, 2002*a,b*, 2003; Rosenthal & Jacobson 1968; Rosenthal & Rubin 1978). One of our hypotheses might be that teachers who expect more from their students treat them more warmly. Furthermore, we may believe that this warmth will be expressed, in part, through tone of voice. Before we can examine the relationship between teachers' expectations and teachers' warmth in tone of voice, however, we must be able to define tonal 'warmth'. One way of defining warmth would be to ask

---

[1] An alternative way of defining 'actual' level of anxiety in terms of test scores is described in a subsequent paragraph on *AC arrows*.

judges to make ratings of the degree of warmth shown in the content-filtered voices of teachers talking to their students. The mean rating of warmth obtained for each stimulus teacher's content-filtered voice becomes the definition of the warmth of the nonverbal behavior.

This particular judgment study, like the one described just above, was conducted for the purpose of estimating parameters (mean warmth) rather than establishing relationships. As such, it might serve as a kind of preliminary study that would be followed up by a study relating the nonverbal behavior to a teacher state or some other type of variable. Such studies have been conducted focusing on the tone of voice shown by, for example, teachers, psychotherapists, counselors, physicians, and mothers (Ambady *et al.* 2002; Ambady & Rosenthal 1992, 1993; Babad 1992; Blanck & Rosenthal 1984; Blanck *et al.* 1990; Eden 1990; Halverson *et al.* 1997; Harris & Rosenthal 1985, 1986; Milmoe *et al.* 1967, 1968; Rosenthal *et al.* 1984). (Though a number of sources have just been listed, it should be noted that they are listed only as illustrations, with no attempt to provide a review of any aspect of the literature of nonverbal communication.)

Decoder judgment

In the case of the two purposes of judgment studies described so far, judges' ratings were employed to provide the definitions of encoder states and encoder nonverbal behavior, usually in the context of a preliminary study or a simple descriptive study; for example, what proportion of experimenters smile at their research subjects? (Rosenthal 1967) Sometimes, however, it is the judgments themselves we want to study. The interpretation of nonverbal cues may depend heavily on personal characteristics of the judges. Thus, we might not be surprised to find that aggressive, delinquent boys will tend to interpret nonverbal cues as more aggressive than would less aggressive boys (Nasby *et al.* 1980). Or we might be interested to learn that blind children may be more sensitive to tone of voice cues (content-filtered and randomized-spliced) than are sighted children (Rosenthal *et al.* 1979). One of the earliest uses of decoders' judgments was to help establish that nonverbal behavior could, in fact, be decoded accurately (Allport 1924; Ekman 1965, 1973).

AB arrows

If we record therapists' expectations for their patients and observe their nonverbal behaviors as they interact with their patients, we have the ingredients of an AB arrow study. Therapists' nonverbal behaviors could be defined in terms of muscle movements in millimeters, or voice changes in hertz, or in terms of warmth, pride, esteem, and expectation, as rated on nine-point scales. In any case, we regard the nonverbal behaviors as the dependent variable, and the therapists' expectations as the independent variable (Blanck *et al.* 1986).

BC arrows

A common type of BC arrow judgment study might experimentally manipulate various encoder nonverbal cues and observe the effects on decoders' ratings of various encoder characteristics (e.g. Friedman 1976, 1978, 1979a; Harrigan & Rosenthal 1983). Questions addressed might include:

- Are smiling faces rated as more friendly?
- Are voices with greater pitch range judged more pleasant?
- Are louder voices judged more extraverted? (Scherer 1970, 1978, 1979a,b, 1982; Scherer et al. 1972; Scherer & Oshinsky 1977)

AC arrows

AC arrow judgment studies are common in the general research domains of clinical diagnosis and person perception. The general paradigm is to ask decoders to assess the encoders' true attributes (e.g. diagnosis, anxiety level, adjustment level) and to correlate decoders' judgments with independently determined definitions of encoders' true traits or states. Thus, for example, clinicians' ratings of adjustment and anxiety might be correlated with encoders' scores on various subscales of such tests as the MMPI, or scores based on the Rorschach, TAT, or life history data.

When AC arrow judgment studies are employed in research on nonverbal communication it is often in the context of 'accuracy' studies. Encoders might, for example, show a variety of posed or spontaneous affects, and judgments of these affects made by decoders are evaluated for accuracy. Sometimes these accuracy studies are conducted to learn the degree to which judges show better than chance accuracy (Allport 1924; Ekman 1965, 1973). At other times, these accuracy studies are conducted to establish individual differences among the judges in degree of accuracy shown. These individual differences in decoding accuracy may then be correlated with a variety of personal attributes of the judges (e.g. gender, age, ethnicity, psychopathology, cognitive attributes, personality attributes) (Rosenthal et al. 1979). It should be noted that such individual difference studies can be meaningfully conducted even when the mean level of accuracy shown by the entire sample of judges does not exceed the chance expectation level as in comparisons of people scoring above chance with those scoring below chance.

ABC chains

Sometimes we are simultaneously interested in the AB arrow and the BC arrow; such studies can be viewed as studies of the ABC chain. Suppose we want to study the mediation of teacher expectancy effects. We begin with a sample of teachers known to vary in their experimentally created expectations for their pupils' intellectual performance (i.e. known to vary in encoder states (A)). These teachers are observed interacting with pupils for whom they hold higher or lower expectations and a sample of judges rates the teachers' behavior on degree of smiling, forward lean, and eye contact (i.e. encoder nonverbal behaviors (B)). Finally, a sample of judges rates the nonverbal behavior of the teachers for degree of overall warmth and favorableness of expectancy (i.e. makes decoder judgments (C) of a fairly molar type). We would now be in a position to examine the effects of experimentally induced teacher expectation on teacher nonverbal behavior and the role of these nonverbal behaviors in predicting outcomes of social consequence, all in the same study (Harris & Rosenthal 1985, 1986).

Designing judgment studies

The particular purpose of any judgment study should determine the particular procedures of any judgment study. Given the diversity of purposes of judgment studies we have discussed above, it is not possible to prescribe the detailed procedures that should be employed for any particular judgment study. However, because judgment studies do have certain communalities, it is possible to discuss methodological issues likely to be confronted in many judgment studies. In the following pages we address three of these issues in some detail:

1. the reliabilities of judgments made;
2. the selection of judges;
3. the combining of judgments to form composite variables.

Issues of reliability

How many judges shall we employ in a judgment study in which our primary interest is in the encoders rather than the judges, and who should they be? The major factors determining the answers to these questions are:

1. the average reliability coefficient (r) between pairs of judges chosen at random from a specified population;
2. the nature of the population of judges to which we want to generalize our results.

Effective reliability

Suppose our goal were to establish the definition of the encoder's state (A) or of some encoder nonverbal behavior (B). We might decide to employ judges' ratings for our definition. As we shall see shortly, if the reliability coefficient (any product moment correlation such as r, point biserial r, or phi) were very low, we would require more judges than if the reliability coefficient were very high. Just how many judges to employ is a question for which some useful guidelines can be presented (Rosenthal 1973, 1982, 1987; Li *et al.* 1996).

If we had a sample of teachers whose nonverbal warmth we wanted to establish, we might begin by having two judges rate each teacher's warmth based on the videotaped behavior of each teacher. The correlation coefficient reflecting the reliability of the two judges' ratings would be computed to give us our best (and only) estimate of the correlation likely to be obtained between any two judges drawn from the same population of judges. This correlation coefficient, then, is clearly useful; it is not, however, a very good estimate of the reliability of our variable, which is not the rating of warmth made by a single judge but rather the mean of two judges' ratings. Suppose, for example, that the correlation between our two judges' ratings of warmth were 0.50; the reliability of the mean of the two judges' ratings (the 'effective' reliability) would then be 0.67, not 0.50. Intuition suggests that we should gain in reliability in adding the ratings of a second judge because the second judge's random errors should tend to cancel the first judge's random errors. Intuition suggests further that adding more judges, all of whom agree with one another to about the same degree, defined by a mean inter-judge correlation coefficient of 0.50 (for this example), should further increase our 'effective' reliability. Our intuition would be supported by a very old and well-known result reported independently and simultaneously by Charles Spearman (1910) and William Brown (1910). With notation altered to suit our current purpose, the well-known Spearman–Brown equation is:

$$R_{SB} = \frac{nr}{1 + (n-1)r} \tag{1}$$

where R_{SB} = 'effective' reliability; n = number of judges; r = mean reliability among all n judges (that is, mean of $\frac{n(n-1)}{2}$ correlations).

Use of this formula depends on two assumptions:

1. a comparable group of judges would show comparable 'mean' reliability among themselves and with the actual group of judges available to us;
2. that all judges have essentially the same variance of their ratings of the same sample.

It should be noted that the 'effective' reliability also can be obtained computationally by means of the Kuder–Richardson '20 equation' or by means of Cronbach's coefficient alpha (Guilford 1954).

When the assumptions underlying the use of the Spearman–Brown equation are not met, as when we can think of two or more different subgroups of judges, adjustments to the equation are available and are described in detail in Li *et al.* (1996).

As an aid to investigators employing these and related methods, Table 5.2 has been prepared employing the Spearman–Brown equation. The table gives the effective reliability, R_{SB}, for each of several values of n (the number of judges making the observations) and r (the mean reliability among the judges). It provides quick, approximate answers to each of the following questions:

1. Given an obtained or estimated mean reliability, r, and a sample of n judges, what is the approximate effective reliability, R_{SB}, of the mean of the judges' ratings? The value of R_{SB} is read from the table at the intersection of the appropriate row (n) and column (r).
2. Given the value of the obtained or desired effective reliability, R_{SB}, and the number, n, of judges available, what will be the approximate value of the required mean reliability, r? The table is entered in the row corresponding to the n of judges available, and is read across until the value of R_{SB} closest to the one desired is reached; the value of r is then read as the corresponding column heading.
3. Given an obtained or estimated mean reliability, r, and the obtained or desired effective reliability, R_{SB}, what is the approximate number (n) of judges required? The table is entered in the column corresponding to the mean reliability, r, and is read down until the value of R_{SB} closest to the one desired is reached; the value of n is then read as the corresponding row title.

Product moment correlations

It should be noted that the mean reliability (r) of Table 5.2 is to be a product moment correlation coefficient such as Pearson's r, the point biserial r, or the phi coefficient. It is often not appropriate to employ such indices of 'reliability' as percentage agreement or multidegree of freedom indices of interjudge agreement.

Some risks in not using Pearson's r-based indices of reliability

Percentage agreement

It has long been common practice for some researchers to index the reliability of judges' categorizations using percentage agreement defined as:

$$\left(\frac{A}{A + D}\right)100 \tag{2}$$

where A represents the number of agreements and D represents the number of disagreements (Rosenthal and Rosnow 1991).

Table 5.2 Effective reliability (R_{SB}) of the mean of judges' ratings

No. of judges (n)	Mean reliability (r)																				
	.01	.03	.05	.10	.15	.20	.25	.30	.35	.40	.45	.50	.55	.60	.65	.70	.75	.80	.85	.90	.95
1	01	03	05	10	15	20	25	30	35	40	45	50	55	60	65	70	75	80	85	90	95
2	02	06	10	18	26	33	40	46	52	57	62	67	71	75	79	82	86	89	92	95	97
3	03	08	14	25	35	43	50	56	62	67	71	75	79	82	85	88	90	92	94	96	98
4	04	11	17	31	41	50	57	63	68	73	77	80	83	86	88	90	92	94	96	97	*
5	05	13	21	36	47	56	62	68	73	77	80	83	86	88	90	92	94	95	97	98	*
6	06	16	24	40	51	60	67	72	76	80	83	86	88	90	92	93	95	96	97	98	*
7	07	18	27	44	55	64	70	75	79	82	85	88	90	91	93	94	95	97	98	98	*
8	07	20	30	47	59	67	73	77	81	84	87	89	91	92	94	95	96	97	98	*	*
9	08	22	32	50	61	69	75	79	83	86	88	90	92	93	94	95	96	97	98	*	*
10	09	24	34	53	64	71	77	81	84	87	89	91	92	94	95	96	97	98	98	*	*
12	11	27	39	57	68	75	80	84	87	89	91	92	94	95	96	97	97	98	*	*	**
14	12	30	42	61	71	78	82	86	88	90	92	93	94	95	96	97	98	98	*	*	**
16	14	33	46	64	74	80	84	87	90	91	93	94	95	96	97	97	98	98	*	*	**
18	15	36	49	67	76	82	86	89	91	92	94	95	96	96	97	98	98	*	*	*	**
20	17	38	51	69	78	83	87	90	92	93	94	95	96	97	97	98	98	*	*	*	**
24	20	43	56	73	81	86	89	91	93	94	95	96	97	97	98	98	*	*	*	**	**
28	22	46	60	76	83	88	90	92	94	95	96	97	97	98	98	98	*	*	*	**	**
32	24	50	63	78	85	89	91	93	95	96	96	97	98	98	98	*	*	*	*	**	**
36	27	53	65	80	86	90	92	94	95	96	97	97	98	98	*	*	*	*	**	**	**
40	29	55	68	82	88	91	93	94	96	96	97	98	98	98	*	*	*	*	**	**	**
50	34	61	72	85	90	93	94	96	96	97	98	98	98	*	*	*	*	**	**	**	**
60	38	65	76	87	91	94	95	96	97	98	98	98	*	*	*	*	*	**	**	**	**
80	45	71	81	90	93	95	96	97	98	98	98	*	*	*	*	*	**	**	**	**	**
100	50	76	84	92	95	96	97	98	98	*	*	*	*	*	**	**	**	**	**	**	**

Note: Decimal points omitted
* Approximately 0.99
**Approximately 1.00

Table 5.3 shows how percentage agreement can be a very misleading indicator of interjudge reliability. In Part A of Table 5.3 we find that two researchers, Smith and Jones, each had two judges evaluate a series of 100 film clips of children for the presence or absence of frowning behavior. Both Smith and Jones found their judges to show 98% agreement, but Smith's 98% agreement was a hollow victory indeed. The correlation between judges A and B was actually slightly negative, $r = -.01$, ($\chi^2_{(1)} = 0.01$). Jones' 98% agreement, on the other hand, was associated with an r of $+ .96$, ($\chi^2_{(1)} = 92.16$).

Part B of Table 5.3 shows two additional cases of percentage agreement obtained by researchers North and West. This time, the two investigators have both obtained an apparently chance level of agreement (i.e. 50%). Both results, however, are very far from reflecting chance agreement, both with $p = 0.0009$. Most surprising, perhaps, is that North obtained a substantial negative reliability ($r = -0.33$) while West obtained a substantial positive reliability ($r = +0.33$); another illustration that percentage agreement is not a very informative index of reliability.

Multi-*df* interjudge reliability

Among the first psychologists to appreciate the problems of percentage agreement as an index of reliability was Jacob Cohen (1960, 1968). He developed an index, kappa, that solved the problem of the percentage agreement index by adjusting for any agreement based simply on lack of variability (e.g. the lack of variability found in Part A of Table 5.3 where both of Smith's judges found 98% of the film clips to show frowning behavior).

Table 5.3 Examples of percentage agreement

A. Two cases of 98% agreement

Smith's results	Judge A		Jones's results	Judge C	
Judge B	Frown	No frown	Judge D	Frown	No frown
Frown	98	1	Frown	49	1
No frown	1	0	No frown	1	49
Agreement = 98% but					
$r_{AB} = -.01$; $\chi^2_{(1)} = 0.01$			Agreement = 98% but		
			$r_{CD} = +.96$; $\chi^2_{(1)} = 92.16$		

B. Two cases of 50% agreement

North's results	Judge E		West's results	Judge G	
Judge F	Frown	No frown	Judge H	Frown	No frown
Frown	50	25	Frown	25	50
No frown	25	0	No frown	0	25
Agreement = 50% but			Agreement = 50%, but		
$r_{EF} = -.33$; $\chi^2_{(1)} = 11.11$			$r_{GH} = +.33$; $\chi^2_{(1)} = 11.11$		

Table 5.4 Results of two diagnosticians' classification of 100 persons into one of four categories

		Judge 1				
		A Schizophrenic	B Neurotic	C Normal	D Brain-damaged	Σ
	A Schizophrenic	13	0	0	12	25
Judge 2	B Neurotic	0	12	13	0	25
	C Normal	0	13	12	0	25
	D Brain-damaged	12	0	0	13	25
	Σ	25	25	25	25	100

$kappa(df = 9) = \frac{O-E}{N-E} = \frac{50-25}{100-25} = .333$

Table 5.4 gives an example of the type of situation in which kappa is often employed. Two clinical diagnosticians have examined the silent videotapes of 100 people in a clinical interview where the interviewer is not shown. Each clinician was asked to assign each interviewee to one of four classifications: schizophrenic, neurotic, normal, and brain damaged. Only three quantities are required to compute kappa:

1. O = observed number on which the two judges have agreed (i.e. the number on the diagonal of agreement). In this example, the observed number is: $13 + 12 + 12 + 13 = 50$.
2. E = expected number under the hypothesis of only chance agreement for the cells on the diagonal of agreement. For each cell, the expected number is the product of the row total and the column total divided by the total number of cases. In this example, the expected number is: $(25 \times 25)/100 + (25 \times 25)/100 + (25 \times 25)/100 + (25 \times 25)/100 = 6.25 + 6.25 + 6.25 + 6.25 = 25$.
3. N = total number of cases classified. In this example, $N = 100$.

Kappa is computed from:

$$kappa = \frac{O - E}{N - E} = \frac{50 - 25}{100 - 25} = .333 \tag{3}$$

in the present example.

Although kappa is clearly an improvement over percentage agreement as an index of reliability, it does raise some serious questions. When kappa is based on tables larger than a 2×2 (e.g. a 3×3, a 4×4 (as in Table 5.4), or larger), as it often is, it suffers from the same problem as does any statistic on $df > 1$. That problem—of diffuse or omnibus procedures—is that for most values of kappa we cannot tell which focused or specific judgments are made reliably and which are made unreliably. Only when kappa approaches unity is the actual interpretation of a value of kappa straightforward (i.e. essentially all judgments are made reliably) (Rosenthal 1991). We illustrate the difficulty in interpreting kappa by returning to Table 5.4.

The 4×4 table we see, based on 9 df, can be decomposed into a series of six pairwise 2×2 tables, each based on a single df, and addressing a very specific, conceptually clear question of the reliability of dichotomous judgments—A vs. B, A vs. C, A vs. D, B vs. C, B vs. D, and C vs. D. Table 5.5 shows the results of computing kappa separately for each of these six 2×2 tables.

Table 5.5 Breakdown of the 9 *df* omnibus table of counts of Table 5.4 into six specific (focused) reliabilities of *df* = 1 each

	A Schiz	B Neurotic	Σ		A Schiz	C Normal	Σ
A Schiz	13	0	13	A Schiz	13	0	13
B Neurotic	0	12	12	C Normal	0	12	12
Σ	13	12	25	Σ	13	12	25
	kappa = 1.00				*kappa* = 1.00		
	A Schiz	D Brain	Σ		B Neurotic	C Normal	Σ
A Schiz	13	12	25	B Neurotic	12	13	25
D Brain	12	13	25	C Normal	13	12	25
Σ	25	25	50	Σ	25	25	50
	kappa = 0.04				*kappa* = −0.04		
	B Neurotic	D Brain	Σ		C Normal	D Brain	Σ
B Neurotic	12	0	12	C Normal	12	0	12
D Brain	0	13	13	D Brain	0	13	13
Σ	12	13	25	Σ	12	13	25
	kappa = 1.00				*kappa* = 1.00		

Schiz = schizophrenic; brain = brain-damaged

Of the six focused or specific reliabilities computed, four are kappas of 1.00, and two are kappas near zero (0.04 and −0.04). The mean of the six 1 *df* kappas is 0.667, and the median is 1.00; neither value being predictable from the omnibus 9 *df* kappa value of 0.33. Tables 5.6 and 5.7 show, even more clearly, how little relation there is between the omnibus values of kappa and the associated 1 *df* kappas (i.e. the focused reliability kappas). Table 5.6 shows an omnibus 9 *df* kappa value of 0.33—exactly the same value as that shown in Table 5.4.

Table 5.7 shows the six focused reliabilities of *df* = 1 associated with the omnibus value of kappa (0.33) of Table 5.6. We see that of these six focused kappas, four are kappas of 0.00, one is a kappa of +1.00, and one is a kappa of −1.00. The mean and median-focused kappa both show a value of 0.00. We can summarize the two omnibus kappas of Tables 5.4 and 5.6, and their associated focused kappas, as follows:

	Example 1	Example 2
Omnibus kappa	0.33	0.33
Mean-focused kappa	0.67	0.00
Median-focused kappa	1.00	0.00

Thus, we have two identical kappas: one made up primarily of perfect reliabilities, the other made up primarily of zero reliabilities.

Although the greatest limitations on kappa occur when kappa is based on *df* > 1, there are some problems with kappa even when it is based on a 2 × 2 table of counts where *df* = 1. The basic problem under these conditions is that very often kappa is not equivalent to the

Table 5.6 Alternative results of two diagnosticians' classification of 100 persons into one of four categories

		Judge 1				
		A	B	C	D	Σ
	A	25	0	0	0	25
Judge 2	B	0	0	25	0	25
	C	0	25	0	0	25
	D	0	0	0	25	25
	Σ	25	25	25	25	100

$kappa(df = 9) = \frac{O-E}{N-E} = \frac{50-25}{100-25} = .333$

Table 5.7 Breakdown of the 9 df omnibus table of counts of Table 5.6 into six specific (focused) reliabilities of $df = 1$ each

	A	B	Σ
A	25	0	25
B	0	0	0
Σ	25	0	25

$kappa = 0.00$

	A	C	Σ
A	25	0	25
C	0	0	0
Σ	25	0	25

$kappa = 0.00$

	A	D	Σ
A	25	0	25
D	0	25	25
Σ	25	25	50

$kappa = 1.00$

	B	C	Σ
B	0	25	25
C	25	0	25
Σ	25	25	50

$kappa = -1.00$

	B	D	Σ
B	0	0	0
D	0	25	25
Σ	0	25	25

$kappa = 0.00$

	C	D	Σ
C	0	0	0
D	0	25	25
Σ	0	25	25

$kappa = 0.00$

product moment correlation computed from exactly the same 2×2 table of counts. This is certainly not a criticism of kappa, since it never pretended to be a product moment correlation. The limitation, however, is that we cannot apply various interpretive procedures or displays to kappa that we can apply to product moment correlations. Examples include the use of the *coefficient of determination*, r^2, (Guilford 1954) and the *binomial effect size display* (Rosenthal & Rubin 1982; Rosenthal & Rosnow 1991)

Here, we need only indicate the conditions under which a 1 df kappa is or is not equivalent to a product moment correlation (referred to as a Pearson r in the general case and sometimes referred to as phi (or ϕ) in the case of a 2×2 table of counts). Kappa and r are equivalent when the row totals for levels A and B are identical to the column totals for levels A and B, respectively. Consider the following example:

		Judge 1		
		A	B	Σ
Judge 2	A	70	10	80
	B	10	10	20
	S	80	20	100

For these data, the marginal totals for level A are identical for Judges 1 and 2 (i.e. 80),

$$kappa(df = 1) = \frac{O - E}{N - E} = \frac{80 - 68}{100 - 68} = .375,$$

and r (or equivalently, phi) yields the identical value of 0.375. Therefore, we could meaningfully compute a coefficient of determination or a binomial effect size display for this particular kappa because it is equivalent to a Pearson r or phi (ϕ).

Now consider the following example in which we have the same four cell entries and the same marginal totals as in the preceding example. The only thing that has changed is the location of the cell with the largest count (70) so that the marginal totals for level A differ for Judges 1 and 2 (20 versus 80).

		Judge 1		
		A	B	Σ
Judge 2	A	10	70	80
	B	10	10	20
	S	20	80	100

In this example,

$$kappa(df = 1) = \frac{O - E}{N - E} = \frac{20 - 32}{100 - 32} = -.176,$$

but r (or ϕ) yields a markedly different value of -0.375. We can, therefore, compute a meaningful coefficient of determination or a binomial effect size display for r, but we cannot do so for kappa.

Other approaches to reliability

Reliability and analysis of variance

When there are only two judges whose reliability is to be evaluated, it is hard to beat the convenience of a product moment correlation coefficient for an appropriate index of reliability. As the number of judges grows larger, however, working with correlation coefficients can become inconvenient. For example, suppose we employed 40 judges and wanted to compute both their mean reliability (r) and their effective reliability (R_{SB}). Table 5.2 could get us R_{SB} from knowing r, but to get r we would have to compute $(40 \times 39)/2 = 780$ correlation coefficients. That is not hard work for computers, but averaging the 780 coefficients to get r can be hard work for investigators or their programmers. There is an easier way, and it involves the analysis of variance.

Table 5.8 Judges' ratings of nonverbal behavior

	Judges			
	A	B	C	Σ
Encoders				
1	5	6	7	18
2	3	6	4	13
3	3	4	6	13
4	2	2	3	7
5	1	4	4	9
Σ	14	22	24	60

Table 5.9 Analysis of variance of judges' ratings

Source	SS	df	MS
Encoders	24.0	4	6.00
Judges	11.2	2	5.60
Residual	6.8	8	0.85

Table 5.8 shows a simple example of three judges rating the nonverbal behavior of five encoders on a scale of 1 to 7, and Table 5.9 shows the analysis of variance of these data.[2] Our computations require only the use of the last column, the column of mean squares (Guilford 1954). Examination of the computational formulas given below shows how well the judges can discriminate among the sampling units (e.g. people) minus the judges' disagreement after controlling for judges' rating bias or main effects (e.g. *MS* encoders – *MS* residuals), divided by a standardizing quantity.

Our estimate of R_{anova} (the effective reliability of the sum or the mean of all of the ratings of the judges) is given by:

$$R_{anova} = \frac{MS\ encoders - MS\ residual}{MS\ encoders} \tag{4}$$

Our estimate of *r* (the mean reliability or the reliability of a *single* average judge) is given by:

$$r_{anova} = \frac{MS\ encoders - MS\ residual}{MS\ encoders + (n-1)\ MS\ residual} \tag{5}$$

where *n* is the number of judges as before (equation 5 is known as the intraclass correlation).

---

[2] In our own research, we typically use seven or nine-point rating scales (1–7 or 1–9) with unipolar rather than bipolar scales (i.e. one scale of 'behaves warmly' and a second scale of 'behaves coldly' rather than a single scale of 'warm–cold'.) Our unipolar scales usually run from 1 (not at all warm) to 7 or 9 (extremely warm). For details on response formats see Rosenthal 1987, Chapter 4.

For our example of Tables 5.8 and 5.9 we have:

$$R_{anova} = \frac{6.00 - 0.85}{6.00} = .858$$

and

$$r_{anova} = \frac{6.00 - 0.85}{6.00 + (3 - 1)0.85} = .669$$

In the present example, it will be easy to compare the results of the analysis of variance approach with the more cumbersome correlational approach. Thus, the correlations (r) between pairs of judges (r_{AB}, r_{BC}, and r_{AC}) are 0.645, 0.582, and 0.800 respectively, and the mean intercorrelation is 0.676, which differs by only 0.007 from the estimate (0.669) obtained by means of the analysis of variance approach.

If we were employing only the correlational approach, we would apply the Spearman–Brown equation (1) to our mean reliability of 0.676 to find R_{SB}, the effective reliability. That result is:

$$R_{SB} = \frac{(3)\,(.676)}{1 + (3 - 1)(.676)} = .862$$

which differs by only 0.004 from the estimate (0.858) obtained by means of the analysis of variance approach. In general, the differences obtained between the correlational approach and the analysis of variance approach are quite small (Guilford 1954).

It should be noted that, in our present simple example, the correlational approach was not an onerous one to employ, with only three correlations to compute. As the number of judges increases, however, we would find ourselves more and more grateful for the analysis of variance approach or for such related procedures as the Kuder–Richardson equations, Cronbach's alpha, or similar methods available in commonly used data analytic packages. Because of its widespread use in software packages, we briefly describe and illustrate the use of Cronbach's alpha (α).

Cronbach's alpha

More than half a century ago, Cronbach (1951) proposed *coefficient alpha* (α) that gives the reliability of a group of judges considered as a set. To compute Cronbach's α we need only three ingredients: n, the number of judges in the set contributing to the 'score' for each encoder rated; S_{judge}^2, the variance of the scores generated by an individual judge; and S_{total}^2, the variance of the total of scores given by the judges to each individual encoder. Cronbach's α is obtained from:

$$\alpha = \left(\frac{n}{n-1}\right)\left(\frac{S_{total}^2 - \sum S_{judge}^2}{S_{total}^2}\right) \qquad (6)$$

Table 5.10 shows the raw data of Table 5.8 but with the addition of the variance for each judge (S_{judge}^2)) and the variance of the sum of the n judges' ratings (S_{total}^2). We find:

Table 5.10 Variances of individual judges and of the sum of judges' ratings of five encoders

Encoders	Judges				Σ
	A	B	C		
1	5	6	7		18
2	3	6	4		13
3	3	4	6		13
4	2	2	3		7
5	1	4	4		9
M	2.8	4.4	4.8		12.0
S^2_{judge}	2.2	2.8	2.7	S^2_{total}	18.0

$$\alpha = \left(\frac{3}{3-1}\right) \left(\frac{18 - (2.2 + 2.8 + 2.7)}{18}\right) = .858$$

—a value that is the same as that reported earlier for R_{anova} (equation 4) and very close to the value (0.862) reported earlier for R_{SB} and obtained from equation 1. All three of these results (R_{anova}, R_{SB}, and α) tend to be quite similar and more so as the judges are more homogenous in their variances (that is, S^2_{judge}) and in their correlations with other judges.

Reliability and principal components

In situations where the ratings made by all judges have been intercorrelated, and a principal components analysis is readily available, another very efficient alternative for estimating the reliability of the total set of judges is available. Armor (1974) has developed an index, *theta*, that is based on the unrotated first principal component (where a principal component is a factor extracted from a correlation matrix employing unity (1.00) in the diagonal of the correlation matrix). The equation for theta is:

$$theta = \frac{n}{n-1} \left(\frac{L-1}{L}\right) \tag{7}$$

where n is the number of judges and L is the latent root or eigenvalue of the first unrotated principal component. The latent root is the sum of the squared factor loadings for any given factor, and can be thought of as the amount of variance in the judges' ratings accounted for by that factor. Factor analytic computer programs generally give latent roots or eigenvalues for each factor extracted, so that theta is very easy to obtain in practice. Armor (1974) has pointed out the close relationship between theta and Cronbach's coefficient alpha.

For an illustration of the use of theta we refer to the standardization of a test of sensitivity to nonverbal cues—the Profile of Nonverbal Sensitivity (PONS) (Rosenthal et al. 1979). When the 220 items of that test were subjected to a principal components analysis, the eigenvalue or latent root (L) of the first (unrotated) component was 13.217. Therefore, from equation 7 we find:

$$theta\ \theta = \frac{n}{n-1}\left(\frac{L-1}{L}\right) = \frac{220}{219}\left(\frac{13.217-1}{13.217}\right) = .929$$

In this particular example, the variables were test items; in other examples, they might have been judges. In general, when reliabilities are being assessed, items of tests and judges of behaviors are equivalent—that is, the term n can refer equally well to judges, items of a test, subtests of a full test, or any other components of a measuring instrument having two or more judges, items, or subtests.

Reporting reliabilities

Assuming we have done our reliability analyses well, how shall we report our results? Ideally, reports of reliability analyses should include both the mean reliability (the reliability of a single judge) and the effective reliability (reliability of the total set of judges or of the mean judgments). Readers of our reports need to know the latter reliability (e.g. R_{SB}, R_{anova}, α, θ) because that is, in fact, the reliability of the variable employed in most cases. However, if this reliability is reported without explanation, the reader may not be aware that the reliability of any one judge's ratings are likely to be lower (often substantially so). Readers may note a reported reliability of 0.80 based on 12 judges and decide that the variable is sufficiently reliable for their purposes. These readers may then employ a single judge, only to find later that this single judge was operating at a reliability of 0.25, not 0.80. Reporting both reliabilities avoids such misunderstandings.

Split-sample reliabilities

A related source of misunderstanding is the reporting of correlations between a mean judge of one type with a mean judge of another type. For example, suppose we had 10 male and 10 female judges, or 10 black and 10 white judges. One sometimes sees in the literature the reliability of the mean male and mean female judge or the mean black and mean white judge. Such a correlation of the mean ratings made by all judges of one type with the mean ratings made by judges of another type can be very useful but they should not be reported as reliabilities without the explanation that these correlations might be substantially higher than the average correlation between any one male and any one female judge or between any one black and any one white judge. The reasons for this are those discussed in the earlier section on effective reliability.

As an illustration of the problem of split-sample reliabilities, consider the following example. Two samples of judges were employed (one week apart) to rate the nonverbal behavior of a set of psychotherapists. There were 10 judges in each of the two groups and the mean ratings assigned to each psychotherapist by the first set of 10 judges were correlated with the mean ratings assigned to each psychotherapist by the second set of 10 judges. The obtained r was 0.818. Reporting this r as 'the reliability' could be misleading to other investigators since it represents *neither* the reliability of the total set of 20 judges *nor* the typical reliability computed from any pair of individual judges.

To obtain the reliability of the total set of 20 judges, we employ the Spearman–Brown equation with $r = 0.818$ and $n = 2$, since there were two *sets* of judges (each with 10 judges whose ratings had been averaged). Our effective reliability, R_{SB}, therefore, is found to be:

$$R_{SB} = \frac{nr}{1 + (n-1)r} = \frac{2(.818)}{1 + (2-1).818} = .900$$

If we want to find the typical reliability of the 20 individual judges, taken one at a time, we rewrite the Spearman–Brown equation to solve not for R_{SB} but for r, as follows:

$$r = \frac{R_{SB}}{n + R_{SB} - nR_{SB}} \tag{8}$$

which, for the present example, yields

$$r = \frac{.900}{20 + .900 - (20).900} = .310$$

To summarize, the group $(n = 10)$ to group $(n = 10)$ reliability was 0.818, the Spearman–Brown 'upped' reliability was 0.900, and the Spearman–Brown 'downed' reliability was 0.310. It should be noted that we could also have obtained this latter r from the original group $(n = 10)$ to group $(n = 10)$ reliability of 0.818, with 0.818 regarded as R_{SB} and with $n = 10$, as follows:

$$r = \frac{R_{SB}}{n + R_{SB} - nR_{SB}} = \frac{.818}{10 + .818 - (10).818} = .310.$$

Trimming judges

It sometimes happens that, when we examine the intercorrelations among our judges, we find one judge who is very much out of line with all the others. Perhaps this judge tends to obtain negative correlations with other judges or at least to show clearly lower reliabilities with other judges than is typical for the correlation matrix. If this 'unreliable' judge were dropped from the data, the resulting estimates of reliability would be biased; that is, made to appear too reliable. If a judge must be dropped, the resulting bias can be reduced by equitable trimming. That is, if the lowest agreeing judge is dropped, the highest agreeing judge is also dropped. If the two lowest agreeing judges are dropped, the two highest agreeing judges are also dropped, and so on.

Experience suggests that when large samples are employed, the effects of trimming judges are small, as is the need for trimming. When the sample of judges is small, we may feel a stronger need to drop a judge, but doing so is more likely to leave a residual biased estimate of reliability. A safe procedure is to do all analyses with and without the trimming of judges and to report the differences in results from the data with and without the trimming. Although the method of trimming judges seems not yet to have been systematically applied, the theoretical foundations for the method can be seen in the work of Barnett & Lewis (1978), Huber (1981), Mosteller & Rourke (1973), and Mosteller & Tukey (1977) and, in particular, in the work of Tukey (1977).

Selection of judges

Individual differences

So far in our discussion of the sampling of judges, we have not considered systematic individual differences among our judges. Typically, there is no special interest in individual differences among judges when we consider issues of reliability. We simply decide on the type of judges we want (e.g. college students, clinical psychologists, linguists, dance therapists, mothers) and then regard each judge within that sample as to some degree equivalent to or interchangeable with any other judge within that sample.

Sometimes, however, our interest focuses directly on individual differences among judges as when we want to know about the relationships of these individual differences with accuracy (or systematic inaccuracy) of encoding and decoding nonverbal behavior. Interest in such relationships has been increasing (e.g. Blanck *et al.* 1986; Buck 1979; DePaulo & Rosenthal 1979*a,b*; DiMatteo 1979; Friedman 1979*a,b*; Hall 1984; Nasby *et al.* 1980; Rosenthal 1979; Rosenthal & DePaulo 1979*a,b*; Rosenthal *et al.* 1979; Uno *et al.* 1972; Weitz 1979; Zuckerman & Larrance 1979; and especially in the valuable collection of contributions brought together by Hall & Bernieri 2001).

The types of variables that have been studied for their degree of relationship to skill in decoding nonverbal cues include judges' age, sex, cultural background, cognitive attributes, psychosocial attributes, special skills and impairments, training, and experience (e.g. Hall & Bernieri 2001; Rosenthal *et al.* 1979).

If we are planning a judgment study and want simply a prototypic sample of judges, we may be content to select a sample of college or high school students. If our aim is simply to define the encoder's state or the encoder's nonverbal behavior by means of the judges' ratings, we need not even be overly concerned about the common problem of volunteer bias (that is, the problem that volunteers for behavioral research may differ systematically from non-volunteers). If our interest, however, is to estimate the average degree of accuracy for the population selected (e.g. students), we should be aware of the potentially large effects of volunteer bias. This problem is addressed in detail by Rosenthal and Rosnow (1975*b*) and Rosenthal (1987).

Recent research with high school students has suggested that the correlation between volunteering for behavioral research and accuracy of decoding nonverbal cues may be on the order of 0.40 (Rosenthal *et al.* 1979). Such a correlation reflects the situation obtained when 70% of the volunteers achieve the median level of accuracy compared to only 30% of the non-volunteers, given that about half the judges were volunteers and half were non-volunteers (Rosenthal & Rubin 1979, 1982).

Maximizing judge accuracy

Sometimes our intent in a judgment study is not to find prototypic judges but the 'best' judges for our purpose. Thus, if we wanted judgments of nonverbal cues to psychoses, we might want clinical psychologists or psychiatrists for our judges. If we wanted judgments of nonverbal cues to discomfort in infants, we might want pediatricians, developmental psychologists, or mothers. If we wanted judgments of nonverbal cues of persuasiveness, we might want trial lawyers, fundamentalist clergy, or salespersons.

If we are seeking no very specialized type of judgment but would like to obtain the highest level of accuracy possible in a general way, we might want to select our judges on the basis of prior research suggesting characteristics of those more sensitive to nonverbal cues. One review of research suggested that to optimize overall sensitivity we might select judges who are female, of college age, cognitively more complex, and psychiatrically unimpaired (Rosenthal *et al.* 1979). Actors, students of nonverbal communication, and students of visual arts tend to perform better than do other occupational groups, and among teachers and clinicians, the more effective teachers and clinicians are likely to be the better decoders of nonverbal cues (Rosenthal *et al.* 1979). Finally, if we were to base our selection of more accurate judges of nonverbal behavior on psychosocial variables, we might want to consider results of the type shown in Table 5.11 (based on research reported elsewhere in detail) (Rosenthal *et al.* 1979).

Users of Table 5.11 should note that the correlations given are medians of varying numbers of studies conducted, so that greater confidence may be placed in those relationships based on a larger number of studies. Even in those cases, however, it is possible for any *one* study to show a much higher or a much lower correlation.

Economic considerations in the selection of judges

Suppose we wanted to assess the degree of anxiety shown by interviewees based only on their nonverbal behavior. We might then show silent videotapes to our judges and have them rate the degree of anxiety shown by each interviewee. Since mental health professionals (e.g. psychiatrists, psychiatric nurses, psychiatric social workers, clinical

Table 5.11 Psychosocial variables likely to be useful in selecting judges of greater sensitivity to nonverbal cues ($r \geq 0.20$)

Variables	No. of studies	Median r	Equivalent to increasing success rate* From	To
Volunteering for research	2	0.40	0.30	0.70
Achievement potential	5	0.31	0.34	0.66
Social/religious values	1	0.28	0.36	0.64
Interpersonal adequacy	5	0.25	0.38	0.62
Democratic orientation	2	0.24	0.38	0.62
Intellectual and interest modes	5	0.23	0.38	0.62
Maturity	5	0.22	0.39	0.61
Interpersonal sensitivity	22	0.22	0.39	0.61
Task orientation	1	0.21	0.40	0.60
Nondogmatic	2	0.20	0.40	0.60
Spouses' report of nonverbal sensitivity	2	0.20	0.40	0.60

Note: For this table, sensitivity to nonverbal cues was defined by performance on the PONS test (Rosenthal *et al.* 1979).
* Based on the binomial effect size display (Rosenthal & Rubin 1982).

Table 5.12 Effective costs as a function of judge cost per task and judge reliability

	Reliability								
	0.10	0.20	0.30	0.40	0.50	0.60	0.70	0.80	0.90
					$\frac{1-r}{r}$				
Cost ($)	9.0	4.0	7/3	1.5	1.0	2/3	3/7	1/4	1/9
5	45	20	12	8	5	3	2	1	1
10	90	40	23	15	10	7	4	2	1
20	180	80	47	30	20	13	9	5	2
30	270	120	70	45	30	20	13	8	3
40	360	160	93	60	40	27	17	10	4
50	450	200	117	75	50	33	21	12	6
100	900	400	233	150	100	67	43	25	11
200	1800	800	467	300	200	133	86	50	22
300	2700	1200	700	450	300	200	129	75	33
400	3600	1600	933	600	400	267	171	100	44
500	4500	2000	1167	750	500	333	214	125	56
1000	9000	4000	2333	1500	1000	667	429	250	111

Note: Effective costs are rounded to the nearest dollar.

psychologists) would seem to be those most expert in evaluating anxiety, we might prefer them as our judges of choice. We might want them, but they might be quite expensive. College sophomores would be a lot less expensive, per hour, but they might not know as much about assessing anxiety. If we had a fixed amount of money with which to employ psychiatrists or sophomores, is there a way by which we could decide whether it would be more economical to choose psychiatrists, or sophomores, or some combination of psychiatrists and sophomores if our goal were to maximize the reliability of our set of judges staying within our fixed budget?

Such a procedure is available and begins by computing the effective cost (*EC*) for each type of judge from the following equation (Li *et al.* 1996):

$$ EC = C_i \left(\frac{1 - r_i}{r_i} \right) \tag{9} $$

where C_i is the cost in dollars of judge type i and r_i is the reliability of a single judge of type i.

Table 5.12 shows the intuitively sensible fact that when costs per judge are low, and reliability per judge is high, we have very low effective costs. The upper right hand corner shows these very low effective costs, while the lower left hand corner shows the very high effective costs of having high-priced judges with low reliability.

The design rule that maximizes reliability is to rank all available judges by their effective cost from lowest cost (our best choice) to highest cost (our worst choice), until we have run out of funds or out of judges. For example, if we had available psychiatrists with reliability 0.80 at a cost of $500, and college sophomores with reliability 0.30 at a cost of $40, we would employ the sophomores because their effective cost is $93 compared to the higher effective cost of $125 for the psychiatrists.

Suppose our budget for judges' time were $500 and we wanted the effective reliability of our judge or judges to be at least 0.80. Selecting a psychiatrist as the judge would precisely meet both of these criteria. However, employing 10 sophomores would cost us less money ($400 instead of $500) and would give us a slightly higher reliability of 0.81 as computed from equation 1 or according to Table 5.2. Staying within our budget, we could actually afford 12 sophomores ($480) whose effective reliability would be higher still ($R_{SB} = 0.84$).

Now suppose we had three kinds of judges available: high school students with reliability 0.20 at a cost of $20; college students with reliability 0.30 at a cost of $40; and graduate students in clinical psychology with reliability 0.60 at a cost of $100. Table 5.12 shows that the effective costs of high school, college, and graduate students are $80, $93, and $67, respectively. Because the effective costs are lowest for the graduate students, we would select them first. If we ran out of graduate students before our funds ran out, and before our reliability was high enough, we would next select high school students, because their effective costs are lower ($80) than those of the college students ($93). In those situations in which two or more types of judges are employed to make the same type of judgments, procedures are available to weight the judges' contributions so as to maximize the overall reliability (Li *et al.* 1996).

Forming composite variables

Suppose that our judges have rated the nonverbal behavior of a set of psychotherapists on three dimensions: warmth, empathy, and positiveness of regard. Suppose, further, that the retest reliabilities and the internal consistency reliabilities of all three variables are 0.70 and that each of our three variables is also correlated with the others 0.70. Under these conditions, when our variables are so highly correlated with each other (as highly correlated as they are with themselves), we may find no advantage to analyzing all our data separately for the three variables.

For most purposes, we might well prefer to form a composite variable of all three. We might, therefore, standard score (Z score) each of the three variables we plan to combine and replace each therapist's three scores by the mean of the three Z scores the therapist earned from the judges. A mean Z score of zero means that the therapist scores as average on our new composite variable; a large positive mean Z score (e.g. + 1.00) means that the therapist scores as quite high on our new composite variable; and a large negative mean Z score (e.g. −1.00) means that the therapist scores as quite low on our new composite variable of warmth, empathy, and positiveness of regard. It should be noted that the means of Z scores are not themselves distributed as Z scores and that if our composite variables are to be employed in the construction of further composites, they should be Z scored again.

Benefits of forming composite variables

For the example given above, and for many more complex cases as well, there are conceptual and practical reasons for forming composite variables. Conceptually, if variables cannot be discriminated from one another (because they are as highly correlated with each other as they are with themselves), it is hard to defend treating them as separate variables. Practically, we are able to obtain more accurate (and usually larger) estimates of the relationship of composites with other variables of interest than we are working with the individual variables before they are combined into a composite. In addition, reducing a larger number of variables to a smaller number of composites makes it easier to interpret appropriately any significance levels we may want to compute.

For example, if we are interested in the relationship between therapists' training and patients' nonverbal behavior, we might have employed 5, or 10, or 20 variables on which patients were to be rated by judges. If we find the relationship between therapists' training and patient behavior to be significant at 0.05 for only one of 10 behaviors, it is difficult to interpret what the 'true' level of significance of that result might be, given that 10 tests of significance were performed. If our 10 patient behaviors had been combined into a single meaningful composite, we would be able to interpret the obtained significance level more appropriately (Rosenthal & Rosnow 1991; Rosenthal *et al.* 2000).

Forming composites and increasing effect sizes

When each of our separate variables shows approximately the same magnitude of correlation with some predictor variable or some outcome variable, and when the correlations among the various separate variables are also fairly homogeneous in magnitude, we can estimate the effects of forming composites on the magnitude of the effect size (correlation) of interest.

For example, suppose we examine the relationship between therapists' training and 10 dependent variables. Suppose further that the correlation (r_i) between therapist training and each of the 10 individual dependent variables is roughly 0.30 and that the average correlation (r) among the 10 dependent variables is 0.50. What would be the new correlation (r_c) of a composite variable with the independent variable of therapist training? We estimate the answer to be a new $r(r_c)$ of 0.40 based on the rearrangement of terms of an equation (14.37) given by Guilford (1954).

The general equation is:

$$r_{composite} = r_{individual} \times F \tag{10}$$

which states simply that the effect size based on the composite variable (r_c) is the product of the typical effect size based on the individual variable (r_i) multiplied by a factor F (Rosenthal 1987).

This factor F is defined as follows:

$$F = \sqrt{\frac{n}{1 + \bar{r}\,(n-1)}} \tag{11}$$

where n is the number of variables entering into the composite and $\bar{r}$ is the mean intercorrelation among the variables entering into the composite.

Table 5.13 shows the values of F for varying levels of n and of $\bar{r}$. Only when the individual variables are perfectly correlated with each other is there no benefit from

Table 5.13 Factors (F) by which effect sizes (r) increase as a function of (a) the number of variables in a composite and (b) the mean intercorrelation among variables

Mean intercorrelation $\bar{r}$	Number of individual variables (n)			
	2	5	10	20
1.00	1.00	1.00	1.00	1.00
0.90	1.03	1.04	1.05	1.05
0.75	1.07	1.12	1.14	1.15
0.50	1.15	1.29	1.35	1.38
0.25	1.26	1.58	1.75	1.87
0.10	1.35	1.89	2.29	2.63
0.00	1.41	2.24	3.16	4.47

forming composites. In general, the more separate variables that are combined into a composite, the greater will be the increase in the effect size r_c obtained. In addition, the *lower* the mean intercorrelation among the individual variables, the greater the increase in the effect size r_c obtained. It should be noted, however, that as the mean intercorrelation becomes lower and lower, it will be rarer and rarer that the effect sizes for the individual variables will be homogeneous. If they are, it means that each individual variable is equivalently related to the external or criterion variable but is 'predicting' an independent portion of that criterion.

The values of F shown in Table 5.13 need only be multiplied by r_i (the typical effect size for individual variables) to yield r_c (the effect size based on the composite variable). There are also situations, however, when r_c is known and we would like to find r_i (the probable value of the typical effect size for individual variables). This is readily accomplished from the following relationship:

$$r_{individual} = \frac{r_{composite}}{F} \qquad (12)$$

Equation 12 would be useful in the following type of situation. Investigator A has reported a correlation between therapists' gender and perceived nonverbal warmth of 0.70. Investigator B feels that r must be too high and tries to replicate, obtaining an r of 0.40. Since both investigators employed large samples, the two rs of 0.70 and 0.40 differ very significantly. Investigator B wonders where A went wrong until she recalls that she used, as her definition of warmth, a single rating scale, whereas A used a composite variable made up of 10 variables with average intercorrelation of 0.25. Using Table 5.13 she finds $F = 1.75$ and, from equation 12:

$$r_i = \frac{r_c}{F} = \frac{.70}{1.75} = .40$$

—a result suggesting that the data of investigators A and B were not discrepant after all. In both cases, the 'per single variable effect size' was 0.40.

Forming multiple composites

So far our discussion of forming composites has focused on the simple case in which the variables are homogeneously related to each other. In such situations, it is reasonable to form only a single composite. There are many situations, however, in which intercorrelations among our variables are not homogeneous, so that we would form two or more composite variables. Consider the intercorrelations among the five variables A, B, C, D, and E of Table 5.14. Variables A, B, and C are ratings of health care providers' warmth, friendliness, and likability, while variables D and E are ratings of the health care providers' self-confidence and professionalism. The mean intercorrelation of the five variables is 0.36 (median = 0.15), with a standard deviation (S) of 0.37. Closer inspection of the correlation matrix of Section A of Table 5.14, however, suggests that combining all five variables would make a poor composite given the great variability of the intercorrelations. Section B of Table 5.14 shows the decomposition of the lower left triangle of the correlation matrix into three groupings. The first grouping shows that the three intercorrelations among variables A, B, and C range between 0.70 and 0.90. The third grouping shows that the correlation between variables D and E is similarly high (0.70). The second grouping in Section B shows that the six correlations between the three variables A, B, and C and the two variables D and E range only from 0.00 to 0.20—correlations that suggest quite strongly that the composite made up of A, B, and C is relatively independent of the composite made up of variables D and E.

Table 5.14 An illustration of the formation of multiple composite variables

A. The correlation matrix

Variables	Variables				
	A	B	C	D	E
A	1.00	0.80	0.70	0.10	0.00
B	0.80	1.00	0.90	0.20	0.10
C	0.70	0.90	1.00	0.10	0.00
D	0.10	0.20	0.10	1.00	0.70
E	0.00	0.10	0.00	0.70	1.00

B. Decomposition of the lower left triangle

	A	B		A	B	C		D
B	0.80		D	0.10	0.20	0.10	E	0.70
C	0.70	0.90	E	0.00	0.10	0.00		

C. The intra/inter matrix of intercorrelations

Composites	Composites	
	I	II
I	0.80	0.08
II	0.08	0.70

The intra/inter matrix

Section C of Table 5.14 shows an intra/inter matrix of mean intercorrelations. The mean r of 0.80 in the upper left cell of the matrix is the *intra*-composite average for composite I; the r of 0.70 in the lower right cell of the matrix is the *intra*-composite average for composite II; and the off diagonal value of 0.08 is the *inter*-composite average characterizing the level of relationship between the ingredient variables of composites with the ingredient variables of other composites.

The value of an intra/inter matrix of mean (or median) intercorrelations is that it tells, at a glance, how justified we are in claiming that we have formed clear, defensible composites (Rosenthal 1966). For example, if our intra/inter matrix were:

	I	II
I	0.75	0.60
II	0.60	0.50

we would not have a strong case for two composites (rather than one) since the typical (mean or median) correlations between the composites ($\bar{r} = 0.60$) is actually higher than the typical correlations within one of the composites ($\bar{r} = 0.50$).

Table 5.15, Section A, shows a larger correlation matrix: the intercorrelations among 14 variables which have been reduced into a set of four composite variables I, II, III, and IV. Section B of Table 5.15 shows the intra/inter matrix with the mean correlations within composites (intra) on the diagonal (shown in boxes), and the mean correlations between composites (inter) off the diagonal. For simplicity, we have omitted the mean correlations below the diagonal since those are simply relistings of mean correlations shown above the diagonals. As the number of variables grows larger, we can get help in the construction of composites by using such procedures as clustering, principal components analysis, factor analysis, and dimensional analysis. If such procedures are used, however, we suggest that they not be used actually to define the composites (as in, for example, 'the factor analysis shows there are five factors'.) We use these procedures only as guides to our judgment about the theoretical and empirical reasonableness of our composite variables. Details of these procedures are given elsewhere (Rosenthal 1987, Chapter 5).

Quantifying the clarity of composites

Two of the most valuable methods of quantifying our degree of success in constructing clear composite variables are the methods of r and of g.

The r method

In the r method, we compute the point biserial correlation between the mean (or median) correlations of the intra/inter matrix with their location *on* the diagonal (coded as 1) versus *off* the diagonal (coded as 0) of the intra/inter matrix. The more positive the correlation, the higher, on average, are the *intra* mean correlations (those on the diagonal) than the *inter* mean correlations (those off the diagonal).

Table 5.16 shows the 10 mean correlations of the intra/inter matrix of Table 5.15, Section B, listed as within composite (intra) or between composite (inter) values. The

Table 5.15 An illustration of the formation of four composite variables

A. The correlation matrix

Composites	Variables	Composite I				Composite II			Composite III				Composite IV		
		a	b	c	d	e	f	g	h	i	j	k	l	m	n
I	a		.40	.60	.50	.30	.25	.20	.15	.20	.20	.25	.25	.30	.25
	b			.50	.40	.25	.20	.15	.20	.25	.15	.10	.30	.25	.30
	c				.60	.10	.15	.20	.30	.15	.15	.10	.20	.30	.25
	d					.30	.20	.25	.25	.10	.15	.20	.30	.20	.20
II	e						.70	.60	.30	.30	.25	.35	.10	.20	.25
	f							.50	.30	.25	.25	.30	.30	.10	.15
	g								.35	.25	.30	.35	.20	.10	.15
III	h									.30	.40	.50	.15	.30	.25
	i										.50	.40	.15	.20	.30
	j											.30	.10	.25	.10
	k												.25	.10	.15
IV	l													.35	.45
	m														.55
	n														

B. The intra/inter matrix

Composites	I	II	III	IV
I	0.50			
II	0.21	0.60		
III	0.18	0.30	0.40	
IV	0.26	0.17	0.19	0.45

Table 5.16 Example of the *r* and *g* methods of quantifying the clarity of composite variables from the intra/inter matrix of Table 5.15B

	Intra-composite mean ($\bar{r}$) On diagonal coded as 1[1]	Inter-composite mean ($\bar{r}$) Off diagonal coded as 0[1]
	0.50	0.21
	0.60	0.18
	0.40	0.26
	0.45	0.30
		0.17
		0.19
Mean	0.49	0.22
S^2	0.0073[2]	0.0026[2]

[1] The correlation between magnitude of mean correlations and their location on (rather than off) the diagonal is 0.92

[2] Weighted value of $S = 0.066$, $g = 4.1$

correlation between the mean correlation and location on the diagonal (rather than off the diagonal) is 0.92, indicating that the average internal consistency of the four composite variables is much greater than the average correlation between the ingredient variables of different composites with one another.

The g method

In the *g* method (named after Hedges' *g* index; Hedges 1981), we find the difference between the mean of the mean *rs on* the diagonal ($\bar{r}_{intra}$) and the mean of the mean *rs off* the diagonal ($\bar{r}_{inter}$) and divide that difference by $S_{aggregated}$ (the weighted *S* combined from the *on* diagonal (intra) and *off* diagonal (inter) values of *r*):

$$g = \frac{\bar{r}_{intra} - \bar{r}_{inter}}{S_{aggregated}} \tag{13}$$

For the data of Table 5.16

$$g = \frac{.49 - .22}{.066} = 4.1$$

indicating that the average relationship of variables within a composite to one another is over four standard deviations larger than the average relationship of variables between composites to one another.

There is no firm rule of thumb to help us decide when the *r* and *g* indexes are large enough to suggest that our composites show clarity of differentiation from one another. Certainly *rs* of 0.25 and *gs* of 0.50 provide suggestive evidence of such clarity (Cohen 1988).

A third method

When we have access to an intra/inter matrix, both the r method and the g method are extremely informative. If it should happen, however, that we know only the mean of the intra-composite (on diagonal) mean rs ($\bar{r}_{intra}$) and the mean of inter-composite (off diagonal) mean rs ($\bar{r}_{inter}$), we cannot use either the r or g methods. An index that can be used in such cases is the *range to midrange ratio* (*rmr*) defined as:

$$rmr = \frac{\bar{r}_{intra} - \bar{r}_{inter}}{(\bar{r}_{intra} + \bar{r}_{inter})/2} \tag{14}$$

which divides the difference between the mean of the intra-composite means ($\bar{r}_{intra}$) and the mean of the inter-composite means ($\bar{r}_{inter}$) by the mean of these two mean rs. Dividing by the mean of these mean rs makes a particular raw difference between $\bar{r}_{intra}$ and $\bar{r}_{inter}$ relatively more meaningful when the mean of these two $\bar{r}s$ is smaller rather than larger.

Table 5.17 shows the *rmr* values obtained for various values of $\bar{r}_{intra}$ and $\bar{r}_{inter}$. Note that when $\bar{r}_{intra} = 0.90$ and $\bar{r}_{inter} = 0.70$, so that $\bar{r}_{intra} - \bar{r}_{inter} = 0.20$, the value of $rmr = 0.25$. When the values of $\bar{r}_{intra}$ and $\bar{r}_{inter}$ are 0.50 and 0.30, respectively, however, $\bar{r}_{intra} - \bar{r}_{inter}$ is still 0.20, but the value of $rmr = 0.50$. For values of $\bar{r}_{intra}$ and $\bar{r}_{inter}$ of 0.30 and 0.10, respectively, *rmr* is 1.00, though the difference between $\bar{r}_{intra}$ and $\bar{r}_{inter}$ is still only 0.20.

No firm guidelines are available for what value of *rmr* should be regarded as strong evidence for the clarity of differentiation of composite variables. Perhaps any value of 0.33 or larger (i.e. the difference between the *intra* and *inter* means of mean intercorrelations is at least one-third of the value of the mean of the *intra* and *inter* mean intercorrelations) can be considered as providing fairly good evidence for the clarity of differentiation of the composite variables.

Table 5.17 Values of the rmr* index for various values of $\bar{r}_{intra}$ and $\bar{r}_{inter}$

		Mean of intra-composite average correlations ($\bar{r}_{intra}$)										
		0.00	0.10	0.20	0.30	0.40	0.50	0.60	0.70	0.80	0.90	1.00
Mean of	0.00	.00	2.00	2.00	2.00	2.00	2.00	2.00	2.00	2.00	2.00	2.00
intercomposite	0.10		0.00	0.67	1.00	1.20	1.33	1.43	1.50	1.56	1.60	1.64
average	0.20			0.00	0.40	0.67	0.86	1.00	1.11	1.20	1.27	1.33
correlations ($\bar{r}_{inter}$)	0.30				0.00	0.29	0.50	0.67	0.80	0.91	1.00	1.08
	0.40					0.00	0.22	0.40	0.55	0.67	0.77	0.86
	0.50						0.00	0.18	0.33	0.46	0.57	0.67
	0.60							0.00	0.15	0.29	0.40	0.50
	0.70								0.00	0.13	0.25	0.35
	0.80									0.00	0.12	0.22
	0.90										0.00	0.11
	1.00											0.00

Note: Values below the diagonal of 0.00 values are negative, indicating no support for the clarity of differentiation of the composite variables considered as a set.

* $rmr = \frac{\bar{r}_{intra} - \bar{r}_{inter}}{(\bar{r}_{intra} + \bar{r}_{inter})/2}$

Other issues to consider in conducting judgment studies

In this chapter, we have discussed a number of methodological issues, but we have been far from exhaustive. For example, we have not discussed the methodological issues to consider in the selection of encoders and the selection and presentation of stimuli. Some of these issues have been discussed in detail elsewhere (Rosenthal 1987), but some others have been raised in more recent research. As an example, it recently has been reported that, in judging dyadic interaction, dyad members in the judge's left visual field are rated systematically differently than are dyad members in the judge's right visual field. Furthermore, dyad members are judged differently when their interaction partner *is*, versus *is not*, visible to the judge (Puccinelli *et al.* 2003, 2004, 2005).

There are also some new developments in the construct validation of standardized stimuli used as measures of individual differences; where construct validity has formerly been thought of only as a qualitative attribute, measures are now available to quantify the degree of construct validity associated with any particular set of stimuli employed as a measure of individual differences (Westen & Rosenthal 2003).

Our final example of recent methodological developments that could not be discussed in this chapter but which may be useful for those conducting judgment studies is the development of a new effect size estimate, $r_{equivalent}$ (Rosenthal & Rubin 2003). With the increased emphasis on the estimation of effect sizes for our research results (American Psychological Association 2001; Wilkinson 1999), it became clear that there were situations in which effect size estimation would be difficult, if not impossible:

1. in meta-analytic research where only sample sizes and p values were reported by the original investigator;
2. research employing nonparametric statistics for which there are no accepted effect size estimates;
3. where directly computed effect size estimates could be very misleading.

The new statistic, $r_{equivalent}$, was designed to deal with any of these circumstances.

To come now to a close, we can venture that a great deal has been learned about conducting judgment studies; but there is a great deal more that we need to know but have not yet learned.

References

Allport, F.H. (1924). *Social psychology.* Boston: Houghton–Mifflin.

Ambady, N. & Rosenthal, R. (1992). Thin slices of expressive behavior as predictors of interpersonal consequences: a meta-analysis. *Psychological Bulletin*, 111, 256–74.

Ambady, N. & Rosenthal, R.(1993). Half a minute: predicting teacher evaluations from thin slices of nonverbal behavior and physical attractiveness. *Journal of Personality and Social Psychology*, 64, 431–41.

Ambady, N., LaPlante, D., Nguyen,T., Rosenthal, R., Chaumeton, N., & Levinson, W. (2002). Surgeon's tone of voice: a clue to malpractice history. *Surgery*, 132(1), 5–9.

American Psychological Association (2001). *Publication manual of the American Psychological Association* (5th edn). Washington, DC: American Psychological Association.

Armor, D.J. (1974). Theta reliability and factor scaling. In *Sociological methodology 1973–1974* (ed. H.L. Costner). San Francisco: Jossey–Bass.

Babad, E. (1992). Teacher expectancies and nonverbal behavior. In *Applications of nonverbal behavioral theories and research* (ed. R.S. Feldman), pp. 167–90. Hillsdale, NJ: Erlbaum.

Barnett, V. & Lewis, T. (1978). *Outliers in statistical data*. New York: John Wiley.

Blanck, P.D. & Rosenthal, R.(1984). Mediation of interpersonal expectancy effects: counselor's tone of voice. *Journal of Educational Psychology*, **76**, 418–26.

Blanck, P.D., Buck, R.W., & Rosenthal, R. (ed.) (1986). *Nonverbal communication in the clinical context*. University Park, PA: Pennsylvania State University Press.

Blanck, P.D., Rosenthal, R., Hart, A.J., & Bernieri, F. (1990). The measure of the judge: an empirically-based framework for exploring trial judges' behavior. *Iowa Law Review*, **75**, 653–84.

Blanck, P.D., Rosenthal, R., & Vanicelli, M. (1986). Talking to and about patients: the therapist's tone of voice. In *Nonverbal communication in the clinical context* (ed. P.D. Blanck, R.W. Buck, & R. Rosenthal), pp. 99–143. University Park, PA: Pennsylvania State University Press.

Brown, W. (1910). Some experimental results in the correlation of mental abilities. *British Journal of Psychology*, **3**, 296–322.

Brunswik, E. (1956). *Perception and the representative design of psychological experiments*. Berkeley: University of California Press.

Buck, R. (1979). Individual differences in nonverbal sending accuracy and electrodermal responding: the externalizing-internalizing dimension. In *Skill in nonverbal communication: individual differences* (ed. R. Rosenthal), pp. 140–70. Cambridge, MA: Oelgeschlager, Gunn and Hain.

Cohen, J. (1960). A coefficient of agreement for nominal scales. *Educational and Psychological Measurement*, **20**, 37–46.

Cohen, J. (1968). Weighted kappa: nominal scale agreement with provision for scaled disagreement or partial credit. *Psychological Bulletin*, **70**, 213–20.

Cohen, J. (1988). *Statistical power analysis for the behavioral sciences* (2nd edn). Hillsdale, NJ: Erlbaum.

Cronbach, L.J. (1951). Coefficient alpha and the internal consistency of tests. *Psychometrika*, **16**, 297–334.

Davitz, J.R. (1964). *The communication of emotional meaning*. New York: McGraw–Hill.

DePaulo, B.M. & Rosenthal, R. (1979a). Ambivalence, discrepancy, and deception in nonverbal communication. In *Skill in nonverbal communication: individual differences* (ed. R. Rosenthal), pp. 204–48. Cambridge, MA: Oelgeschlager, Gunn and Hain.

DePaulo, B.M. & Rosenthal, R. (1979b). Telling lies. *Journal of Personality and Social Psychology*, **37**, 1713–22.

DiMatteo, M.R. (1979). Nonverbal skill and the physician–patient relationship. In *Skill in nonverbal communication: individual differences* (ed. R. Rosenthal), pp. 104–34. Cambridge, MA: Oelgeschlager, Gunn and Hain.

Eden, D. (1990). *Pygmalion in management: productivity as a self-fulfilling prophecy*. Lexington, MA: Heath.

Ekman, P. (1965). Communication through nonverbal behavior : a source of information about an interpersonal relationship. In *Affect, cognition, and personality* (ed. S.S. Tomkins & C. Izard), pp. 390–442. New York: Springer.

Ekman, P. (1973). Cross-cultural studies of facial expression. In *Darwin and facial expression: a century of research in review* (ed. P. Ekman), pp. 169–222. New York: Academic Press.

Ekman, P., Friesen, W.V., O'Sullivan, M., Chan, A., Diacoyanni–Tarlatzis, I., Heider, K., *et al.* (1987). Universals and cultural differences in the judgments of facial expressions of emotion. *Journal of Personality and Social Psychology*, 53, 712–17.

Friedman, H.S. (1976). *About face: the role of facial expressions of emotion in the verbal communication of meaning.* Unpublished doctoral dissertation, Harvard University.

Friedman, H.S. (1978). The relative strength of verbal versus nonverbal cues. *Personality and Social Psychology*, 4, 147–50.

Friedman, H.S. (1979*a*). The interactive effects of facial expressions of emotion and verbal messages on perceptions of affective meaning. *Journal of Experimental Social Psychology*, 15, 453–69.

Friedman, H.S. (1979*b*). The concept of skill in nonverbal communication: implications for understanding social interaction. In *Skill in nonverbal communication: individual differences* (ed. R. Rosenthal), pp. 2–27. Cambridge, MA: Oelgeschlager, Gunn and Hain.

Guilford, J.P. (1954). *Psychometric methods* (2nd edn). New York: McGraw–Hill.

Hall, J.A. (1984). *Nonverbal sex differences.* Baltimore, MD: The Johns Hopkins University Press.

Hall, J.A. & Bernieri, F.J. (ed.) (2001). *Interpersonal sensitivity: theory and measurement.* Mahwah, NJ: Erlbaum.

Halverson, A.M., Hallahan, M., Hart, A.J., & Rosenthal, R. (1997). Reducing the biasing effects of judges' nonverbal behavior with simplified jury instruction. *Journal of Applied Psychology*, 82, 590–8.

Harrigan, J.A. & Rosenthal, R. (1983). Physicians' head and body positions as determinants of perceived rapport. *Journal of Applied Social Psychology*, 13, 496–509.

Harrigan, J.A., Harrigan, K.M., Sale, B.A., & Rosenthal, R. (1996). Detecting anxiety and defensiveness from visual and auditory cues. *Journal of Personality*, 64, 675–709.

Harris, M.J. & Rosenthal, R. (1985). The mediation of interpersonal expectancy effects: 31 meta-analyses. *Psychological Bulletin*, 97, 363–86.

Harris, M.J. & Rosenthal, R.(1986). Four factors in the mediation of teacher expectancy effects. In *The social psychology of education* (ed. R.S. Feldman), pp. 91–114. New York: Cambridge University Press.

Hedges, L.V. (1981). Distribution theory for Glass's estimator of effect size and related estimators. *Journal of Educational Statistics*, 6, 107–28.

Huber, P.J. (1981). *Robust statistics.* New York: John Wiley.

Li, H., Rosenthal, R., & Rubin, D.B. (1996). Reliability of measurement in psychology: from Spearman–Brown to maximal reliability. *Psychological Methods*, 1, 98–107.

Milmoe, S., Novey, M.S., Kagan, J., & Rosenthal, R. (1968). *The mother's voice: postdictor of aspects of her baby's behavior. Proceedings of the 76th Annual Convention of APA*, pp. 463–464.

Milmoe, S., Rosenthal, R., Blane, H. T., Chafetz, M. E., & Wolf, I. (1967). The doctor's voice: postdictor of successful referral of alcoholic patients. *Journal of Abnormal Psychology*, 72, 78–84.

Mosteller, F. & Rourke R.E.K. (1973). *Sturdy statistics.* Reading, MA: Addison–Wesley.

Mosteller, F. & Tukey, J.W. (1977). *Data analysis and regression.* Reading, MA: Addison–Wesley.

Nasby, W., Hayden, B., & DePaulo, B.M. (1980). Attributional bias among aggressive boys to interpret unambiguous social stimuli as displays of hostility. *Journal of Abnormal Psychology,* **89**, 459–68.

Puccinelli, N.M., Tickle–Degnen, L., & Rosenthal, R. (2003). Effect of dyadic context on judgments of rapport: dyad task and partner presence, *Journal of Nonverbal Behavior,* **27**, 211–36.

Puccinelli, N.M., Tickle–Degnen, L., & Rosenthal, R. (2004). Effect of target position and target task on judge sensitivity to felt rapport. *Journal of Nonverbal Behavior,* **28**, 211–20.

Puccinelli, N.M., Tickle–Degnen, L., & Rosenthal, R. (2005). *Stage left, stage right? Position effects on perception of an agent.* Manuscript submitted for publication.

Rogers, P.L., Scherer, K.R., & Rosenthal, R. (1971). Content-filtering human speech: a simple electronic system. *Behavior Research Methods and Instrumentation,* **3**, 16–18.

Rosenthal, R. (1966). *Experimenter effects in behavioral research.* New York: Appleton–Century–Crofts.

Rosenthal, R. (1967). Covert communication in the psychological experiment. *Psychological Bulletin,* **67**, 356–67.

Rosenthal, R. (1969). Interpersonal expectations. In *Artifact in behavioral research* (ed. R. Rosenthal & R.L. Rosnow), pp. 181–277. New York: Academic Press.

Rosenthal, R. (1973). Estimating effective reliabilities in studies that employ judges' ratings. *Journal of Clinical Psychology,* **29**, 342–5.

Rosenthal, R. (1974). *On the social psychology of the self-fulfilling prophecy: further evidence for Pygmalion effects and their mediating mechanisms, Module 53.* New York: MSS Modular Publications.

Rosenthal, R. (1976). *Experimenter effects in behavioral research* (enlarged edn). New York: Irvington Publishers.

Rosenthal, R. (ed.) (1979). *Skill in nonverbal communication: individual differences.* Cambridge, MA: Oelgeschlager, Gunn and Hain.

Rosenthal, R. (1982). Conducting judgment studies. In *Handbook of methods in nonverbal behavior research* (ed. K.R. Scherer & P. Ekman), pp. 287–361. New York: Cambridge University Press.

Rosenthal, R. (1985). From unconscious experimenter bias to teacher expectancy effects. In *Teacher expectancies* (ed. J.B. Dusek, V.C. Hall, & W.J. Meyer). Hillsdale, NJ: Erlbaum.

Rosenthal, R. (1987). *Judgment studies: design, analysis, and meta-analysis.* New York: Cambridge University Press.

Rosenthal, R. (1991). Some indices of the reliability of peer review. *The Behavioral and Brain Sciences,* **14**, 160–1.

Rosenthal, R. (2002a). Covert communication in classrooms, clinics, courtrooms, and cubicles. *American Psychologist,* **57**, 838–49.

Rosenthal, R. (2002b). The Pygmalion effect and its mediating mechanisms. In *Improving academic achievement* (ed. J. Aronson), pp. 25–36. New York: Academic Press.

Rosenthal, R. (2003). Covert communication in laboratories, classrooms, and the truly real world. *Current Directions in Psychological Science,* **12**, 151–4.

Rosenthal, R. & DePaulo, B.M. (1979*a*). Sex differences in accommodation in nonverbal communication. In *Skill in nonverbal communication: individual differences* (ed. R. Rosenthal), pp. 68–103. Cambridge, MA: Oelgeschlager, Gunn and Hain.

Rosenthal, R. & DePaulo, B.M. (1979*b*). Sex differences in eavesdropping on nonverbal cues. *Journal of Personality and Social Psychology*, 37, 273–85.

Rosenthal, R. & Jacobson, L. (1968). *Pygmalion in the classroom: teacher expectation and pupils' intellectual development.* New York: Holt, Rinehart & Winston.

Rosenthal, R. & Rosnow, R.L. (1975*a*). *A primer of methods for the behavioral sciences.* New York: John Wiley.

Rosenthal, R. & Rosnow, R.L. (1975*b*). *The volunteer subject.* New York: Wiley–Interscience.

Rosenthal, R. & Rosnow, R.L. (1991). *Essentials of behavioral research: methods and data analysis* (2nd edn). New York: McGraw–Hill.

Rosenthal, R. & Rubin, D.B. (1978). Interpersonal expectancy effects: the first 345 studies. *The Behavioral and Brain Sciences*, 3, 377–86.

Rosenthal R. & Rubin, D.B. (1979). A note on percent variance explained as a measure of the importance of effects. *Journal of Applied Social Psychology*, 9, 395–6.

Rosenthal, R. & Rubin, D.B. (1982). A simple, general purpose display of magnitude of experimental effect. *Journal of Educational Psychology*, 74, 166–9.

Rosenthal, R. & Rubin, D.B. (2003). $r_{equivalent}$: a simple effect size indicator. *Psychological Methods*, 8, 492–6.

Rosenthal, R., Blanck, P.D., & Vannicelli, M. (1984). Speaking to and about patients: predicting therapists' tone of voice. *Journal of Consulting and Clinical Psycology*, 52, 679–86.

Rosenthal, R., Hall, J.A., DiMatteo, M.R., Rogers, P.L., & Archer, D. (1979). *Sensitivity to nonverbal communication: The PONS test.* Baltimore, MD: The Johns Hopkins University Press.

Rosenthal, R., Rosnow, R.L., & Rubin, D.B. (2000). *Contrasts and effect sizes in behavioral research: a correlational approach.* New York: Cambridge University Press.

Scherer, K.R. (1970). *Non-verbale Kommunikation.* Hamburg: Helmut Buske Verlag.

Scherer, K.R. (1971). Randomized-splicing: a note on a simple technique for masking speech content. *Journal of Experimental Research in Personality*, 5, 155–9.

Scherer, K.R.(1978). Personality inference from voice quality: the loud voice of extraversion. *European Journal of Social Psychology*, 8, 467–87.

Scherer, K.R. (1979*a*). Acoustic concomitants of emotional dimensions: judging affect from synthesized tone sequences. In *Nonverbal communication: readings with commentary* (2nd edn) (ed. S. Weitz), pp. 249–53. New York: Oxford University Press.

Scherer, K.R. (1979*b*). Voice and speech correlates of perceived social influence in simulated juries. In *Language and social psychology* (ed. H. Giles and R. St.Clair), pp. 88–120. Oxford: Basil Blackwell.

Scherer, K.R. (1982). Methods of research on vocal communication: paradigms and parameters. In *Handbook of methods in nonverbal behavior research* (ed. K.R. Scherer and P. Ekman), pp. 136–98. New York: Cambridge University Press.

Scherer, K.R. & Oshinsky, J.S. (1977). Cue utilization in emotion attribution from auditory stimuli. *Motivation and Emotion*, 1, 331–46.

Scherer, K.R., Koivumaki, J.H., & Rosenthal, R. (1972). Minimal cues in the vocal communication of affect: judging emotions from content-masked speech. *Journal of Psycholinguistic Research*, 1, 269–85.

Scherer, K.R., Scherer, U., Hall, J.A., & Rosenthal, R. (1977). Differential attribution of personality based on multi-channel presentation of verbal and nonverbal cues. *Psychological Research*, 39, 221–47.

Spearman, C. (1910). Correlation calculated from faulty data. *British Journal of Psychology*, 3, 171–95.

Tukey, J.W. (1977). *Exploratory data analysis*. Reading, MA: Addison–Wesley.

Uno, Y., Koivumaki, J.H., & Rosenthal, R. (1972). Unintended experimenter behavior as evaluated by Japanese and American observers. *Journal of Social Psychology*, 88, 91–106.

Weitz, S. (1979). Commentary. In *Skill in nonverbal communication: individual differences* (ed. R. Rosenthal), pp. 28–30. Cambridge, MA: Oelgeschlager, Gunn and Hain.

Westen, D. & Rosenthal, R. (2003). Quantifying construct validity: two simple measures. *Journal of Personality and Social Psychology*, 84, 608–18.

Wilkinson, L. & Task Force on Statistical Inference (1999). Statistical methods in psychology journals: guidelines and explanations. *American Psychologist*, 54, 594–604.

Zuckerman, M. & Larrance, D.T. (1979). Individual differences in perceived encoding and decoding abilities. In *Skill in nonverbal communication: individual differences* (ed. R. Rosenthal), pp. 171–203. Cambridge, MA: Oelgeschlager, Gunn and Hain.

Appendix

List of equations

$$R_{SB} = \frac{nr}{1 + (n-1)r} \tag{1}$$

$$\left(\frac{A}{A+D}\right)100 \tag{2}$$

$$kappa = \frac{O-E}{N-E} \tag{3}$$

$$R_{anova} = \frac{MS\ encoders - MS\ residual}{MS\ encoders} \tag{4}$$

$$r_{anova} = \frac{MS\ encoders - MS\ residual}{MS\ encoders + (n-1)\ MS\ residual} \tag{5}$$

$$\alpha = \left(\frac{n}{n-1}\right)\left(\frac{S^2_{total} - \Sigma S^2_{judge}}{S^2_{total}}\right) \tag{6}$$

$$theta = \frac{n}{n-1}\left(\frac{L-1}{L}\right) \tag{7}$$

$$r = \frac{R_{SB}}{n + R_{SB} - nR_{SB}} \tag{8}$$

$$EC = C_i\left(\frac{1 - r_i}{r_i}\right) \tag{9}$$

$$r_{composite} = r_{individual} \times F \tag{10}$$

$$F = \sqrt{\frac{n}{1 + \bar{r}(n-1)}} \tag{11}$$

$$r_{individual} = \frac{r_{composite}}{F} \tag{12}$$

$$g = \frac{\bar{r}_{intra} - \bar{r}_{inter}}{S_{aggregated}} \tag{13}$$

$$rmr = \frac{\bar{r}_{intra} - \bar{r}_{inter}}{(\bar{r}_{intra} + \bar{r}_{inter})/2} \tag{14}$$

RESEARCH APPLICATIONS IN NONVERBAL BEHAVIOR

CHAPTER 6

NONVERBAL BEHAVIOR AND INTERPERSONAL SENSITIVITY

JUDITH A. HALL, FRANK J. BERNIERI, AND DANA R. CARNEY

Although questions about how people respond to others' nonverbal cues have always been central to the study of nonverbal communication, the study of individual differences in accuracy of nonverbal cue processing, or interpersonal sensitivity, is a more recent endeavor. This chapter focuses on assessment of individual differences, emphasizing the major paradigms and instruments for assessing accuracy of nonverbal cue processing, and discussing characteristics of the stimuli and judgment methodologies (e.g. what state or trait is being judged, who is being judged, what cue channels are available, whether the cues are posed or spontaneous, whether judgment is done in live interaction or from standard stimuli, what judgment format is used, what criteria and methods are used for scoring). Relative advantages of different approaches are discussed in terms of psychometric qualities, validity, and utility.

Introduction

Interpersonal sensitivity is a complex concept that is subject to many definitions and many methods of measurement. This chapter describes approaches to the measurement of accuracy in processing interpersonal, mostly nonverbal, cues. By 'cues' we mean perceptible behaviors, such as facial expressions and tones of voice, that have the capacity to give insight into the expressor's attributes or condition. We define interpersonal sensitivity as accuracy in judging the meanings of cues given off by expressors, as well as accuracy in noticing or recalling cues. We discuss methods of measuring such accuracy at both the group level (i.e. mean level of accuracy for a particular social group or in a particular experimental condition) and at the level of the individual test taker (i.e. for assessing individual differences).

One could argue that a proper definition of interpersonal sensitivity would also include behavior that is emitted in response to another's cues, on the grounds that such responses are crucial to truly sensitive interpersonal interaction (Bernieri 2001). For example, empathy defined as the ability to commiserate effectively with a sad friend can be seen as a manifestation of interpersonal sensitivity. However, such a broad definition of the construct cannot be handled in the space allowed. This chapter is limited to the study of the receptive aspect of interpersonal sensitivity. In this research, perceivers make judgments about cues or about people whose cues they see and/or hear, and such judgments are then scored for accuracy.

In daily life, we are constantly processing and evaluating cues that are conveyed by others through the face, body, and voice or embodied in their appearance, and we can do so with surprising accuracy based on fairly small amounts of information (e.g. Ambady & Gray 2002; Ambady *et al.* 2001; Carney *et al.* 2004; Lippa & Dietz 2000). Unless we are very distracted, it is likely that we are continuously monitoring and processing cues emanating from the people around us, but even when we are distracted or not consciously attending, cues in the periphery of our attention are often processed unconsciously. Research shows that when people are subliminally shown different facial expressions, their behavior varies in keeping with the affective connotations of the primed cues (Murphy & Zajonc 1993). Thus, cues of which people have no awareness appear to be processed accurately. Strangers are capable of making personality judgments of each other at levels greater than chance within minutes of laying eyes on each other for the first time and without hearing each other say anything (Marcus & Leatherwood 1998). Infants respond to nonverbal cues in ways that suggest at least rudimentary comprehension, for example by noticing when the affective tone is similar or different between visual and auditory modalities (Phillips *et al.* 1990). As further evidence for infants' attunement to nonverbal cues, they mimic adults' facial expressions shortly after birth (Meltzoff & Moore 1977) and show categorical perception of faces (Bornstein & Arterberry 2003).

Animals, of course, also respond to cues conveyed by each other and by human beings. The communication of information on sex, age, health, vulnerability, attractiveness, mating readiness, affiliation and reconciliation, territoriality, dominance, and threat, conveyed by static cues such as size and by dynamic cues such as facial expressions, vocalizations, or body movements, is crucial to social life throughout the animal kingdom (de Waal 2001). The biological value of being able to make such discriminations is obvious, as life, death, and reproductive success may hang in the balance (McArthur & Baron 1983). One can hardly imagine a functional social order in which the members are not supremely sensitive to information of this sort.

Lest one assume that the cues animals can respond to are all simple, gross, or wired in, one needs only talk to dog trainers and owners to hear many accounts of their dogs' (sometimes excessive) sensitivity to each other and to humans. In social psychology, the most famous demonstration of the subtlety of nonverbal cue processing by an animal was the horse, Clever Hans. In the early 1900s in Berlin, Clever Hans attracted a wide following for his apparent ability to count, solve mathematical problems, and answer apparently any question to which he could answer by tapping his hoof the appropriate number of times, even if his owner was not the questioner and even if the questioner did not know the answer (see Spitz 1997 for an excellent account). Hans' abilities were so prodigious that many careful observers, including his owner, were persuaded that he possessed conceptual thinking.

Under attack as a fraud, Hans' owner agreed to let a commission of experts (including experimental psychologists) conduct an investigation. Their experiments led to the conclusion that Hans was not a fraud, and that he was indeed a remarkable horse. However, what made him remarkable was not that he could solve mathematical problems (he could not), but rather that he combined uncanny sensitivity to cues with a quick intelligence for learning reward contingencies. Hans could perceive changes in the questioner's (or audience member's) face, head, eyes, posture, and respiration that were often not visible to the naked human eye, and he learned how to respond to them in ways that earned him food snacks and approval. Thus, he knew that he would be rewarded if he started tapping after hearing a question and then stopped when the questioner, or someone in the audience who knew the answer, inadvertently cued him by moving his or her head by as little as one millimeter, or by some other tiny cue. The relevance of the Clever Hans phenomenon to the development of interpersonal sensitivity in human beings and to our appreciation of the ubiquity of nonverbal cue processing in everyday life cannot be overstated.

But how do we measure something as intangible as our sensitivity to each other? In Clever Hans' case, experimentation determined that he was sensitive, indeed very sensitive. But *how* sensitive? How do we put numbers on such accuracy? And how do we even define what it is we are interested in?

Overview of chapter

In this chapter, we deal both conceptually and practically with methodologies for measuring interpersonal sensitivity. On the conceptual side, we discuss definitional and methodological issues that are generic to this area of research, such as the definition of interpersonal sensitivity and the determination of scoring criteria. On the practical side, we describe specific instruments, including their psychometric characteristics, validity (as much as space permits), and utility. We describe measurement approaches in terms of characteristics of the stimuli and judgment methodologies, including what state or trait is being judged, who is being judged, what cue channels are available, whether the cues are posed or spontaneous, whether judgment is done live or from standard stimuli, what judgment format is used, what operational criteria are used for scoring, and what techniques are used for scoring accuracy.

Conceptual issues

Sensitivity to what?

It takes only a little thought to recognize that sensitivity involves numerous processes and cues that vary along multiple dimensions (Bernieri 2001; Hall & Bernieri 2001). Such variations include:

- the depth of cue processing that one engages in (attentional versus inferential);
- the degree of awareness of cue processing (not conscious versus conscious);
- stimulus dynamism (static, such as physiognomic; semi-static, such as clothing style; or dynamic, such as hand gestures);
- stimulus channel (such as face versus voice);
- spontaneity of encoding (posed versus spontaneous);
- construct domain (such as states versus traits);
- what specific construct is being measured (such as different specific emotions).

It is important to state at the outset that distinctions such as given in these examples are oversimplifications. Awareness, for example, is a continuum, not a dichotomy, and the same is true for stimulus dynamism (a given cue may appear static only because it does not change rapidly enough for the change to be evident in short behavioral samples). Below we discuss these dimensions, as well as various qualifications, in broad terms, leaving the specifics of measurement to a later section.

Depth of processing

As the Clever Hans example indicated, one kind of sensitivity is simply noticing. This *attentional accuracy* (Hall *et al.* 2001), which can apply to either behavior or appearance, is typically the first step in making accurate interpretations of the meanings or significance of cues. Interpretation can occur right away ('From the way she is looking at me, I can tell she knows I'm lying!'). Sometimes, however, what is noticed takes on significance at a later date: 'Oh, you didn't get the job. That's why you were so quiet at breakfast' or 'Now that I think of it, I realize my boss doesn't talk to me as much as he used to'. Sometimes it's the noticing itself that matters, rather than a higher order interpretation: 'I've noticed that my friend has pierced ears, so I will buy her that kind of earring' or 'Remember Jane? She's the one who smiles all the time'.

Though the concept of noticing cues appears to be very simple, conceptually one can distinguish between paying attention, noticing, and recalling cues. These three processes, listed in the order of likely occurrence in practice, are not synonymous. A person may be paying attention but might still miss cues, or may notice cues but not remember them later (or may remember them incorrectly). The field of eyewitness testimony demonstrates how fallible the recall of behavior that is seen and heard can be (Fruzzetti *et al.* 1992).

In contrast to attentional accuracy, the term *inferential accuracy* refers to judgments made about the meaning or significance of cues (Hall *et al.* 2001). Empirically, almost all research on interpersonal sensitivity, at both the group and individual level, has been based on inferential accuracy. The range of different things about which people can draw inferences will be discussed later.

Awareness of processing

In the example of a priming experiment in which expressive cues are presented subliminally, one can be sure that the cues were processed without conscious awareness. It is common to read that the processing of others' nonverbal cues is, by nature, tacit and out of awareness (e.g. Ambady & Gray 2002; Gilbert & Krull 1988). Edward Sapir famously referred to nonverbal communication as 'an elaborate secret code that is written no where, known by none, and used by all' (Sapir 1949). In other words, people are very skillful in their use and interpretation of nonverbal cues, but they have little or no explicit insight into cue usages and meanings (e.g. Grahe & Bernieri 2002).

However, in daily life we process cues with different *degrees* of awareness, from unaware to completely aware. Sometimes people are aware that they are processing specific cues: 'I could tell from the tears in his eyes that my husband was very moved by the movie'. Other times, they are aware that they are processing cues, but they are not very aware of the specific cues they are using: 'I don't know why, but I was sure she was telling the truth'. Of course, even if we are very deliberate about noticing and are very sure of what we think we saw or what cues we think we relied on, we might still be wrong. People might have judgment policies (rules for decoding meaning; Bernieri 2001) that they consciously apply, but the judgment policies may be wrong and, therefore, their judgments will be wrong (Hall and Braunwald 1981). Or, the judgment policy may be wrong but their judgments wind up being generally correct because the erroneous cue happens to covary with a cue that is valid for the judgment in question.

In daily life, as well as in the research laboratory, it is very difficult to know how aware people are of the process of judging cues. Research on self-fulfilling prophecies generally assumes that neither party in an interaction is aware of the biasing cues being conveyed and responded to (Rosenthal 1976; Rosenthal & Rubin 1978; Snyder *et al.* 1977) and, of course, any study using subliminally presented stimuli demonstrates unconscious processing. In the tradition of measuring sensitivity to cues (the subject of this chapter), the problem of determining awareness is usually skirted by making perceivers fully aware that they are judging cues and then focusing on accuracy of judgment rather than the process of judgment. Thus, whether perceivers use an implicit or explicit process is not of concern to the researcher.

But people do undoubtedly possess many beliefs about nonverbal communication (e.g. Carney *et al.* (2005); Rosip & Hall 2004) and these beliefs, independent of their application in the judgment of actual nonverbal stimuli, can be considered an explicit kind of interpersonal sensitivity so long as the investigator can score them for accuracy. An example of a correct belief would be that a facial expression of genuine enjoyment is likely to involve the muscles at the outer corners of the mouth and eyes (Ekman *et al.* 1990). (Of course, one could also have an implicit understanding of such a relation that one could apply in practice even if one could not articulate it explicitly.) Explicitly held beliefs about the meanings of nonverbal cues may certainly contribute to the accurate processing of nonverbal cues. To what extent such explicit knowledge contributes to accurate judgment of others is an empirical question about which not much is known at present (Rosip & Hall 2004). One study that begins to explore this general issue distinguished between cues that were abstract, subjective, and molar (e.g. apparent dominant behavior, nervousness) and cues that were more concrete, objective, and molecular (e.g. proximity, eye contact) in determining judgments of dyad rapport based on exposure to short excerpts of interaction (Grahe & Bernieri 2002). Judgments of rapport were influenced equally by both categories of cues. However, whereas perceivers were generally aware of how their judgments were influenced by abstract cues, they were much less aware of how the concrete, objective, molecular cues affected their judgments.

Stimulus characteristics

The question of what form the cues presented to perceivers should take is a complex one. In principle, one could develop a typology of interpersonal sensitivity measurements that represents the crossing of many factors including those already mentioned and those still to be discussed. A given method would represent a cell in this many-celled matrix. Here, we will be content with listing different conceptual factors.

1.   Cue dynamism

Here again, a continuum is present but, pragmatically, one can talk about different categories of dynamism. Some cues are intrinsically static, at least within reasonable time frames, height being an example. Others can vary gradually over time (weight, hair length while it grows), while others that seem intrinsically static can actually change abruptly with surgical or cosmetic intervention (body shape, facial features, haircuts). Some cues are relatively static within an interaction (seated distance from an inter-action partner), while others are likely to change very often (mouth or hand movements). Sometimes 'static' versus 'dynamic' is artificially defined by varying how long the perceiver is allowed to view the stimulus. A still photograph isolated from the ongoing behavioral stream is thus made into an artificially static stimulus, or posture may seem static only because the video clips are short and the person's posture did not change during the time allowed.

2.   Channels

The concept of channel is useful heuristically, as a way of dividing up the sources of nonverbal information, but its specific definition may vary. Thus, 'face' may be a convenient channel for one researcher but regions of the face may be conceptualized as different channels by another researcher. Commonly discussed channels are facial expressions, eye behavior, head movements, upper body movements, lower body movements, hand/arm movements, posture, proxemic variables, touch (self and other), vocal behavior, face or body physiognomy, hair and make-up, and clothing and accessories (Knapp & Hall 2005). Within each of these categories, multiple sub-categories can be identified.

The distinction between the verbal and nonverbal behavior channels, seemingly an easy one, can actually be unclear. Hand emblems such as the A–OK sign or the 'gun-to-temple' gesture in U.S. culture (Ekman & Friesen 1972) have such distinct verbal translations that they might almost be considered verbal, even though technically they are not. Manual sign language systems are generally considered so far toward the linguistic end of the continuum that nonverbal communication researchers typically do not study them. Fluid hand movements emitted during speech are closely tied to the language encoding process (McNeill 1985). Behaviors such as interruptions and back-channel responses (e.g. 'mm-hmm', 'yeah', 'I see') are often considered to be functionally nonverbal because their significance does not depend on the linguistic content per se.

Pragmatically, researchers of interpersonal sensitivity sometimes keep the verbal and nonverbal channels integrated, so that perceivers are exposed to both at once (e.g. Costanzo & Archer 1989; Ickes 2001; Vogt & Colvin 2003), and sometimes they separate them (e.g. silent video, content-masked speech, transcript) (Gesn & Ickes 1999; Murphy et al. 2003; Rosenthal et al. 1979; Scherer et al. 1977).

3.   Spontaneity

Cues to be noticed or judged may vary in how spontaneously or deliberately they occur. This too is a continuum, with totally spontaneous, unrehearsed, and unplanned behavior at one end (e.g. facial expressions one doesn't even know one is making) and completely deliberate, planned, or posed behavior at the other (e.g. putting on a display of good cheer when you actually feel sad, displaying hand emblems such as the 'A–OK' sign, deliberately looking at your watch to indicate to someone that you need to leave). This dimension corresponds roughly to the conscious–unconscious distinction made earlier with respect to the perceiver's awareness of the nonverbal perception process. There has been debate over whether one can ever be sure that expressions are unplanned or unintended (Fridlund 1997).

4. Construct domain

Bernieri (2001) identified numerous categories of meaning about which a perceiver can be interpersonally sensitive. Inferences can be about *states* or *traits* (another distinction that has an underlying continuum). Most commonly studied is sensitivity to *states* and, within this, affective states have received the most attention. These can be measured directly (is the person showing disgust on his face?) or indirectly (is the person using the kind of cues she would use if she was talking about her divorce/thanking someone/ talking to a lost child?). Another state commonly studied is truth versus falsehood, which also can be inquired about directly (is she lying?) or indirectly (does this person make me feel uncomfortable?).

Many other states can, of course, be the objects of sensitivity, though affect and deception have received the most research attention. We often make judgments about others' thoughts, intentions, needs, physical states, and likely future behavior from observing their outwardly expressed behavior (Bernieri 2001).

The domain of *traits* that may be judged from nonverbal cues is also large. In this category, ability to judge personality traits has been studied most often. Other individual differences that people judge in daily life include intelligence, specific competencies, status or dominance, ethnicity, prejudice, culture, sexual orientation, mental health, and social adjustment.

As alluded to above, when we introduced the concept of 'attentional accuracy', another kind of sensitivity is memory for (relatedly, noticing or attending to) cues. Such cues can be static (e.g. appearance; Horgan *et al.* 2004) or dynamic (e.g. nonverbal behavior; Hall & Murphy 2004).

Table 6.1 shows (not exhaustively) specific interpersonal sensitivity constructs that have been measured, with illustrative studies cited for each.

What is the accuracy criterion?

In daily life, when we make the kinds of judgments listed above, sometimes we find out whether the judgments are right or wrong: 'I can't believe I fell for his lies' or 'You're 21? You look so much younger'. But much of the time, we never know for sure. However, researchers who set out to measure accuracy *must* know or else they cannot score their instruments. Deciding what is the 'right answer' to an interpersonal sensitivity question has been called the criterion problem (Archer *et al.* 2001; Bernieri 2001; Kenny 1994; Rosenthal *et al.* 1979).

Kenny (1994) categorized criteria used in sensitivity research as self-report, consensus, expert judgments, behavioral observations, and operational criteria. Establishing a

Table 6.1 Constructs assessed in interpersonal sensitivity research

Construct	Illustrative research
Situationally determined affect	Costanzo & Archer 1989; Rosenthal *et al.* 1979
Emotions	Matsumoto *et al.* 2000; Nowicki & Duke 1994
Relationships	Barnes & Sternberg 1989; Costanzo & Archer 1989
Love	Aloni & Bernieri 2004
Rapport	Bernieri *et al.* 1996
Deception	Ekman & O'Sullivan 1991; deTurck 1991
Personality	Blackman 2002; Borkenau & Liebler 1995
Status	Barnes & Sternberg 1989; Schmid Mast & Hall 2004
Others' interpersonal sensitivity	Carney & Harrigan 2003
Intelligence	Murphy *et al.* 2003; Reynolds & Gifford 2001
Thoughts and feelings	Ickes 2001; Thomas & Fletcher 2003
Prejudice	Carney 2004; Rollman 1978; Richeson & Shelton 2005
Sexual orientation	Ambady *et al.* 1999
Ethnic group	Allport & Kramer 1946; Dorfman *et al.* 1971
Recall of appearance	Horgan *et al.* 2004
Recall of nonverbal behavior	Hall *et al.* 2001; Hall & Murphy 2004
Explicit knowledge of nonverbal cues	Rosip & Hall 2004; Vrij & Semin 1996
Explicit knowledge of gender differences	Hall & Carter 1999; Swim 1994

valid criterion can be a difficult epistemological enterprise because often there is not an unimpeachable 'gold standard'. We will mention some of these difficulties as we proceed. The summary below is brief and the reader should consult the sources named above for an expanded discussion.

Self-report

Self-report, or what the target (i.e. the person being judged) says about him/herself, is mostly used when the target is deemed to have valid knowledge about the state, trait, or characteristic in question. Examples of each of these would be 'my current mood', 'my extraversion', and 'my age'. Sometimes such self-reports are measured using well-validated instruments (such as for measuring personality). Setting aside the possibility that the target would fabricate the answer, self-report criteria are fallible to the extent that the target may not actually know the correct answer. The tendency to engage in self-enhancing distortions is ubiquitous and may not always involve a cynical attempt to deceive (Colvin *et al.* 1995).

Consensus

Consensus, or what observers agree is the right answer, is often used as the criterion for labeling emotional expressions (e.g. Ekman *et al.* 1987; Zuckerman *et al.* 1975). Consensus judgments are fallible to the extent that observers share an erroneous judgment policy (association between the cue and its attributed meaning) even when they show high inter-observer reliability of judgment. For example, observers may agree, but erroneously, that if a woman speaks relatively loudly she is more likely to be addressing a woman than a man (Hall & Braunwald 1981).

The desirability of consensus as a criterion may depend on the nature of the construct being judged. If the construct is defined as something residing within the target person, observers' consensus may not be a good criterion. For example, physical pain exists within the target and is defined independently of what observers think. However, if the construct is socially defined (e.g. expressed hostility or politeness), consensus may be the most appropriate criterion.

Expert judgments

Expert judgments may be provided by respondents who are considered to have the best possible knowledge about the target's state or trait. For example, a clinical psychologist's opinion of a target's degree of psychoticism would likely be more trustworthy than the target's own opinion. Of course, such 'experts'(whether they be clinicians, teachers, supervisors, parents, or friends) can still be biased or ignorant.

Behavioral observations

Behavioral observations are especially relevant for sensitivity defined as attentional accuracy. Thus, trained coders or a computer might provide data on a target's length of gaze or average fundamental vocal frequency and this could then serve as the basis for determining whether perceivers are accurate in their recall of gaze or pitch. Trained coders can also be used to establish the criterion for perceivers' judgments of personality (Funder *et al.* 2000). The reliability and validity of such criteria are obviously relevant here (as is always the case, no matter what the criterion). If behavioral observations are highly impressionistic or inferential (e.g. if a group of naïve judges were to rate the friendliness of the targets), such a criterion might better be called consensus.

One important illustration of behavioral observation as criterion is the application of the Facial Action Coding System or FACS (Ekman *et al.* 2002). The FACS produces a detailed identification of what facial muscles have moved, in what combinations, and how much. By itself, the FACS is simply a descriptive system. However, when paired with empirical findings indicating what muscle activity is associated with what kind of emotional experience or intention, the FACS can be used to establish scoring criteria for expressions. For example, if a given configuration of facial movements is deemed, according to FACS research, to show 'disgust', then those movements are the criterion against which judgments of that expression are scored (Ekman & Rosenberg 1997; Ekman *et al.* 2002).

Behavioral observations have the appeal of being relatively concrete to define but they become problematic if the researcher wants to draw a higher-order inference about the behavior in question (Bernieri 2001). For example, it might be easy to count interruptions, but not easy to know whether interruptions mean dominance or simply active participation.

Operational criteria

Finally, operational criteria are used when some externally verifiable fact can be identified as the operational definition of the target's state or trait. If the researcher chooses when the target will lie or tell the truth, then the researcher's choice is the operational criterion to be used when scoring the accuracy of perceivers' lie–truth judgments. As other illustrations, Buck (1979) showed emotionally evocative pictures to the target and then asked perceivers to guess what pictures were being shown just from watching the target's face (thus, the pictures are the operational criterion). Costanzo and Archer (1989) arranged for a (real) boss and subordinate to interact and then asked perceivers to guess which person was the boss.

In early research, some experimenters created unexpected experiences for participants as a controlled method of producing specific emotional states. So, for example, having to cut the head off a dead rat was assumed to produce disgust and being told (falsely) that one's loved one had died was assumed to produce grief (Dunlap 1927; Landis 1924). The common technique of asking targets to deliberately pose the expression of certain emotions (Noller 1980, 2001; Nowicki & Duke 1994; Rosenthal *et al.* 1979) and then using the posed intention as the criterion, can also be included in this category. In the assessment of explicit cue knowledge (Rosip & Hall 2004), the scoring criterion is also operational in nature because it treats findings available in previous research as the 'gold standard' against which people's beliefs are compared and scored for accuracy.

Each of these criterion definitions has limitations, some of which we have identified. Each criterion definition is likely to have its own construct validity problems. Sometimes, researchers combine more than one of these criterion-setting methods in order to reduce error to a minimum. As examples, Vogt and Colvin's (2003) criteria for targets' personality included self-reports, parental reports, peer reports, and direct observation; and Scherer and Ceschi's (2000) criteria for targets' emotions included self-reports, independent observers, and behavioral measures. What to do when criteria conflict remains a problem. In practice, the best test of the validity of accuracy criteria may be whether the accuracy scores generated by a given method or instrument produce findings suggestive of construct validity.

Questions at the intersection of theory and method

We started with general observations about the nature of interpersonal sensitivity and then progressed toward empirical issues by discussing different kinds of criteria that can be used for determining accuracy. Now we move further into empirical territory by asking several questions that relate to actual research on interpersonal sensitivity. It is not our intention to review all, or even much, of what is known from this body of research. But it is essential to ask several fundamental questions about this research in order to set the stage for a description of specific methodologies.

Can cues be judged accurately?

If researchers could not obtain above-chance levels of accuracy with their measuring instruments, one could justifiably challenge the tests' adequacy. If, for example, perceivers trying to identify a 'fear' expression are systematically wrong in their judgments or are no more accurate than they would be if they were just guessing, one might question whether accuracy of judging 'fear' had adequately been tested. Therefore, most researchers look for overall accuracy at above-chance levels.

Numerous techniques can be applied to manipulate difficulty level and thereby achieve a desired overall level of accuracy. These include varying the amount of the stimulus the perceiver is exposed to (e.g. 2 seconds vs. 10 seconds); altering the wording of item alternatives on a multiple choice response to make discriminations easier or harder (e.g. a choice between 'happy' and 'fear' as opposed to 'surprise' and 'fear'); or manipulating signal clarity (e.g. high vs. low-intensity vocal expressions; Baum & Nowicki 1998). Sometimes, researchers calibrate their instruments to achieve a level of accuracy that is not merely better than chance but that falls at a level that optimizes variance in scores in order to create the best opportunity for detecting individual differences (Guilford 1954). For example, if the guessing level is 50%, then optimal accuracy is around 75% (Rosenthal *et al.* 1979; Rosip & Hall 2004).

Because investigators can exercise a great deal of control over the mean level of accuracy obtained on a given test (and also because the judged stimuli, judgment task, and scoring methods can be noncomparable between tests), interpretations of absolute levels of accuracy and comparisons of accuracy across different constructs or tests must be undertaken with great caution. To help researchers compare across studies, Rosenthal and Rubin (1989) developed an effect-size index for standardizing mean percentage accuracy across studies that differ in the number of response alternatives provided to perceivers.

Broadly speaking, perceivers have above-chance levels of accuracy, though the range is great. Judgments of deception are not much above the guessing level (Malone & DePaulo 2001), whereas accuracy in identifying prototypical facial expressions of emotion is often extremely high (e.g. Biehl *et al.* 1997; Ekman *et al.* 1987). Whether the overall level is 'too high' or 'too low' depends on the purposes of the research. It is important to note, however, that obtaining levels above chance is not necessarily required in order to have a valid test. When researchers cannot obtain above-chance levels it is important to ascertain whether the observed scores contain true-score variance or are due completely to random error. It is entirely possible for a measure to have a large true-score variance component even when the sample mean is below chance levels of accuracy. For example, imagine a Spanish reading comprehension test that is given to a sample of 100 people of whom only 10 or so know the language. By the same token, individual items on a test that fall below the chance level may still be valid items if they correlate with other items on the test. Such an item, though difficult for most people, is still likely to be judged correctly by good decoders (Rosenthal *et al.* 1979). Demonstrating the validity of such a test or item requires carrying out construct validity studies to show (for example) that the test or item correlates as predicted with other variables.

Are group effects worth studying?

Showing an adequate level of interpersonal sensitivity at the group level may be comforting to a researcher, but it does not answer the question of whether such sensitivity is an interesting social psychological variable. This question depends on whether sensitivity, as it is measured in research, is related to other real-world or experimentally manipulated group-level variables. This should not be considered a foregone conclusion. Perhaps interpersonal sensitivity in 'real life' does not vary with situational, task-specific, or group-based factors; or, perhaps the instruments that researchers have devised fail to capture that sensitivity even if such relations actually exist.

Research has, in fact, produced many group-level results—far too many to review here. Based on reviews and primary sources (e.g. Ambady et al. 2000, 2001; Ambady & Gray 2002; Baum & Nowicki 1998; Carney et al. 2004; Elfenbein & Ambady 2002; Hall 1978, 1984; Malone & DePaulo 2001; Rosenthal et al. 1979), it has been shown that accuracy varies with the channel being judged (e.g. face vs. voice), the length of stimulus exposure, the intensity of the cues being expressed, the specific construct being judged, the gender of perceivers and targets, the culture and ethnicity of perceivers and targets, perceivers' occupational characteristics, and perceivers' manipulated mood. This sampling of results indicates that interpersonal sensitivity is a meaningful social psychological construct.

Do individual differences exist?

Many researchers of interpersonal sensitivity are interested in questions relating to individual differences, such as where such differences come from and their cognitive, social, and personal correlates. Therefore it is crucial to demonstrate that research instruments and methods are capable of detecting individual differences. This question takes us to questions about the psychometric adequacy of measurement approaches, because individual differences that are not associated with reliable measurement are due to random error (noise) and are therefore not true individual differences. Also related to the question of reliability is the question of how intercorrelated different tests are. We address both of these questions in this section.

Reliability

One index of true individual difference variance is retest reliability: do test takers maintain their relative rank compared to each other when tested again? Established tests report adequate retest reliability, with median retest correlations of 0.69 across six samples taking the PONS test (Rosenthal et al. 1979), and retest correlations of 0.80 for the CARAT (Buck 1976), 0.70 for the IPT (Costanzo & Archer 1989), 0.80 and above for the DANVA (Nowicki & Duke 2001), and 0.88 for an omnibus paper-and-pencil test of nonverbal cue knowledge (Rosip & Hall 2004). These figures indicate that there is considerable stability in measured interpersonal sensitivity. (The full names of tests and details on individual tests are given at the end of the chapter).

Another index of reliability is internal consistency, which is a joint function of the strength of inter-item correlations and the number of items on the test. The widely used PONS test (Rosenthal et al. 1979) has good internal consistency (KR-20 = 0.86), but this good reliability is achieved by having a large number of items on the test (220 to be exact) that in fact have an average inter-item correlation of only about 0.03. Therefore, though the full-length test has good internal consistency, the short forms of the PONS (such as the 40-item face and body test, or the 40-item voice test), as well as several other tests, including the IPT (Costanzo & Archer 1989), have poor internal consistency—typically, Cronbach's alphas of less than 0.40 and, sometimes, much less (see review in Hall 2001). On the other hand, some tests, including the DANVA (Nowicki & Duke 1994) and the JACBART (Matsumoto *et al.* 2000), have internal consistency (alpha) in the 0.70–0.80 range. Rosip and Hall's (2004) test of explicit nonverbal cue knowledge also has internal consistency in this range.

It is interesting that nonverbal decoding tests (that is, tests involving the judgment of cues emitted by targets) with the best internal consistency tend to be those testing a single content domain, namely emotions. Decoding tests with weak inter-item correlations (e.g. PONS and IPT) cover a much broader domain of content, in that the test taker must judge cues that are associated with a range of affective, role, and situational circumstances.

In principle, the problem of weak inter-item correlations in sensitivity instruments can be rectified as long as the inter-item correlations are greater than zero and there is a sufficient number of items (as on the full-length PONS test for which internal consistency is acceptable). Unfortunately, however, real-world constraints can limit the realization of psychometric goals. The full-length PONS test is often foregone in exchange for shorter but less reliable forms of the test, and some tests with questionable internal consistency are already rather long (e.g. the full-length IPT test). Because it is typically not feasible in practice to use extremely long tests, low internal consistency may remain an issue.

Another intriguing possibility that sensitivity researchers and theoreticians may need to deal with is that the various components, skills, and competencies that constitute global sensitivity—sometimes even as they exist within a single instrument such as the IPT or PONS—are simply orthogonal to one another. To the extent that this is true, the internal consistency of a single test instrument becomes less relevant, as will be discussed below.

Intercorrelations among tests

Repeatedly, correlations between different interpersonal sensitivity tests have been found to be very low or even close to zero (reviewed by Bernieri 2001; Colvin & Bundick 2001; Hall 2001). Furthermore, analysis of the factor structure of the PONS test suggested that the major channels of face, body, and voice are relatively orthogonal on that test (Rosenthal *et al.* 1979). At present, it is not known whether this pattern of low intercorrelations stems from weak psychometric qualities of the instruments (i.e. weak internal consistency) or reflects the true structure of the interpersonal sensitivity domain. It is quite possible that the domain of interpersonal sensitivity consists of several, perhaps many, discrete skills that are not well predicted one from another, as proposed by one prescient writer in the early days of interpersonal sensitivity research (Buck 1976). Thus, ability to detect lies may be unrelated to ability to judge emotion in the voice, and these may both be independent of many other abilities (e.g. to judge the kind of relationship two people have, or to judge someone's personality traits).

Alternatively, there may exist a structure to the sensitivity domain that can only be detected with larger test batteries and latent variable analysis. Possible structures could be based on channels, the types of constructs being judged (e.g. state vs. trait), the breadth or specificity of test content, specific design methodologies or scoring systems, and so forth. (For discussion of the structure of the emotional intelligence construct, see Mayer *et al.* 2003 and Roberts *et al.* 2001.)

Are poor internal consistency and poor between-test correlations necessarily bad?

As we have noted, the domain of interpersonal sensitivity may include quasi-independent discrete variables that collectively define the higher-order construct. One might think of either whole tests or items within tests in this way. To think in this manner is analogous to seeing income, education, and occupational prestige as collectively defining socioeconomic status (Bollen & Lennox 1991). Socioeconomic status is the empirical consequence of one's standing on these indices rather than being a latent construct of which each index is simply an indicator. Thus, the fact that income, education, and occupational prestige are not strongly intercorrelated would not lead one to conclude that these variables are flawed indicators of the latent construct or that one had created a psychometrically bad scale of socioeconomic status. Rather, socioeconomic status is *defined* by the component variables, which might even have a compensatory relation to each other (e.g. high income may compensate for less education).

Applying the same logic to the case of interpersonal sensitivity, one could argue that tests that are more omnibus in their content may actually gain validity by including items that represent a number of different skills. The IPT (Costanzo & Archer 1989), for example, includes items relating to deception, kinship, competition, status, and intimacy. On the other hand, a test that includes items from distinct meaning domains could have attenuated correlations with external variables if not all of the meaning domains actually bear a relation to those variables. For example, total score on a test that includes items on lie detection as well as role relations might correlate weakly with success as a police interrogator if only the lie-detection component of skill is relevant to police interrogation skills. Thus, there may be both good and bad aspects to tests with diverse content.

Do individual differences matter?

Good reliability does not necessarily mean that what is measured is meaningful or useful. Conversely, as discussed above, poor internal consistency does not necessarily mean that nothing meaningful or useful is being measured. To ask whether something meaningful is being measured is to ask about construct validity. Fortunately, tests of interpersonal sensitivity have many correlates that both support the claim that interpersonal sensitivity is being measured and reveal a great deal about the place of interpersonal sensitivity in the daily lives of children and adults. This chapter is too short to do justice to this literature, but a brief summary based on reviews as well as primary sources will demonstrate how rich the network of findings is (e.g. Ambady *et al.* 2001; Archer *et al.* 2001; Bernieri 1991; Carney & Harrigan 2003; Costanzo & Archer 1989; DiMatteo *et al.* 1979; Funder & Harris 1986; Hall 1998 (Table 7–4); Hall & Carter 1999; Hall *et al.* 1997, 2000; Knapp & Hall 2002; Nowicki & Duke 2001; Rosenthal *et al.* 1979). We limit this summary to research based on decoding tests (i.e. inferential accuracy) because nearly all research is on that topic.

Better interpersonal sensitivity, as measured with inferential tests, has been found to be associated with increasing age through childhood; better mental health; more well adjusted personality; less shyness and social anxiety; more dominant personality; higher self-esteem; higher social competence based on sociometric ratings, as well as peer, teacher, and parent ratings; higher ratings of sensitivity by peers or supervisors; better ability to judge a friend's interpersonal sensitivity; more democratic attitudes among teachers; more social inclusion needs; more cognitive complexity; more self-monitoring; more internal locus of control; more popularity; less aggression; higher academic achievement (when test takers are children); better supervisor ratings of job performance (when test takers are clinicians, foreign service officers, and teachers); more satisfaction among medical patients (when test takers are the patients' physicians); quicker ability to learn in a dyadic teaching situation; possession of more accurate knowledge of differences between men's and women's behavior; higher reports of marital satisfaction; and being rated by peers as more likeable, honest, and open, and less hostile and manipulative. However, self-assessment of one's own sensitivity (including confidence in one's performance) shows little relationship to measured accuracy (Aloni & Bernieri 2004; Carney & Harrigan 2003; DePaulo *et al.* 1997; Riggio & Riggio 2001; Smith *et al.* 1991; Zuckerman & Larrance 1979).

The discriminant validity of interpersonal sensitivity tests also requires examination. The variable of most concern in this regard is overall intelligence as measured by IQ or achievement measures. Correlations with such measures range from negligible to moderate in magnitude (Davis & Kraus 1997; Halberstadt & Hall 1980; Nowicki & Duke 2001; Rosenthal *et al.* 1979; Rosip & Hall 2004), with the trend suggesting a satisfactorily small contribution of general cognitive ability to interpersonal sensitivity. Thus, tests of interpersonal sensitivity are not simply measuring overall cognitive ability.

Although the range of correlates listed above indicates that individual differences do matter, it is important to acknowledge that many of the correlations are modest in magnitude, and sometimes they do not support predictions. It is also important to note that in listing correlates of interpersonal sensitivity, we are not making claims about causal relations. Not much is known about the causal antecedents and consequences of interpersonal sensitivity.

Major paradigms

Standard cue sets

By far the most common paradigm for assessing interpersonal sensitivity involves the use of standard cue sets, by which we mean stimuli that are stored in the form of photographs, drawings, audiotapes, or videotapes and which can therefore be judged by groups of perceivers and re-used on more than one occasion. The cue set contains multiple items showing one or more targets (the term 'target' is synonymous with 'encoder' or 'expressor'). Structuring the cue set involves many choices including the number of targets, length of clips, what channels to include, and what constructs to include. At this stage, researchers can only speculate about the implications of these choices (Colvin & Bundick 2001).

Sometimes a researcher creates a stimulus set for a particular study and does not use it again (e.g. Zuckerman *et al.* 1975), and sometimes a researcher invests much time and energy in developing, refining, and standardizing stimuli for repeated use. When stimuli are standardized and the researcher also wants to promote the stimulus set as the basis for a standardized test, he or she is also likely to conduct psychometric and normative analyses as well as undertake to demonstrate convergent and discriminant validity. Other sources can be consulted on psychometric theory and the design of tests (e.g. Cronbach 1990; Kline 2000*a,b*; Loewenthal 2001).

The validity of using standard cue sets is well established through empirical research. The term 'thin slices' was coined by Ambady and Rosenthal (1992) to describe cue sets containing very brief excerpts of behavior (less than five minutes in length but often less than one minute). In addition to a wealth of research showing that accuracy judgments made from thin slices have construct validity as predictors of personal characteristics, states, and outcomes (as indicated by the partial list offered earlier), research shows that accuracy of judgments based on thin slices can significantly predict accuracy based on a longer stream of the same behavior (Archer & Akert 1980) and that accuracy based on a thin slice may be as high as accuracy based on a longer slice (Carney *et al.* 2004).

There are many advantages to using standard cue sets. The stimuli are easily transportable, and administering the test can typically be done with simple equipment in a group setting. A scoring key needs to be developed only once. If the research question requires the researcher to code the stimuli for different cues (e.g. how much the targets smiled or details of the targets' clothing), the behavior needs to be coded only once (e.g. Borkenau & Liebler 1995; Hall & Murphy 2004; Schmid Mast & Hall 2004). Using a standard cue set also facilitates valid comparisons among perceivers and between groups because accuracy is measured against a common stimulus. Finally, with this approach one can easily separate verbal from nonverbal cues as well as different nonverbal channels of communication, as described later.

There are also limitations to using standard cue sets. One is ecological validity, because the behavior represented in a standard cue set is likely to be shown briefly and out of context, which could have a negative impact on the accuracy of judgments. Also, there are limitations to the researcher's ability to generalize beyond the specific features of the measurement paradigm used. The extent to which validity is jeopardized by design features of the stimulus set is an empirical question. Though the PONS test was criticized for having only one target (LaFrance & Henley 1994), the accumulated results for the test suggest that it has validity (e.g. Funder & Harris 1986; Hall 2001; Rosenthal *et al.* 1979). Whether it would have even more validity if it had more targets, or had different content, or used a different criterion as the basis of scoring, is not known.

Face-to-face assessment

Much more rarely undertaken is the assessment of interpersonal sensitivity between people who interact *with each other*. There are two reasons for doing this kind of research. One is that one can achieve a higher level of 'real lifeness' than can be obtained using standard cue sets. Communication that occurs during live interaction entails cognitive and motivational processes that are difficult, perhaps impossible, to create in a standardized decoding paradigm (Bernieri 2001; Patterson 1995). The second reason is that the live paradigm permits the investigation of theoretical questions not easily handled in the standardized paradigm—for example, the accuracy of husbands' and wives' communication with each other (Noller 1980) or the accuracy of superior-subordinate communication (Hall *et al.*, in press; Snodgrass 1985, 1992; Snodgrass *et al.* 1998).

Because assignment of roles controls for pre-existing skills and experiences, the live interaction paradigm is especially suited to studying the impact of motivational processes on accuracy. To illustrate, Hall *et al.* (in press) adapted the dyadic communication task of Noller (1980) by randomly assigning dyad members to high- and low-power roles and then having them deliberately send nonverbal affective messages to each other. Accuracy of decoding was scored by comparing judgments to the affect being intentionally communicated.

However, there are significant difficulties with this research paradigm. The first is the labor intensiveness of recruiting and running participants in live interactions. The second is interpretational ambiguity that is intrinsic to a within-dyad communication situation. In the Hall *et al.* (in press) study, as in Snodgrass (1985, 1992), it was not clear whether a difference in the decoding accuracy of the assigned power groups was due to one group making special efforts to decode well or to the other group producing messages that were especially easy to judge. These sources of accuracy are fully confounded in a dyadic situation.

To understand the source of this difference, Hall *et al.* (in press) showed the videotaped expressions to naïve judges (as did Noller 1980 and Snodgrass *et al.* 1998). Comparison of the naïve group's accuracy to the original groups' accuracy makes it possible to disentangle the confounded sender and receiver effects because the naïve group's performance can be considered a pure indicator of the accuracy with which the original expressions could be decoded. Thus, the dyadic communication methodology has significant ambiguities, the resolution of which can have substantial theoretical importance (in the example case, whether low-power individuals' accuracy of judging superiors' cues was due to their decoding efforts or to the intrinsic clarity of the messages sent by the superiors).

If the researcher is able to gather judgment data (with appropriate criteria for scoring) from several people in a round-robin or other appropriate design (in which each person in a group serves as both target and judge; Kenny 1994; Kenny *et al.* 1996; Kenny & Winquist 2001), then well-developed statistical methods, based on Kenny's Social Relations Model, are capable of separating different sources of variance. Specifically, perceiver, target, and perceiver X target effects (analogous to main effects and interaction in the analysis of variance) can be isolated for both judgments and criteria and compared to derive different kinds of accuracy scores. Difficulties with this approach include the logistics of recruiting participants in groups and running enough groups for meaningful analysis, and mastering the requisite statistical tools. It is, furthermore, a method best suited to the study of judgment processes among strangers. However, as Bernieri (2001) argues, the intrinsically componential nature of measured accuracy is a fact to be reckoned with, though some researchers may be more interested than others in decomposing an accuracy score into different sources of variance such as rating biases, general knowledge of people and situations, and accuracy of judging specific targets with other (artifactual) influences removed.

The hybrid paradigm: retrospective tape review

Another methodology for measuring interpersonal sensitivity is the retrospective tape review ('empathic accuracy') paradigm developed by Ickes and colleagues (Ickes 1997, 2001; Ickes *et al.* 1990). We refer to this paradigm as 'hybrid' because participants both engage in face-to-face interaction and make judgments of recorded behavior. After participants interact in live interaction, each participant individually reviews the videotape of the interaction two times. The first time, the participant stops the tape whenever he or she remembers having had a 'thought or feeling' and writes down the content of the thought or feeling. The second time, the participant watches his or her partner, with the experimenter stopping the tape at each of the partner's previously identified thoughts and feelings, at which point the participant guesses what the partner's thought or feeling was. Then the two lists of thoughts and feelings (the partner's self-reports and the participant's guesses) are compared and scored for accuracy. Findings to date suggest that accuracy in this paradigm depends more on verbal than on nonverbal cues (Gesn & Ickes 1999).

As with the face-to-face accuracy paradigm, dyadic retrospective tape review confounds perceiver and target effects (Ickes 2001). However, it is possible to avoid this difficulty by enlisting naïve viewers to make judgments, as well as the original interactants. It is also possible to use videotape clips from this paradigm as a standard cue set that shows multiple targets, for which each target's self-reported thoughts and feelings serve as the criteria of accuracy (Gesn & Ickes 1999; Marangoni *et al.* 1995).

Explicit knowledge assessment

As mentioned earlier, a potentially interesting approach to measuring interpersonal sensitivity consists of assessing people's explicit knowledge about social behavior. In this approach, the test taker is asked directly (on a paper-and-pencil test) about the meanings or correlates of nonverbal cues or about a domain of social behavior. Vrij and Semin (1996) measured knowledge of cues to deception, Murphy (2003) measured knowledge of cues to intelligence, Hall and Carter (1999) measured knowledge of a range of gender differences, including gender differences in nonverbal communication, and Rosip and Hall (2004) measured knowledge about a wide range of nonverbal cues and usages. In each case, the explicit knowledge test was scored by comparing responses to a 'gold standard' developed from the research literature.

This approach may have utility in itself, and is likely to expand understanding of the proximal determinants of sensitivity as measured with a performance test. For example, Rosip and Hall (2004) found that women scored higher on their 81-item Test of Nonverbal Cue Knowledge (TONCK) and that scores on the TONCK had a modest but significant correlation with performance on nonverbal decoding tests (PONS and DANVA). Recent work is emerging to demonstrate that performance on the IPT is also predicted by one's explicit knowledge of the relevant cues related to the interpersonal domains highlighted in that video task (McLarney–Vesotski 2003). How strong the correlations are likely to be between explicit knowledge and performance-based sensitivity could depend on many factors, including the degree of overlap in item content between the tests (i.e. whether tests are concerned with similar or different domains of meaning), perceivers' ability to describe explicitly the tacit knowledge base they use when making judgments of people, the adequacy of the 'gold standard' used for scoring accuracy on the paper-and-pencil test, and the contribution of transient factors such as motivation and distraction.

Operational issues

Separating channels

If only visual behavior is to be judged, it is easy to use photographs or silent videotapes. Visible features can be selectively obscured using electronic masking (e.g. obscuring facial expressions so that the viewer can see only body movements). When words only are to be judged, transcripts of what is said can be prepared for perceivers to read and judge (e.g. Murphy *et al.* 2003). When vocal nonverbal characteristics are to be judged, it is necessary to obscure the verbal content. This has been done in several ways, including the following (see Scherer *et al.* 1985; Scherer 2003; and Chapter 3 for more detailed descriptions and comparisons). *Randomized splicing* consists of dividing the voice sample into short segments, rearranging the segments, and playing the new sample to perceivers (Rosenthal *et al.* 1979). The meaning of a spoken sentence is no longer evident but the voice retains many of its acoustic properties. The use of a low bandpass filter produces what is known as *electronically filtered speech* by removing the highest tones, thereby making consonants hard to identify and making the voice sound muffled and the words unintelligible (Rosenthal *et al.* 1979). Both of these methods can be used with naturalistically recorded voice samples.

Standard-content methodology consists of asking targets to read something with neutral affective content such as the alphabet, a weather report, or a standard sentence (e.g. Borkenau & Liebler 1995; Dimitrovsky 1964; Noller 1980; Nowicki & Duke 1994). If emotional meaning is to be judged, the targets may be asked to deliberately vary their voices to convey the desired emotions. If traits (e.g. intelligence, extraversion) of the targets are to be judged, targets may be asked to behave in their normal way while reading or reciting the standard content.

Instruments vary in whether they are designed to be scored in only one channel (e.g. facial expressions on the JACBART; Matsumoto *et al.* 2000), whether they can be scored in multiple channels (e.g. face, body, and voice on the PONS test; Rosenthal *et al.* 1979), or whether verbal and nonverbal channels (and various nonverbal channels) are typically not distinguished (e.g. IPT of Costanzo & Archer 1989; empathic accuracy task of Ickes 2001). However, even in the latter case, the researcher can still experimentally separate the channels if this is desired. Doing so brought Costanzo and Archer (1989) to the conclusion that verbal information contributes little to accuracy on the IPT, while a similar analysis led Gesn and Ickes (1999) to conclude that verbal information matters more than nonverbal information in the empathic accuracy paradigm.

Response formats

The most common response format for testing interpersonal sensitivity is *multiple choice*, with the number of options ranging from two to approximately seven. As examples, for each item on the PONS test there are two (out of a total of 20) situational labels (e.g. 'talking about the death of a friend' and 'expressing jealous rage'), with the pairings varying from item to item (Rosenthal *et al.* 1979). The DANVA presents the options 'anger, fear, sadness, or happiness' for all items (Nowicki & Duke 1994). The JACBART lists seven emotions as the choices (Matsumoto *et al.* 2000). Most lie detection tasks involve two choices (truth or lie) (Malone & DePaulo 2001). The TONCK (omnibus explicit knowledge test) presents a 'true–false' option for all items (Rosip & Hall 2004).

Corrections have been offered to control for different numbers of response options (Rosenthal & Rubin 1989), similarities and differences among response alternatives (e.g. more negative than positive emotion options; Ekman 1994), and response bias (Wagner 1993, 1997). Studies that compare results with and without such corrections are much needed (e.g. Elfenbein & Ambady 2002; see Scherer *et al.* 2003 for a discussion of corrections).

When the responses are dichotomous, signal detection methods (Green & Swets 1966) may be applied to distinguish response bias from accuracy, as was done in Dorfman *et al.*'s (1971) study of accuracy in distinguishing Jewish from non-Jewish faces. This method has good potential applicability to research on lie detection, in that it distinguishes among hits (correctly saying truth when the item does indeed show truth), false alarms (saying truth when it is actually a lie), misses (saying lie when it is actually truth), and correct rejections (correctly calling a lie a lie) (Malone & DePaulo 2001). Accuracy (sensitivity) is the excess of hit rate over false alarm rate after standardization of the relevant percentages. Sometimes the biases themselves are of theoretical interest as, for example, the so-called truth bias whereby people tend to overestimate how often targets are telling the truth or biases in how romantic partners view each other (Kenny & Acitelli 2001).

Less often used are dimensional response formats, whereby perceivers can respond on a rating scale. Sometimes the purpose of using a rating scale is to assess accuracy indirectly, as for example in lie detection research, by asking perceivers to rate how ambivalent a target seems rather than to state explicitly whether the communication is truthful or not (Malone & DePaulo 2001). Accuracy is higher to the extent that the average ambivalence rating for deceptive messages is higher than that for truthful messages.

An implicit rating scale methodology is used in some research on judging personality, wherein perceivers perform a Q-sort on adjectives describing a target (Colvin & Bundick 2001; Vogt & Colvin 2003). In a Q-sort, the perceiver places descriptive statements or adjectives into ordered piles to reflect how much each one describes the target. One can think of a Q-sort as a rating task on which mean and variance are controlled at the outset. More explicit ratings are also sometimes made—for example, when perceivers rate the extraversion of each target represented in the stimulus set (Borkenau & Liebler 1995; Lippa & Dietz 2000), or partners in a face-to-face interaction rate the other's feelings about the self and other (Snodgrass 1985, 1992), or perceivers rate facial expressions on the degree to which each of seven emotions is present (Hall & Matsumoto 2004).

Scoring methods

On first glance, it would seem that scoring interpersonal sensitivity tasks would be a straightforward matter of comparing responses to the criterion of accuracy. For example, did the perceiver say 'anger' to an expression that actually is 'anger' according to the researcher's criterion? However, scoring accuracy tasks is not always simple, because there are alternative ways of scoring the same set of data and one way may be no more 'correct' than another. Also, the scoring options often depend on the structure of the dataset. Finally, some statistical methods for scoring accuracy are very complex and not fully accessible to many researchers. Below are some of the scoring choices facing researchers.

Percentage or mean (sum) accuracy

Using this approach, accuracy is represented by the percentage correct or the mean (or sum) of correct items. To maximize interpretability and usefulness to other researchers, whenever possible the confusion matrices should be included in research reports. To illustrate, if the stimuli consisted of six facially depicted emotions and the response alternatives consisted of the same six emotions, then the confusion matrix shows the data for all cells of this six by six array of responses. Accuracy is determined by comparing the diagonal values to off-diagonal values.

The great majority of studies of interpersonal sensitivity use percentage or mean (or sum) accuracy, without the correction (e.g. they count up the number of correct answers). The guessing or chance level of accuracy depends, of course, on how many response options are provided. For analysis of individual differences, accuracy is calculated for individual perceivers, and for group-based analysis, the mean accuracy across perceivers is used. Investigators may have further choices to create subtotal scores. For example, at the group level, accuracy can be calculated across perceivers and separately for each target, yielding encoding accuracy scores for use in analysis of individual differences among targets in how accurately they were judged. How far to subdivide accuracy scores according to individual targets or according to other variables such as sex or the different constructs being judged (e.g. different emotions) is a decision based on theoretical goals as well as the impact on reliability of decreasing the number of items included in an accuracy score. Assessment of overall accuracy typically consists of comparing the mean accuracy against the guessing level by a one-sample t-test. As with any such test, assuming a mean that deviates at all from the null hypothesis value, the p-value will become smaller with increasing sample size.

Absolute discrepancy

Early accuracy researchers often calculated accuracy as the absolute difference between a perceiver's rating of a target and the criterion (typically, the target's self-rating). Cronbach (1955) and others pointed out hazards with this method, identifying several distinct reasons relating to the use of rating scales for why accuracy might be artifactually high or low. Researchers have not often used this approach in recent years. Hall *et al.* (2001) used discrepancy scores in a somewhat different way, calculating the absolute difference between how much a perceiver said the partner displayed a certain cue (rated on a scale) and how much the partner actually displayed that cue (as counted or timed by coders), after each was Z-scored. With this method, more accuracy is defined as smaller absolute discrepancy between these two values.

One cannot employ this metric to address the question of whether there is, or is not, a significant level of accuracy. The problem is that testing the null hypothesis that people have no accuracy tests whether a sample of judgments differs significantly from *perfect* accuracy (e.g. $|d| = \phi$), which is a null hypothesis of little scientific value. Testing whether judgments have some accuracy is not the same as testing whether judgments have perfect accuracy. Another problem with the difference metric is that there is no value for it that corresponds to *zero* accuracy. The point at which one moves from less than perfect accuracy (difference > zero) to zero accuracy is not addressable quantitatively. However, significance tests between sample means can be meaningfully interpreted, allowing one to use this metric to determine whether accuracy increases or decreases significantly (e.g. over time, after intervention, or between groups).

Range scoring

Hall and Murphy (2004) measured accuracy of recalling the nonverbal behavior of a person being interviewed on videotape by asking perceivers to estimate how often each of 16 nonverbal behaviors were emitted. Because scoring an estimate as 'correct' only if it was an exact match with the criterion value would make the test prohibitively difficult, ranges were established such that approximately 50% of the participants' estimates fell within the range for a given behavior. To illustrate, if the exact count of hand gestures was 16, the range of estimates scored as accurate might fall between 13 and 19. One advantage of this method is that the investigator has good control over the difficulty level of items. Range scoring suffers from the same limitation as absolute discrepancy scoring in the sense that there is no defined 'zero-accuracy' value against which tests can be made.

Profile correlation

Profile correlation (Bernieri *et al.* 1994; Blackman 2002; Funder 1980; Lippa & Dietz 2000; Vogt & Colvin 2003)—also called sensitivity correlation (Judd & Park 1993) and idiographic analysis (Kenny & Winquist 2001)—is defined as the correlation between judgments and criterion values for a given decoder. Choice is required between calculating the profile correlation across items (e.g. traits/states being judged) within targets in order to generate a separate decoding accuracy coefficient for each target, or across targets within traits/states in order to generate a separate decoding accuracy coefficient for each trait/state. Either way, the resulting correlation is used as an accuracy score that can range from -1.0 to $+1.0$. (Typically, for any statistical analysis, it is normalized using the Fisher-z transformation.)

The profile correlation across items indicates how well the profile of item judgments made by the perceiver matches the profile of criterion values in the target. Using this approach, Vogt and Colvin (2003) had perceivers make Q-sorts of 100 personality-relevant adjectives after seeing a target on videotape. The perceivers' ratings (determined by which pile each trait was sorted into) were then correlated with the target's criterion values for the same 100 items, producing a separate profile accuracy correlation for each combination of perceiver and target. In this case, the N for the correlation was the number of traits in the analysis, or 100.

Although the metric calculated is a Pearson r and is interpreted as such, significance testing is problematic in that the units of analysis (items within target) are not independent. Therefore, researchers do not use this trait profile correlation to answer the question 'is *this* perceiver significantly accurate in judging this target?'. Instead, it is most often used as an effect size estimate to track how accuracy might be influenced by various other things. The present authors are not aware of any investigations that have described the precise distribution of this metric calculated in this manner, but we have little reason to doubt that the sample means of this statistic are distributed normally. Therefore, as with any other quantitative measure of accuracy, sample means can be subjected to parametric tests of significance. For example, an appropriate test of whether group mean accuracy is significantly greater than $r = 0$ is simply a one-sample t-test against zero, with N being the number of perceivers in the group. (For an alternative method for testing whether overall accuracy exceeds chance, see Kenny & Winquist 2001.) Note that for all such tests against zero, the p-value associated with any given non-zero value will become smaller as the number of perceivers increases.

The choice of a null hypothesis reflecting 'no accuracy' for the trait profile correlation statistic, however, is anything but straightforward. The most obvious null value for the profile correlation would be $r = 0$. Generally, a perceiver would be accurate to the extent he or she judged traits correctly as high or low. A significantly negative profile correlation would indicate a perceiver attributed the *opposite* or complementary personality to the target. But as Cronbach (1955) and others (Bernieri *et al.* 1994; Kenny & Winquist 2001) have pointed out, positive profile correlations will be achieved, in part, by some variance components that are not associated with rating a specific target uniquely. Consider the case where a perceiver is judging a target on the traits warmth, honesty, laziness, and hostility. We might assume that across the general population, the traits of warmth and honesty are more pronounced than are laziness and hostility. Without reading a target uniquely, a perceiver would register a positive profile accuracy correlation merely by rating the target more highly on the positive traits than on the negative ones. Under these circumstances, perceivers would be accurate against a null hypothesis of $r = 0$ but only because of an appreciation of how traits are manifest across the population and not because they perceived the given target accurately. In other words, they would be accurate due to the accuracy of their implicit theory of personality or *stereotype* accuracy (Bernieri *et al.* 1994; Cronbach 1955; Kenny & Winquist 2001). Psychologically mature and emotionally stable perceivers who believe people generally like social contact and are not severely neurotic will tend to produce positive trait profile accuracy correlations across all targets. Psychotic or emotionally unstable perceivers who believe that people are generally sadistic and misanthropic would likely generate trait profile accuracy correlations that are negative or near zero, no matter who they may be judging. For this reason, it is likely that an ill-timed review of accuracy that did not consider the impact of variance components concluded that, in fact, the good judge of personality was psychologically healthy and mature (Taft 1955). (Interestingly, this conclusion appears to be correct even if it was based on questionable methodology.)

Procedures to measure and/or remove this contributing source of variance to trait profile accuracy correlations can be found in Bernieri *et al.* (1994) and in Kenny and Winquist (2001). The common theme behind these procedures is to determine the extent to which the profile correlation found is significantly higher than that which can be attributed to a generic reading of the typical human being's trait profile. The null hypothesis for these tests shifts from $r = 0$ to a correlation value that is somewhere above zero. Exactly where above zero one sets the null will differ depending on the design of the study.

In a 'perception of roommate' study where all perceivers judged one target—their own roommate—Bernieri *et al.* (1994) calculated the average trait values across all targets for each trait in the study. This generated a 'mean target trait profile'. The extent to which the perceivers' judgments happened to correlate with this mean target trait profile represented a kind of *chance* accuracy and served as a null hypothesis. In that context, a perceiver (let us say it is a female) would be accurately judging her roommate only to the extent that her judgments correlated more strongly to the target profile than to the statistically derived pseudo roommate.

A problem with this particular technique is that if a target happens to have a very typical trait profile (i.e. it happens to match closely the statistically derived pseudo target trait profile), then a perceiver will not be able to show any accuracy above the null even when her judgments match the target criterion perfectly. In other words, perceivers only have the potential for accuracy above the null to the extent that the target personality differs from the norm.

Yet another approach would be to compare the trait profile correlation to the target with all of the other profile correlations that could be statistically derived from the nontargets. In the roommate study described above, one would correlate a perceiver's single set of trait judgments made of her roommate to each of the other target profiles recorded in the study. If there were N roommate pairs in the entire sample, then each perceiver would have one trait profile correlation for her roommate, and N -1 trait profile correlations with the remaining pseudo roommates. The central tendency of the distribution of pseudo roommate trait profile correlations would represent a null value above which accuracy for reading the true roommate would be inferred.

Earlier we said the profile correlation can be calculated across targets within a trait or other construct. This correlation indicates how well a perceiver's profile of ratings of targets matches the actual profile of the targets on the trait. To illustrate, Lippa and Dietz (2000) correlated perceivers' ratings of extraversion for each of 32 targets (seen on videotape for approximately 30 seconds each) with those targets' self-reported extraversion. In this case, the N for the correlation was the number of targets (or 32), with each perceiver receiving one correlation (i.e. accuracy score) which represented his/her accuracy across all targets for the trait of extraversion. For this design, the null value of $r = 0$ is appropriate.

As noted by Bernieri et al. (1994), Kenny and Winquist (2001), and others, profile correlations and many other scoring methods can be subjected to componential analyses (conceptually, if not empirically) to acknowledge different sources of variance in the accuracy scores (see Cronbach 1955). Methods for correcting or adjusting scores for stereotype accuracy and elevation are discussed by Bernieri et al. (1994) as well as by Kenny (1994; Kenny & Winquist 2001) and others.

Group accuracy correlations

All of the preceding methods begin by computing interpersonal accuracy for individual perceivers before averaging or summarizing them to arrive at a group mean estimate. Accuracy can also be computed at a sample level directly, without ever calculating any one perceiver's level of accuracy. Such metrics can be appropriate for exploring group-level hypotheses (e.g. investigating gender, age, and role effects). For example, Hall et al. (2001) compared the accuracy of high-status versus low-status participants in their recall of their partner's nonverbal behaviors using such a method.

When group-level effects are of primary concern and individual differences within groups are considered error variance, then group accuracy correlations are the appropriate metric. In some instances, a sample or group of individuals might only generate one single judgment outcome, as in the case of a search committee's final assessment of a job candidate. The group in essence becomes a single perceiver. Group correlations of this type are conceptually similar to those formed for any single perceiver. Below we describe two different kinds of group accuracy scoring methods.

Pooled consensus accuracy: group accuracy correlations reflecting the accuracy of a group's mean judgment

In this method, the ratings made by perceivers are averaged before any other calculations are made. Conceptually, a group, committee, or sample is considered 'the perceiver', from which a single judgment is generated. The group consensus can be derived by simply averaging the individual ratings or it could conceivably be the outcome of a group discussion. When a group judges either a sample of targets on one item or judges one target across a set of items (i.e. profile), a correlation is computed with the criterion values where the null hypothesis of no accuracy is defined as $r = 0$. As illustration of this method, Borkenau and Liebler (1995) averaged perceivers' ratings of extraversion for each of 50 targets and then correlated these mean ratings with the criterion values derived from targets' self-ratings of extraversion. (For further illustrations of this method, see Zebrowitz et al. 2002 and Hall & Carter 1999.)

A notable feature of this method is that the magnitude of the resulting group correlation tends to be larger than the average of the accuracy correlations individually calculated (Ambady *et al.* 2000; Kunda 1999). As examples, Bernieri *et al.*(1996) found that pooled consensus judgments of target rapport correlated around $r = 0.29$ with targets' own ratings of rapport, whereas the average accuracy for individual perceivers was only around $r = 0.20$. Watson (1989) found that perceivers' ratings of target persons' personality traits correlated with the targets' self-ratings more strongly when five perceivers' ratings were pooled before calculating the profile correlation than when profile correlations were calculated for individual perceivers and then averaged (e.g. for agreeableness, $r = 0.16$ vs. $r = 0.10$). Finally, Hall and Carter (1999), in studying the accuracy of people's beliefs about sex differences, found the profile accuracy of pooled judgments to be $r = 0.70$, whereas the average individual profile accuracy correlation was only around $r = 0.45$.

The relative gains in accuracy attained by pooled consensus judgments will be driven by reliability issues. In general, these group accuracy correlations will increase as the N of perceivers within the group increases, due to the cancellation of random error. They might also increase to the extent that the different perceivers in the group are accurately detecting different sources of criterion variance from each other. For example, imagine a five-member committee where each member's judgment across targets correlates $r = 0.30$ with the criterion but they each employ a different and orthogonal cue or strategy to achieve this degree of accuracy. The resulting consensus judgment might then be understood as a composite of five orthogonal valid predictors. The gain in accuracy from pooling in this case would result more from the combination of orthogonal sources of true accuracy variance than it would from simply increasing N (i.e. the cancellation of random errors) (Guilford 1954).

The group accuracy correlation with perceivers as the units of analysis

This approach has been referred to as nomothetic analysis because one focuses primarily on the situational factors that influence the accuracy of a given sample of perceivers (Kenny & Winquist 2001). The judgments of a sample of perceivers are correlated with the criterion values for a set of targets, items, or relationships, with each perceiver–target dyad being a unit of analysis and N being the number of such dyads. Examples of this are studies that investigate accuracy of roommates' or friends' perceptions of one another or accuracy of doctors' and patients' impressions of how much they are liked by the other (e.g. Bernieri *et al.* 1994; Funder *et al.* 1995; Hall *et al.* 2002).

In this method, a single correlation coefficient assesses the degree of correspondence between perceiver judgment and criterion across the sample of perceivers. The group accuracy correlation is a sample statistic. There is no component of it that relates to the accuracy of any individual perceiver. The null hypothesis reflecting no accuracy is represented by $r = 0$, where the *df* is $N-2$ perceivers. For any given positive non-zero value of r, the *p*-value for the significance test against zero will decrease as a function of N.

Lens model analysis

Brunswik (1956) was concerned with modeling the accuracy with which perceivers could assess their physical environments. He proposed a methodology where, after a perceiver judged a set of stimuli, his or her judgments would be subjected to a regression analysis to learn how they correlated with the criterion as well as with a series of potential judgment mediators or cues. The correlation between a perceiver's judgment of an attribute (e.g. size) over a series of stimuli and the criterion values for those stimuli constitute a perceiver's accuracy, which Brunswik termed *achievement*.

Heider (1958) was the first to embrace the lens model as a conceptual framework with which to describe interpersonal perception. However, it was not until many years later that the employment of the lens model for interpersonal perception began in earnest (e.g. Funder & Sneed 1993; Gifford 1994; Scherer 1982). This model has been useful in documenting not only how accurately people make judgments, but also what cues influence a perceiver's judgments and how the cues themselves are related to the criterion (i.e. ecological validity).

The lens model has been applied to study vocal behavior (Scherer 1978), personality traits (Borkenau & Liebler 1995; Gifford 1994; Lippa 1998), intelligence (Borkenau & Liebler 1995; Murphy *et al.* 2003; Reynolds & Gifford 2001), and rapport (Bernieri & Gillis 2001; Bernieri *et al.* 1996; Gillis & Bernieri 2001; Gillis *et al.* 1995). To apply this model, the researcher:

1. establishes criterion values of the state or trait in question for each target in the stimulus set;
2. gathers perceivers' judgments of the targets on the state or trait in question, and;
3. codes or otherwise assesses the targets on cues that may be relevant to the state or trait.

(See Chapter 3 for more detailed description.)

To illustrate, Gifford (1994) established the personality dominance of 60 targets through self-ratings and had perceivers rate the targets on dominance from videotaped interactions. He also measured how much the targets gestured and how much they manipulated an object (e.g. jewelry, shirt sleeve, pen). The correlation between perceiver judgments and the targets' true dominance, as defined by the criterion, constituted their level of achievement (i.e. dominance judgment accuracy) and was around $r = 0.26$. The correlation between target dominance and coded behavior constituted the ecological validity of the cues examined and was $r = 0.29$ for gestures and $r = -0.46$ for object manipulation. This suggested that target dominance could be perceived by observers looking for more gestures and little object manipulation. In fact, perceiver judgments of dominance correlated highly with gestures ($r = 0.66$), suggesting that this is precisely how perceivers looked for dominance. Interestingly, perceiver judgments did not correlate significantly with object manipulation, indicating that observers overlooked an important cue, given that this cue had the strongest relationship to the dominance criterion (Gifford 1994).

The lens model can be constructed either for a perceiver group as a whole or for individual perceivers whose coefficients (accuracy correlations and correlations indicating their judgment policies) can be averaged for purposes of summary display (Bernieri *et al.* 1996; Bernieri & Gillis 2001). A few critical points need to be made when a lens model analysis is performed on pooled consensus judgments. First, pooling perceiver judgments before correlating them with a target criterion defines a group accuracy correlation (see p. 261). Therefore, increases in the reliability of the perceiver judgment should increase achievement (accuracy) as the number of perceivers being pooled increases. Second, the cue utilization output of the lens model analysis based on pooled consensus judgments cannot be taken as representative or typical of the individual perceivers that contributed to it. There is no mathematical reason to necessitate that any *one* perceiver utilized the cues in the manner consistent with the apparent cue utilization of the pooled judgment to which they contributed. To illustrate, suppose there were three perceivers who were all judging the dominance of a set of targets. Imagine further that all had a different single-cue judgment such that perceiver A was influenced by head nods, perceiver B by gestures, and perceiver C by forward lean. The lens model of their pooled judgments in this case would likely reveal a complex judgment policy consisting of all three cues—a policy employed by no one. Finally, to the extent that individual perceivers have judgment policies that consist of *opposite* cue dependencies (i.e. some perceivers are tracking in a positive direction while others are tracking the same cue in a negative direction), lens models of pooled consensus judgments will not reflect the actual judgment policies being employed at the individual perceiver level.

Sometimes, investigators using the lens model are interested in determining which cues can account for accuracy—in other words, which cues can be called mediators of the judgment–accuracy link. Inspection of the corresponding correlations associated with a cue (e.g. The gesture correlations of 0.29 and 0.66 associated with dominance in the Gifford example above) gives an indication if that cue is a mediator. Cues that have corresponding correlations that are extreme in magnitude and similarly signed are good candidates for mediation. Two points must be made about such a conclusion. First, an eyeball conclusion is not as sound as a statistical test. For this purpose, statistical tests are available—for example, the Sobel test (Kenny *et al.* 1998; for applications in the context of the lens model, see Murphy *et al.* 2003 and Zebrowitz *et al.* 2002). Second, even if such a test shows that accuracy can be statistically accounted for with a given cue, because of the correlational nature of such data, there is no way to know for sure that this cue was actually used. An alternative possibility is that perceivers used a different (possibly unmeasured) cue, but that cue was highly correlated with the measured cue. In the Gifford example of gestures described above, such a correlated cue might have been speaking time. Because people gesture when speaking and hardly at all when not, perceivers may have been making their judgments based on seeing how much the targets spoke and not on their gesturing.

Variance components approach

The final scoring method we will discuss is the variance components or Social Relations Model (SRM) approach developed by Kenny (Kenny 1994; Kenny & Winquist 2001). Among all the methods described, the variance components approach has the most potential for comprehensiveness in that the analysis is limited only by the amount and quality of the data available. Inspired by Cronbach's (1955) admonition that accuracy researchers should be mindful of the sources of variance that contribute to a given accuracy metric, the approach attempts to identify and partition, exhaustively, all of the variance components possible, given the data matrix.

Perhaps the best way to understand the SRM is to imagine what the ideal or perfect data set for learning about interpersonal perception accuracy would look like from an analysis of variance (ANOVA) framework. If one could imagine every person in a population rating every other person in that population, on every possible attribute, in every possible situation/role, over an infinite number of trials, then one could theoretically identify precisely what contributed to a given perceiver's accuracy in any single cell within that perfect data matrix, given one had the corresponding criterion data. One would be able to partition perfectly the extent to which the accuracy was due to such things as:

1. this particular perceiver's judgment biases;
2. the perceiver's general knowledge of how various traits and other attributes hang together in humans;
3. how well this particular perceiver accurately perceives this particular target, trait, or situation/time uniquely.

In this hypothetical data matrix, no significance testing would be needed because we would simply be describing the parameters of the population and individual score components.

In essence, the various statistical procedures developed from the SRM are all designed to estimate as many sources of variance as possible given the completeness of the data matrix provided (Kenny & Winquist 2001). Although the general method is expandable to allow the examination of almost any theoretical effect on accuracy one could conceive, its most representative form partitions accuracy into the four components identified by Cronbach (Cronbach 1955; Kenny 1994; Kenny & Albright 1987). When multiple targets are judged by multiple perceivers on a single measure, and the criterion data are recorded on a similar scale, then one can determine accuracy due to:

1. *elevation*—the degree of correspondence between the perceiver's judgment grand mean and the criterion grand mean;
2. *differential elevation*—the degree of correspondence between a target's variation from the sample target mean and the variation of the perceiver's judgment of that target from the perceiver's mean;
3. *stereotype*—understood in terms of a perceiver's knowledge of the population mean value of the trait/attribute in question;
4. *dyad*—the extent to which a perceiver's judgments of a target correspond to that target's behavior as it is uniquely expressed towards the perceiver.

Calling the variance components approach a 'scoring method' hardly does it justice, as it essentially attempts to marry the proper statistical analysis to any given experimental design and item scaling, and results in a unique output of variance components for that particular paradigm. The most notable feature of this approach is that the interpretation of the outputs from these analyses can vary greatly in their utility. To date, the SRM has been employed primarily for determining the relative magnitudes of accuracy components (e.g. when people are accurate is it because they know the generic person stereotype or is it because they perceive the uniqueness of the target?). It was not developed to assess an individual perceiver's accuracy. It describes accuracy at the level of a sample and, thus, is conceptually similar to *group accuracy* discussed earlier. As such, this approach is not well suited to exploring trait moderators of an individual's accuracy. However, SRM should be ideal for exploring situational and role moderators of accuracy, although this particular use for this technique has yet to be fully exploited.

Another issue influencing the utility of this approach involves the assumption and necessary interpretation of accuracy as being componential. Although the various sources of variance are mathematically defined and easily discussed in terms of the rows and columns of a data matrix, some have wondered whether the decomposition of accuracy undermines the integrity and interpretability of the accuracy construct itself (Funder 2001; Vogt & Colvin 2003). What one researcher might label artifact, another might consider accuracy. The theoretical utility and validity of an accuracy construct that is left after several of its variance components have been removed will have to be defended.

Nevertheless, ways of analyzing accuracy within the SRM are evolving to fit the increasing number of experimental designs (Kenny & Winquist 2001). But, more importantly, the framework is expanding to handle an increasing number of factors that were never before incorporated into accuracy theory. For example, Kenny and Winquist (2001) describe the procedures one would use if targets were judged on multiple measures instead of one. The analysis of this design extension doubles the number of accuracy components from four to eight. The potential of this method is great because there are other factors not yet explored (e.g. roles, situation, time, medium, domain of attribute being assessed) that could be incorporated into this model, generating even more variance components. For example, in the future, one might use SRM to address the questions 'to what extent is a perceiver accurate in judging Professor Jones because of an intuitive understanding of how professors typically behave?' and 'are people more accurate in assessing traits, states, or the behavioral cues that express them?'. The SRM is flexible enough to be modified to handle many such research questions not yet framed.

Instruments for measuring interpersonal sensitivity

Thus far, we have led the reader from broad conceptual issues to more concrete, operational issues (and problems) in the assessment of interpersonal sensitivity. It is now time to describe specific instruments in more detail, some of which we have mentioned in the preceding pages. These instruments vary greatly in how frequently they have been used in published research. (Methodological descriptions of other measurement paradigms that we described earlier can be found in the citations provided with those descriptions.)

Profile of Nonverbal Sensitivity Test (PONS; Rosenthal *et al.* 1979)

This test measures accuracy of inferring the emotional tone of scenes acted out by one female expressor. The full-length PONS test consists of 220 2-second audio clips, video clips, or combined audio and video, and a printed answer sheet containing 220 pairs of brief verbal descriptions that are responded to in multiple-choice style. The PONS test has an *a priori* structure consisting of 11 channels: three visual channels alone, with no voice; two vocal channels alone, with no visual cues; and six combinations of the three visual and two vocal cues. These 11 channels are crossed by 20 affective scenes (e.g. returning a faulty item to a store, expressing jealous rage) which themselves fall into a two-by-two configuration (with five scenes each) representing the dimensions of positivity (positive vs. negative) and dominance (more dominant vs. less dominant). The test was made in 1971, and the monograph describing the test's development and validation was published in 1979 (Rosenthal *et al.* 1979). Internal consistency (KR-20) for the full-length test is 0.86, and test–retest reliability is 0.69 (median over six samples). Short forms of the test include the 40 audio-only items, the 40 face and body items, and the 60 face, body, and face-plus-body items shown as still photographs.

Among the many validity results published in Rosenthal *et al.* 1979, and since, are the following: people who scored higher on the PONS had healthier, more well-adjusted personalities, were rated as more interpersonally sensitive by peers or supervisors, were more democratic teachers, and were rated as better in their job performance as clinicians and teachers. The test also shows developmental and sex differences (females score higher).

Empathic acccuracy standard-cue methodology (Ickes 1997, 2001)

Empathic inference is the 'everyday mind reading' that people do whenever they attempt to infer other people's thoughts and feelings, and empathic accuracy is the extent to which such inferences are accurate. The basic methodology was described earlier in this chapter. In the standard-cue variant of this methodology, a collection of videotaped expressors can be shown to perceivers who were not the original interaction partners (e.g. Gesn & Ickes, 1999). The tape is stopped at the precise moments that the expressor indicated that he or she thought or felt something, and perceivers indicate, in an open-ended fashion, what the expressor was feeling at that moment. Responses are then scored for accuracy on a 0 (*not accurate at all*) to 2 (*maximally accurate*) response scale. A perceiver's responses can then be summed across judged expressors and used as an individual difference measure of empathic accuracy. Inter-rater alphas tend to be around 0.90 and the general empathic accuracy paradigm shows predictive validity (Marangoni *et al.* 1995; Stinson & Ickes 1992).

Interpersonal Perception Task (IPT; Costanzo & Archer 1989)

The IPT shows videotaped clips of varying lengths (approximately one minute) in which people are shown in interaction or speaking to the camera. Both nonverbal and verbal cues are presented in a full-channel audiovisual mode (verbal cues, though present, are designed not to be informative). The IPT has both 30-item and 15-item versions (Archer *et al.* 2001). Criteria for scoring this multiple-choice test are objective facts about the expressors or the circumstances under which their cues were expressed. An example would be a videotaped clip of a woman talking to someone on the telephone—is she talking to her mother or her boyfriend? Or, a person is telling aspects of her life story—is it a true story? For each IPT scene there is an interpretive question, and, for each question, there is an objectively correct answer. Each of the IPT scenes taps one of five interpretive domains: kinship, lie-telling, competition, status, and intimacy. Test–retest reliability is $r = 0.70$ (Costanzo & Archer 1989).

Diagnostic Analysis of Nonverbal Accuracy (DANVA; Nowicki & Duke 1994, 2001)

Several tests to measure sensitivity to nonverbal cues of emotion are collectively called the DANVA. The basic test stimuli of the DANVA are predominantly posed photographs and audio recordings (of a single standard sentence). The DANVA measures are 24-item measures which tap four different emotions: happy, sad, angry, and fearful. In the most widely used test, perceivers view pictures of 24 adults posing a facial expression of emotion for 2 seconds and then choose the emotion word that best represents the facial expression. The audio version of the task is the same except that the stimuli are voices reading the standard sentence. Responses are then scored for accuracy against the scoring key. Additional versions of the DANVA include tests with children and African Americans as expressors. Internal consistency is usually higher than 0.70 for all DANVA tests, and the tests have predictive validity and correlations with an array of personality constructs and aspects of social and mental adjustment (Nowicki & Duke 2001).

Missing Cartoons Test (deMille et al. 1965)

This test is a 28-item measure of social situation decoding ability in which respondents are asked to choose the missing cartoon segment that belongs in a four-segment cartoon strip. Each four-segment strip depicts an ambiguous social situation where one of the four segments is missing and the correct cartoon segment that completes the sequence is listed below the strip along with three incorrect choices. The ambiguous social situations contain overt cues such as those associated with behavior, and less overt cues such as those associated with thoughts and feelings. The number of items answered correctly is the accuracy score. This measure has shown adequate internal consistency (alpha = 0.76) and predictive validity (e.g. Carney & Harrigan 2003).

Child and Adolescent Social Perception Measure (CASP; Magill–Evans et al. 1995)

The CASP consists of 10 naturalistic scenes acted out by children and adolescents, presented on videotape with electronic filtering of the soundtrack to prevent verbal comprehension. Test takers do not mark a preprinted answer sheet but, rather, respond in an open-ended fashion to probes about which emotions they perceive. A standardized scoring system is used. This test shows age and gender differences in a normative sample of children, differentiates normally functioning adolescents from a sample with Asperger's syndrome, and correlates with parent and teacher ratings of functioning (Koning & Magill–Evans 2001). Internal consistency is 0.88 (Magill–Evans et al. 1995).

Communication of Affect Receiving Ability Test, (CARAT; Buck 1976)

The 'slide-viewing technique' (Buck 1979) measures spontaneous expression of emotional cues (i.e. cues that are revealed on the target's face without awareness or intention). Although variations on this technique exist, the basic paradigm consists of showing affectively arousing color slides to individuals whose faces are surreptitiously recorded on a videotape as they watch the slides. The videotape is then shown to naïve judges, who are typically asked which slide was being viewed. If the slide can be accurately identified, one can infer that the expressor unintentionally revealed his or her emotional response to the slide. Test–retest reliability is 0.80 (Buck 1976).

Most research using the slide-viewing technique is concerned with accuracy of expressing, not accuracy of judging. However, Buck (1976) incorporated one set of these facial expressions into a judgmental accuracy test. Test takers view a series of faces and can respond either categorically, as described earlier (i.e. which slide was being viewed), or dimensionally, by rating how pleasant the expressor rated his or her own experience. Accuracy for the dimensional measure (which Buck called the 'pleasantness' measure) consists of correlating these ratings with the original expressor's ratings across the different expressor's expressions. Thus, there are two different criteria for accuracy: the category of the slide (sexual, unusual, scenic, and unpleasant) and the expressor's self-ratings of pleasant affect.

The CARAT has not been extensively used in individual difference research, though validational findings have been reported (Buck 1976; Hall *et al.* 1997).

Japanese and Caucasian Brief Affect Recognition Test (JACBART; Matsumoto *et al.* 2000)

The JACBART was developed as an improved version of the Brief Affect Recognition Test (BART; Ekman & Friesen 1974). The BART consists of photographs of faces showing 'basic' emotions identified in the research program of Paul Ekman (happiness, sadness, disgust, fear, surprise, and anger), presented tachistoscopically (e.g. less than 1/25 second; Ekman & Friesen 1974). Test takers choose which emotion was shown from a multiple choice. The JACBART (Matsumoto *et al.* 2000) is similar to the BART, except that it contains equal numbers of Japanese and Caucasian, and male and female, expressions of seven different emotions (happiness, sadness, disgust, fear, surprise, anger, and contempt) and each expression is 'sandwiched' between two neutral expressions made by the same expressor. The entire test is on videotape (not requiring special equipment). Exposures are 1/5 second or shorter.

Reliability is high (internal consistency >0.80, retest r = 0.78), and scores correlate with an array of personality measures. Scoring can be done categorically or using individual profile correlations (a separate correlation for each perceiver for each item, where the correlation is between the perceiver's ratings of how much each of seven emotions was shown in the expression and how much a normative sample who viewed the expressions for 10 seconds said each emotion was shown in the expression; Hall & Matsumoto 2004).

Pictures of Facial Affect (POFA; Ekman & Friesen 1976)

The POFA is a set of 110 black and white photographs of 14 different individuals (eight female and six male) expressing six different 'basic' emotions—happy, sad, angry, fearful, surprised, and disgusted, plus a neutral picture for each individual expressor. The development and validation of the POFA was based on Ekman and Friesen's Facial Action Coding System (FACS; Ekman & Friesen 1978). FACS is a coding system that maps facial muscle configurations to different emotional experiences, and was used to select photographs for the POFA—that is, FACS-determined muscular configurations were used as criteria in choosing stimuli that accurately represent each of the six basic emotions.

The POFA is considered to be more of a stimulus set than a standardized test of emotion decoding ability. However, it can be used as an individual difference measure of emotional sensitivity and has been used in a large number of studies. When the POFA is used in research, a selection of the photographs (or sometimes the whole set) is presented to participants either in photograph, slide, or digitized (i.e. on a computer screen) form. Participants are then asked to judge the emotion being expressed in the photograph and respond on a forced-choice scale (e.g. McAndrew 1986; Niit & Valsiner 1977). In some studies, though, participants were allowed to respond in an open-ended response format (e.g. Boucher & Carlson 1980).

The validity of the POFA expressions is supported by the numerous studies that have shown consensus within and across cultures (see Russell 1994). Generally, the psychometric properties of the POFA are largely assumed, since its construction was based on an extremely elaborate and highly reliable and valid system for determining and labeling the intensity of facial expressions of affect (i.e. FACS). Recent work has added validity data as described in the following sampling of results.

The POFA shows developmental effects (Lenti *et al.* 1999), relations to personality (Larkin *et al.* 2002), and differences between psychiatric and learning disabled groups and normally functioning groups (Holder & Kirkpatrick 1991; Rojahn *et al.* 2002). Wallbott (1991) showed that people could accurately identify which of the POFA slides they were viewing from videotapes of themselves while viewing the pictures. Dimberg and Thunberg (1998) showed that the POFA predicted facial activity (measured with EMG) consistent with the POFA pictures shown at 300–400 milliseconds (almost subliminal) of exposure. (Also see Dimberg 1997 and Dimberg *et al.* 2000 for additional evidence of this effect.)

Mayer–Salovey–Caruso Emotional Intelligence Test (MSCEIT; Mayer *et al.* 2003)

Emotional intelligence (EI) is defined as a set of skills concerned with the processing of emotion-related information, with emotion decoding accuracy at its theoretical (Mayer & Salovey 1997) and measurement (Mayer *et al.* 2003) core. The construct of EI is most reliably and validly measured with the MSCEIT, Version 2.0 (Mayer *et al.* 2003). The MSCEIT measures each component and associated sub-components of the four-branch model proposed by Mayer and Salovey (1997):

1. the accurate perception of emotion;
2. the use of emotion to facilitate cognitive activities;

3. the ability to understand emotion;
4. regulation/management of emotion.

Because Mayer and Salovey's (1997) model of EI hypothesized that emotional knowledge is embedded within a social context of communication and social interaction, the criterion scores, or 'right answers', for each of the items on the MSCEIT are based on hundreds of raters' average scores on each item. Split-half reliabilities for each of the four MSCEIT branches and associated subtests ranged from 0.64 to 0.93 on a large diverse sample of individuals (Mayer *et al.* 2003). The test–retest reliability of the total MSCEIT score has been reported as $r = 0.86$ (Brackett & Mayer 2003). The components of the MSCEIT are moderately intercorrelated yet distinct. Indeed, confirmatory factor analytic results support Mayer and Salovey's (1997) four-component EI model (Mayer *et al.* 2003).

Although the MSCEIT has been the subject of considerable development and reliability work, the validity of this test is just beginning to emerge. Theoretically, EI should be related to a number of adaptive interpersonal consequences, and the usefulness of the MSCEIT in attempting to predict such positive outcomes is without question. However, whether such relations exist is only beginning to receive attention now that the MSCEIT has been fully developed.

For our purposes, the emotion-decoding aspect of the MSCEIT has the greatest relevance, as only this portion of the test is concerned with interpersonal sensitivity as opposed to other emotion-related traits and tendencies.

Conclusions

Researchers wanting to measure interpersonal sensitivity have many choices to make, both conceptual and operational. It is obvious that theory should guide method—in this case, that the questions one wants to ask should guide the choice of instruments and methods. However, this is easier said than done. Not enough is yet known about the landscape of interpersonal sensitivity to know with any certainty how research questions do map onto instruments and methods. If we want to measure the impact of some variable on interpersonal sensitivity, how do we choose which domain of sensitivity to examine? If we know what domain we want (e.g. sensitivity to emotions), which of the several available instruments should we pick? Which emotions should we include? Should we use still photos or moving video, or posed or spontaneous expressions? Is it all right to develop one's own instrument? Which of many possible criteria and scoring methods should we pick? Regrettably, research at this stage in the field's development does not offer good answers to such questions. Therefore, researchers can hardly be faulted if they just use the instrument they are most familiar with, or that someone recommends to them, or that is most often cited, or that is most convenient to acquire and use. Often we lack the empirical knowledge on which to make a more empirically grounded choice.

With the passage of time, this situation should improve. In the meantime, we would caution researchers not to generalize too much beyond the instruments, methods, and operational definitions that they have used. Findings for one kind of accuracy (e.g.

domain, method) may not apply to another kind of accuracy. If resources allow, multiple methods should be used. Meta-analyses that examine results for different methodologies are especially valuable (Elfenbein & Ambady 2002; Hall 1978; McClure 2000). Understanding the impact of methodology on results is, of course, an important step toward developing a theory of interpersonal sensitivity (Zebrowitz 2001).

References

Allport, G.W. & Kramer, B.M. (1946). Some roots of prejudice. *Journal of Psychology*, 22, 9–39.

Aloni, M. & Bernieri, F.J. (2004). Is love blind? The effects of experience and infatuation on the perception of love. *Journal of Nonverbal Behavior*, 28, 287–96.

Ambady, N. & Gray, H.M. (2002). On being sad and mistaken: mood effects on the accuracy of thin-slice judgments. *Journal of Personality and Social Psychology*, 83, 947–61.

Ambady, N. & Rosenthal, R. (1992). Thin slices of expressive behavior as predictors of interpersonal consequences: a meta-analysis. *Psychological Bulletin*, 111, 256–74.

Ambady, N., Bernieri, F., & Richeson, J.A. (2000). Towards a histology of social behavior: judgmental accuracy from thin slices of the behavioral stream. *Advances in Experimental Social Psychology*, 32, 201–71.

Ambady, N., Hallahan, M., & Conner, B. (1999). Accuracy of judgments of sexual orientation from thin slices of behavior. *Journal of Personality and Social Psychology*, 77, 538–47.

Ambady, N., LaPlante, D., & Johnson, E. (2001). Thin-slice judgments as a measure of interpersonal sensitivity. In *Interpersonal sensitivity: theory and measurement* (ed. J.A. Hall & F.J. Bernieri), pp. 89–101. Mahwah, NJ: Erlbaum.

Archer, D. & Akert, R.M. (1980). The encoding of meaning: a test of three theories of social interaction. *Sociological Inquiry*, 50, 393–419.

Archer, D., Costanzo, M., & Akert, R. (2001). The Interpersonal Perception Task (IPT):alternative approaches to problems of theory and design. In *Interpersonal sensitivity: theory and measurement* (ed. J.A. Hall & F.J. Bernieri), pp. 161–82. Mahwah, NJ: Erlbaum.

Barnes, M.L. & Sternberg, R.J. (1989). Social intelligence and judgment policy of nonverbal cues. *Intelligence*, 13, 263–87.

Baum, K.M. & Nowicki, S., Jr. (1998). Perception of emotion: measuring decoding accuracy of adult prosodic cues varying in intensity. *Journal of Nonverbal Behavior*, 22, 89–107.

Bernieri, F.J. (1991). Interpersonal sensitivity in teaching interactions. *Personality and Social Psychology Bulletin*, 17, 98–103.

Bernieri, F.J. (2001). Toward a taxonomy of interpersonal sensitivity. In *Interpersonal sensitivity: theory and measurement* (ed. J.A. Hall & F.J. Bernieri), pp. 3–19. Mahwah, NJ: Erlbaum.

Bernieri, F.J. & Gillis, J.S. (2001). Judging rapport: employing Brunswik's lens model to study interpersonal sensitivity. In *Interpersonal sensitivity: theory and measurement* (ed. J.A. Hall & F.J. Bernieri), pp. 67–88. Mahwah, NJ: Erlbaum.

Bernieri, F., Gillis, J.S., Davis, J.M., & Grahe, J.E. (1996). Dyad rapport and the accuracy of its judgment across situations. *Journal of Personality and Social Psychology*, 71, 110–29.

Bernieri, F.J., Zuckerman, M., Koestner, R., & Rosenthal, R. (1994). Measuring person perception accuracy: another look at self-other agreement. *Personality and Social Psychology Bulletin*, 20, 367–378.

Biehl, M., Matsumoto, D., Ekman, P., Hearn, V., Heider, K., Kudoh, T., *et al.* (1997). Matsumoto and Ekman's Japanese and Caucasian Facial Expressions of Emotion (JACFEE): reliability data and cross-national differences. *Journal of Nonverbal Behavior,* 21, 3–21.

Blackman, M. (2002). The employment interview via the telephone: are we sacrificing accurate personality judgments for cost efficiency? *Journal of Research in Personality,* 36, 208–23.

Bollen, K. & Lennox, R. (1991). Conventional wisdom on measurement: a structural equation perspective. *Psychological Bulletin,* 110, 305–14.

Borkenau, P. & Liebler, A. (1995). Observable attributes and manifestations and cues of personality and intelligence. *Journal of Personality,* 63, 1–25.

Bornstein, M.H. & Arterberry, M.E. (2003). Recognition, discrimination and categorization of smiling by 5-month-old infants. *Developmental Science,* 6, 585–99.

Boucher, J.D. & Carlson, G.E. (1980). Recognition of facial expression in three cultures. *Journal of Cross-Cultural Psychology,* 11, 263–80.

Brackett, M. & Mayer, J.D. (2003). Convergent, discriminant, and incremental validity of competing measures of emotional intelligence. *Personality and Social Psychology Bulletin,* 29, 1147–58.

Brunswik, E. (1956). *Perception and the representative design of psychological experiments.* Berkeley, CA: University of California Press.

Buck, R. (1976). A test of nonverbal receiving ability: preliminary studies. *Human Communication Research,* 2, 162–71.

Buck, R. (1979). Measuring individual differences in nonverbal communication of affect: the slide-viewing paradigm. *Human Communication Research,* 6, 47–57.

Carney, D.R. (2004). *In the face of prejudice: nonverbal expression and accurate detection of explicitly and implicitly measured anti-Black attitudes.* Unpublished doctoral dissertation, Northeastern University, Boston, MA.

Carney, D.R. & Harrigan, J.A. (2003). It takes one to know one: interpersonal sensitivity is related to accurate assessments of others' interpersonal sensitivity. *Emotion,* 3, 194–200.

Carney, D.R., Hall, J.A., & Smith LeBeau, L. (2005). Beliefs about the nonverbal expression of social power. *Journal of Nonverbal Behavior,* 29, 105–123.

Colvin, C.R., Block, J., & Funder, D.C. (1995). Overly positive self-evaluations and personality: Negative implications for mental heath. *Journal of Personality and Social Psychology,* 68, 1152–1162.

Colvin, C.R. & Bundick, M.J. (2001). In search of the good judge of personality: some methodological and theoretical concerns. In *Interpersonal sensitivity: theory and measurement* (ed. J.A. Hall & F.J. Bernieri), pp. 47–65. Mahwah, NJ: Erlbaum.

Costanzo, M. & Archer, D. (1989). Interpreting the expressive behavior of others: the Interpersonal Perception Task. *Journal of Nonverbal Behavior,* 13, 225–45.

Cronbach, L.J. (1955). Processes affecting scores on 'understanding of others' and 'assumed similarity'. *Psychological Bulletin,* 52, 177–93.

Cronbach, L.J. (1990). *Essentials of psychological testing,* 5th edn. New York: Harper Collins.

Davis, M.H. & Kraus, L.A. (1997). Personality and empathic accuracy. In *Empathic accuracy* (ed. W. Ickes), pp. 144–68. New York: Guilford.

deMille, R., O'Sullivan, M., & Guilford, J.P. (1965). *Missing Cartoons—Form A*. Beverly Hills: Sheridan Supply Company.

DePaulo, B.M., Charlton, K., Cooper, H., Lindsay, J.J., & Muhlenbruck, L. (1997). The accuracy-confidence correlation in the detection of deception. *Personality and Social Psychology Review, 1*, 346–57.

deTurck, M.A. (1991). Training observers to detect spontaneous deception: effects of gender. *Communication Reports, 4*, 79–89.

de Waal, F.B.M. (ed.). (2001). *Tree of origin: what primate behavior can tell us about human social evolution*. Cambridge, MA: Harvard University Press.

DiMatteo, M.R., Friedman, H.S., & Taranta, A. (1979). Sensitivity to bodily nonverbal communication as a factor in practitioner–patient rapport. *Journal of Nonverbal Behavior, 4*, 18–26.

Dimberg, U. (1997). Facial reactions: rapidly evoked emotional responses. *Journal of Psychophysiology, 11*, 115–23.

Dimberg, U. & Thunberg, M. (1998). Rapid facial reactions to emotional facial expressions. *Scandinavian Journal of Psychology, 39*, 39–45.

Dimberg, U., Thunberg, M., & Elmehed, K. (2000). Unconscious facial reactions to emotional facial expressions. *Psychological Science, 11*, 86–9.

Dimitrovsky, L. (1964). The ability to identify the emotional meaning of vocal expressions at successive age levels. In *The communication of emotional meaning* (ed. J.R. Davitz). New York: McGraw–Hill.

Dorfman, D.D., Keeve, S., & Saslow, C. (1971). Ethnic identification: a signal detection analysis. *Journal of Personality and Social Psychology, 18*, 373–9.

Dunlap, K. (1927). The role of eye muscles and mouth muscles in the expression of the emotions. *Genetic Psychology Monographs, 2*, 199–233.

Ekman, P. (1994). Strong evidence for universals in facial expressions: a reply to Russell's mistaken critique. *Psychological Bulletin, 115*, 268–87.

Ekman, P. & Friesen, W.V. (1972). Hand movements. *Journal of Communication, 22*, 353–74.

Ekman, P. & Friesen, W.V. (1974). Nonverbal behavior and psychopathology. In *The psychology of depression: contemporary theory and research* (ed. R.J. Friedman & M.M. Katz). Oxford, UK: Wiley.

Ekman, P. & Friesen, W.V. (1976). *Pictures of Facial Affect*. Palo Alto, CA: Consulting Psychologists' Press.

Ekman, P. & O'Sullivan, M. (1991). Who can catch a liar? *American Psychologist, 46*, 913–20.

Ekman, P. & Rosenberg, E. (1997). *What the face reveals: basic and applied studies of spontaneous expression using the Facial Action Coding System (FACS)*. New York: Oxford University Press.

Ekman, P., Davidson, R.J., & Friesen, W.V. (1990). The Duchenne smile: emotional expression and brain physiology II. *Journal of Personality and Social Psychology, 58*, 342–53.

Ekman, P., Friesen, W.V., & Hager, J.C. (2002). *Facial Action Coding System*. Salt Lake City, UT: A Human Face.

Ekman, P., & Friesen, W.V. (1978). *The Facial Affect Coding System: A technique for the measurement of facial movement*. Palo Alto, CA: Consulting Psychologists Press.

Ekman, P., Friesen, W.V., O'Sullivan, M., Chan, A., Diacoyanni–Tarlatzis, I., Heider, K., *et al.* (1987). Universals and cultural differences in the judgments of facial expressions of emotion. *Journal of Personality and Social Psychology*, 53, 712–17.

Elfenbein, H.A. & Ambady, N. (2002). On the universality and cultural specificity of emotion recognition: a meta-analysis. *Psychological Bulletin*, 128, 203–35.

Elfenbein, H.A. & Ambady, N. (2003). When familiarity breeds accuracy: cultural exposure and facial emotion recognition. *Journal of Personality and Social Psychology*, 85, 276–90.

Fridlund, A.J. (1997). The new ethology of human facial expressions. In *The psychology of facial expression* (ed. J.A. Russell & J.M. Fernández–Dols), pp. 103–29. Paris: Cambridge University Press.

Fruzzetti, A.E., Toland, K., Teller, S.A., & Loftus, E.F. (1992). Memory and eyewitness testimony. In *Aspects of memory, practical aspects* (2nd edn) (ed. M.M. Gruneberg & P.E. Morris), pp. 18–50. Florence, KY: Taylor & Frances.

Funder, D. C. (1980). On seeing ourselves as others see us: self-other agreement and discrepancy in personality ratings. *Journal of Personality and Social Psychology*, 48, 473–493

Funder, D. (2001). Three trends in current research on person perception: positivity, realism, and sophistication. In *Interpersonal sensitivity: theory and measurement* (ed. J.A. Hall & F.J. Bernieri), pp. 319–31. Mahwah, NJ: Erlbaum.

Funder, D.C. & Harris, M.J. (1986). On the several facets of personality assessment: the case of social acuity. *Journal of Personality*, 54, 528–50.

Funder, D.C. & Sneed, C.D. (1993). Behavioral manifestations of personality: an ecological approach to judgmental accuracy. *Journal of Personality and Social Psychology*, 64, 479–90.

Funder, D.C., Furr, R.M., & Colvin, C.R. (2000). The Riverside Behavioral Q-Sort: a tool for the description of social behavior. *Journal of Personality*, 68, 451–89.

Funder, D.C., Kolar, D., & Colvin, R.C. (1995). Agreement among judges of personality: interpersonal relations, similarity, and acquaintanceship. *Journal of Personality and Social Psychology*, 69, 656–72.

Gesn, P.R. & Ickes, W. (1999). The development of meaning contexts for empathic accuracy: channel and sequence effects. *Journal of Personality and Social Psychology*, 77, 746–61.

Gifford, R. (1994). A lens-mapping framework for understanding the encoding and decoding of interpersonal dispositions in nonverbal behavior. *Journal of Personality and Social Psychology*, 66, 398–412.

Gilbert, D.T. & Krull, D.S. (1988). Seeing less and knowing more: the benefits of perceptual ignorance. *Journal of Personality and Social Psychology*, 54, 193–202.

Gillis, J.S. & Bernieri, F.J. (2001). The perception and judgment of rapport. In *The essential Brunswik: beginnings, explications, applications* (ed. K.R. Hammond & T.R. Steward), pp. 380–83. New York: Oxford University Press.

Gillis, J., Bernieri, F., & Wooten, E. (1995). The effects of stimulus medium and feedback on the judgment of rapport. *Organizational Behavior and Human Decision Processes*, 63, 33–45.

Grahe, J.E. & Bernieri, F.J. (2002). Self-awareness of judgment policies of rapport. *Personality and Social Psychology Bulletin*, 28, 1407–18.

Green, D.M. & Swets, J.A. (1966). *Signal detection theory and psychophysics*. New York: Wiley.

Guilford, J.P. (1954). *Psychometric methods*, 2nd edn. New York: McGraw–Hill.

Halberstadt, A.G. & Hall, J.A. (1980). Who's getting the message? Children's nonverbal skill and their evaluation by teachers. *Developmental Psychology,* 16, 564–73.

Hall, J.A. (1978). Gender effects in decoding nonverbal cues. *Psychological Bulletin,* 85, 845–57.

Hall, J.A. (1984). *Nonverbal sex differences: communication accuracy and expressive style.* Baltimore: The Johns Hopkins University Press.

Hall, J.A. (1998). How big are nonverbal sex differences? The case of smiling and sensitivity to nonverbal cues. In *Sex differences and similarities in communication: critical essays and empirical investigations of sex and gender in interaction* (ed. D.J. Canary & K. Dindia), pp.155–77. Mahwah, NJ: Erlbaum.

Hall, J.A. (2001). The PONS test and the psychometric approach to measuring interpersonal sensitivity. In *Interpersonal sensitivity: theory and measurement* (ed. J.A. Hall & F.J. Bernieri), pp.143–60. Mahwah, NJ: Erlbaum.

Hall, J.A. & Bernieri, F.J. (ed.) (2001). *Interpersonal sensitivity: theory and measurement.* Mahwah, NJ: Erlbaum.

Hall, J.A. & Braunwald, K.G. (1981). Gender cues in conversations. *Journal of Personality and Social Psychology,* 40, 99–110.

Hall, J.A. & Carter, J.D. (1999). Gender-stereotype accuracy as an individual difference. *Journal of Personality and Social Psychology,* 77, 350–9.

Hall, J.A. & Matsumoto, D. (2004). Sex differences in judgments of multiple emotions from facial expressions. *Emotion,* 4, 201–6.

Hall, J.A. & Murphy, N.A. (2004). *Recall of nonverbal and verbal cues: exploring a new definition of nonverbal sensitivity.* Manuscript submitted for publication.

Hall, J.A., Carter, J.D., & Horgan, T.G. (2000). Gender differences in the nonverbal communication of emotion. In *Gender and emotion: social psychological perspectives* (ed. A.H. Fischer), pp. 97–117. Paris: Cambridge University Press.

Hall, J.A., Carter, J.D., & Horgan, T.G. (2001). Status roles and recall of nonverbal cues. *Journal of Nonverbal Behavior,* 25, 79–100.

Hall, J.A., Halberstadt, A.G., & O'Brien, C.E. (1997). 'Subordination' and nonverbal sensitivity: a study and synthesis of findings based on trait measures. *Sex Roles,* 37, 295–317.

Hall, J.A., Horgan, T.G., Stein, T.S., & Roter, D.L. (2002). Liking in the physician–patient relationship. *Patient Education and Counseling,* 48, 69–77.

Hall, J.A., Rosip, J.C., Smith LeBeau, L., Horgan, T.G., & Carter, J.D. (in press). Attributing the sources of accuracy in unequal power dyadic communication: who is better and why? *Journal of Experimental Social Psychology.*

Heider, F. (1958). *The psychology of interpersonal relations.* Hillsdale, NJ: Erlbaum.

Holder, H.B. & Kirkpatrick, S.W. (1991). Interpretation of emotion from facial expressions in children with and without learning disabilities. *Journal of Learning Disabilities,* 24, 170–7.

Horgan, T.G., Schmid Mast, M., Hall, J.A., & Carter, J.D. (2004). Gender differences in memory for the appearance of others. *Personality and Social Psychology Bulletin,* 30, 185–96.

Ickes, W. (ed.). (1997). *Empathic accuracy.* New York: Guilford.

Ickes, W. (2001). Measuring empathic accuracy. In *Interpersonal sensitivity: theory and measurement* (ed. J.A. Hall & F.J. Bernieri), pp. 219–41. Mahwah, NJ: Erlbaum.

Ickes, W., Stinson, L., Bissonnette, V., & Garcia, S. (1990). Naturalistic social cognition: empathic accuracy in mixed-sex dyads. *Journal of Personality and Social Psychology,* **59**, 730–42.

Judd, C.M. & Park, B. (1993). Definition and assessment of accuracy in social stereotypes. *Psychological Review,* **100**, 109–28.

Kenny, D.A. (1994). *Interpersonal perception: a social relations analysis.* New York: Guilford.

Kenny, D.A. & Acitelli, L.K. (2001). Accuracy and bias in the perception of the partner in a close relationship. *Journal of Personality and Social Psychology,* **80**, 439–48.

Kenny, D.A. & Albright, L. (1987). Accuracy in interpersonal perception: a social relations analysis. *Psychological Bulletin,* **102**, 390–402.

Kenny, D.A. & Winquist, L. (2001). The measurement of interpersonal sensitivity: consideration of design, components, and unit of analysis. In *Interpersonal sensitivity: theory and measurement* (ed. J.A. Hall & F.J. Bernieri), pp. 265–93. Mahwah, NJ: Erlbaum.

Kenny, D.A., Kashy, D.A., & Bolger, N. (1998). Data analysis in social psychology. In *The handbook of social psychology* (4th edn) (ed. D.T. Gilbert, S.T. Fiske, & G. Lindzey), pp. 233–65. Boston: McGraw–Hill.

Kenny, D.A., Kieffer, S.C., Smith, J.A., Ceplenski, P., & Kulo, J. (1996). Circumscribed accuracy among well-acquainted individuals. *Journal of Experimental Social Psychology,* **32**, 1–12.

Kline, P. (2000*a*). *A psychometrics primer.* London: Free Association Books.

Kline, P. (2000*b*). *A handbook of psychological testing.* London: Routledge.

Knapp, M.L. & Hall, J.A. (2002). *Nonverbal communication in human interaction* (5th edn). Belmont, CA: Wadsworth/Thomson Learning.

Koning, C. & Magill–Evans, J. (2001). Validation of the Child and Adolescent Social Perception Measure. *Occupational Therapy Journal of Research,* **21**, 49–67.

Kunda, Z. (1999). *Social cognition: making sense of people.* Cambridge, MA: MIT Press.

LaFrance, M. & Henley, N.M. (1994). On oppressing hypotheses: or differences in nonverbal sensitivity revisited. In *Power/gender: social relations in theory and practice* (ed. L. Radtke & H. Stam). London: Sage.

Landis, C. (1924). Studies of emotional reactions: 2. General behavior and facial expression. *Journal of Comparative Psychology,* **4**, 447–509.

Larkin, K.T., Martin, R.R., & McClain, S.E. (2002). Cynical hostility and the accuracy of decoding facial expressions of emotions. *Journal of Behavioral Medicine,* **25**, 285–92.

Lenti, C., Lenti–Boero, D., & Giacobbe, A. (1999). Decoding of emotional expressions in children and adolescents. *Perceptual and Motor Skills,* **89**, 808–14.

Lippa, R. (1998). The nonverbal display and judgment of extraversion, masculinity, femininity, and gender diagnosticity: a lens model analysis. *Journal of Research in Personality,* **32**, 80–107.

Lippa, R.A. & Dietz, J.K. (2000). The relation of gender, personality, and intelligence to judges' accuracy in judging strangers' personality from brief video segments. *Journal of Nonverbal Behavior,* **24**, 25–43.

Loewenthal, K. (2001). *An introduction to psychological tests and scales* (2nd edn). Hove, UK: The Psychology Press.

Magill–Evans, J., Koning, C., Cameron–Sadava, A., & Manyk, K. (1995). The Child and Adolescent Social Perception Measure. *Journal of Nonverbal Behavior,* **19**, 151–69.

Malone, B.E. & DePaulo, B.M. (2001). Measuring sensitivity to deception. In Interpersonal sensitivity: Theory and measurement (ed. J.A. Hall & F. J. Bernieri), pp. 103–24. Mahwah, NJ: Erlbaum.

Marangoni, C., Garcia, S., Ickes, W., & Teng, G. (1995). Empathic accuracy in a clinically relevant setting. *Journal of Personality and Social Psychology*, **68**, 854–69.

Marcus, D.K. & Leatherwood, J.C. (1998). The interpersonal circle at zero acquaintance: a social relations analysis. *Journal of Research in Personality*, **32**, 297–313.

Matsumoto, D., LeRoux, J., Wilson–Cohn, C., Raroque, J., Kooken, K., Ekman, P., *et al.* (2000). A new test to measure emotion recogition ability: Matsumoto and Ekman's Japanese and Caucasian Brief Affect Recognition Test (JACBART). *Journal of Nonverbal Behavior*, **24**, 179–209.

Mayer, J.D. & Salovey, P. (1997). What is emotional intelligence? In *Emotional development and emotional intelligence: implications for educators* (ed. P. Salovey & D. Sluyter), pp. 3–31. New York: Basic Books.

Mayer, J.D., Salovey, P., Caruso, D.R., & Sitarenios, G. (2003). Measuring emotional intelligence with the MSCEIT V2.0. *Emotion*, **3**, 97–105.

McAndrew, F.T. (1986). A cross-cultural study of recognition thresholds for facial expression of emotion. *Journal of Cross-Cultural Psychology*, **17**, 211–24.

McArthur, L.Z. & Baron, R.M. (1983). Toward an ecological theory of social perception. *Psychological Review*, **90**, 215–38.

McClure, E.B. (2000). A meta-analytic review of sex differences in facial expression processing and their development in infants, children, and adolescents. *Psychological Bulletin*, **126**, 424–53.

McLarney–Vesotski, A. (2003). *Trait predictors of the good judge: three proposed underlying mediators*. Unpublished doctoral dissertation, University of Toledo, Toledo, OH.

McNeill, D. (1985). So you think gestures are nonverbal? *Psychological Review*, **92**, 350–71.

Meltzoff, A.N. & Moore, M.K. (1977). Imitation of facial and manual gestures by human neonates. *Science*, **198**, 75–8.

Murphy, N.A. (2003). *Intelligence in social interaction*. Unpublished doctoral dissertation, Northeastern University, Boston, MA.

Murphy, N.A., Hall, J.A., & Colvin, C.R. (2003). Accurate intelligence assessments in social interaction: mediators and gender effects. *Journal of Personality*, **71**, 465–93.

Murphy, S.T. & Zajonc, R.B. (1993). Affect, cognition, and awareness: affective priming with optimal and suboptimal stimulus exposures. *Journal of Personality and Social Psychology*, **64**, 723–39.

Niit, T. & Valsiner, J. (1977). Recognition of facial expressions: an experimental investigation of Ekman's model. *Acta et Commentationes Universitatis Tarvensis*, **429**, 85–107.

Noller, P. (1980). Misunderstandings in marital communication: a study of couples' nonverbal communication. *Journal of Personality and Social Psychology*, **39**, 1135–48.

Noller, P. (2001). Using standard content methodology to assess nonverbal sensitivity in dyads. In *Interpersonal sensitivity: theory and measurement* (ed. J.A. Hall & F.J. Bernieri), pp. 243–64. Mahwah, NJ: Erlbaum.

Nowicki, S., Jr. & Duke, M.P. (1994). Individual differences in the nonverbal communication of affect: the Diagnostic Analysis of Nonverbal Accuracy Scale. *Journal of Nonverbal Behavior*, 18, 9–35.

Nowicki, S., Jr. & Duke, M.P. (2001). Nonverbal receptivity: the Diagnostic Analysis of Nonverbal Accuracy (DANVA). In *Interpersonal sensitivity: theory and measurement* (ed. J.A. Hall & F.J. Bernieri), pp. 183–98). Mahwah, NJ:Erlbaum.

Patterson, M.L. (1995). A parallel process model of nonverbal communication. *Journal of Nonverbal Behavior*, 19, 3–29.

Phillips, R.D., Wagner, S.H., Fells, C.A., & Lynch, M. (1990). Do infants recognize emotion in facial expressions? Categorical and 'metaphorical' evidence. *Infant Behavior and Development*, 13, 71–84.

Reynolds, D.J. & Gifford, R. (2001). The sounds and sights of intelligence: a lens model channel analysis. *Personality and Social Psychology Bulletin*, 27, 187–200.

Richeson, J. A. & Shelton, J. N. (2005). Thin slices of racial bias. *Journal of Nonverbal Behavior*, 29, 75–86.

Riggio, R. E., & Riggio, H. R. (2001). Self-report measurement of interpersonal sensitivity. In *Interpersonal sensitivity: theory and measurement* (ed. J.A. Hall & F.J. Bernieri), pp. 127–42. Mahwah, NJ: Erlbaum.

Roberts, R.D., Zeidner, M., & Matthews, G. (2001). Does emotional intelligence meet traditional standards for an intelligence? Some new data and conclusions. *Emotion*, 1, 196–231.

Rojahn, J., Singh, N.N., Singh, S.D., Baker, J.A., Lawrence, M.A., & Davis, C.M. (2002). Concurrent validity studies of the Facial Discrimination Task. *Journal of Child and Family Studies*, 11, 203–15.

Rollman, S.A. (1978). The sensitivity of Black and White Americans to nonverbal cues of prejudice. *Journal of Social Psychology*, 105, 73–7.

Rosenthal, R. (1976). *Experimenter effects in behavioral research* (enlarged edn). New York: Irvington.

Rosenthal, R. & Rubin, D.B. (1978). Interpersonal expectancy effects: the first 345 studies. *Behavioral and Brain Sciences*, 3, 377–86.

Rosenthal, R. & Rubin, D.B. (1989). Effect size estimation for one-sample multiple-choice-type data: design, analysis, and meta-analysis. *Psychological Bulletin*, 106, 332–7.

Rosenthal, R., Hall, J.A., DiMatteo, M.R., Rogers, P.L., & Archer, D. (1979). *Sensitivity to nonverbal communication: the PONS test*. Baltimore: The Johns Hopkins University Press.

Rosip, J.C. & Hall, J.A. (2004). Knowledge of nonverbal cues, gender, and nonverbal decoding accuracy. *Journal of Nonverbal Behavior*, 28, 267–86.

Russell, J.A. (1994). Is there universal recognition of emotion from facial expressions? A review of cross-cultural studies. *Psychological Bulletin*, 115, 102–41.

Sapir, E.A. (1949). Communication. In *Selected writings of Edward Sapir in language, culture, and personality* (ed. D.G. Mandelbaum). Berkeley and Los Angeles: University of California Press.

Scherer, K.R. (1978). Inference rules in personality attribution from voice quality: the loud voice of extraversion. *European Journal of Social Psychology*, 8, 467–87.

Scherer, K.R. (1982). Methods of research on vocal communication: paradigms and parameters. In *Handbook of methods in nonverbal behavior research* (ed. K.R. Scherer & P. Ekman), pp. 136–98. Cambridge, UK: Cambridge University Press.

Scherer, K.R. (2003). Vocal communication of emotion: a review of research paradigms. *Speech Communication,* 40, 227–56.

Scherer, K. R. & Ceschi, G. (2000). Criteria for emotion recognition from verbal and nonverbal expression: studying baggage loss in the airport. *Personality and Social Psychology Bulletin,* 26, 327–339.

Scherer, K.R., Feldstein, S., Bond, R.N., & Rosenthal, R. (1985). Vocal cues to deception: a comparative channel approach. *Journal of Psycholinguistic Research,* 14, 409–25.

Scherer, K.R., Johnstone, T., & Klasmeyer, G. (2003). Vocal expression of emotion. In *Handbook of the affective sciences* (ed. R.J. Davidson, H. Goldsmith, & K.R. Scherer), pp. 433–56. New York: Oxford University Press.

Scherer, K.R., Scherer, U., Hall, J.A., & Rosenthal, R. (1977). Differential attribution of personality based on multi-channel presentation of verbal and nonverbal cues. *Psychological Research,* 39, 221–47.

Schmid Mast, M., & Hall, J.A. (2004). Who is the boss and who is not? Accuracy of judging status. *Journal of Nonverbal Behavior,* 28, 145–66.

Smith, H.J., Archer, D., & Costanzo, M. (1991). 'Just a hunch': accuracy and awareness in person perception. *Journal of Nonverbal Behavior,* 15, 3–18.

Snodgrass, S.E. (1985). Women's intuition: the effect of subordinate role on interpersonal sensitivity. *Journal of Personality and Social Psychology,* 49, 146–55.

Snodgrass, S.E. (1992). Further effects of role versus gender on interpersonal sensitivity. *Journal of Personality and Social Psychology,* 62, 154–8.

Snodgrass, S.E., Hecht, M.A., & Ploutz–Snyder, R. (1998). Interpersonal sensitivity: expressivity or perceptivity? *Journal of Personality and Social Psychology,* 74, 238–49.

Snyder, M., Tanke, E.D., & Berscheid, E. (1977). Social perception and interpersonal behavior: on the self-fulfilling nature of social stereotypes. *Journal of Personality and Social Psychology,* 35, 656–66.

Spitz, H.H. (1997). *Nonconscious movements: from mystical messages to facilitated communication.* Mahwah, NJ: Erlbaum.

Stinson, L. & Ickes, W. (1992). Empathic accuracy in the interaction of male friends versus male strangers. *Journal of Personality and Social Psychology,* 62, 787–97.

Swim, J.K. (1994). Perceived versus meta-analytic effect sizes: an assessment of the accuracy of gender stereotypes. *Journal of Personality and Social Psychology,* 66, 21–36.

Taft, R. (1955). The ability to judge people. *Psychological Bulletin,* 52, 1–23.

Thomas, G. & Fletcher, G.O. (2003). Mind-reading accuracy in intimate relationships: assessing the roles of the relationship, the target, and the judge. *Journal of Personality and Social Psychology,* 85, 1079–94.

Vogt, D.S. & Colvin, C.R. (2003). Interpersonal orientation and the accuracy of personality judgments. *Journal of Personality,* 71, 267–95.

Vrij, A. & Semin, G.R. (1996). Lie experts' beliefs about nonverbal indicators of deception. *Journal of Nonverbal Behavior,* 20, 65–80.

Wagner, H.L. (1993). On measuring performance in category judgment studies of nonverbal behavior. *Journal of Nonverbal Behavior,* 17, 3–28.

Wagner, H.L. (1997). Methods for the study of facial behavior. In *The psychology of facial expression* (ed. J.A. Russell & J.M. Fernández–Dols), pp. 31–54. New York: Cambridge University Press.

Wallbott, H.G. (1991). Recognition of emotion from facial expression via imitation? Some indirect evidence for an old theory. *British Journal of Social Psychology,* 30, 207–19.

Watson, D. (1989). Strangers' ratings of the five robust personality factors: evidence of a surprising convergence with self-report. *Journal of Personality and Social Psychology,* 57, 120–8.

Zebrowitz, L.A. (2001). Groping for the elephant of interpersonal sensitivity. In *Interpersonal sensitivity: theory and measurement* (ed. J.A. Hall & F.J. Bernieri), pp. 333–50. Mahwah, NJ: Erlbaum.

Zebrowitz, L.A., Hall, J.A., Murphy, N.A., & Rhodes, G. (2002). Looking smart and looking good: facial cues to intelligence and their origins. *Personality and Social Psychology Bulletin,* 28, 238–49.

Zuckerman, M. & Larrance, D.T. (1979). Individual differences in perceived encoding and decoding abilities. In *Skill in nonverbal communication* (ed. R. Rosenthal), pp. 171–203. Cambridge, MA: Oelgeschlager, Gunn & Hain.

Zuckerman, M., Lipets, M.S., Koivumaki, J.H., & Rosenthal, R. (1975). Encoding and decoding nonverbal cues of emotion. *Journal of Personality and Social Psychology,* 32, 1068–76.

CHAPTER 7

NONVERBAL BEHAVIOR IN EDUCATION

ELISHA BABAD

The purpose of this chapter is to acquaint the reader with the various ways nonverbal (NV) research is used in education. 'Research' is taken here in a global and loose manner, covering the entire range of fact-seeking activities, from controlled experimental studies at one extreme, to informal gathering of NV information for purposes of teacher reflection and improvement at the other extreme. The chapter is intended to be descriptive and analytical. Various methods, instruments, and ways of using NV information in education are delineated, and relevant methodological issues concerning NV research in education are discussed. But the chapter does not provide a critical evaluation of the various methods, and it does not judge any of the applications it describes.

The significance of nonverbal behavior in education

Chapters on NV behavior in education usually begin with a discussion of the importance of NV research to education, just as chapters on NV behavior in other areas typically expand on the significance of NV behavior to each of those areas (e.g. De Paulo 1992). If the main objectives of schooling are cognitive development and scholastic achievement, then it is the *verbal* domain that is most significant in education. It might be said that the NV domain gains its significance by *mediating* the success of the verbal domain in achieving the central goals of education. How the teacher 'delivers' instruction in the classroom has strong affective components. Indeed, critical aspects of teacher–student interaction are nonverbal. NV communication can facilitate and improve the quality of the teaching/learning process, but it often hinders the process either for the entire student body or for defined groups of students.

Teacher–student interactions are continuous and cumulative, conducted repeatedly over long periods of time. These interactions include both verbal and NV aspects, the latter carrying much of the affective tone of the exchange and often conveying to the students information about the 'real nature' of the situation. Subtle, repetitive, and systematic nuances of teachers' NV behavior toward specific students can affect the students' self-concepts and school experiences substantially.

Another reason for the significance of NV behavior in education is the high frequency of deception in teachers' classroom behavior. Controlling an entire classroom of energetic youngsters for long hours every day, and dealing with numerous obstacles to effective teaching and learning are formidable tasks, likely to create frustration and negative feelings. But, teachers' negative feelings toward their classes, and toward individual students or groups of students in particular, are not considered to be legitimate, and their direct expression is rarely permitted. Therefore, there is much deception, pretense, and even lying in teacher behavior, especially in their treatment of low-achieving, low-expectancy students (Babad 1998; Weinstein 2002).

The literature on NV leakage (Babad *et al.* 1989*b*; De Paulo & Rosenthal 1979; Ekman 1985; Ekman & Friesen 1969*a*) teaches us that analysis of NV behavior via separation of channels makes it possible to trace concealed negative affect. If hidden negative affect is exposed, perhaps steps can be taken to prevent or remedy its negative consequences.

Brief historical review of trends in nonverbal research in education

Research on NV behavior did not originate in education, and even today, it is not central to it. NV research is conducted mostly in those areas of the behavioral sciences focused on affect, expression, personality, and social perception. Educators, on their part, are more concerned about issues of thinking, teaching, cognitive development and learning. As a result of technological advances, such as the invention of video recording, computerization, and progress in the investigation of NV behavior, NV research was imported to education, and today it is a central topic in educational research. The following review should acquaint the reader with the major topics of NV research in education.

Microteaching

Microteaching (MT) followed the technological advances in video recording. The method was developed in the 1960s by Dwight Allen and his colleagues at the Stanford University Teacher Education Program, and its popularity spread very quickly (Allen & Ryan 1969; Brown 1975; Perrott 1977). Today, MT is one of the major methods/ instruments in teacher training and teacher development programs worldwide. However, the overenthusiasm of the 1970s, with MT as a panacea, has subsided somewhat. Most practitioners now take a more cautious and realistic view of its potential for increasing teaching effectiveness. However, almost all prospective and in-service teachers have participated at least once in a feedback session based on a videotaped lesson, which is the essence of MT.

MT is essentially a data-based feedback intervention for teachers' self-inquiry ('reflection') and skills training. A teaching session is videotaped in a classroom or studio, and the recording serves as the raw 'empirical' data for analysis. The videotaped materials are supposed to provide the most reliable and unbiased evidence of teacher behavior and the most complete coverage of all aspects of the teaching situation. In the MT session, the videotaped material is viewed together by the videotaped teacher-in-training, the supervisor, and often by the teacher's peers as well, and the teacher receives personal feedback and supervision. The analysis of the videotaped data can take many forms, from open impressionistic discussion to more exacting analysis of pre-selected aspects. Statistical treatment of operationally defined and measured variables might be included.

MT was not intended initially to focus on NV aspects, but was conceived as a tool for pedagogic and didactic examination and reflection. Thus, the verbal components and the actual teaching process, which were considered to be fully reconstructed in the recording, were the main focus of analysis. MT was not associated with any particular theory of instruction, and supervisors could utilize the recorded materials to foster and teach whichever theory of learning they preferred. However, because of the salience of the visual aspects in the video recorded material, NV aspects inadvertently gained importance.

In teacher training, even those who are primarily interested in the didactic and instructional aspects of teachers' conduct, could not ignore the fact that the NV delivery of instruction and the ways teachers handle students in the classroom must affect the teaching/learning process. As a result, MT sessions have eventually focused more and more on teacher–student interaction and teachers' NV behavior. Teachers received feedback on how to improve their conduct in their teaching and in their interactions with students. The analyses related, among other aspects, to the teacher's position toward the entire classroom, focusing on appearance, dress, poise, use of voice, body and hands, movement in the classroom, teacher's enthusiasm, eye contact, etc. Other parts of the analysis focused on the most difficult and critical aspect of teaching:

1. How to deal with weak, low-achieving, and often unmotivated students?
2. How to handle disciplinary problems and other obstacles to effective teaching?

If MT were to be categorized as a 'research method', it would probably be described as mostly qualitative, reflective action research. Its main advantage is the reconstruction (collection) of the fullest and most accurate 'data base' for subsequent analysis. Its main weakness is the lack of systematic methods for analyzing data, for making inferences, and for reaching data-based conclusions.

In any event, MT made an important contribution by emphasizing the importance of teachers' NV behavior in education. MT also opened the door for developing more rigorous methodologies for empirical analysis of video recordings of classroom interaction.

Noncognitive and expressive aspects in the delivery of instruction

As mentioned above, the raison d'être for focusing on NV processes in education is the weight of NV behaviors in the delivery of teaching material and in the teachers' conduct toward students. Researchers began to search for particular teacher behaviors that might have measurable effects on the products of the educational process (students' attitudes and motivation, academic achievement, students' evaluation of teachers). Thus, side by side with developments in the measurement of teaching effectiveness and students' ratings of teachers (SRT), advances were made in the analysis of verbal and NV behaviors and their contributions to educational outcomes.

The 'Doctor Fox' studies

The original Doctor Fox study was published three decades ago (Naftulin *et al.* 1973) and caused intense controversy. A charismatic, interesting, and funny lecturer (actually an actor) delivered a lecture to an audience of in-service teachers. The lecture was devoid of any consequential content, but the delivery was gripping and enjoyable. Doctor Fox received very high evaluations from his audience, who praised him for academic aspects and learning no less than for his expressive style. The Doctor Fox studies were written up as a critique of SRT research, presented as a threat to the validity of SRT measurement, and casting doubt on students' ability to evaluate 'real' teaching effectiveness. Studies by Doctor Fox supporters and opponents were published in the 1970s and 1980s, and these studies were very widely cited. The advocates of SRT (Abrami *et al.* 1982; Marsh 1984, 1987) concluded that Doctor Fox studies did not constitute a threat to SRT validity.

The main point concerning the history of NV research in education is that the importance of teachers' expressive style (with its heavy NV components) was illuminated very intensely, and more researchers began to conduct investigations on teachers' NV behavior.

Teacher immediacy and teacher enthusiasm

In recent years, two parallel lines of research examined the manifestations and effects of teachers' expressive style, by focusing on teacher immediacy and teacher enthusiasm. Quite strangely, the two fields have developed independently, despite their conceptual affinity. This independence may stem in part from the fact that researchers of teacher enthusiasm (Murray 1983; Schonwelter *et al.* 1994; Wood 1998—all in Canada) came from the tradition of SRT measurement in higher education, whereas the investigators of teacher immediacy (e.g. Andersen & Andersen 1982; Titsworth 2001) were interested in elementary and high-school students and focused on teaching and learning processes. Both teacher immediacy and teacher enthusiasm emphasize the role of teachers' expressive style and NV behavior in affecting their students (although both verbal *and* NV immediacy are measured in some studies).

Teacher immediacy is the NV behavior generating the perception of 'psychological closeness' with students (Titsworth 2001). Andersen and Andersen (1982) characterized highly immediate teachers by eye contact, movement, leaning forward, vocal variety, gestures, humor, and smiling. Non-immediate teachers were described as reading from notes, standing behind a podium, and using monotone delivery and abstract examples. Similarly, Wood (1998, following Murray 1983) summarized the characteristics of enthusiastic teachers as speaking in a dramatic and expressive way, showing variation in pitch, volume, and vocal inflection, smiling and laughing, moving about while lecturing, gesturing with hands and arms, using facial gestures, eye contact, and humor. The two descriptions are virtually identical, except that perhaps in the university environment, the feature of 'psychological closeness' is not as relevant as in elementary and high-school teaching.

In both fields, the accumulating results (Andersen & Andersen 1982; Ikeda & Beebe 1992; Wood 1998) generally indicate that teacher immediacy (with many more published studies) and teacher enthusiasm, are indeed related to better outcomes of the learning process (perhaps even in a proven causal relationship). Positive relationships were reported for measures of motivation, positive SRT, and high evaluations of teaching effectiveness, students' selective attention, and sometimes even better learning outcomes. (Incidentally, these findings are quite consistent with the findings of the famous, or *notorious*, Doctor Fox studies.)

Various methodological advances were made in order to measure teacher immediacy and teacher enthusiasm. (In fact, advances had to be made in the measurement of teachers' NV behavior on the one hand and in the measurement of educational products on the other.) The range of studies regarding these phenomena included surveys, field studies of various types, quasi-experimental and experimental studies, and projects of applied intervention. However, teacher immediacy and teacher enthusiasm were most often measured by students' high-inference reports and ratings of their teachers' behavior (e.g. 'Does your teacher move around in the class while lecturing? Does your teacher establish eye contact with students?'). Fewer studies used low-inference observational methods, recording actual teacher behavior in the classroom. (See later discussion of the issue of high- versus low-inference measurement.)

Thin slices research

A recent development in NV research (not necessarily in education) is the investigation of thin slices of NV behavior. Thin slices research continues the trend of measuring decoding sensitivity via judgments of brief instances of NV behavior in the Profile of Nonverbal Sensitivity (PONS) test (Rosenthal *et al.* 1979). In thin slices research, judges are exposed to extremely brief samples of NV behavior (e.g. of trial judges, job applicants, doctors, TV interviewers, psychological experimenters, and recently, also of teachers), and asked to rate their impressions of these target figures. These ratings are then correlated with a variety of criteria characterizing these target people, with a diagnostic and/or predictive objective (e.g. judges' verdicts, applicants' success in job interviews, SRT). The macro-level analysis (i.e. raters' global reactions to a brief NV clip) can be accompanied by a micro- (or molecular-) level analysis, where each movement, expression, and gesture in any given clip, is scrutinized and quantified, in an attempt to discover exactly what contributed to raters' macro ratings (see later discussion of micro analysis).

Thin slices research is based on the assumption that people absorb a great deal of interpersonal information from very brief exposure to target persons, and their judgments can be accurate and predictive of defined criteria no less than judgments made on the basis of much longer acquaintance and/or mutual interaction (Ambady & Rosenthal 1992; Ambady *et al.* 2000; Milmoe *et al.* 1967). Several thin slices studies in high-school and university settings indicated that students' evaluations of their teachers can indeed be predicted from thin slices of teachers' NV behavior in the classroom (Ambady & Rosenthal 1993; Babad *et al.* 2003, 2004; see p. 288).

By nature, thin slices research is quite complicated and expensive to run, especially compared to administering a short questionnaire to students about their teachers' NV behavior. In thin slices research, appropriate samples of teacher behavior must be videotaped in the classroom, following strict procedures. The necessary lab work must then be done to select clips and record them on master cassettes. Next, these clips are administered to groups of judges/raters who are unfamiliar with the video-taped teachers. Still, despite these difficulties, thin slices research can demonstrate, in the most dramatic and clear manner, the tremendous informational value of NV behavior, even with the briefest exposure.

Thin slices research usually involves a minimal context because of the brief exposure. In some studies (Babad *et al.* 1989*a*,*b*, 1991), the context was minimized not only by the brief exposure but also by separation of channels (face, body, voice, verbal content). The issue of using only minimal-context research in the absence of the full-classroom context has been debated among educational researchers (Galloway 1984; Woolfolk 1985; Woolfolk & Galloway 1985). Some educationalists criticized the value of context-minimal research in education (e.g. Doyle 1977; see discussion in Galloway 1984 and in Babad 1992). They argued that the true meanings of an educational situation are embedded *only* in its fullest context, and therefore a minimized context cannot be considered to represent the actual classroom situation. Some studies on teacher immediacy could probably be considered acceptable even by the purest full-context advocates, but thin slices research, almost by definition, involves a minimal context.

Another issue related to context in NV research was presented by Archer and Akert (1980), concerning the sampling of clips to be judged. Would any sample of NV behavior be equal in its informational value to other samples taken from the same overall situation, or would a given NV behavior acquire its meaning only in its *specific* situational context? Archer and Akert showed that behavior samples were replaceable. However, this issue has a special twist in NV research in education, because within one classroom session, teachers are involved in a variety of unique and distinct activities (e.g. administrative issues, disciplining students, teaching the entire class, interacting with individual students of different abilities). Recent research (Babad *et al.* 2003, 2004) indicates that the predictive power of judgments based on thin slices of teachers' NV behavior in the classroom indeed varies greatly (sometimes even reverses its direction) among the specific teacher activities.

Predicting student evaluations from thin slices of teachers' NV classroom behavior

The recent educational thin slices studies (Ambady & Rosenthal 1993; Babad *et al.* 2003, 2004), where attempts were made to predict students' evaluations of their teachers (SRT) from very brief instances of teachers' NV behavior in the classroom, highlighted three important issues. First, these studies indicated that even 10 seconds of teachers' NV, content-free, expressive behavior has sufficient informational value to predict students' end-of-course evaluations of their teachers. In studies of teacher immediacy and teacher enthusiasm, the predictor variable (that is, NV behavior) is based on long-term impressions and judgments of teachers' expressive style by their actual classroom students. Here, 10 seconds of isolated NV behavior could provide sufficient information with potential predictive value.

Second, the more recent studies by Babad *et al.* (2003, 2004) showed that the patterns of NV–SRT relations vary between educational contexts (i.e. different patterns in university and in high school) and within specific classroom situations. Being judged by foreign judges as more competent, friendly, and interesting in one situation might predict SRT positively; in another situation, these judgments can be related negatively to SRT; and, they might be completely unrelated to SRT in yet another educational situation. For example, in the university study (2004), judges' positive ratings of instructors' NV behavior while lecturing was a positive predictor of SRT. But, being judged more positively in NV behavior while interacting with university students was related negatively to SRT! (Babad *et al.* argued that this negative relation was moderated by course difficulty: instructors tried harder to have better interactions with their students in difficult courses. Nevertheless, these courses received lower evaluations.) In high school, positive SRTs were predicted from positive judgments of teachers' NV behavior while disciplining students and while interacting with low-achieving students, whereas negative relationships with SRT were found for frontal lecturing and for positive interactions with high-achieving students. Babad *et al.* (2003) reasoned that the negative predictions were probably moderated by students' extremely negative reactions to teachers' differential behavior (TDB) toward high-versus low-achieving students (and it appears that highly successful frontal lecturing *is* associated with teachers also being more differential to high- versus low-achieving students).

The external, foreign judges make their ratings only on the basis of the 10 seconds of viewing time, and they are not aware of the context. For actual students, teachers' NV behavior acquires its particular meaning within the context in which it is enacted, along with and in comparison to their knowledge of the teacher in other situations.

Third, microanalysis of the thin slices of university lecturing (2004) provided a detailed and specific behavioral profile of successful lecturers. This profile, based on 10 short seconds of lecturing by each instructor, supported the conceptions of teaching excellence in the teacher immediacy and teacher enthusiasm literature. The latter were, of course, based on students' long-range exposure to teachers without limiting them to context. Most readers would probably not be surprised by this empirical confirmation, but it is always helpful to find confirmation for conceptual ideas from rigorously designed studies, and it is doubly important because of some salient views that context-free educational events cannot be considered as truly representative of classroom reality.

Multiculturalism

With growing waves of immigration to almost all Western countries in Europe and America, concerns about multiculturalism and cultural differences among students of different racial and ethnic groups have intensified among educationalists and behavioral scientists. The major concern about multiculturalism focuses on teaching and learning processes and the degree to which particular approaches or interventions might be more appropriate and beneficial to particular groups. But the issue is also highly relevant for NV behavior, because students of different backgrounds might differ from the mainstream in both decoding and encoding capacities, and problems in communication may arise due to a different understanding (or lack of understanding) of culturally-dependent NV cues (see Feldman 1985, 1992; Galloway 1984).

Teachers cannot automatically assume that their behavior toward particular students is perceived and understood as they intend it, and particular gestures and NV behaviors may not have universal meanings for all groups of recipients. Multicultural research on NV behavior aims to trace and illuminate cultural differences in decoding NV behaviors. One commonly known example can illustrate the issue, and it concerns the behavior of 'looking someone straight in the eye'. In Western cultures, this behavior usually carries a positive meaning of honesty and straightforwardness, and people are praised for this kind of eye contact. But in some cultures, looking someone straight in the eye is not considered positive at all, but rather aggressive, daring, and impolite. Understanding such cultural differences in meaning can help teachers avoid miscommunication with some of their students.

Teacher expectancy research

'Pygmalion in the classroom' (Rosenthal & Jacobson 1968), which demonstrated that teachers' expectations of students' academic potential might affect student performance, had a tremendous impact on research in educational psychology. The possibility that teachers' judgments of students' abilities and their expectations for them might become self-fulfilling prophecies had wide-range implications that stimulated several extensive lines of research. Educational implications had more to do with naturally occurring expectations than with experimentally fabricated expectations, due to real differences among students. Educators have been very concerned about negative expectations and their potential to damage and hinder weak and minority group students (Weinstein 2002). The overriding trend worldwide to integrate different groups of students in heterogeneous classrooms intensified the issue of teacher expectancies because, today, teachers are facing a wide range of individual differences in their classrooms. Inevitably, there is greater variability in their expectations and prophecies in a heterogeneous classroom. Therefore, more differential behavior is likely to occur (Babad 1993).

For teacher expectations to affect students' performance, these expectations must be transmitted via differential behavior, which would be perceived and internalized by the students. Thus, the study of the mediation of teacher expectancies via teachers' differential behavior (TDB) gained momentum from the 1970s, and numerous specific differential behaviors have been identified and investigated (Babad 1993, 1998; Brophy 1983, 1985; Harris & Rosenthal 1985). With the accumulation of research findings, it became evident that the transmission of expectancies is not accomplished by gross and obvious behaviors, but rather through very fine and often hidden nuances of affective behavior. Most of those differential behaviors are NV, and teachers are most often unaware of their differential affective transmissions. The potential effects of TDB lie in the systematic accumulation and repetition of such fine nuances over long periods of teacher–student interaction.

One example of a NV behavior that has been studied quite extensively and can illustrate the issue of TDB, is the measured duration of teacher's eye contact with different students. When a student fails to answer a teacher's question, the teacher would continue to be in eye contact with that student for a brief period (measured in seconds or milliseconds) before turning his/her eyes away. It turns out (Brophy 1983; Harris & Rosenthal 1985) that the duration of this eye contact following failure varies as a function of teacher expectancy: the duration would be longer if the teacher expects the student to be capable of answering the question, and shorter in the case of a low expectancy. The difference in duration is most often not even noticeable to a casual observer, yet students are extremely sensitive in perceiving and interpreting the hidden message, especially because such behaviors are repeated over time (Weinstein 2002).

A colleague of mine in Philadelphia, Norman Newberg, tried many years ago to train teachers to intentionally prolong such eye contact with low-expectancy students. The (informal) results he reported in a changed atmosphere and increased student motivation were very positive.

The numerous studies investigating the mediation of teacher expectancies via TDB employed a wide range of methods and instruments, including behavioral observations in classrooms, reports of teachers and students, and video recordings, in both field studies and controlled experiments. Some studies dealt with global behavioral trends, whereas other studies focused on specific behaviors, to the extreme of microanalyzing molecular teacher behaviors. Babad *et al.* (1987, 1989a,b, 1991) and Babad and Taylor (1992) conducted a series of studies on expectancy-related NV behavior in short exposure and separation of NV channels.

Teachers' interpretations of students' NV behavior

Throughout the years, there has been a steady flow of investigations of teachers' interpretations of their students' NV behavior (Brooks & Woolfolk 1987; Halberstadt & Hall 1980; Kagan & Tippins 1991; Webb *et al.* 1997; Woolfolk & Brooks 1983; see also Smith 1984). The interpretation of students' differential NV cues is an important component of the teaching–learning process, as it provides the teacher with information about a student's comprehension, motivation, and involvement at a given time, enabling him/her to handle the student in the most appropriate and effective way.

As the writings of Woolfolk, Brooks, and Smith indicate, such studies have largely been associated with teacher expectancy research. Teachers' continuous observations and their interpretations of students' behavior determine their expectations for each student and influence their own expectancy-related differential behavior toward their students. The term 'determine', as used in the previous sentence, refers both to the formation of new expectancies and to the maintenance of existing expectancies (self-fulfilling prophecies vs. self-maintaining expectations; see Darley & Fazio 1980). In Brophy's (1985) terms, 'student effects on teachers' are teacher expectations based on real differences among students, which, in this case, are reflected in students' differential NV behavior.

But at times, the focus on students' NV behavior is more momentary. In the flow of the teaching process, teachers must use NV cues to provide them with necessary information about a student's comprehension at a given moment in a specific interaction. The student's facial expression and gestures can tell the teacher whether the student understands, how difficult the task is for the student, and whether specific interventions might or might not be effective.

Skill training in NV behavior

The applied part of the focus on NV behavior in education should, of course, be expressed in NV skill training for improving teacher effectiveness. And indeed, sporadic articles in the literature describe, evaluate, and promote skill training to facilitate improved teacher delivery (see Smith 1984).

Those who are familiar with training for prospective teachers and in-service training for teachers know that such efforts are very common and widely applied in the field. In fact, NV training is part and parcel of the supervisory component of teacher training, be it in microteaching or other training methods. However, such efforts are usually not published in the scientific journals because of their applied (and uncontrolled) nature. Interventions focusing on NV behavior are usually not based on research findings but rather on the natural intuition and experience of the supervisors. The training efforts are most often rather sporadic and non-systematic. Their effectiveness is not measured by conventional tools in methodologically designed studies.

A few examples of reports on applied interventions in NV skills include the works of Knizling and Jackson (1987) and Talbert–Johnson and Beran (1999), who reported attempts to train teachers to improve their verbal and NV immediacy. Minskoff (1980a,b) provided examples of NV skill training given to students.

NV skill training (like other applied interventions for changing teacher behavior and conduct) has two main components: feedback and practice. The feedback can be based on empirical research findings, on specific observations, or on video recording of the participating teachers. It provides teachers with the relevant behavioral information, highlighting and specifying what needs to be changed (see Babad 1990 on empirically based feedback to teachers concerning their students' perceptions of their differential classroom behavior). The practice component follows the awareness brought about by the feedback: teachers are actually trained how to behave, how to respond to students in given situations, and how better to monitor and control their own NV behavior.

Applied interventions would, most likely, vary between the two major domains of NV research in education discussed above, namely, teacher immediacy and teacher expectancies. To improve teacher immediacy and teacher enthusiasm, the purpose of NV skill training would be to *increase* teachers' use of certain behaviors: to be more expressive; to show more variation and changes in NV behavior; to increase movement and gesturing; to smile and laugh; etc. On the other hand, to deal with the negative effects of teacher expectancies, the purpose of NV skill training would be to *decrease* the occurrence of differential behaviors and to treat students more equitably (and, if possible, to treat all students more positively). An example mentioned earlier was the anecdotal report of Newberg's attempt to train teachers to prolong their eye contact with all students following students' failure to respond to teachers' questions.

Methodological and measurement issues in nonverbal research in education

This chapter was intended to present methodological and measurement issues in NV research in education, but was not intended to be a review article. Therefore, I do not present systematically the various studies and their results, nor do I provide full coverage of all areas of NV research in education. Specific studies and results are presented as a function of their relevance to the discussion of methodological issues and measurement methods.

Low-inference and high-inference measurement in educational research

In conventional empirical research, methodologically based data collection is the heart of a research project. Preparatory theoretical and conceptual work leads to the definition of research questions, and these are operationalized in terms of measurable variables. The researchers then measure these variables by whatever methodology they selected—rates of occurrence, simple or complex frequencies, levels of intensity, etc. Next, the data are analyzed by the proper and most appropriate statistical methods, and the researchers proceed to evaluate the results and reach conclusions about the research question(s). This traditional approach is now labeled in educational research, 'low-inference measurement'. The variables must be operationally defined so that the data can be collected with the utmost reliability and unbiased accuracy. The observer (i.e. data collector) simply records specific behaviors of the target person (most often teacher) in an objective way, without making any judgment.

Until the 1960s, complex social phenomena in classrooms were investigated via low-inference measurement. An important influence on the study of classroom climates was the classic work of Lewin *et al.* (1939) who investigated the impact of three types of leadership. To measure the effects on classroom climate, complex observational scales and instruments had to be constructed (e.g. Amidon & Hough 1967, 1982; Flanders 1970), and observers were trained how to conduct behavioral observations in classrooms and how to record the data in a reliable manner.

The demands of low-inference measurement made educational research less practical and less feasible, because data collection was very costly and required highly trained observers. These difficulties were exacerbated by a frequent demand in educational research that the number of sampling units (N) should be of classrooms rather than of students. Cronbach (1976) and Cooper and Good (1983) emphasized that, for the study of many classroom and/or teacher-focused phenomena, the appropriate N for statistical analysis is not the total number of students. Rather, the N should consist of the number of classrooms or teachers, with averaged variables serving as the data for analysis. To conduct a reasonable study on a classroom phenomenon and expect to reach statistically significant results, the number of classrooms to be included must be quite substantial. Coupled by the demands of complex and expensive low-inference data collection in each classroom, Cooper and Good (1983) lamented that classroom research would almost not be conducted at all.

Since the 1960s, high-inference measurement has become the acceptable and legitimate alternative to low-inference measurement. It is far more practical and less costly, and makes it possible to conduct large-scale educational research with relatively modest means (see Chavez 1984; Fraser & Walberg 1991). In high-inference measurement, the observer not only records the classroom behaviors but also makes inferences and judgments about their meaning and about what occurred in the classroom. For example, to measure teacher friendliness or classroom cohesion, instead of defining sets of operationalized behavioral variables, measuring their frequencies and then defining a statistically weighted index to assess each construct, observers are simply asked to rate teacher friendliness directly or to assess how cohesive the classroom is. Today, a variety of scales and questionnaires is available to assess classroom climate

(Fraser & Fisher 1983) and practically nobody bothers to use the cumbersome, low-inference measures any more.

The shift from low- to high-inference measurement involved not only the insertion of inference and judgment into the measurement, but also replaced outside observers by the actual participants. In high-inference measurement of classroom climate (Fraser & Fisher 1983; Fraser & Walberg 1991), the students complete a self-report questionnaire about their classroom, and their averaged responses represent the classroom's climate. The ease of administering short self-report questionnaires to entire classrooms without employing outside observers at all makes it possible to conduct large-scale educational research with relative ease. An additional conceptual justification for this method emphasized that this type of measurement captures the subjective experience of the students, which is really the essence of classroom climate. The judgments of adult observers and educators might be more 'objective' by some criteria, but do not necessarily reflect how the students actually feel in their classroom.

This argument may be quite compelling, but one cannot escape the suspicion of bias in subjective self-report. In studying TDB via high-inference self-report of students and teachers, Babad (1990) found that students reported that their teachers gave more emotional support to high-achieving than to low-achieving students. The teachers, however, described their behavior in the opposite pattern, that is, giving more emotional support to low achievers. A comparison with a host of low-inference findings indicated that the students were right and the teachers were wrong. Thus, in that case, the teachers' subjective sense of providing more emotional support to low achievers was not borne out by objective empirical data.

High-inference, self-report data might be more acceptable when the numerous respondents (students) show agreement and consensus. When they disagree in their judgments of the classroom reality, the measurement becomes more problematic. For example, Babad (1996) showed that low-achieving and high-achieving students differed in how they reported their teachers' differential behavior. In such cases, great caution is required in interpreting questionnaire results.

To connect this issue to NV research in education, it must be pointed out again that research on NV behavior is usually exceptionally expensive and complex, because it involves more stages than other types of research—videotaping, lab work to prepare master cassettes, employing outside judges, etc. Perhaps the required effort and cost drives potential researchers away, to conduct research in other fields through simple administration of questionnaires.

Much of recent NV research follows the overall trend in educational research. More and more studies on NV behavior in education are conducted via high-inference measurement, where teachers' students or external observers judge and rate the teachers' expressive style. High-inference measurement is indeed appropriate if we want to measure teachers' consistent traits or behavioral style rather than focusing on specific behaviors. Indeed, much of the research on teacher enthusiasm (Wood 1998) and teacher immediacy is based on high-inference measurement (e.g. Frymier & Thompson 1995; McCroskey et al. 1996; Rocca 2001; Rocca & McCroskey 1999).

How can NV behavior be measured?

Essentially, one can measure NV behavior in educational settings in three major ways:

1. ask participants (students, teachers) about their impressions;
2. conduct behavioral observations in the classroom;
3. videotape ongoing NV behavior in the classroom.

The most economical and practical method in NV research in education today is simply to ask students about their teacher's behavior. All students in a given classroom are asked to rate, describe, or assess aspects of their teacher's behavior (preferably when the teacher is not present in the classroom), and the data consist of their averaged evaluations. This is a high-inference measurement method, and it invites students to make summative judgments about the relative frequency or intensity of any given behavior. Even if the behavior in question is very specific (such as 'makes eye contact with students'), its frequency is not quantitatively measured but rather assessed as reflecting students' conclusions about its rate of occurrence. Of course, many of the NV behaviors evaluated in this method by students are initially generalized and inferred rather than behaviorally specific—has a relaxed body position; has a tense expression; moves around; etc.

In fact, when students are asked about their impressions of their teacher's behavior, the appropriate behaviors to be assessed are the most salient molar behaviors. This method cannot be readily used to measure specific nuances or molecular behaviors. Students' judgments are not specific to a given behavior at a particular moment but are, rather, long-term impressions based on the accumulation of their exposure to the teacher for many hours. Thus, the students actually provide their generalizations about the teacher's typical behavior (or 'traits' or 'teaching style') across situations.

Variations of this method have been successfully and appropriately used in research on teacher immediacy and teacher enthusiasm, where the focus is intended to be on the overall characterization of the teacher. It would be less useful for research intended to uncover specific behavioral nuances in particular instructional situations (e.g. teachers' NV reactions to wrong answers by high- or low-achieving students or their reactions to interruptions or noise in the classroom).

For several decades, from the 1950s to the 1980s, it was commonplace to conduct classroom research via systematic behavioral observations. The development of VCR technology changed this trend, as will be discussed later. Numerous observational methods and instruments were constructed in those years to analyze interaction processes, mostly teacher–student interaction (e.g. Amidon & Hough 1967; Bales 1965; Flanders 1970). Each system involved its unique methodology (concerning time sampling strategies, operational definitions of each specific behavior, coding systems, aggregating behavioral clusters, etc.). In-service systems were devised to train observers how to use each method in the classroom and how to make meaning of the observational data. (*Mirrors for behavior* edited by Simon & Boyer (1974) is an encyclopedia of the classroom observational systems of that period.) In different instruments, the judgments ranged from very minute and specific behaviors (e.g. raised eyebrow) to global attributional generalizations (e.g. flexible, anxious).

NV behavior was not a central aspect of these systems of classroom observations. However, the very fact that a multitude of teacher behaviors was systematically measured (especially in those instruments focusing on specific behaviors) implied that NV behaviors must have been included. For instance, how could an observer analyze and characterize teacher behavior without including NV behaviors such as smiling, eye contact, physical distance, or touch (and on a secondary level, voice inflections, facial expressions, hand and body movements, etc.)? However, no research tradition or sustained interest in NV behavior had existed in those years in educational research. Thus, despite the great contribution of behavioral observation systems to classroom research in general, a focused educational research interest in NV behavior, especially within the framework of teacher expectancy research, was developed only in later years.

Despite their contributions to educational research, the use of systematic classroom observation systems began to wane toward the end of the twentieth century. High-inference measurement gained popularity, and advances in video recording made it possible to reproduce classroom interaction on videotape, without sending trained observers to conduct repeated observations in the classroom. It is much easier to videotape a class session than to conduct behavioral observations. Videotaped material is considered to be an accurate representation of the ongoing process, and it has the advantage of the possibility of playback, which can improve the reliability of ratings.

The main difference between classroom observations and VCR recording is in the potential flexibility in coding and data analysis. Classroom observations require an a priori measurement model and a fixed set of coding definitions and procedures, because the ongoing process is not reproducible. VCR recording does not require a fixed system, and the researcher has much more flexibility in data analysis. The same videotaped material can be coded and analyzed in different ways, variables can be added with ease, and different measurement perspectives and paradigms can be applied simultaneously. As far as NV research is concerned, video recordings have additional advantages. First, the visual nature of the VCR makes some NV aspects of teacher and student behavior more salient and amenable for analysis. Second, the video recording makes it possible to focus on particular channels and even ignore other channels, thus reducing the influence of the overall context.

For training purposes in microteaching, the full context is preferred, and meaning of particular gestures and behaviors is made in context. For judgment research purposes, usually segments are preferred, and they are isolated and separated from the overall context. The segments might represent random sampling of all 'classroom conduct' but, most often, they are samples designed to represent particular instructional situations (e.g. frontal teaching, interaction with students, handling disciplinary interruptions, explaining difficult material). In thin slices research (Ambady & Rosenthal 1992; Ambady et al. 2000; Babad et al. 2003, 2004), exposure time is intentionally minimized, so that judges are exposed to extremely brief samples of target's NV behavior. The context is further removed by preventing judges' comprehension of the verbal content (either by lowering the audio volume, as in Ambady & Rosenthal 1992, or by employing foreign judges who cannot understand teachers' speech, as in Babad et al. 2003, 2004).

From a methodological point of view, students' global judgments are less effective than ratings of videotaped material, because judgments based on full context and a long history of acquaintance and interaction can be more biased and influenced by a variety of 'irrelevant' factors. In fact, students' judgments might be biased even if the reliability of their judgments is high (that is, they show high agreement), because *all* students in a given classroom might be influenced by commonly held stereotypes or rumors about particular teachers. On the other hand, students' judgments have higher ecological validity, as they represent the 'classroom reality' as experienced by the real participants in school. In judgment studies, the judges who rate the videotaped clips are often demographically different from the students who are the recipients of teacher behavior, and sometimes that might in itself be a source of bias.

Types of judgments of NV behavior in educational research

When conducting NV research in education in the form of judgment studies, judges could be asked to rate the smallest units of observed behavior, and would be involved as little as possible with global impressionistic judgments. The reduction of a collection of specific behaviors (facial expressions, hand, body and head movements, audio variables, intonations, etc.) to a meaningful integrated meaning reflecting a given affective state, could be made by the researcher using conceptual and/or statistical means (including theory, previous findings, factor analysis).

It turns out, however, that people (including young students) usually form generalized and global impressions about affective states. They 'know', quite confidently, the extent to which a given teacher is relaxed, excited, angry, warm, critical, loving, or upset at a given time. It also turns out that such judgments can be reliable to an acceptable degree. Throughout years of conducting NV research in education, it has been my experience that judges don't like the task of making multiple judgments on isolated, minute samples of teacher behavior, especially when NV channels are separated. For instance, imagine that judges are shown a clip depicting several seconds of a teacher's body, without hearing what the teacher is saying and without seeing the student with whom he/she is interacting. Subsequently, they are asked to make 12 judgments about that teacher. The judges often feel that they do not really know anything, their ratings are no more than blind guesses, and they find the job very cumbersome when multiple ratings must be made about numerous context-minimal clips. On the other hand, methodological considerations sometimes require the use of many behavioral samples and numerous rating variables.

Actually, most researchers give high-inference measurement assignments to judges in judgment studies, asking them to make global judgments on the basis of their impressions. Only in microanalysis is the measurement focused on the frequencies and intensities of specific nuances and molecular behaviors. Even microanalysis, however, can include more global judgments such as anxious, relaxed, or even 'sarcastic'.

The list of variables in judgment studies can be theory-based, employing variables derived from the relevant theory. Another way of constructing a variable list for judgment studies is to make use of variables that have been used in previous NV studies of various types. Subsequent to data collection, factor analysis or principal components analysis can reduce the data and help to define factor-based composite scores.

In theory-based variable construction, when the research is directly focused on a particular phenomenon, the relevant variables are derived almost directly from the operational definition of the phenomenon to be investigated. For example, in teacher immediacy research, McCroskey *et al.* (1996) defined the following list of 10 variables:

- gestures while talking to the class;
- uses monotone/dull voice when talking to the class;
- looks at the class while talking;
- smiles at the class while talking;
- has a very tense body position while talking to the class;
- moves around the classroom while teaching;
- looks at the board or notes while talking to the class;
- has a very relaxed body position while talking to the class;
- smiles at individual students in the class;
- uses a variety of vocal expressions when talking to the class.

These variables obviously 'define' teacher immediacy as a teacher's 'trait' or consistent expressive style.

Another example of a theory-based variable list is taken from research on teachers' NV expectancy-related 'teacher differential behavior' (TDB) (Babad 1993; Babad *et al.* 1989*a*). In that series of studies, judges viewed teachers' NV behavior while talking about and to high- and low-expectancy students. The 10 variables to be judged for each clip were: warm; dominant; task-oriented; tense/nervous/anxious; condescending; hostile; clear; active/energetic/enthusiastic; democratic; and flexible. Following principal components analysis, these variables were reduced into three composite scores:

1. *non-dogmatic behavior* (flexible, democratic, and warm);
2. *negative affect* (hostile, condescending, and tense/nervous/anxious);
3. *active teaching behavior* (task-oriented, clear, dominant, and active/energetic/enthusiastic).

These composite scores reflected the major elements consistently involved in the mediation of positive and negative teacher expectancies.

A third, interesting example of constructing a theory-based list of judgment variables concerns Ekman and Friesen's (1969*b*) theory of the central modalities in the repertoire of NV behavior. These theoretical constructs (regulators, illustrators, adaptors, etc.) can be rated by judges who have been trained to understand and identify them. In that case, the judgments could be labeled 'conceptual judgments'. Babad (1999; Babad *et al.* 2004) used some of these constructs in microanalysis and found, as predicted in Ekman and Friesen's theory, that 'adaptors' indeed hindered social interaction and led to negative ratings. A similar finding was reported by Ambady & Rosenthal (1993).

When judges are asked to make multiple ratings for each video clip and the data are subsequently reduced by principal components analysis, it often turns out that all ratings load very highly on the unrotated first component. This indicates that all ratings have a strong common denominator, probably reflecting an overall negative or positive reaction or general impression of the videotaped person. Despite the discussion above about variable lists, this finding might indicate that the specific content of a particular rating is perhaps not so important, because judges are expressing, in their multiple ratings again and again, their overall reaction to the target person. Thus, the various ratings could be averaged into an overall composite for data analysis.

Such a strong unrotated first component was systematically found in four studies predicting student ratings of teachers (SRT) from thin slices of teachers' NV behavior in the classroom (Ambady & Rosenthal 1993 (two studies); Babad *et al.* 2003, 2004). In all four studies, a composite averaging all ratings was used in data analysis. In a study examining fair versus preferential NV behavior of a TV interviewer toward different interviewees (Babad 1999), in which a very large number of video clips had to be rated, I initially chose to ask judges *only* for their general impression. For each clip, they were asked to provide their judgment on a single nine-point rating scale, from 'very negative' to 'very positive'. The decision to employ only one global rating per clip may be particularly helpful when the number of NV clips to be judged is very large.

Microanalysis: molar versus molecular judgments

When people hear about dramatic predictions made from judgments of thin slices of NV behavior, such as students' post-course evaluations of their teachers predicted from a few seconds of teachers' NV classroom behavior, the question that immediately pops up in their minds is: 'What *did* this teacher do in those few seconds that could be predictive of important future outcomes?' Microanalysis is the attempt to answer this question, to uncover the molecular determinants of global impressions.

In microanalysis, a few judges view again and again each short clip of the target's NV behavior, and rate the clip on a long list of specific, isolated variables, judging each gesture and movement. In the judgment study itself, judges view each clip only once, and their ratings are used as predictor variables in correlations with some outcome measure (SRT, student learning, etc.). In microanalysis, the judges' ratings after one viewing become the criterion variables, to be predicted from the ratings of the molecular variables. A successful microanalysis reveals a pattern of correlations indicating which particular molecular elements in the video clips contributed to the global positive or negative impressions. In this way we can potentially uncover the NV profile of good lecturers, TV interviewers, trial judges, etc.

But microanalysts are often disappointed, because these analyses can be quite elusive, and frequently they do not yield meaningful and important results. Sometimes, attempts to discover specific NV elements contributing to the overall impression uncover only a few universal components (such as smiling, adding to positive judgments; and Ekman-type adaptors, leading to negative judgments) or sporadic predictors that do not form a meaningful pattern.

The utility and contribution of the microanalytic method is enhanced if it can lead to the formulation of differential predictions and distinct profiles. In Babad's (1999) investigation of six TV interviewers (where multiple NV clips were available for each interviewer), microanalyses made it possible to delineate (in addition to the generalized profile for all interviewers combined) the personal profile of each interviewer, highlighting the specific NV behaviors which predicted his unique positive or negative global impression. Potentially, each interviewer in that study could have been provided with empirical feedback of exactly what he does, in his body language and NV behavior, to create positive or negative impressions. Determination of personal style is more difficult in studies where only one very short clip is available for each target person (such as the professors and high-school teachers in the Ambady & Rosenthal 1993 and the Babad *et al.* 2003, 2004 studies).

In the Babad *et al.* (2004) study of the NV behavior of university professors, we used the same set of molecular variables as in Babad's (1999) study of TV interviewers. Thus, we were able to compare the NV profile of positively rated professors to that of positively rated TV interviewers. This comparison of the microanalyses for professors and TV interviewers was quite instructive. A substantial number of variables systematically predicted the global (negative–positive) judgment in the same direction in both analyses: some correlations were positive and contributed to positive judgments (e.g. smiling, relaxed face, round hand movements); and other correlations were negative (e.g. frowning, gazing down, blinking, and several adaptors, such as fidgeting with self and with objects). *However,* a substantial number of microanalytic variables that were found to be negative predictors of judgments of interviewers' behavior, were found to be positive predictors for lecturers. In other words, the same behavior that was related to (or 'perceived' as) a negative judgment, in the case of TV interviewers, contributed to a positive impression in the case of college lecturers. The list of variables following this pattern included sarcasm, head shaking, hand movement and gestures, beating hand movements, body mobility, body and posture shifts, changes in intensity, and several voice variables such as volume and change.

Thus, in the tense and emotionally loaded atmosphere of the TV interview, 'strong' gestures, changes in NV behavior and shifts in intensity are negative indicators, but in the more relaxed, less dramatic, and perhaps boring 'educational' atmosphere of the university lecture, these changes and shifts become positive indicators. Universal interpretations of NV behaviors as being 'positive' or 'negative' (commonly made in the popular mass media) must therefore be avoided. It is important to understand that—except for a few really universal NV indicators such as smiling, shouting, and crying—a specific behavior acquires its unique meaning only in the context within which it is enacted.

Some readers might be interested in the specific list of variables used in those microanalyses, because an adapted list might be useful for other content domains as well. The list (Babad 1999; adapted for the college setting) consisted of the following variables:

- *Face:* smile, frown, gaze down (usually at notes), eye contact, blinking, narrow/wide eyes, tense/relaxed face, sarcasm, general expressiveness of face.
- *Head:* movement and expression, nod, shake, thrust, touch head.
- *Hands:* hold, movement and expression, beating movement, round movement, hands in pockets, hands folded together.
- *Body:* position (standing/sitting), movement in space, body expressiveness, shrug; in sitting position—leaning forward, backward, and sideways; in standing position—orientation toward audience, fidgeting with body, fidgeting with object.
- *Changes:* body and posture shift, change in NV expression, change in intensity.

- *Global variables* from Ekman and Friesen's (1969*b*) conceptualization: regulators, illustrators, adaptors, and also relaxed/tense, overall emphasis.
- *Voice:* volume, soft/hard voice, voice change, emphasis, tempo, intent to make students understand.

As can be seen in the above list, most variables consisted of observable behaviors that could be counted, whereas a few were impressionistic judgments of specific aspects (e.g. gesture, expression of the head) or global (high-inference) impressionistic judgments (e.g. sarcasm, emphasis).

Separation of channels, leakage, and deception

As mentioned earlier, the issue of classroom context is quite controversial among educational researchers, and some 'educationalists' object to NV research in education because it violates the demand to maintain full context. They (Berliner 1983; Doyle 1977, 1981, Fenstermacher 1979) see danger in applying research methods and findings from settings outside the classroom. They advocate the use of various ecological approaches that consider all relevant characteristics of the classroom (certainly including verbal content of classroom interactions) for investigating classroom phenomena. Naturally, NV research *must* ignore many components of the context, otherwise the research could not focus on NV aspects.

But even within the field of NV research, one finds different opinions about the role of the context. A context-minimal approach (Babad 1992; Rosenthal *et al.* 1979) aims at separating every element and every NV channel and examining each independently of other channels. A more contextual approach aims at maintaining the context to the fullest extent possible within the NV framework. This difference is saliently represented in the basic approaches of the central tests of NV sensitivity and NV decoding skills— the PONS and the IPT. The PONS test (Rosenthal *et al.*, 1979) presents very brief instances of NV behavior, separated into different channels and combinations of channels (visual and audio channels, face, body, content-filtered and randomly spliced voice, etc.). On the other hand, the tests designed by Dane Archer and his colleagues (SIT—Archer & Akert 1977; IPT—Archer & Costanzo 1988) present longer stimuli, depicting actual social scenes.

Babad *et al.* (1987, 1989*a,b*, 1991; Babad & Taylor 1992; see Babad 1992) conducted a series of studies on the mediation of teacher expectancies, separating NV channels and employing a context-minimal approach.

The trend has changed in the last decade, because of the rise of thin slices research (Ambady *et al.* 2000; Ambady & Rosenthal 1992). In thin slices research, the critical variable is the length of video clip presented to judges (really, its brevity), but judges are exposed to the full NV context in their brief exposure, and only verbal comprehension is denied. (Most American researchers prevent verbal comprehension by presenting the clips with the volume turned down. By doing this, they lose the NV information inherent in the voice. The present author, operating from Israel and using Hebrew-speaking target persons, takes the clips abroad, to be judged by raters who do not understand the Hebrew language. Thus, the audio NV information is not lost.)

In NV research in education, separation of channels is critical to the investigation of an influential classroom phenomenon, namely, teachers' transmission of negative affect despite their deceptive efforts. Studies on self-fulfilling prophecies, on the mediation of teacher expectancies, and on teacher differential behavior (TDB), consistently show the existence of differential behavior toward different groups of students, strongly concentrated in teachers' affective transmissions (Babad 1998). Most of these transmissions are implicit, expressed in very fine nuances of NV behavior. The students are angry at their teachers for their differential conduct and what they perceive as lack of fairness, and this affects the classroom atmosphere and the way the students experience their teachers (Babad 1995, 1998; Babad *et al.* 2003). Teachers tend to deny their differential affect, and they try to hide negative affect and transmit false positive affect instead (Babad 1990, 1993, 1998).

The conceptualization of *NV leakage* is highly relevant to this issue and makes it possible to examine affective deception empirically (DePaulo & Rosenthal 1979; Rosenthal & DePaulo 1979; Zuckerman *et al.* 1986). Leakage as a process was first introduced by Ekman and Friesen (1969a, 1974), who found differences between face and body channels in the likelihood of giving away deception. Leakage is caused by differential controllability of communication channels: when people try to conceal their true affect and transmit deceitful affect instead, their deceit might be more successful in more controllable channels (speech content, followed by face) and less successful in less controllable channels (e.g. body, content-filtered speech). A 'leakage hierarchy' orders the various channels according to the degree of control available to the encoder.

Babad *et al.* (1989b) investigated leakage effects in the NV behavior of elementary school teachers. They predicted that biased teachers (those more susceptible to stereotypically biasing information and more likely to demonstrate TDB) would have to conceal more negative affect than unbiased teachers. Using a three-stage leakage hierarchy (transcript, face, and body), the hypothesis was indeed supported. Biased teachers demonstrated clear, linear leakage effects. Of course, such research on affective deception cannot be carried out without separation of verbal and NV channels.

Between-teacher and within-teacher designs

In most studies on NV behavior in education, a between-teacher design is used. A sample of teachers is usually investigated and their NV behavior is measured. For each given behavior (e.g. use of smiling toward students, voice inflection) or cluster (e.g. teacher immediacy), each teacher receives a score representing his/her relative standing in the sample, and that score is correlated with another score(s) representing some educational outcome (e.g. teaching effectiveness, student learning). The purpose of such research is to predict educational outcomes from teachers' NV behavior (in brief or long exposure). This design is a between-teacher design because each teacher appears once in the computation of the correlation (in the scale for the predictor variable and in the scale of the criterion variable).

In studies on the mediation of teacher expectancies and TDB, researchers are interested in the differences between teacher behavior in certain situations and other situations, and then a within-teacher design is used. In that design, the score representing the difference between situations within each teacher is the focus of the investigation, most often the difference between teacher's behavior in interaction with high-expectancy and low-expectancy students.

The within-teacher design is also relevant for research, comparing teacher behavior in different teaching situations (see Babad *et al.* 2003, 2004). As mentioned, NV behavior attains its meaning within the context in which it is enacted. Therefore, the same NV behavior (even a positive universal like smiling) might be perceived in a certain meaning in one context (say, in interaction with an excellent student) than in another context (say, in interaction with a disruptive low achiever). To use another example, raising one's voice for emphasis in lecturing has a different meaning from the same behavior in dealing with discipline problems.

As mentioned earlier, students are extremely sensitive to differences in teacher behavior toward different students (Babad 1990, 1998; Weinstein 1985, 1989). Classroom climate and students' satisfaction are more negative in classrooms of highly differential elementary school teachers (Babad 1995), and differential teachers receive much lower evaluations from their high-school students than fair and equitable teachers (Babad *et al.* 2003). In her recent book, Weinstein (2002) argued that teachers' negative treatment of low-achieving, minority groups and special needs students is the central source of school failure in America.

The differences in teachers' NV behavior toward high and low achievers, measured in a within-teacher design in thin slices judgment research, are significantly related to TDB reported by the actual students in high-inference questionnaires (Babad *et al.* 2003). Students' sensitivity to teachers' differential conduct is so keen that they can make accurate attributions about TDB from teachers' behavior toward the *entire class*. In a sequel to the above study, (Babad 2005), high-school students viewed short clips depicting the frontal teaching behavior of teachers unknown to them (when the teachers were addressing their entire classrooms) and were asked to make guesses about each teacher's differentiality. Amazingly, the accuracy of their guesses/predictions exceeded $r = 0.40$.

Children as judges of NV behavior: judgment versus detection

In educational research, most of the data are usually 'provided' by adults, teachers, classroom observers, judges, or experimenters, even if the tested variables pertain to the children/students. The shift to more ecologically valid research meant, among other things, that the children's own perceptions, underlying schemas and reactions, based on their own subjective experience, should be the target of the research.

That was the nature of the shift in the measurement of classroom climate, which was mentioned earlier (Fraser & Walberg 1991)—researchers moved from low-inference measurement of behavioral observations made by adult observers to a high-inference definition of classroom climate through the perceptions and judgments of the children themselves. A similar 'sub-trend' took place in teacher expectancy research. Weinstein (1985, 1989; Weinstein & Middlestadt 1979) and Babad (1990) decided to investigate teachers' expectancy-related differential behavior through the eyes of the students, as subjectively experienced by them in the classroom. Both discovered that young students were aware of, and extremely sensitive to TDB, and could describe and rate it reliably.

A shift to the children as the direct providers of social information requires a change in measurement methods and practices. The investigated behaviors must be defined in a simple and concrete language, and removed from the more conceptual and abstract adult language. For example, 'classroom cohesiveness' must be replaced by simple statement such as 'students like each other' and/or 'students don't quarrel with each other in this classroom'. In addition, certain methods of questioning are not appropriate for use with young children. This is particularly true when children are asked about their own classroom teachers. Children do not think about their teachers in analytical terms, and they often shy away from 'judging' their teachers (or other adults), especially in the alien, formal context of having to fill in a research questionnaire. (In contrast, high-school students seem to love to judge their teachers, especially in formal questionnaires!)

The same ideas apply in the measurement of NV behavior, with some additional difficulties. In measurement of classroom climate or TDB, the children report about their own classroom, their own teacher, and their own experiences in the classroom. In NV judgment studies, children employed as judges must evaluate the behaviors of teachers who are unknown to them and they must form their judgments on the basis of limited information. The task itself (viewing video clips of teachers and subsequently rating these teachers) is foreign to young children and some of the scales seem quite strange (e.g. is the teacher critical of students? Is the teacher relaxed?). Thus, the judgment task must be changed and adapted for the children.

In two studies, we used a detection design as an alternative to the usual judgment design, employing young children to evaluate the investigated teachers, who were, of course, unknown to them (Babad *et al.* 1991; Babad & Taylor 1992). Children in New Zealand and Israel, as young as third and fourth graders, viewed brief video clips of Israeli teachers in interaction with (or talking about) a high-expectancy and a low-expectancy student. Only the teachers were seen and heard in those clips, and the student with whom the teacher was interacting always remained invisible. The children/ judges were told that a different unseen student was involved in each clip, and their task was to make guesses about that student. Thus, the original judgment task was converted into a detection task, when the only information available for making attributions about the invisible student was the teacher's conduct. Following each clip, the children rated, on a nine-point scale, the extent to which the invisible student was an excellent (9) or weak (1) learner, and the degree to which that student was liked (9) or disliked (1) by the teacher. Differences in excellence and teacher liking in favor of the high-expectancy invisible student served as evidence of expectancy-related TDB. In both studies, the young raters did an excellent job of detection and accurately identified each of the two students. In the 1991 study, the detection design was compared to the conventional judgment design and we found, as expected, that young judges could not handle the judgment task with the adult-type rating scales (warm, dominant, task-oriented, flexible, etc.).

It seems that evaluation of teachers' NV behavior via guessing/attributing about something that does not appear at all in the videotape clip but is hypothesized to be related to it, might have potential when the judges are young students. First, the detection task might, for them, be easier to handle than the regular judgment task. And second, they probably bring some of their implicit notions about covariation among aspects of teacher behavior to bear upon the guessing task. This was also the case in Babad's 2005 study mentioned above, where students provided accurate guesses about TDB from clips depicting their lecturing behavior to the entire class.

The shift from judgment to detection and from adult judges to younger students adds to the ecological validity of the research, because the younger judges are more similar to the students who are the recipients of teachers' NV behavior. It also offers an interesting investigative variation and allows the researchers to be more flexible. Finally, it allows the researchers to come closer to an understanding of the underlying schemas that enable children to process social information in the classroom. On the other hand, detection studies might be a bit more risky than judgment studies, because they introduce some unknown factors (and perhaps additional sources of variance) into the research.

The unmeasurable influence of rare events

The final methodological issue in this discussion is really a warning about an unmeasurable factor that might limit the generalizability of NV research in education. In empirical, low-inference NV research, samples of NV behavior are videotaped and subsequently judged. Assuming that the samples are drawn expertly and without bias, they still may not be reliably representative of the actual students' experiences. This is due to the influence of dramatic, intense events that occur very infrequently, and almost *never* when the camera is in the classroom. These events are the rare occasions when teachers lose control and let loose some behaviors or reactions that are usually well under control. Although these events are very infrequent, students weigh them heavily in 'knowing' what the teacher really thinks and feels about particular students or about the classroom in general. Weinstein (2002) interviewed students to find out how they know how smart they are. She reported that very often their knowledge was based on a rare (negative or positive) event that did not necessarily represent the teacher's usual daily conduct.

Because rare events are not represented in behavioral samples, students' experiences and attributions might differ to a smaller or greater extent from the conclusions drawn in the empirical studies, thus potentially reducing the predictability of educational outcomes. In a way, measurement via actual students' reports rather than foreign judges' ratings may provide a partial solution to this problem, because the students weigh *all* information available to them from their accumulating interactions with their teachers, and they know how to give the 'proper' weight to rare events.

The future of nonverbal research in education

Chapters like this one usually end with the author's assessment of future research, either of what directions the field *should* take or what directions are most likely to actually develop. I, personally, have been involved for many years in research on expectancies and on wishful thinking, and therefore I am aware of the possibility that subjective preferences might well affect presumably objective predictions, and no less aware of the self-fulfilling nature of expectations. Thus, a look into the future is probably not really objective, yet it might affect future research to some small degree.

First, NV research in education will probably be strongly influenced by the developments in NV research in other areas. In a way, education is a field of application of NV research, and thus influenced by the more global trends in NV research, as reflected in the other chapters in this book.

Because thin slices research is gaining momentum in NV research at this time, I believe that we will see more thin slices research in education. The findings of the educational studies conducted thus far were quite dramatic. That kind of research is usually very appealing to doctoral students and other investigators, and thin slices research can be applied to many important aspects of teaching and classroom interaction. Probably we may expect to see more investigations of specific instructional situations and their impact on students (e.g. research on teachers' disciplinary behavior). There is also much room to study the NV behavior of *students*, as there has been relatively little NV research focusing on students. Of special interest might be research of students' NV behavior in conjunction with teachers' NV behavior. Burgoon and her associates (Burgoon *et al.* 1995; Burgoon & White 1997) have studied patterns of mutual influences in dyadic interaction.

In my opinion, research on teacher immediacy and teacher enthusiasm has reached a peak in recent years. Therefore, I tend to think that there will be a certain decline in the future, unless new research questions within this field emerge. On the other hand, the relative ease of conducting teacher immediacy and teacher enthusiasm research, together with the strong intuitive appeal of this topic, might lead to sustained interest in the future.

With regard to teacher expectancy research, there has been a noticeable decline in researchers' interest over the last decade, and this would probably affect NV research on TDB. On the other hand, recent writings on expectancy-related issues might rekindle interest in this field of research. I refer mostly to Weinstein's (2002) book on the effects of negative expectations in education and to the Babad *et al.* (2003) findings on students' intense anger about teachers' lack of fairness and absence of equitable treatment of all students. Given that students are so sensitive in picking up TDB and preferential treatment, we might see more NV research focusing on this issue.

Finally, the area where we *should* see more progress in the future is the application of NV research to teacher training. As pointed out earlier, actual research on data-based skills training for improving teachers' classroom conduct is missing. Thus, the very extensive applied efforts invested by numerous educators in the field are based on the intuitive notions of individual practitioners, with no dissemination of systematic, data-based knowledge. Despite the methodological difficulties discussed earlier, one should really hope to see further developments in applied NV research in education.

References

Abrami, P., Leventhal, L., & Perry, R. (1982). Educational seduction. *Review of Educational Research*, **52**, 445–64.

Allen, D. & Ryan, K. (1969). *Microteaching*. Reading, MA: Addison–Welsey.

Ambady, N. & Rosenthal, R. (1992). Thin slices of behavior as predictors of interpersonal consequences: a meta-analysis. *Psychological Bulletin,* **111,** 256–74.

Ambady, N. & Rosenthal, R. (1993). Half a minute: predicting teacher evaluations from thin slices of behavior and physical attractiveness. *Journal of Personality and Social Psychology,* **64,** 431–41.

Ambady, N., Bernieri, F., & Richeson, J. (2000). Toward a histology of social behavior: judgmental accuracy from thin slices of the behavioral stream. In *Advances in experimental social psychology, Vol. 32* (ed. M. Zanna), pp. 201–71. Boston: Academic Press.

Amidon, E.J., & Hough, J. (Eds.) (1967). *Interaction analysis: theory, research and application.* Reading, MA: Addison-Wesley.

Amidon, E.J. & Hough, J. (1982). A search for school climate: a review of the research. *Review of Educational Research,* **52,** 368–420.

Andersen, P. & Andersen, J. (1982). Nonverbal immediacy in instruction. In *Communication in the classroom* (ed. L. Barker), pp. 98–120. Engelwood Cliffs, NJ: Prentice–Hall.

Archer, D. & Akert, R.M. (1977). Words and everything else: verbal and nonverbal cues in social interpretation. *Journal of Personality and Social Psychology,* **35,** 443–9.

Archer, D. & Akert, R.M. (1980). The encoding of the meaning: a test of three theories of social interaction. In *Language and social interaction* (ed. D. Zimmerman & C. West). *A special issue of Sociological Inquiry,* **50,** 393–419.

Archer, D. & Costanzo., M. (1988). *The Interpersonal Perception Task.* Berkeley, CA: University of California Extension Media Center.

Babad, E. (1990). Measuring and changing teachers' differential behavior as perceived by students and teachers. *Journal of Educational Psychology,* **82,** 683–90.

Babad, E. (1992). Teacher expectancies and nonverbal behavior. In *Applications of nonverbal theories and research* (ed. R.S. Feldman), pp. 167–90. Hillsdale, N.J.: Erlbaum.

Babad, E. (1993). Teachers' differential behavior. *Educational Psychology Review,* **5,** 347–76.

Babad, E. (1995). The 'teachers pet' phenomenon, teachers' differential behavior, and students' morale. *Journal of Educational Psychology,* **87,** 361–74.

Babad, E. (1996). How high is 'high inference'? Within classroom differences in students' descriptions of classroom interaction. *Journal of Classroom Interaction,* **31,** 1–9.

Babad, E. (1998). Preferential affect: the crux of the teacher expectancy issue. In *Advances in research on teaching, Vol. 7: expectations in the classroom* (ed. J. Brophy), pp. 183–214. Greenwich, CT: JAI Press.

Babad, E. (1999). Preferential treatment in television interviewing: evidence from nonverbal behavior. *Political Communication,* **16,** 337–58.

Babad, E. (2005). Guessing teachers' differential treatment of high- and low-achievers from thin slices of their public lecturing behavior. *Journal of Nonverbal Behavior,* **29,** 125–134.

Babad, E. & Taylor, P. (1992). Transparency of teacher expectations across language, cultural boundaries. *Journal of Educational Research,* **86,** 120–5.

Babad, E., Avni–Babad, D., & Rosenthal, R. (2003). Teachers' brief nonverbal behaviors in defined instructional situations can predict students' evaluations. *Journal of Educational Psychology,* **95,** 553–62.

Babad, E., Avni–Babad, D., & Rosenthal, R. (2004). Prediction of students' evaluations from professors' nonverbal behavior in defined instructional situations. *Social Psychology of Education*, 7, 3–33.

Babad, E., Bernieri, F., Rosenthal, R. (1987). Nonverbal and verbal behavior preschool, remedial, and elementary school teachers. *American Educational Research Journal*, 24, 405–15.

Babad, E., Bernieri, F., & Rosenthal, R. (1989*a*). When less information is more informative: diagnosing teacher expectancies from brief samples of behavior. *British Journal of Educational Psychology*, 59, 281–95.

Babad, E., Bernieri, F., & Rosenthal., R. (1989*b*). Nonverbal communication and leakage in the behavior of biased and unbiased teachers. *Journal of Personality and Social Psychology*, 56, 89–94.

Babad, E., Bernieri, F., & Rosenthal, R. (1991). Students as judges of teachers' verbal and nonverbal behavior. *American Educational Research Journal*, 28, 211–34.

Bales, R.F. (1965). *Small groups: studies in social interaction* (revised edn). New York: A.A. Knopf.

Berliner, D. (1983). Developing concepts of classroom environment: some light on the T in classroom studies of ATI. *Educational Psychologist*, 18, 1–13.

Brooks, D. & Woolfolk, A.E. (1987). The effects of students' nonverbal behavior on teachers. *Elementary School Journal*, 88, 51–63.

Brophy, J. (1983). Research on the self-fulfilling prophecy and teacher expectations. *Journal of Educational Psychology*, 75, 631–61.

Brophy, J. (1985). Teacher–student interaction. In *Teacher expectancies* (ed. J. Dusek), pp. 303–28. Hillsdale, NJ: Erlbaum.

Brown, G. (1975). *Microteaching: a program of teaching skills*. London: Methuen & Co.

Burgoon, J. & White, C. (1997). Researching nonverbal message production: a view from interaction adaptation theory. In *Message production: advances in communication theory* (ed. J. Greene), pp. 279–312. Mahwah, NJ: Erlbaum.

Burgoon, J., Stern, L., & Dillman, L. (1995). *Interpersonal adaptation: dyadic interaction patterns*. New York: Cambridge University Press.

Chavez, R.C. (1984). The use of high-inference measures to study classroom climates: a review. *Review of Educational Research*, 54, 237–61.

Cooper, H. & Good, T. (1983). *Pygmalion grows up: studies in the expectation communication process*. New York: Longman.

Cronbach, L. (1976). *Research on classroom and schools: formulation of questions, design and analysis*. Stanford evaluation consortium, Eric document no. ED 135 801, Stanford University, CA.

Darley, J. & Fazio, R. (1980). Expectancy confirmation processes arising in the social interaction sequence. *American Psychologist*, 35, 867–81.

DePaulo, B. (1992). Nonverbal behavior and self presentation. *Psychological Bulletin*, 111, 203–43.

DePaulo, B. & Rosenthal, R. (1979). Ambivalence, discrepancy and deception in nonverbal communication. In *Skill in nonverbal communication* (ed. R. Rosenthal), pp. 204–48. Cambridge, MA: Oelgeschlager, Gunn, & Hain.

Doyle, W. (1977). Paradigms for teacher education research. In *Review of research in education*, *Vol. 5* (ed. L. Shulman), pp. 163–98. Itasca, IL: Peacock.

Doyle, W. (1981). Research on classroom contexts. *Journal of Teacher Education*, 32, 3–6.

Ekman, P. (1985). *Telling lies*. New York: Norton.

Ekman, P. & Friesen, W. (1969a). Nonverbal leakage and clues to deception. *Psychiatry*, 32, 88–106.

Ekman, P. & Friesen, W. (1969b). The repertoire of nonverbal behavior: categories, origins, usages and coding. *Semiotica*, 1, 49–98.

Ekman, P. & Friesen, W. (1974). Detecting deception from the body and face. *Journal of Personality and Social Psychology*, 29, 288–98.

Feldman, R.S. (1985). Nonverbal behavior, race, and the classroom teacher. *Theory into Practice*, 24, 45–9.

Feldman, R.S. (ed.) (1992). *Applications of nonverbal behavior theories and research*. Hillsdale, NJ: Erlbaum.

Fenstermacher, G. (1979). A philosophical consideration of recent research on teaching effectiveness. *Review of Research in Education*, 6, 157–85.

Flanders, N.A. (1970). *Analyzing teacher behavior*. Reading, MA: Addison–Wesley.

Fraser, B. & Fisher, D. (1983). *Assesment of classroom psychological environment*. Research seminar and workshop series. Beutley, Australia: Western Australian Institute of Technology.

Fraser, B.J. & Walberg H.J. (1991). *Educational environments: evaluation, antecedents, and consequences*. Oxford/New York: Pergamon Press.

Frymier, A.B. & Thompson, C.A. (1995). *Using students reports to measure immediacy: is it a valid methodology?* Paper presented at the annual meeting of the Speech Communication Association, November 1995

Galloway, C. (1984). Nonverbal behavior and teacher–student relationships: an intercultural perspective. In *Nonverbal behavior: perspectives, applications, intercultural insights* (ed. A. Wolfgang). Toronto: Hogrefe.

Halberstadt, A.G. & Hall, J.A. (1980). Who's getting the message? Children's nonverbal skill and their evaluation by teachers. *Developmental Psychology*, 16, 564–73.

Harris, M. & Rosenthal, R. (1985). Mediation of interpersonal expectancy effects: 31 metaanalyses. *Psychological Bulletin*, 97, 363–86.

Ikeda, T. & Beebe, S.A. (1992). *A review of teacher nonverbal immediacy: implications for intercultural research*. Paper presented at the annual meeting of the International Communication Association. Miami, May 1992.

Kagan, D.M. & Tippins, D.J. (1991). Helping student teachers attend to student cues. *Elementary School Journal*, 91, 343–56.

Knizling, H.G. & Jackson, I. (1987). Training teachers in nonverbal sensitivity and nonverbal behavior. *International Journal of Educational Research*, 11, 589–600.

Lewin, K., Lippit, R., & White, R.K. (1939). Patterns of aggressive behavior in experimentally created social climates. *Journal of Social Psychology*, 10, 271–99.

Marsh, H. (1984). Student evaluation of university teaching: dimensionality, reliability, validity, potential biases, and utility. *Journal of Educational Psychology*, 76, 707–54.

Marsh, H. (1987). *Students' evaluation of university teaching: research findings, methodological issues and directions for future research*. Elmford, NY: Pergamon.

McCroskey, J.C., Sallinen, A., Fayer, J., Richmond, V.P., & Barraclough, R.A. (1996). Nonverbal immediacy and cognitive learning: a cross-cultural investigation. *Communication Education,* 45, 200–10.

Milmoe, S., Rosenthal, R., Blane, H.T., Chafetz, M.E., & Wolf, I. (1967). The doctor's voice: postdictor of successful referral of alcoholic patients. *Journal of Abnormal Psychology,* 72, 78–84.

Minskoff, E.H. (1980*a*). Teaching approach for developing nonverbal communication skills in students with social perception deficits: part 1. The basic approach and body language clues. *Journal of Learning Disabilities,* 13, 118–24.

Minskoff, E.H. (1980*b*). Teaching approach for developing nonverbal communication skills in students with social perception deficits: part 2. Proxemic, vocalic, and artifactual cues. *Journal of Learning Disabilities,* 13, 203–8.

Murray, H. (1983). Low-inference classroom teaching behaviors and students' ratings of college teaching effectiveness. *Journal of Educational Psychology,* 75, 138–49.

Naftulin, D., Ware, J., & Donnelly, F. (1973). The Doctor Fox lecture: a paradigm of educational seduction. *Journal of Medical Education,* 48, 630–5.

Perrott, E. (1977). *Microteaching in higher education: research, development and practice.* Surrey, GB: Society for Research into Higher Education.

Rocca, K.A. (2001). *Participation in the college classroom: the impact of instructor immediacy and verbal aggression.* Paper presented at the annual meeting of the national communication association, Atlanta, GA, November 2001.

Rocca, K.A. & McCroskey, J.C. (1999). The interrelationship of student ratings of instructors' immediacy, verbal aggressiveness, homophily, and interpersonal attraction. *Communication Education,* 48, 308–16.

Rosenthal, R. & DePaulo, B. (1979). Sex differences in eavesdropping of nonverbal cues. *Journal of Personality and Social Psychology,* 37, 273–85.

Rosenthal, R. & Jacobson, L. (1968). *Pygmalion in the classroom.* New York: Holt, Rinehart & Winston.

Rosenthal, R., Hall, J.A., Archer, D., DiMatteo, M.R., & Rogers, P.L. (1979). *The PONS test manual: Profile of Nonverbal Sensitivity.* New York: Irvington Publishers.

Schonwetter, D., Perry, R., & Struthers, C. (1994). Student perceptions of control and success in college classroom: affects and achievement in different instructional conditions. *Journal of Experimental Education,* 61, 227–46.

Simon, A. & Boyer, E. (Eds.) (1974). *Mirrors for behavior III: An anthology of observation instruments.* Research for Better Schools Inc., Philadelphia: Pennsylvania.

Smith, H. (1984). Nonverbal behavior aspects of teaching. In *Nonverbal behavior: perspectives, applications, intercultural insights* (ed. A. Wolfgang), pp. 171–202. Toronto: Hogrefe.

Talbert–Johnson, C. & Beran, D. (1999). Higher education and teacher immediacy: creating dialogue for effective intercultural communication. *Journal for a Just and Caring Education,* 5, 430–1.

Titsworth, B.S. (2001). The effects of teacher immediacy, use of organizational lecture cues, and students' notetaking on cognitive learning. *Communication Education,* 50, 283–97.

Webb, J.M., Diana, E.M., Luft, P., Brooks, E.W., & Brenna, E.L. (1997). Influence of pedagogical expertise and feedback on assessing student comprehension from nonverbal behavior. *Journal of Educational Research*, **91**, 89–97.

Weinstein, R. (1985). Student mediation of classroom expectancy effects. In *Teacher Expectancies* (ed. J. Dusek), pp. 329–50. Hillsdale, NJ: Erlbaum.

Weinstein, R. (1989). Perceptions of classroom processes and student motivation: children's views of self-fulfilling prophecies. In *Research on motivation in education: volume 3. Goals and cognitions* (ed. C. Ames & R. Ames), pp. 187–221. New York: Academic Press.

Weinstein, R. (2002). *Reaching higher: the power of expectations in schooling.* Cambridge, MA: Harvard University Press.

Weinstein, R. & Middlestadt, S. (1979). Student perceptions of teacher interactions with male high and low achievers. *Journal of Educational Psychology*, **71**, 421–31.

Wood, A. (1998). The effects of teacher enthusiasm on student motivation, selective attention, and text memory. Doctoral dissertation, University of Western Ontario. *Dissertation abstracts International, Section A: Humanities & Social Sciences.* US, 1999 March 59 (9-A): p. 3355.

Woolfolk, A. (1985). Research perspectives on communication in classroom. *Theory Into Practice*, **24**, 3–7.

Woolfolk, A. & Brooks, D. (1983). Nonverbal communication in teaching. In *Review of research in education, Vol. 10* (ed. E. Gordon), pp. 103–50. Washington, DC: American Educational Research Association.

Woolfolk, A. & Galloway, C. (1985). Nonverbal communication and the study of teaching. *Theory Into Practice*, **24**, 77–84.

Zuckerman, M., DePaulo, B., & Rosenthal, R. (1986). Humans as deceivers and lie detectors. In *Nonverbal communication in the clinical context* (ed. P. Blanck, R. Buck, & R. Rosenthal). University Park, PA: Pennsylvania State University Press.

Notes

Elisha Babad is the Anna T. Lazarus Professor of Educational Social Psychology and Head of the School of Education at the Hebrew University of Jerusalem. The author is thankful to the United States–Israel Binational Science Foundation (BSF) for supporting his research on NV behavior in education for several years (Grant No. 1997053). The author is grateful to Robert Rosenthal for almost three decades of productive and satisfying collaboration, and to Dinah Avni–Babad for her encouragement and participation in NV research.

CHAPTER 8

NONVERBAL BEHAVIOR AND PSYCHOPATHOLOGY

ANN M. KRING AND BARBARA K. STUART

The study of nonverbal behavior has captured the imagination and interest of researchers across a number of disciplines, including psychology, sociology, anthropology, ethology, and linguistics to name but a few. At least since Darwin's 1872 publication of *The Expression of Emotion in Man and Animals* (see also Ekman 1998), the study of nonverbal behavior has been particularly central to researchers interested in emotion. Indeed, contemporary conceptualizations of emotion all include reference to nonverbal behaviors, particularly facial expressions, as integral to emotional responding, due not only to Darwin but also to the pioneering work of Tomkins, Izard, and Ekman in the 1960s and early 1970s.

However, it has only been in the last two decades that research on the nature of emotion and psychopathology has illuminated the important role that nonverbal behaviors play in a variety of disorders (for reviews see Berenbaum *et al.* 2003; Keltner & Kring 1998; Kring 2001). This is somewhat surprising given the ubiquity of emotion problems in different psychological disorders. Indeed, emotion disturbances figure prominently in many different forms of psychopathology, whether they are 'excesses' in emotion, 'deficits' in emotion, or the lack of coherence among emotional components. As illustrated in Table 8.1, many of the disorders found in the current *Diagnostic and Statistical Manual* (DSM-IV-TR; American Psychiatric Association 2000) include one or more symptoms reflecting an emotion disturbance.

Much of the progress towards understanding the nature of emotion disturbances in psychopathology has been aided by the use of methods pioneered by basic emotion researchers. Indeed, basic research on the components of emotional responding in nonclinical populations has proven useful and relevant for the study of emotional dysfunction in clinical populations. However, considerably less research has been conducted on understanding how nonverbal behaviors outside the context of emotion may be related to the symptoms, etiology, or course of different psychological disorders. In this chapter, we focus on the methods, complexities, and promises of studying emotional behavior in different forms of adult psychopathology. After first defining emotion, we next consider in some detail some of the special considerations associated with studying emotional behavior in psychological disorders.

Nonverbal behavior and emotion

Drawing from over a century of theory and research, there is fairly good consensus that emotions are adaptive and serve important functions. Broadly defined, emotions are

Table 8.1 Emotion-related symptoms in DSM–IV–TR

Disorder	Emotion-related symptom
Schizophrenia, schizoaffective, schizophreniform	Affective flattening, anhedonia
Major depressive episode	Depressed mood, anhedonia
Manic episode	Elevated, expansive, or irritable mood
Dysthymia	Depressed mood
Hypomanic episode	Elevated, expansive, or irritable mood
Panic disorder	Intense fear or discomfort
Agoraphobia	Anxiety
Specific phobia, social phobia	Marked and persistent fear
Obsessive–compulsive disorder	Marked anxiety or distress
PTSD	Irritability, anger, physiological reactivity, distress, anhedonia, restricted range of affect
Acute stress disorder	Symptoms of anxiety or increased arousal
Generalized anxiety disorder	Excessive anxiety and worry, irritability
Hypochondriasis	Preoccupation with fears of having disease
Anorexia nervosa	Fear of gaining weight
Sleep terror disorder	Intense fear and signs of autonomic arousal
Pathological gambling	Irritability, dysphoric mood
Adjustment disorder	Marked distress
Paranoid personality disorder	Quick to react angrily
Schizoid personality disorder	Emotional coldness, detachment, flattened affectivity
Schizotypal personality disorder	Inappropriate or constricted affect, excessive social anxiety
Antisocial personality disorder	Lack of remorse, irritability
Borderline personality disorder	Affective instability due to marked reactivity of mood, inappropriate intense anger or difficulty controlling anger
Histrionic personality disorder	Rapidly shifting and shallow expressions of emotion
Narcissistic personality disorder	Lacks empathy
Avoidant personality disorder	Fear of criticism, disapproval, or rejection
Dependent personality disorder	Fear of being unable to care for self or being left alone
Alcohol intoxication	Mood lability
Alcohol withdrawal	Anxiety
Amphetamine intoxication	Euphoria or affective blunting, anxiety, tension, anger
Amphetamine withdrawal	Dysphoric mood
Caffeine intoxication	Nervousness, excitement
Cannabis intoxication	Euphoria, anxiety
Cocaine intoxication	Euphoria or affective blunting, anxiety, tension, anger
Cocaine withdrawal	Dysphoric mood
Hallucinogen intoxication	Anxiety or depression
Inhalant intoxication	Belligerence, euphoria
Nicotine withdrawal	Dysphoric or depressed mood, irritability, frustration, anger, anxiety
Opioid intoxication	Euphoria followed by dysphoria
Opioid withdrawal	Dysphoric mood
Phencyclidine intoxication	Belligerence
Sedative etc. intoxication	Mood lability
Sedative etc. withdrawal	Anxiety

complex systems that developed through the course of human evolutionary history to prepare an organism to act in response to environmental stimuli and challenges. Furthermore, emotions are comprised of a number of components, including (but not limited to) behavioral or expressive, feeling or experiential, and physiological, that are typically coordinated within the individual. Indeed, the coordination of these components, under most circumstances, serves a number of important intra- and interpersonal functions (e.g. Ekman 1994; Frijda 1986; Keltner & Kring 1998; Lang *et al.* 1990; Levenson 1992), although across different contexts, these components may only be loosely connected (Russell *et al.* 2003).

In our view, advances in the understanding of emotion disturbances in psychopathology will be best advanced by adopting the conceptualizations, definitions, and methods for assessing emotion posited by basic emotion researchers. As we have argued elsewhere (Kring & Bachorowski 1999), the functions of emotion in persons with various psychopathological disorders are comparable to those for nondisordered individuals. In many different disorders, however, one or more components of emotional processing are impaired in some respect, thus interfering with the achievement of emotion-related functions. For example, schizophrenia patients' absence of facial expressions may evoke negative responses from others (Krause *et al.* 1992) and have a number of other consequences for social relationships and interactions (Keltner & Kring 1998).

We submit, then, that the study of emotion in psychopathology does not require different methods than those used to study emotion in nonpathological populations. Indeed, the promise of translating basic emotion theory and methods into the study of emotion and psychopathology has been realized in many areas of research, as we review later in the chapter. Although similar methods for assessing emotion in psychological disorders can and should be used, researchers must nevertheless take into consideration issues and characteristics of particular patient populations that may render interpretations of emotional behavior difficult. For example, when studying patients with schizophrenia, researchers must be mindful of possible medication side-effects that may manifest themselves as emotional disturbances (Kring & Earnst 1999).

Special considerations in the study of emotion and psychopathology

Conducting research with psychopathological populations requires special consideration with respect to a number of issues, including sample issues, diagnosis, treatment or medication effects, illness course, and comorbidity. Full review of these issues is beyond the scope and topic of this chapter; for additional exposition on these important considerations we refer interested readers to the chapter by Sher and Trull (1996) in the *Annual Review of Psychology*. We nevertheless believe it is important to discuss these issues in brief as they have enormous bearing on study design and the interpretation of findings from studies assessing emotional behavior and psychopathology.

Sampling issues

In psychopathology research, true experiments cannot be conducted due to the fairly obvious fact that persons cannot be randomly assigned to have a psychological disorder such as schizophrenia. Instead, most psychopathology researchers employ convenience or nonprobability samples by, for example, including patients from a particular hospital or outpatient clinic or recruiting nonpatient controls by accepting volunteers from the community (Sher & Trull 1996). Recruiting patients for a research study is difficult, fraught with special ethical considerations, and labor intensive, and thus convenience samples are often the most feasible. However, this approach is not without problems as selection biases can affect the generalizability and interpretability of the findings.

An additional sampling issue of relevance is the use of clinical versus subclinical samples. Clinical samples are typically defined as individuals who meet diagnostic criteria for a particular disorder. Subclinical samples may comprise individuals at risk for a particular disorder or individuals who exhibit a number of symptoms of a disorder but do not meet the diagnostic criteria for that disorder. Studies using subclinical populations are also referred to as analogue studies. In many studies using subclinical populations, college students scoring high on a symptom measure are compared to college students who do not score high on the measure. For example, many studies have examined college students selected on the basis of scores on the Beck Depression Inventory (BDI; Beck *et al.* 1961). However, this inventory was not designed to diagnose depression, only to assess its severity in a clinically diagnosed group. Some evidence indicates that selecting subjects solely on the basis of elevated BDI scores does not yield a group of people who can serve as a good analogue for those with clinical depression (Coyne 1994). High scorers may not be clinically depressed (Santor & Coyne 2001). Further, Hammen (1980) found that high scorers declined markedly when retested just two to three weeks later. On the other hand, other evidence suggests that individuals who score high on symptoms measures and yet do not meet diagnostic criteria do not differ markedly from individuals who meet diagnostic criteria (Gotlib *et al.* 1995). Kendall *et al.* (1987) provided a set of guidelines for investigators to follow when using the BDI in order to maximize comparability between studies using individuals scoring high on the BDI and studies using individuals who meet diagnostic criteria for depression.

Researchers interested in schizophrenia have studied individuals believed to be at risk for developing schizophrenia, sometimes referred to as 'psychosis prone'. In the 1970s, Loren and Jean Chapman developed self-report scales of characteristics believed to reflect the precursors for schizophrenia, including physical and social anhedonia, perceptual aberrations, and magical thinking (Chapman *et al.* 1976; Eckblad & Chapman 1983; Mishlove & Chapman 1985). These investigators conducted a longitudinal study of college students at the University of Wisconsin by following, for 10 years, over 500 students who scored high on these measures to ascertain how many students would go on to develop schizophrenia (Chapman *et al.* 1994). The results of the 10-year follow-up indicated that a number of the students exhibited psychiatric symptoms, though very few actually developed schizophrenia, leaving some to wonder whether this is a useful analogue for schizophrenia research. However, other follow-up studies have indicated that social anhedonia is a significant predictor of the later development of schizophrenia spectrum disorders (Kwapil 1998).

Trull and colleagues (e.g. Trull 1995; Trull *et al.* 1997) have studied emotional, cognitive, and interpersonal features of borderline personality disorder (BPD) among nonclinical college students who were not seeking treatment for BPD but who nonetheless demonstrated a number of BPD features. Individuals with a high number of BPD features reported greater trait-negative affect, hostility, anxiety, and depression, and less trait-positive affect than control participants who had no BPD features. What is unclear is whether these individuals with BPD features differ in important ways from patients with the diagnosis of BPD.

Decisions about whether to use patients who meet diagnostic criteria for a particular disorder versus individuals with a number of symptoms should be made on both theoretical and empirical grounds. The current diagnostic systems are works in progress and, thus, considering as valid only those studies that use patients meeting diagnostic criteria would be a mistake. On the other hand, studies that define 'patient' groups by identifying college students with a very small number of symptoms (e.g. a score of 7 on the BDI) are not likely to advance our understanding of a particular disorder. What needs to be done is work that integrates both clinical and subclinical samples to broaden our understanding of emotional features and disturbances associated with the various psychological disorders.

Diagnostic issues

Choosing to study individuals who meet diagnostic criteria for a particular disorder still leaves a number of decisions for the researcher. First, decisions about which diagnostic system to adhere to must be considered. Most often, the American diagnostic system, currently DSM-IV-TR (APA 2000) is used. However, international researchers often follow the International Statistical Classification of Diseases and Related Health Problems (ICD-10; World Health Organization 1992). Although the two systems do not differ tremendously, there are subtle differences, which may render comparison across studies using the different diagnostic systems difficult. Furthermore, both of these diagnostic systems have undergone a number of revisions over the past 30 years. For example, depending upon the disorder of interest, it can be difficult to compare findings from studies conducted in the 1970s (DSM-II), early 1980s (DSM-III), and today (DSM-IV).

Beyond decisions about the diagnostic system, procedures for assigning diagnoses must be delineated. In some studies, diagnoses are obtained from reviewing patients' records. This is problematic in that clinical practices for assigning diagnoses vary quite a bit from hospital to hospital and clinic to clinic, with some diagnoses made following a 10-minute conversation with a patient, others made from prior patient records, and still others made from a systematic interview and treatment team case conference. Given this variability, the stability and reliability of diagnoses across such sites is likely quite low. Most research studies use structured clinical interviews, such as the Structured Clinical Interview for DSM-IV (SCID-IV; First et al. 1994). The advantages to using such structured interviews are many. First, the questions and scoring system in the interview are standardized so that differences between investigators are minimized. Second, training materials are available to increase the likelihood that different investigators use the interviews in a similar fashion. Third, these interviews have been used in a large number of studies of different psychological disorders and the reliability and validity of the instruments have been well established.

So as not to unnecessarily reify the diagnostic criteria for particular disorders, some investigators choose to study a spectrum of disorders. For example, many studies of schizophrenia may include patients with schizophrenia, schizoaffective disorder, schizophreniform disorder, and delusional disorder. Those who study autism may include patients with Asperger's Syndrome and perhaps other pervasive developmental disorders. Those interested in studying depression may include persons who meet criteria for major depressive disorder and dysthymia. The reasoning behind such an approach is that any one set of diagnostic criteria is a fallible indicator of what is undoubtedly a broader range of pathology. On the other hand, hypotheses about emotion and a particular disorder (e.g. schizophrenia) cannot be as unequivocally tested with a broad-spectrum sample.

To be sure, the diagnostic criteria are a 'work in progress' and will likely continue to change. However, the specificity of a particular emotion disturbance cannot be tested with a sample that cuts across many (similar) disorders. At the least, researchers should be clear when describing the sample used in a study. Furthermore, inclusion of sufficient numbers of patients in each diagnostic group in order to systematically test for any differences in the dependent variables of interest is ideal.

Treatment issues

When studying patient groups, information about current and past treatment must be gathered and taken into consideration. Interpretation of findings about emotion disturbances in psychopathology may vary depending upon treatment status. For example, if an emotion disturbance exacerbates when patients are no longer receiving treatment, one might conclude that the treatment was effective in resolving the emotion disturbance. By contrast, an emotion disturbance that persists regardless of treatment status, as is the case with diminished expressiveness in schizophrenia (Kring & Earnst 1999), suggests that the disturbance is a stable aspect of the disorder that may be relatively resistant to treatment. Finally, if an emotion disturbance remits when patients are withdrawn from treatment, particularly medication, the emotion disturbance is likely a medication side-effect.

Indeed, in some disorders such as schizophrenia, side-effects from medication may present like the emotional phenomena of interest. For example, one of the most common and troubling side-effects of neuroleptic medication is akinesia (Blanchard & Neale 1992; Carpenter *et al.* 1985; Marder *et al.* 1991; Sommers 1985; Van Putten & Marder 1987; Van Putten *et al.* 1980). Although clinical descriptions of akinesia vary, it is typically defined by characteristics that are virtually identical to descriptions of the schizophrenia symptom of affective flattening, including diminished facial expression, nonspontaneous speech, and few gestures. Thus, it is often difficult to determine whether the diminished expressiveness seen in some schizophrenia patients is a symptom of the disorder or a side-effect of the medication.

A number of strategies have been employed to assess medication effects on various performance measures. Perhaps the most common method has been to examine the correlation between equated medication dosage levels and the dependent variables of interest. Although this approach provides useful descriptive information about medication dosage, it does not take into account the differential effect of different types of medications (Blanchard & Neale 1992). A second common approach is to assess medication side-effects with clinical rating scales and then to include these scores as a covariate in statistical analyses to partial out the effects of side-effects on performance. However, as discussed later, some rating scales for medication side-effects contain items that are virtually identical to items on scales designed to assess the emotion disturbance. Thus, relying solely on clinical rating scales will provide an incomplete assessment.

In order to assess the effects of medication on emotional behavior, one of the most powerful designs is a within-subjects design (Blanchard & Neale 1992) referred to by Spohn and Strauss (1989) as a counterbalanced crossover design. In this design, the same patients are tested both on and off medication, with roughly half of the sample being off medication at the first testing and then retested while on medication, and the other half of the sample being on medication at the first testing and then retested while off medication. The within-subjects aspect of the design allows patients to serve as their own controls, and the counterbalancing aspect of the design controls for order effects. Although this is a powerful design to detect medication effects on a dependent variable of interest, withdrawing medication from patients for research purposes is no longer possible in many hospitals and clinics. Thus, many investigators will be unable to clearly assess what, if any, effects medications may have on emotion behavior and instead note this as a possible alternative account for the findings reported.

Testing patients receiving treatment (medication or psychotherapy) is not without advantages. Indeed, in many respects this is a more ecologically valid assessment of patients with a particular disorder given that a large number of individuals do indeed receive treatment.

Course of illness

In their seminal review of cognitive theories of depression, Barnett and Gotlib (1988) distinguished between the concepts of antecedents, concomitants, and consequences. Briefly, for a variable such as nonverbal behavior to be considered an antecedent of a psychological disorder, it must be shown to precede the onset of the disorder. Features that are observed during an episode of a psychological disorder may be more accurately construed as concomitants, and those features that persist after the episode has abated might be considered consequences.

To interpret findings regarding emotional behavior and different psychological disorders, it is necessary to review the evidence in the context of the temporal course of the disorder. Specifically, evidence showing that emotion disturbances precede the onset of a given disorder would support the role of an observed emotion disturbance as antecedent to the disorder and allows for a clearer claim about the causal status of that disturbance. A prospective, longitudinal study is the best design to determine whether or not emotional disturbances precede the onset of a disorder; however, few such studies have been conducted. Evidence that emotional disturbances are present only during an active symptomatic state suggests that the disturbances are better construed as concomitants. Indeed, most of the research on emotional disturbances in psychopathology has employed cross-sectional designs that are ideally suited to evaluate whether particular emotional features can be construed as concomitants.

Finally, if the evidence indicates that emotion disturbances persist after symptomatic recovery or predate a relapse, the disturbances may be construed as consequences of the disorder. Prospective, longitudinal designs again are the best method for ascertaining whether emotional features can be considered to be a consequence of the disorder. Understanding where, in the course of a disorder, certain emotional features or disturbances appear has important implications for treatment development as well as for theories of etiology (for a review see Kring 2001).

Comorbidity

Comorbidity refers to co-occurrence of more than one disorder. This is very common across all disorders. For example, 50% or more of patients with schizophrenia also have a substance-related disorder (Blanchard *et al.* 2000); anxiety and mood disorders exhibit a tremendous amount of comorbidity (Mineka *et al.* 1998). Given that comorbidity is so common, findings from studies that examine a particular disorder (e.g. depression) that is not comorbid with another disorder (e.g. generalized anxiety disorder) may not generalize well to the larger population of individuals with depression. For example, there is some evidence to indicate that nonverbal behaviors observed in comorbid anxiety and depression (e.g. distressed facial expressions, hostility, agitation) differ from observations of depression (Katz *et al.* 1993). On the other hand, if researchers are interested in isolating a specific emotion disturbance for depression, then the place to begin is with a sample of patients with depression only. Later studies could include patients with depression and anxiety to test the generalizability of the particular emotion disturbance.

Why study emotion in psychopathology?

Although it may seem obvious that the study of emotion in psychopathology is of critical importance, since emotion is so central to many different disorders (see Table 8.1), we submit that it is important to be clear about the goals of such research. For example, in our view, research on emotional behavior or other nonverbal behavior in psychopathology will not supplant current diagnostic assessments. In other words, we doubt that different psychological disorders can be diagnosed by nonverbal or emotional behavior 'signatures' independent of other measures.

Furthermore, it is unlikely that emotion clearly distinguishes different psychological disorders (see also Pansa–Henderson *et al.* 1982). For example, findings by Watson *et al.* (1988), indicating that heightenened levels of negative affect (NA) could characterize both anxiety and depression, while lowered levels of positive affect (PA) uniquely characterized depression, suggest that emotion might serve as a means for distinguishing among psychological disorders. However, subsequent research has shown that other disorders, including schizophrenia and social phobia show the same pattern of heightened NA and lowered PA (e.g. Berenbaum & Fujita 1994; Blanchard *et al.* 1998; Wallace & Alden 1997), casting doubt on the specificity of this pattern to depression.

Nonetheless, we do believe that findings on emotion and psychopathology will be a useful augmentation to diagnostic assessments, and we concur with Berenbaum and colleagues (2003) that the development of a taxonomy of emotion disturbances in psychopathology may have much clinical utility. While we are less optimistic that such a taxonomy may provide greater predictive power than current diagnostic systems (as nonverbal behavior is not necessarily indicative of gross psychopathology), it can nevertheless highlight subtle dysfunctional processes.

Numerous descriptive studies on nonverbal behavior and psychopathology have been conducted over the last 40 years; however, there has been little cumulative benefit from these studies. As highlighted above, changes in diagnostic systems and practices makes comparison across studies from different diagnostic 'eras' difficult, if not impossible. However, descriptive studies have also failed to advance our knowledge of emotion disturbances in psychopathology due to the overly descriptive nature of the research. A typical study may begin with a small sample of patients (e.g. 7–10) and then try to identify variables (e.g. facial expression, vocal expression, gestures, eye contact) that distinguish these patients from a nonpatient control group. Many of these studies are conducted without advancing hypotheses about how or why groups may differ and without sufficient conceptual or theoretical underpinnings to constrain such hypotheses. Thus, the literature is replete with several mini-findings that neither advance our understanding of a particular disorder (with respect to symptoms, course, etiology, or treatment) nor advance our understanding of the ways in which emotion disturbances are manifest within a particular disorder or constellation of symptoms.

As noted above, it is important to discover where emotion disturbances are situated in the temporal course of a given disorder, and this is a laudable goal for research on emotion and psychological disorders. For example, finding particular emotion behaviors prior to the onset of an illness would suggest that these behaviors have the potential to be construed as a marker for the illness or a vulnerability indicator (Nuechterlein & Dawson 1984). Finding a constellation of emotion disturbances concomitant with an episode of a disorder points to the possibility that changes in this disturbance can be used as an indicator of treatment effectiveness. Addressing these questions requires prospective, longitudinal designs.

An additional goal for researchers interested in emotion and psychopathology might be to develop newer, more effective interventions. The theorizing of Marsha Linehan about the role of emotion regulation deficits in borderline personality disorder (BPD) led to the development of dialectical behavior therapy (DBT; Linehan, 1993) for this disorder. Theories posited by Linehan and others (Linehan 1987; Snyder & Pitt 1985; but see Farchaus–Stein 1996) have suggested that individuals with BPD have difficulty returning to an 'emotional baseline' following an emotional event. Furthermore, empirical evidence suggests that BPD patients report chronic and intense feelings of a number of negative emotions, including anger, hostility, depression, loneliness, and anxiety (e.g. Coid 1993; Farchaus–Stein 1996; Gunderson *et al.* 1975; Gunderson & Phillips 1991; Kruedelbach *et al.* 1993; Soloff 1981; Soloff & Ulrich 1981; Snyder & Pitt 1985).

Portions of DBT involve training patients in a number of emotion regulation skills, including reorientating of attention, changing facial and body language, perspective taking, inhibition of mood-dependent actions, and experiencing emotion without escalating or blunting the feelings (Linehan 1993; Linehan & Schmidt 1995; Robins *et al.* 2001). Although there are several studies showing the effectiveness of this intervention, little work has yet been conducted to confirm the emotion mechanisms believed to be central to the disorder. The development of DBT followed from theory, and the attendant empirical work to support the hypothesized emotion regulation deficits is now being conducted (e.g. Lynch *et al.* 2001).

An alternative approach would be to build an intervention based on accumulated findings about a particular emotional behavior disturbance in a disorder. For example, accumulated evidence shows that schizophrenia patients are less emotionally expressive than nonpatients (see Kring 1999 for a review). Certainly, expressive behavior is an important part of socially skilled behavior. However, recent evidence suggests that the emotional deficits in schizophrenia are distinct from social skills deficits (Salem & Kring 1999), and thus interventions aimed at improving social skills may not necessarily change expressive behavior. These interventions could be strengthened by including components that specifically target emotional disturbances (e.g. expressing emotion at the right time in the appropriate contexts; interpreting emotions in others) as well as the performance of socially skilled behavior.

Approaches to studying emotion and nonverbal behavior in psychopathology

A number of different approaches to studying emotion and nonverbal behavior in psychopathology have been used. Some of these methods are more specific to psychopathology (e.g. symptom rating scales), whereas others are commonly used in other areas of research (e.g. facial expression coding systems such as FACS). This diversity of methods is both a blessing and a curse. Some of the methods are designed with the complexities associated with different disorders in mind. However, the sheer number of different methods throughout the literature makes comparisons across studies quite difficult. In this section, we present a cross-section of these methods, highlighting the strength and weaknesses of each along the way.

Symptom rating scales

Symptom rating scales are not typically derived to assess nonverbal behavior or emotion. However, to the extent that a particular disorder involves emotional or nonverbal behavior symptoms, they will be included in these rating scales. Most generally, symptom rating scales are completed following an interview with a patient. These interviews typically focus on the signs and symptoms of a particular illness. Table 8.2 includes a description of some commonly used clinical rating scales for adult psychopathology. These interviews were designed to assess specific symptoms and their severity and as an aid to diagnosis. Individual subscales may contain items relevant to emotion or nonverbal behavior, and other research suggests that these measures are related to other indices of emotion. For example, Kring *et al.* (1994a) found that the affective flattening subscale of the Schedule for the Assessment of Negative Symptoms

Table 8.2 Selected clinical rating scales

Scale	Relevant disorders	Items relevant to emotion and nonverbal behavior
BPRS	Schizophrenia, mood disorders	Anxiety, emotional withdrawal, guilt feelings, tension, mannerisms and posturing, depressive mood, hostility, motor retardation, blunted affect, excitement
HAM–D	Major depressive disorder	Depressed mood, feelings of guilt, slowed speech or decreased motor activity, agitation, anxiety
HAM–A	Anxiety disorders	Anxious mood, tension, fears, depressed mood, twitching, stiffness, fidgeting, restlessness, tremor of hands, furrowed brow, strained face, sighing
PANSS	Schizophrenia	Blunted affect, emotional withdrawal, anxiety, guilt, tension, mannerisms and posturing, depression, motor retardation, hostility, excitement
SANS	Schizophrenia	*Affective flattening*: unchanging facial expression, decreased spontaneous movements, poor eye contact, affective nonresponsivity, paucity of expressive gestures, lack of vocal inflections; *avolition-apathy*: physical anergia; *anhedonia-asociality*
SAPS	Schizophrenia	*Bizarre behavior*: aggressive and agitated behavior, repetitive or stereotyped behavior
ADI	Autism	Anticipatory gestures, vocal expression, range of facial expression, appropriate facial expression, pleasure/excitement

Note: BPRS = Brief Psychiatric Rating Scale (Ventura *et al.* 1993); HAM–D = Hamilton Rating Scale for Depression (Hamilton 1960); HAM–A = Hamilton Rating Scale for Anxiety (Hamilton 1959); PANSS = Positive and Negative Syndrome Scale (Kay *et al.* 1986); SANS = Scale for the Assessment of Negative Symptoms (Andreasen 1984); SAPS = Scale for the Assessment of Positive Symptoms (Andreasen 1984); ADI = Autism Diagnostic Interview (Le Couter *et al.* 1989).

(SANS; Andreasen 1984) was related to coded facial expressions of positive and negative emotion and an acoustic assessment of vocal prosody.

Although these interviews and rating scales are quite effective in assessing specific symptoms of a disorder, they are not a particularly effective means for assessing emotion and nonverbal behavior. First, the behavioral sample upon which they are based may not be representative because the ratings are typically made at one particular time, usually while the patient is in the hospital. Second, the format of these interviews also relies on a certain degree of clinical skill that may systematically fail to elicit emotional material, and thus may not provide an opportunity for patients to express a wide range of emotions. Third, the items on most rating scales do not differentiate between reduced expression of positive versus negative emotions but, rather, assess overall reduced expressiveness, therefore resulting in data that are uninformative with respect to particular emotions. Finally, most uses of the rating scales require a tabulation of a total score rather than specific subscale scores. Thus, knowing the overall total on the BPRS is informative with respect to overall symptomatology, but it does not provide any specific information about emotional symptoms.

A special type of clinical rating scale often of interest to researchers studying the emotional features of schizophrenia is one that assesses medication side-effects. As noted above, akinesia can appear virtually identical to flat affect. Unfortunately, the items on clinical rating scales used to rate akinesia are often the same items used to assess flat affect. This suggests the need for a more comprehensive and fine-grained behavioral assessment of expressive behavior and emotional responding that goes beyond rating scales for symptoms and medication side-effects.

Self-report measures of symptoms or diagnosis

Many symptom self-report measures have been developed. Review of these measures far exceeds the scope of this chapter. In almost all cases, these measures were not developed to assess emotion or nonverbal behavior associated with a particular disorder. Rather, they were developed to assess symptoms of disorders. Like the clinical interviews discussed above, these measures include items related to emotion only if emotion-related symptoms are part of the disorder. Taken alone, then, these measures are not a good measure of emotion in psychopathology. Taking out emotion-relevant items to form a new 'subscale' may violate the integrity of the measure and is therefore not recommended. These measures may be used to augment other measures of emotion and psychopathology but, like clinical interviews, the primary purpose of these measures is to provide information about diagnosis, symptom severity, or both.

Observational ratings

Other methods for assessing emotion and nonverbal behavior include direct observational ratings. Most often, these studies have been conducted with patients who are inpatients. For example, Brown *et al.* (1979) observed and rated overt changes in facial expression associated with pleasurable activities that were exhibited by six schizophrenia and five depressed inpatients; schizophrenia patients exhibited significantly more such changes than did depressed patients.

The Autism Diagnostic Observation Schedule—Generic (ADOS–G; Lord *et al.* 2000) is a combination of clinical interview/rating scale and observational method. The generic version of this measure was developed for use with a broader age range of individuals, including adults, following the success of the ADOS (Lord *et al.* 1989; Lord *et al.* 1999) in diagnosing autism in children ranging from 5–12 years old. The ADOS–G involves a number of activities and interactions that allow an examiner to assess social–emotional and other disrupted behaviors, as well as language capabilities. Activities include conversational interactions/interviews, examining cartoons, creating a story, describing a picture, and telling a story from a book. Some of the emotional behaviors assessed by the ADOS–G include unusual eye contact, whether or not facial expressions are directed towards others, empathetic or emotional gestures, empathy/comments on others' emotions, shared enjoyment, mannerisms, negative behaviors, and anxiety. Like most clinical interviews, a good bit of training is necessary in order to administer the measure accurately and competently.

Other descriptive, observational approaches come from the ethological psychiatry tradition (Troisi 1999). From this perspective, nonverbal behaviors are observed, catalogued, and conceptualized from an evolutionary standpoint (e.g. Pederson *et. al* 1988). Nonverbal behaviors are not necessarily presumed to reflect emotion, consistent with other ethological approaches to nonverbal behavior (e.g. Birdwhistell 1970;

Mitchell & Thompson 1986; Smith 1985). These studies typically include very small numbers of patients and describe a very large number of behaviors, most usually during an inpatient hospital stay.

One goal of the ethological psychiatry approach is to describe the behavior of the 'typical patient'. This implies that a psychological disorder can be identified by a particular nonverbal behavior 'signature'. However, this assumption does not leave much room for individual variation—yet individual differences are widespread in both patient and nonpatient populations. Additionally, since most of these studies include such a small sample of patients (due largely to the labor-intensive work associated with observing hundreds of behaviors), generalizations to larger groups of patients cannot be clearly made.

Findings from this approach have suggested that certain nonverbal behaviors may change over the course of a hospital stay for patients with depression and schizophrenia. For example, Pederson et al. (1988) observed and recorded the presence or absence of 142 different behaviors exhibited by five hospitalized depressed patients. Observations were conducted for four hours each day during the entire hospital stay (ranging from 4 to 11 weeks). Analyses were concerned with identifying behaviors that changed from the first to last week of hospitalization and how these behaviors correlated with symptom ratings of depression. Patients who improved the most during their hospital stay tended to display greater activity towards the end of the stay (e.g. more communication, getting out of bed, greater eye contact). Yet, there were widespread individual differences even among just five patients.

Similar findings were reported by Fossi et al. (1984) who observed 110 different behaviors among 29 hospitalized depressed patients. After treatment, patients exhibited greater eye contact, more exploration in the environment, and more frequent facial expressions of emotion. Towards the end of the hospital stay, patients spent less time in their rooms and more time in common areas compared with the early part of the hospital stay. Schelde (1998) also found behavior changes in 11 patients with depression following an inpatient stay of between 3 and 15 weeks. Specifically, patients showed less withdrawal, nonspecific gaze, more mouth movements, more social interest, more smiles, and more verbal social behavior. Other findings show that depressed individuals exhibited more excitement, gestures, and head movement following recovery (Bos et al. 2002; Geerts & Bouhys 1998; Geerts et al. 1996).

Although findings such as these may be informative with respect to generating hypotheses for future studies about nonverbal behavior and depression, they are limited by numerous methodological issues, including:

- small sample sizes;
- variations in treatment;
- insufficient information about patients' symptoms;
- lack of a control group.

More recent ethological studies have attempted to predict prognosis and treatment response (Troisi 1999). The Ethological Coding System for Interviews (ECSI) was developed to rate behaviors occurring in the context of a clinical interview. Thirty-seven different behaviors are rated using this system, and seven subscales are then created: affiliation (e.g. smile, eye raise); submission (e.g. nod, lips in and pressed together); prosocial (affiliation and submission combined); flight (e.g. look away, look down, shut eyes); assertion (e.g. lean forward, head shake, thrust, frown); displacement (e.g. scratch, fumble, yawn, hands on face); and relaxation (e.g. relax, settle, laugh, arms across chest). In a sample of 18 male schizophreniform patients, Troisi *et al.* (1991) found that patients with a poor prognosis had less eye contact and more eye closures during an interview than patients with a good prognosis. Troisi *et al.*(1998) found that 28 drug-free, male schizophrenia patients showed less prosocial behavior and displacement and fewer gestures than 12 healthy controls or 13 medical students. Troisi *et al.* (1989) found that 14 depressed individuals who responded to medication (amitriptyline) showed more affiliation and assertion. These findings, though based on small sample sizes, support the use of this system for assessing nonverbal behaviors in the context of an interview, but not emotional behavior per se.

Laboratory paradigms and coding systems

Borrowing directly from the basic emotion literature, researchers have used a number of laboratory paradigms to elicit emotion in persons with different psychological disorders. These studies typically involve presenting patients with emotionally evocative stimuli (e.g. film clips, pictures, slides, odors) and asking them to rate their experience of emotion following the presentation. Facial expressions are often videotaped and later coded and, in some cases, psychophysiological measures are also employed. The advantages to this approach are many. First, stimuli often have been used in a number of studies, thus bolstering confidence in their emotion-eliciting capabilities. Furthermore, a number of studies have also used these stimuli with patient populations, further confirming their applicability to psychopathology research. Second, these studies are conducted in laboratory settings where a number of extraneous variables can be brought under experimental control, thus making interpretation of findings more clear. Third, these studies typically involve assessments of multiple components of emotion allowing for a more comprehensive understanding of emotion function (or dysfunction) in a particular patient group. Fourth, methods used to assess emotion behaviors, such as facial expression, are often well-validated systems used in a number of studies.

This approach is not without limitations, however. For example, the ecological validity is less than ideal. Knowing how patients respond to emotionally evocative films clips does not necessarily translate into knowing how patients respond to emotional events in daily life. In addition, certain emotions (e.g. anger) are more difficult to elicit in a laboratory context than others (e.g. happiness), limiting the range of emotions that can be studied. Finally, these studies often examine emotional behavior in the individual, without regard to contextual influences (e.g. social interaction).

A range of emotionally evocative stimuli have been used in laboratory studies of emotion and psychopathology. While all laboratory inductions of emotion are somewhat artificial in nature, viewing film clips is a relatively common activity for most people. This method is also not reliant on subjects' ability to recall past experiences. Slides or still photographs present momentary emotional scenes, whereas film clips present a more realistic context in which emotional experiences typically develop over time. Additionally, this procedure has been used successfully with different patient populations (e.g. Berenbaum & Oltmanns 1992; Kring & Earnst 1999; Kring *et al.* 1993; Kring & Neale 1996; Litz *et al.* 2000; Rottenberg *et al.* 2002). Finally, film clips ensure that the nature of emotional stimuli is consistent across all subjects. Other widely used stimuli in laboratory research include pictures of facial expression (e.g. Kring *et al.* 1999; Sloan *et al.* 2002) and emotionally evocative slides (e.g. Allen *et al.* 1999; Sloan *et al.* 1997, 2001)

Studies that videotape facial expressions for later coding have used a variety of coding systems, such as the Facial Action Coding System (FACS: Ekman & Friesen 1978; Ekman *et al.* 2002) and the Facial Expression Coding System (FACES: Kring & Sloan 1992). These systems have been developed with nonpatient populations and used in several studies of basic emotion processes in both patient and nonpatient populations. Other studies have created a coding scheme for a particular study and not for widespread use by other investigators. Decisions about which method of measurement to adopt should be driven by both theoretical and practical considerations.

Widely considered the standard in observational coding systems, FACS was designed to provide a comprehensive assessment of all visible facial muscle movements without explicitly making reference to the meaning of those movements. FACS coders are trained to identify 44 anatomically distinct muscle movements (e.g. lip corner puller), labeled action units (AUs), but they are not asked to make inferences about underlying emotional state (e.g. happy expression). Directions for identifying particular AUs believed to be signs associated with emotional expressions is provided with FACS. FACS is theoretically aligned with a discrete emotions perspective, whereby a set of biologically based and functionally significant basic emotions are postulated (e.g. Ekman 1992). The emphasis, therefore, is on identifying AUs that are relevant to seven basic emotions: fear, anger, disgust, happiness, sadness, surprise, and contempt.

Kring and Sloan (1992) developed FACES as a systematic method for rating dimensional expressivity. Rather than assessing discrete emotions associated with specific muscle movements, FACES coders rate the changes in facial musculature that are associated with valence and intensity. We adopted the assumption that coders will be culturally familiar with facial expressions and, thus, will be able to identify facial muscle changes of positive and negative valence. FACES has been used in studies of emotional responding in various patient populations (e.g. Aghevli *et al.* 2003; Kring *et al.* 1993; Kring & Neale 1996; Wagner *et al.* 2003) and college students (e.g. Kring *et al.* 1994*b*; Kring & Gordon 1998).

Other laboratory approaches to assessing nonverbal behavior in psychopathology include the role play test (RPT: e.g. Bellack *et al.* 1990*b*). Patients are given a number of different scenarios (e.g. someone asks to borrow money and you were planning to spend the money on something for yourself) and are asked to act out how they would respond in the scenario. These role plays are videotaped and later rated for verbal and nonverbal behaviors. The impetus for the development of the RPT was to develop a system upon which objective assessment of social competence among psychiatric patients could be based. In the RPT, the videos are rated for gaze appropriateness, speech duration, meshing (smooth conversation), and affect. Other RPTs include the Assessment of Interpersonal Problem Solving Skills (AIPSS; Donahoe *et al.* 1990).

Approaches in action: emotion and psychopathology

In this section, we review selected findings on emotional behavior in adult psychopathology. This review is intended to highlight the promise of adopting basic emotion paradigms to the study of emotion in psychopathology, despite the numerous complexities associated with psychopathology research.

Schizophrenia

A number of investigators have used methods for eliciting emotion and measuring emotion behavior that were developed by researchers studying basic emotion in order to investigate emotional responding among patients with schizophrenia. These studies, most of which were conducted in the last 12 years, have yielded a consistent and well-replicated set of findings.

Schizophrenia patients are less expressive (both facially and vocally) than nonpatients in response to a variety of contexts and stimuli, including emotionally evocative films (Berenbaum & Oltmanns 1992; Kring & Earnst 1999; Kring & Neale 1996; Kring *et al.* 1993; Mattes *et al.* 1995), cartoons (Dworkin *et al.* 1996), and social interactions (Borod *et al.* 1989; Krause *et al.* 1989; Martin *et al.* 1990; Kring *et al.* 1994*a*; Mattes *et al.* 1995). In addition, schizophrenia patients' pattern of facial and vocal expression have been distinguished from other patient groups with symptoms that bear resemblance to flat affect, including depression, Parkinson's disease, and patients with right hemisphere brain damage (Borod *et al.* 1989; Levin *et al.* 1985; Martin *et al.* 1990; Berenbaum & Oltmanns 1992). Despite their diminished expressive behavior, schizophrenia patients reported experiencing similar and, in some cases, greater amounts of emotion compared to nonpatients (Berenbaum & Oltmanns 1992; Earnst & Kring 1999; Kring & Earnst 1999; Kring & Neale 1996; Salem & Kring 1999).

It is important to point out that we, and others, have found this same pattern both when patients were on medication (Berenbaum & Oltmanns 1992) and when they were off medication (Kring *et al.* 1993; Kring & Neale 1996; Kring & Earnst 1999). Moreover, we have found that both facial expression and subjective experience are remarkably stable across time and medication status (Kring & Earnst 1999). Additional evidence shows that schizophrenia patients exhibit very subtle, microexpressive displays in a manner consistent with the valence of the stimuli (Mattes *et al.* 1995; Earnst *et al.* 1996; Kring *et al.* 1999; Kring & Earnst 2003). For example, we have shown that in response to positive stimuli, schizophrenia patients exhibit more zygomatic (cheek) muscle activity, which is typically associated with positive emotion, than corrugator (brow) muscle activity, which is typically associated with negative emotion. By contrast, in response to negative stimuli, patients exhibit more corrugator activity than zygomatic activity (Kring & Earnst 2003).

Although schizophrenia patients may exhibit subtle facial expressions, these displays are not observable to others, and this relative inexpression has a number of interpersonal consequences. For example, spouses of schizophrenia patients with negative symptoms, including flat affect, reported greater marital dissatisfaction (Hooley et al. 1987). Healthy individuals reported experiencing more fear and sadness and were themselves less expressive when they interacted with a schizophrenia patient than when they interacted with another healthy individual (Krause et al. 1992). Using symptom rating scales to measure diminished expressivity, Bellack et al. (1990a) found that patients who were the least expressive had poorer interpersonal relationships and poorer adjustment at home and in other social domains. Without the benefit of overt signs of emotion, others may misinterpret the ongoing emotional state of a patient with schizophrenia. Moreover, there is some evidence indicating that schizophrenia patients may not be aware of how unexpressive they are (Kring 1991). Thus, patients may not understand others' reactions in ongoing interactions, and they may not take alternate measures to make their emotional state known.

There is some evidence to suggest that schizophrenia patients may display fewer facial expressions (particularly positive expressions) prior to the onset of the illness. For example, Walker and colleagues (1993) obtained home movies of adults with schizophrenia that were made before these adults developed schizophrenia. They coded facial expressions from the home movies of pre-schizophrenic boys and girls and found that girls displayed fewer joy expressions and that both boys and girls displayed *more* negative facial expressions compared to their healthy siblings. Findings from prospective, high-risk studies have reported similar findings. High-risk studies identify a group of children at risk for developing schizophrenia (typically defined as having a biological parent with schizophrenia) and then follow them from childhood through the period of risk (Neale & Oltmanns 1980). Teacher ratings from the Copenhagen High-Risk Study indicated that boys and girls who were later diagnosed with schizophrenia were more emotionally labile, socially withdrawn, socially anxious, and relatively unexpressive than children who did not develop schizophrenia (Olin et al. 1995; Olin & Mednick 1996). Findings from the New York High-Risk Project indicated that flat affect was greater among adolescents at risk for developing schizophrenia than adolescents at risk for developing affective disorders (Dworkin et al. 1991).

Mood disorders

Accumulated evidence indicates that individuals with major depressive disorder (hereafter referred to as depression) exhibit dampened facial, vocal, and gestural expressive behavior (Berenbaum & Oltmanns 1992; Ekman & Friesen 1974; Gotlib & Robinson 1982; Hargreaves et al. 1965; Jones & Pansa 1979; Kaplan et al. 1999; Murray & Arnott 1993; Scherer 1986; Schwartz et al. 1976; Ulrich & Harms 1985; Waxer 1974). In addition, dampened expressive behavior among individuals with depression may be specific to positive expressions, though this needs additional study. For example, Berenbaum and Oltmanns (1992) found that depressed individuals showed fewer facial expressions in response to positive stimuli (but not to negative stimuli) than nonpatients and schizophrenic patients with flat affect.

In other studies, researchers examining emotion and other nonverbal behavior in social interactions found that currently depressed individuals exhibited less eye contact than recovered depressed individuals (e.g. Hinchliffee *et al.* 1971; Waxer 1974, 1976) or nonpatients (Troisi & Moles 1999) and that greater eye contact and gaze were associated with a reduction in symptoms over the course of inpatient treatment (Ellgring 1986). Other findings suggest that depressed individuals exhibit less eye contact in more interactions that are unobtrusively observed than in laboratory paradigms (Segrin 1992). In a review of social functioning and depression, Feldman and Gotlib (1993) noted a number of studies that found depressed individuals to exhibit little eye contact, few smiles, and monotonous speech in interactions with unfamiliar others, yet exhibited more negative emotions and disruptions with spouses.

Expressive vocal deficits have also been studied in depression. Broadly, the speech of depressed individuals has been qualitatively described as flat, dull, and slow in tempo (Buck 1984; Hargreaves *et al.* 1965; Levin *et al.* 1985; Murray & Arnott 1993; Scherer 1986). Acoustic analyses, such as those derived through the analysis of digitized waveform representations of speech, have also proven useful in distinguishing between the speech of depressed and nondepressed individuals. For example, Bettes (1988) reported that mothers with self-reported symptoms of depression produced infant-directed speech with narrower pitch contours than were observed in the infant-directed speech of control mothers. Similarly, Kaplan *et al.* (1999) also noted different patterns of pitch modulation and variability in the infant-directed speech of mothers with symptoms of depression. Other researchers have shown that depressed individuals exhibit less affection, fewer gazes, flat affect, and less playing with their infants (reviewed in Feldman & Gotlib 1993).

Even fewer researchers have examined emotional behavior in bipolar disorder. Simoneau and Miklowitz (1991) developed a coding system for nonverbal behaviors exhibited during family interactions called the Nonverbal Interactional Coding System (NICS). Using this system, bipolar patients have been found to exhibit greater affiliative behaviors (e.g. gestures, leaning) yet similar amounts of distancing behaviors (e.g. looking away, leaning away) in interactions with parents than schizophrenia patients (Simoneau *et al.* 1996). Bipolar patients from families rated low in expressed emotion (EE) displayed more positive nonverbal behaviors in a family interaction than bipolar patients from families rated high in EE (Simoneau *et al.* 1998). There is also some evidence to suggest that an empirically supported psychosocial intervention for bipolar disorder, family focused treatment (FFT: Miklowitz & Goldstein 1990; Miklowitz *et al.* 2003), has an effect on emotional behavior in bipolar patients. Compared to pre-treatment, patients exhibited more positive nonverbal behavior after receiving FFT (Simoneau *et al.* 1999).

Anxiety disorders

Surprisingly, little is known about emotional behavior among patients with anxiety disorders, with the most research on nonverbal behavior and anxiety being conducted with social phobia. Social phobia is characterized by anxiety, fear, and avoidance of social situations, performance, and evaluations. Indeed, individuals with social phobia do not experience such anxiety when alone, but rather experience extreme anxiety when confronted with a social situation that involves interaction or presumed evaluation (Barlow 2002).

Findings from one study suggest that individuals with social phobia display non-verbal behaviors characteristic of anxiety. Marcus and Wilson (1996) studied social anxiety among college women during an observed speaking task. Observers' ratings of anxiety were significantly related to speakers' reports of anxiety, even though speakers rated themselves as more anxious than they were rated by observers. These findings indirectly suggest that social anxiety is comprised of relatively easily recognizable nonverbal behaviors and cues. Fydrich *et al.* (1998) developed the Social Performance Rating Scale (SPRS) to assess verbal and nonverbal behaviors exhibited by social phobia patients during a role play test. Items rated include voice quality, gaze, discomfort, and talk time, and these items distinguished socially phobic adults from a non-patient control group. Wallace and Alden (1997) found that individuals with social phobia exhibited fewer positive nonverbal behaviors and less warmth and interest during a dyadic social interaction. Socially phobic individuals also were rated as more visibly anxious than their non-anxious counterparts.

Conclusions

Given the central role emotion plays in several psychological disorders, the assessment of nonverbal and emotion behaviors can be of tremendous benefit to furthering our understanding of the symptoms, course, and treatment of psychopathology. We have suggested that the methods developed to study emotion in nonpatient populations are extremely useful for psychopathology research. Indeed, as briefly reviewed here, adopting methods from basic emotion research has allowed investigators to study multiple components of emotional response in emotionally evocative situations and has revealed a number of important findings about emotional behavior in psychopathology.

Laboratory-based measures of emotional responding can provide important information that is not easily accessed with clinical rating scales. For example, ratings of flat affect might be misinterpreted to mean that a schizophrenia patient is without feeling. Indeed, studies that rely solely on clinical rating scales that typically assess only one component of emotion may fail to adequately capture the essence of the emotional disturbance in schizophrenia, which appears to be the lack of coordinated engagement of emotion response components. Although the experimental control offered by a laboratory manipulation of emotion answers important questions, its generalizability is limited. Results from these laboratory studies can suggest a number of hypotheses that can then be tested in a more ecologically valid (but less well-controlled) setting. For example, examining emotional response tendencies in contexts such as social interaction with family members is a direction that deserves further empirical attention. Thus, a combination of both laboratory and naturalistic research, augmented with information from self-report and clinical rating scales, will likely yield the most complete picture of emotion disturbances in psychopathology.

There is no question that emotional disturbances figure prominently in psychopathology. Additional research is needed, however, to more fully illuminate the manner in which emotional behaviors may contribute to the onset, maintenance, and long-term consequences of the disorders. Research that encompasses a wide variety of methods and multiple levels of analysis is the most promising approach not only to understanding emotion dysfunction, but also to developing effective interventions.

References

Aghevli, M.A., Blanchard, J.J., & Horan, W.P. (2003). The expression and experience of emotion in schizophrenia: a study of social interactions. *Psychiatry Research, 119*, 261–70.

Allen, N.B., Trinder, J., & Brennen, C. (1999). Affective startle modulation in clinical depression: preliminary findings. *Biological Psychiatry, 46*, 542–50.

American Psychiatric Association (2000). *Diagnostic and statistical manual of mental disorders* (4th edn, text revision). Washington, DC: APA.

Andreasen, N.C. (1984). *The Scale for the Assessment of Negative Symptoms (SANS)*. The University of Iowa, Iowa City, Iowa.

Andreasen, N.C. (1984). *The Scale for the Assessment of Positive Symptoms (SAPS)*. The University of Iowa, Iowa City, Iowa.

Barlow, D.H. (2002). *Anxiety and its disorders* (2nd edn). New York: Guilford.

Barnett, P.A. & Gotlib, I.H. (1988). Psychosocial functioning and depression: distinguishing among antecedents, concomitants, and consequences. *Psychological Bulletin, 104*, 97–126.

Beck, A.T., Ward, C.H., Mendelson, M., Mock, J., & Erbaugh, J. (1961). An inventory for measuring depression. *Archives of General Psychiatry, 4*, 651–71.

Bellack, A.S., Morrison, R.L., Wixtead, J.T., & Mueser, K.T. (1990*a*). An analysis of social competence in schizophrenia. *British Journal of Psychiatry, 156*, 809–18.

Bellack, A.S., Morrison, R.L., Mueser, K.T., Wade, J.H., & Sayers, S.L. (1990*b*). Role play for assessing the social competence of psychiatric patients. *Psychological Assessment, 2*, 248–55.

Berenbaum, H. & Fujita, F. (1994). Schizophrenia and personality: exploring the boundaries and connections between vulnerability and outcome. *Journal of Abnormal Psychology, 193*, 148–58.

Berenbaum, H. & Oltmanns, T.F. (1992). Emotional experience and expression in schizophrenia and depression. *Journal of Abnormal Psychology, 101*, 37–44.

Berenbaum, H., Raghavan, G., Le, H.–N., Vernon, L.L., & Gomez, J.J. (2003). A taxonomy of emotional disturbances. *Clinical Psychology: Science and Practice, 10*, 206–26.

Bettes, B. (1988). Maternal depression and mothers: temporal and intonational features. *Child Development, 59*, 1089–96.

Birdwhistell, R.L. (1970). *Kinesics and context*. Philadelphia, PA: University of Pennsylvania Press.

Blanchard, J.J. & Neale, J.M. (1992). Medication effects: conceptual and methodological issues in schizophrenia research. *Clinical Psychology Review, 12*, 345–61.

Blanchard, J.J., Brown, S.A., Horan, W.P., & Sherwood, A.R. (2000). Substance use disorders in schizophrenia: review, integration, and a proposed model. *Clinical Psychology Review, 20*, 207–34.

Blanchard, J.J., Mueser, K.T., & Bellack, A.S. (1998). Anhedonia, positive and negative affect, and social functioning in schizophrenia. *Schizophrenia Bulletin, 24*, 413–24.

Borod, J.C., Alpert, M., Brozgold, A., Martin, C., Welkowitz, J., Diller, L., et al. (1989). A preliminary comparison of flat affect schizophrenics and brain-damaged patients on measures of affective processing. *Journal of Communication Disorders*, 22, 93–104.

Bos, E.H., Geerts, E., & Bouhys, A.L. (2002). Non-verbal interaction involvement as an indicator of prognosis in remitted depressed subjects. *Psychiatry Research*, 113, 269–77.

Brown, S., Sweeney, D.R., & Schwartz, G.E. (1979). Differences between self-reported and observed pleasure in depression and schizophrenia. *The Journal of Nervous and Mental Disease*, 167, 410–15.

Buck, R. (1984). *The communication of emotion*. New York: Guilford Press.

Carpenter, W.T. Jr., Heinrichs, D.W., & Alphs, L.D. (1985). Treatment of negative symptoms. *Schizophrenia Bulletin*, 11, 440–52.

Chapman, L.J., Chapman, J.P., Kwapil, T.R., Eckblad, M. & Zinser, M.C. (1994). Putatively psychosis-prone subjects 10 years later. *Journal of Abnormal Psychology*, 103, 171–83.

Chapman, L.J., Chapman, J.P., & Raulin, M. (1976). Scales for physical and social anhedonia. *Journal of Abnormal Psychology*, 85, 374–82.

Coid, J.W. (1993). An affective syndrome in psychopaths with borderline personality disorder. *British Journal of Psychiatry*, 162, 641–50.

Coyne, J.C. (1994). Self-reported distress: analog or ersatz depression? *Psychological Bulletin*, 116, 29–45.

Darwin, C. (1872). *The expression of the emotions in man and animals*. Oxford, England: Murray Press.

Donahoe, C.P., Carter, M.J., Bloem, W.D., Hirsch, G.L., Laasi, N., & Wallace, C.J., (1990). Assessment of interpersonal problem-solving skills. *Psychiatry*, 53, 329–39.

Dworkin, R.H., Bernstein, G., Kaplansky, L.M., Lipsitz, J.D., Rinaldi, A., Slater, S.L., et al. (1991). Social competence and positive and negative symptoms: a longitudinal study of children and adolescents at risk for schizophrenia and affective disorder. *American Journal of Psychiatry*, 148, 1182–8.

Dworkin, R., Clark, S.C., Amador, X.F., & Gorman, J.M. (1996). Does affective blunting in schizophrenia reflect affective deficit or neuromotor dysfunction? *Schizophrenia Research*, 20, 301–6.

Earnst, K.S. & Kring, A.M. (1999). Emotional responding in deficit and nondeficit schizophrenia. *Psychiatry Research*, 88, 191–207.

Earnst, K.S., Kring, A.M., Kadar, M.A., Salem, J.E., Shepard, D., & Loosen, P.T. (1996). Facial expression in schizophrenia. *Biological Psychiatry*, 40, 556–8.

Eckblad, M. & Chapman, L.J. (1983). Magical ideation as an indicator of schizotypy. *Journal of Consulting & Clinical Psychology*, 51, 215–25.

Ekman, P. (1992). Facial expression and emotion. *American Psychologist*, 48, 384–92.

Ekman, P. (1994). Strong evidence for universals in facial expression: a reply to Russell's mistaken critique. *Psychological Bulletin*, 115, 268–87.

Ekman, P. (1998). *Charles Darwin's 'The expression of the emotions in man and animals'.* London, England: Harper Collins/New York, NY: Oxford University Press.

Ekman, P. & Friesen, W.V. (1974). Nonverbal behavior and psychopathology. In *The psychology of depression: contemporary theory and research* (ed. R.J. Friedman & M.M. Katz), pp. 203–32. Washington, DC: John Wiley.

Ekman, P. & Friesen, W.V. (1978). *The Facial Action Coding System*. Palo Alto, CA: Consulting Psychological Press.

Ekman, P., Friesen, W.V., & Hager, J.C. (2002). *The Facial Action Coding System*. Salt Lake City, UT: A Human Face.

Ellgring, H. (1986). Nonverbal expression of psychological states in psychiatric patients. *Acta Psychiatrica Scandinavia*, **236**, 31–4.

Farchaus–Stein, K. (1996). Affect instability in adults with a borderline personality disorder. *Archives of Psychiatric Nursing*, **10**, 32–40.

Feldman, L.A. & Gotlib, I.H. (1993). Social dysfunction. In *Symptoms of depression* (ed. C.G. Costello), pp. 85–111. New York: John Wiley.

First, M.B., Spitzer, R.L., Gibbon, M., & Williams, J.B.W. (1994). *Structured Clinical Interview for Axis I DSM–IV disorders – Patient Edition (SCID-I/P, version 2.0)*. New York: Biometrics Research Department.

Fossi, L., Faravelli, C., & Paoli, M. (1984). The ethological approach to the assessment of depressive disorders. *Journal of Nervous and Mental Disease*, **172**, 332–41.

Frijda, N. (1986). *The emotions*. Cambridge, England: Cambridge University Press.

Fydrich, T., Chambliss, D.L., Perry, K.J., Buergener, F., & Beazley, M.B. (1998). Behavioral assessment of social performance: a rating system for social phobia. *Behaviour Research and Therapy*, **36**, 995–1010.

Geerts, E. & Bouhuys, N. (1998). Multi-level prediction of short-term outcome of depression: non-verbal interpersonal processes, cognitions, and personality traits. *Psychiatry Research*, **79**, 59–72.

Geerts, E., Bouhuys, N., & Van den Hoofbakker, R.H. (1996). Nonverbal attunement between depressed patients and an interviewer predicts subsequent improvement. *Journal of Affective Disorders*, **40**, 15–21.

Gotlib, I.H. & Robinson, L.A. (1982). Responses to depressed individuals: discrepancies between self-report and observer-rated behavior. *Journal of Abnormal Psychology*, **91**, 231–40.

Gotlib, I.H., Lewinsohn, P.M. , & Seeley, J.R. (1995). Symptoms versus a diagnosis of depression: differences in psychosocial functioning. *Journal of Consulting and Clinical Psychology*, **63**, 90–100.

Gunderson, J.G. & Phillips, K.A. (1991). A current view of the interface between borderline personality disorder and depression. *American Journal of Psychiatry*, **148**, 967–75.

Gunderson, J.G., Carpenter, W.T., & Strauss, J.S. (1975). Borderline and schizophrenic patients: a comparative study. *American Journal of Psychiatry*, **132**, 1259–64.

Hamilton, M. (1959). The assessment of anxiety states by rating. *British Journal of Medical Psychology*, **32**, 50–5.

Hamilton, M. (1960). A rating scale for depression. *Journal of Neurology, Neurosurgery and Psychiatry*, **12**, 56–62.

Hammen, C.L. (1980). Depression in college students: beyond the Beck Depression Inventory. *Journal of Consulting and Clinical Psychology*, **48**, 126–8.

Hargreaves, W., Starkweather, J., & Blacker, K. (1965). Voice quality in depression. *Journal of Abnormal Psychology*, **70**, 218–29.

Hinchliffe, M.K., Lancashire, M., & Roberts, F.J. (1971). A study of eye contact changes in depressed and recovered psychiatric patients. *British Journal of Psychiatry*, **119**, 213–15.

Hooley, J.M., Richters,J.E., Weintraub, S., & Neale, J.M. (1987). Psychopathology and marital distress: the positive side of positive symptoms. *Journal of Abnormal Psychology*, **96**, 27–33.

Jones, I.H. & Pansa, M. (1979). Some nonverbal aspects of depression and schizophrenia occurring during the interview. *Journal of Nervous and Mental Disease*, **167**, 402–9.

Kaplan, P.J., Bachorowski, J.–A., & Zarlengo–Strouse, P. (1999). Infant-directed speech produced by mothers with symptoms of depression fails to promote learning in four-month-old infants. *Child Development*, **70**, 560–70.

Katz, M.M., Wetzler, S., Cloitre, M., Swann, A., Secunda, S., Mendels, J., et al. (1993). Expressive characteristics of anxiety in depressed men and women. *Journal of Affective Disorders*, **28**, 267–77.

Kay, S.R., Opler, L.A., & Fiszbein, A. (1986). *Positive and negative syndrome scale (PANSS) rating manual*. Albert Einstein College of Medicine/Montefiore Medical Center and Schizophrenia Research Unit, Bronx Psychiatric Center, Bronx, NY.

Keltner, D. & Kring, A.M. (1998). Emotion, social function, and psychopathology. *Review of General Psychology*, **2**, 320–42.

Kendall, P.C., Hollon, S.D., Beck, A.T., Hammen, C.L., & Ingram, R.E. (1987). Issues and recommendations regarding use of the Beck Depression Inventory. *Cognitive Therapy & Research*, **11**, 289–99

Krause, R., Steimer, E., Sanger–Alt, C., & Wagner, G. (1989). Facial expressions of schizophrenic patients and their interaction partners. *Psychiatry*, **52**, 1–12.

Krause, R., Steimer–Krause, E., & Hufnagel, H. (1992). Expression and experience of affects in paranoid schizophrenia. *Revue européenne de Psychologie Appliquée*, **42**, 131–8.

Kring, A.M. (1991). *The relationship between emotional expression, subjective experience, and autonomic arousal in schizophrenia*. Unpublished doctoral dissertation.

Kring, A.M. (1999). Emotion in schizophrenia: old mystery, new understanding. *Current Directions in Psychological Science*, **8**, 160–3.

Kring, A.M. (2001). Emotion and psychopathology. In *Emotions: current issues and future directions* (ed. T.J. Mayne & G.A. Bonanno), pp. 337–60. New York: Guilford Press.

Kring, A.M. & Bachorowski, J.–A. (1999). Emotion and psychopathology. *Cognition and Emotion*, **13**, 575–99.

Kring, A.M. & Earnst, K.S. (1999). Stability of emotional responding in schizophrenia. *Behavior Therapy*, **30**, 373–88.

Kring, A.M. & Earnst, K.S. (2003). Nonverbal behavior in schizophrenia. In *Nonverbal behavior in clinical settings* (ed. P. Philippot, E. Coats, & R.S. Feldman), pp. 263–86. New York: Oxford University Press.

Kring, A.M. & Gordon, A.H. (1998). Sex differences in emotion: expression, experience, and physiology. *Journal of Personality and Social Psychology*, **74**, 686–703.

Kring, A.M. & Neale, J.M. (1996). Do schizophrenic patients show a disjunctive relationship among expressive, experiential, and psychophysiological components of emotion? *Journal of Abnormal Psychology*, **105**, 249–57.

Kring, A.M. & Sloan, D. (1992). *The facial expression coding system (FACES): a users guide.* Unpublished manuscript.

Kring, A.M., Alpert, M., Neale, J.M., & Harvey, P.D. (1994*a*). A multichannel, multimethod assessment of affective flattening in schizophrenia. *Psychiatry Research,* 54, 211–22.

Kring, A.M., Kerr, S.L., & Earnst, K.S. (1999). Schizophrenic patients show facial reactions to emotional facial expressions. *Psychophysiology,* 36, 1–7.

Kring, A.M., Kerr, S.L, Smith, D.A., & Neale, J.M. (1993). Flat affect in schizophrenia does not reflect diminished subjective experience of emotion. *Journal of Abnormal Psychology,* 102, 507–17.

Kring, A.M., Smith, D.A., & Neale, J.M. (1994*b*). Individual differences in dispositional expressiveness: development and validation of the Emotional Expressivity Scale. *Journal of Personality and Social Psychology,* 66, 934–49.

Kruedelbach, N., McCormick, R.A., Schultz, S.C., & Grueneich, R. (1993). Impulsivity, coping styles, and triggers for craving in substance abusers with borderline personality disorder. *Journal of Personality Disorders,* 7, 214–22.

Kwapil, T. (1998). Social anhedonia as a predictor of the development of schizophrenia-spectrum disorders. *Journal of Abnormal Psychology,* 107, 558–65.

Lang, P.J., Bradley, M.M., & Cuthbert, B.N. (1990). Emotion, attention, and the startle reflex. *Psychological Review,* 97, 377–95.

Le Couteur, A., Rutter, M., Lord, C., Rios, P., Roberston, S., Holdgrafer, M., *et al.* (1989). Autism diagnostic interview: a standardized investigator-based instrument. *Journal of Autism and Developmental Disorders,* 19, 363–88.

Levenson, R.W. (1992). Autonomic nervous system differences among emotions. *Psychological Science,* 3, 23–7.

Levin, S., Hall, J.A., Knight, R.A. & Alpert, M. (1985). Verbal and nonverbal expression of affect in speech of schizophrenic and depressed patients. *Journal of Abnormal Psychology,* 94, 487–97.

Linehan, M.M. (1987). Dialectical behavior therapy for borderline personality disorder. *Bulletin of the Menninger Clinic,* 51, 261–76.

Linehan, M.M. (1993). *Cognitive behavioral treatment of borderline personality disorder.* New York: Guilford Press.

Linehan, M.M. & Schmidt, H. (1995). The dialectics of effective treatment of borderline personality disorder. In *Theories of behavior therapy: exploring behavior change* (ed. W.T. O'Donohue & L. Krasner), pp. 553–84. Washington, DC: American Psychological Association.

Litz, B.T., Orsillo, S.M., Kaloupek, D., & Weathers, F. (2000). Emotional processing in posttraumatic stress disorder. *Journal of Abnormal Psychology,* 109, 26–39.

Lord, C., Risi, S., Lambrecht, L., Cook, E.H., Leventhal, B.L., DiLavore, P.C., *et al.* (2000). The Autism Diagnostic Observation Schedule – Generic: a standard measure of social and communication deficits associated with the spectrum of autism. *Journal of Autism and Developmental Disorders,* 30, 205–23.

Lord, C., Rutter, M., DiLavore, P.C., & Risi, S. (1999). *Autism Diagnostic Observation Schedule– WPS (ADOS–WPS).* Los Angeles, CA: Western Psychological Services.

Lord, C., Rutter, M., Goode, S., Heemsbergen, J., Jordan, H., Mawhood, L., *et al.* (1989). Autism Diagnostic Observation Schedule: a standardized observation of communicative and social behavior. *Journal of Autism and Developmental Disorders,* 19, 185–212.

Lynch, T.R., Robins, C.J., Morse, J.O., & MorKrause, E.D. (2001). A mediational model relating affect intensity, emotion inhibition, and psychological distress. *Behavior Therapy*, 32, 519–36.

Marcus, D.K. & Wilson, J.R. (1996). Interpersonal perception of social anxiety: a social relations analysis. *Journal of Social and Clinical Psychology*, 15, 471–87.

Marder, S.R., Wirshing, W.C., & Van Putten, T. (1991). Drug treatment of schizophrenia: overview of recent research. *Schizophrenia Research*, 4, 81–90.

Martin, C.C., Borod, J.C., Alpert, M., Brozgold, A., & Welkowitz, J. (1990). Spontaneous expression of facial emotion in schizophrenic and right brain-damaged patients. *Journal of Communication Disorders*, 23, 287–301.

Mattes, R.M., Schneider, F., Heimann, H., & Birbaumer, N. (1995). Reduced emotional response of schizophrenic patients in remission during social interaction. *Schizophrenia Research*, 17, 249–55.

Mineka, S., Watson, D., & Clark, L.A. (1998). Comorbidity of anxiety and unipolar mood disorders. *Annual Review of Psychology*, 49, 377–412.

Miklowitz, D.J. & Goldstein, M.J. (1990). Behavioral family treatment for patients with bipolar affective disorder. *Behavior Modification*, 14, 457–89.

Miklowitz, D.J, George, E.L., Richards, J.A., Simoneau, T.L., & Suddath, R.L. (2003). A randomized study of family-focused psychoeducation and pharmacotherapy in theoutpatient management of bipolar disorder. *Archives of General Psychiatry*, 60, 904–12.

Mishlove, M. & Chapman, L.J. (1985). Social anhedonia in the prediction of psychosis proneness. *Journal of Abnormal Psychology*, 94, 384–96.

Mitchell, R.W. & Thompson, N.S. (1986). Deception: perspectives on human and nonhuman *deceit*. Albany, NY: State University of New York Press.

Murray, I.R. & Arnott, J.L. (1993). Toward the simulation of emotion in synthetic speech: a review of the literature on human vocal emotion. *Journal of the Acoustical Society of America*, 93, 1097–108.

Neale, J.M. & Oltmanns, T.F. (1980). *Schizophrenia*. New York, NY: John Wiley.

Nuechterlein, K.H. & Dawson, M.E. (1984). A heuristic vulnerability/stress model of schizophrenic episodes. *Schizophrenia Bulletin*, 10, 300–12.

Olin, S.S. & Mednick, S.A. (1996). Risk factors of psychosis: identifying vulnerable populations premorbidly. *Schizophrenia Bulletin*, 22, 223–40.

Olin, S.S., John, R.S., & Mednick, S.A. (1995). Assessing the predictive value of teacher reports in a high risk sample for schizophrenia: an ROC analysis. *Schizophrenia Research*, 16, 53–66.

Pansa–Henderson, M., De L'Horne, D.J., & Jones, I.H. (1982). Nonverbal behaviour as a supplement to psychiatric diagnosis in schizophrenia, depression, and anxiety disorders. *Journal of Psychiatric Treatment and Evaluation*, 4, 489–96.

Pederson, J., Schelde, J.T.M., Hannibal, E., Behnke, K., Nielsen, B.M., & Hertz, M. (1988). An ethological description of depression. *Acta Psychiatrica Scandinavia*, 78, 320–30.

Rifkin, A., Quitkin, F., & Klein, D.F. (1975). Akinesia: a poorly recognized drug-induced extrapyramidal behavioral disorder. *Archives of General Psychiatry*, 32, 672–4.

Robins, C.J., Ivanhoff, A.M., & Linehan, M.M. (2001). Dialectical behavior therapy. In *Handbook of personality disorders: theory, research, and treatment* (ed. J.W. Lively) pp. 437–59. New York, NY: Guilford Press.

Rottenberg, J., Kasch, K.L., Gross, J.J., & Gotlib, I.H. (2002). Sadness and amusement reactivity predict concurrent and prospective functioning in major depressive disorder. *Emotion*, 2, 135–46.

Russell, J.A., Bachorowski, J.–A., & Fernández–Dols, J.–M. (2003). Facial and vocal expressions of emotion. *Annual Review of Psychology*, 54, 329–49.

Salem, J.E. & Kring, A.M. (1999). Flat affect and social skills in schizophrenia: evidence for their independence. *Psychiatry Research*, 87, 159–67.

Santor, D.A. & Coyne, J.C. (2001). Evaluating the continuity of symptomatology between depressed and nondepressed individuals. *Journal of Abnormal Psychology*, 110, 216–25.

Schelde, J.T.M. (1998). Major depression: behavioral markers of depression and recovery. *Journal of Nervous and Mental Disease*, 186, 133–40.

Scherer, K.R. (1986). Vocal affect expression: a review and model for future research. *Psychological Bulletin*, 99, 143–65.

Schwartz, G.E., Fair, P.L., Salt, P., Mandel, M.R., & Klerman, G.L. (1976). Facial muscle patterning to affective imagery in depressed and nondepressed subjects. *Science*, 192, 489–91.

Segrin, C. (1992). Specifying the nature of social skill deficits associated with depression. *Human Communication Research*, 19, 89–123.

Sher, K.J. & Trull, T.J. (1996). Methodological issues in psychopathology research. *Annual Review of Psychology*, 47, 371–400.

Simoneau, T.L. & Miklowitz, D.J. (1991). *Nonverbal behavior in high and low expressed emotion families of schizophrenic and bipolar patients.* Paper presented at the 6th annual meeting of the Society for Research in Psychopathology, Cambridge, MA.

Simoneau, T.L., Miklowitz, D.J., Goldstein, M.J., Nuechterlein, K.H., & Richards, J.A. (1996). Nonverbal interactional behavior in the families of persons with schizophrenic and bipolar disorders. *Family Process*, 35, 83–102.

Simoneau, T.L., Miklowitz, D.J., Richards, J.A., Saleem, R., & George, E.L. (1999). Bipolar disorder and family communication: effects of a psychoeducational treatment program. *Journal of Abnormal Psychology*, 108, 588–97.

Simoneau, T.L., Miklowitz, D.J., & Saleem, R. (1998). Expressed emotion and interactional patterns in the families of bipolar patients. *Journal of Abnormal Psychology*, 107, 497–597.

Sloan, D.M., Bradley, M.M., Dimoulas, E., & Lang, P.J. (2002). Looking at facial expressions: dysphoria and facial EMG. *Biological Psychology*, 60, 79–90.

Sloan, D.M., Strauss, M.E., Quirk, S.W., & Sajatovic, M. (1997). Subjective and expressive emotional responses in depression. *Journal of Affective Disorders*, 46, 135–41.

Sloan, D.M., Strauss, M.E., & Wisner, K. (2001). Diminished response to pleasant stimuli by depressed women. *Journal of Abnormal Psychology*, 110, 488–93.

Smith, W.J. (1985). Consistency and change in communication. In *The development of expressive behavior* (ed. G. Zivin), pp. 51–76. San Diego, CA: Academic Press.

Snyder, S. & Pitt, W.M. (1985). Characterizing anger in the DSM–III borderline personality disorder. *Acta Psychiatrica Scandinavica*, 72, 464–9.

Soloff, P.H. (1981). A comparison of borderline with depressed and schizophrenic patients on a new diagnostic interview. *Comprehensive Psychiatry*, 22, 291–300.

Soloff, P.H. & Ulrich, R.F. (1981). Diagnostic interview for borderline patients: a replication study. *Archives of General Psychiatry*, 38, 686–92.

Sommers, A.A. (1985). Negative symptoms: conceptual and methodological problems. *Schizophrenia Bulletin*, 11, 364–79.

Spohn, H.E. & Strauss, M.E. (1989). Relation of neuroleptic and anticholinergic medication to cognitive functions in schizophrenia. *Journal of Abnormal Psychology*, 98, 367–80.

Troisi, A. (1999). Ethological research in clinical psychiatry: the study of nonverbal behavior during interviews. *Neuroscience and Biobehavioral Reviews*, 23, 905–13.

Troisi, A. & Moles, A. (1999). Gender differences in depression: an ethological study of nonverbal behavior during interviews. *Journal of Psychiatric Research*, 33, 243–50.

Troisi, A., Pasini, A., Bersani, G., Grispini, A., & Ciani, N. (1989). Ethological predictors of amitriptyline response in depressed outpatients. *Journal of Affective Disorders*, 17, 129–36.

Troisi, A., Pasini, A., Bersani, G., Di Mauro, M., & Ciani, N. (1991). Negative symptoms and visual behavior in DSM–III–R prognostic subtypes of schizophreniform disorder. *Acta Psychiatrica Scandinavia*, 83, 391–4.

Troisi, A., Spalleta, G., & Pasini, A., (1998). Non-verbal behavior deficits in schizophrenia: an ethological study of drug-free patients. *Acta Psychiatrica Scandinavia*, 97, 109–15.

Trull, T.J. (1995). Borderline personality disorder features in nonclinical young adults: 1. Identification and validation. *Psychological Assessment*, 7, 33–41.

Trull, T.J., Useda, J.D., Conforti, K., & Doan, B.T. (1997). Borderline personality disorder features in nonclinical young adults: 2. Two-year outcome. *Journal of Abnormal Psychology*, 106, 307–14.

Ulrich, G. & Harms, K. (1985). A video analysis of the nonverbal behavior of depressed patients and their relation to anxiety and depressive disorders. *Journal of Affective Disorders*, 9, 63–7.

Van Putten, T. & Marder, S.R. (1987). Behavioral toxicity of antipsychotic drugs. *Journal of Clinical Psychiatry*, 48 (9, Suppl.), 13–19.

Van Putten, T., May, P.R.A., & Wilkins, J.N. (1980). Importance of akinesia: plasma chlorpromazine and prolactin levels. *American Journal of Psychiatry*, 137, 1446–8.

Ventura, J., Lukoff, D., Nuechterlein, K.H., Liberman, R.P., Green, M.F., & Shaner, A. (1993). Manual for the Expanded Brief Psychiatric Rating Scale. *International Journal of Methods in Psychiatric Research*, 3, 227–43.

Wagner, A.W., Roemer, L., Orsillo, S.M., & Litz, B.T. (2003). Emotional experiencing in women with posttraumatic stress disorder: congruence between facial expressivity and self-report. *Journal of Traumatic Stress*, 16, 67–75.

Walker, E.F. , Grimes, K.E., Davis, D.M., & Smith, A.J. (1993). Childhood precursors of schizophrenia: facial expressions of emotion. *American Journal of Psychiatry*, 150, 1654–60.

Wallace, S.T. & Alden, L. (1997). Social phobia and positive social events. The price of success. *Journal of Abnormal Psychology*, 106, 416–24.

Watson, D., Clark, L.A., & Carey, G. (1988). Positive and negative affectivity and their relation to anxiety and depressive disorders. *Journal of Abnormal Psychology*, 97, 346–53.

Waxer, P.H. (1974). Nonverbal cues for depression. *Journal of Abnormal Psychology*, 83, 319–22.

Waxer, P.H. (1976). Nonverbal cues for depth of depression: set versus no set. *Journal of Consulting and Clinical Psychology*, 44, 493.

World Health Organization (1992). *International statistical classification of diseases and related health problems* (1989 revision) (10th edn). Geneva: WHO.

CHAPTER 9

RESEARCH METHODS IN DETECTING DECEPTION RESEARCH

MARK G. FRANK

The methodology involved in nonverbal deception research has recently come under scrutiny due to the importance of catching liars in real-world counter-terrorism efforts. This chapter will examine the pros and cons associated with the design of a deception scenario, particularly in terms of ecological validity, the execution of the scenario, as well as later judge and behavioral scoring studies. From here, the relative merits of various video, audio, and observational methods for capturing the data are discussed.

> Truth exists; only lies are invented.   Georges Braque

Nonverbal behavior in deception

One of the after-effects of the September 11 terrorist attacks was a renewed interest in human intelligence gathering. Counter-terrorism professionals escalated their efforts to obtain accurate threat information through face-to-face interviews with suspected terrorists, witnesses, and informants. This interpersonal form of information gathering is replete with obstacles that affect its accuracy, such as the well-documented short-comings of human memory, honest differences of opinion, and even outright deception (e.g. Hauggard & Repucci 1992). Although most of these factors are inadvertent, outright deception (i.e. telling a lie) involves an *intentional* effort to generate false information or to actively conceal the truth (Ekman 1985/2001). Because a lie involves a deliberate, conscious behavior, we can speculate that this effort may leave some trace, sign, or signal that may betray that lie. It is these signs or signals that, if and when they occur, counter-terrorism professionals hope to recognize so as to allow them to weigh accurately the information they gather to aide their future counter-terrorism efforts.

What interests the scientist, as well as society at large, is how well our counter-terrorism professionals can make these judgments accurately, as well as whether they can do this in real time, without technological assistance. Terrorism has thus renewed interest in the two most basic questions ever asked of human deception research. First, what clues betray deception, if any? Second, if these clues are present, can people detect them?

Deception research is certainly more than verbal and nonverbal clues to lying and our abilities to catch lies. Research programs have looked at deception as a means to understanding other topics such as interpersonal communication, through the strategic use of deception in interpersonal encounters (Feldman *et al.* 2002); cognitive development, through the study of children's abilities to develop a theory of mind (Hala *et al.* 1991); comparative cognition, through the observation of other animals' abilities to engage in behaviors that look remarkably similar to human deception (Suddendorf & Whiten 2001); and, more recently, the evolution of human signaling systems, through the co-evolution of signs of deception and 'cheater detectors' (Shackleford 1997).

Although deception is a large topic, for this chapter we will focus on the methodology employed in studying nonverbal aspects of a specific subset of deception research—humans telling lies. These nonverbal behaviors include facial expressions, eye movements, and other actions; head, hand, leg, and other body movements, gestures, or postures; and voice tones and other paralinguistic information. We will examine the choices an investigator can make in terms of defining what they mean by a lie, what sorts of lie situations they wish to study, how they mirror the structural features of those situations, the implications that has for the variables studied and the techniques used to analyze those variables, and the possible implications for judge studies of people's abilities to detect lies and truths. Although many of the factors that will be discussed apply to both liars and truthtellers, and thus should not make a difference in the search for behaviors that do distinguish liars and truthtellers, they can generate so much behavioral noise that they make it difficult for researchers to pull out any behavioral signal (type II errors). Other factors that will be discussed apply more strongly to a liar or truthteller and thus can generate type I errors.

Finally, nonverbal detection of deception research is simply a subset of nonverbal behavior research in general. It draws from other areas that seem to be studied more autonomously, as in research on the voice, the face, body movements, and judge studies. In fact, one might even consider it an applied aspect of nonverbal behavior research. Therefore, many of the methodological issues associated with studying the voice, face, or body are discussed in more detail elsewhere in the volume (e.g. see Chapters 2, 3, and 4). This chapter will be devoted to amplifying those aspects of nonverbal behavior research most strongly affected by conducting deception research that are not raised elsewhere in this book.

Theoretical background

Scientists studying deception over the past century have noted one thing—that, unlike the fictional Pinocchio, whose nose grew in response to telling a lie, there is no specific verbal or nonverbal deception clue that appears in people in all situations to indicate deception (see recent review by DePaulo *et al.* 2003). However, this same review concluded that there do seem to be some clues that, on the aggregate, predict deception, particularly when liars are motivated. So, for example, liars appear to be less forthcoming, their accounts are less compelling, they appear to be more tense, and their accounts are a bit too polished.

The variables that comprise 'less forthcoming' or compelling have been studied at a number of levels. Some studies involve investigating behavior at the most elemental *physical* units of measurement, such as logging the movements in the hands, feet, arms, legs, torso, head, eyebrows, lips, eyelids; or counting eyeblinks, measuring pupil dilation, fundamental frequency, amplitude, jitter in the voice; or counting words, number of pauses, response latency, or time spent talking in the speech.

Other studies investigate behavior at the most elemental *psychologic meaning* level which, although often comprised of composites of the physical units described above, has its own types and patterns of movement. Researchers have identified empirical or conceptual reasons for examining these as distinct units. Some of these variables include manipulators or adaptors (which involve touching, rubbing, etc., of various body parts), illustrators (which accompany speech to help keep the rhythm of the speech, emphasize a word, show direction of thought, etc.), emblems (gestures that have a speech equivalent, such as a head nod meaning 'yes'; see Ekman *et al.* 1976), particular emotions represented in facial expressions (e.g. Ekman *et al.*1988) or in the voice (Scherer 1984), or other composite speech measures such as speech rate and speech errors.

Other studies investigate behavior at the most *interpretative* level by measuring variables such as immediacy, cognitive complexity, or plausibility of an account (again, see review by DePaulo *et al.* 2003).

It seems that part of the reason so many different levels of variables have been studied in deception research is that most theorists have described clues to deception as falling into those that represent additional cognitive activity, or those that represent emotional activity, or those that represent efforts to conceal either or both cognitive and emotional activity (e.g. Ekman 1985/2001; Hocking & Leathers 1980; Zuckerman *et al.* 1981). Thus, a researcher who is trying to fully unpack the variety of clues that might demonstrate one is engaged in excess cognitive activity, or that one is having an emotion, will probably end up looking at all these levels of specificity described earlier.

The real problem with all these levels is that, at times, the variables may be perfectly understood, but at other times conceptually confused. For example, researchers studying deception and the smile have never defined in their reports what they meant by a smile, and yet coders have always showed extremely high inter-rater reliability (above 0.90) when scoring the number of smiles (see Frank 2003 for a review). In contrast, researchers have often proposed a role for 'arousal' in detecting deception, yet in different reports arousal has meant something as variable as an orienting response (e.g. deTurck & Miller 1985) to a full-blown emotional expression of fear (e.g. Frank 1989), along with certain (apparently to some) indeterminate points in between (e.g. Burgoon & Buller 1994; see also discussion by Waid & Orne 1982). Arousal in the physiological detection of deception literature has also been used to describe physiological states as different as stress, anxiety, embarrassment, and even anger (Steinbrook 1992). This definitional looseness may account for why only the least precisely measured variables found at the interpretive level seem to show any consistent relationship to deception.

Another reason why patterns in deception detection seem to occur only in the most interpretive level of variables may be due to the differences between the paradigms used to study deception, and their ability to generate cognitive and emotional clues or motivate subjects to conceal such clues. Although the first mission of a researcher who plans on studying deception is to clearly identify the components and assumptions behind any verbal or nonverbal variable used to investigate deception, the second and less obvious mission is to clearly outline the assumptions behind the paradigms used to study deception. Both are required to insure adequate comparability and identification of trends across studies, and yet only recently have systematic efforts been made to fulfill the first mission (DePaulo *et al.* 2003). So now we turn to the second mission.

Designing laboratory deception scenarios

The first thing to consider when designing a paradigm is that not all lies are the same. It is clear from observing the world that a lie about the attractiveness of someone's new tie is not of the same magnitude as a lie about whether someone has murdered their best friend. In a more controlled setting, it is an error to assume that a lie about which card one drew from a deck of 52 is the same as a lie involving terrorist activities. In one sense, the former is a game, whereas the latter is deadly serious; this, in all likelihood, will affect the nonverbal behaviors, strategies, and findings derived from each paradigm, with a resulting cap on the generalizability of the results to the real-world situations in which one is interested. We also note the ethics of experimentation are such that it may be impossible to create a perfect scenario capturing all the elements of a situation involving lying to a police officer about one's involvement in a homicide, or lies involved in terrorism activity. However, the steps described below may at least allow the researcher to get closer to his or her target of creating a paradigm to adequately assess the type of lies one is interested in studying.

Step 1: Defining deception and lying

The first critical step is to be clear about what sort of deception one is exploring. According to Ekman (1985/2001), a lie is a deliberate attempt to mislead, without prior notification of the target. This means that a lie is a subcategory of deception, as some deception does not involve a deliberate activity on the part of the deceiver. For example, Ekman (1985/2001) discusses how a tiger does not deliberately choose its stripes, yet relies upon those stripes to conceal its location in high grass and thus deceive its prey.

Some other forms of deception are authorized and involve an explicit or implied prior notification of the target, so that what is seen or heard is not quite the reality. In some situations the deception is explicit, as when actors in a play or movie are giving explicit notification that they are pretending to be someone else, or when a poker player engages in bluffing. In other situations, the deception is more implicit, as when a polite dinner guest expresses enjoyment over a meal he or she may not have liked, or when a home seller lists the price of the home that is not the only price they will accept. What is important here is that the decision a researcher makes about what sort of deception they will study—whether passive deception (such as the tiger) or an active deception (such as in a situation which involves an active unauthorized misleading of another)—may have implications for the behaviors they might observe or the situations to which they may generalize their results (see Ekman 1985/2001 for a more thorough discussion of these and other examples).

It is not an error to study any of these situations, but the researcher must be cautious in what he or she can generalize based upon the type of lie used in the experiment.

Caution!

One could argue that most laboratory deception research features sanctioned behavior, thus prior notification is given. This means that one cannot study lies in the laboratory. In our own work, like all mock theft research, the theft is authorized as part of the procedure. Although the situation appears to be a crime, it is explained to subjects and is part of the procedure (e.g. Frank & Ekman 1997). Likewise, the paradigms that involve describing someone they like as if they dislike them (e.g. DePaulo & Rosenthal 1979), pretending to be the Soviet Ambassador misleading a TV interviewer(e.g. Druckman *et al.* 1982), falsely stating one's opinion (Mehrabian 1971; Frank & Ekman 1997), stabbing a mannequin (Pavlidis *et al.* 2002), and so forth, all involve explaining exactly how to carry out the lie.

However, there have been a few studies to examine unsanctioned lies. The best scenario for this is the stealing information paradigm, where a subject observes a teammate improperly obtaining a correct answer to a dot estimation task and then lying to the experimenter when asked to explain how they came up with their answer (e.g. Exline 1971; Feeley & deTurck 1998). Although one might argue that the lie may be sanctioned as part of an ethic of not being a tattle-tale, typically these lies are not part of the informed consent process. This makes it unclear to the subject as to whether lying to cover up for this teammate is authorized.

Another example of an unsanctioned lie is the capture of spontaneously uttered white lies. For example, Feldman *et al.* (2002) videotaped a situation in which male and female subjects were getting acquainted, and then asked the subjects to indicate which statements were truthful and which were lies. The subjects identified some lies they told to the other, ranging from a fabricated record deal for their band to feigning interest in a story told by the other. Although these are spontaneous lies (i.e. the subject is not instructed to lie), the researcher is still at the mercy of the subject to report honestly which statements were lies. In other words, the *ground truth* (i.e. what really happened, what someone really thinks or feels) is not perfectly confirmable. In contrast, one can observe the ground truth as to whether a subject took a ring or a check. This same principle of reliance upon the subject for ground truth applies to the diary studies of deception as well (e.g. DePaulo *et al.* 1996*b*; Kashy & DePaulo 1996). However, these studies typically did not examine the nonverbal behaviors that may accompany the spontaneous lies.

But this is about as close as we can come to real-life lies in the laboratory without violating ethical standards. It would be very interesting to drop a $20 dollar bill, surreptitiously observe a subject to see whether he or she took it, and then interview them about it whilst secretly videotaping the interrogation. But this would be unethical. Indeed, if this were done by a police officer, it would be illegal in many jurisdictions due to laws on police entrapment. An antidote to this involves observing some real-life lies captured on video, but that too has problems that we will discuss later. Regardless, research has not systematically manipulated all these variables save sanctioned/ unsanctioned—which does show some differences in behavior (Feeley & deTurck 1998)—so, to some extent, we cannot be confident as to how they might affect the behaviors displayed by the subjects. It is reasonable that researchers should consider this issue and spell it out in their methodology, so that future researchers can interpret any trends that emerge based upon these variables.

Step 2: Consider the subjects

Who will be the liars or lie catchers? Of course one must consider the usual information—age, sex, occupation, experience, education, language, and other life and personal characteristics. But one should consider these in the light of what implications they have for the sort of information one wishes to gather, for recording behavior, or for later judge studies when these videotapes are shown to observers. For example, if studying children, one should be cautious about the setting, as things like a lavaliere or other types of microphones, flashing red lights from video cameras, and so forth can distract children to a greater degree than adults. Moreover, given that most researchers posit a cognitive overload as one of the mechanisms behind behavioral clues (e.g. Ekman 1985/2001; Hocking & Leathers 1985; Zuckerman *et al.* 1981), these distractions may have a stronger effect on the liars than the truthtellers, if done in a between-subject design.

It is also true that the types of lies in which one's subjects engage will be more limited in children, as research shows a specific developmental progression of different lie motives (e.g. DePaulo 1982; Ekman 1989). Or, if one is examining subjects who have disabilities that render communication with the subjects difficult (e.g. left hemisphere brain damage; Etcoff *et al.* 2000), one must make sure to create tasks that enable effective communication without giving tip-offs to either the subjects, the coders who will score the behaviors, or judges who may later make ratings.

Caution!

For some cultures, it is reputed that lying to strangers is socially acceptable; although almost all cultures consider lies told within their extended family group unacceptable (Bond & Atoum 2000). This cultural approval of lying would suggest different findings when studying these cultures versus cultures that have norms prohibiting lying in almost all situations. Another possible confound involves examining subjects who are lying/telling the truth in their non-native language, as attempts to speak in another language should generate more clues purported to be related to lying (DePaulo *et al.* 2003 for a review) such as hesitations, latencies, speech errors—all independent of the actual lie or truth. Although these factors would apply equally to liars and truthtellers, they may cause so much additional noise so as to render any potential significant difference undetectable.

This also means one that must consider how the type of subject may limit the information gleaned from a judge study where these truthful/lying subjects are stimulus materials. We can try to create situations that are as realistic as possible using undergraduate subjects, but if we use them as stimulus material that test the skills of law enforcement professionals, we will always have to exercise some caution in our interpretation of the actual day-to-day skills of law enforcement, which may involve dealings with murderers and rapists; activities that, thankfully, most undergraduates do not carry out. Research does suggest that criminal inmates are more informed about how to execute deception than non-inmates (Vrij & Semin 1996). So this must be factored into any design planning.

Step 3: Consider the relationship between the subject–liar/truthteller and experimenter–interviewer–lie catcher, including physical presence and the presence of a script

The type of lie one is studying should dictate whether the interviewer is in an oppositional, confrontational, or informational relationship with the subject, or even whether there is an interviewer physically present at all. For example, mock theft scenarios usually attempt to extrapolate to law enforcement situations, and thus the interviewer is often more of an interrogator who is oppositional and confrontational to subjects by trying to catch their lies (e.g. Frank & Ekman 1997). Other scenarios involve an informational interviewer who asks the subject how they came up with a particular answer (e.g. Feeley & deTurck 1998; even though these studies can manipulate suspicion as well), or to describe people they know and like (where the subject may lie about this) (e.g. DePaulo & Rosenthal 1979), or to describe how a certain scene makes them feel (e.g. Ekman & Friesen 1974).

The reason that this structural feature matters is that this relationship can affect the motivation of subjects, along with the type and intensity of emotions experienced by the subject. For example, results derived from a neutral interviewer may not be generalizable to actual law enforcement situations where the interviewers are seen as the opposition, as this opposition may arouse emotions not present in an informational type interview (for both the liar and the truthteller) (see Ekman 1985/2001 for a more detailed theoretical rationale). Likewise, an oppositional lie catcher/interviewer may limit what one might generalize about real-life, day-to-day type lies where people do not interrogate others on politeness-type statements.

Finally, the physical presence of an interrogator must be considered. First, work on human emotion suggests that stronger emotions will be more aroused by the physical presence of a person than by talking to a camera (e.g. Detenber & Reeves 1996). This may be due to human evolution, as our emotional system evolved to deal with three-dimensional animate situations including conspecifics, rather than two-dimensional video representations (Ekman 2003), or that the 'mere presence' of an individual has measurable affects on another's arousal (Zajonc et al. 1965; Schmitt et al. 1986). Second, if an interrogator is present, his or her appearance must be noted, as a particularly intimidating interrogator may cause emotions and behaviors that would not be elicited by a friendlier looking interrogator.

In other scenarios, the lie catchers may not be present—they are presented as an individual or a panel who will be viewing the interaction (either concurrently or later, via videotape) and making a judgment (e.g. DePaulo et al. 1983). More recent work is now looking at computer-mediated communication and how that may or may not affect deception as a strategy or the possible behavioral signs exhibited under these circumstances (e.g. Burgoon & Nunamaker 2004). As in all these designs, the experimenter should consider carefully the ecological validity of this interaction for generalizability, as the presence of an interrogating individual seems to create a very different psychological state, giving feedback to the subjects as they attempt to truthfully or deceptively offer their account. In contrast, if a researcher wanted to examine the effect of remote technologies on deception, as in a child victim's testimony over closed circuit TV, this would be the right paradigm (e.g. Davies 1999). However, most lies, according to diary studies (e.g. DePaulo *et al.* 1996b), are told to people, not to faceless others. Either way this must be carefully considered.

At this step, one needs also to consider whether the interaction between interviewer and subject is scripted or spontaneous. The advantage of the scripted interview is that one can eliminate, or at least reduce, a potentially huge source of variance in the behaviors one may see in the subjects. This will mean scripting not just the words but, at some level, the delivery of those words and the behaviors that correspond to them. One would not want one interrogator being a smiling, happy-go-lucky sort, whereas the second is a scowling, mad sort. The disadvantage of the script is that you may sacrifice some external validity—but again, it depends upon the situation you are hoping to mirror in the laboratory. If you are looking at a checkpoint situation (e.g. 'have you packed your own bags?'), then the script is most appropriate.

The advantage of the spontaneous interview is that it allows the interviewer to follow up questions, and permits the give and take that may be more typical of a law enforcement interview or any other in which lying is suspected (e.g. parent questioning a red-eyed child about the smell of marijuana smoke on their clothes). It also provides information on what a good versus a bad lie catcher might do. The disadvantage is the loss of experimental control; so much so that it may make it impossible to test falsifiable hypotheses about the subject's behaviors, thus rendering any conclusions about behavior when lying uninterpretable (DePaulo *et al.* 1996a). It also means that a researcher should probably record all the behaviors of that interrogator to allow more fine-tuned analyses later, including parsing out what subject behaviors are driven by the interrogator's behavior and which are due to the lie or truth of the subject. For example, if the interrogator leans into the subject whilst making a strong accusation, it could be that all subjects will show some withdrawal behavior or emotional reaction to the lean in, and not to the lie or truth they tell.

Moreover, if the interrogation is not tightly scripted, the words chosen by the interrogator may generate very divergent results. To use an absurd example, an interrogator who says to one subject 'are you lying about what you did?' may get a different response than if he/she were to ask 'are you a lying scumbag?'. We can presume that subtler differences would have a differential effect as well. For example, an interrogator who asks closed questions will generate much less verbal information than an interrogator who asks open-ended questions. Moreover, it would appear to be easier to lie with a one-word answer than to have to generate a narrative (Frank & Ekman 1997, in preparation). For example, 'did you take the money?' may be easier than 'tell me about what you did with the money?'. The first question will likely generate no word usage differences between liars and truthtellers (its either 'yes' or 'no', although our experience is that some will say a complete sentence such as 'no I did not'), whereas the second question is more likely to generate some usage differences. Differences in the interrogator's voice tone with identical word structure, and differences in facial expressions (e.g. an angry look vs. pleasant) and body postures (relaxed vs. with clenched fists) will have differential effects on the subject.

Because we don't know what sort of effects these differences will have, it seems reasonable for a researcher who intends to use an interrogator to try to minimize these problems by scripting the words and behaviors of the interrogator as tightly as possible. If not, it seems apparent that a researcher must videotape the behavior of the interrogator as well as the subject and have some system for synchronizing the behaviors of the interrogator and subject to identify any cause and effect.

Finally, the interrogators should be blind as to whether the subject is lying. Otherwise, their knowledge may subtly affect their body posture, facial expression, voice tone, etc., which may have a differential effect on the behavior of the subject—even if the interrogators are scripted. Moreover, if later, these videos are shown to other subjects to test how well they detect deception, these observer subjects may end up picking up some subtle disdain or other clue in the voice tone of the *interrogator* that causes the observer to judge the subject's deception, rather than judging it entirely on the behavior of the subject. One way to help insure this is to ask the interrogator to make a 'seat of the pants' judgment, on a form, as to whether they thought the subject was lying. This will give the researcher some basis for estimating the possible bias within the interrogator that may affect the behavior of the subject. But it comes at a cost, since if the interrogator becomes too concerned about making correct judgments, it may make it harder for them to follow their script or control their behavior, thus generating more behavioral information than the researcher had hoped for. One way to reduce this possibility is to spend some time assuring the interrogator that their judgment of truth or lie is no indication of their true levels of accuracy, but simply needed as a check, and that they are to remain as neutral as possible. Hopefully, this will reduce their motivation to catch the liars, which may spill into their behaviors in an unknown but subtle way.

Caution!

Although one can design paradigms where the interviewers are confrontational or oppositional, to actually conclude that they are *as* confrontational or *as* oppositional as the real world may be a mistake. First, our own observations of real police interviews suggest that some very good detectives are not all that confrontational or even oppositional. One must guard against basing one's procedures in the experiment upon a stereotype of how a professional may function. Second, although a researcher may have designed their interviewer to not be confrontational, in fact the subject may think this interviewer is confrontational. A quick assessment of the subject's perceptions at the end of the experiment—either in the form of a checklist or a debriefing question—will ascertain how confrontational, oppositional, or informational the interviewer was seen.

Conversely, the lack of a human interrogator has the advantage of offering much tighter experimental control. Questions can be printed and presented to subjects or shown on a television screen/computer monitor, or subjects may be instructed prior to entering the interview room to offer a free-flowing narrative. This may be ecologically valid as well, because there are occasions in life where one may tell a lie to a faceless other. One example might be a phone call; a second might be during remote testimony in child sex abuse cases using closed-circuit television (e.g. Davies 1999); and a third and increasingly common example are remote television interviews with celebrities or politicians, where the potential liar is listening to the interviewer in an earpiece, yet speaking only to a television camera with no access to the visual image of the inter-viewer. Either way involves the classic internal/external validity trade-offs that re-searchers wrestle with daily (see Carlsmith *et al.* 1976).

Step 4: Consider the type of lie

Ekman (2001) describes a number of ways to lie—to fabricate, distort, conceal (i.e. not saying anything), as well as a 'telling the truth falsely' lie (i.e. telling a factual truth in a sarcastic or other way so as to make a target disbelieve the fact). The vast majority of the lies studied in the nonverbal deception literature have been the fabrication lies (i.e. the subject says something that is contradicted by reality). Concealment-type lies have been more popular in some of the physiological measurement deception studies such as the P300 brain response work (e.g. Farwell & Donchin 1991), but these studies have not focused on the nonverbal correlates of deception.

Within the category of fabrication lies, one can lie about a committed or witnessed action, an opinion, a feeling, a viewed image, and so on. This means that researchers should carefully consider what it is they are asking subjects to lie about, as each situation described above may generate lies that differ in structure, verbiage, emotion generation, and so forth. For example, if the type of lie is such that the subject simply has to deny an action he or she committed, this may produce fewer words and may be less cognitively challenging than a lie about why the subject has a certain opinion (e.g. Frank & Ekman 2004b). We also don't know whether someone lying about how they feel (e.g. Ekman & Friesen 1974) will generate more or fewer words than the action or an opinion or information they know, and so forth. These choices may also affect the length of video and audio material that will be analyzed later.

If the type of lie affects the length of behaviors to be analyzed, that in turn will affect the relationship between a post-interview self-report emotion questionnaire and other emotional measures such as facial expressions. This we know because research shows that the longer the period covered by a self-report emotion checklist, the weaker the relationship between the nonverbal behavior and the emotion (e.g. Rosenberg & Ekman 1994). Moreover, if the reduction in the number of words available for later analysis is severe enough, then many of the techniques that examine paralinguistic information or even word choice will not be able to be used (e.g. Newman *et al.* 2003; Porter & Yuille 1995). Finally, one must be careful that the behaviors executed by the liar are not physically more demanding than those by the truthteller. If a liar stabs a mannequin repeatedly, whereas a truthteller does not, the extra physical effort may be artifactually raising the arousal levels of the deceptive subjects relative to the truthtellers (cf. Pavlidis *et al.* 2002).

Caution!

One should also consider the issue of the reliability of ground truth. If the subjects are to do the identical acts (e.g. enter a room, search for a ring or some money, and then come back to the lab), then the only practical issue a subject will lie about is whether they took the money or object; they will in all likelihood be truthful about all else. This limits the amount of their interrogation behavior that is an actual lie. Yet in real crimes, often there is information revealed by the guilty person that only the guilty person knows, or that places him or her at the crime scene and in possession of the murder weapon that the innocent person will not be able to generate. So the script that instructs the subject on how to conduct their mission may artificially constrain the number of word clues that a real law enforcement person might rely upon to judge whether the subject is lying.

Second, often in deception work the ground truth is not directly observable. In these instances, steps need to be taken to increase the researcher's confidence in the ground truth. For example, in the dot estimation paradigm (e.g. Exline 1971; Feeley & deTurck 1998), the liars often tell partial lies and/or partial truths. This makes it difficult to determine which segment should be analyzed in order to measure any clues to deceit, or even whether the statement uttered by the subject is actually a lie or not. In other lie scenarios, the ground truth is entirely in the head of the subject. In the false opinion (e.g. Frank & Ekman 1997; Mehrabian 1971), or the favorable description of someone you actually dislike (e.g. DePaulo & Rosenthal 1979), or the spontaneous lie study (Feldman et al. 2002), the researcher is dependent upon the subject honestly indicating their actual opinion, or the fact that they really like a certain person, or which of their just uttered statements were lies. This is in contrast to those other scenarios in which researchers can confidently measure ground truth such as the false description of a photo, concealing knowledge they provided, or mock crime scenarios—as the researcher knows what the picture looks like, or how the subject found out the number of dots, or whether the subject actually took the money or headphones.

The reasons we warn about this are twofold. First, a subject may be truly ambivalent about an opinion they hold about a topic or person. In this instance, one should allow subjects the ability to select an issue they—not the experimenter, nor a general survey of campus opinions—feel strongly about. One can give a number of issues for the subject to discuss, but later one must use some check to ascertain how strongly the subject believed a particular opinion. Second, in a (hopefully) rare turn of events, a particularly savvy (and deceptive) subject may decide to increase their odds of being seen truthful by falsifying their true opinion when asked by the researcher prior to the lie, so that when the time comes to 'lie', the subject will actually be telling the truth. To reduce the chances of this occurring, the researcher has to ascertain the subject's true opinion before the subject is fully cognizant of their need to deceive someone. In our own work using a false opinion scenario (Frank & Ekman 1997, 2004a), we dealt with this problem by advertising for a two-part 'communication skills experiment'. When the subject arrived, we had them fill out an initial consent form that described a questionnaire study in which we gathered information on a variety of personality indices and issues, including their true opinions. When this was finished, we then gave the second consent form that describes assessing the communication skill of deception, including falsifying opinions. We also double-checked this reality by asking the subject to reconfirm the ground truth when the debriefing is over and they have been paid. Of course, this means you should assure the subject that their credit and/or money and/or esteem from the experimenter are secure and will not withdrawn by any eleventh-hour confession on their part. Explain how important it is to the experiment that the real truth be known. None of these techniques guarantees a researcher will get the truth, but it increases the odds that the information provided by the subject to establish a ground truth is accurate.

Step 5: Decide whether to assign subjects to conditions or to allow them to choose whether to lie

On the surface, this seems to be a simple issue. Of course, in an empirical study one would randomly assign a subject to conditions. How else could one infer causality? However, the ecological validity question intervenes to make this question not as straightforward as it seems. One can argue that in day-to-day life, most people choose whether or not to lie. Some people who are poor liars, and know they are poor liars, may avoid deception as an interpersonal strategy (e.g. Zuckerman *et al.* 1981). Conversely, some who are 'natural performers' (Ekman 1985/2001) seem to know they are effective liars and may choose deception as an interpersonal strategy more often in their lives. Routine use of lying as an interpersonal strategy is one of the hallmarks of psychopathy (e.g. Hare 1999). Indirect data supporting this assertion comes from the dot estimation paradigm. In this paradigm, subjects observe another subject (actually a confederate) cheat on a task in order to obtain some reward. The subject is then questioned about how they did so well to obtain the reward. One of the things the researchers note in this paradigm is a significant attrition of subjects who will not engage in this deceptive task in the first place and withdraw their participation (Feeley & deTurck 1998). Thus, the results from this paradigm are based upon a selected sample, which of courses limits its generalizability.

However, if the researcher is interested in the characteristics of people who will lie, then this may not be such a problem. For example, in our mock crime paradigm, we were also interested in the people who might choose to take the money and then lie about it. So once again, having a clear sense of what issues you wish to address will dictate whether you randomly assign or not.

Caution!

The causality question does not go away because we recognize it. One will have to couch his or her results in terms of the people who choose to lie, rather than factors involved in lying itself. Also, it could be that the laboratory situation may be artificial enough that choosing whether to lie in a laboratory experiment may not have any bearing on whether one would lie in the real world. It may be the case that a person who is fearful of lying in the real world due to the consequences involved may suddenly feel disinhibited in the laboratory setting—similar to a person who feels it is OK to shoot characters in a video game, whereas they would not in real life. We do not know the answer to this. Regardless, careful wording is needed in any write up.

Step 6: Decide how long your subject has to concoct his or her lie, or how long they have to maintain the lie

The time allotted to craft a lie will affect how convincing a lie might be, as research has shown that planned lies (where the subject has plenty of time to work out their falsehood) are often harder to detect than spontaneous lies (where the subject has a very brief period of time in which to work out their falsehood) (Zuckerman *et al.* 1981). The choices one makes here will affect a number of variables—the amount of verbiage, the accompanying paralinguistic information, the presence of emotions, illustrators, and so forth. For example, research shows that subjects searching for words (as may happen in more spontaneous lies) are aided by increasing hand movements (Krauss 1998). Again, deciding what sort of situation one is interested in mirroring will help determine the time allotted for lie creation.

The length of the entire session should also be considered. Certainly the section of the interview in which the lie is spoken is important. For example, the difference between a one-word denial lie and an extended 20-minute interview where the subjects play the Russian Ambassador in a mock 'meet the press' type interview (Druckman *et al.* 1982) may create very different demands on the subject's ability to lie. It would appear to be harder to maintain a lie of longer duration; the odds that someone will contradict themselves would seem to increase with the amount of information they provide. The length of the entire session should also be considered, as subject fatigue may make it harder for them to maintain a convincing lie if they've been under interrogation for one hour, rather than 15 minutes.

Caution!

It is important that one considers when and where in the interview sequence a subject might lie, as an additional factor in determining how long a subject has to concoct his or her lie. This period of time should be as long as the amount of time a truthteller has to mull over the issue that he or she will truthfully describe. Each of these issues is affected by the cognitive complexity of the lie (i.e. simple denial versus fabricating an opinion) which, based on most models of how lies are betrayed, will affect the behavioral information that follows (e.g. Ekman 1985/2001; Hocking & Leathers 1985).

Step 7: Decide how many lies a subject is to tell and in what order

Many paradigms feature just a single lie about a single event (as in the mock crime tradition). Others assign subjects to lie about some of the photos they're looking at, and tell the truth about what they believe about their friends and enemies (e.g. DePaulo & Rosenthal 1979; Manstead *et al.* 1984). When should the researcher alternate lies and truths, or randomly assign the location of the lies, or allow the subject to choose when or whether to lie or how often? As usual, it depends upon what situation one wishes to generalize. If one is interested in studying what happens when a person is confronted suddenly with the possibility of lying, then procedures where a card is drawn that assigns them to lie on the very next question may be appropriate. The order in the interview sequence in which the lie appears matters, as recent work by Vrij *et al.* (2004) found that lie catchers were more accurate judging a lie that occurred as the fourth question asked rather than the first question asked.

But note that in this situation, like most experimental situations, it is not the subject's choice when to lie—whereas in the real world, it would more likely be their choice. It is also the case that in the real world, lies and truths are often intertwined, and not imposed from external sources. Allowing the subject to choose when to lie in the sequence of questions can overcome that problem. However, one loses experimental control and, thus, order effects would need to be partialed out, or some other statistical adjustment made, to account for the irregularity of the position of the lie or lies in the sequence of questions.

If one chooses a one-shot, between-subject designed lie or truth, one has the advantage of ecological validity for some situations (like a crime), but suffers from a lack of within-subject comparison criteria for the behaviors. Given some of the small effect sizes one deals with in nonverbal clues to deception (DePaulo *et al.* 2003), one gives up quite a bit of power by employing only between-subject comparisons. One may also have to be more reticent about inferences across other one-shot lie situations. For example, it is harder to generalize to a real world lie about a theft if one asks research subjects to lie about their intended area of study, versus asking them to lie about a mock theft.

To obtain some sort of comparison, ideally one should insert, somewhere in the sequence, an equally anxiety-provoking truth told along with the lie. Thus, allowing a subject to lie about the theft of either a watch or a ring, and also to tell the truth, would provide a more controlled sample of truth in which to compare a specific person's lie. Likewise, if a subject lies and tells the truth about a photo, the stakes and complexity of the photos should be similar. The order of the lie and truth, and ring versus watch, should be counterbalanced as well, which should hopefully iron out any differences due to the complexity of the material.

Caution!

One must remember that in the real world, the things most people lie about are those that they have some relationship or experience with, and thus there may be some emotional/attachment aspect or particular knowledge aspect that goes with it. A picture that one is seeing for the first time and asked to lie about has no day-to-day, easily drawn out justification, nor any emotional/attachment aspect. In contrast, everyone can relate to the temptation of taking something that wasn't theirs. In other words, in our attempts to try to control our stimuli we may be leaving out some yet to be known critical element. However, the researcher can make these pallid lies come to life, and thus engage the subject more, by using a cover story that discusses how a criminal might have to create an alibi, etc.

A second concern is that one must be careful when alternating truth/lie that the discomfort or other behavioral indications associated with deception don't bleed into the behaviors of the truthful items and thus cloud the nonverbal displays of the subjects. This is particularly true when the lie involves concealing powerful emotions. For example, Ekman & Friesen (1974) showed films to nursing students, first of ocean waves, then of burn victims and a leg amputation. In each instance, the nurse was to claim they were viewing pleasant ocean waves. Ekman & Friesen (1974) did not counterbalance the truths and lies in their experiment because they found, in their pilot testing, that when they showed the gory film first, the strong emotions generated by that film stayed with the subjects and were manifest in the 'truth' films of ocean waves that came afterward. If a researcher wishes to counterbalance a strong, emotion-eliciting type lie, then a cooling off period, or some other distracting task, should be inserted between truths/lies, as we have done in some recent work (Frank & Ekman, in preparation). But again, keep in mind that a person does not have the opportunity to counterbalance his or her lies in the real world, even though it is easily defensible and appropriate from a research methods perspective.

Step 8: Decide what stakes are involved in successful or unsuccessful lies

In real life, some scenarios don't feature many stakes if the lie is caught, mainly because the lies are told so often (e.g. politeness lies; DePaulo *et al.* 1996b). Other lies feature high stakes, where the unsuccessful liar may be killed and the successful liar may get away with murder. In the laboratory, we cannot create these sorts of high stakes, but we can include some stakes if that is what the researcher is interested in exploring. Many experiments try to provide incentives for successful lying, such as a monetary reward for either the best liar (e.g. Kraut & Poe 1980) or for all successful liars, or a benevolent inference about one's intelligence (DePaulo *et al.* 1983) or others. However, fewer studies provide punishments for unsuccessful deception. We used withdrawal of money and threat of loud, startling blasts of noise for unsuccessful deception (Frank & Ekman 1997). Others have used threat of mild electric shock (Mehrabian 1971). Again, understanding what sort of situation one is interested in will determine what the researcher is to do.

Caution!

One other thing to consider is whether punishment should be extended to the truthful person who is misjudged. The real world is replete with instances of innocent people who have been wrongly imprisoned—so this is not just a theoretical possibility (Dwyer *et al.* 2000). We would argue that in a real-life context, any person accused of a serious crime (innocent or not), who is interrogated by skeptical police, would feel nervous. So, again the situation a researcher attempts to mirror in the laboratory will determine whether one employs a punishment for the innocent, falsely judged.

Although we might be able to create high stakes in the laboratory, for ethical reasons, we will never be able to create stakes that match serious real-world situations like counter-terrorism or crimes. Even though we can get closer to understanding these situations by employing fairly high stake paradigms (Frank & Ekman, 1997), we don't know whether these lower stakes are just linearly related to the higher stakes in terms of number and types of emotions or paralinguistic information or body actions, or whether there is a curvilinear relation. Part of the rationale for DePaulo *et al.*'s (1983, 1988) motivational impairment effect was that small amounts of motivation can help the liar control his or her nonverbal behavior, whereas larger amounts of motivation can cause more nonverbal clues to exude from the subject. These motives were not quite as high a stake as some other paradigms, but it does highlight the fact that we should not assume linear relationships between any of these variables and their effects on nonverbal behavior.

Examining real-world examples of lying

On the surface, it would seem that the best way to understand lying in the real world is to look at lies told in the real world (e.g. videos of actual police interrogations; dramatic appeals from a person to find the person who killed his or her spouse, when we now know the person issuing the appeal was the real killer). Methodologically and conceptually, there are a number of problems with using data derived from real-world lies. First and foremost is the identification of ground truth. This is important for both the purported lie and the purported comparison truths. A researcher must clearly identify the criteria he or she used to determine which statements are truthful, which are lies, and which might be a partial truth or lie because, like lots of things in social science, it is never as simple as it appears. For example, if a suspect denies involvement in a crime whilst being interrogated, and they are convicted by a jury despite that denial, does this mean their denial of the crime was a lie? We do know that hundreds of people in the United States have been exonerated by DNA, although they were convicted by juries (Dwyer *et al.* 2000). So conviction cannot be the gold standard.

But what if the suspect confessed? That too is not without problems, as researchers have documented that people have confessed falsely, be it due to mental illness, police pressure, disorientation, or naivety (Dwyer *et al.* 2000). What if, in later interviews, the person admits certain statements originally claimed to be truthful were actually lies? That is better, but not foolproof. There may be motivational or self-image factors that may cause the person to admit part of the truth, but not all of it, thus rendering their new 'truth' a lie (Inbau *et al.* 1986). For example, a suspect under interrogation may admit, after initial denials, that they did molest a child, but they molested this child just once—when, in fact, it may have been repeated molestations over months. What if there is a video of the suspect committing the crime or DNA evidence that the suspect had sex with the victim? That is even better, but if the suspect actually believes they did not commit the crime, due to drug or alcohol blackouts or mental illness (despite evidence that any reasonably sane person would not deny), they would not be lying because they would not be *deliberately* misleading anyone.

A similar process exists for determining the ground truth of any comparison truthful statement chosen for analysis by the researcher. What may seem to be an inconsequential event described by a suspect, and thus assumed to be the truth, may not be the truth. For example, a suspect may describe a seemingly innocuous lunch with a friend. To the researcher, this does not seem to be all that relevant to the crime, so there is no motive for the suspect to mislead about this lunch, so it is chosen as an example of the suspect telling the truth. Yet maybe that lunch story was a lie because the suspect was hiding a romantic affair that had nothing to do with the crime under investigation. Likewise, one must be very careful about using the actual confession as a truthful item. Although one can do behavioral analysis on this statement (but see above about concerns about a 'partial' confession), if one then chooses to show it to judges who are tasked with identifying truths and lies, then this item may be so obviously a truth to the observers (i.e. why would someone lie about admitting the crime?) that it would artifactually inflate observer–subjects' judgment accuracy rates (e.g. Vrij & Mann 2001). Likewise, if a subject's admission is a false confession, many of the problems stated above would apply. So, a number of criteria can be enlisted to insure that any piece of a real-world lie or truth is actually a lie or truth, although there may not be a 100% guaranteed way to determine the ground truth. But as always, a researcher must stipulate this in any report, and not assume that convictions, video/DNA evidence, and such like, are sufficient.

A second consideration in using real-life lies is the quality of the video. Our experience with real-world police interrogation video is that the quality is so poor that one can only do the most rudimentary nonverbal analyses. Most involve a camera in a corner that captures the entire interrogation room, badly illuminated and focused, and the face is so small as to prohibit using most of the facial coding systems such as FACS (Ekman & Friesen 1978) or Izard's MAX (e.g. Malatesta & Haviland 1986). Moreover, often the suspect is behind a desk or table, thus eliminating any measurements of behaviors occurring below the waist. Finally, the audio quality may preclude any analysis of fundamental frequency or other paralinguistic clues.

A third consideration is the role of the type and frequency of questions and other contextual factors. For example, a video of an interrogation that is a result of eight hours of relentless police questioning, where the subject has not taken his or her diabetes medication or has been denied access to cigarettes that feed their nicotine habit, may generate some misleading clues to deception. An interrogation of a suspect that is a second, or third interview, with either similar or different interviewers, may be different than the first interview because the suspect has now had a chance to rehearse his or her story a few times. An interview where the interrogator has been hostile and cuts off the suspect's attempted responses will, in all likelihood, generate different responses from the suspect than if the interrogator allows the suspect to fully explain his or her position without interruption (certain variables such as response length will certainly be affected). An interrogator who is hostile, but does not cut off the suspect, may also generate different responses than a more supportive, information-seeking style interrogator—in particular, in the responses of a truthtelling suspect. Moreover, if an interrogator starts out being supportive, but periodically verges into hostility, they will affect the nonverbal behaviors of the subject/suspect independent of truth or lie as the subject reacts to these periods of hostility. In fact, Ekman (1985/2001) referred to how a hostile interviewer can generate fear clues, and then incorrectly infer these as lie clues, as the 'Othello error'.

A researcher may try to put in some sort of measures of the interrogator's hostility to help control for them in later analyses, but deciding on the exact criteria for this hostility in real-life data may be difficult. Should one use the researcher's impression, that of a panel of judges, or do they have access to the subject to ask him or her? Maybe what seems mild to an observer may be felt as harsh by the subject (or vice versa). Finally, as with laboratory based interrogations, the predispositions, biases, feelings, etc., of the interrogator may leak into his or her verbal and nonverbal behavior. This can also have a differential effect on the suspect.

The fourth consideration is the sample size and/or subjects under consideration. One published real-life criminal study (Vrij & Mann 2001) involves a single subject/suspect who tells multiple lies and truths. This is a good beginning to studying lies in the real world, but it suffers from the reality that there is only one subject (their later work included some more examples; Mann et al. 2002).

We know, from other work, that people differ so drastically in their abilities to perpetrate a lie (e.g. DePaulo & Rosenthal 1979; Frank & Ekman 2004a) that we have to be extra cautious in what we infer about what this means for people's abilities to lie or their behaviors when lying in the real world, or in what we infer about people's abilities to spot such lies. For example, if the subject/suspect was a poor liar, then we would be misled into thinking that real-life lies have many more obvious clues than the laboratory lie, or that people are more accurate in identifying real-life lies than laboratory lies. Or, if the subject/suspect was an excellent liar, then we would be misled into thinking that there are no clues to lying in the real world, or that people are very poor at detecting real-world lies.

The fifth consideration is the privacy and notoriety concerns for the suspects, be they found guilty or not guilty. In terms of privacy, a researcher must be sure to obtain the proper consents from either the subject or from the television station that originally showed the piece in the media, if this is an issue. In terms of notoriety, if this case is a high-profile case, then the public's knowledge of the case can bias both the coders who score the behaviors and the judges who make observations of the suspect, as it is hard for people who may have developed strong preconceived notions of the character of the subject/suspect/defendant to code their nonverbal behaviors in as unbiased a manner as possible. This same bias may apply to people asked to judge the truth or innocence of a video clip taken from one of these high-profile cases—not to mention knowing the outcome of the case if it was adjudicated. In coding both the behavior and perception of this person, one can expect these raters to bring their biases to their judgments, producing misleading evidence about behavioral clues or perceptions of lying.

Hybrid studies

There are very few studies that have elements of both the real world and some laboratory controls. For example, Feldman et al. (2002) had subjects engage in a 'get acquainted' conversation, and then asked them later which statements were lies. Although he and his colleagues were not as interested in the nonverbal components of the lies, and these were mainly low-stake white lies that subjects were willing to admit to a researcher, these were still unauthorized deceptions and, thus, provide good insight into the strategic aspects of deception in the real world. One of the best high-stake lie experiments was also not interested in measuring the nonverbal elements, but was a polygraph and behavioral judgment study (Ginton et al. 1982). This study involved Israeli police cadets improperly changing their answers on an exam that determined their admittance to the police and their level in that organization. This scenario featured a real lie, with real implications for the lives of the liars. It also had a clear, measurable ground truth. It had multiple subjects, not a single good or bad liar. Thus, it combined some of the best features of a real-world high-stake situation, with enough experimental control to help make inferences about behaviors. However, attempting to do this study today may be problematic due to ethical concerns.

General procedural considerations

Recruitment

Once an investigator has determined his or her paradigm, there are still other decisions that need to be made about the execution of the experiment. The first issue concerns recruiting subjects. As in any experiment, one needs to direct recruitment towards the groups of interest. But in a lie experiment, this takes on a slightly different twist. If one advertises a 'lying' experiment, the first risk one runs is generating a biased sample of good liars who feel the need to rise to that challenge, or possibly bad liars interested in how to lie better. We do not know whether this will actually happen, but given the uncontroversial finding that some people are much better liars than others, one should be alert to this possibility.

The second risk in recruitment involves using scenarios in which the ground truth is in the head of the subject (see p. 350). To repeat briefly, if the subject knows it is a 'lying' experiment, he or she may be more tempted to cheat by claiming the opposite of their true opinion to be their true opinion or to like/dislike someone they actually dislike/ like, to increase their perceived odds at lying and getting away with it (as they would actually be telling the truth). The way to reduce this possibility is to recruit using other titles that do not raise the issue of lying (e.g. 'communication skills experiment'). This will increase the odds of a more typical sample of subjects. Of course, subjects should be fully informed when they arrive that lying is one communication skill that the researcher is now interested in studying.

Assessments

Whatever sorts of inventories a researcher uses to measure current states (e.g. emotions, thoughts, impressions), he or she should administer these as soon as possible after the incident or behavior of interest to the researcher to try to get as fresh a judgment from the subject as possible, before other instructions or considerations may confound the subject. Although this applies to all psychological studies, it is especially important for a lie study because in some lie paradigms (e.g. the mock crime scenarios) there are many detailed instructions for the subjects to follow that can be confusing and confounding (e.g. going down the hall, looking for the object, making sure not to disturb anything, what to say to people who may run into the subject). However, one must be careful that taking too many measures throughout the paradigm may artificially disrupt the flow of the interaction between subject and interviewer/interro-gator, thus rending it too artificial to be extrapolated to real-world behavior. And, this may affect the liars more than truthtellers, as almost all models of human deception acknowledge that they have more to keep in their head than a truthteller (e.g. Ekman 1985/2001). There is no hard and fast rule here, but thinking through exactly what aspects of the experiment the researcher wishes to emphasize will, in all likelihood, drive his or her decision.

Judging deception

Judge studies in interpersonal deception are conducted to either gather some information about the liars/truthtellers (as in judging the confidence, mood, or simple ability to be a good or bad liar) or to gather some information about people's abilities to detect lies and their resultant judgment processes. Many of the variables and decisions that one would make in the process of collecting deception data apply to any nonverbal behavior judge study, so the reader is referred to Chapter 5 for more detailed information. This section will focus on those aspects of conducting judge studies that are uniquely relevant to issues in the nonverbal study of human deception.

Judges as coders

Judges can be used to test a variety of nonverbal hypotheses related to deception. For example, channel studies (which show judges' samples of just facial behavior, just transcripts, just the body, just the content-filtered voice) have been used numerous times in deception work to examine where clues to deceit may be located (e.g. Zuckerman *et al.* 1985). Using groups of judges to identify these characteristics can be a less costly way to derive data on variables than the slow motion, back and forth coding. However, one must be cautious that, because judges cannot see a clue, it does not mean other methods of close examination conducted by trained coders may not reveal some important clues overlooked by the judges. This is particularly true when trying to observe the often subtle clues deceptive subjects emit in their active efforts to conceal such clues.

Judges as subjects

More often, judge studies are used to determine the processes by which judges detect deception. This shifts the role of the judge from that of coder to actual subject of study. As the subjects of study, we can ask many of the same questions of these judge-subjects as we would in the experiments that test people's abilities to perpetrate the lie. Typically, the general processes involved in doing deception judge studies are similar to those in any other judge study, particularly in terms of order of items, number of items, using Likert versus nominal variables, and so forth (again, see Rosenthal 1982, Chapter 5). However, one of the advantages of doing judge studies of deception is that most people feel they are pretty good at it, and, with experience, some professionals feel they get better and better—without showing actual improvement (DePaulo & Pfeifer 1986). This means, compared to most judge studies, a deception judge study seems to have more enthusiastic and motivated judges who enjoy the challenge of 'catching liars'. This is particularly so if looking at professional groups whom we as a society depend upon to catch liars (e.g. Ekman *et al.* 1999). However, there are a number of factors that one might have to overcome with other judge groups and, in particular, if they are not typical university students.

Groups with organic/social communication obstacles

One may be interested in studying groups that, due to their life circumstance or culture, may not understand the language of the experiment or be able to communicate adequately their decisions. For example, we studied patients with left hemisphere brain damage, to examine their ability to detect deception (Etcoff *et al.* 2000). Due to damage in the speech processing centers of their brains, they could not comprehend speech. The lead author, a clinical neuropsychologist, had to work through a communication strategy involving hand signals to obtain their judgments, rather than simple judgments of 'lie' or 'truth' delivered on a sheet of paper. Similar problems may also be encountered when dealing with children who come from an abused background (e.g. Bugental *et al.* 2001), inmates (e.g. Vrij & Semin 1996), those who are hearing or sight impaired, or even non-educated, non-English speakers.

Groups with language communication obstacles

We had to abandon a project looking at lie-catching skills of non-English speaking subjects—Russian, Lebanese Arabic, and Vietnamese—who judged lies and truths told in English. Our hypothesis was that by not understanding English, they would be forced to rely upon nonverbal clues and, thus, may be more accurate lie catchers than native English speakers. We translated our basic response form which asked questions about confidence, numbered 1 to 20, with the words 'lie' and 'truth' after each number. Judges were to circle one of these responses for each stimulus subject shown, depending upon whether they thought that subject was lying or telling the truth. Of course, we had the form translated back to make sure that it read in Russian, Arabic, and Vietnamese the way we intended it to read. The Vietnamese and Arabic immigrants to Australia that we used had little formal education, and even though the three experimenters were native speakers of these three languages, the subjects found it bizarre to be circling words to represent a judgment, or were afraid that this was a test that could affect their status in Australia (despite our reassurances). Some felt it was impolite to cast such a negative assertion about another person (i.e. to call someone a liar). Thus many of the responses were unanswered, or they circled in between the words, and so forth. The data we did obtain showed no difference between them and native-born Australian subjects, although we had less than five useable data forms across 50 subjects.

Groups with age-related communication obstacles

The last issue to discuss about the types of judge subjects is to factor in their maturity and attention span. In some studies looking at children's abilities to recognize the concept of lying, they have often used puppet shows to demonstrate a deceptive act and then asked children to judge the behaviors of the character (e.g. Hala *et al.* 1991). Children may also be more likely to offer spontaneous outbursts about the person they may be judging. Finally, one must make very sure that the child subject truly understands what a lie is (usually by around age three or four) before they embark upon the judge study.

Cautions!

Independence of observations

One essential assumption of a judge study is that the subjects' judgments are independent. This means that they do not influence each other in any way. Given the number of judges that can be used in a judge study (hundreds at times), it seems impractical to literally run one subject at a time, so researchers often resort to running groups of judges at a time. In a deception judge study, this poses an additional challenge. There appears to be some macho value associated with being a good lie catcher, and our experience conducting judge studies on deception suggests that it is a lot harder for subjects to keep quiet, and not snort, giggle, or offer some pejorative comment on the stimulus subjects when judging whether they are lying compared to almost any other judgment we could ask. So an experimenter must take the appropriate steps, including explaining to subjects why it is important to maintain independence, and how their snort or giggle can affect the judgments of others.

Assumptions about base rate in the judge task

It is also our experience that some professional groups are biased toward judging deception (Ekman *et al.* 1999). Some police officers will judge all stimulus items as deceptive, as their beliefs are that it is worse for a liar to get away with the lie than to falsely judge a truthteller. With these groups, we warn them that the test is not a trick, and that there are at least one, two, or three liars and one, two, or three truthtellers in the set they are about to see and judge (the exact number depending upon the total number of stimulus items). The reason for this is that we have found that some subjects engage in a mental calculus if they know the actual base rate of lying (usually 50%), so when they feel they are circling the word 'lie' too much, they will compensate and start circling the word 'truth'. What this means is that they are basing their judgments on some artifactual decision rule driven entirely by the artificial nature of the task and independent of the stimulus items. This, of course, would render any conclusion on perceptual abilities null at worst, suspect at best.

Fatigue

Judging item after item is a tiring process for subjects. But it seems to be even more so for judging deception, as compared to simply judging how a subject feels. This may be due to the complexity of the behaviors for subjects to be mindful of, or possibly the pressure a subject feels under to be a good lie catcher (which seems to be a badge of honor for subjects). Our experience suggests that a deception judge study should be limited to about 30 minutes. After that, subject fatigue seems to set in and subjects become more careless in their responses and researchers will begin to lose their ability to draw conclusions about the judgment process outside of the effects of fatigue.

Technical issues in display

Image size

In deception experiments, there are a few variables in the technical display of the items to be considered. First is the size of the image. We know that the size does seem to affect the emotional impact of the image (Detenber & Reeves 1996). However, in terms of later generalizability of people's abilities to judge deception in face-to-face encounters, this means the head size in the image shown to judges should be the same as that one sees in the situation to which they wish to generalize. If it is a face-to-face encounter, the image should be big enough to capture that. If it is from a distance (e.g. across a room), then the image should capture that as well. Although we are unaware of any studies showing judgment accuracy differences with increasing stimulus subject head size, it is reasonable to conclude that there will be a point at which the head size is too small to see subtle movements. As mentioned earlier, many images on police videos are too small to do facial analysis.

Today, a researcher is not limited to displaying video images on a TV; one can show items on a computer, on the web, or whatever. However, it still seems important to make sure the items are of adequate size to enable one's conclusions to match the hypotheses.

Room set-up

Given the engaging nature of a deception judgment task, it becomes imperative to make sure that the room is set up properly, with subjects having adequate sight lines to the stimulus material and being able to see their response forms properly. This also means that the audio must be adequate to capture a voice properly (particularly if one is interested in studying voice tone clues), and that the room is acoustically sound. Moreover, the subject seating should be such that no matter where they sit, the subject can see a facial close-up that will be approximately the same as that in a face-to-face encounter.

The judgment test

When testing judge subjects, as in any judge study, one must consider the number of items, the length of the items, the order of truth/lie items, the base rate of deception across the items, and how to control for guessing.

As mentioned earlier, the number of items is important as it affects judge fatigue. But another issue to consider is the length of the item. One can choose to show judges a five-minute segment of an interview, and ask them to decide whether the stimulus subject has committed the act they are denying, or to listen to a stimulus subject describe their opinion and decide how much of that is truthful and how much deceptive. This latter type judgment appears to be more fatiguing to a subject than a simpler judgment as to whether the stimulus subject engaged in the act they are denying.

Often, researchers will decide to show judges a segment of the interview. The question is which segment to choose. If the deception paradigm is about an act they are denying (as in the typical mock-crime experiment or in describing their opinion), there is often much truth in the stimulus subject's assertions. In this instance, the researcher should make sure to select a segment that has the most verifiable ground truth to make sure judges are seeing actual deception, not assumed deception.

If this situation is one where subjects are telling multiple truths and lies, then all the rules about good counterbalancing and selection within the sequence apply (see Rosenthal 1982).

Another issue is the base rate of deception in the test. Usually, researchers simplify later analysis by having half the items deceptive and half, truthful. This means that a person guessing on a categorical choice response form (i.e. 'truth' or 'lie') would, on average, get 50% of the items correct. This also controls for other phenomena, such as the 'truth bias', found in undergraduates (Levine *et al.* 1999) or the 'more lie bias' found in law enforcement (Ekman *et al.* 1999). At times, this base rate cannot be achieved, or it can be that the researcher would like to examine the effect of base rate changes. In this case, using other measures of accuracy, besides percentage of items correct (e.g. signal detection theory; see Stanislaw & Todorov 1999 for a current conceptualization), should be employed to adequately control for guessing.

Finally, one should consider whether to show a single person twice—once lying, once truthful (a within-stimulus subject judgment; e.g. Ekman & Friesen 1974)—or show different people, each contributing one stimulus item (a between-stimulus subject judgment; e.g. Frank & Ekman 1997). This has particular import for deception experiments because most deception researchers have argued that the specific clues to deceit are more idiopathic (e.g. DePaulo 1994) and, thus, the within-subject task may inflate accuracy rates compared to between-subject taks. A researcher should be aware of this when comparing results across different studies.

Conclusion

Much of the research on deception and nonverbal behavior is similar to nonverbal research in general. Issues in design, counterbalancing, accounting for ecological validity, as well as internal validity, are as relevant to deception as any other topic in nonverbal behavior. However, the specifics of deception often interact with these concepts in a way that the researcher must be aware of. A failure to do so may create untenable conclusions and results that may not be relevant to the real-world understanding of deception.

Regardless of the decisions made by a researcher, this chapter suggests that some of these apparently trivial decisions can have an enormous effect on what can be concluded from the study. This is especially true in deception research because, unlike other nonverbal research (e.g. a facial expression of emotion work), no researcher has ever identified anything approaching a specific response or pattern of response that is the equivalent to the nonverbal behavior patterns seen in fear, anger, and so forth (Ekman 1994). In other words, this lack of a 'Pinocchio' deception response in humans (i.e. a response in all people in all situations indicates a lie) implies there is still much work remaining to identify any signal or pattern of signals that may betray deception— if any exist at all (Ekman 1985/2001).

So, given our state of knowledge on deception, and given its re-emergence as a topic worthy of study due to its importance in the face of current terrorist-driven threats, it is more imperative than ever that deception researchers spell out carefully all their apparently minor paradigm decisions. This allows researchers to more carefully compare new findings with old data, as one cannot adequately compare without being able to render some judgment on the equivalence of various paradigms. In this way, we can move more quickly down a path toward unraveling the processes involved in deception, so we can understand it at a level that enables the discovery of truths or refutation of myths.

Acknowledgments

The author gratefully acknowledges that some of the ideas in this chapter are based upon work supported by the Office of Naval Research Grant # N0014–02–1–0709 and # N00014–03–1–0847, and National Science Foundation Grant # 0220230. Any opinions, findings, and conclusions or recommendations expressed in this material are those of the author and do not necessarily reflect the views of the Office of Naval Research or the National Science Foundation. Finally, special thanks go out to Paul Ekman, as many of these ideas have come from hours of joint discussions and, odds are, that all the good ideas were his but have seeped into my thought patterns such that I now think they're mine.

References

Bond, C.F. Jr. & Atoum, A.O. (2000). International deception. *Personality & Social Psychology Bulletin*, 26, 385–95.

Bugental, D.B., Shennum, W., Frank, M.G., & Ekman, P. (2001). 'True lies': children's abuse history and power attributions as influences on deception detection. In *Attribution, communication behavior, and close relationships* (ed. V. Manusov & J.H. Harvey), pp. 248–65. Cambridge, UK: Cambridge University Press.

Burgoon, J.E. & Buller, D.B. (1994). Interpersonal deception: III. Effects of deceit on perceived communication and nonverbal behavior dynamics. *Journal of Nonverbal Behavior*, 18, 155–84

Burgoon, J.E. & Nunamaker, J. (2004). Computer-aided support of the detection of deception. *Journal of Group Decision and Negotiation*, 13, 107–10.

Carlsmith, J.M., Ellsworth, P.C., & Aronson, E. (1976). *Methods of research in social psychology.* New York: Random House.

Davies, G. (1999). The impact of television on the presentation and reception of children's testimony. *International Journal of Law & Psychiatry*, 22, 241–56.

DePaulo, B.M. (1982). Age changes in the detection of deception. *Child Development*, 53, 701–9.

DePaulo, B.M. (1994). Spotting lies: can humans learn to do better? *Current Directions in Psychological Science*, 3, 83–6.

DePaulo, B.M. & Pfeifer, R.L. (1986). On-the-job experience and skill at detecting deception. *Journal of Applied Social Psychology*, 16, 249–67.

DePaulo, B.M. & Rosenthal, R. (1979). Telling lies. *Journal of Personality and Social Psychology*, 37, 1713–22.

DePaulo, B.M., Ansfield, M.E., & Bell, K.L. (1996a). Theories about deception and paradigms for studying it. *Communication Theory*, 6, 297–310.

DePaulo, B.M., Lanier, K., & Davis, T. (1983). Detecting the deceit of the motivated liar. *Journal of Personality and Social Psychology*, 45, 1096–103.

DePaulo, B.M., Lindsay, J.J., Malone, B.E., Muhlenbruck, L., Charlton, K., & Cooper, H. (2003). Cues to deception. *Psychological Bulletin*, 129, 74–112.

DePaulo, B.M., Kashy, D.A., Kirkendol, S.E., Wyer, M.M., & Epstein, J.A. (1996*b*). Lying in everyday life. *Journal of Personality and Social Psychology*, **70**, 979–95.

DePaulo, B.M., Kirkendol, S.E., Tang, J., & O'Brien, T.P. (1988). The motivational impairment effect in the communication of deception: replications and extensions. *Journal of Nonverbal Behavior*, **12**, 177–202.

Detenber, B.H. & Reeves, B. (1996). A bio-informational theory of emotion: motion and image size effects on viewers. *Journal of Communication*, **46**, 66–84.

deTurck, M.A. & Miller, G.R. (1985). Deception and arousal: isolating the behavioral correlates of deception. *Human Communication Research*, **12**, 181–201.

Druckman, D., Rozelle, R.M., & Baxter, J.C. (1982). *Nonverbal communication*. Beverly Hills, CA: Sage.

Dwyer, J., Neufeld, P., & Scheck, B. (2000). *Actual innocence: five days to execution and other dispatches from the wrongly convicted*. New York: Doubleday.

Ekman, P. (1985/2001). *Telling lies: clues to deceit in the marketplace, politics, and marriage*. New York: Norton.

Ekman, P. (1989). *Why kids lie*. New York, NY: Charles Scribners.

Ekman, P. (1994). Strong evidence for universals in facial expression: a reply to Russell's mistaken critique. *Psychological Bulletin*, **115**, 268–87.

Ekman, P. (2003). *Emotions revealed: recognizing faces and feelings to improve communication and emotional life*. New York: Times Books/Henry Holt and Co.

Ekman, P. & Friesen, W.V. (1974). Detecting deception from body or face. *Journal of Personality and Social Psychology*, **29**, 288–98.

Ekman, P. & Friesen, W.V. (1978). *The facial action coding system*. Palo Alto, CA: Consulting Psychologists Press.

Ekman, P., Friesen, W.V., & O'Sullivan, M. (1988). Smiles when lying. *Journal of Personality and Social Psychology*, **54**, 414–20.

Ekman, P., Friesen, W.V., & Scherer, K.R. (1976). Body movement and voice pitch in deceptive interaction. *Semiotica*, **16**, 23–7.

Ekman, P., O'Sullivan, M., & Frank, M.G. (1999). A few can catch a liar. *Psychological Science*, **10**, 263–6.

Etcoff, N.L., Ekman, P., Magee, J.J., & Frank, M.G. (2000). Superior lie detection associated with language loss. *Nature*, **405**, 139.

Exline, R.V. (1971). Visual interaction: the glances of power and preference. *Nebraska Symposium on Motivation*, 163–206.

Farwell, L.A. & Donchin, E. (1991). The truth will out: interrogative polygraphy ('lie detection') with event-related brain potentials. *Psychophysiology*, **28**, 531–47.

Feeley, T.H & deTurck, M.A. (1998). The behavioral correlates of sanctioned and unsanctioned deceptive communication. *Journal of Nonverbal Behavior*, **22**, 189–204.

Feldman, R.S., Forrest, J.A., & Happ, B.R. (2002). Self-presentation and verbal deception: do self-presenters lie more? *Basic & Applied Social Psychology*, **24**, 163–70.

Frank, M.G. (1989). *Human lie detection ability as a function of the liar's motivation*. Unpublished doctoral dissertation, Cornell University, Ithaca, NY.

Frank, M.G. (2003). Smiles, lies, and emotion. In *The smile: forms, functions, and consequences* (ed. M. Abel). New York, NY: The Edwin Mellen Press.

Frank, M.G. & Ekman, P. (1997). The ability to detect deceit generalizes across different types of high stake lies. *Journal of Personality and Social Psychology*, 72, 1429–39.

Frank, M.G. & Ekman, P. (2004*a*). Appearing truthful generalizes across different deception situations. *Journal of Personality and Social Psychology*, 86, 486–95.

Frank, M.G. & Ekman, P. (2004*b*). Nonverbal detection of deception in forensic contexts. In *Handbook of forensic psychology* (ed. W. O'Donohue & E. Levensky), pp. 635–53. New York, NY: Elsevier.

Frank, M.G. & Ekman, P. (in preparation). *A new twist on a false opinion paradigm*. Unpublished data, Rutgers University.

Ginton, A., Daie, N., Elaad, E., & Ben–Shakhar, G. (1982). A method for evaluating the use of the polygraph in a real-life situation. *Journal of Applied Psychology*, 67, 131–7.

Hala, S., Chandler, M., & Fritz, A.S. (1991). Fledgling theories of mind: deception as a marker of three-year-olds' understanding of false belief. *Child Development*, 62, 83–97.

Hare, R.D. (1999). *Without conscience: the disturbing world of the psychopaths among us*. New York: Guilford Press.

Haugaard, J.J. & Repucci, N.D. (1992). Children and the truth. In *Cognitive and social factors in early deception* (ed. S.J. Ceci, M. DeSimone–Leichtman, and M.E. Putnick). Hillsdale, NJ: Erlbaum.

Hocking, J.E. & Leathers, D.G. (1980). Nonverbal indicators of deception: a new theoretical perspective. *Communication Monographs*, 47, 119–31.

Inbau, F.E., Reid, J.E., & Buckley, J.P. (1986). *Criminal interrogation and confessions*. Baltimore: Williams and Wilkins.

Kashy, D.A. & DePaulo, B.M. (1996). Who lies? *Journal of Personality and Social Psychology*, 70, 1037–51.

Krauss, R.M. (1998). Why do we gesture when we speak? *Current Directions in Psychological Science*, 7, 54–60.

Kraut, R.E. & Poe, D. (1980). Behavioral roots of person perception: the deception judgments of customs inspectors and laymen. *Journal of Personality and Social Psychology*, 39, 784–98.

Levine, T.R, Park, H.S., & McCornack, S.A. (1999). Accuracy in detecting truths and lies: documenting the 'veracity effect'. *Communication Monographs*, 66, 125–44.

Malatesta, C.Z. & Haviland, J.M. (1986). Measuring change in infant emotional expressivity: two approaches applied in longitudinal investigation. In *Measuring emotions in infants and children, Vol. 2. Cambridge studies in social and emotional development* (ed. C.E. Izard & P.B. Read), pp. 51–74. New York: Cambridge University Press.

Mann, S., Vrij, A., & Bull, R. (2002). Suspects, lies and videotape: an analysis of authentic high-stakes liars. *Law and Human Behavior*, 26, 365–76.

Manstead, A.S., Wagner, H.L., & MacDonald, C.J. (1984). Face, body, and speech as channels of communication in the detection of deception. *Basic & Applied Social Psychology*, 5, 317–32.

Mehrabian, A. (1971). Nonverbal betrayal of feeling. *Journal of Experimental Research in Personality*, 5, 64–73.

Newman, M.L., Pennebaker, J.W., Berry, D.S., & Richards, J.M. (2003). Lying words: predicting deception from linguistic styles. *Personality & Social Psychology Bulletin*, 29, 665–75.

Pavlidis, I., Eberhardt, N.L., & Levine, J.A. (2002). Seeing through the face of deception. *Nature*, 415(6867), 35.

Porter, S. & Yuille, J.C. (1995). Credibility assessment of criminal suspects through statement analysis. *Psychology, Crime & Law*, 1, 319–31.

Rosenberg, E.L. & Ekman, P. (1994). Coherence between expressive and experiential systems in emotion. *Cognition & Emotion*, 8, 201–29.

Rosenthal, R. (1982). Conducting judgment studies. In *Handbook of methods in nonverbal behavior research* (ed. K.R. Scherer & P. Ekman), pp 287–361. New York, NY: Cambridge University Press.

Scherer, K. (1984). On the nature and function of emotions: a component process approach. In *Approaches to emotion* (ed. K. Scherer & P. Ekman), pp. 293–317. Hillsdale, NJ: Lawrence Erlbaum.

Schmitt, B.H., Gilovich, T., Goore, N., & Joseph, L. (1986). Mere presence and social facilitation: one more time. *Journal of Experimental Social Psychology*, 22, 242–8.

Shackleford, T.K. (1997). Perceptions of betrayal and the design of the mind. In *Evolutionary social psychology* (ed. J.A. Simpson & D.T. Kenrick), pp. 73–108. Hillsdale, NJ: Lawrence Erlbaum.

Stanislaw, H. & Todorov, N. (1999). Calculation of signal detection theory measures. *Behavior Research Methods, Instruments & Computers*, 31, 137–49.

Steinbrook, R.(1992). The polygraph test: a flawed diagnostic method. *New England Journal of Medicine*, 327, 122–3.

Suddendorf, T. & Whiten, A. (2001). Mental evolution and development: evidence for secondary representation in children, great apes, and other animals. *Psychological Bulletin*, 127, 629–50.

Vrij, A. (2004). Interrogation and interviewing. In C. Spielberger (Ed.), *Encyclopedia of Applied Psychology*, volume 2, 415–426. London: Elsevier Ltd.

Vrij, A. & Mann, S. (2001). Telling and detecting lies in a high-stake situation: the case of a convicted murderer. *Applied Cognitive Psychology*, 15, 187–203.

Vrij, A. & Semin, G.R. (1996). Lie experts' beliefs about nonverbal indicators of deception. *Journal of Nonverbal Behavior*, 20, 65–80.

Waid, W.M. & Orne, M.T. (1982). The physiological detection of deception. *American Scientist*, 70, 402–9.

Zajonc, R.B., Heingartner, A., & Herman, E.M. (1965). Social enhancement and impairment of performance in the cockroach. *Journal of Personality and Social Psychology*, 13, 83–92.

Zuckerman, M. & Driver, R.E. (1985). Telling lies: verbal and nonverbal correlates of deception. In *Multichannel integration of nonverbal behavior* (ed. W.A. Siegman & S. Feldstein), pp. 129–47. Hillsdale, NJ: Erlbaum.

Zuckerman, M., DePaulo, B.M., & Rosenthal, R. (1981). Verbal and nonverbal communication of deception. In *Advances in experimental social psychology, Vol. 14* (ed. L. Berkowitz), pp. 1–59. San Diego, CA: Academic Press.

CHAPTER 10

NONVERBAL COMMUNICATION CODING SYSTEMS OF COMMITTED COUPLES

DAN K. YOSHIMOTO, ALYSON SHAPIRO, KELLY O'BRIEN, AND JOHN M. GOTTMAN

Introduction

As discussed in previous chapters, the study and understanding of a single modality of nonverbal behavior, such as vocal or facial action, is rich in information regarding specific individual behavior. While this approach is useful, it is also somewhat artificial when it comes to understanding the complexities of real behavior. Generally, the expression of an emotion or other behavior involves the coordination of multiple modalities working concurrently, which requires an integrated approach for quantifying nonverbal behavior. Thus, the meaning of behavior is based on the configuration of these specified modalities and their function relative to each other.

One of the drawbacks of studying singular modalities of expression is that this usually involves the study of a single individual rather than how an individual interacts with others. Gottman and his research team have developed nonverbal behavioral coding systems to study both the various modalities an individual uses to express specific positive and negative emotions, as well as how individuals express these emotions during interaction. This more comprehensive approach of studying nonverbal behavior is exemplified best in observational studies assessing dyadic interaction in intimate relationships, such as between couples and parents with their children.

The study of these couple and parent–child relationships within the family are important because they are some of the most influential and defining relationships we establish in our lives. These systems generally begin with the formation of a wide array of dyadic-committed relationships beyond heterosexual married couples, such as gay, lesbian, bisexual, transgendered, and (as a recent epidemiological Fragile Families Survey reported) unmarried cohabiting mothers (Sigle–Rushton & McLanahan 2002). These primary dyadic relationships establish a foundation for family formation and play powerful roles in the lives of each person within these systems.

Research suggests that poor dyadic adjustment has been linked to immunosuppression of women in heterosexual married couples and increased physiological arousal, increased negative affect, and negative affect reciprocity, which are predictive of future relationship dissatisfaction and dissolution. Hostility and marital discord also are associated with poor outcomes for children developing in these families (Gottman & Katz 1989; Gottman *et al.* 1997; Hetherington *et al.* 1982; Hooven *et al.* 1995).

Considering how dyadic relationships influence individual physical, psychological, and emotional well-being, it is astounding to consider the rate at which these relationships end in divorce. The divorce rate in the United States continues to soar, with 67% of all first marriages and nearly half of all second marriages ending in divorce (Martin & Bumpass 1989). Therefore, research continues to explore the predictors and active mechanisms involved in relationship quality and instability over time.

A common methodological approach used in studying couples is self-report questionnaires, which provide valuable insider reports by each partner. While subjective ratings of behaviors and experiences play an essential role in enhancing our understanding of dyadic interaction, this information is biased and influenced by relationship quality and the cognitive attributes each person associates with their partner. These positive or negative attributes influence the way individuals interpret their partner's behavior, such that in happily married couples, individuals rate neutral behaviors more positively than individuals in unhappy relationships. Unhappy couples tend to rate neutral behaviors more negatively (Weiss 1980). This phenomenon has been termed 'sentiment override'.

The integration of self-report and observer ratings of behavior are especially important when studying interaction. The implementation of observational coding of behavior during conflict resolution tasks provides an opportunity to assess the active mechanisms involved in breaking marriages apart. Some of the most powerful predictors of relationship dissolution are derived from our objective observation of specific affect occurring during conflict resolution, such as contempt, defensiveness, criticism, and stonewalling. Additionally, another type of objective measurement is psychophysiology, where research suggests that distressed couples are best characterized by a greater overall state of heightened physiological arousal than happy couples, and this greater arousal during baseline and during conflict resolution is predictive of future dissolution and poorer relationship satisfaction at four-year follow-up (Levenson & Gottman 1985).

Considering the variety of data collected and results produced, the objective assessment of nonverbal behavioral communication in committed relationships has been an essential part of the multi-method approach implemented by Gottman and his research team.

This chapter will focus on various nonverbal behavioral coding systems used in our laboratory when studying committed relationships. The following coding systems will be presented: Specific Affect Coding System (SPAFF), Triadic Interaction Coding System (TICS), and psychophysiological assessment. The discussion of each coding system will be organized into sections providing information about the background and evolution of these coding systems, equipment required to implement these systems into your laboratory, guidelines for training, some significant findings as a result of the implementation of these coding systems, and some recommendations for future research.

Specific Affect Coding System[KRO1]

The Specific Affect Coding System (SPAFF) is designed to code specific emotions in marital and family interactions. This coding system categorizes affect at the level of the emotion and yields codes that are descriptive of the emotional communication in any interaction over time. SPAFF is a gestalt coding system, which uses a holistic approach to recognize and categorize affect, through integrating a physical features approach with a cultural informant approach. The physical features approach allows detailed recognition and categorization of facial, physical, and verbal cues currently known to be associated with specific emotions. The cultural informant approach allows the coder to use his or her subjective understanding of emotions in identifying specific affects. The synthesis of these two approaches allows the coding system to draw on the wealth of research information on emotional expression, training observers to become aware of cues typically associated with discrete emotions, while also inviting the observer to bring to the coding the wealth of his/her experience as an emotional being as a further aid in accurately identifying specific affects.

SPAFF can be used to examine any discussion between two (or more) people. Although it has been used most extensively to capture emotional communication when couples are discussing an area of disagreement, it has also been used to study parent–child interactions, sibling interactions, couples discussing the events of the day or a positive topic, and couples naturally interacting in an unstructured, apartment laboratory setting.

Background

The idea behind the development of SPAFF is that emotions are expressed in a variety of ways. They are not only evident in the face or the voice, or the content of a conversation, but in all of these ways. Affect is often most evident when a person is freely expressing, but emotions may even be evident when an individual is trying to conceal them (e.g. a trembling chin in a person trying to hold back tears).

Emotions are expressed in ways that are culturally universal and quantifiable through affective cues (Ekman & Friesen 1975), and in ways that are culturally specific, and can only readily be recognized and coded by a cultural informant. Categorizing emotions goes beyond the quantification of physical cues such as the action of a facial muscle or a movement in the body. Thus, SPAFF categorizes specific affects at the level of the emotion itself, rather than the level of the verbal or nonverbal cues. Furthermore, emotions do not occur naturally in categories of negative, positive, and neutral, but in the form of specific affects like anger or joy (Gottman et al. 1996a). By coding them this way, many of the nuances that distinguish qualitatively different relationships from each other are revealed. For example, one may have positive interactions with both a co-worker and a spouse, but the affection expressed towards the spouse is likely to be very different from the encouragement given to the co-worker.

The SPAFF grew out of the Couples Interaction Scoring System (CISS) and Ekman and Friesen's (1978) Facial Action Coding System (FACS). The CISS was designed to have coders scan hierarchically for a set of specific cues to determine whether units of the interaction were negative, neutral, or positive (Gottman 1979). The observer looks first for facial actions, then at voice tone, and, finally, movements in the body, ignoring the content of the conversation and focusing on the nonverbal communication. The observer codes speaker and listener behaviors during each speaker turn in a conversation.

Through careful examination of couples' conflict discussions, Gottman became convinced that the CISS system was not sensitive enough to capture all the affective content of the interactions that were being coded. The cues it relied on were not extensive enough to capture all of the emotion moments in a conversation. Second, he was convinced that the content of a couple's conversation, as well as their nonverbal cues, communicated emotion, and the CISS system did not capture the emotion in the script a couple used. Finally, Gottman believed that labeling emotions as only positive, neutral, and negative was too rudimentary to adequately describe and examine family interactions. Negative affect in the CISS, for example, assigned anger, sadness, contempt, disgust, and fear to the same category, despite the different impact the expression of any of these emotions could have on the relationship. Similarly, negative reciprocity in the CISS system would be coded any time a negative code from one spouse was followed by a negative code for the other spouse, despite the fact that a relationship in which anger is followed by contempt is clearly different from one in which anger is followed by fear or sadness. The development of a new coding system was essential to capture these important differences.

In 1980, Gottman consulted with Ekman and Friesen about their new Facial Action Coding System (FACS). The FACS is designed to categorize the action units (AUs) produced by each facial muscle. These AUs represent the changes in facial appearance seen during what we recognize as expressions of emotion (Ekman & Friesen 1978). This system is very detailed and objective and can be used to describe any set of facial actions, and the combination of several of these AUs typifies the expression of basic emotions. As Gottman continued to observe couples' interactions, however, he realized that the FACS codes alone were inadequate to describe specific emotional moments expressed only in the voice, physical features, or verbal content of the conversation. He started noting additional cues that he saw couples using to communicate affect.

The task of listing all possible physical features that could serve as cues of emotional expression, however, proved to be virtually impossible. One example illustrates this dilemma particularly well. A husband and wife were discussing a disagreement in which he accused her of being jealous of all the women in his car pool. She responded in a very interesting and compelling way. She gently rubbed her face against her soft-looking white cashmere sweater, tilted her head, and looking at her husband with wide eyes said, 'That's not true'. This was clearly a request for love and affection, and her husband responded with affection and reassurance saying, 'Now you know, none of those women are as beautiful to me as you are'. She was reassured and beamed with joy.

This wife's request for support and affection could be recognized by other cultural judges but could not easily be coded by defining specific cues used to express emotions. In this instance, what was the critical cue or set of cues to be coded? Was it the rubbing of the face against the sweater, the tilting of the head, the head-to-shoulder velocity, or the wide eyes? Any of these things alone, however, could be part of other emotional expressions or completely unrelated to emotional expression. Scratching one's face against one's shoulder, for example, could be part of a request for affection such as the one described above but is more likely to reflect that someone has an itch.

The infinite number of gestures that could be used to express emotion and the infinite meanings of physical features of actions that could reflect gestures of emotions (or gestures that were not emotional) simply made the task of categorizing all cues of emotional expression unwieldy. Cultural informants, in contrast, could be used to identify culturally clear gestures of specific emotions. This approach is typically used by anthropologists studying new cultures and can be validated by the use of independent judges to establish reliability.

In revising the CISS system, Gottman endeavored to include the verbal content of a couple's conversation into the coding of emotional expression, as well as recognizing a gestalt of cues including the voice, facial expression, gestures, timing of words, stress, and movement. The final result was the development of SPAFF, which bridges an objective and subjective approach through the synthesis of a physical features and a cultural informant approach. The SPAFF system was designed to systematically teach coders to recognize verbal content and vocal and facial cues that typically indicate specific affects, while going beyond these cues and coding a specific emotion, if they feel it is justified by their background as cultural judges.

Specific affect codes

Several versions of SPAFF have been developed. The most recent is the 20-code version which includes 13 negative, one neutral, and six positive categories (Gottman *et al.* 1998). The negative codes are: disgust, contempt, belligerence, domineering (with a high- and a low-intensity level), criticism, anger, tension, tense humor, defensiveness, whining, sadness, and stonewalling. The positive codes are: interest, validation (with a high- and a low-intensity level), affection, humor, and surprise/joy. The one neutral code categorizes affect that appears neither clearly positive nor clearly negative in nature. Each of these specific emotion codes is described briefly below.

Disgust reflects the underlying feeling of revulsion and includes the verbal and nonverbal rejection of something the person considers noxious. This disgust is in response to something the partner does or says he/she likes. This code is different from contempt in that it reflects more of a physiological revulsion rather than an attitude of superiority towards one's spouse. This is usually an involuntary reaction and demonstrates distaste or an aversion. Verbally, disgust is expressed through statements such as 'yuck' or 'oh, that makes me sick'. Physically, the expression of the disgusted spouse is one of nausea and can take the form of a gagging gesture or the wrinkling up of one's nose.

Contempt is an attempt to insult or otherwise communicate a lack of respect towards one's partner. It tends to have an icy quality with a sense of superiority and can be communicated verbally or facially. Verbal expressions of contempt include sarcasm, mockery, insults, and hostile humor. Examples of these include a person repeating something their partner has said with disrespectful exaggeration or making comments like 'you're so boring'. Facially, contempt can be expressed by a dimpling on one side of the mouth (the muscle buccinator pulls the left or right lip corner laterally and creates a dimple) and/or an eye roll.

Belligerence is coded when a person appears to be trying to provoke a fight with his or her partner. This is often done by challenging one's partner or delighting in that person's discomfort. Examples of this include: asking taunting questions that only confuse and irritate the partner, using humor that the partner does not think is funny, and testing the agreed-upon limits of the relationship using dares like 'What would you do if I did?' and 'What are you going to do about it?' A belligerent individual may also thrust their jaw forward or raise both eyebrows while saying these things.

Domineering is the act of trying to control the conversation or the partner's actions. This can be seen through attempts to force compliance, to get the other person to withdraw, retreat, or submit to their own views. Physically, the person may lower their head and chin, shake their finger, or glower. *Low-intensity domineering* includes: patronizing, lecturing, talking incessantly to try to maintain the floor, invalidation of things the partner may say, and low-balling. (Low-balling involved getting one's partner to say 'yes' to the simplest facts, and then slowly escalating, like a salesman, in an attempt to draw the partner into agreeing to things that are far from the person's initial point of view.) *High-intensity domineering* consists of threats like 'if you ever do that again, I'll . . .' or ultimatums such as 'if you don't improve, I'm leaving'.

Criticism involves attacking one's partner's personality or character rather than a specific behavior, and almost always involves blaming or the insinuation of blame. It is important to distinguish this code from a complaint, which usually involves a particular situation and is a statement of anger, displeasure, or distress. Criticism makes a complaint global and pervasive. Someone airing a complaint may say, 'It upset me when I came home and there were dirty dishes in the sink', but a critical partner may say 'You left dirty dishes in the kitchen again. I just can't trust you, can I?' Criticism can be distinguished from contempt in that it is usually focused around a global issue (such as never helping around the house) rather than directly putting down one's partner (such as saying that they are a slob).

Anger is coded when the person sounds or looks like he or she is 'fed up'. This can include irritation or annoyance, using a raised voice, direct statements of anger, and signs of constrained anger. Physical cues associated with anger include involuntary twitches, having a tight jaw or clenched teeth, one's voice being lowered or raised beyond the limits of normal tone, and short sighs. Note that anger is often blended with other negative emotions such as belligerence and contempt, but that it is only coded in the absence of these negative emotions.

Tension results from feeling worried, anxious, or fearful, and is usually the result of an uncomfortable topic being brought up in conversation. A tense person may have a hard time speaking, with several unfinished thoughts, or repeatedly say 'ah'. They may also fidget, pluck at their clothes, rub their face, or bite their nails. Shifting and nervous smiling or laughter that does not seem appropriate to the situation are also indicators of tension.

Tense humor is coded when both partners in a conversation share in a brief bout of nervous laughter or tense joking. The laughter is used as a release of tension or to avoid an unpleasant topic. The smiles on the partners' faces may seem fake or forced if they do not involve the wrinkling around the outer corner of the eyes that a genuine smile produces.

Defensiveness is coded when people deny personal responsibility or blame for the problem being discussed. Defensiveness usually communicates an innocent victim stance as if to say, 'It's not my fault, why are you picking on me?'. It can take the form of excuses for the behavior; 'yes...but' statements in which the partner starts to agree with their spouse but ends up disagreeing; counter-criticisms; and evenly aggressively defensive statements such as a strong, loud, 'No, I did NOT do that'. A person who is acting defensively may also fold their arms across their chest and raise their eyebrows.

Whining is coded when the voice quality (while airing a complaint) has a very nasal, high-pitch, sing-song sound. This whining sound is often drawn out as in the example, 'Whyyy? I like watching that show.' If there is any defensiveness included in the content of the person's speech, it should not be coded whining.

Sadness is characterized by a marked decrease in energy, passivity or seeming resigned, slow sighing, pouting or sulking, crying, or expressing hurt feelings through words, vocal quality, or facial expression. The underlying feeling that accompanies this affect is one of depression, hopelessness, dejection, regret, or grief. Sometimes the partner's voice will lower, they may frown, or the eyebrows may come together and raise.

Stonewalling refers to the total lack of listening behaviors in a couple's interaction. Usually a listener watches the speaker, nods from time to time, and gives occasional verbal assents to the speaker, such as 'Uh-huh, yeah, um'. When someone is stonewalling, that person gives none of these listener cues, looking like stonewalling rather than an interactive partner in the conversation. Often one will focus on something trivial to avoid eye contact (such as playing with hair or hands) and have a monitoring gaze, where the person glances at the partner occasionally and quickly looks away, as if to see if the ogre is still there. Stonewalling is often an active way of communicating to the partner, 'I'm not listen to you', and is usually in response to something aversive the partner is doing.

The *neutral* code is the dividing line between negative and positive and is typically characterized as being non-emotional in nature. Any behavior that does not fit into any of the other SPAFF categories is also coded as neutral to satisfy the requirement of a mutually exclusive and exhaustive coding system.

Interest is reflected in the involvement and positive energy of the listener. The interested partner may ask a question in order to understand what their partner is saying or ask for additional information or opinions. Genuine interest involves concern about a partner's thoughts and feelings.

Validation involves acceptance and openness to a partner's views and feelings that communicates respect, even if the person disagrees. SPAFF codes both low-level and high-level validation. Low-level validation involves giving backchannels or positive listening behaviors. These consist of keeping eye contact with the speaker and occasionally responding with head nods or verbal assent, to let the speaker know the listener is following him/her (e.g. 'umm-hum', 'yeah', 'um'). **High-level validation** requires a higher level of expressing understanding, including direct expressions of acceptance, apologies, paraphrasing what one's partner has said, or finishing a partner's sentence to express that he/she is 'on the same page'.

Affection is coded when a direct expression of caring is clear. These expressions can include direct statements of loving and caring, tenderness or closeness such as reminiscing about shared moments, compliments, empathy, and supporting one's partner in a common cause. The voice tone is often warm when affection is present.

Humor is characterized by the sharing of laughter with the underlying feeling of shared happiness rather than tension. Joking, good-natured teasing, and exaggeration, such that both partners think the joke is funny enough to laugh at, can characterize these moments. This shared humor (or having something be funny enough that both people enjoy the joke) is very important in distinguishing this positive affect from the derisive teasing that can be seen in contempt.

Positive surprise or joy involves a happy, positive, or emphatic reaction to something in the conversation. Joy can often been seen through a broad, warm smile that appears on one's face after receiving a compliment. Positive surprise is often evident through big smiles and exclamations in reaction to an unanticipated event or remark.

Training

As a preparatory step in learning SPAFF, coders in our laboratory are first taught Ekman and Friesen's FACS (as described above). Training in this coding system involves studying the muscles of the face and which of these muscles cause each AU. Coders learn the outward changes that are produced when an AU is performed, including how these might differ slightly from one face to another. After becoming familiar with single AUs, observers learn combinations of AUs, including those that form facial expressions signifying emotion. For example, during AU4 (the 'brow lowerer'), the eyebrows are pulled down and together. This facial movement may be an expression of anger by itself but, combined with AU23 (the 'lip tightener'), in which the lips narrow and are pulled inward, the emotion is even more apparent.

We recommend coders become certified in FACS before learning SPAFF. Information about FACS training and certification is available through Dr Paul Ekman[1]. Completing the FACS training process ensures coders are able to detect emotional expression in slight facial movements. It will also help sensitize coders to subtle changes in affect and provide a solid base for learning the other vocal and verbal cues that will be integrated with facial information when coding specific affects.

Once coders have learned FACS, training in the actual SPAFF system begins. Coders are taught to draw on the wealth of information we have about what physical features are typically clues of specific emotions based on research. They are also taught that we want them to go beyond simply using these physical features in their coding and to make judgments as socially competent cultural informants when coding specific affects.

Coders in our laboratory learn vocal and verbal cues simultaneously during their SPAFF training, which complements the knowledge they already have about facial actions. During training meetings, coders watch videotape clips containing examples

---

[1] FACS training materials can be obtained by visiting *paulekman.com*

of each code taken from couple interactions. Observers also view and discuss entire interactions during class and are assigned tapes to code on their own. From the start of the training, the focus of the class is on integrating all the cues the coder observes to define the specific affect present. However, it may instead be useful to teach coders by building on each cue, so that they first concentrate on content, then vocal information, and, finally, facial actions. In this case, coders may read and code affect from written transcripts, learn vocal cues by listening to and coding from a set of training audiotapes, and finally work to recognize and code facial actions on videotape.

Once the training class is complete, observers are required to complete a reliability training process. They code several previously coded tapes alongside an experienced SPAFF coder and several on their own, that are later compared to the coding of an experienced observer. Newly trained coders are required to reach reliability with the trainer on a predetermined number of tapes before coding actual study data.

We also recommend regular meetings to review and discuss coded tapes after coders are trained and reliable. These meetings help to ensure that all coders are using the coding system in the same way and not succumbing to coder drift over time. We also suggest that observers periodically recode tapes that they completed several months ago. Comparing the two coding passes allows coders to check if they have maintained reliability with themselves over time.

A SPAFF training manual is available in the book, *What predicts divorce: the measures*, and audiotapes and videotapes are available through our laboratory (see Gottman *et al.* 1996*b*). This book features both the 10-category version of SPAFF and the 16-category version (which is very similar to the 20-category system focused on here).

We have found that actors tend to be skilled SPAFF coders due to their extensive familiarity with specific emotions. Graduate students, staff, and undergraduate students, however, can all make excellent SPAFF coders. The important thing is that the coders are sensitive to emotions and can act as socially competent cultural informants about those emotions. We have found that some people simply cannot seem to recognize and categorize emotions. To ensure that the people selected as coders can function as emotionally sensitive cultural judges, we recommend having coding candidates watch, with the trainer, a video of the type of interaction that will be coded and discuss the emotions they see. If they can distinguish between basic positive, neutral, and negative emotions, they will likely be able to learn and become reliable in using SPAFF.

Data collection for both the SPAFF and the Triadic Interaction Coding System (TICS) are virtually identical. Thus, this process is described in a combined data collection section following the description of the TICS below.

Results

SPAFF has been used for a variety of purposes across many studies. Although it has been used most extensively to capture emotional communication during conflict discussions, it has also been used to examine everyday conversations and positive conversations in marriages (Gottman & Levenson 1999; Gottman *et al.* 2003*a*). In addition, it has been employed with parent–child and sibling interactions (Gottman 1994; Shortt &

Gottman 1997). It has been used for examining specific affects by assigning weights to each affect and grouping positive and negative coding together (Gottman 1994; Gottman *et al.* 1999), and has been used both inside and outside of our laboratory (Dufore 2000). Summaries of a small selection of studies utilizing SPAFF coding are presented below.

A study predicting martial happiness and stability in newlyweds used SPAFF coding of conflict discussions to examine several types of process models of marriage (Gottman *et al.* 1998). The models explored were:

- anger as a dangerous emotion;
- active listening as important for the marriage;
- negative affect reciprocity;
- negative wife start-up;
- husband physiological soothing;
- de-escalation.

Results did not support an active listening model, a negative affect reciprocity model, or a model that posits that anger is a dangerous emotion. Indeed, this research revealed that anger does not appear to have any negative outcomes longitudinally, provided that the anger is not blended with other negative emotions such as contempt, domineering, or belligerence. Active listening exchanges rarely occurred and were not predictive of differential marital outcomes, and reciprocation of high-level negative affect did not predict marital instability or unhappiness

Support was found for the negative wife start-up, positive affect, de-escalation, and physiological soothing models tested. Specifically, harsh start-up by the wife, absence of de-escalation on the part of either the husband or the wife, lack of physiological soothing of the husband, and the husband rejecting his wife's influence all predicted divorce. Marital satisfaction was predicted with 80% accuracy, and divorce with 83% accuracy (Gottman *et al.* 1998). Through the use of SPAFF, this research identified specific affects that were problematic, such as anger. Additionally, the sequential nature of the coding enabled the researchers to examine dynamics of the conflict discussion such as how the discussion was started and whether or not influence was accepted by the partner.

The ability of SPAFF to capture the dynamics in couples with abusive relationships was illustrated by a 1996 study examining the longitudinal course of these relationships (Jacobson *et al.* 1996). Again, coding from marital conflict discussions was used to predict the course of the marriage. This study revealed that husbands who tended to be highly domineering, emotionally abusive, and globally negative during their initial visit tended to remain severally abusive if they were still married two years after their initial visit to our laboratory.

The utility of the SPAFF across populations is illustrated by a study conducted by Shortt to examine the closeness of sibling relationships (Shortt & Gottman 1997). Adult siblings were videotaped while having both a conflict discussion and a discussion of an enjoyable nature. This study revealed that close sibling relationships were characterized by empathy as well as overall higher positive affect and fewer power struggles.

Finally, we have used SPAFF coding in conjunction with non-linear dynamic modeling to describe the dynamics of the couple's relationship and to predict relationship success (Gottman *et al.* 1999, 2002). The advantages of using mathematical modeling are:

- this approach provides a new language for thinking about the changing dynamics of the couple's interaction over time;
- once a model has been created for the marriage, it can be used to simulate a variety of situations to test the model and the corresponding theory (Cook *et al.* 1995);
- the parameters yielded from modeling each couple's interaction provides valuable information about the quality of the couple's relationship and has the potential to inform clinicians, as well as researchers, about what type of intervention is needed to help couples improve their relationships.

SPAFF coding can be analyzed through the use of non-linear mathematical modeling which assigns theoretically based weights to each code such that there is a numerical value for each time. These numerical codes can then be analyzed using a model we have developed specifically to describe marriage. This technique was used in a study to predict divorce in a sample of newlyweds. Factors that predicted divorce were:

- both husband and wife having more negative predispositions, or uninfluenced steady states;
- husbands being influenced negatively by their wives, or having more negative-influenced steady states;
- having a lower negativity threshold, or having a lower tolerance to negativity before a change in affect is seen (Gottman & Levenson 1999).

Future research

In theory, the SPAFF should be generalizable across cultures, with the stipulation that the coder is a cultural informant for the culture he/she is coding. This is necessary as the coding system utilizes the physical cues of universal emotional expressions with the judgments of a cultural informant. This premise is supported by the fact that the SPAFF has been successful in describing the interactions of various types of relationships and ethnicities we have attempted to code to date. Further research, however, is needed to confirm the validity of using SPAFF across cultures.

The SPAFF system has been used to code emotions in married heterosexual couples, gay and lesbian couples, parents and children, and adult siblings (Gottman *et al.* 1996*a*, 2003*b*; Shortt & Gottman 1997). It has been used not only to code conflict discussions, but also neutral or positive conversations (Gottman & Levenson 1999). These studies not only support the validity of the SPAFF but also illustrate that the SPAFF codes are generalizable across all of these groups and types of interactions. This summary is based on six different longitudinal studies with a total of 667 married couples. Each of these studies matched the major racial and ethnics groups of the area in which the research was conducted. These samples included a largely Caucasian Midwestern sample, more diverse and representative samples from the Seattle area, and diverse and representative samples from the San Francisco Bay Area. Approximately 30% of the total sample across all six studies was from non-white ethnic groups. Although our sample includes ethnic minorities, we do not make racial distinctions in our summary. This kind of future research would require over-sampling a particular ethnic group to observe differing patterns in couple interactions. Although the ethnic diversity we have been able to include in our samples suggests that the SPAFF coding is generalizable across ethnic groups within the United States, this is an area where further study is needed.

Triadic Interaction Coding System

The Triadic Interaction Coding System (TICS) is designed to index the interactive intent of each member of the mother–father–baby triad across several dimensions to describe the dynamics within families. This particular coding system focuses on the mother–father–baby triad, but could be adapted to capture the dynamics within other triads or larger groups. The mother, father, and baby are coded individually over time for facial affect, direction of gaze, and vocalization. Parents are additionally coded for giving their infant space versus over-stimulating them, and for co-parenting. We will focus on the co-parenting dimension in this chapter because it examines the way partners interact with each other, as well as how they interact with their baby as a couple through nonverbal and verbal behavior. Understanding how couples respond to each other and their baby in the context of triadic interactions enriches our understanding of their dyadic interactions and, ultimately, the quality of their relationship.

Similar to SPAFF, TICS is a gestalt coding system, which recognizes and categorizes affect through the integration of observed physical features and the specific cultural experiences of the observer. A detailed recognition and categorization of facial, physical, and verbal cues currently known to be associated with interactive intent comprise the physical features used in the TICS. Additionally, coders use their subjective understanding of emotions to help them identify codes of specific affect. This synthesis allows TICS to draw on what is known about emotional expression and an observer's wealth of experience as a social being who was raised with a particular set of family dynamics to enhance and refine their coding ability. Each TICS dimension is a mutually exclusive and exhaustive coding system. Coding is continuous, yielding one code per second to allow for sequential analysis of family interactions.

Background

Social relationships, whether they are romantic, parent–child, or friendships, have all traditionally been studied at the level of the dyad, especially when systematic observational coding is employed. While research of dyadic relationships is important, focusing only on the dyad has limitations. A wealth of research supports a bi-directional relationship between the marital dyad and their child, such that the birth of the first baby tremendously impacts the relationship quality of the parents (Belsky & Pensky 1988; Belsky *et al.* 1983; Cowan & Cowan 1992; Shapiro *et al.* 2000), and marital discord within a family negatively impacts child development (Davies & Cummings 1995; Emery 1982; Gottman & Katz 1989; Rutter 1990).

Despite the historical neglect of research examining the dynamics within the family at the family level, recent research shows how analysis at the family level produces important contributions, enriching our understanding of how the family subsystems influence each other and the family as a whole (Fivaz–Depersinge 1991; Fivaz–Depersinge & Corboz–Warnery 1999). TICS attempts to fill this methodological gap in the study of interactions at the family level—in this case, the mother–father–infant triad, using several dimensions that index each person's interactive intent with respect to the other two family members involved in the interaction.

In 1995, Shapiro and Gottman developed the TICS in an effort to capture the nonverbal and verbal communication of each member of the mother–father–baby triad through a series of coding dimensions. Coding dimensions are designed along a spectrum from positive to negative. Each code can be weighted and summed at each moment in time resulting in one composite code for each moment. Combining dimensions increases variability, which is especially important, since we use non-linear dynamic modeling to examine family dynamics. Multiple coding dimensions enable us to examine aspects of interaction as they relate to each other, such as the relationship between co-parenting and parents' tendency to over-stimulate their baby.

In designing the TICS, Shapiro drew on the Tronick Monadic Phases Coding System,[2] Gottman's SPAFF, Ekman and Friesen's (1978) FACS, and Oster and Rosenstein's Baby FACS (in press). Similar to the Monadic Phases Coding System, TICS coding is done along multiple dimensions that are examined separately, assigned weights, and combined. The facial affect dimension, in particular, draws upon facial AU codes in the FACS and Baby FACS systems. Finally, TICS draws upon SPAFF in utilizing a cultural informant and specific features approach, allowing observers to act as a social expert to make judgments in their coding. A unique aspect of TICS, when compared with coding systems that focus on the behavior of an individual, is the interactive component of the inclusion of the co-parenting and over-stimulation dimensions, making it important to take into account the interactive intent of all family members when coding a specific person. This is particularly true of the co-parenting dimension since co-parenting requires the effort of both parents to coordinate play. For example, an action that may be supportive of a partner in one context (e.g. when the baby is fussy) may be intrusive or competitive in another context, where the baby is actively enjoying the interaction.

The TICS is designed to code mother–father–baby interactions specifically during the Lausanne triadic play paradigm (Corboz–Warney et al. 1993), where parents take turns playing separately and together with their baby, who is in a special infant seat between them. Although TICS was specifically designed for this triadic interaction, it also has the ability to code interactions among a number of family members (i.e. more than three) within diverse settings.

---

[2] The Tronick Monadic Phases Coding System captures aspects of both infant and adult contributions to face-to-face dyadic interaction along a number of dimensions including affect, gaze, and posture. (Tronick, Brazelton and Als, 1982).

Family triad setting

Families participate in Lausanne triadic play (LTP) when their infant is between three and nine months old. In our laboratory, we typically schedule visits with families when their infants are three months old. LTP is a videotaped, semi-structured situation that facilitates the examination of the triad as a whole as well as the organization of its parts (Corboz–Warnery *et al.* 1993). Parents are to play with their infant as naturally as possible in four phases:

1. In the first phase, one parent plays with the infant while the other parent watches.
2. Parents switch roles in the second phase.
3. In the third phase, both parents play with their infant as a threesome.
4. Parents then interact with each other while ignoring the baby as much as possible.

Parents must determine by themselves, who will begin the first phase and how to make the transition from each of the four phases. They are asked to use toys and pacifiers as little as possible during interactions with their infant. Parents also have the prerogative to take breaks as they see fit, if their child becomes upset, and then resume the interaction once they feel ready. Parents sit on chairs that are equidistant from the table with the infant seat attached. Facilitators are not present in the room during the interactions, but may occasionally interrupt sessions when babies are extremely distressed and parents do not take a break of their own accord. In our laboratory, we also hooked each family member up to physiological sensors designed to measure and record electrocardiogram (ECG).

Co-parenting

The co-parenting TICS dimension is designed to capture a couple's ability to co-parent, operationalized/defined as working together and supporting each other during interactions with their infant. The mother and father are coded separately throughout their interaction. This coding dimension is designed to tap the couple's co-parenting both when they are interacting together with their baby (as a threesome), and when one parent is playing with their baby (and their spouse is asked to be 'simply present').

When coding parents playing together with their baby in the third phase, the dimensions are divided into inclusion and exclusion dimensions. The positive codes are inclusion, coordinated play, and complimentary play. The negative codes are exclusion and separate play. The first two phases of LTP are focused on coding the passive partner using the following codes: one positive (supportive), one negative (intrusive), one neutral, and an unscorable code.

Inclusion versus exclusion

The inclusion versus exclusion TICS dimension is coded separately for each parent during a family play interaction that includes both parents and their infant. Although this system is designed to describe parent–infant interactions in which infants are seated in a baby seat between the parents, it can be adapted for other parent–infant or parent–child interactions.

Inclusion is coded any time one parent makes an active effort to include his or her partner in family play. You may observe a verbal explicit invitation or subtle suggestion, or a nonverbal gesture. Examples of this include: the mother saying, 'Let's sing a song that daddy knows'; the father holding one of the baby's arms and handing the mother the other arm; and mother saying, 'Daddy makes great noises, why don't you make some of your noises for us, Daddy?'

Coordinated play is coded when the mother and father appear to be doing the same or very similar things at the same time or, in other words, are coordinated in the way they are playing with their baby. This is one instance where both parents should be coded as coordinated play, since this code implicitly implies involvement by both parents. When watching coordinated play, you may often get the feeling that their movements could have been choreographed, as in a dance, because of the synchrony the parents reflect. Examples of coordinated play include: both parents singing the same song together; both parents doing the same actions to a song; both playing the same game with the baby and taking turns with game actions; and one parent swinging one arm while the parent swings the other arm at the same time (i.e. in synchrony).

Complementary play is coded any time one parent appears to be interacting with their baby and/or partner in a way that supports or compliments what their partner is doing. The actions of the person given this code must appear to be tied into the actions of the other parent in some way for this to be coded. Often one person is more active during complementary play, but it seems clear that the other parent is temporarily taking a more passive role to support his/her partner. Examples of complementary play include: one parent making funny faces at the baby while the other is laughing and commenting on the funny faces; one parent talks to the baby while the other softly strokes the baby; and one parent plays with one of the baby's arms while the other parent plays with the opposite leg (but not doing the same action at the same time, which would be coded as coordinated).

The *neutral* code is the dividing line between coordination with one's partner and competition or withdrawal. This code is typically characterized as being nonemotional in nature and actions that appear outside the goal of the interaction. Care-taking activities such as wiping drool off the baby's face are usually coded neutral because they are usually short, utilitarian, and outside of the playful intent of the interaction. Behaviors that do not fit into any of the other categories in this dimension are also coded as neutral to satisfy the requirement of a mutually exclusive and exhaustive coding system.

Unscoreable is coded whenever the observer cannot tell what is going on in an interaction because they cannot see or hear well enough to make a judgment about it. This is usually due to video or audio problems, and should be treated as missing data during data analysis.

Separate play is coded when the mother and father are both playing with the baby, but in ways that seem completely unrelated. Often this will happen when parents play specific, unrelated games with their baby during dyadic play, and then use those same unrelated games during family play (where both parents are playing with their baby at the same time) without modifying them to include or even compliment their partner. Examples of this include: mother plays a 'zooming in' game while the father wiggles the baby's foot; father does 'wheels on the bus' actions with the baby's legs while the mother talks to the baby and strokes his hand; and the mother attempts to play a peek-a-boo game with the baby while the father is engaging the baby in a tickle game.

Note that, although both parents can be engaging in separate play at the same time, seprate play can be coded for a single parent. For example, one parent may start a new unrelated activity such as a tickle game that would be coded as separate play, while the other parent engages in complimentary play by commenting on the play and withdrawing slightly. In this case, only the second partner would be coded as engaging in complimentary play since the other parent appears to make no effort to compliment or support them, a least at that moment in the play.

Exclusion is coded when one of the parents actively excludes his/her partner, monopolizing the interaction. This can be done either verbally or nonverbally. One common way that one parent will exclude their partner through their posture alone is to lean in close enough to their baby that the other parent can no longer see the baby. Other examples of this code include: mother says, 'Let's play pat-a-cake now' to the baby and takes both of the baby's arms; and the father says 'Yes, Daddy's fun, Mummy isn't' while playing with the baby.

Supportive versus intrusive

The supportive versus intrusive TICS dimension codes only the passive person during each dyadic play phase. For example, the father is coded during the mother–baby play phase when asked to be 'simply present'. Although this coding dimension is designed specifically to examine interactions within the Lausanne triadic play paradigm, it is adaptable for coding a parent in the same room while his/her partner is actively interacting with their baby.

The *supportive* code captures the appreciation and support reflected by the passive parent of their partner's interactions with the baby. Some subtle supportive behaviors include: active watching of the playing dyad; smiling when one's partner is having a successful play experience; making an empathetic face or noise when their partner is having difficulty; or re-directing the baby's attention to their partner if the baby looks at him/her. Other more explicit behaviors are helpful acts such as getting a pacifier that has fallen on the floor so one's partner can use it. All helpful acts are not necessarily supportive, but can sometimes be intrusive. Therefore, observers must act as a cultural informant to judge whether or not the intent of the action is to support or detract from their partner's play experience with their infant.

The *neutral* code is characterized as non-emotional in nature and may seem outside the goal of the interaction. Neutral codes index behaviors that do not fit into any other category in this dimension. Neutral is often coded when the passive parent is visibly not attending to the interaction, evidenced by their looking around the room or filling out questionnaires, and is therefore not supportive or intrusive.

Unscoreable is coded whenever the observer cannot make a judgment about a person's behavior, usually due to video or audio problems, and should be treated as missing data during data analysis.

The passive parent is *intrusive* any time he or she acts in a way to detract from, or intrude upon, the interaction between their partner and baby. Examples of this code include: laughing at an inappropriate time; making remarks about how the other person isn't having a successful experience; making faces or comments to attract the baby's attention away from the parent who is actively playing; and even strongly suggesting playing strategies to the parent who is playing with the baby. Again, observers should distinguish between supportive and intrusive behaviors in helpful acts, paying close attention to actions that detract from the playing/interactive experience of the active parent, which is coded as intrusive. An example of an intrusive behavior is reaching into the dyadic interaction to wipe the baby's mouth. The alternative non-intrusive behavior is handing the drool cloth to the other parent, which is less disruptive and coded supportive.

Training

Each of the TICS dimensions is a mutually exclusive and exhaustive coding system and can be taught separately. We recommend giving each potential observer an overview of all the TICS coding dimensions but, to expedite the process of training and reliability, having each focus on learning only one or two. A general awareness of the TICS dimensions enables observers to more succinctly focus on one coding dimension, rather than attempting to capture all of the diverse interactions occurring during a specific interaction.

Training of observers should emphasize the importance of recognizing physical features that are typically associated with specific emotions, over-stimulation in infants, vocal and verbal cues, and other nonverbal communication. Watching videotape clips of examples of each code taken from family play sessions are a general part of training meetings. Discussion focuses on the videotape clips and a conceptualization of the entire interaction. Videotapes are assigned for independent coding outside of the training meetings.

It is important that TICS observers become familiar with both videos focused on the parents and the infant, and should be trained using videos of both views. In our laboratory, we videotape a view of the infant and one of both parents onto two separate tapes or DVDs that can be viewed either separately or simultaneously through adjacent monitors. It is possible to videotape the parents and the infant together using a split screen, but this had the disadvantage of making each family member appear smaller, making some of the coding more difficult. It is important for observers to note the spatial orientation of all family members in relation to each other, so they can make judgments about when one parent is blocking their partner's view of the baby, or when each person is looking at another's face.

The view of the baby and the parents should be used in training, such that observers become familiar with the best view for coding each dimension and knowing when it is important to watch one view or both views simultaneously. For most TICS dimensions, the best view for coding is the frontal view of the target individual. In the case of the co-parenting and infant over-stimulation dimensions, it is helpful to view the parents and the baby simultaneously so that the nonverbal signals of each family member are considered when making a judgment about the interactive intent of the parent.

One example illustrates this need to view the infant and parents clearly. During the father–infant interaction phase, the mother spent the first two minutes actively watching her husband play with their baby. At one point during this interaction, the mother turned her head to look at her husband, and then away from both her husband and baby, clearly avoiding eye contact. By viewing only the parent view it was unclear as to the intent of the mother turning away from the interaction. After watching the baby view, it was clear that the baby turned towards the mother and smiled, inviting her to join the interaction. The mother, however, mindful that it was her husband's turn to play with the baby, attempted to redirect the baby's attention toward the father by looking directly at him, and then away. In this case, incorporating the parent and baby views provided a more comprehensive understanding of the interaction, revealing that she is trying to be supportive of her husband.

As with SPAFF training, coders should become certified in FACS and familiar with Baby FACS (Oster & Rosenstein, in press) before learning TICS. It also will help sensitize coders to subtle changes in affect and provide a solid base for learning the other vocal and verbal cues that will be integrated with facial information when coding specific affects.

Following the initial training process, observers then must become reliable. Trainees code several tapes alongside an experienced TICS coder, and then a few more tapes on their own. Reliability is determined by achieving a kappa greater than 0.70. Training is complete once a coder has reliably coded five tapes by themselves (for each individual). In order to maintain reliability and prevent coder drift, weekly meetings are set up for reviewing and discussing tapes. Additionally, coders are asked to recode the same family they coded three to four months prior as another check of coder drift.

A TICS training manual is available through our laboratory (Shapiro 1996). Graduate students, staff, undergraduate students, parents, and non-parents can all make excellent TICS coders. The important thing is that the coders are sensitive to people's nonverbal, as well as verbal, cues and can act as socially competent cultural informants about social communication that takes place within families. One difficulty common to beginning coders is the tendency to perceive and report the best in parent's interactions. For example, it is common for a beginning coder to want to categorize a parent who is being enthusiastic with their child but competitive with their spouse as being complimentary in their co-parenting, even though this behavior should be coded as 'separate play'. Explaining to coders that even the best parents usually have instances of separate play and over-stimulation can help observers to get past their initial positive bias and to recognize more negative codes.

As with SPAFF training, we have found that, despite in-depth training, some people simply cannot recognize and categorize some nonverbal communication cues critical to coding the co-parenting dimension, distinguishing between giving space and over-stimulating an infant, and in various types of emotional communication. To ensure that potential coders are sensitive cultural judges, candidates watch a videotape of the type of interaction they will be coding and discuss what they observe with a trained coder. If they can distinguish between basic positive cooperation between parents and competition, they will likely be able to learn and become reliable using the co-parenting dimension of the TICS.

Results

The TICS is a relatively recent coding system, and thus few results are available using this coding system to date. In this section, we summarize one study that uses the TICS coding to examine the dynamics within the mother–father–infant triad. The goal of this study was to examine the impact of marital satisfaction on this triad, the role of the father with respect to the mother and baby in triadic play, and the overall dynamics within the triad through non-linear mathematical modeling (Shapiro *et al.* 1998; Shapiro & Swanson 1999).

An initial sample of 130 couples were recruited within the first nine months of marriage and followed longitudinally. Ten high marital satisfaction and ten low marital satisfaction couples who became parents, chosen based on the Marital Adjustment Test scores (Locke & Wallace 1959), were identified for the current study. Three of these families were eliminated from the study due to short family play sessions, leaving 17 families. These families were invited into our laboratory when their first infant was approximately three months old to participate in LTP (see p. 381). We focused on a phase of LTP in which parents are asked to play together with their baby naturally. The mother, father, and baby in each triad were coded individually over time for facial affect and direction of gaze. Parents were additionally coded for giving their infant space versus over-stimulating them, and for co-parenting with their partner. Codes were assigned weights and summed, resulting in one score for each second. Marital satisfaction was assessed using the Marital Adjustment Test.

The mutual influence of the mother, father, and baby within the triad was examined in two steps. First, the mother–infant interaction was examined through non-linear dynamic modeling when the father was exerting two different types of influence: a relatively positive influence (father's score above his median); and a relatively negative influence (father's score below his median). Then the parameters yielded from the mother–baby model were examined with respect to both marital satisfaction and the father's influence through using repeated measures multivariate analysis of variance (MANOVA).

Results indicated that both marital satisfaction and the role of the father have a significant influence on the overall dynamics in the family triad. Infant affect was significantly more negative both in unhappily married families overall, and when the father's influence was relatively negative. There was also a significant trend for mothers in happily married families to have a more positive baseline affect (or uninfluenced steady state) when their husbands were relatively positive, and unhappily married mothers to have relatively negative baseline affect (or uninfluenced steady state) when their husbands were relatively positive. Thus, happily married mothers are in synchrony with their husbands, while mothers with low marital satisfaction are out of sync with their husbands. This may reflect competition between the parents or enmeshment of one and withdrawal of the other. Babies also had a significantly more negative influence on the mother when the father was relatively negative, without regard to marital satisfaction, and there were also trends in the direction of the mother's affect being more negative when the father was relatively negative that did not reach significance.

Overall, both marital satisfaction and the role of the father have an impact on the mother and baby within the family triad, and thus the family dynamics. It appears to be particularly problematic when there is low marital satisfaction and the father is relatively negative. Fathers and their babies, in particular, appear to be in sync during triadic play. Significant findings relating father and baby affect, but not mother and father affect, in low marital satisfaction families may indicate that parents are more attuned to their baby than to each other during triadic play. Since the relatively negative influence from the father is related to the infant exerting a more negative influence on the mother, parents may influence each other indirectly rather than directly when all three family members are interacting together. Further experimental research is needed to confirm the directions in which the mother, father, and baby influence each other.

Data collection

Both SPAFF and TICS coding, in our laboratory, has traditionally been done in real time using an 'affect wheel' developed by the Instrument Development Lab of the Center for Human Development and Disabilities at the University of Washington and supporting computer software developed by Catherine Swanson, in our laboratory, specifically for this purpose.

Coders first do a preparatory viewing of the interaction they are planning to code to familiarize them with the couple and their conversation or the family and their play session. The supporting computer program is started, and coders sit in front of their own video monitor and the dial that we call an 'affect wheel' (see Figure 10.1). A template that reflects either SPAFF codes or any of the five TICS dimensions can be used with this 'affect wheel' set-up. While watching the videotape, observers code each spouse or family member separately by turning the affect wheel dial which, in turn,

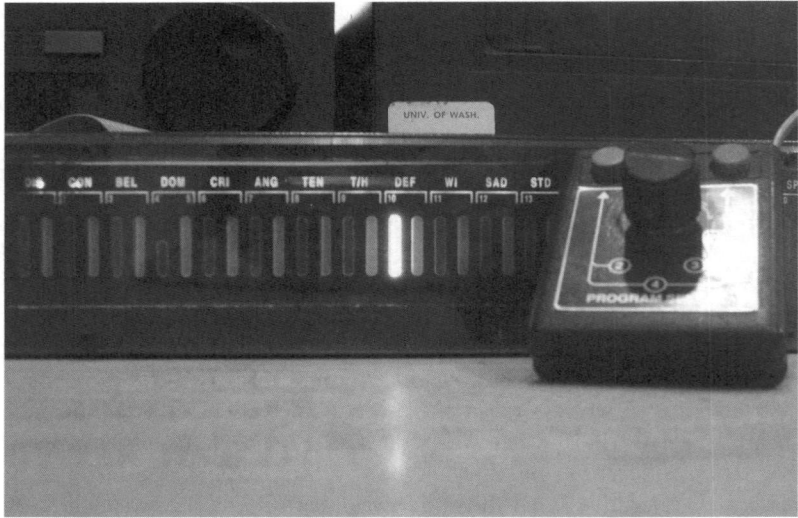

Figure 10.1 Each column on the Specific Affect (SPAFF) Coding Wheel shown in this picture refers to a specific positive, negative, or neutral affect. Only one column or affect may be selected at a time. While illuminated, SPAFF information is collected second-by-second.

changes a light display on a panel that is labeled with each SPAFF or TICS code (depending on which template is being used). Each change in the position of the display reflects a change in code. The code indicated on the display is automatically entered into the computer through the affect wheel, preventing data entry errors, as well as saving data entry time.

This system for collecting data allows codes to be recorded sequentially and records the duration of each code. These coding stations are equipped with dual monitors and 'affect wheel dials', allowing two users to enter codes simultaneously on their ownkeyboards while viewing the same interaction on separate monitors. This increases our coding efficiency and allows coders to check their reliability at the end of each session they code. We calculate reliability for both SPAFF and TICS using the kappa programs designed by Catherine Swanson. This Kappa program is not available outside of our lab.

The entire coding process described here takes as little as 45 minutes for SPAFF coding. That includes 15 minutes for the initial viewing of a conflict discussion, and an additional 15 minutes to code each spouse. TICS coding requires substantially more time than SPAFF coding because each family play interaction must be coded for each coding dimension for each target person you code. Deciding to use only specific TICS dimensions can cut down coding time. Coding a 30-minute family play session using only the TICS co-parenting dimension takes as little as one and a half hours. We also believe that this real-time coding is theoretically sound as emotions in the real world are communicated in real time rather than slow motion.

Two coders independently code each interaction to ensure reliability whenever possible, and at least 25% of our interactions are always coded. In our laboratory, coders can code either at separate times or simultaneously, so that they can instantly check their reliability using a kappa program. To ensure that coding is reliable for sequential analysis, we need to demonstrate that observes are coding the same affect at the same time. We use a three to five second window in the confusion matrix from which the kappa is calculated for this purpose. This means that a code is considered as being coded reliably if the second rater records the same code, plus or minus one to two seconds (plus or minus one second for the three-second window, and plus or minus two seconds for the five-second window). If the coders have a kappa of 0.6 or above, the coding file is kept for later analysis. If the coders were not able to obtain a kappa of 0.6 or above, however, that interaction is re-coded by a different set of coders.

Although we currently do SPAFF and TICS coding exclusively in real time, SPAFF has been used in many ways. It has been used for coding with only audiotapes, as well as with videotapes. Initially, verbatim transcripts were used as a coding tool, and the coding was done on paper and later entered into a computer. This system worked well and yielded good reliability, but it took 25 hours on average to code a 15-minute discussion. SPAFF coding has also been done without transcripts using a computer-assisted coding station designed by the James Long Company.[3] Similar to our affect wheel system, this system allows for continuous coding and automates the timing such

---

[3] James Long software and hardware can be obtained from: James Long Company, 45 Woodland Road, Bedford Hills, NY 10207–1713; tephone (518) 835–3734. This software is very general and could be used for any observational coding system.

that the code entered into the computer is synchronized with the corresponding point on the video to which the computer is connected. This allowed for computing duration of codes as well as recording the sequence of codes, which makes the use of diverse statistics, including sequential analysis and non-linear dynamic modeling, possible. The use of this system for coding and recording the SPAFF also speeded up the coding, making it about 75% faster than the older system using transcripts, whilst coding reliability remained reasonable. This hardware and software is available through the James Long Company.

Psychophysiological assessment of committed relationships

As previously discussed in this chapter, the SPAFF coding system focuses on specific affective behavior that occurs during a 15-minute conflict discussion in couples. While SPAFF provides a unique perspective from which to approach the study of dynamic interactions of couples, an equally unique and complementary aspect of interaction to consider is each person's physiology. Psychophysiological data is a window into the inner world of each person's experience and how they internally respond to each other during conflict. Similar to SPAFF, physiological data is sampled second by second. SPAFF coding and physiological data are synchronized, starting and ending at the same time. The synchronization of data collection allows us to later line up these two streams of data, matching their behavior as coded by SPAFF and their physiological experience of these behaviors.

A multi-method approach for understanding couples interaction is necessary, since research consistently supports the relationship between behavior and physiology. Integrating psychophysiological information into our study of interactions is vital to a comprehensive understanding of the dynamics in committed relationships. Porges and his associates (1994, 1996) demonstrated that a variable called 'vagal tone', which is commonly measured by respiratory sinus arrhythmia (RSA), is highly correlated with attention and self-regulatory processes in children. Different styles of emotion regulation such as cognitive reappraisal and emotional suppression are also associated with effective interpersonal functioning, such that emotional suppression is related to poorer interpersonal functioning (Gross & John 2003). Additional research on affect regulation examined the effects of suppressing emotional displays induced by film, suggesting that physiological responses are heightened by suppression, showing a direct and specific linkage between behavior and physiology (Gross & Levenson 1993, 1997).

Background

Since behavior and physiology are consistently observed to have a bi-directional relationship, it is important to incorporate physiology for a thorough understanding of dynamic interactions within committed relationships. Gottman began implementing psychophysiological methodology in his early research of dyadic relationships looking at parent–child and child–peer interactions. The integration of psychophysiological measures allowed for a more comprehensive understanding of the mechanisms involved in social and emotional development of children. Research continues to support the predictive validity of vagal tone and a child's social and emotional development (Calkins 1997; Gottman & Katz 1995; Gottman *et al.* 1996*a*; Porges *et al.* 1994, 1996).

Vagal tone is a measure of vagus nerve functioning. The vagus nerves the tenth cranial nerve of the parasympathetic nervous system, located in the medulla and consisting of afferent and efferent fibers that innervate a number of autonomic systems throughout the body. Specifically, these fibers innervate the heart at the sinoatrial node, which mediates heart rate. While there is no direct way to measure vagal tone, RSA (the ebbing and flowing of blood flow in the heart) serves as a commonly used indirect measure of vagal functioning (Doussard–Roosevelt & Porges 1999). Research in the area of emotion regulation, child development, and psychophysiological research continues to support the use of RSA as the most accurate measure of vagal tone, but with some controversy (Beauchaine 2001).

Gottman continued his exploration of the intricacies of vagal tone and emotion regulation and competency by administering a Meta-Emotion Interview (Katz & Gottman 1991) to parents and collecting psychophysiological data. The Meta-Emotion Interview assessed how parents' thoughts and feelings about emotions affected parental socialization. Gottman identified a form of parental socialization, which he termed 'emotion coaching', that seemed to mediate vagal tone functioning and emotional and social development in children (Gottman *et al.* 1996*a*, 1997). Emotion coaching consists of a number of components: an awareness of low-intensity emotions in themselves and their children; viewing the negative emotions as an opportunity for intimacy or teaching; validating the child's emotions; labeling the child's emotions; and problem solving with the child; as well as setting limits on the behavior (Gottman *et al.* 1996*a*).

In an effort to understand parent–child relationships and the family system more fully, Gottman expanded his scope of research to encompass an assessment of the parent's relationship satisfaction and stability and its effects on child development. A multi-method approach, incorporating SPAFF and psychophysiological data, was implemented to study couples' interactions during conflict resolution and its association with relationship satisfaction and stability. The inextricable link between behavior and physiology as it relates to interactions is consistently seen in the literature. When attempting to suppress emotions, especially negative ones, individuals become more physiologically aroused and have less functional interpersonal connections (Gross & Levenson 1993; Gross & John 2003). Suppression of emotion is also associated with disrupting communication (Butler *et al.* 2003). During conflict discussions, partners both express and suppress a variety of emotions. These interactions are comprised of interspersed behavioral responses to their partner, as well as voluntary and involuntary affective displays. Psychophysiological research quantifies individual physiological reactions to their partner's behavior.

Studying psychophysiology allows us to assess overall autonomic arousal, and specifically identify parasympathetic versus sympathetic activation. This behavioral and physiological integrative method provides an opportunity for us to examine the intricacies of relationship dynamics. Physiological assessment is the window to the inner world of individuals during conflict. We are able to assess the degree to which individuals engage or withdraw from conflict in reaction to feeling physiologically stressed, and determine whether individuals are able to soothe themselves and their partner whilst in the midst of conflict. Therefore, specific and diverse psychophysiological measures of autonomic nervous system activation during conflict provide a vast array of information that enhances our comprehension of behavior and relationship dynamics.

Equipment and software

There are a variety of psychophysiological software packages and equipment to select from, depending on the specific research question. The following physiological channels are collected using BIOPAC equipment[4], and allow us to distinguish between sympathetic and parasympathetic functioning of the autonomic nervous system, deriving specific indices such as vagal tone: electrocardiogram, impedence, respiration, skin conductance, finger pulse transit time, and amplitude.

BIOPAC provides a MINDWARE software program that converts the signals received into a viewable format on the computer screen for each individual. All physiological channels (i.e. one channel for ECG for one partner) for each person will be displayed, allowing you to run a signal test ensuring that each person's signal is clear prior to initiating data collection. The amount of physiological data collected for each person may vary in the number of channels, length, or types of physiology you collect.

While collecting physiological data in the laboratory is ideal, there are times when going to the study participant's home may make the difference between the individual or couple participating in the study or not. In such cases, portable units manufactured by J and J Engineering are used.[5] These units are capable of collecting the same physiological measures (e.g. electrocardiogram, skin conductance) and are incredibly portable and convenient, requiring a laptop and a small bin containing the converter box, leads, and electrode kit.

Results

Integrating physiological assessments with the SPAFF coding system in the study of couples' interactions has produced a wealth of information, adding to our comprehensive understanding of the dynamics within couples. By assessing general physiological arousal in marital couples, Levenson and Gottman (1983) discriminated between distressed and non-distressed couples, such that distressed couples were characterized by overall physiological arousal and physiological linkage.

Physiological linkage consisted of comparing each partner's heart rate (ECG), skin conductance, and respiration. The more closely these somatic measures of each person's physiology mirrored each other, the more physiologically linked they were, and the more distressed they were as a couple. Physiological linkage alone accounted for 60% of the variance in relationship satisfaction. Additionally, higher levels of physiological

---

[4] BIOPAC Systems Inc. may be contacted at: 42 Aero Camino, Santa Barbara, CA 93117; telephone (805) 685–0066. Further information about BIOPAC Systems may be obtained at: www.biopac.com

[5] J and J Engineering Inc. may be contacted at: 22797 Holgar Ct. NE, Poulsbo, WA.

arousal before and during conflict are highly predictive of declines in marital satisfaction over a three-year period (Levenson & Gottman 1985; Gottman & Levenson 1992).

Interestingly, research of same-sex committed relationships suggests that higher levels of general physiological arousal are indicative of more satisfied couples, and less satisfied couples tend to be less aroused during conflict discussions (Gottman *et al*, 2003*a*; Levenson & Gottman 1985). These results suggest a fundamental difference between same-sex committed relationships and heterosexual married couples and indicate that much could be learned from the further study of same-sex couple dynamics.

While research comparing same-sex and heterosexual married couples using questionnaires has consistently found that heterosexual, gay male, and lesbian couples are very similar in levels of satisfaction, quality, and commitment in their relationships, the active mechanisms involved were not identified (Blumstein & Schwartz 1983; Kurdek 2003; Kurdek & Schmitt 1986; Peplau & Cochran 1990). Implementing our multi-method approach to further understand these dynamics, results indicated that while relationship satisfaction was similar across groups, same-sex couples were much more effective in their communication during conflict. Same-sex couples started their discussions about an area of disagreement more positively and continued these discussions with more affection and humor than heterosexual married couples, and with less negative affect such as belligerence (Gottman *et al.* 2003*b*). These specific behavioral and physiological differences suggest that further investigation of the specific mechanisms driving these interactions may provide beneficial information to help all committed relationships, regardless of sexual orientation.

Future directions/implications

While including psychophysiological assessment in research is difficult, especially if constrained by financial and staff resources, it provides a vast amount of knowledge and a unique perspective from which to approach and study dyadic interaction. We have primarily presented research focused on romantic relationships, yet these psychophysiological procedures may be useful in a variety of studies that assess the dynamics of other relationships such as friendships, parent–child, and parent–child–sibling interactions.

Psychophysiological assessment, while not a specific nonverbal behavioral coding system, is a measure that truly complements the information derived from the SPAFF or TICS coding systems. The exceptional quality of these two coding systems is that they do not focus merely on a specific mode of expression, but rather a variety of modalities, which offers an understanding of how, in combination, they function as one coherent system. SPAFF and TICS truly assess behavior in context.

Another advantage of using SPAFF or TICS, or collecting psychophysiology, is that these methods resolve the potential problem of common method variance, which plagues purely self-report studies. As reviewed in the research presented in this chapter, implementation of nonverbal behavioral coding systems surveys an array of factors influencing behavior. This sets the stage for building stronger theory from which more novel and innovative questions can be developed.

Advancements in technology have also contributed greatly to our ability to successfully develop, implement, and analyze data from studies that assess nonverbal behavior.

The diversity of information now available through nonverbal behavioral coding systems, and the technology to collect this information, affords us the opportunity to formulate more complicated, interesting, and possibly more accurate theories. In whichever population or type of relationship being studied, the implementation of behavioral and psychophysiological components will provide essential information that will assist in developing a comprehensive understanding of active mechanisms involved in these relationships. With greater accessibility to nonverbal behavioral coding systems and psychophysiological equipment, the implementation of more complex multi-method research is encouraged, which can only help to advance/improve/develop future research and our understanding of human behavior.

References

Beauchaine, T. (2001). Vagal tone, development and Gray's motivational theory: toward an integrated model of autonomic nervous system functioning in psychopathology. *Development and Psychopathology*, **13**, 183–214.

Belsky, J. & Pensky, E. (1988). Marital change across the transition to parenthood. *Marriage and Family Review*, **12**, 133–56.

Belsky, J., Spanier, G., & Rovine, M. (1983). Stability and change in a marriage across the transition to parenthood. *Journal of Marriage and the Family*, **45**, 567–77.

Blumstein, P. & Schwartz, P. (1983). *American couples: money, work, sex*. New York: Pocket Books.

Butler, E.A., Egloff, B., Wilhelm, F.H., Smith, N.C., Erickson, E.A., & Gross, J.J. (2003). The social consequences of expressive suppression. *Emotion*, **3**, 48–67.

Calkins, S.D. (1997). Cardiac vagal tone indices of temperamental reactivity and behavioral regulation in young children. *Developmental Psychobiology*, **31**, 125–35.

Cook, J., Tyson, R., White, J., Rushe, R., Gottman, J., & Murray, J. (1995). Mathematics of marital conflict: qualitative dynamic mathematical modeling of marital interaction. *Journal of Family Psychology*, **9**, 110–30.

Corboz–Warney, A., Fivaz–Depersinge, E., Bettens, C.G., & Favez, N. (1993). Systemic analysis of father–mother—baby interactions: the Lausanne Triadic Play. *Infant Mental Health Journal*, **14**, 298–316.

Cowan, C.P. & Cowan, P.A. (1992). *When partners become parents*. New York: Basic Books.

Davies, P.T. and Cummings, E.M. (1995) Marital conflict and child adjustment: an emotional security hypothesis. *Psychological Bulletin*, **116**, 387–411.

Doussard–Roosevelt, J.A. & Porges, S.W. (1999). The role of neurobehavioral organization in stress responses: a polyvagal model. In *Soothing and stress* (ed. M. Lewis & D. Ramsay), pp. 57–76. Mahwah, NJ: Lawrence Erlbaum Associates.

Dufore, D.S. (2000). Marital similarity, marital interaction and couple shared view of their marriage. *Dissertations Abstracts*.

Ekman, P. & Friesen, W.V. (1975). *Unmasking the face: a guide to recognizing emotions from facial clues*. Palo Alto, CA: Prentice-Hall.

Ekman, P. & Friesen, W.V. (1978). *Facial Action Coding System*. Palo Alto, CA: Consulting Psychologist Press.

Emery, R.E. (1982). Interparental conflict and the children of discord and divorce. *Psychological Bulletin*, 92, 310–30.

Fivaz–Depersinge, E. (1991). Documenting a time-bound circular view of hierarchies: a micro-analysis of parent–infant dyadic interaction. *Family Process*, 30, 1010–120.

Fivaz–Depersinge, E. and Corboz–Warnery, A. (1999). *The primary triangle: a developmental systems view of mothers, fathers, and infants*. New York: Basic Books.

Gottman, J.M. (1979). *Marital interaction: experimental investigations*. New York: Academic Press.

Gottman, J.M. (1994). *What predicts divorce? The relationship between marital processes and marital outcomes*. Hillsdale, NJ: Lawrence Erlbaum Associates.

Gottman, J.M. & Katz, L.F. (1989). The effects of marital discord on young children's peer interaction and health. *Developmental Psychology*, 25, 373–81.

Gottman, J.M. & Katz, L.F. (1995). Vagal tone protects children from marital conflict. *Development and Psychopathology*, 7, 83–92.

Gottman, J.M. & Levenson, R.W. (1992). Marital processes predictive of later dissolution: Behavior, physiology, and health. *Journal of Personality and Social Psychology*, 63, 221–33.

Gottman, J.M. & Levenson, R.W. (1999). What predicts change in marital interaction over time? A study of alternative models. *Family Process*, 38, 143–58.

Gottman, J.M., Coan, J., Carrere, S., & Swanson, C. (1998). Predicting marital happiness and stability from newlywed interactions. *Journal of Marriage and the Family*, 60, 1–18.

Gottman, J.M., Katz, L.F., & Hooven, C. (1996a). Parental meta-emotion philosophy and the emotional life of families: theoretical models and preliminary data. *Journal of Family Psychology*, 10, 1–26.

Gottman, J.M., Katz, L.F., & Hooven, C. (1997). *Meta-emotion: how families communicate emotionally*, pp. 214–26. Mahwah, NJ: Lawrence Erlbaum Associates.

Gottman, J.M., Levenson, R.W., Gross, J., Fredrickson, B.L., McCoy, K., Rosenthal, L., *et al.* (2003a). Correlates of gay and lesbian couples' relationship satisfaction and relationship dissolution. *Journal of Homosexuality*, 45, 23–43.

Gottman, J.M., Levenson, R.W., Swanson, C., Swanson, K., Tyson, R., & Yoshimoto, D. (2003b). Observing gay, lesbian and heterosexual couples' relationships: mathematical modeling of conflict interaction. *Journal of Homosexuality*, 45, 65–91.

Gottman, J., McCoy, K., Coan, J., & Collier, H. (1996). The specific affect coding system (SPAFF) for observing emotional communication in marital and family interaction. In J. H. Gottman (Ed.), What predicts divorce: The measures. Nahwah, NJ: Lawrence Erlbaum Associates.

Gottman, J.M., Murray, J.D., Swanson, C.C., Tyson, R., & Swanson, K.R. (2002). *The mathematics of marriage: dynamic nonlinear models*. Cambridge, MA: MIT Press.

Gottman, J., Swanson, C., & Murray, J. (1999). The mathematics of marital conflict: dynamic mathematical nonlinear modeling of newlywed marital interaction. *Journal of Family Psychology*, 13, 13–19.

Gottman, J.M., Woodin, E.M., & Coan, J.A. (1998). *Specific affect coding system manual, 20-code version (4.0)*. Unpublished laboratory manual.

Gross, J.J. & John, O.P. (2003). Individual differences in two emotion regulation processes: implications for affect, relationships, and well-being. *Journal of Personality and Social Psychology*, 85, 348–62.

Gross, J.J. & Levenson, R.W. (1993). Emotional suppression: physiology, self-report, and expressive behavior. *Journal of Personality and Social Psychology*, **64**, 970–86.

Gross, J.J. & Levenson, R.W. (1997). Hiding feelings: the acute effects of inhibiting negative and positive emotion. *Journal of Abnormal Psychology*, **106**, 95–103.

Hetherington, E.M., Cox, M., & Cox, R. (1982). Effects of divorce on parents and children. In *Nontraditional families* (ed . M. Lam), pp. 233–88. Hillsdale, NJ: Lawrence Erlbaum Associates.

Hooven, C., Gottman, J.M., & Katz, L.F. (1995). Parental meta-emotion structure predicts family and child outcomes. *Cognition and Emotion*, **9**, 229–64.

Jacobson, N.S., Gottman, J.M., Gortner, E., Berns, S., & Shortt, J.W. (1996). Psychological factors in the longitudinal course of battering: when do the couples split up? When does the abuse decrease? *Violence & Victims*, **11**, 371–92.

Katz, L.F. & Gottman, J.M. (1991). *The meta-emotion interview*. Unpublished manuscript, University of Washington, Department of Psychology. Seattle, WA.

Kurdek, L.A. (2003). Differences between gay and lesbian cohabiting couples. *Journal of Social and Personal Relationships*, **20**, 411–36.

Kurdek, L.A. & Schmitt, J.P. (1986). Relationship quality of partners in heterosexual married, heterosexual cohabiting, and gay and lesbian relationships. *Journal of Personality and Social Psychology*, **51**, 711–20.

Levenson, R.W. & Gottman, J.M. (1983). Marital interaction: physiological linkage and affective exchange. *Journal of Personality and Social Psychology*, **45**, 587–97.

Levenson, R.W. & Gottman, J.M. (1985). Physiological and affective predictors of change in relationship satisfaction. *Journal of Personality and Social Psychology*, **49**, 85–94.

Locke, H.J. & Wallace, K.M. (1959). Short marital-adjustment and prediction tests: their reliability and validity. *Marriage and Family Living*, **21**, 251–5.

Martin, T.C. & Bumpass, L. (1989). Recent trends in marital disruption. *Demography*, **26**, 37–51.

Oster, H. & Rosenstein, D. (in press). *Baby FACS: analyzing facial movement in infants*. Palo Alto, CA.

Peplau, L.A. & Cochran, S.D. (1990). A relationship perspective on homosexuality. In *Homosexuality/heterosexuality: concepts of sexual orientation* (ed. D.P. McWhirter, S.A. Sanders, & J.M. Reinisch). New York: Oxford University Press.

Porges, S.W., Doussard–Roosevelt, J.A., Portales, A.L., & Greenspan, S.I. (1996). Infant regulation of the vagal 'brake' predicts child behavior problems: a psychobiological model of social behavior. *Developmental Psychobiology*, **29**, 697–712.

Porges, S.W., Doussard–Roosevelt, J.A., Portales, A.L., & Suess, P.E. (1994). Cardiac vagal tone: stability and relation to difficultness in infants and 3-year-olds. *Developmental Psychobiology*, **27**, 289–300.

Rutter, M. (1990). Psychosocial resilience and protective mechanisms. In *Risk and protective factors in the development of psychopathology* (ed. R.J. Rold, A.S. Masten, D. Cicchetti, *et al.*), pp. 181–214. Cambridge, England: Cambridge University Press.

Shapiro, A.F. (1996). *The Triadic Interaction Coding System*. Unpublished laboratory manual. University of Washington, Department of Psychology, Seattle, WA.

Shapiro, A.F. & Swanson C. (1999). *The role of the father in the dynamics of the mother–father–infant triad*. Society for Research in Child Development, Albuquerque, NM.

Shapiro, A.F., Gottman, J.M., & Carrère, S. (2000). The baby and the marriage: identifying factors that buffer against decline in marital satisfaction after the first baby arrives. *Journal of Family Psychology,* **14,** 59–70.

Shapiro, A.F. Gottman, J.M., Lubkin, S., Tyson, R., & Swanson, C. (1998). *The influence of the marital relationship on interactions within the mother–father–baby triad.* International Society for the Study Behavioral Development, Bern, Switzerland.

Shortt, J.W. & Gottman, J.M. (1997). Closeness in young adult sibling relationships: affective and physiological processes. *Social Development,* **6,** 142–64.

Sigle–Rushton, W. & McLanahan, S. (2002). The living arrangements of new unmarried mothers. *Demography,* **39,** 415–33.

Tronick, E., Brazelton, T.B., and Als, H. (1982). Monadic phases: A structural descriptive analysis of infant-mother face to face interaction. *Merrill-Palmer Quarterly,* **26,** 3–24.

Weiss, R.L. (1980). Strategic behavioral marital therapy: toward a model for assessment and intervention. In *Advances in family intervention, assessment theory, Vol. 1* (ed. J.P. Vincent), pp. 229–71). Greenwich, CT: JAI press.

CHAPTER 11

MACROVARIABLES IN AFFECTIVE EXPRESSION IN WOMEN WITH BREAST CANCER PARTICIPATING IN SUPPORT GROUPS

JANINE GIESE–DAVIS, KAREN ALTREE PIEMME, CAROLINE DILLON, AND SUZANNE TWIRBUTT

The goals of this chapter are to present a rationale and methodology for closely examining emotional expression and verbal narratives from videotape of group therapy sessions. Emotional expression is often assumed to be a mechanism necessary for change processes to take place in therapy (Greenberg 1993), though change in emotional expression is rarely documented or tested as an outcome variable (Giese–Davis *et al.* 2002*b*).

Although many of the techniques we present for coding group therapy would be generalizable across populations and settings, our design was implemented to study breast cancer support groups in particular. Empirical evidence about the role of emotional expression in breast cancer survival has accumulated over many years, and provides a justification for the careful study we have designed. We will begin with a general discussion of behavioral research on group therapy and the rationale and hypotheses that have generated our particular study of emotion in breast cancer support groups. We will then proceed to describe our methodology for coding these naturally occurring groups, to present some sample data from our work, and to offer the emotion coding and verbal narrative definitions we use for coding in Appendix 1 and 2.

Coding emotional expression in group sessions

Research on groups began in the late 1800s, and by the 1930s included behavioral observation (Hare 1976). Many observational coding systems evolved for examining specific group behavior, group dynamics, and group process, with perhaps the most well-known early coding system being the Bales system (Bales 1950, 1983). This system allowed coding of who acts, toward whom, whether it is an action or a nonverbal expression, the direction of the action, description of the behavior, and the image visualized by the actor (image of self, other, group, etc.). Although the Bales system was very thorough in describing group processes, it did not focus on specific emotional expressions. It was used to study many different kinds of group settings and was followed by the development of so many different coding schemes that, today, few studies have replicated their use in small group research (Trujillo 1986).

Observational research on group therapy has also included many coding schemes. Nine process coding systems described in a recent publication summarizing successful process evaluations underestimates the number available (Beck & Lewis 2000*a,b*). Coding of emotional expression using videotape, audiotape, or transcripts of group therapy sessions has occurred in a number of studies, but previous coding of emotion has never allowed a frame by frame analysis. Some examples include:

- the coding of hostility/affection (Cytrynbaum 2000);
- hostility/support (Lewis *et al.* 2000);
- positive–negative statements (Davis *et al.* 2000);
- affirmation (Marziali 2000);
- congruence between affect and content (Simon & Agazarian 2000);
- hate–love (Benjamin 2000);
- levels of anxiety using the Gottschalk–Gleser text analysis method (Gottschalk & Gleser 1969) examining transcriptions (Grabhorn 1998);
- expression versus suppression of feelings (Farrell 1976);
- therapist ratings of inadequate or adequate emotional expression (Flowers & Booraem 1991);
- hostility, affection, depression, anxiety, happiness (Koch 1983);
- emotional tone from transcriptions (Budman *et al.* 1993);
- presence and intensity of love, joy, surprise, anger, sadness, or fear (Rosner *et al.* 2000).

Unlike this previous research, our choice of the Specific Affect Coding System (SPAFF; Gottman 1995) has allowed us to code specific emotion categories across a wide range of natural behavior and emotions. The coding categories of SPAFF closely matched our hypotheses to be discussed later in this chapter. In combination with the James Long System (JLC) (a hardware/software link between the computer and VCR), our system allows us to sample continuous data at the frame by frame level of analysis and to output the duration of emotional expression data that was important to our hypotheses.

Coding emotional expression in supportive–expressive (SET) groups

We began our current studies using SPAFF (Gottman 1995) to code emotional expression in breast cancer support groups. Our research was based on a long history of speculation about the role of expression in cancer progression. The goal of coding emotional expression was particularly interesting because of a previous finding that metastatic breast cancer patients randomized to supportive–expressive therapy (SET) group lived significantly longer than those randomized to a control group (Spiegel *et al.* 1989). A main goal of SET is emotional expression.

Our lab group was in the process of conducting an 'attempt to replicate' trial of SET and survival in women with metastatic breast cancer and was videotaping the group sessions (videotape was not available from the 1989 study). SET specifically encourages expression of fear, anger, and sadness and utilizes an existential focus that likely increases emotional and physiological arousal in the therapy room (Spiegel & Classen 2000; Spiegel & Spira 1991). We predicted that change over time in women's emotional expression in SET sessions might be associated with cortisol level, immune function, and survival. We wanted to examine how emotional expression in group sessions related to emotion regulation self-report, and we also wanted to examine the role of emotional expression in social interaction. We predicted that expression of positive and primary negative affect would increase social support both within the group and in the women's daily lives.

As researchers had not coded emotional expression at this level in cancer support groups, we had to invent ways to use the video material available to us in order to accomplish the task. We set up our data so that, in addition to emotional expression, we could study backchanneling responses (i.e. short utterances or phrases that listeners make as someone is talking, such as 'uh-huh', 'oh my', 'wow') to each woman's expression. We also developed a topics coding system so that we could examine topics more likely to enhance the therapeutic process or the range of emotional expression. We also created a narrative coding system to study differences in emotional expression when the women are talking in narrative form ('story coding') compared to talking directly to each other. We present in Appendix 1, the coding definitions for our SPAFF for Breast Cancer and, in Appendix 2, our story coding system.

In this chapter, we use our coding of SET sessions for women with metastatic breast cancer to illustrate our methods. This study is a randomized clinical trial for women with recurrent and metastatic breast cancer (see Giese–Davis *et al.* 2002*b* for complete demographic and medical information). Of 125 women recruited into the study, 64 were randomized to the treatment group and received at least one year of SET, unless they died or dropped out of the group. The goals of the study were to attempt to replicate a prior study with women who had metastatic breast cancer in which researchers found that mood disturbance (Spiegel *et al.* 1981) and pain (Spiegel & Bloom 1983) were significantly decreased, and that survival (Spiegel *et al.* 1989) was significantly extended compared to a nontreatment control group. In the current study from which our data are derived, women were randomized to one of three SET groups over a seven-year rolling enrollment. Women in the control group and the treatment group all received educational materials.

Coding, read-up, and analysis of our coded data takes much time, so we will present data from the number of tapes currently available to us to illustrate our methods. The number of tapes will therefore vary, depending on the point illustrated.

Rationale for the study of emotional expression in breast cancer

Even as early as the second century, Galen observed that women with cancer were more dysphoric, melancholy, and/or emotionally reserved (Galen 1966). Since that time, greater emotional inhibition has been linked empirically with greater incidence and faster progression of cancer (see Giese–Davis & Spiegel 2003; McKenna *et al.* 1999; Spiegel & Kato 1996 for reviews). Most studies have focused on negative emotions, particularly anger, and found that greater anger suppression (Fox *et al.* 1994; Greer & Morris 1975; Greer & Watson 1985), restraint of assertive behavior (Derogatis *et al.* 1979; Goldstein & Antoni 1989; Kune *et al.* 1991), repression (Bahnson 1981; Dattore *et al.* 1980; Hahn & Petitti 1988; McKenna *et al.* 1999), and denial (Bahnson & Bahnson 1969; Derogatis *et al.* 1979; Schonfield 1975) were associated with poorer prognosis. Though some researchers have found null or reverse associations between these constructs and cancer incidence or progression (Greer *et al.* 1979; Persky *et al.* 1987; Watson *et al.* 1999), the most consistent findings involve inhibited or dysregulated emotional expression (Gross 1989) and repression (Giese–Davis & Spiegel 2003).

However, due to methodological and conceptual inconsistencies in these many studies, it remains unclear which emotion regulation styles may be related to physiological vulnerability in cancer patients and whether those styles are related to particular kinds of emotional expression. Because this lack of clarity has hampered researchers' ability to draw firm conclusions, we have sought to distinguish types of emotion regulation and specify types of emotional expression in our research studies with cancer patients. Here, we review the rationale for evaluating emotional expression among cancer patients and present a methodology for reliably doing so.

Are distinctions among emotion regulation constructs clear?

A cancer literature has developed that combines several emotion inhibition constructs under the rubric of the 'type C personality'. This combination was created, in part, due to the lack of evidence about the associations among these constructs and the lack of finely tuned measurement instruments for capturing subtle differences (Greer & Watson 1985; Temoshok 1987). More recently, however, empirical evidence both outside and within the cancer domain has begun to support distinctions (Giese–Davis & Spiegel 2001; King *et al.* 1992) among the awareness or clarity of felt emotions (Salovey *et al.* 1995; Taylor *et al.* 1985; Watson & Clark 1992), suppression of negative emotions (King & Emmons 1991; Pettingale *et al.* 1985; Roger & Nesshoever 1987; M. Watson & Greer 1983), restraint of aggressive or hostile actions (King & Emmons 1991; Roger & Nesshoever 1987; Weinberger & Schwartz 1990), confidence in one's skill with emotional expression (Giese–Davis *et al.* 2004; Kring *et al.* 1994), and repressive defensiveness (Weinberger 1990; Weinberger & Davidson 1994). Greater clarification of the components of the phenomenon and measurement instruments should bring about more careful empirical tests of the role of emotion inhibition in cancer progression.

We demonstrated that the constructs of suppression, repressive defensiveness, restraint of hostility, and distress were separable in a factor analysis utilizing metastatic breast cancer patients enrolled in a randomized trial of SET, and that these emotion inhibition dimensions remained relatively stable over one year in a multi-trait, multi-occasion matrix utilizing the control group (Giese–Davis & Spiegel 2001). We also demonstrated that SET (an emotion-focused group therapy), for metastatic breast cancer patients, significantly reduced suppression while increasing restraint of hostility, though it had a marginal effect on maintaining emotional self-efficacy and did not impact repressive defensiveness (Giese–Davis *et al.* 2002*b*). Though we were able to demonstrate these changes using self-report instruments of emotion regulation, it remains unclear how these constructs relate to observed change over time in emotional expression during group sessions.

There were a number of reasons for examining emotional expression directly in these group sessions. We were interested in testing specific hypotheses about change in emotional expression behavior and how it related to change in emotion regulation constructs. We were also interested in examining the associations between change in specific affective expressions and change in physiological and psychological well-being. Also, we wanted to specify the kind of emotional expression associated with change so that therapists might more readily be trained to recognize this expression and facilitate it in real time. The desire for therapists to be able to recognize these expressions in real time, and the long history of application of SPAFF to natural social interaction, led us to utilize this macrocoding system.

SPAFF as a macrocoding system

Many researchers have explored the role of facial expressions (Ekman & Friesen 1978), voice tone (Scherer 1982, 1988), language (Pennebaker & King 1999; Pennebaker & Stone 2003; Pennebaker *et al.* 2003), and body movements (Hall *et al.* 1995) as separate behavioral channels. We have chosen to study emotional expression in our group therapy setting using SPAFF (Gottman 1995) in which codes are a 'gestalt' (Gottman 1993, p. 484) or combination of these four channels.

SPAFF codes have the added advantage that they can be recognized and coded in (close to) real time. Many coding systems require a few hours of coding for just a few minutes of video. SPAFF coding typically takes about one to three times the number of minutes of video. This real-time aspect of the coding allows us to more readily complete this complex task of coding expression in a group, and it also allows us to more readily transfer what we learn to the training of therapists.

SPAFF is a 'cultural informant' system in which emotion coding categories and thresholds must be modified to reflect the context of the research data. Gottman argues that researchers ought to consider an action emotional 'if in this culture, at this time, cultural informants can reliably tell us that this action means, say 'sadness'' (Gottman 1993, p. 479). With this kind of a coding system, it is important to ensure that the thresholds and affects coded in a given context are not simply transferred from another wholly different context, and that those people most familiar with the context can identify those emotions reliably. In our case, we chose to utilize that SPAFF system, but it had been constructed to assess marital arguments. Cancer support groups generally do not generate the heightened level or intensity of hostility that occur in marital arguments.

Yoshimoto and colleagues (Chapter 10) describe SPAFF as it was developed and utilized to examine marital interaction (Gottman 1995). In their latest 20-code version (Gottman *et al.* 1998), they include 13 negative affect codes: disgust, contempt, belligerence, domineering (with a high- and a low-intensity level), criticism, anger, tension, tense humor, defensiveness, whining, sadness, and stonewalling. They also include neutral and six positive codes: interest, validation (with a high- and a low-intensity level), affection, humor, and surprise/joy. We used extensive piloting to take Gottman's original SPAFF into our breast cancer support group context. In our SPAFF for Breast Cancer modification there are 23 emotion codes. We have elected to summarize these codes into categories of primary negative affect, positive affect, defensive/hostile affect, constrained anger, and neutral in much of our work, to represent the goals and hypotheses of our emotion-focused SET. A complete description of these codes and summary variables will follow the specific hypotheses that generated this study.

Specific SET hypotheses

> I was angry with my friend;
> I told my wrath, my wrath did end.
> I was angry with my foe;
> I told it not, my wrath did grow.
>
> William Blake

> Anger ventilated often hurries toward forgiveness;
> anger concealed often hardens into revenge.
>
> Edward G. Bulwer–Lytton (Baron Lytton)

In our SET model, therapists particularly facilitate the expression of the primary emotions of fear, anger, and sadness (Giese–Davis *et al.* 2002*b*; Spiegel & Classen 2000). These are emotions often felt by these women as they cope with an average prognosis of 18 months to live. Our hypotheses are that, at the individual level, in SET, women will increase the mean duration of expression of primary negative affect. It is also likely that this expression of primary negative affect will be accompanied by a reduction in the mean duration of constrained anger and defensive/hostile affect and an increase in the duration of positive affect over time.

The goals of SET are to facilitate clients' expression of primary emotions so that we can access their cognitive schemas, making them available for restructuring (Foa & Kozak 1986; Greenberg & Foerster 1996) and so that transformation of these emotions can take place allowing cancer patients to make clear choices with their remaining time. A cognitive schema is a cognitive system or way of thinking that helps one to organize and make sense of information. Chronically distressed individuals often have stable and self-defeating schemas that keep them from recovering from depression or trauma. Encouraging expression in the group allows participants to quickly become aware of their distress and the cognitions associated with it. Through expression of underlying primary negative affect and the processing of the thoughts associated with it, transformation of these affective experiences is possible, including a gradual reduction in defensive, hostile, or constrained emotion (Daldrup *et al.* 1994; Greenberg 1993; Greenberg & Webster 1982), greater understanding of self and other (Greenberg & Foerster 1996; Greenberg & Webster 1982; Koch 1983), and reduction of distress or an increase in positive affect (Koch 1983; McCallum *et al.* 1995; Orlinsky & Howard 1986).

These individual goals are also complemented by the interpersonal goals of facilitating support in SET.

In particular, we have been interested in testing whether our therapy lengthens the moments of time women can tolerate sitting with or expressing primary negative affect (i.e. fear, anger, and sadness) in the SET group (Giese–Davis *et al.* 2002*b*; Giese–Davis & Spiegel 2003). Therapists in our groups actively work with clients to allow expression of fear, anger, and sadness. They encourage the women to imagine and express those feelings in the moment, without defensively turning from them so quickly that thera-peutic processing of those emotions in the group cannot occur. From our perspective, it is better for a woman to be able to sit with the expression of fear, anger, and sadness for longer moments in the group and really have a chance to experience, label, express, process, and integrate that emotion while receiving support in the group setting. These moments are really only seconds long. A woman who takes time to express these vulnerable emotions for a long enough duration to allow these therapeutic processes to take place is likely, theoretically, to receive the most therapeutic benefit, even if the expression occurs only a few times in a session. By contrast, a woman who expresses short, frequent moments of the same affect may not receive the same benefit because therapeutic processing is unlikely to take place.

We hypothesize that the ability to sink into those affective expressions for longer moments allows both an individual and a social benefit. The woman herself will be more likely to know and process how she feels, allowing greater decision-making potential to come of this knowledge. It is likely to be more cathartic as well (although no research documents this assertion). In addition, it is more likely that others in her support group or social environment will know how she is feeling and can respond supportively or help with decisions that might be made based on these feelings. Because we are interested in the length of moments of affective expression, as opposed to the total amount of time in session or proportion of time compared with other emotions, we have used the mean duration of a moment of affect as our metric in most of our studies with emotion coding.

Although this metric is correlated with total amount of time talking, and frequency of time talking in a group session, it is a better metric for our studies for several reasons. In addition to the reasons listed above, we do not violate assumptions when using statistical tests that require that one observed variable should not preclude another (Johnson 2002), since it is theoretically possible to have a mean duration of a moment of each affect within a woman's total speaking time in a group session. Also, many studies that can appropriately use frequencies or total durations of SPAFF codes as dependent measures use standardized tasks with set time periods. Because the time each woman speaks in any group session varies considerably ($M = 10.71$, $SD = 5.43$, $R = 3.08$–21.56 minutes per $1\frac{1}{2}$ hour session based on 177 tapes coded for our metastatic study), it is also important, in our context, to use mean duration of affects. Researchers can easily use this type of system when their hypotheses focus, instead, on the metrics of frequency or total duration of emotional expression in groups.

In the next section, we describe the steps we took to transfer the SPAFF coding utilized to study marital conflict to our setting, give background for our summary codes, and specify both the 23 specific codes and summary variables.

Transferring SPAFF to the breast cancer support group context

In order to implement the use of this coding system in a breast cancer support group context, it was necessary to learn SPAFF. In a one-week training workshop (delivered through John Gottman's lab in Seattle), we each learned the Facial Action Coding System (FACS; Ekman & Friesen 1978) codes that form the basis for the facial muscle movement cues, and also learned the voice tone, body movement, and content cues necessary to code reliably. Ekman and Friesen mapped all the muscles of the human face and gave each muscle movement a number or action unit (AU). There are about 15 of these muscle movements that are part of SPAFF codes. All examples of videotape used in this training process were from marital interaction studies. Using videotapes of men and women having a marital dispute, we were trained to see and hear the coding cues (i.e. face, voice, body, and content), and to establish coding thresholds. A coding threshold is the level at which the cues need to be present in order to reliably give the behavior each code. There are many instances in which several of the cues for a particular code will be present briefly (as part of a blend of emotion) or at a low enough level that coders cannot, with assurance, code that affect. Setting these thresholds for coders and keeping them consistent across coders is one of the most difficult tasks of obtaining reliable data. We also hired Gottman's coding trainer to come to Stanford to initially train our first coding cohort.

As discussed earlier, SPAFF is context sensitive. In order to insure that both range of emotion and coding thresholds matched our context, we initially piloted the SPAFF coding thresholds and categories just as they existed in the marital research in Gottman's laboratory at that time (1996). We utilized videotape from a pilot metastatic breast cancer group that had been conducted for a year prior to the start of the randomized 'attempt to replicate' trial of SET. By using the pilot group for development of SPAFF for Breast Cancer, we avoided the research design mistake of inappropriately developing our system to match only the women on whom we would test our hypotheses. We applied this coding system to the speaking turns of 10 women during pilot group sessions. We utilized multiple coders (six) and compared coded segments with Cohen's kappa. We also met as a group and replayed segments of each woman's code and discussed at length how well the coding system, as it existed, matched the affect expression we were seeing. Based on this process, we modified the code in ways that better matched the material. We then conducted a second round of coding 10 women's speaking turns during group sessions (different sessions than in the first phase of piloting).

We began an iterative process of examining kappas, discussing as a group, and honing the definitions of each code until we could all code reliably. We also created example videotapes for each code that presented segments showing each emotion, as well as examples of similar emotional states that would not fit into our coding categories due to being below the threshold or blended with other emotions in which another emotion was dominant.

Coded emotion categories

People who experience a threat to their life often feel strong emotions, but their expression of these strong feelings is often difficult for family members, friends, and social acquaintances to handle well. Many family members or friends unfortunately constrain cancer patients' emotional expression due to their own discomfort (Wortman & Lehman 1985). In our experience, the expression of genuine fear, anger, and sadness often has the paradoxical effect of making the emotion real but transitory, a step to the next emotion rather than a preserved state, more like a storm passing through than chronic overcast. But the constraint of this expression increases both the level and length of distress (Lepore & Helgeson 1998).

Unfortunately, expression through venting or hostile expression, or expressions of overwhelming sadness or fear may lead to emotional isolation of the cancer patient at a time when they really need support (Wortman & Lehman 1985). Research on social rules for emotional displays indicates that often the strongest rules govern the strongest emotions (Gallois 1993) and that it is important not to reveal vulnerability to a possible source of danger (Scherer 1985). People experiencing cancer or other life crises are often the unfortunate recipients of the social stigma related to experiencing and expressing strong vulnerable emotions, and they often believe that to express these feelings in most social contexts may only cause them greater pain (Wortman & Lehman 1985). In support groups, where people are experiencing similar kinds of life crises, it is much safer and more acceptable to express these feelings (Lieberman & Borman 1980).

As an emotion-focused and existential psychotherapy, SET uses the focus on these vulnerable emotions to help women understand and express what touches them most deeply. Group norms support the tolerance of this expression. Therapists encourage women to use the practice and modeling of direct and better-modulated expression in the group to increase effective affect expression with their loved ones and caregivers. We modified Gottman's SPAFF codes to better capture these hypotheses.

Our coding system modification, SPAFF for Breast Cancer, contains 23 coding categories. This represents an expansion of the 16-code SPAFF taught to us in Seattle. Our modifications were made to accommodate specific hypotheses and to better reflect our material. In SET (Spiegel & Classen 2000; Spiegel & Spira 1991), our aim, as therapists, is to encourage the expression of 'primary negative affect' or direct fear, anger, and sadness (Giese–Davis *et al.* 2002*b*). In addition, a longstanding hypothesis in the breast cancer literature links suppressed anger with higher cancer incidence and faster progression (Giese–Davis & Spiegel 2003). We were especially attentive to ensuring that these emotions would be captured accurately in our coding process, and this led to 23 codes. We have 16 negative codes: fear (two levels), direct anger, constrained anger, sadness (two levels), tension, tense humor, verbalized contempt, micromoment contempt, domineering, belligerence, defensiveness, whining, disgust, and stonewalling. We also code neutral and six positive codes: affection (two levels), validation, interest, delight/excitement/surprise, and genuine humor.

In our piloting process, we became aware that the women in our groups expressed more sadness than was present in the marital interaction tapes. We made a decision to separate the sadness code into a high and low level (high when a woman is choked up or crying, low being coded when the rest of the coding cues for sadness are present) so that we could more readily test exploratory hypotheses about degree of expression. Likewise, fear presented itself somewhat differently in our groups. We separated the fear code into a high and low level to capture moments when women were simply talking about being afraid (low level fear) with no facial or voice tone cues for fear, from moments when both facial and voice tone cues were present (high level fear). It is much more common for women to talk about being afraid with very neutral affect in the group than to express high fear.

We also decided to separate direct anger (high-level burst of anger with voice, facial, body movement and content cues) from constrained anger or frustration (lips pressed, snort of air out the nose, slapping of arm of chair, irritation in voice that does not culminate in a direct anger expression). Constrained anger is also much more common in the groups than direct anger. Last of the negative code changes from the original SPAFF, we separated contempt into two categories—micromoment contempt (a purely nonverbal code of just a dimpler movement, with or without an eyeroll) from verbalized contempt (when a woman verbalized this emotion). In addition to these changes, we also separated the affection code into two categories, including high (affection with touch) and low (affection without touch), to examine in more detail what we saw commonly as women reached out to touch each other in response to a moment of empathy or concern. With these coding categories in place, we also created summary variables to more readily test our primary hypotheses.

Summary variables

We have chosen to create a summary variable of the vulnerable emotions, that we call 'primary negative affect'—fear (two levels), sadness (two levels), and direct anger—because of the goals of SET. We have separated the other coded negative affects into 'constrained anger' (a stand-alone code) and a summary variable called 'defensive/ hostile affect'. We examine constrained anger separately in our data because of the longstanding hypothesis that suppressing or repressing anger is associated with greater incidence or faster progression of cancer (Giese–Davis & Spiegel 2003). We will eventually examine the association of coded emotional expression with survival. We have included codes that are avoidance or defensive expressions (disgust, defensiveness, tension, tense humor, whining) and hostile expressions (verbalized contempt, micro-moment contempt, belligerence, domineering, stonewalling) into one summary code 'defensive/hostile'. This summary code is also based on SET hypotheses. Many types of therapy, including psychodynamic and emotion-focused therapies such as SET, seek to reduce both defensive and hostile behavior (Greenberg 1993; Hessle 1975; Kinseth 1982; Taurke *et al.* 1990; Truax & Wittmer 1973).

Restraint of hostility is generally associated with positive psychosocial outcomes. Restraint of hostile expression within families has been correlated with positive outcomes including lower risk for emotional abuse of children (Calam *et al.* 2002), lower levels of distress (Honig *et al.* 1997), lower marital distress, fewer ill health effects from marital conflict, and less husband-to-wife aggression (Heyman 2001; Notarius & Markman 1989). High levels of hostility have also been associated with negative health effects (Adams 1994; Barefoot *et al.* 1983, 1989; Dembroski *et al.* 1989; Koskenvuo *et al.* 1988; Shekelle *et al.* 1983; Williams *et al.* 1980). The expression of overt anger, fear, and sadness by an individual may diminish 'holding a grudge' and increase empathy— leading to less aggression (Snyder *et al.* 2003).

As samples of our data, we present the means for these summary variables (Table 11.1) and the associations between the mean durations of our summary variables (Table 11.2). We have presented primary negative affect (fear, anger, sadness); positive affect (affection—two levels, validation, interest, delight/excitement/surprise, and genuine humor); defensive/hostile affect (disgust, defensiveness, tension, tense humor, whining, verbalized contempt, micromoment contempt, belligerence, domineering, stonewalling); a division of defensive/hostile into defensive (disgust, defensiveness, tension, tense humor, whining) and hostile (verbalized contempt, micromoment contempt, belligerence, domineering, stonewalling); constrained anger; and neutral. We also present the total duration of each of our summary codes collapsed across all participants for nine random SET sessions in the first year and a half of one of three SET groups in the 'attempt to replicate' study (Fig. 11.1). Because of rolling enrollment, it is not possible to track well the development of the group or change in emotional expression at the group level. Our goal in presenting these data is for the reader to get a sense of the mean durations, range of emotional expression in SET group sessions, as well as the associations among our summary variables.

Cancer support groups in different modalities: face-to-face and online synchronous groups

Our work has now gone beyond the traditional face-to-face (f2f) context of support groups for women with breast cancer to include a set of studies designed to create and to examine the impact of online synchronous cancer support groups (OSGs) (Lieberman *et al.* 2003). An OSG is a group that is facilitated (similar to our work with therapist-facilitated f2f SET groups), closed to new members, meets at a certain time each week, and offers simultaneous chat between members and facilitators online over the internet. In doing this work, we also became aware that researchers who examine emotional expression from transcripts of f2f groups may be missing some of the richness of the emotional expression available when all the voice, face, body, and content cues are available from videotape. We have therefore created SPAFF for Breast Cancer–Text in order to facilitate the examination of transcripts and OSGs.

Table 11.1 Mean duration of a moment for SPAFF for Breast Cancer for the first session for women with metastatic breast cancer randomized to supportive–expressive group therapy ($N = 36$) in seconds

Summary variable	Mean (*SD*)
Primary negative affect	3.92 (3.68)
Positive affect	2.93 (1.37)
Defensive/hostile affect	1.66 (0.64)
Defensive affect	1.54 (0.61)
Hostile affect	1.60 (1.66)
Constrained anger	2.47 (2.22)
Neutral	9.13 (2.64)

Table 11.2 Spearman correlations among summary variables for SPAFF for Breast Cancer for the first session for women with metastatic breast cancer randomized to supportive–expressive group therapy ($N = 36$)

Summary variable	PNAF	PSAF	D/HAF	DFAF	HOAF	CANG	NEU
Primary negative affect	—						
Positive affect	−0.05	—					
Defensive/hostile affect	−0.23	0.31	—				
Defensive affect	0.07	0.27	0.78***	—			
Hostile affect	−0.11	0.22	0.50***	0.09	—		
Constrained anger	0.01	0.19	0.31	0.16	0.37*	—	
Neutral	0.11	0.13	0.20	0.26	0.07	0.10	—

Note: * $p < 0.05$, *** $p < 0.001$.

These correlations are based on mean durations of a moment of affect in this first session. PNAF = primary negative affect; PSAF = positive affect; D/HAF = defensive/hostile affect; DFAF = defensive affect; HOAF = hostile affect; CANG = constrained anger; NEU = neutral affect.

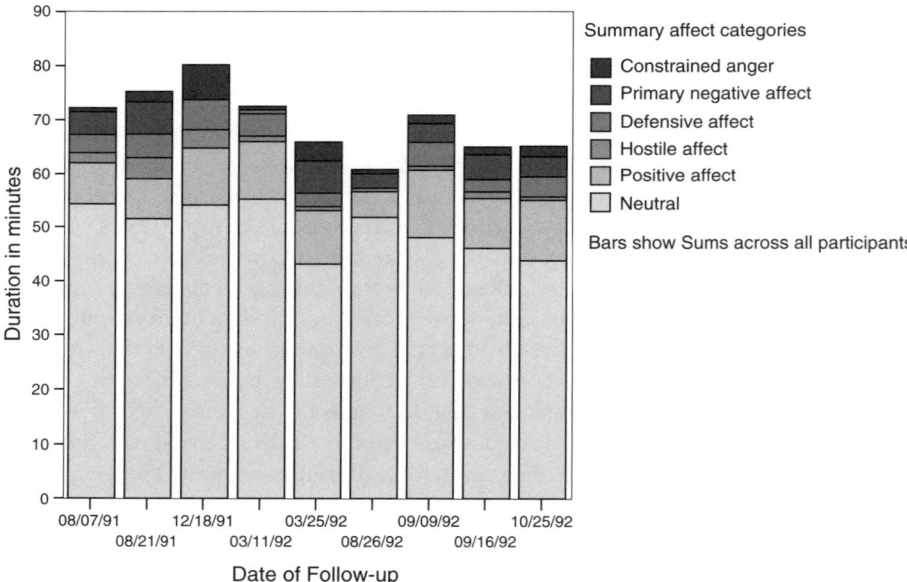

Figure 11.1 Total duration of each summary variable coded in our supportive–expressive group for metastatic breast cancer, collapsed across all the women participants in one of three groups, during nine random group sessions in the first year and a half of this randomized trial. This is presented to allow a visual sense of total affect expression in a group session.

SPAFF for Breast Cancer–Text

Many of the studies examining emotional expression in therapy groups have utilized transcripts rather than video or audiotape (Budman *et al.* 1993; Cytrynbaum 2000; Grabhorn 1998; Lewis *et al.* 2000). Observational researchers who utilize video and audiotape cues are not generally the same researchers who utilize text as data. Assumptions about emotional expression and experience may be quite different between the two methodologies, leading to inconsistency in the literature examining whether emotional expression in therapy sessions is an important process. We have therefore also extended our SPAFF for Breast Cancer to a text format to complete studies comparing emotion coded from video to that for text, and to have a tool for examining text-only group therapy contexts (Liess *et al.* 2004). We have applied this SPAFF for Text to both transcripts of f2f and OSGs to examine, from an observational coding perspective, whether certain emotions are more difficult to detect in text-only compared with f2f support-group settings.

SPAFF for Text differs somewhat depending upon whether it is applied to OSGs versus transcripts of f2f groups. When there is an online discussion, those participating seem to understand that the only avenue for expressing themselves is what appears in print on the screen. For this reason, they tend to use much more punctuation, abbreviations of understood online catch phrases, and even emoticons (:), ;), >:(etc.—and some computers now allow for the input of such symbols as ☺, ☻, etc.). When SPAFF for Text is applied to transcripts of f2f discussions, some of the emotion is missed by coders simply because the speakers are expressing themselves vocally/phys-ically/facially in ways that are not picked up when the discussion is transferred to the typed page. We are able to capture many emotions in the text, but there may be more emotion expressed than the coder is able to capture simply because s/he is not privy to the vocal/physical/facial context.

In coding emotional expression in text of OSGs, as opposed to transcripts of f2f groups, it is important to note the phenomenon of time lag. In a f2f group, response/reaction to an individual is almost immediate. However, in an online/text-analyzed group, multiple people are responding simultaneously. For this reason, a response can only be registered as quickly as a participant in the group types. In order to understand the thread of a conversation (and its corresponding emotional expression), one must often backtrack through the transcript before assigning a code to the emotion. For example, someone may type 'yes' which, if taken to be a response to the line immedi-ately before theirs, could be seen as validation (affirming someone's summary) when, in fact, it may be a response to a question that was posed to them half a page before and may therefore actually be neutral. Likewise, someone may type something of a poten-tially humorous nature, but may not seem to have a genuine (if any) response from the group and may therefore come across as tense humor. However, further down the page, someone may indicate 'That was funny', but the humor response may have been delayed by the virtual time lag. It is, therefore, essential when coding text to continually read forward and back, forward and back, to capture both content and context and to pinpoint expressions and responses to adequately and accurately reflect the emotions being expressed within the conversation.

During each of our studies examining the process of emotional expression in both f2f and OSG groups, we became aware that the women talked to each other for a substantial amount of time in each group session by telling stories . These stories were often about how they interacted with their physicians, their spouses, their children, or their friends. It seemed that often women practiced a stronger emotional expression during these story-telling moments than they may have actually been able to express in the moment described. We wondered whether expressing emotion in the context of a story might help women to practice emotional expression and generalize this expression to their daily lives. We began to believe that it was important for us to examine the use of these story-telling moments by creating a coding system to indicate whether women were telling a story and what kind of story. Although much research documents the usefulness of written narratives, the use of spoken narratives in groups has received far less attention.

Narrative content in SET groups

The guiding presence of the present work is that the act of constructing stories is a natural human process that helps individuals to understand their experiences and themselves. This process allows one to organize and remember the events in a coherent fashion while integrating thoughts and feelings. In essence, this gives individuals a sense of predictability and control over their lives. Once an experience has structure and meaning, it would follow that the emotional effects of that experience are more manageable. Constructing stories facilitates a sense of resolution, which results in less rumination and eventually allows disturbing experiences to subside gradually from conscious thought.

(Pennebaker & Seagel 1999)

An integral part of support groups may be the stories told by participants (Rappaport 1993). Narratives are one of the most common ways that memories are stored, and their retelling helps people to feel as though their life is under control and has some larger purpose. Narratives fulfill four basic psychological needs: purposiveness, justification, efficacy, and self-worth (Baumeister 1994). When telling a story, it is much easier to present a sequence of events as being intentionally and causally related to one's life goals (purposiveness). Specifically, many cancer patients may use narratives as a way to put a positive spin on their disease (e.g. by talking about the positive and desirable long-term effects of having cancer). Narratives also allow people to interpret events in a way consistent with personal values and standards (justification) while bolstering their sense of self-worth. Also, by downplaying luck and emphasizing control while telling the narrative, the speaker maximizes her sense of efficacy.

In overcoming the shock of diagnosis with a terminal disease such as metastatic breast cancer, patients may develop an 'illness narrative' which aids in the recollection and re-examination of their life. Illness narratives commonly involve an epiphany of discovery in which the patient realizes 'who I always was' or 'who I might become' (Frank 1993). An illness narrative may return life control to the patient and help uncover the 'silver lining' of the cancer diagnosis.

Some research supports the importance of the role of community or group narratives in creating individual change over time. Support groups may be effective to the extent that they help a person to learn a new story, reflecting the collective group reframing of traumatic events (Kennedy & Humphreys 1994; Rappaport, 1993, 1995, 1998, 2000).

Written narratives are important ways that people consolidate their traumatic experiences (Pennebaker & Beall 1986) and work through unresolved feelings (Lepore

& Greenberg 2002), with interventions using written narratives associated with numerous health outcomes including fewer medical center visits (Pennebaker & Seagel 1999; Pennebaker *et al.* 1988*b*), greater immunocompetence (Pennebaker *et al.* 1988*a*), and measurable change in arthritic joints (Smyth *et al.* 1999). Spoken narratives have also been associated with increased health benefits (Pennebaker & Susman 1988), but so far the spoken narratives in group psychotherapy have not been investigated.

Emotional expression in verbal narratives in group sessions may differ from the emotional expression of group participants talking directly to each other. Caroline (Perry) Dillon created our story coding system as part of her Senior Honors thesis at Stanford University. We have conducted two examinations of our data utilizing this coding system (Giese–Davis *et al.* 2003; Perry *et al.* 2002). We present this coding system in Appendix 2.

To code either emotional expression or narratives from videotapes of group therapy sessions, we needed to invent a way to utilize video material that was easily obtained in a therapy session and that was not so costly as to make this task prohibitive. This method included a number of technical aspects of the coding, the use of sampling strategies, and the use of coding speaking turns that we will describe below.

Technical aspects of coding emotional expression in therapy groups

My colleagues and I have created a new type of system for coding emotion and behavior in group settings by layering separate levels of coding. In the next few sections, we will describe the technical aspects of how we utilize the James Long System, that links a computer with a VCR, to allow us to code our tapes. We will describe a layered system of coding, the videography of the groups we code, sampling strategies for coding ongoing groups, and the detailed aspects of how we code.

In our system, depending on the research question, we can make multiple passes through each videotape to code each of the six levels of our system (speaker, emotion of speaker, backchanneler, emotion of backchanneler, topics, story). This system was set up to create a dataset in which we could examine not only emotional expression, but social interaction. We code through a software/hardware connection created by the James Long System. The software samples from keyboard macros at 30 times per second, making the collection of sampled continuous data possible. We therefore have frame-by-frame coded data, but the task of the coder is merely to strike the key associated with a particular code. Layering of the data is accomplished through merging time-synchronized codes in the multiple layers.

We were not able to have a separate camera focused on each woman in the group therapy studies we have examined so far. Instead, these groups were taped by a videographer who was either in an observation room (next to the therapy room), controlling mounted cameras in the therapy room, or in the room during the therapy session. The videographer, in either position, focuses on the person who is speaking. Since we do not have women on camera at all times, our data are limited to examination of the emotional expression of the women who are speaking. Because we are coding a group interaction, women sometimes talk over each other, there are back-channel responses as others talk, and, occasionally, the entire group is either silent or all talking at once ('overtalk'). We account for each of these possibilities.

Sampling for group therapy study of metastatic breast cancer patients

Unlike studies in which participants are brought in for standardized experimental procedures in several follow-up increments, such as in John Gottman's marital inter-action task (Gottman 1995), therapy groups must be sampled over time. Sampling strategies must match hypothesized questions. In the 'attempt to replicate' SET trial, there was rolling enrollment in the study over a period of seven years. We sampled 16 sessions for each woman, matching the dates of sessions as those closest to her self-report follow-ups in the first year of study participation: four at baseline and four at each of four months, eight months, and twelve months. Some women dropped out of the group or died before they attended 16 sessions.

To examine social interaction, we sampled a random tape from each of the four tapes at each of the four sessions and coded emotional expression for all participants (usually three to ten in each session) and therapists (usually one or two in each session). For these four tapes per woman, we also have been in the process of coding the topics discussed on the entire tape ('topics coding'). In addition, for the four tapes targeted for each woman, we code whether, in her talk turns, she is telling a story or narrative or is instead directly responding to the other women ('story coding'). The emotion coding, backchanneling coding, and story coding systems each rely on already having the coding of speaking turns to pull up into the JLC coding editor. The JLC editor allows us to show, on the computer screen, an identifying ID number or initials for each person in the session as they speak and the timing of (in hours:minutes:seconds:frames) their talk turns.

Coding procedure

We first lay a code for who is speaking (and whether they are on or off camera) for each entire videotape (SET sessions are one and a half hours) on which we will code emotional expression (even if we will only emotion code one woman on the videotape). This is necessary in order to calculate the woman's speaking time relative to the other women in the group and also to facilitate merging the coding of speaking turns with emotional expression, backchanneling, and story coding. Coders of speaking turns indicate the time when each person's talk turn begins and ends by hitting keyboard macros associated with each participant and therapist. This code also includes categor-ies for uncodable sounds, silence, and overtalk. Coding emotional expression onto the coding of speaking turns ('speaker coding') is accomplished by bringing the speaker code into the edit window of the JLC. We code emotional expression of one woman at a time because it is difficult for coders to maintain appropriate thresholds while coding multiple people in one pass through the data. Coders can fast forward to each talk turn for the woman they are coding and insert emotion codes.

Specifics: time for coding and reliabilities

As an estimate, for 210 videotapes (each 1 ½ hours long), speaker coding took $M = 4.14$ hours ($SD = 1.39$) and coders rated the difficulty of coding them at $M = 3.03$ ($SD = 0.96$) on a Likert-type scale of 1 to 5 (1 = least difficult; 5 = extremely difficult). We randomly select 10% of our speaker-coded videotapes for double coding and reliability comparisons: on 27 tapes mean $K = 0.91$ ($SD = 0.03$). By comparison, for 854 tape-by-woman segments, it took coders of emotional expression, using SPAFF, $M = 1.65$ ($SD = 0.99$) hours to code one woman for a 1 ½-hour therapy session. Emotion coders rated the difficulty at $M = 2.70$ ($SD = 1.03$).

We also indicate whether these speakers are on or off camera, so that we can analyze whether there are differences in our coding for the off-camera speaking turns. Because SPAFF focuses heavily on voice tone, most of the codes are still possible from vocal content. To examine some of the correlations among our coded variables, and whether time off camera makes a noticeable difference in the coded data, we examined the very first session for 36 women with metastatic breast cancer randomized to receive SET. In this first session, each woman told her 'cancer story'. We chose this session, in part, because each woman was engaged in a similar expressive task. We examined whether percentage of time off camera for each woman was correlated with our summary codes and each specific affect. For our summary codes, no correlation was significant between time off camera and neutral, positive affect, primary negative affect, defensive/hostile affect, and constrained anger (Pearson $r = -0.27$–0.08). Neither was there any significant correlation between percentage of time off camera and any specific affect we code (Spearman $r = -0.26$–0.23).

Our goal is to preserve the length of the natural talk turn without interrupting it with backchanneling responses (e.g. 'oh', 'uh huh', 'great', 'right'). All backchannelling responses are coded at a separate level ('listener code'). In the listener code, we indicate who is backchanneling and whether they are on or off camera. Because much of the backchanneling happens off camera, we have an 'unidentified backchanneler' code. Similar to emotion coding on speaker code, listener code is brought into the JLC edit window; however, we code all participants' backchanneling in one pass through the data. Because our primary questions to date involve primary speaking turns, and coding backchanneling responses is time-consuming ($M = 7.07$ hours for listener and 6.25 hours for listener emotion for 1 ½-hour sessions), we have no representative analysis of our listener code. Analysis of our data, to date, has focused on the primary speaking turns (Ellis *et al.* 2002; Giese–Davis *et al.* 2001, 2002c, 2003; Liess *et al.* 2004; Perry *et al.* 2002).

Finally, it is crucial to this process of coding group therapy sessions to have a clear, replicable, and reliable selection and training procedure for coders. Coding so many group sessions means that no single training cohort of coders will complete the entire task. Coders must be reliable when compared across cohorts to guarantee that the thresholds they use are not changing over time. We present below our selection and training procedure for our coders.

Selection and training of coders

The success of the Emotion Coding Lab—Stanford, would not be possible without the hard work, dedication, and commitment of our many volunteers. Students from various college and university campuses are recruited twice a year, once in September (for the entire school year) and also in May (for our summer internship program). Students are asked to first attend an information session that details the internship program and outlines the criteria and commitment requirements. At the end of the session, we request that they think about the obligation and respond back after a 24-hour period if they are interested in obtaining an interview slot. During the interview process students are assessed thoroughly to identify their natural strengths to determine for which coding team they are better suited—emotion or topics coding. Upon completion of the interview, they are instructed again to think about the commitment required for 24 hours and, only after this time, to let us know their decision.

Many students apply for this internship program (and over 200 have completed the internship since 1996). We have found that by simply asking them to wait 24 hours and consider their commitment twice during the selection process, we eliminate most coders whose attendance to complete their required time would be unreliable. We have between 10 and 20 undergraduate intern coders, in addition to two paid staff positions (a coding lab liaison who trains and manages topics coders and handles all programming and technical assistance, and an emotion coding trainer) in our lab at any given time.

We have developed a reliable mechanism for the selection of our coders. We interview each potential coder and they watch a 10-minute segment of videotape from one of our groups. We ask them to respond to the videotape by telling us what they saw. The videotape segment is chosen specifically because the woman speaking for much of the 10 minutes hardly moves her facial muscles and has a rather quiet voice. Nevertheless, her voice tone conveys primarily verbalized contempt and domineering throughout the segment. If potential coders cannot hear emotion in the voice, they will miss the level of contempt she is expressing. SPAFF codes rely heavily on voice tone, so if potential coders cannot accurately tell us the emotions expressed on this tape, we have found that we are unlikely to be successful training them to be reliable. The very best coders will be those who, within just a few minutes, will say that the woman is 'bitter' or 'very angry' or 'controlling'. These coders are readily trained and maintain extremely high kappas throughout their coding tenure.

If potential coders do not readily report that the woman is expressing anger, we ask them to look down our quick summary list of SPAFF for Breast Cancer emotions and indicate whether they saw her express each emotion. This method ensures that the potential coder is not simply too shy to indicate that a woman with breast cancer is expressing a negative emotion. If coders can indicate the appropriate expressions by going down our list, then they are also likely to be trainable. In addition, we ask each person how they can tell that the woman is expressing these emotions. If they are using facial, body, and voice cues to determine what she is expressing, they will likely make excellent emotion coders.

Some people simply do not hear or see these emotions. These people are unlikely to be skilled at emotion coding. In addition, if they report that the way that they discriminate emotions is primarily through content, they are unlikely to become skilled emotion coders. Fortunately, within our lab there is a good match for one of our coding systems for these individuals who do not hear emotion readily. They code the topics the women are discussing in the groups. We have found that those people who either do not see or hear emotion, or focus primarily on the content of the discussion as a way to take in information, will make excellent and reliable 'topics coders'. It is also true, in our experience, that we have difficulty training those people who hear and see emotion quickly to code topics. They miss much of the content, usually due to their perceptual skew toward focus on emotion.

Because it is very costly and time-consuming to train coders, it is crucial to have a solid screening procedure in place that predicts success coding in a particular setting and with a particular population. In the several instances when we have attempted to train a content-focused person to code emotion, it is very clear that the cost to us was much higher than the return in usable reliable data.

All emotion coders begin by learning facial action units (Ekman & Friesen 1978). Actions units (AUs) are taught not just by description or by looking at photographs, but by working in the mirror to recreate the AUs on their own faces. This is important for a couple of reasons. First, while the facial/muscular expression of a given emotion may be relatively standard, the physical structure of people's faces varies widely. It is, therefore, important for coders to see the same expression that they are creating on their own faces as it appears on the faces of their fellow coders. This method ensures that they can recognize that it is still the same expression, despite any physical/structural differences (more narrow eyes, fuller lips, etc.). Secondly, emotion works both from the inside out and the outside in. If a person feels a particular emotion, that emotion is reflected on their face. The reverse is also true—if an individual makes a particular face, they can feel, to some degree, the corresponding emotion. As coders begin to see this connection, they can use it to their benefit in coding. If they are not sure how a subject is feeling, they can look at their expression, replicate it, and get a sense of how the person is feeling.

Coders take a test on the AUs. They learn our coding categories through focus on four quadrants: facial muscle movement, voice tone, body movement, and content. An actor/director/educator from the San Jose Repertory Theatre, Karen Altree Piemme, teaches these codes. Coders view videotape segments and fill in a four-quadrant grid with what they saw and indicate the emotion they would code. They code practice segments of videotape and compare their coding with printed transcripts of those segments that have been coded by consensus of our group (so that we believe them to be accurate). They code six entire group videotapes (one woman on each tape) and are compared for Cohen's kappa with:

1. coders from the original cohort of coders in our lab (who helped to define the codes and set the standards);
2. our current emotion coding trainer;
3. all the coders in the current training cohort.

These particular tapes were chosen because, on each tape, coders from the original cohort had acheived above a 0.80 kappa. A range of women is also represented on those six tapes, including several women who are very emotionally expressive and several who are not. Our trainer meets with each emotion coder and goes over the pattern of the results of those kappas. She views videotape of their coding where there are problems and clarifies with them cues they may be missing. It is most difficult for new coders to gauge the threshold that takes a code from neutral to a positive or negative emotion. If their coding is not accurate, they may then be required to code a further set of tapes and go through these same procedures.

Each week our trainer meets with coders, as a group, to 'consensus code' tapes as a method of ongoing continuing education to reinforce the accuracy of the coding system and cut down on any tendency for coders to change coding thresholds when they are coding without real-time feedback. Consensus coding is accomplished by having a hardware/software link (JLC) between two coding stations that are physically next to each other that allows us to play a videotape and show two coders' coding streams simultaneously as the tape plays (on separate monitors). The coding cohort and trainer fast forward to any section of code where the two coders have disagreed. The section of videotape is played and the group decides together what the codes should be for that particular section. During this consensus training, each coder's opinion in determining the code is required so that our trainer understands both the strengths and problem areas for each coder.

All coders are blind to hypotheses. We have been particularly careful to guard against hypothesis-savvy coders in the following ways:

1. Coders are prohibited from knowing any hypotheses while being an active coder.
2. Because we intend to test hypotheses related to change over time, we assign random numbers to each videotape so that coders are less likely to know the order, date, or even the year when the videotape was made.
3. Tapes are assigned randomly in ways that would make it difficult to establish an order for the sequence of events in the group.
4. Coders are prohibited from sharing with each other the knowledge of a specific group member's death, or to name specifically events discussed on tape.
5. Coders are unaware with whom their tapes will be compared for kappa.

To reduce secondary post-traumatic stress reactions, coders discuss emotional reactions to the viewing of these videotapes as a regular part of weekly lab meetings. During these discussions, coders can talk about their reactions to events on tape, but cannot name a particular woman or discuss her disease course. Upon leaving the lab, coders are debriefed as to specific hypotheses—none have guessed the hypotheses.

In the Emotion Coding Lab—Stanford, all tape segments coded for emotion, topics, and story are coded by two coders and compared for kappa using a two-second $+/-$ window and the stream of duration-coded data. If the tape segment passes above a 0.60 kappa, it is entered into our dataset. A coin flip determines which coder's file is entered. If it does not pass 0.60, it is recoded. Some files that have passed above a 0.55 kappa (0.55–0.59) but have not yet been recoded are used for consensus coding training (described above). Our consensus-coded file is then entered as data. In our first session of SET in the metastatic study dataset referred to earlier, mean durations of affect were not significantly different when comparing those files that were consensus coded versus those that passed 0.60 kappa.

Summary

In summary, we have successfully implemented emotion and story coding at a frame-by-frame level of data collection and duration of affect data analysis in our lab. Our layered arrangement of coding systems allows us to examine both individual and group interaction variables in trying to understand therapeutic mechanisms in SET groups. We have begun to expand into coding in other contexts:

- coding other group therapy styles (Ellis *et al.* 2002; Liess *et al.* 2004);
- coding training exercises in listening and disclosing for women with breast cancer being trained to be peer counselors (Giese–Davis *et al.* 2002*a*);
- coding of behavior in the Trier Social Stress Task (Kirschbaum *et al.* 1993).

In the Trier Social Stress Task, participants take part in an experimental paradigm designed to induce social stress in order to examine physiological reactions (autonomic and cortisol) to acute stress. Participants give a short speech and calculate difficult math subtractions in front of an audience of several people who do not provide facial feedback or encouragement. Although this is a standard physiological stress paradigm, the observed emotional expression of participants during the task has not previously been investigated using SPAFF. SPAFF coding in a group setting is labor intensive, and completing the sample of tapes for a group therapy study with rolling enrollment over seven years has required the coding of over 500 videotape segments. We look forward to the near-future completion of this sample and the testing of our primary hypotheses.

It has been important for this research inquiry that SPAFF as a macrocoding system was available. For a number of reasons, it would not be possible to test these hypotheses using many of the single-channel coding systems. For instance, it requires many more hours per videotape segment to code facial affect using FACS. In addition, much of the richness of this data can be heard in the voice and seen in the body movement. Lastly, the content of what the women express is equally an important aspect of processing emotion from a therapeutic standpoint. Only a coding system that marries these aspects of the therapy context is capable of accurately reflecting our primary hypotheses in doing this work. In addition, as social creatures, we experience the emotional expression of others as a macrosystem including voice tone, facial expression, body movement, and content. We use multiple cues to assess the meaning of emotional expression as we hear it in our day-to-day lives. Our research context is a fairly natural one, in that women with cancer are simply talking to each other in a therapy group rather than engaging in an experimental task designed to elicit a particular emotion. We are grateful that the method of our research matches this naturalistic context.

Although it is interesting to study emotional expression in basic research, we do not want our work to stop there. We would like to be able to translate this basic research into the practice of psychotherapy, making therapists better able to identify emotional expressions and learn techniques for encouraging them in support groups. Only such a macrosystem allows for this translation to practice.

Authors' note

The work in the Emotion Coding Lab—Stanford, was created with funding from a postdoctoral fellowship to Janine Giese–Davis from the Breast Cancer Research Program of California (BCRP) 1FB-0383, with additional funding from the John D. and Catherine T. MacArthur Foundation. Continued funding has been provided by NIMH grant MN47226, with additional funding from NCI, BCRP grants 4BB-2901, 5FB-0036, 7BB-2400, and NIA/NCI Program Project AG18784 for the data presented in this chapter. Thanks also to the Kozmetsky Global Collaboratory at Stanford, for funding for narrative coding We would also like to thank Helena Kraemer (biostatistician) for advice on sampling strategy for rolling enrollment in support groups, Sue DiMiceli (data manager and programmer), and Jennifer Boyce, Casey Alt, Sanjay Chakrapani, Barbara Symons, Diana Edwards, David Weibel, Caryn Bernstein, Wendy Ellis, and Bita Nouriani, who helped to shape our system. We would also like to thank all the coding interns who have contributed valid data to our studies, videographers (particularly Catherine Byers White), and the women with breast cancer who have been willing to be videotaped.

References

Adams, S.H. (1994). Role of hostility in women's health during midlife: a longitudinal study. *Health Psychology*, 13, 488–95.

Bahnson, C.B. (1981). Stress and cancer: the state of the art, part 2. *Psychosomatics*, 22, 207–20.

Bahnson, M.B. & Bahnson, C.B. (1969). Ego defenses in cancer patients. *Annals of the New York Academy of Science*, 164, 546–59.

Bales, R.F. (1950). *Interaction process analysis reading*. MA: Addison–Wesley.

Bales, R.F. (1983). SYMLOG: a practical approach to the study of groups. In *Small groups and social interaction, Vol. 2* (ed. H.H. Blumberg, A.P. Hare, V. Kent & M. Davies). New York: John Wiley.

Barefoot, J.C., Dahlstrom, W.G., & Williams, R.B. (1983). Hostility, CHD incidence, and total mortality: a 25-year follow-up study of 255 physicians. *Psychosomatic Medicine*, 45, 59–63.

Barefoot, J.C., Dodge, K.A., Peterson, B.L., Dahlstrom, W.G., & Williams, R.B. (1989). The Cook–Medley hostility scale: item content and ability to predict survival. *Psychosomatic Medicine*, 51, 46–57.

Baumeister, R.F. (1994). How stories make sense of personal experiences: motives that shape autobiographical narratives. *Personality and Social Psychology Bulletin*, 20, 676–88.

Beck, A.P. & Lewis, C.M. (2000a). Comparison of the systems of analysis: concepts and theory. In *The process of group psychotherapy: systems for analyzing change* (ed. A.P. Beck & C.M. Lewis), pp. 415–42. Washington, DC: American Psychological Association.

Beck, A.P. & Lewis, C.M. (ed.) (2000b). *The process of group psychotherapy: systems for analyzing change*. Washington, DC: American Psychological Association.

Benjamin, L.S. (2000). Use of structural analysis of social behavior for interpersonal diagnosis and treatment in group therapy. In *The process of group psychotherapy: systems for analyzing change* (ed. A.P. Beck & C.M. Lewis), pp. 381–412. Washington, DC: American Psychological Association.

Budman, S.H., Soldz, S., Demby, A., Davis, M., & Merry, J. (1993). What is cohesiveness? An empirical examination. *Small Group Research*, 24, 199–216.

Calam, R., Bolton, C., Barrowclough, C., & Roberts, J. (2002). Maternal expressed emotion and clinician ratings of emotional maltreatment potential. *Child Abuse and Neglect*, 26, 1101–6.

Cytrynbaum, S. (2000). The member–leader scoring system. In *The process of group psychotherapy: systems for analyzing change* (ed. A.P. Beck & C.M. Lewis), pp. 175–218. Washington, DC: American Psychological Association.

Daldrup, R.J., Engle, D., Holiman, M., & Beutler, L.E. (1994). The intensification and resolution of blocked affect in an experiential psychotherapy. *British Journal of Clinical Psychology*, 33, 129–41.

Dattore, P.J., Shantz, R.C., & Coyne, L. (1980). Premorbid personality differentiation of cancer and noncancer groups: a test of the hypothesis of cancer proneness. *Journal of Consulting and Clinical Psychology*, 43, 388–94.

Davis, M.S., Budman, S.H., & Soldz, S. (2000). The individual group member interpersonal process scale. In *The process of group psychotherapy: systems for analyzing change* (ed. A.P. Beck & C.M. Lewis), pp. 283–308. Washington, DC: American Psychological Association.

Dembroski, T.M., MacDougall, J.M., Costa, P.T., & Granditis, G.A. (1989). Components of hostility as predictors of sudden death and myocardial infarction in the Multiple Risk Factor Intervention Trial. *Psychosomatic Medicine*, 51, 514–22.

Derogatis, L.R., Abeloff, M.D., & Melisaratos, N. (1979). Psychological coping mechanisms and survival time in metastatic breast cancer. *Journal of the American Medical Association*, 242, 1504–8.

Ekman, P. & Friesen, W.V. (1978). *Facial action coding system: a technique for the measurement of facial movement.* Palo Alto, CA: Consulting Psychologists Press.

Ellis, W., Giese–Davis, J., Lieberman, M., Golant, M., Simon, J., & Spiegel, D. (2002). *Emotional expression and therapist behavior in online vs. face-to-face breast cancer support groups: a comparative study.* Paper presented at the annual meeting of the Society for Behavioral Medicine, Washington DC, April 2002.

Farrell, M.P. (1976). Patterns in the development of self-analytic groups. *Journal of Applied Behavioral Science*, 12, 523–42.

Flowers, J.V. & Booraem, C.D. (1991). Focusing on emotion in group therapy: what clients, what problems, and what for. *Psychological Reports*, 69, 369–70.

Foa, E.B. & Kozak, M.J. (1986). Emotional processing of fear: exposure to corrective information. *Psychological Bulletin*, 99, 20–35.

Fox, C.M., Harper, P., Hyner, G.C., & Lyle, R.M. (1994). Loneliness, emotional repression, marital quality, and major life events in women who develop breast cancer. *Journal of Community Health*, 19, 467–82.

Frank, A.W. (1993). The rhetoric of self-change: illness experience as narrative. *The Sociological Quarterly*, 34, 39–52.

Galen. (1996). *On the passions and errors of the soul* (P. Harkins, Trans.). Columbus: Ohio state University Press.

Gallois, C. (1993). The language and communication of emotion. *American Behavioral Scientist*, 36, 309–38.

Giese–Davis, J. & Spiegel, D. (2001). Suppression, repressive-defensiveness, restraint, and distress in metastatic breast cancer: separable or inseparable constructs? *Journal of Personality*, **69**, 417–49.

Giese–Davis, J. & Spiegel, D. (2003). Emotional expression and cancer progression. In *Handbook of affective sciences* (ed. R.J. Davidson, K.R. Scherer, & H. Hill Goldsmith), pp. 1053–82. Oxford: Oxford University Press.

Giese–Davis, J., Bliss–Isberg, C., Carson, K., Donaghy, J., Star, P., Batten, C., *et al.* (2002*a*). *Peer counselors in a training session provide accurate predictions of who will be an effective peer navigator.* Paper presented at the annual meeting of the Society for Behavioral Medicine, Washington DC, April 2002.

Giese–Davis, J., Koopman, C., Butler, L. D., Classen, C., Cordova, M., Fobair, P., *et al.* (2002*b*). Change in emotion regulation strategy for women with metastatic breast cancer following supportive–expressive group therapy. *Journal of Consulting and Clinical Psychology*, **70**, 916–25.

Giese–Davis, J., Koopman, C., Butler, L. D., Joss, J., Classen, C., Roberts, J., *et al.* (2004). The Stanford Emotional Self-Efficacy Scale–Cancer: reliability, validity, and generalizability. In *Emotional expression and health: advances in theory, assessment and clinical applications* (ed. I. Nyklícek, L. Temoshok & A. Vingerhoets), pp. 204–22. Hove, UK/New York: Brunner–Routledge.

Giese–Davis, J., Perry, C.J., Abercrombie, H., & Spiegel, D. (2002*c*). *Steeper diurnal cortisol rhythm associated with greater primary negative affect and greater positive affect within spoken narratives in cancer support groups.* Paper presented at the Society for Psychophysiological Research 42nd Annual Meeting, Washington DC, October 2002.

Giese–Davis, J., Perry, C.J., Abercrombie, H., & Spiegel, D. (2003). *Steeper diurnal cortisol rhythm associated with greater coded primary negative affect and greater positive affect within spoken narratives.* Paper presented at the Society of Behavioral Medicine's 24th Annual Meeting, Salt Lake City, March 2003.

Giese–Davis, J., Sephton, S., & Spiegel, D. (2001). *Less expression of primary negative affect associated with flattened diurnal slope of cortisol.* Paper presented at the Annual Conference for the Society for Psychophysiological Research, Montreal, Canada, 10–14 October 2001.

Goldstein, D. & Antoni, M. (1989). The distribution of repressive coping styles among non-metastatic and metastatic breast cancer patients as compared to non-cancer patients. *Psychology and Health,* **3**, 245–58.

Gottman, J.M. (1993). Studying emotion in social interaction. In *Handbook of emotions* (ed. M. Lewis & J.M. Haviland), pp. 475–88. New York: Guilford Press.

Gottman, J.M. (1995). *What predicts divorce: the measures.* Hillsdale, NJ: Lawrence Erlbaum Associates.

Gottman, J.M., Woodin, E.M., & Coan, J.A. (1998). *Specific affect coding system manual, 20-code version (4.0).* Unpublished manuscript.

Gottschalk, L.A. & Gleser, G.C. (1969). *The measurement of psychological states through the content analysis of verbal behaviour.* Berkeley: University of California Press.

Grabhorn, R. (1998). Affective experience in a case of group therapy with psychosomatic inpatients. *Psychoanalytic Inquiry,* **18**, 490–511.

Greenberg, L. (1993). Emotion and change processes in psychotherapy. In *Handbook of emotions* (ed. M. Lewis & J.M. Haviland), pp. 499–519. New York: Guilford Press.

Greenberg, L.S. & Foerster, F.S. (1996). Task analysis exemplified: the process of resolving unfinished business. *Journal of Consulting and Clinical Psychology*, 64, 439–46.

Greenberg, L.S. & Webster, M.C. (1982). Resolving decisional conflict by Gestalt two-chair dialogue: relating process to outcome. *Journal of Counseling Psychology*, 29, 468–77.

Greer, S. & Morris, T. (1975). Psychological attributes of women who develop breast cancer: a controlled study. *Journal of Psychosomatic Research*, 19, 147–53.

Greer, S. & Watson, M. (1985). Towards a psychobiological model of cancer: psychological considerations. *Social Science Medicine*, 20, 773–7.

Greer, S., Morris, T., & Pettingale, K.W. (1979). Psychological response to breast cancer: effect on outcome. *Lancet*, 2(8146), 785–7.

Gross, J. (1989). Emotional expression in cancer onset and progression. *Social Science and Medicine*, 28(12), 1239–48.

Hahn, R.C. & Petitti, D.B. (1988). Minnesota Multiphasic Personality Inventory-rated depression and the incidence of breast cancer. *Cancer*, 61, 845–8.

Hall, J.A., Harrigan, J., & Rosenthal, R. (1995). Nonverbal behavior in clinician–patient interaction. *Applied and Preventive Psychology*, 4, 21–37.

Hare, A.P. (1976). *Handbook of small group research*. New York: Free Press.

Hessle, S. (1975). The Defense Mechanism Test: a personality test for studying change in defense organization and self-identity with clients in psychotherapy. *Cognitive Therapy and Research*, 8, 559–78.

Heyman, R.E. (2001). Observation of couple conflicts: clinical assessment applications, stubborn truths, and shaky foundations. *Psychological Assessment*, 13, 5–35.

Honig, A., Hofman, A., Rozendaal, N., & Dingemans, P. (1997). Psycho-education in bipolar disorder: effect on expressed emotion. *Psychiatry Research*, 72, 17–22.

Johnson, M.D. (2002). The observation of specific affect in marital interactions: psychometric properties of a coding system and a rating system. *Psychological Assessment*, 14, 423–38.

Kennedy, M. & Humphreys, K. (1994). Understanding worldview transformation in members of mutual help groups. *Prevention in Human Services*, 11, 181–98.

King, L.A. & Emmons, R.A. (1991). Psychological, physical, and interpersonal correlates of emotional expressiveness, conflict, and control. *European Journal of Personality*, 5, 131–50.

King, L.A., Emmons, R.A., & Woodley, S. (1992). The structure of inhibition. *Journal of Research in Personality*, 26, 85–102.

Kinseth, L.M. (1982). Spontaneous nonverbal intervention in group therapy. *International Journal of Group Psychotherapy*, 32, 327–38.

Kirschbaum, C., Pirke, K.M., & Hellhammer, D.H. (1993). The 'Trier Social Stress Test'—a tool for investigating psychobiological stress responses in a laboratory setting. *Neuropsychobiology*, 28, 76–81.

Koch, H.C. (1983). Correlates of changes in personal construing of members of two psychotherapy groups: changes in affective expression. *British Journal of Medical Psychology*, 56, 323–7.

Koskenvuo, M., Kaprio, J., Rose, R.J., Kesaniemi, A., Sarna, S., Heikkila, K., *et al.* (1988). Hostility as a risk factor for mortality and ischemic heart disease in men. *Psychosomatic Medicine*, 50, 330–40.

Kring, A.M., Smith, D.A., & Neale, J.M. (1994). Individual differences in dispositional expressiveness: development and validation of the Emotional Expressivity Scale. *Journal of Personality and Social Psychology,* **66**, 934–49.

Kune, G.A., Kune, S., Watson, L.F., & Bahnson, C.B. (1991). Personality as a risk factor in large bowel cancer: data from the Melbourne Colorectal Cancer Study. *Psychological Medicine,* **21**, 29–41.

Lepore, S.J. & Greenberg, M.A. (2002). Mending broken hearts: effects of expressive writing on mood, cognitive processing, social adjustment and health following a relationship breakup. *Psychology & Health,* **17**, 547–60.

Lepore, S.J. & Helgeson, V.S. (1998). Social constraints, instrusive thoughts, and mental health after prostate cancer. *Journal of Social and Clinical Psychology,* **17**, 89–106.

Lewis, C.M., Beck, A.P., Dugo, J.M., & Eng, A.M. (2000). The group development process analysis measures. In *The process of group psychotherapy: systems for analyzing change* A. (ed. P. Beck & C.M. Lewis), pp. 221–62. Washington, DC: American Psychological Association.

Lieberman, M. & Borman, L. (1980). Self-help groups for coping with crises: origins, members, processes, and impact. San Francisco: Jossey–Bass Inc.

Lieberman, M.A., Golant, M., Giese–Davis, J., Winzelberg, A., Benjamin, H., Humphreys, K., *et al.* (2003). Electronic support groups for breast carcinoma: a clinical trial of effectiveness. *Cancer,* **97**, 920–5.

Liess, A., Ellis, W., Giese–Davis, J., Gruenstein, A., Golant, M., & Spiegel, D. (2004). *Emotional information available from videotapes vs transcripts.* Paper presented at the 25th Meeting of the Society of Behavioral Medicine, Baltimore, 24–27 March 2004.

Marziali, E. (2000). Three complementary systems for coding the process of therapeutic dialogue. In *The process of group psychotherapy: systems for analyzing change* (ed. A.P. Beck & C.M. Lewis), pp. 311–56. Washington, DC: American Psychological Association.

McCallum, M., Piper, W.E., & Morin, H. (1995). Affect and outcome in short-term group therapy for loss. *International Journal of Group Psychotherapy,* **43**, 303–18.

McKenna, M.C., Zevon, M.A., Corn, B., & Rounds, J. (1999). Psychosocial factors and the development of breast cancer: a meta-analysis. *Health Psychology,* **18**, 520–31.

Notarius, C.I. & Markman, H.J. (1989). Coding marital interaction: a sampling and discussion of current issues. *Behavioral Assessment,* **11**, 1–11.

Orlinsky, D.E. & Howard, K.I. (1986). Process and outcome in psychotherapy. In *Handbook of psychotherapy and behavior change: an empirical analysis* (3rd edn) (ed. S.L. Garfield & A.E. Bergin), pp. 311–81. New York: John Wiley.

Pennebaker, J. & Seagel, J. (1999). Forming a story: the health benefits of narrative. *Journal of Clinical Psychology,* **55**, 1243–54.

Pennebaker, J.W. & Beall, S.K. (1986). Confronting a traumatic event: toward an understanding of inhibition and disease. *Journal of Abnormal Psychology,* **95**, 274–81.

Pennebaker, J.W. & King, L.A. (1999). Linguistic styles: language use as an individual difference. *Journal of Personality & Social Psychology,* **77**, 1296–312.

Pennebaker, J.W. & Stone, L.D. (2003). Words of wisdom: language use over the life span. *Journal of Personality & Social Psychology,* **85**, 291–301.

Pennebaker, J.W. & Susman, J.R. (1988). Disclosure of traumas and psychosomatic processes. *Social Science Medicine,* **20**, 327–32.

Pennebaker, J.W., Kiecolt–Glaser, J.K., & Glaser, R. (1988*a*). Confronting traumatic experience and immunocompetence: a reply to Neale, Cox, Valdimarsdottir, and Stone. *Journal of Consulting and Clinical Psychology,* **56**, 638–9.

Pennebaker, J.W., Kiecolt–Glaser, J.K., & Glaser, R. (1988*b*). Disclosure of traumas and immune function: health implications for psychotherapy. *Journal of Consulting and Clinical Psychology,* **56**, 239–45.

Pennebaker, J.W., Mehl, M.R., & Niederhoffer, K.G. (2003). Psychological aspects of natural language use: our words, our selves. *Annual Review of Psychology,* **54**, 547–77.

Perry, C.J., Giese–Davis, J., & Spiegel, D. (2002). *Emotional expression during narratives in a breast cancer support group.* Paper presented at the Annual Meeting of the Society for Behavioral Medicine, Washington DC, April 2002.

Persky, V.W., Kempthorne–Rawson, J., & Shekelle, R.B. (1987). Personality and risk of cancer: 20-year follow-up of the Western Electric Study. *Psychosomatic Medicine,* **49**, 435–49.

Pettingale, K.W., Watson, M., & Greer, S. (1985). The validity of emotional control as a trait in breast cancer patients. *Journal of Psychosocial Oncology,* **2**, 21–30.

Rappaport, J. (1993). Narrative studies, personal stories, and identity transformation in the mutual help context. *Journal of Applied Behavioral Science,* **29**, 239–56.

Rappaport, J. (1995). Empowerment meets narrative: listening to stories and creating settings. *American Journal of Community Psychology,* **23**, 795–807.

Rappaport, J. (1998). The art of social change: community narratives as resources for individual and collective identity. In *Addressing community problems: psychological research and intervention* (ed. X.B. Arriaga & S. Oskamp), pp. 225–46. Thousand Oaks, CA: Sage.

Rappaport, J. (2000). Community narratives: tales of terror and joy. *American Journal of Community Psychology,* **28**, 1–24.

Roger, D. & Nesshoever, W. (1987). The construction and preliminary validation of a scale for measuring emotional control. *Personality and Individual Differences,* **8**, 527–34.

Rosner, R., Beutler, L.E., & Daldrup, R.J. (2000). Vicarious emotional experience and emotional expression in group psychotherapy. *Journal of Clinical Psychology,* **56**, 1–10.

Salovey, P., Mayer, J.D., Goldman, S.L., Turvey, C., & Palfai, T.P. (1995). Emotional attention, clarity, and repair: exploring emotional intelligence using the trait meta-mood scale. In *Emotional disclosure and health* (ed. J.W. Pennebaker), pp. 125–54. Washington, DC: American Psychological Association.

Scherer, K.R. (1982). Methods of research on vocal communication: paradigms and parameters. In *Handbook of methods in nonverbal behaviour research* (ed. K.R. Scherer & P. Ekman), pp. 136–98. Cambridge: Cambridge University Press.

Scherer, K.R. (1985). Vocal affect signalling: a comparative approach. In *Advances in the study of behavior, Vol. 15* (ed. J. Rosenblatt, C. Beer, M.–C. Busnel, & P.J.B. Slater), pp. 189–244. New York: Academic Press.

Scherer, K.R. (1988). On the symbolic functions of vocal affect expression. *Journal of Language and Social Psychology,* **7**, 79–100.

Schonfield, J. (1975). Psychological and life-experience differences between Israeli women with benign and cancerous breast lesions. *Journal of Psychosomatic Research,* **19**, 229–34.

Shekelle, R.B., Gale, M., Ostfeld, A.M., & Paul, O. (1983). Hostility, risk of coronary heart disease, and mortality. *Psychosomatic Medicine,* **45**, 109–14.

Simon, A. & Agazarian, Y. (2000). The system for analyzing verbal interaction. In *The process of group psychotherapy: systems for analyzing change* (ed. A.P. Beck & C.M. Lewis), pp. 357–80. Washington, DC.: American Psychological Association.

Smyth, J.M., Stone, A.A., Hurewitz, A., & Kaell, A. (1999). Effects of writing about stressful experiences on symptom reduction in patients with asthma or rheumatoid arthritis: a randomized trial. *Journal of the American Medical Association,* **281**, 1304–9.

Snyder, J., Stoolmiller, M., Wilson, M., & Yamamoto, M. (2003). Child anger regulation, parental responses to children's anger displays, and early child antisocial behavior. *Social Development,* **12**, 336–60.

Spiegel, D. & Bloom, J.R. (1983). Group therapy and hypnosis reduce metastatic breast carcinoma pain. *Psychosomatic Medicine,* **45**, 333–9.

Spiegel, D. & Classen, C. (2000). *Group therapy for cancer patients: a research-based handbook of psychosocial care.* New York: Basic Books.

Spiegel, D. & Kato, P. (1996). Psychosocial influences on cancer incidence and progression. *Harvard Review of Psychiatry,* **4**, 10–26.

Spiegel, D. & Spira, J. (1991). *Supportive/expressive group therapy: a treatment manual of psychosocial intervention for women with recurrent breast cancer.* Stanford University School of Medicine, unpublished manuscript.

Spiegel, D., Bloom, J.R., Kraemer, H.C., & Gottheil, E. (1989). Effect of psychosocial treatment on survival of patients with metastatic breast cancer. *Lancet,* **2(8668)**, 888–91.

Spiegel, D., Bloom, J.R., & Yalom, I. (1981). Group support for patients with metastatic cancer. A randomized outcome study. *Archives of General Psychiatry,* **38**, 527–33.

Taurke, E.A., Flegenheimer, W., McCullough, L., Winston, A., Pollack, J., & Trujillo, M. (1990). Change in patient affect/defense ratio from early to late sessions in brief psychotherapy. *Journal of Clinical Psychology,* **46**, 657–68.

Taylor, G.J., Ryan, D., & Bagby, R.M. (1985). Toward the development of a new self-report alexithymia scale. *Psychotherapy and Psychosomatics,* **44**, 191–9.

Temoshok, L. (1987). Personality, coping style, emotion and cancer: towards an integrative model. *Cancer Survival,* **6**, 545–67.

Truax, C.B. & Wittmer, J. (1973). The degree of the therapist's focus on defense mechanisms and the effect on therapeutic outcome with institutionalized juvenile delinquents. *Journal of Community Psychology,* **1**, 201–3.

Trujillo, N. (1986). Toward a toxonomy of small group interaction-coding systems. *Small Group Behavior,* **17(4)**, 371–94.

Watson, D. & Clark, L.A. (1992). Affects separable and inseparable: on the hierarchical arrangement of the negative affects. *Journal of Personality and Social Psychology,* **62**, 489–505.

Watson, M. & Greer, S. (1983). Development of a questionnaire measure of emotional control. *Journal of Psychosomatic Research,* **27**, 299–305.

Watson, M., Haviland, J.S., Greer, S., Davidson, J., & Bliss, J.M. (1999). Influence of psychological response on survival in breast cancer: a population-based cohort study. *The Lancet,* **354**, 1331–6.

Weinberger, D.A. (1990). The construct validity of the repressive coping style. In *Repression and dissociation: implications for personality theory, psychopathology, and health* (ed. J.L. Singer), pp. 337–86. Chicago: University of Chicago Press.

Weinberger, D.A. & Davidson, M.N. (1994). Styles of inhibiting emotional expression: distinguishing repressive coping from impression management. *Journal of Personality*, **62**, 587–612.

Weinberger, D.A. & Schwartz, G.E. (1990). Distress and restraint as superordinate dimensions of self-reported adjustment: a typological perspective. *Journal of Personality*, **58**, 381–417.

Williams, R.B., Haney, T.L., Lee, K.L., Kong, Y., Blumenthal, J.A., & Whalen, R.E. (1980). Type A behavior, hostility, and coronary atherosclerosis. *Psychosomatic Medicine*, **42**, 539–49.

Wortman, C.B. & Lehman, D.R. (1985). Reactions to victims of life crisis: support attempts that fail. In *Social support: theory, research, and applications* (ed. I.G. Sarason & B.R. Sarason), pp. 463–89. Dordecht: Martinus Nijhoff Publishers.

Appendix 1

SPAFF for Breast Cancer for videotape and text

Neutral

Attributes

Code neutral when no affect is being expressed or when the emotion expressed is below our codable threshold. Look for information exchange or other non-emotional content and the absence of physical cues. Sometimes what seems like emotional content will be delivered with neutral affect—code neutral.

This is important because, though the participant may have experienced a particular emotion, if their emotional response is something that has happened in the past and they are only now discussing it, or they are able to objectively examine their feelings and are therefore expressing neutral affect in present time, it is important to note that distinction. In order to accurately capture emotional expression, we must reflect the emotion that is being expressed in the moment. We are not in the business of speculating about what emotions they may have experienced or expressed heretofore, and an examination of their feelings on a particular subject is not the same as the expression of the feelings themselves. If we do not make this distinction we are in danger of sliding down the slippery slope of presumption or analysis in which we presume/think we may know what is/was happening with a particular individual. In that case, reliability cannot be consistently achieved. It is for this reason that we must strictly adhere to coding what we see in present time. In addition, when a speaker is off camera and silent, we code neutral.

Physical cues

None.

Dialogue examples

- Participant #1: Talking about crying but expressing neutral affect (emotional content but neutral affect)
- Participant #2: So that would be what date? (neutral content, neutral energy)

Interest

Attributes

Interest involves responding with positive energy to another member of the group. Positive energy is genuine engagement with what is being said and/or active curiosity. They may finish each other's sentences, comment positively on what someone has just said, or seek elaboration from the speaker. Interest must either have emotional content (how do you feel about that?) or positive energy. If the content and the voice tone of a question are neutral, code neutral. Remember that interest may not always take the form of a question.

When interest does appear as a question, there is a distinctive upsweep in the tone of voice at the end of the phrase. This tonal shift, which indicates that the person is genuinely looking for a response to their question, is a distinct indicator of interest. Occasionally, participants will ask questions to which they already know the answer or the answer to which does not particularly interest them (this is sometimes done to shift the focus from them if they are feeling uncomfortable). These kinds of questions do not have the tell-tale upsweep in the voice and would not be coded as interest. Likewise, rhetorical questions are not coded as interest.

The term 'interest' is sometimes used to indicate interest (e.g. 'that's interesting' or 'I would be interested to know...'). When interest is being expressed, the speaker may continue to seek additional information. The vocal pattern is sometimes staccato with positive energy and a higher pitch. Low-level excitement is also coded as interest.

With the exception of truly introspective statements in which the speaker is really looking to examine a personal situation/thought or behavior pattern etc., we do not code interest as a self-directed emotion.

Physical cues

Look for action units (AUs; Ekman & Friesen 1978) 6, 7, and 12 (attentiveness). Listen for increased volume and tempo of speech and decrease in pauses between talk turns.

Dialogue examples

- Therapist #1: What did it feel like when you told her you loved her?
- Therapist #2: So when you were driving home, how did you feel?
- Participant #2: Did she ask you to come back again? Responding to Participant #4's account of her visit to Participant #9 when she was very ill (positive energy).
- Participant #1: So how old are you? Responding to Participant # 8 who has just told the group that it is her birthday (positive energy).
- Participant #3: Could anyone stay after group next week so I could interview you?
- Participant #3: It's chemotherapy? Inquiring about Participant # 11's treatment.

Text interest

(Here and following, 'text' refers to our modification of SPAFF as it is used to code videotape to our SPAFF for Text used to code transcripts.)

- Questions are assumed to be true interest as we have elected to assume that no one would waste their time typing a question if they weren't actually interested.
- Be careful, because participants do not always type ? marks; the exception to questions being coded as interest is when the questions are asked in relation to technical difficulties with the online chat process (such as 'Is anybody else having difficulty logging on . . . ?') which does not indicate interest as emotional content, but seeks to solve a logistical problem.
- Also, look for single exclamation points ('Wow!') that indicate low-level excitement, which is coded as interest.

Validation

Attributes

Validation communicates openness, acceptance, and respect. It involves affirmation and openness to another's point of view, even if they disagree. It communicates understanding and support. Validation is often expressed by summarizing the point of view or story another person has just talked about. It is important to note that validation is delivered with a neutral voice tone and yet involves more than information exchange. Compliments delivered with neutral voice tone and expressions of pride (self-directed) usually indicate validation. (If there is empathy in the content or the voice tone, look for a lot of warmth in the voice or mirroring of another's feelings—code affection.)

Counter-validation is often seen in these participants' groups. This occurs when an individual whose idea was just summarized may often say 'yes' as if to affirm that the individual had an accurate understanding of what they were saying. For this reason, the word 'yes', when not expressed as an answer to a question, is coded validation (unless it is followed by '. . . but').

One must be careful when coding validation if it occurs when an individual is summarizing another person's thoughts/feelings because, for it to be validation, it must be an *accurate* summary. If an individual has summarized for someone and that person's response is 'well, that's not exactly what I was trying to say . . .' then, in fact, they did not 'get' what was being said and therefore did not validate them with their summary.

Validation does not need to be expressed exclusively toward members of the group. Positive comments made about family members, co-workers, etc., are common. Even experiences and resources can be validated. For example, a group member returning from a pilgrimage may describe the experience as 'profoundly moving', thereby validating it. Likewise, someone may suggest that a particular book 'held a lot of valuable information for me' and, in that expression, is essentially validating the author.

Physical cues

Look for a head nod with eye contact. Listen for backchannels, such as 'mmm hmm', and neutral voice tone.

Dialogue examples

- Therapist #2: Low energy (echoes/summarizes Participant #4)
- Therapist #2: You could be more natural (echoes/summarizes Participant #4)
- Therapist #2: That sounds very comfortable (affirmation)
- Therapist #1: It strikes me in listening to what you say that the most touching moment was when you acknowledged to her that you might not see her again (summarizing)
- Participant #3: You said before... (summarizing Participant #4)
- Participant #4: That was really special (compliment; neutral voice tone)

Text validation

- Content: caring/affirmation/accurate summary of another's feelings you will sometimes encounter 'textual backchanneling'—things like 'wow' (without an exclamation point) and 'really' (without a question mark)—that participants will throw in as acknowledgment and to let the 'speaker' know that they are really 'listening' and 'got' what was expressed.
- Greetings, when punctuated by a single exclamation point ('Margaret!' or "Hi, Margaret!'), as if to say 'I'm happy you're here', would be coded as validation. This is different from the generic 'Hi everybody' that is used when someone 'enters' the chatroom simply to announce their 'arrival'.

Affection/caring

Attributes

Affection/caring involves warmth and closeness as well as empathy. Verbally, affection/caring may be demonstrated by direct compliments or expressions of support. It may also take the form of a concerned question or statement (e.g. were worried about you) delivered in a warm voice. Nonverbal cues are very important. Facial expressions and a warm voice tone should match the content of what they are saying. There are two levels of affection

1. *Low level*—affection/caring without touching
2. *High level*—affection/caring with touching

Physical cues

Look for facial expressions of concern or looks that express the same feeling being expressed by another member or the group as a whole. Concerned eyes often look squinty. An individual expressing affection may often lean in toward the person to whom they are speaking, and might tilt their head to the side and/or back. Listen for a warm voice tone (lowered volume and legato (smooth and connected without breaks) meter) or a voice tone that mirrors (i.e. expresses the same affect, tone, cadence) that of the woman they are responding to. Mirroring is tricky to catch in that if it were an isolated expression it would appear to be whatever emotion is actually being mirrored but, in this context, the expression of solidarity with the other person presents itself as affection.

Dialogue examples

- Participant #1: I want to thank you for talking with me last week. It was really helpful because... (warm voice tone; closeness; becomes high level when they hold hands)
- Participant #4: I had a real good visit with her (warm voice tone)
- Participant #4: Describing holding Participant #9's hand during a visit to her home (warmth, closeness)
- Participant #5: Thanks to another participant who has come over to comfort her (warmth, closeness)

Text affection/caring

- Content: complementary/supportive
- Exclamation points can often upgrade statements to low affection
- High affection: participants sometimes type 'big hugs for Karen!' or ((((Karen)))) which indicates a hug; concerned/caring questions ('How have you been?'), especially if the content/context indicates that the person to whom they are speaking has been experiencing some challenges. This is different from a casual 'How are you?' as a standard greeting. The use of superlatives moves the text into affection/caring. For example, 'That's wonderful' would be validation but 'That's really wonderful' would be affection. Likewise, 'I'm sorry to hear that' would be coded validation, whereas 'I'm so sorry...' would be affection.

Excitement/joy/delight

Attributes

This code is characterized by a high level of positive energy. The speaker will often exhibit rapid fluctuations in pitch, volume, and rate of speech; place exaggerated emphasis on certain words; and seem buoyant. If you could use an exclamation point to punctuate the person's speech and if their content is positive, then you should probably use this code. This code is differentiated from interest by the level of intensity and by the delight associated with this code. Look for this code especially when people are coming in and greeting each other and also during storytelling. Surprise (in a positive context) also falls within this code.

Physical cues

Look for AUs 1+2+5+25 or 26 and often 12.

Dialogue examples

- Participant #4: I walked in and said, [Participant #9]! (high level of positive energy)

- Participant #4: I've never seen anything like it! (high level of positive energy)
- Participant #1: It's absolutely amazing!—Describing a place where she went on a trip (high level of positive energy)

Text delight/excitement/surprise

- Lots of !!!'s, ?!?!?, etc.
- Sometimes capitalized

Also, look for key words of excitement or incredulity/surprise (e.g. 'You're kidding or That's amazing).

Humor

Attributes

Humor is coded only when it is shared by two or more members of the group. There is an underlying tone of happiness and a genuine sense of something being funny. Do not confuse this code with tense humor which serves primarily as an expression of tension. When in doubt about whether to code humor or tense humor, code tense humor. Begin coding when the speaker delivers the punch line of a joke, unless they are laughing already. To be clear, a 'punch line' is whatever final phrase or statement elicits a humor response on the part of the listener(s). That is to say, there doesn't need to be a set-up followed by a traditional punch line (as if to a joke).

Physical cues

Look for the AUs (6) of happiness and especially for warmth around the eyes. Look around the eyes for movement of the muscles that cause crows' feet wrinkles as the person laughs. The AU is called the 'cheek raiser and lid compressor'.

Dialogue examples

- Participant #4: Even Billy?! Relating Participant #9's surprise over something her son did.
- Participant #1: If they want something interesting... Goes on to describe all the things she could do during her interview with 'Good Morning America'.
- Participant #1: How about letting my husband do it? There's a statement!

Text humor versus tense humor

- Has to do with content and a somewhat subjective 'ringing true' feeling.
- Participants may respond with 'lol' (lots of laughs), 'rotfl' (rolling on the floor laughing), typed laughter like 'hee hee', 'ha ha', etc.

Typically, when the humor is genuine, there is a great degree of group participation—an immediate flurry of 'lol' or 'ha ha' etc. that springs up from the rest of an OSG, for instance. With tense humor, a participant will often make a joke and there is no response—the rest of the group ignores it or, at least, does not refer to it/respond to it. Sometimes a participant will often say something and then follow it with their own 'ha ha'—which would be coded as tense humor. Also, while 'hee hee' and 'ha ha' are most often genuine, 'har har' is typically tense and, if it comes from another or other members of the group, can indicate a shared tense humor.

Be careful that tense humor/unfunny jokes are not confused with sarcasm which is coded as contempt.

Tense humor

Attributes

Tense humor is often preceded by a tense moment and often serves to defuse a tense situation. It may occur in short spurts and then go back to a negative emotion. Tense humor may occur during a speaker's talk turn as little giggle that appears to let off steam. Tense humor lacks an underlying tone of happiness; it is not truly enjoyed the way genuine humor is. When tense humor is shared, it tends to take on a 'fox in the henhouse' quality. If we are not sure whether to code tense humor or humor, we code tense humor.

Physical cues

Look for a nervous laugh (must be more than a smile) which does not appear to express genuine happiness or humor. Tense humor can often be distinguished from real humor by the absence of smiling eyes and by tension around the mouth. Start coding tense humor at the moment the tense laughter starts.

Dialogue examples

- Participant #3: Is that what I sounded like? (short spurt of laughter; not shared)
- Participant #2: After last week, I didn't want to be late! (shared laughter; tense subject)
- Participant #4: They see us going into the psychiatry building and figure they don't want to get us upset! (not shared)

Tension

Attributes

Tension often arises when an uncomfortable subject is introduced into conversation. A tense speaker will have difficulty expressing what they want to say. They may start several incomplete or unfinished thoughts or say 'uh' and 'ah' repeatedly without being able to communicate what they mean. (This is different from searching for words or pausing to compose their thoughts.) They may fidget excessively or bite their lip.

Tension typically presents itself as a kind of friction within the speaker. As if engaged in some isometric exercise, the speaker will press against themselves physically—either pressing their lips or hands together, pressing their hands to another part of their body (rubbing their face, etc.), smacking their lips, or some other unrelaxed gesture—or vocally. Stuttering or finding some kind of verbal filler (uh, um, er) is a kind of vocal friction and should be coded as tension. Vocal/verbal tension is coded when the speaker emits a *triple* stutter/placeholder.

Physical cues

Look for AUs 20, 1+2+4, 1+2+4+5, as well as unfelt smiles, frequent eye movements, lip biting, and fidgeting. Fidgeting often includes touching their face, wiggling their legs, and wrinkling their forehead.

Dialogue examples

- Therapist #1: Stopping and starting a sentence when describing heightened security at psychiatry building due to threats from a former patient.
- Participant #3: Having trouble expressing herself when asked how it feels to hear Participant #4 say she hasn't learned anything from the group.

Text tension

Tough to pick up in text unless person actually types 'um', 'er', etc. in context of a difficult topic.

Fear

Attributes

Fear is an emotion that is rarely expressed openly. Women may express fear related to their disease, as well as in response to a difficult subject being discussed in the group. There are two levels of fear—verbalized and high-level. Be careful not to confuse fear with tension. Fear is much more intense, and less common, than tension, which is described below. There are two levels of fear:

1. *Verbalized fear:* code verbalized fear when someone is talking about being afraid (e.g. I'm really scared of the pain). There are no physical cues.
2. *High-level fear:* code high-level fear when someone looks as if they are in imminent danger, like a deer caught in headlights. They must show physical cues but may or may not verbalize their fear.

Be careful when coding verbalized fear that what is being expressed is truly fear—look for fear words (e.g. scared, afraid, terrified, petrified). The term 'worried' most often expresses concern or preoccupation rather than fear (as in 'I'm worried that I might have left the coffee pot on') and is, therefore, seldom coded as fear.

Physical cues

Look for AUs 20, 1+2+4, 1+2+4+5, frequent eye movements, and fidgeting.

Dialogue examples

- Participant #6: The fear of not being alert is a big issue for me (verbalized fear)
- Participant #7: That's why I'm here in this group. I'm scared! (verbalized fear)
- Participant #5: When I think of some of us getting sicker and not getting better, it's very frightening (verbalized fear)

Text fear

Can only pick up verbalized fear

Sadness

Attributes

Sadness is expressed in many forms by members of the group. In some cases, a woman may act resigned and helpless, as if all energy has drained from her. In other cases, women may be full of energy while expressing grief and loss. There are two levels of sadness:

1. *Low-level:* all sadness that is not high-level is coded low-level.
2. *High-level:* high-intensity sadness is coded when there are tears or when a woman's voice clearly sounds as if she is crying. Also code high sadness if she is too choked up to speak.

Physical cues

Look especially for AUs 1, 4, and 15. Sad eyes (often cast downward) and drooping around the corners of the mouth (pouting) are important clues for sadness. Listen for a lowered or wavering voice and long, low-energy sighs.

When a person moves in and out of low sadness, the cues most often work together —downcast eyes work in tandem with a lowered voice tone. More often than not, when the gaze comes back up, so does the vocal energy level, moving the speaker out of sadness.

Dialogue examples

- Participant #8: Breaks into tears while talking about her friend potting pansies for her.
- Therapist #1: [Participant #11] died last night at 11:15.
- Participant #8: I'm glad her friend from Denver was able to see her before she died (downcast eyes; tearful voice).

- Participant #8: I have this feeling that if I go away for four days some of these people won't be here (tears).
- Participant #1: I feel sad and relieved . . . relieved that her struggle is over (low energy; grief).
- Participant #1: I feel very sad and unsatisfied about my work as a nurse (resigned; low energy; downcast eyes).
- Participant #5: Sobbing while talking about husband's diagnosis with an incurable brain disease.
- Participant #9: I don't think you understand how hard it must be for your mother (tears).
- Participant #6: I don't feel very in charge of my life (resigned).

Text sadness

- Content: expressions of sadness, loss
- Make sure participant is referring to present or continuing feeling rather than past sad feelings
- High sadness: participant must actually say she is crying

Contextually, look for someone who has not participated much in the conversation. They may subsequently refer to having had 'a rough week' and may refer to themselves as being 'down', 'blue', or 'low'. People who are sad typically say/type less, don't give a lot of details/information, may give a brief context, and then simply say, 'it's been hard', etc.

Frustration/constrained anger

Attributes

When expressing frustration, the speaker sounds as if she is irritated, annoyed, fed up, exasperated, at the end of her rope. Frustration is often characterized by an inner conflict that is not being resolved. It may look like a mixture of anger and tension, as if the person is flustered and not able to get beyond this point.

Frustration/constrained anger is different from tension in that, rather than being exclusively fricative (a consonant type: as the sound is pronounced, friction is produced, hence fricative), the expression comes out in small bursts that are then stopped short. Listen for a staccato musicality to the voice, or certain words being punctuated. Look for a combination of tension and expression (such as speaking through clenched teeth).

Physical cues

Look for AUs 4, 5, and 7, as well as tightening around the mouth and pressing the lips together. Sometimes an 'unfelt' smile can indicate repressed frustration. Often a telltale sign of a speaker who is exhibiting frustration is a slight (or pronounced) bobble of the head as they are speaking. Listen for stuttering and changes in the rhythm of speech and in the way certain words are stressed. Also listen for sighs that come out in short bursts.

Dialogue examples

- Participant #6: I realized I had some anger (irritated voice tone).
- Participant #10: I'm so sick of having cancer. Hits the arms of her chair with her palms.
- Participant #6: It's little dumb things like knowing I'll be in chemo for 14 days (irritated voice tone).

Text frustration/constrained anger

- Content: expressions of irritation/annoyance, exasperation
- Often capitalized
- May actually type phrases like 'argggh!'

People who are frustrated tend to say/type more. The musicality of the word choice is more staccato. If you were to read the text aloud, you would notice punctuated speech. Look for short-burst phrases/sentences (though sometimes quite a lot of them). Also, there is often a great deal of punctuation used (especially exclamation points). This is different from the punctuation that is used with excitement and is distinguished by the content/context.

Direct anger

Attributes

Compared with other emotions, anger is direct and pure. There is a purposefulness to anger as if something is being accomplished just by expressing the anger. An angry speaker may be scolding or accusing someone else, and she may sound irrational. Her words are likely to be biting and abrupt. Anger often feels like an explosion or release (in contrast to frustration which is constrained).

Physical cues

Look for AUs 4, 5, 7, 23, and 24, along with lip presses, involuntary twitches or jerks, tightened jaw, and clenched teeth. Listen for a voice tone raised or lowered out of its normal range and for changes in the way words are stressed.

Dialogue examples

- Participant #7: Pow! Pow! Pow! Slams her fist into her other palm over and over again while discussing her anger at the rapid progression of her disease.
- Participant #2: Nothing in this whole damn world is inevitable! I wanted to hit him. Talking about a doctor who told her it was inevitable her lung cancer would return.
- Participant #6: I felt not taken seriously... Telling the group why she is angry at them for creating false distinctions between primary and metastatic disease.

Text direct anger

- Most of the direct anger we code in the face-to-face groups is based on nonverbal cues, so there would have to be a blatant outburst among group members or something equivalent to code direct anger.

With direct anger, you will see someone express only the anger statement. Direct anger tends to have nothing other than the feeling itself expressed. If they can say/type more (and often a lot more), it's probably constrained anger. Direct anger, on the other hand, looks something like this: 'Aaarrghh!! I'm furious!!!!!!!', and that would be all that is said/typed during that 'talk turn'.

Contempt

Attributes

Contempt is a direct communication of lack of respect toward someone or something—a group member, a relative, a doctor, the cancer. It is very different from a simple disagreement with another point of view. There are two types of contempt:

1. *Micromoment contempt:* this code applies when only physical cues for contempt are present.
2. *Verbalized contempt:* this code involves verbal cues with or without physical cues. There is a suggested superiority in verbalized contempt, an icy quality, a looking down one's nose.

Look for sarcasm, hostile humor, mockery, name calling, and insults. This may be an important code to look for during storytelling. If someone is acting the part of another person during storytelling and is expressing negative affect, contempt is the most likely code. In addition, contempt can be self-directed.

Physical cues

Look for AU 14 (unilateral or bilateral, with mouth open or closed) and eye rolls. Eye rolls are always coded contempt.

Dialogue examples

- Participant #3: That can really be annoying—talking about crying for no reason (AU 14).
- Participant #4: Mocking visitors of Participant #9 who whispered at her bedside (does a facial 'whatever').
- Participant #1: Telling group about the stupid questions a reporter asked her.

Text contempt

- Content: hostile humor, insults
- Micromoment contempt cannot be coded from text

Look for sarcasm and be careful not to code it as tense humor. Responses to sarcasm that are also sarcastic are considered mirroring and would be coded as low affection.

Domineering

Attributes

The goal of domineering behavior is to dominate another person (or the group) in no uncertain terms. Someone who is domineering is trying to force compliance and to get someone else to withdraw, retreat, or submit to their point of view. Domineering often involves a patronizing tone, the invalidation of another's point of view, and a lecturing quality. A person who is being domineering will often cite authorities and/or use cliches and platitudes to support their own position. A domineering person will most likely insist on maintaining the floor and will interrupt others or speak over them. When in doubt about coding domineering, use the two out of three rule—at least two of the following three attributes must be present to code domineering: voice tone, content, and physical cues.

Physical cues

Look for AUs 4+7, 4+5+7, 1+2+7, 1+2+5, along with chin down, body leaning forward, finger shaking, head cocked to one side, and glowering. Eyebrow raising is an important cue. Listen for incessant speech with a staccato, lilting rhythm and a patronizing tone. (If you feel as if this person is treating you like a small child, domineering is the most likely code.)

Dialogue examples

- Participant #3: In a lecturing (but positive) tone, telling the group 'This is what I get from you...'
- Participant #4: Telling the group about her conversation with Bill Moyers in a patronizing tone.
- Participant #2: I'm not going to *not* plan! (adamant; forceful)
- Participant #2: Talking about misdiagnosis of pericardial involvement in breast cancer patients (patronizing).

Text domineering

- Can't apply 'two out of three' rule, so must find alternate way to pick up.
- Content: preaching, lecturing, or has a patronizing tone—someone who is 'on their high horse' about something. Look for unsolicited advice being given that is not followed by the recipient(s) feeling appreciative or that the speaker was actually being helpful.
- We didn't see any in the pilot groups.

Belligerence

Attributes

Belligerence functions to provoke a response, as if trying to pick a fight or challenge another person. The intent behind belligerence is to get a rise out of someone else by pushing their buttons. (This is in contrast to domineering which involves stifling someone else's point of view in order to get their compliance.) Look for taunting questions, questions which seem impossible to answer without placing yourself in an untenable position, and dare statements that seem to say 'Well, what would you do if I did?'

Physical cues

Look for AUs 1 and 2, jaw thrust forward, and head cocked back. Often, the speaker will thrust their head forward and then pull it back (either in a down/up sweep or a side-to-side sweep). Voice tone may be lilting and sing-songy and may go up in pitch at the end of a sentence.

Dialogue examples

- Participant #3: Why don't you call your doctor? Challenging Participant #11 who is having symptoms but has yet to discuss them with her doctor.
- Participant #8: But you must have had to talk about it since this episode in the hospital. Taunting Participant #2 by suggesting that she must have had to talk with her children about her cancer in light of recent progression.
- Participant #5: Don't you think so? Challenging Therapist #1 about views on suicide.
- Participant #12: What are your objectives for your groups? Challenging the expertise of Therapist #1.

Text belligerence

Content: taunting questions, challenges, dare statements, provocation

Defensiveness

Attributes

Defensiveness communicates feigned blamelessness, as if to say 'Leave me alone. What are you picking on me for?' Look for 'Yes, but...' statements and excuses, cross-complaining, and counter-criticism, which serve to deflect the criticism initially directed at the speaker. Picture the speaker holding up her arms in front of her face as if to defend herself from attack. Be aware that it may not always be clear what the speaker views as a threat (you may wonder why she feels defensive). She may be defending someone other than herself.

Defensiveness is generally directly related to some individual and that is reflected in the content of the defensive statement (such as 'well, I didn't know about it' or 'she never told me') or phrased with a question as part of it ('how were we supposed to know...?').

Physical cues

Listen for a whiny voice tone. Look for arms folded across the chest and possibly a false smile (lacking AU 6).

Dialogue examples

- Participant #5: Apologizing for bringing up non-cancer-related concerns.
- Participant #3: Telling Participant #4 she fears depressing her.
- Therapist #1: Suggests that Participant #1's sadness may relate to grief over something of herself that he doesn't know yet.
- Participant #2: Responds to Participant #8's probing that her family talks about her breast cancer but doesn't dwell on it.

Text defensive

- Content: cross-complaining, counter-criticism

A lot of defensiveness begins with 'I' statements—'I didn't know...' or 'I just thought...' and sometimes takes the form of a question 'How was I supposed to...?' or 'How are we expected to...?'

Whining

Attributes

Whining is coded only when a whiny tone of voice is not accompanied by content that indicates another code, most likely defensiveness. Look for content that is emotionally neutral, such as trivial complaints about the weather.

Physical cues

Listen for a whiny, sing-songy tone of voice with a higher pitch than normal.

Text whining

- Content: trivial complaints

Often about logistical/technical difficulties with the online chatroom process. Quite often about the weather.

Disgust

Attributes

Disgust is an involuntary reaction to a noxious stimulus. It is a physical aversion to and active rejection of something one finds repulsive. The offending stimulus could be an unpleasant treatment, the advancing disease itself, or a specific behavior on the part of a group member, doctor, or someone else. The reaction is involuntary, as if the urge to gag is uncontrollable. This tends to be an infrequent code because it is so strong and because it is physical rather than emotional. Occasionally, it can be seen in group members who, as a part of their treatment, have become particularly sensitive to smell. Be careful not to confuse this code with contempt. (Code disgust when physical cues are present but content cues do not indicate contempt.)

Physical cues

Look for AUs 9 and 10, comments such as 'eeww' and 'yuck', and physical cues suggesting nausea.

Dialogue examples

- Participant #7: Talking about spread of her disease.

Text disgust

- Participants sometimes type disgust words such as 'UGH!' or 'yuck;
- Often capitalized

Look for all manner of disgust words: 'ugh', 'yuck', 'gross', 'eeeew', 'disgusting', etc.

Stonewalling

Attributes

Stonewalling involves a total lack of listening behavior and an active tuning out of the conversation. Look for away behavior, such as looking away and automanipulation, which conveys the message, 'I'd rather not be here right now'. This is likely to be a rare code in these groups.

Physical cues

Look for a stiff and frozen face with clenched jaws. Also look for automanipulation and looking away.

Text stonewalling

Cannot code from text.

Overtalk

It does occur, in the course of a group session, that there are times when there is no one individual 'speaker' because multiple people are speaking simultaneously and no one person can be determined to have the focus of the group. This often happens as people are arriving and simultaneous parallel conversations are taking place. It may also happen if a particular topic elicits simultaneous response from multiple group members. These moments are referred to as 'overtalk' and are coded as though they are their own subject/group member.

Emotion coding overtalk involves picking out the dominant emotion in the room at any given time. Because of the multiple simultaneous shifts in emotion, the code does not usually stay on any one emotion for very long, nor does it tend to capture whole sentences (or even phrases). Instead, it rides the peaks of emotional expression as they segue between dominant emotions. The most reliable, then, of the 'four quadrants' of emotion coding, where coding overtalk is concerned, is voice tone. Because you are not coding an individual subject/group member but are, instead, coding the entire group (or, at least, everyone involved in conversation) as though they are a single subject, FACS is not particularly helpful—both because the camera is almost never positioned in such a way as to capture the faces of every group member, and because trying to synthesize facial cues from multiple group members on a microsecond basis to determine a dominant emotion would not be a viable (or reliable) process.

Additionally, the body 'quadrant' can be helpful insofar as it provides confirmation of the emotions perceived through voice tone or, for example, when it occurs at the beginning or end of a session wherein the physical contact of group members (perhaps hugging with greetings) may be the dominant emotional content in the room. Content/context is helpful in the broadest sense—to know whether one conversation is a fairly neutral exchange of information, while a completely separate and simultaneous conversation may be a person relaying an amusing story/anecdote; or, in the case of the entire room erupting in conversation rather than the structure of separate simultaneous conversations, it helps to be aware of whether participants are responding/reacting to a joke/humorous statement or whether the simultaneity of response has risen out of disagreements/differing opinions about a particular subject on the part of group members, etc.

Aside from this broad context, the codes shift too quickly to rely to any large extent, on a second by second basis, on content. Therefore, beyond the assistive nature of the other 'quadrants', one must listen with great acuity to the change in voice tone across all conversations to find the dominant emotion. Such changes may occure from one second to the next—a burst of frustration from one person may almost immediately be overshadowed by the laughter from someone else in the room, only to be overtaken by the long slow sigh of a sad participant. These auditory cues are what permeate the environment, which is why they are the greatest determining factor in the dominant emotion of the room. One must be careful, however, in coding overtalk, that the reliance on voice tone does not depend exclusively (or even primarily) on volume. It may be, for example, that one person is laughing and, while they may be the loudest emotion expressed, there may be more participants expressing validation (just at a lowered volume). The dominant emotion in the room is the one being *most* expressed (not just expressed the loudest).

Appendix 2

Coding stories or narratives in breast cancer support groups

Story coding summary

Generally, to make the distinction between 'story' (any kind—story, cancer story, history story, or childhood story) and 'no story', distinguish between things that have *happened* (actions, events, occurrences, experiences) and things that do not fall into this category (thoughts, feelings, responses/reactions, justifications). In order to be aware of this general distinction, look for 'I' or 'me' (or 'we') in relation to the action/event/ occurrence (even if someone else is involved). For example: '*I* went to the store...' is something that happened; 'She told *me* that...' is something that happened; '*We* used to go to...' is something that happened. Be careful not to confuse a past tense emotion/thought/etc. with an event. That is to say, 'I wondered if I was doing the right thing...' is an expression of a thought/consideration that was in the past—it is not an event.

Also, in realizing that past tense is used in telling a story, be clear that that is a grammatical distinction, even if it is a relatively current event. For example, saying 'I went in for my biopsy today...' is a cancer story: 'Went' is (grammatically) past tense, so even though she is talking about 'today', she is relating an event that has happened— definition of a story.

There is, then, a shift in the I/me/we when it is a history story. Look for the connection to the speaker ('my mother', 'my aunt', etc.) that may then be replaced with the pronoun 'she' for the duration of the story. For example, 'When my mother was first diagnosed with cancer, she didn't want anyone to know and she hid it from us for a long time...' would be a history story.

Examples of codes

Story off : used for women who are not being story coded on a particular assignment.
No story: coded when the woman is not telling a story.
Story: used when the story being told does not fall into one of the three more specific categories.

- A story is usually told in the past tense.
- Must be about a personal experience (this includes past group sessions) or relationships with others.
- Example: 'She called me and told me about her chemo...', 'She told me she wouldn't be coming today...' (Note: when talking about relationships with others, it must be directly tied to the woman in some way. For example, saying 'She told me...' or 'She had chemo today...' is not a story.)
- Answering a question without any elaboration is not a story.
- Personal observations are not a story unless the observation was the result of or leads to an action.

- Example: 'I feel sad', 'I wondered if that was the best thing to do', and 'I thought that was unfair' are not stories. 'When my doctor told me I had to have more chemo, I felt really sad' or 'When I visited Joan and saw her in so much pain, I thought it was just really unfair' are both stories.
- If the woman uses a general 'you' subject instead of 'I', but the subject is so specific that it is obviously a personal experience, this is a story.
- Example: 'When you're standing by the side of your broken car and no one's around, you suddenly realize how alone you are'.
- An explanation of why a woman told a story is not a story.
- Example: '... that's why I came to group today' or 'I'm telling you this so you can learn from it...'

Cancer story: a story in this category deals with the woman and her cancer (e.g. treatments, doctor visits, things the doctor has said). Stories about personal experiences with other people with cancer do not fall into this category.

Family history story: stories in this category are about relatives who have had cancer. (It must be a relative, not a friend or someone else in the group.)

Childhood story: these stories are those that deal with the woman's childhood.

SUPPLEMENTARY
MATERIALS

CHAPTER 12

TECHNICAL ISSUES IN RECORDING NONVERBAL BEHAVIOR

MARK G. FRANK, PATRIK N. JUSLIN, AND
JINNI A. HARRIGAN

From the early days of recording nonverbal behavior using 16mm film or paper and pencil reports, significant technological strides have been made. Such advances include the use of video and audio tapes, digital and 8mm recording, computer-driven data collection and analysis, scanning devices—all of which offer greater visual and auditory capture of the nonverbal data; greater clarity, precision, and comparability of data; and improved data storage and analysis than 20 years ago. The intent of this chapter is to provide information on the best methods of securing and maintaining audiovisual data. This review is not intended to be comprehensive but to allow researchers the opportunity to consider the technical methods most appropriate for collecting data to answer their research questions (see Berger 1970; Wallbott 1982).

General considerations

Several basic questions must be addressed by the researcher prior to choosing a method of recording behavior. Athough some research questions can be answered without making a permanent record, and others can be modified in such a way as to make recording unnecessary, most will require a permanent record. Recording can be costly not only in terms of materials (e.g. videotape), but also in terms of designing the research setting; obtaining and training the necessary recording personnel; the additional time spent during each experiment in recording the information; the time spent storing and maintaining the recorded materials; and, later, retrieval of data previously recorded.

It is not uncommon for nonverbal behavior researchers who have toiled in the field for years to have amassed boxes and boxes (or shelves and shelves) of recorded material. Obviously, recorded material permits repeated viewing and comparison among behaviors and across modalities, and among research laboratories. Recorded data permit slow-motion viewing of minute behaviors and, often, researchers will discover relationships and patterns that were not originally considered at the time of recording. This can yield significant information related to the research question, or old research questions, or to the development of new research questions.

Permanent records, accessed after the recording, are vital for allowing observers or raters to make assessments and judgments about the participants' behavior. For example, recording participants as they describe a highly anxious experience permits not only analysis of the participants' nonverbal, vocal, and verbal behavior, but offers opportunities for independent raters to evaluate the participants' behavior in selected scenes aggregated onto a stimulus tape showing many participants (Harrigan *et al.* 2004). In addition, the participants' behaviors can be compared with respect to their scores on various personality measures, skills, and abilities.

Not surprisingly, the decision to record imposes constraints on the research set-up, and often recording areas require significant modification, particularly when recording studios or facilities are not available to the researcher. The latter often determines the type of equipment used to record. Researchers may dream of ideal settings where several unobtrusive cameras and microphones can be operated by several recording personnel in an environment with soundproofing, adjustable lighting, etc., but often the reality is considerably more modest. Typically, a researcher struggles to figure out where to put a camera, in a generic room, that will provide the most visible and audible record of the behaviors he/she is after.

Besides the location issue, other constraints in the recording process include the number of participants recorded (e.g. a dyad, family, group); whether an interactant will be recorded with the participants; how close or far should the cameras and microphones be to the participants; the effects of the recording apparatus on the naturalness of the participants' behaviors; and so forth. Inevitably, compromises will be made in the recording process, but some specific questions need to be considered:

- What is to be the recording medium (e.g. digital or analogue video format)?
- What are the logistics and obtrusiveness involved in using the various technologies?
- How will one light, frame, and choose segments of the behaviors to study?
- How will one store the behavioral data?

Many of these questions are addressed in the following more specific discussion and recommendations.

Specific considerations—the recording media

Video issues

Most studies that examine nonverbal behavior have opted for videotape as the recording medium. But, there are many types of video available now that a researcher should consider, that vary in format, each with pros and cons. The primary issue for anyone doing behavioral research is to choose a format that will provide as clear an image as possible, one that is easy to use, and, ideally, that enables one to dub without losing information and/or quality.

Format

The first issue that a researcher must deal with is the videotape format used in his or her home country. The analogue recording standard in North America, the Caribbean, much of South America, and Japan is called NTSC (National Television Systems Committee), whereas most of Europe, Asia, and Australia use the PAL (Phase Alternate Line) standard. Other individual places such as France or Russia use SECAM (Sequential Couleur Avec Memoire i.e. sequential color with memory). Typically, PAL generates the best image as defined by lines of resolution (525 for NTSC versus 625 for PAL). Within both NTSC and PAL, one can obtain SuperVHS versions that offer a better image still.

However, the NTSC and PAL also differ in the number of frames per second they generate; NTSC runs almost 30 frames a second (actually 29.94), whereas PAL runs at 25 frames a second. By contrast, movie cameras employing film run at 24 frames a second. The frame rate is not a trivial problem as it means a researcher cannot be confident of uncovering any micro behavior that happens in less than $1/30^{th}$ of a second ($1/25^{th}$ for PAL). To give an example, at one point we thought we had discovered some new phenomenon where individuals were blinking but not closing their eyelids entirely. It turned out that the blinks happened so quickly that a frame rate of 30 frames a second was not fast enough to always capture the moment the lids came together.

Digital vs. analogue

The second issue is whether to use the analogue or digital format. The standard VHS video cameras available on the market feature analogue recording methods; more modern cameras use digital formats. Digital is a bit more expensive than analogue, but worth the price when it comes to dubbing, because the main disadvantage of analogue techniques is that each dub one makes from a master tape will look less sharp than the master, and each copy from a copy will have a worse image still. Digital entirely stops this dubbing drubbing of images, so the original, sharp images are preserved from copy to copy.

Within this issue of digital vs. analogue is an issue of how to record digitally. There are affordable cameras today that will record directly to a computer hard disk, rather than to a digital videotape. These have the advantage of not needing to buy videotape. They also have the advantage of being almost immediately accessible to editing with some computer-based editing package. The disadvantage is that many of the straight-to-computer digital cameras do not feature very high-quality images. Another disadvantage is that one must have a computer that is fast enough to keep up with the camera's frame rate, otherwise one gets dropped frames (i.e. the system fails to record a frame or two whilst it catches up) that can disrupt an analysis, and particularly one in which timing is important. A final disadvantage is that a crashed hard disk can cost one all data in a flash. This means one would most definitely have to back-up those materials, and probably on CDs or some other material, after recording directly onto the hard disk. And, most of the compression algorithms used for these digital images still mean that a single frame can take up quite a bit of space (almost 1 megabyte per frame). So, a 2-minute video can take up to 3.5 gigabytes.

Interlaced vs. progressive scan

A third issue with these analogue methods is that they usually involve using interlaced images. What this means is that for each scan of the video image, only the odd or even lines of the picture are transmitted consecutively. For the next pass, the other lines are shown. This is imperceptible to the human eye as the images flicker—not too dissimilar to how the old 24 frames a second movie film didn't show every position of movement, but when the images are run consecutively the human eye sees it as smooth movement without noticeable jumps. (The fact that films of Charlie Chaplin's era do look jumpy is only because they ran at 16 frames a second.) But keep in mind that, in an interlaced image, only half the image is changing at any given time.

Interlaced images have a few advantages. First, interlacing is usually the default option in any sort of video camera, thus a researcher can buy more affordable cameras. Second, for most gross behavioral coding one might do, interlacing will not make a difference. Third, one can use these interlaced images in very basic videorecorder to videorecorder style editing. Thus, one does not need very expensive editing packages to make copies or to generate smaller clips to analyze. Finally, interlaced images can look very clear to the human eye.

Interlacing has some disadvantages. First, a researcher will lose some of the sharpness of the images when examined in fine-grained frame-by-frame analysis because half of the image is moving at any time, causing the image to blur slightly in a freeze frame. It does not preclude doing fine-grained analyses, but it just makes it a bit harder, which can reduce some of the inter-coder reliability essential to behavioral coding. This becomes particularly problematic if a participant is making a big behavioral movement, like a sweeping gesture of the hands, and so forth. Second, current advances in computer vision technology have produced a number of computer algorithms that can score videotaped behavior such as hand or head movements, eye blinks, and even facial behavior (e.g. Bartlett *et al.* 2005). To take advantage of this technology, the video data must be digitized, and many algorithms cannot adequately analyze interlaced images without dubbing them into a different format with progressive scan.

In contrast to interlaced images are non-interlaced or progressive scan images. These images are not interlaced but are more like the old movie films, where each frame is like a distinct digital photograph. They have the advantage of being clearer images than interlaced, particularly in slow motion when the participant is moving. They are also amenable to most editing packages. Finally, most computer vision algorithms work best with the progressive scan images, thus allowing any possible future uses. The only disadvantage is that cameras with the progressive scan options are often a little more expensive than those with interlaced image only. Given where we might be heading with some automated coding systems (e.g. Bartlett *et al.* 2005), our recommendation is clearly to use digital images, in progressive scan, at a minimum 30 frames a second.

Audio issues

The art of recording voices is a complex topic, and we are only able to offer some general suggestions in this chapter (the reader is encouraged to consult more extensive sources; e.g. Ballou 1991; Wallbott 1982; Yewdall 1999). There are many reasons for making sound recordings in studies of nonverbal behavior and affect expression. The voice samples may be used for repeated presentations in judgment studies (Harrigan *et al.* 1996) or for detailed acoustic analyses (Juslin & Laukka 2001). Researchers may also want to manipulate the samples in various ways; see Modules D and G of Chapter 3). Moreover, recordings may be used to create larger databases that can be used in several studies by various researchers.

The extent to which one can achieve these goals depends on the recording quality, among other things. As a rule, high-quality recording is required, but the precise requirements obviously depend on the goals of the study. If the goal is mainly to obtain information about what is happening in a particular situation, the sound quality is not critical. However, if the goal is to conduct sophisticated acoustic or perceptual analyses of the voice sample, it is absolutely necessary to use high-quality recordings. Some voice measures are very sensitive with regard to sound quality (e.g. jitter), whereas others can be obtained fairly reliably even with samples of poor quality. However, as emphasized by Juslin and Scherer (Chapter 3), voice researchers need all the cues they can get, so the aim should always be to obtain the best recordings possible. Achieving this requires detailed planning of the recording and careful consideration of everything that could potentially go wrong.

A first choice facing the voice researcher is whether to record only sound or both sound and picture. Visual recording obviously introduces a number of additional problems (Wallbott 1982), and it may seem preferable for practical and economical reasons to record sound only. Yet there is something to be said for recording the visual channel as well: it makes it possible to examine possible interactions between the two channels (Harrigan *et al.* 2004). For instance, facial expressions may affect voice characteristics (Tartter & Braun 1994), and it may be very useful to have visual information as well when analyzing the voice. The use of both sound and video will probably become more common as equipment becomes cheaper and easier to use. In addition, researchers increasingly try to develop large databases of emotional expression samples that can be used for a variety of aims (e.g. Douglas–Cowie *et al.* 2003). Therefore, if it is practically and economically feasible, researchers are encouraged to record visual as well as auditory information.

A second choice concerns recording equipment. As a rule, we recommend the use of digital recording equipment. First, good digital recorders are often cheaper than good analogue recorders. Secondly, digital recordings are more durable than analogue recordings. Thirdly, digital recorders require less maintenance than analogue recorders. Finally, unlike analogue recorders, digital recorders are capable of full dynamic range. In digital recording, the sound is stored as a stream of discrete numbers that each represents the air pressure at a particular time. The numbers are generated by an *analog to digital converter* (ADC). Each number is called a sample, and *sample rate* refers to the number of such samples taken per second. The most commonly used sample rate when recording sound is 48 kHz. However, if you require synchronization between video and sound recording, it may be better to use 44.1 kHz. The quality of built-in microphones in video recorders is typically poor, and speech samples should therefore be recorded on a digital audio tape (DAT) recorder of superior quality, or directly onto a hard disk. There is a variety of professional DAT recorders on the market, including some that are small and portable and that can easily be used for field recordings using battery power.

Digital recording may involve storage of information on plastic tapes (DAT tapes), compact flash (CF) memory cards, or computer hard disks. Such recordings can easily be transferred to software for acoustic measurement (see Module D, Chapter 3) There are still analogue recorders out there (e.g. many of the analogue VHS cameras), but digitizing is definitely the way to go—in particular, due to the ability to dub the audio without losing quality.

A major problem in recording is what type of microphone to use and how to set it up. A microphone is a *transducer* that converts sound waves (or acoustic energy) to electrical energy. There are two general types of microphone: *dynamic* (which have no active electronics involved in amplifying the signal) and *condenser* (which require an external power supply, either batteries or so-called 'phantom power') microphones. Condenser microphones are generally preferred in laboratory settings because they have a broader and more uniform frequency response that gives a natural sound. On the other hand, they are more fragile and sensitive to transient sounds than are dynamic microphones. Although one should strive to obtain a microphone with a *flat frequency response* (i.e. one that reproduces all frequencies more or less equally), it must be noted that all microphones color the sound to some extent. One further aspect of microphone choice concerns its *directivity* (i.e. the relative sensitivity of the microphone to sounds that come from different directions, as indexed by its *polar pattern*). Which direction characteristics are desired depends on the distance between the microphone and the speaker, as well as on whether the speaker will be stationary or moving.

The researcher must decide whether to use a large, stationary microphone or a small microphone attached to the speaker. The choice obviously depends on the specific goals of the study, but each type of microphone has its pros and cons. The advantage of a traditional stationary microphone is that it is easy to set up, it may be hidden from the speaker (if that is a desirable requirement), and it does not invite handling by the speaker. On the other hand, a smaller microphone attached to the speaker is less obtrusive to the speaker, allowing him or her to move around freely, which means that it may be preferable to record speech samples in natural environments. However, this kind of microphone is not always easily attached to the speaker and it invites handling by the speaker that may produce unwanted noise. Moreover, if using a wireless microphone, there is the potential problem of signal interference in certain environments (Wallbott 1982).

There are a number of good methods to gather the audio stream that vary in their conspicuousness to the participant. The most conspicuous would be to use a headset or ear clip microphone that typically attaches to the head or ear of the participant, with a microphone that extends out toward the mouth. A constant distance to the participant's mouth is thus maintained, regardless of head movements. The next most conspicuous is to use a microphone which has a hard wire connection to the video camera or other recording medium or a lavaliere microphone, which is a small microphone that attaches to a participant (usually their lapel or similar location on their shirt) and transmits the audio via a sender pack to a receiver where it is actually recorded. A shotgun microphone, as the name states, looks a bit like a shotgun and points directly at the participant, but can be concealed more readily in the room. Finally, the least conspicuous is to use a hidden-room microphone. These are often hidden in a vase or a light socket or similar place where a participant cannot see them. Just as with decisions regarding which camera arrangement to use, each type of microphone has different advantages and disadvantages.

There are some unique aspects to consider when deciding what microphone to use in nonverbal behavior experiments. First, a researcher should consider how obtrusive this microphone will be to the participant. If it is too obtrusive, it will remind the participant that they are being recorded, which may change their self-awareness and, thus, their behaviors, in known or unknown ways (e.g. Kleck *et al.* 1976). For example, in deception research, this may have a particularly strong effect on the 'liars' versus the truthtellers, as they have the additional cognitive load caused by deception to which this further addition of self-awareness may exacerbate this overload. Second, a researcher should consider the quality of the recording in light of the participant's anticipated movements. For example, if a participant moves his or her head quite a bit, that may take him or her in and out of the effective range of a shotgun microphone, unless someone is aiming the microphone at all times. Again, this may also affect 'liars' and truthtellers differentially, as research has shown 'liars' tend to have fewer head movements than truthtellers (Ekman *et al.* 1976). Thus, one might obtain more reliable audio from the 'liars' rather than the truthtellers. Likewise, a participant who faces away from a microphone hidden in a light socket will not be recorded as well as a participant who faces the light socket. If the microphone is planted in a vase or object in front of the participant, it may enter the video shot that is later shown to coders or judges, which may distract them.

In some nonverbal studies, one can instruct participants to sit still, but in some types of emotion or deception research, behavior will be more active, so the audio recording should be prepared to follow the participants. In all nonverbal behavior work, it may be useful to make sure that if there is an interviewer, interrogator, or confederate interactant (e.g. in clinical, deception, or similar studies), that his or her interview or interaction be captured on audio to permit later analyses or as a check to make sure they are following their script or to check on unanticipated variables in this interactant's behaviors. This permits the researcher to more accurately measure things like a participant's response latency, as the researcher can note exactly when the question was finished being asked, and when the participant started his or her response.

The main issue with all recording decisions is obtaining the best possible record of the participant's audible behavior that will enable a researcher to examine the greatest number of variables. Most of the microphones described above will capture much of the essential information. However, one variable—amplitude, or loudness (see Box 3.2, Chapter 3)—is very elusive to capture reliably because most of the above solutions permit variability in the distance between participant's mouth and the microphone. The headset or ear clip microphones solve that problem, but at a cost. First, they make the participant more aware that he or she is being recorded because of this direct physical attachment of the microphone to the head. Second, the presence of these microphones in the facial shots of the participant may block some critical facial movement that a coder might score, or may simply be distracting to later raters or observers who will make judgments about the participants. Again, the researcher will have to weigh these options and decide what variables are most important.

Finally, some general advice when recording sound. First, record in as quiet a setting as possible and use sound-absorbing materials to reduce the sound reflections, since in

DAT recorders there is no tape hiss that will cover up the sounds of background noise (e.g. a fan, traffic noise). Secondly, pay attention to the recording level: use a fixed recording level, if at all possible, to make possible inter-individual comparisons of voice intensity; generally avoid using automatic recording level control, because it may amplify background noise in speech pauses, or otherwise influence acoustic measurements; and note that on digital recorders, too high a recording level will result in a 'clipped' signal, rather than a gradual limiting. Thirdly, listen back to the tapes to make sure that the sound is OK, and make back-ups of all tapes and check that they are identical to the original (even digital audio tapes may fail).

Specific considerations—getting the shot

Once the audio and video recording format has been decided, now the researcher must decide how to best capture the participants' behavior.

Lighting the shot

Another important feature of recording video is to make sure the lighting is adequate, and does not generate shadows or blurs or other problems that will make later interpretation of the behavior difficult. The main problem seems to occur with the use of overhead lights. Overhead lights can create shadows under the eyes of the participants, making some sorts of facial analyses difficult to conduct. A variety of techniques can be used to 'fill in' those shadows. One is to use some floor lighting— either like footlights used in the theater, or to simply put desk lamps or other light sources onto the floor of the recording room. One should be careful as to the eye level of those lights, because if they shine directly into the eyes of the participants they can distract the participant, or generate some behaviors that may mask a significant behavioral finding (e.g. if they squint a lot, this may hide some other potentially interesting findings in the subtle eye or brow movements or blinking). A second technique is to use a white table (if the participant is sitting at a table) or other white materials (rugs, sheets, etc) to reflect the light from the ceiling upward under the eyes. This is often less obtrusive to the participant and less expensive for the researcher.

A second issue is the blur and pixilation that can occur when the lighting is too bright, or not color-balanced. This means that if a participant moves his or her head too quickly, a frame-by-frame analysis will reveal an unfocused streak that will be difficult to analyze in terms of subtle behavioral clues. Pixilation means that the contours and borders between shadows, bumps, and ridges on a face caused by muscle movement may expand in such a way as to eliminate many of these clues to muscle movement. We have had to deal with pixilation when the color balance in the lighting is not right, as it reduces the quality of the image noticeably.

A final consideration with lighting is to decide between incandescent or fluorescent lights. Fluorescent have the advantage of being cheaper to run than incandescent, and they tend not to generate the additional heat that incandescent bulbs do, which may cause the participant to sweat or wipe his or her brow or generate other clues that may confound the actual clues associated with emotion or deception. However, the disadvantage of fluorescent lights is that, unlike incandescent lights, they flicker, and that can be a problem with some of the higher-end cameras. In addition, they often emit low buzzing sounds that can become problematic when doing later voice contour analyses. This is why most TV and other media use incandescent lighting.

Framing the shots

It seems obvious that a researcher must decide what sort of information he or she is most interested in and, of course, design the data collection to maximize the quality of those variables. The difficulty as usual is in the details. The first issue that must be addressed is the type of shot, or better yet, the framing of the shot of the participant. There are a number of options in terms of the frame. Typically, many researchers since Ekman & Friesen (1974) have opted to use two separate cameras—one to shoot a facial close-up, and a second to shoot a full-body image. The separate cameras were important in identifying the leakage hierarchy of controllable behaviors in deception situations (Ekman & Friesen 1969). A researcher can keep these separate shots as separate videotapes taken from two cameras, or use a mixer to put the images on a split screen with the full body on one half and the facial close-up in the other half. If there is an interactant, a researcher may want to include them in the shot, depending upon whether they are unconstrained in their interacting or questioning or are given a behavioral and questionnaire script. If they are sufficiently trained to behave a certain way and are scripted in their questions, it is less imperative to video record them (but very important to audio record them).

A second issue related to the frame is the zoom of the shot on the face. How close in to the face does one want to be? This is an important issue in terms of the generalizability of the eventual findings. If the researcher is interested in extrapolating to face-to-face encounters, then the size of the head in the image should approximate to the size of a head in a face-to-face encounter. This will typically mean a frame from the mid-shoulders (above the armpit) to the top of the head. Moreover, if the researcher is doing microanalyses of the facial expressions along the lines of Ekman & Friesen's Facial Action Coding System (FACS; 1978), he or she must have a fairly close-in shot, framed as above. These facial scoring systems can use shots framed farther away, but this may cause a drop in intercoder reliability as the facial size shrinks. For most reliable results with systems like FACS, the face should be minimum quarter of the screen, although smaller shots can still be used. The other problem is that if the shot is framed farther away (i.e. the head size is smaller), not only will details in the expressions of participants be lost, reducing reliability in coding microbehaviors, but also it will reduce the researcher's abilities to draw conclusions about what happens in people's facial expressions during deception, anxiety, embarrassment, or other emotions, or about people's abilities or lack of abilities to detect deception or emotion from facial expressions in general.

If the shot is framed such that the entire participant as well as the room is in the shot, then the researcher is limited to generalizing his or her results to spotting emotion and deception from across the room, rather than in terms of normal conversational distances (which Hall (1966) argues is approximately 0.45–1.2m). Likewise, zooming in too close also produces problems because a small head movement on the part of the participant may take them out of the shot. So we recommend that a researcher leave enough room to allow at least normal head movement activity, and our experience is that a shot from the mid-shoulders to the top of the head usually keeps the participant in frame for most of the movements they may make, but also is detailed enough to permit any facial analysis one may wish.

These issues with zoom also apply to the full-body shot. Because of space constraints in laboratory settings, cameras may be so close to the participant that, even when fully zoomed out, one cannot get the entire participant into the shot. Thus, choices have to be made. If a researcher wants to measure the effect of the body independent of the face, then he or she can leave the participant's head out of frame (but be careful, as often during their interviews they move around enough that the head may dip back into the shot). Sometimes, one may want a full-body shot—then one may have to cut off the feet of the participant. This of course sacrifices information about foot movements (as different from leg movements, which is more typically studied). The recommendation is to get in as close as one can on the body whilst retaining as much information as possible.

A caution at this point may be warranted. A researcher should keep in mind what they may be doing with their video recorded shots in the future. By putting the facial close-up and full-body shot on a split screen, one may have to use some crude techniques to separate them later. For example, if a researcher plans on coding the facial behavior without any potentially biasing information from the body, then one may have to block the body half of the screen with a sheet of thick paper. Likewise, if later one decides to show these videos to a judge or groups of judges to assess their abilities to detect emotion, deception, or other characteristics of the participants, then again one may have to block out half the screen with some paper or other opaque object. There probably is some sort of technique that can digitally disentangle these images, but one should become aware of them, and their costs, prior to making the decision on recording.

The converse problem can also be true. One may originally be interested in the body movements independent of the head, but later may want to understand what happens when both are available. Thus, to reassemble both the facial close-up and the full-body shot into a single shot later may be very difficult.

One solution is to convert the video to digital media with enough compression where one can show both images simultaneously in different computer windows. The key to this, of course, is to have very accurate frame counting and/or time coding so that these windows are showing the same point in time accurate to, at least, plus or minus one frame.

This caveat applies to all techniques in nonverbal research. There may be valuable information that a researcher excludes unwittingly by sacrificing certain bits of data in his or her shots or audio recording. This may only become apparent later. So, the general recommendation is to get as much data as one can in each data collection to provide the greatest number of analysis/hypothesis options later.

Auto-focus warning

For all video recording—but in particular facial close-ups—it is imperative to switch the video camera to a manual focus. If one leaves it on auto-focus, when the participant moves his or her head (as they often do in these unconstrained scenarios), the infra-red auto-focus beam will hit the wall behind the participant rather than the participant's head, thus rendering the shot out of focus temporarily. The basic technique to prevent this is to switch to manual focus, then zoom in as close to the participant as possible, focus the shot, and then zoom out to the required shot size. This way if the participant now moves forward, back, or to the side, they will stay in focus.

To hide or not hide the camera

Another issue to consider is whether or not to use a hidden camera. Research going back to the 1970s (Kleck *et al.* 1976) showed that the presence of a camera does seem to alter people's behaviors in measurable ways. Again, the researcher must decide which level of camera presence is acceptable for ecological validity. A variety of options exist: one can leave the camera, on its tripod, in the room with the participant; one can bury and/or hide the camera in a bookshelf or other object within the room; or one can put the camera behind a one-way mirror or smoked glass.

Each technique has its advantages and disadvantages. The main advantage of putting the camera in the room is that there is nothing between the participant and the lens, allowing the researcher to get the highest quality image possible. Other advantages only apply if having a camera in the room is the ecologically valid thing to do. For example, a researcher may be studying the effects of the camera on a remote parole board hearing—where the inmate in prison talks to the camera whilst addressing the parole evaluation panel, who is in a remote location observing this testimony and responding. Or, one may be interested in the situation where a person is being interviewed remotely (e.g. a talk show where numerous guests debate a topic from various locations) where, in this instance, although the interviewees do not see but only hear the interviewer, the interviewees are actually speaking to a camera.

The main disadvantage of a camera in the room is that if there is an interactant, the presence of the camera can distract a participant away from the interactant. This may or may not lower the ecological validity, depending upon what situation the researcher is hoping to model. As shown above, this would not be such an issue if the participant were speaking directly to the camera, to unseen observers viewing at the other end. In other situations, this may generate differential effects on participants in some conditions. For example, in deception research, this might have a stronger differential effect on the 'liars', who are already being more taxed cognitively by attempting to lie than the truthtellers.

The second technique is to keep the camera in the room, but employ various forms and levels of camouflage for it. At the most basic level, one can reduce its salience by simply putting some black electrical tape over the red light on the camera, as the flashing or brightness of that light may be a constant reminder to the participant that they are being recorded. A better technique, that allows one to keep the pristine unimpeded shot but reduces the salience even more, is to hide the camera. Given the size of cameras today (as small as a few centimeters), they can be placed almost anywhere—in the overhead air ducts, in the light switch, in a plant in the room, under a table, and so forth. If one has a larger, higher quality camera that cannot be buried into a light switch, one can at least reduce its salience by putting it into a bookcase or other location in the room so that it blends into the background (this also means covering the red light that indicates recording). One technique we have used successfully is to put the camera behind a bookcase, line the back of the bookshelf with black felt, and then cut out a hole in the back of the bookcase and the felt and put just the camera lens through the hole. This does not fully hide the camera, but in a scenario where a participant is being interviewed about their truthfulness, almost all participants report that they forget about the camera once the interrogation begins. This is despite participants' observations that they can readily find the cameras if they are asked to look for them.

The disadvantage of using these techniques depends upon the camera one uses. Most of the tiny 'lipstick' cameras that can be hidden in light switches generate fairly poor images, often only in black and white. Moreover, often these cameras have limited zooming power that precludes one from obtaining a facial close-up adequate to score subtle muscle movements. Higher quality digital cameras are usually larger, thus harder to hide. However, many of the higher-end models do allow for remote aiming, focusing, and zooming, so once they are hidden or buried, one can still have some control over the image as the interaction proceeds.

The third technique is to put the camera behind a one-way mirror or smoked glass of some sort. This eliminates the camera salience issue, but does reduce the quality of the image somewhat because of the glass/mirror filter the image must pass through. Moreover, one must use a remote microphone (attached or wireless) to transmit audio to the camera. However, this gives a great deal of leeway to the camera operator to make sure the participant stays in frame and focus, because now this operator can simply stand behind the tripod and move the camera without worrying about being seen by the participant. Another advantage is that the camera operator can make a bit more noise without it being heard by the participant or distracting them. However, using one-way mirrors or smoked glass also means that the room housing the camera must be dark, with no residual light, as that will illuminate the camera and operator so that they become visible to the participant on the other side of the mirror or glass. And don't throw away the black electrical tape—an observant participant will be able to see the red flashing light of the recording camera through the one-way mirror, even if the lights are out. And finally, the sophisticated research participant of today will assume, when they see a mirror in a laboratory, that someone is behind it observing them, which may alter their behavior in some way—even if there is no camera behind it. One technique to reduce the distracting effect of a very large mirror in the room is to place a curtain or some other material to block off as much of the one-way mirror as one can, whilst still permitting the necessary observational field of view.

Ethics of recording

An important research issue raised by the use of a hidden camera is informed consent. In the USA, some University Ethics Committees (or Institutional Review Boards or

IRBs) may prohibit a researcher from not disclosing the audio-video recording of the participant prior to the deception scenario. Some IRBs may allow a researcher to not inform before the videotaping, but then require the researcher to inform the participant afterwards and, at the same time, to provide the participant an opportunity to have that videotape erased now that they are fully informed. We have found that in a paradigm where participants are being interviewed about whether they have lied, we always obtain *a priori* informed consent about the audio-video recording, but hide the cameras. Given the attention-grabbing power of the interview/interrogations we do, almost all participants report that they forget about the cameras quite quickly. But, for us, *a priori* consent is not a big issue because we are interested in generalizing to real-life law enforcement situations. Prior to their interrogation, real suspects are, by law, informed that they are being recorded. We note that we are unsure whether these issues apply to other countries.

Finally, the more sophisticated university student of today will probably assume they are being videotaped anyhow. By withholding that information until the debriefing, a researcher may cause a participant to wonder where the cameras are, which may turn out to be a distraction in and of itself—although we don't have any data that directly addresses this.

Even though we provide *a priori* informed consent (e.g. Frank & Ekman 1997), we also extend an opportunity for the participant to erase the video afterward. Rarely, however, has a participant exercised that right (only twice in about 500 participants). In some ways, one can argue that a participant is not fully informed even with *a priori* informed consent. They are, of course, fully informed that they are being recorded but, if one stretches the concept of informed consent, one could argue that participants are not fully informed until after the interview is over. So this *ex post facto* consent seems like a reasonable and fair procedure to both the researcher and the participant.

A final IRB issue involves what sorts of consent a researcher obtains. Often, in nonverbal research, one will wish to either examine various behaviors or to assess the ability of judges to detect emotion or deception or evaluate personality characteristics. In deception work, this means the videotapes of the 'liar' and truthteller participants are going to be shown to other judge participants. At times, this may mean people who know the participant. Moreover, a researcher may later wish to post something on the web or a representative of the media may wish to show an example for the nightly news. To fully cover the researcher, it makes sense to obtain consent from the participant to show their videotapes in a variety of other settings, ranging from judge studies all the way to the nightly news on TV. We use a step-by-step consent, where we ask participants to consent to a variety of uses, starting with just allowing the research team to analyze the behaviors, to asking about judge studies with other participants, to classroom teaching examples, scientific conferences, public presentations, and ending with the media (newspapers, radio, TV, and the internet). This particular consent is fairest to the participants if it is obtained after the experiment is over.

Ethics of public presentation

Researchers should be mindful, when presenting these materials in some public forum, that they keep identifying information about participants to a minimum, unless participants consent otherwise. In deception work, researchers should also be mindful about describing a participant as a 'liar' as, although to the researcher it is their experimental condition, to others, it rings pejorative about the participant's character. If this were an experiment where participants were randomly assigned to conditions, then making sure to mention often that they were assigned to steal or lie would be good form. If the video came from an experiment where the participant was allowed to choose whether to lie, then one should make sure to explain whatever artificial constraints applied to the situation, and that lying was a sanctioned behavior in the experiment, and so forth.

Prior to analysis

Before engaging in any analysis, there is a variety of information a researcher may want to encode including, on the videotape itself, details about participants, date, time, and condition. A time code will localize behaviors of interest in the sequence. There are a number of methods one can use to accomplish these goals.

Logging information

One should have the participant number somewhere on a participant's videotape or audiotape. This does not need to stay on the video for the entire duration of their recorded behaviors, but it is usually a good idea to have it somewhere so that researchers do not have to rely upon their memory as to which participant is which. Most videotape cameras will allow additions of text right onto the screen with some sort of caption or titling command. However, if a researcher does not have this option, one can do this the old-fashioned way—use a director's clapboard or simply make up a sign that lists the participant number, condition if appropriate, date, time, experiment, interactant, or whatever other information one might want. (For one study, 14 years ago, we used two blank videotapes with paper wrapped around them on which we wrote the participant number, date, time, etc. We then slapped the two videotapes together like a clapboard.) Thus, one's finances should not be an obstacle to recording this information. It is always preferable to have this information on the videotape itself, and not to rely on simply the labels on the videotape or other recording medium. Likewise, for audio-only recording, a researcher should read into the file the participant number, etc., prior to the recording of the participant.

These techniques do not mean it is not important to label the tapes/recording medium immediately, so as to not confuse tapes—it is. A researcher may want to use Polaroid or digital still photos with the participant numbers, conditions, and so forth, as well as to help distinguish one participant from another (since muddling participants is an unrecoverable error).

Time coding

In order to reliably score nonverbal or other behaviors in a videotape, a researcher must know where these behaviors occurred in the behavioral stream. This means inserting some sort of frame/time counter. There are a number of solutions to this problem—from using a VITC time code that is often built into video cameras, to inserting a separate frame counter after the initial recording, to simply using the numbered frames generated by some digital media. The key here is to get some sort of system that will enable you to reliably count frames, as that will be the smallest unit of time you will be able to identify using video (in NTSC, this means about 30 frames a second, or 1/30th of a second; whereas PAL will be 1/25th of a second). Ideally, these measures should be tied to the actual frames, and then one can estimate durations of various nonverbal and verbal measures accurately within 1/30th of a second by simply counting the frames.

Another way to keep track of time is to have a digital clock that is accurate to at least 1/30th of a second behind the head of the participant and thus out of his or her view. This clock will not distract, but will keep accurate time and will insure the ultimate goal—that each frame of the video, for each participant, has a unique marking.

Other ways for frame marking include tapping into a Global Positioning System (GPS) clock, although that clock typically runs only as fine as whole seconds—so unless everything one is interested in occurs for longer than one second, then one ought to consider another solution. But for a GPS, one needs a receiver and to lay the signal into the audio track of the videotape. Finally, it is possible to create your own time-code generator, to lay into the audio signal as well, but this means hiring someone with the skill to build this device.

Time coding is also essential for coordinating multiple cameras so a researcher can track back when a behavior occurred in the head or body. There are a number of ways to coordinate separate cameras. Some low-tech solutions to synchronization include blocking the shots by using a header or director's clapboard that lists the participant number and other important information (see above). This clapboard should be in all camera shots, which means typically it will be in front of the participant's face or where the participant's face will be when they enter the recording room. One simply snaps the top board down onto the base. Thus, when one is editing the raw video, there is now a clear visual signal on the video (when the boards connect), as well as an audio signal (the clap) that will assist in identifying start and stop times for analyses. Or, if one is going to enter a time code after the initial recording, then this clapboard visual (as well as audio) signal becomes a clear point in time in which to start the time-code generator. Instead of a clapboard, a simple hand clap may accomplish the same function. However, one will not have the participant number, etc., on the video, unless this is shot earlier, using a poster board or the titling functions of the video camera.

Using these methods will insure that the time code will be 'almost' identical on each video: 'almost' because with some time code or frame counters, one must physically press the start button as the tape is rolling. Thus, human skill is involved to ensure that the counter starts at the same frame on different tapes. Unless one's hand–eye skills are exceedingly poor, most people can have their time codes on different tapes within a few frames. Our experience is that if you don't have an unambiguous signal, this error range expands considerably and may even be off by as much as 30 frames (one second in NTSC).

Clapboards are now available that also generate a flash—yet another visible signal as to an exact frame in which to start the frame counting on all cameras. There are other technical solutions to coordinating cameras; some involve using what is referred to as 'genlock', where the cameras share the same timing mechanism so that each camera is shooting the same frame at the exact same moment in time. However, many high-quality cameras with this feature can be quite expensive. There are less expensive cameras that do this, but they tend to suffer from a poorer visual image.

Back-up issues

An important consideration is what to do with the raw data once it has been recorded. If scoring these data for nonverbal behaviors, one should not use the original or master video. If for some reason that videotape got corrupted, the entire nonverbal data set would be lost. Our recommendation is to dub the originals onto a copy master (first-generation dub). In fact, it is at this dubbing stage that one can impose an external frame counter so that the copy master is also the frame counter master. Then, make a second-generation dub from this copy master (rather than from the actual master), in which to do the more laborious, back-and-forth movements associated with nonverbal scoring. The main reason for this is that the back-and-forth viewing of nonverbal behaviors can be especially tough on videotape, making damage (and the permanent loss of data) more likely. Using a second-generation dub means that even if the videotape wears out or gets corrupted, one can simply make another copy from the time-code master and start again. The downside of this approach (with analogue, but not digital video) was mentioned earlier—that one loses sharpness with each generation of video dub.

If the data are on digital videotapes, and the analysis is played on a computer-based video viewing platform, then the digital video tape is a back-up, and the digital image that the researcher loads into his or her computer is the first-generation copy. It can make sense, at this point, to copy this first-generation copy onto a different hard drive or computer as another back-up. The biggest problem with the digital media is the size of these digital files, as one frame using a 5:1 compression ratio (in essence making each frame like a jpeg) can be up to 1 Mb in size (again, it depends upon the compression algorithm used). Thus, a three-minute video can take 1 Mb × 30 frames/second × 60 seconds/minute × 3 minutes = 5400Mb of space (or approximately 5.3Gb). If a researcher has 40 participants, it means they would need to have 212Gb of storage space on their computer. If a researcher has two camera shots, it means they need 424Gb of storage space (almost half a Terabyte!). Converting to DVDs (which use MPEG-2 compression) would save more space but, with more compression, one will lose more information and the video quality will be slightly less (but typically still superior even to original analogue video).

Long-term storage issues

Having audio/video recorded the data, one must consider how to store it to ensure maximum utility for both the current project and any future projects. There are some basic rules here. If using tapes of any sort (video, audio—be they digital or analogue), they should be stored upright and away from sunlight and high humidity. Within a few years, videotape will degrade. Some videophiles recommend fast-forwarding videotapes all the way to the end, and then rewinding to the beginning, once a year to maintain the integrity of the video. Given APA ethical guidelines that state one should preserve data for five years, post publication, this is not a trivial issue.

If data is recorded digitally, there are some other issues to consider. One can store data on CD-ROMS or DVDs. If the data was originally analogue, this requires a digital conversion. There are various products that allow this conversion, through a number of different computer operating systems or platforms, and they have come down in price such that, at the time of writing, one can obtain the software for under $1000. Regardless, the CD-ROMS and DVDs should provide better, more robust long-term storage than the videotapes, whilst taking up less space in the lab. However, these solutions are not impervious to dust, light, heat, and so forth, so one would still need to store them upright and away from those environmental factors that degrade material in general. Moreover, there is some competition over which type of DVD format is best (e.g. DVD-R, DVD+RW, DVD-RW; not unlike the Beta vs. VHS videotape controversy in the 1980s), so one should keep an eye toward which format might offer the best long-term access.

Data can also be stored on a big computer hard disk with its own controller, known as a RAID (Redundant Array of Inexpensive Drives). Many of the computer servers used by academic departments or businesses are RAIDs, and they are being used increasingly in research labs themselves. These RAIDs allow for an enormous amount of storage in a relatively small space; for example, one can get 1 Terabyte (1024Gb) of space into a piece of hardware about the size of a desktop computer. (RAIDs can generate more heat than a desktop, so adequate ventilation/climate control is needed.)

There are a number of ways to configure this RAID to create automatic back-ups or even to allow direct recording onto the RAID. For example, one can configure the RAID to 'RAID 0', 'RAID 1', 'RAID 0 + 1', 'RAID 5', or 'RAID 10'. (There are others, but these are the most popular.) In our work, we use RAIDs that have 10 drives each. If we set it to RAID 0, this means the data being recorded goes across all 10 of the drives (called 'striping'). This allows fast recording which reduces the chance of dropping frames. However, it also means that an error in processing or retrieval may be a permanent error. Thus, for more safe recording and later storage/retrieval, one can consider RAID 1. In RAID 1, the computer (through its controller) will record to two disks at the same time, thus making a copy (sometimes called 'mirroring') as it records. Thus, if one disk becomes corrupted, an automatic back-up exists within the RAID which can be accessed and, in many cases, depending upon the type of data corruption, can be used to repair the corrupted disk. The downside of RAID 1 is that one's total disk space is actually halved; functionally, it is like having only five drives to record and five that back-up. In RAID 10, the disks are blocked so that some are mirrored and some are striped, giving good reliability and speed, but at the cost of even more storage space.

The other RAID configurations described above all trade-off the variables of speed of recording/retrieval, space available for storage, and tolerance for disk failures. If one is simply storing digital data, then the safer options like RAID 1 seem appropriate. If recording, then one would need to experiment with the controller cards and RAID configuration to be sure that all the data is captured safely, without dropping frames.

There are a number of on-line sources that describe the relative costs for each (e.g. *http://www.utexas.edu/cc/vms/about/raid.html*).

Finally, if one is going to store data on a RAID and would like to access it over a few years, then consider making back-up copies of the data to store away from the RAID (known as 'offsite back-ups'). This may be important in that if a fire or some other catastrophe occurs (e.g. the sprinkler system accidentally goes off) and all the material is stored in one location, then even back-ups will be ruined. 'Offsite back-ups' can be on CD-ROMS or DVDs, or one can buy a tape back-up system that can store 100s of gigabytes of data on a tape smaller than a VHS videotape.

Analysis

Having prepared the analogue images for coding, it is best to analyze them on an industrial quality VCR with a jog/shuttle wheel. The reason for this is that most home-use VCRs (even with jog/shuttle wheels) have a rollback feature that causes it to go forward first when one tries to rewind. This becomes a problem when a researcher is trying to locate a specific frame number for when a behavior occurs, as this feature will cause one to overshoot the specific period of time one is trying to analyze. Moreover, with some VCRs, the images will jump and be harder to follow. An industrial grade VCR will smoothly go forward and backward one frame at a time, without any rollback or jump that can slow down the isolation of a particular frame.

When it comes to digital images being played by some computer-based viewer, one can usually go back and forth smoothly, without rollback. The problem is that some of the viewers do not have a slow-motion or frame advance backward command in either their version of a media player or DVD player. Other publicly available media viewers do have frame advance, and that is what we would strongly recommend. Various research teams have created their own players that also allow recording and scoring behaviors on a frame-by-frame basis (e.g. I-Code—Cohn *et al.* 2000).

What to analyze?

At this point, the behaviors, emotions, paralinguistic information, and so forth, are measured as in any nonverbal behavior experiment. Included in this decision might be to determine which segment of the interview to analyze—particularly if the interview is 10 minutes or so long. Whatever the decision, a researcher should be consistent and choose the same segment in time for each participant. So, if they choose the first minute, they should do so for all participants. If they chose the participant's response to the first four questions, or responses to questions 2, 3 5, and 9, they should do that for all participants. In deception research, a researcher must be able to clearly identify which segments spoken by the participant are deceptive, which are true, and which cannot be determined. So, if a participant in a mock theft refers to some incident that happened to him or her on the way to the lab prior to the experiment, researchers may not be able to know whether that actually happened. Likewise, with an emotion study, the researcher should have some independent evidence confirming the presence of the emotion to be more confident that what one is coding is an emotion or the behavior of interest (Levenson 1988).

Reliability

As with any behavioral coding, having a second independent coder is essential to good science. There are a number of techniques to determine reliability and Rosenthal (1982; see also Chapter 5) has discussed the pros and cons of using Pearson's r, Spearman's r, percentage agreement, number of agreements divided by agreements plus disagreements, and so forth. The exact statistic one uses will depend upon the nature of the data, the types of measures, the distribution of scores, etc., so a hard and fast blanket rule cannot be issued.

A cautionary note is in order. One thing to keep in mind is that the data should be time-corrected (i.e. one should look at each variable in terms of the rate per minute, rather than simply report a count). The reason for doing this is that some speakers talk longer than others. A participant who takes longer to answer a question may just simply have the time to generate more of the other behaviors of interest. This then makes it difficult to compare patterns across participants.

A second issue, closely related to the above, is to watch out for multi-collinearity. This means many variables will be naturally correlated and may create artifactual findings unless they are controlled. For example, many researchers will find speech length correlated with speech errors; the most parsimonious explanation is that the more one talks, the more the odds of committing a speech error, independent of anxiety, deception, etc. In deception work, if a researcher finds 'liars' talk more and have more speech errors, he or she cannot determine whether the speech errors are simply an artifact of speech length.

A third issue, related to the one above, is correcting for multiple comparisons. We have heard a number of talks given by researchers who examined 80 comparisons, and reported three significant findings, and then go on to report a different study looking at the same 80 comparisons on a separate sample, and reported three significant results— with none replicating the results of the first experiment. Given the scientific acceptance of an alpha of 0.05, this means that we accept 5 in 100 odds that our results are determined by chance. In an experiment with 80 comparisons, 5% chance means that, by chance alone, we would allow four significant findings. So, at this point, the most parsimonious explanation of the results of an experiment with 80 comparisons that has not made a very strong correction for chance is that they are noise.

One should keep in mind, however, the APA's Task Force on Statistical Inference would have a very different view of how to tackle a problem like this (Wilkinson & Task Force on Statistical Inference 1999). The Task Force would recommend one employ an effect size estimation with confidence intervals. Also, they would recommend that when the same 80 comparisons are made a second time, meta-analytic procedures should be employed. The bottom line is that one should be cautious about just piling in as many variables as one can think of without considering proper adjustments and techniques for isolating effects from noise.

Field recordings

Recording nonverbal behavior in the field presents a myriad of complex problems. But there are some research questions that can be best solved by recording outside the laboratory (e.g. proxemic seating arrangements in public settings, interactions with baggage handlers at airports). In these settings, it is often not possible to control for lighting, background noises, unexpected intrusions, and so forth. Placement of the recording apparatus may not be ideal to capture visual and auditory behavior and may be intrusive for the participants. Lighting and sound are the most crucial variables and need be considered carefully when planning outdoor recording in particular. For example, the optimal camera-to-participant distance must be calculated in advance, especially if a hidden camera is used.

Audio recording out of doors is often not feasible because of background noise and the sensitivity of most microphones, but a wind shield for the microphone may be useful. Recent years have seen important developments in small, portable sound recorders that may be triggered automatically by voice input. Such devices are likely to be very useful in increasing our understanding of real-life vocal expression, as long as the recording quality is not compromised. Debriefing procedures may be required for participants. Eibl–Eibesfeldt (1979) developed an ingenious method of mirrors and camera angles to film his participants without their awareness of being directly recorded. Recording outdoors can be accomplished but the researcher's goals should be modest, particularly if facial, vocal, or small behaviors are of interest.

Finally, while we wish to point out the difficulties encountered in recording nonverbal behavior outside of the laboratory, we do not wish to discourage researchers who are interested in making such field recordings. Clearly, an interplay between laboratory and field studies provides a more convincing basis for generalization of effects in studies of nonverbal behavior, and some phenomena, such as the time-course of nonverbal behaviors in everyday life, may be almost impossible to study in the laboratory.

Conclusion

As technology advances, the trend is always to increase the quality of recording and decrease the cost and size of equipment. This presents interesting challenges to researchers, as sometimes it may make sense to hold off on a project for a few months so one can obtain a better piece of equipment for lesser cost. For example, in 2002, senior author, Mark Frank, requested a RAID for storing and recording data that, at the time the grant proposal was submitted, cost $12,000. However, by the time the grant was awarded, four months later, it cost $8990 (and, at the time of writing, costs less than $6000). However, if one waits to optimize equipment in terms of quality and price, one may become paralyzed with indecision and put off the project indefinitely. Metaphorically, this flow of technology change and costs are like a fast-moving stream, and one must eventually jump into the stream! Luckily, today, there exists affordable equipment that is of such high quality that one can do any sort of nonverbal research without breaking the bank. So, a researcher should jump into that stream as soon as he or she has solidified their ideas. But always keep in mind that the quality of research will be based foremost on the quality of the ideas and its execution, and no technological bell or whistle can overcome a bad design.

Author's note

Senior author, Mark Frank, gratefully acknowledges that some of the ideas in this chapter are based upon work supported by the Office of Naval Research Grant # N0014–02–1–0709 and # N00014–03–1–0847, and National Science Foundation Grant # 0220230. Any opinions, findings, and conclusions or recommendations expressed in this material are his and do not necessarily reflect the views of the Office of Naval Research or the National Science Foundation.

References

Ballou, G.M. (ed.) (1991). *Handbook for sound engineers* (2nd edn). Carmel, IN: SAMS/Macmillan.

Bartlett, M.S., Movellan, J.R., Littlewort, G., Braathen, B., Frank, M.G., & Sejnowski, T.J. (2005). Toward automatic recognition of spontaneous facial actions. In *What the face reveals: basic and applied studies of spontaneous expression using the Facial Action Coding System (FACS)* (ed. P. Ekman). London: Oxford University Press.

Berger, M.M. (ed.) (1970). *Videotape techniques in psychiatric training and treatment.* New York, NY:Brunner–Mazel.

Cohn, J.F, Zlochower, A., Lien, J., Hua, W., & Kanade, T. (2000). Automated face analysis. In *Progress in infancy research, Vol. 1* (ed. C. Rovee–Collier & L. Lipsitt), pp. 155–82. Mahwah, NJ: Lawrence Erlbaum Associates.

Douglas-Cowie, E., Campbell, N., Cowie, R. & Roach, P. (2003). Emotional Speech: Towards a new generation of databases. *Speech Communication*, 40, 33–60.

Eibl–Eibesfeldt, I. (1979). Similarities and differences between cultures in expressive movements. In *Nonverbal communication: readings with commentary* (2nd edn) (ed. S. Weitz). New York, NY: Oxford University Press.

Ekman, P. & Friesen, W.V. (1969). Nonverbal leakage and clues to deception. *Psychiatry*, 32, 88–105.

Ekman, P. & Friesen, W.V. (1974). Detecting deception from body or face. *Journal of Personality and Social Psychology*, 29, 288–98.

Ekman, P. & Friesen, W.V. (1978). *The facial action coding system.* Palo Alto: Consulting Psychologists Press.

Ekman, P., Friesen, W.V., & Scherer, K.R. (1976). Body movement and voice pitch indeceptive interaction. *Semiotica*, 16, 23–7.

Frank, M.G. & Ekman, P. (1997). The ability to detect deceit generalizes across different types of high stake lies. *Journal of Personality and Social Psychology*, 72, 1429–39.

Hall, E. (1966). *The hidden dimension.* Garden City, NY: Doubleday.

Harrigan, J.A., Harrigan, K.M., Sale, B.M., & Rosenthal, R. (1996). Detecting anxiety and defensiveness from visual and auditory cues. *Journal of Personality*, 64, 675–708.

Harrigan, J.A., Wilson, K., & Rosenthal, R. (2004). Detecting state and trait anxiety from auditory and visual cues: a meta-analysis. *Personality and Social Psychology Bulletin*, 30, 56–66.

Introduction to RAID Technology (May 96). University of Texas at Austin, ACITS OpenVMS Services. *http://www.utexas.edu/cc/vms/about/raid.html*

Juslin, P.N. & Laukka, P. (2001). Impact of intended emotion intensity on cue utilization and decoding accuracy in vocal expression of emotion. *Emotion, 1*, 381–412.

Kleck, R.E., Cartwright, D., & Lanzetta (1976). Effects of being observed on expressive, subjective, and physiological responses to painful stimuli. *Journal of Personality and Social Psychology, 34*, 1211–18.

Levenson, R.W. (1988). Emotion and the autonomic nervous system: a prospectus for research on autonomic specificity. In *Social psychophysiology and emotion: theory and clinical applications* (ed. H.L. Wagner), pp. 17–42. New York, NY: Wiley.

Rosenthal, R. (1982). Conducting judgment studies. In K.R. Scherer & P. Ekman (Eds.) *Handbook of Methods in Nonverbal Behavior Research*, 287–361, London: Cambridge.

Tartter, V.C. & Braun, D. (1994). Hearing smiles and frowns in normal and whisper registers. *Journal of the Acoustical Society of America, 96*, 2101–7.

Wallbott, H.G. (1982). Technical appendix. Audiovisual recording: procedures, equipment, and troubleshooting. In *Handbook of methods in nonverbal behavior research* (ed. K.R. Scherer & P. Ekman), pp. 542–79. Cambridge, UK: Cambridge University Press.

Wilkinson, L. & Task Force on Statistical Inference (1999). Statistical methods in psychology journals: guidelines and explanations. *American Psychologist, 54*, 594–604.

Yewdall, D.L. (1999). *The practical art of motion picture sound.* Boston: Focal Press.

METHODOLOGICAL ISSUES IN STUDYING NONVERBAL BEHAVIOR

KLAUS R. SCHERER AND PAUL EKMAN

With comments and additions from Klaus R. Scherer and Jinni A. Harrigan

A selective historical sketch of methodological development in nonverbal behavior research

Interest in the actions of the voice, the face, and the body can be traced back to the writings of the earliest philosophers. The expression of emotion and intention and the role of nonverbal behavior in rhetoric have occupied some of the major thinkers over the centuries (see Key 1977; Laver 1980). Much of the relevant writing, however, is characterized by speculation and introspection. In some cases, a primitive type of systematic observation constituted the basis for inference (Bell 1806; Duchenne 1862; Piderit 1867). Yet, despite some systematic experimental work on expression by anatomists and physiologists during the eighteenth and early nineteenth centuries, the history of the empirical study of nonverbal behavior begins with Charles Darwin and his monumental study, 'The expression of the emotions in man and animals' (1872/1965)[1]. In this seminal book, Darwin not only introduced some of the major substantive and theoretical issues that still guide much of the research in this area, but also pioneered some of the methods of research.

Two theoretical issues posed by Darwin are at the root of much of the recent controversy in the field. The first issue, central to Darwin's interest in evolution, concerns the issue of the innateness versus the social learning of nonverbal behavior. Although Darwin did not deny that culture and social structure strongly affect nonverbal behavior, he was convinced that facial expressions are biologically determined and, furthermore, that there is phylogenetic continuity in their evolution. This central notion of biological determinism has strongly affected the choice of methods used in collecting evidence for its support. An important aspect of Darwin's methods is the comparative approach (i.e. comparing expressive behavior in many animal species, including man). The basis for such comparison is systematic observation in the form of repeated, close scrutiny of the behavior of an organism in different states and the detailed and careful description of even minute observable changes in action and appearance.

---

[1] See the revised version of this book, Darwin (1872/1998).

Darwin meticulously observed expressive behavior patterns and, in many cases, used drawings and photographs to obtain a permanent iconic image of the behavior under study. As objects of study, he used naturally occurring expressions as well as experimentally induced ones and expressions posed by actors. He also drew extensively on anecdotal reports in the literature, on the visual arts, and on reports by acquaintances and fellow scientists, particularly about facial expression in different cultures. Although Darwin was impressed, on the voyage of the *Beagle,* with his ability to understand the facial expressions of individuals from many countries, he obtained more systematic data later. From England, he sent a list of questions to 36 people living or working in other countries. He asked, for example, 'Is astonishment expressed by the eyes and mouth being raised?' (Darwin 1872/1965, p. 15)[2].

The second theoretical issue, which is closely related to the first, is the communicative use of expressive signs. In many ways, Darwin pioneered the functional analysis of behavior that characterizes modern ethology. Most of his theoretical efforts consisted of attempts to derive the underlying functional significance of the observable expressive behavior. Darwin clearly acknowledged the fact that some nonverbal behaviors, specifically symbolic gestures, serve primarily communicative functions, and that these are used 'voluntarily and consciously' in a culturally shared code—although he was convinced that all of these movements had 'some natural and independent origin' (Darwin, 1872/1965, p. 355)[3]. Whilst conventional gestures that varied across cultures might have communication as their main function, Darwin maintained that the innate facial expressions did not originate in a need to communicate, although they provided important information to others[4].

---

[2] In Darwin (1872/1998), this citation is located on p. 22.

[3] In Darwin (1872/1998), this citation is located on p. 356.

[4] The functions of nonverbal behavior are often misunderstood. Some authors suggest an exaggerated distinction between nonverbal behavior as an *expression* of some internal state versus the *communication* of a message to a receiver. Thus, Fridlund (1994) makes a strenuous effort to argue that the facial movements usually considered as expressions of emotions have not evolved to 'express' an individual's emotion but rather to signal a message to potential observers. However, ever since Aristotle (e.g. the strategic use of anger expression in 'Ethica Nicomachea', Aristotle, 1962 edition), many authors, including Darwin, have insisted on the social-communicative value of emotional expressions. Ekman (1997) discusses features which distinguish 'expression' from 'communication'. The multifunctionality of nonverbal expression is most elegantly captured by an adaptation of Karl Bühler's 'Organon' model of signs (Bühler 1934/1965; see Scherer 1988 or Krampen *et al.* 1987 for a more detailed description). The model postulates that any sign always has three functions — as a *symptom* (of the expresser's state), as a *symbol* (of a socially shared meaning category), and as an *appeal* (a social message toward others). Bühler insisted that a sign is all of these things at the same time. Nothing could be more true of nonverbal expressions of emotion — they function as a symptom (of the underlying emotional state), as a symbol (of a meaningful social category, in this case the emotion concept), and as an appeal (signaling reaction, action intentions, and requests for responses from others). Due to this multifaceted nature of nonverbal expression, researchers in this area are well advised to adopt a combination of etic and emic approaches (see Kappas *et al.* 1991, pp. 200–4; see also Chapter 3).

Darwin was the first to study observers' judgments of facial expression, noting that observers who did not know the context in which an expression occurred still agreed about the emotion shown. The judgment method has become one of the most commonly used in studies of nonverbal behavior (see Rosenthal 1982). Darwin also experimented, often with his own children, to observe reactions to a variety of sounds, gestures, and facial expressions. Clearly, modern-day methodologists would have many objections to details of Darwin's procedures; these would reflect the nascent state of most methods during the last half of the nineteenth century. Yet, at the same time, Darwin's approach compares very favorably with that taken in modern single-shot studies, so far as comprehensiveness, appropriateness of the methods, and detail of observation are concerned.

Darwin's contemporaries in other disciplines, particularly the early German anthropological psychologists (see Allport 1968, pp. 48–50), also showed much interest in nonverbal behavior. In the process of examining differences and similarities between different races and cultures, they paid much attention to communication systems such as language, gestures, and facial expression (Kleinpaul 1888/1972; Wundt 1900–1920). However, their writings, which were mostly compilations of reports from ethnographic studies and of anecdotes, did not spawn much of a research tradition. Such a tradition was established at the beginning of the twentieth century, when the psychology of expression *(Ausdruckspsychologie)* attained a dominant position in German psychology and quickly spread to other countries (without, however, achieving a similar importance). The basic tenet of this tradition was the assumption that individual differences between persons manifest themselves in a particular style of expressive movement, which homomorphically affects all aspects of motor activity, such as facial and bodily movement, handwriting, vocalization, and so on.

Whereas many of the representatives of this approach were given to no empirical pursuits like introspection and phenomenology, others did use more empirical, quantitative methods. In many cases, they produced fairly precise observations and descriptions of nonverbal phenomena, often using induction methods (e.g. producing an emotion by imagination or by exposing subjects to arousing stimuli). Furthermore, they introduced systematic behavior sampling methods, obtaining, as a result, different behavior samples, from several persons, sometimes at several points in time (e.g. Allport & Vernon 1933; Bühler 1933; Pear 1931; Wolff 1943). In this tradition, we also find the first consistent attempts to use quantitative measurement and statistical analysis.

Under the influence of Nazism, segments of German psychology degenerated into an ideology of racial determinism. Some German psychologists attempted to show that the superiority of the Aryan races was manifest, even in expressive behavior patterns. In an attempt to procure evidence that would prove these claims wrong, a young social scientist at Columbia University, David Efron, conducted a classic study (published in book form in 1941) which is still counted among the best studies in the field of nonverbal behavior, both in theoretical rigor and in development of appropriate methodology (Efron 1941/1972).

Efron used both naturalistic observation and some experimental induction in his study of the gestures of Jewish and Italian immigrants in New York. He was one of the first to use film extensively to document sequences of nonverbal behavior (see also Bateson & Mead 1942), and he made much use of the frame-by-frame analysis methods that have become one of the hallmarks of nonverbal behavior analysis. In addition, Efron used drawings to code, iconically, the most important aspects of the movement patterns, thus developing a rudimentary transcription system. He also recognized that the functional classification of movement patterns is an important part of an analysis of bodily movement as an element of expression and communication systems. His distinction of types of hand movements was adopted and further developed in later studies (Ekman & Friesen 1969, 1975; Rosenfeld 1982)[5]. Finally, Efron used observers to determine how particular gestures would be decoded, in order to assess their role in a nonverbal signaling system. Interestingly, Efron ignored the face almost entirely, focusing his efforts primarily on body movement. Many of the classes of behavior he noted for the body, such as speech emphasis, can also be seen in facial actions (see Ekman 1979).

It is difficult to overestimate the important role of David Efron as a pioneer for both conceptual and methodological development in the field (Rosenfeld 1982)[6]. Unfortunately, many researchers have remained ignorant of his work or have not acknowledged its influence; often, methods used by Efron were 'rediscovered' many years later.

Another pioneer who has had much influence on the field both conceptually and methodologically, although his work has generated curiously little empirical research, is Ray Birdwhistell. An anthropologist by training, Birdwhistell was heavily influenced by structural linguistics (particularly the work of Harris, Bloomfield, Trager, and Smith)[7] and introduced this way of thinking and its methodology to the analysis of movement behavior. Proceeding from the assumption that human movement is organized in a code with a design similar to that of language (see Hockett 1960), Birdwhistell (1952)[8] attempted to create a science of 'kinesics' in analogy to phonetics. Accordingly, he attempted to define movement units within a hierarchically organized code, which he believed to be almost entirely determined by cultural convention and learning.

Birdwhistell, along with other researchers, advocated the use of cinematic techniques and the microanalysis of the filmed behavior, with slow motion and frame-by-frame analysis (as Efron had recommended 10 years earlier); Birdwhistell also developed a transcription system that was one of the first instances of an attempt at exhaustive symbolic transcription of nonverbal behavior (apart from attempts at dance notation; see Hutchinson 1970). Though this system has never been used extensively (only for illustrative purposes on very short behavior samples), it has had a strong impact on discussion about the transcription and analysis of nonverbal behavior. Kendon (1982, Section 8.2) provides a detailed description of Birdwhistell's approach and an appreciation of his role. Critical evaluations of the system can be found in Ekman (1957, p.146, Section 2.2) and Rosenfeld (1982, Section 5.7).

---

[5] See also Ekman 1977 and work by Krauss and colleagues and Freedman and colleagues in Chapter 4.
[6] See Box 4.1 in Chapter 4 for more cross-cultural studies involving gestures.
[7] See reference list for these citations.
[8] See also Birdwhistell (1970).

One of the most notable developments of the fifties and sixties was the strengthened concern of psychiatrists and clinical psychologists with nonverbal behavior—a concern resulting in the establishment of many new approaches and methods. Even though most of these researchers were concerned with mental patients, the rationales for studying nonverbal behavior and the approaches used differed widely, depending on the goals of the inquiry (evaluating the diagnostic value of nonverbal behavior, tracing the etiology of the illness in patterns of social communication, or studying the process of clinical interviews) as well as on the theoretical persuasion of the clinician (psychoanalysis, transactional analysis, behavior therapy, and so on). It would be most interesting to trace the development of interests and the mutual influences of the major researchers in this period in detail. Here, only some of the major strands of research can be taken into account.

One distinctive approach, sometimes referred to as the *natural history* approach (reviewed in detail by Kendon 1982, Section 8.2), represents the confluence of ideas from anthropology, structural linguistics, information theory, and psychiatry, and is associated with the names of Bateson, Birdwhistell, Brosin, Fromm–Reichmann, Hockett, and McQuown. This group was particularly concerned with a structural analysis of the communication patterns between patients and therapists, using phonetic, paralinguistic, and 'kinesic' transcription techniques. One of the problems that have plagued this approach is that it is never quite clear what rules control the identification of structural units and hierarchical organization. More recently, Scheflen (1966, 1973) and Kendon (1970, 1973) have attempted to indicate with greater specificity how to proceed in order to identify the structural organization of behavior.

Another approach to the analysis of nonverbal behavior stemming from clinical concerns is the psychoanalytic approach. Freud, and some of his contemporaries, commented on the fact that nonverbal behavior might reveal unconscious processes that are repressed and consequently not verbalized (Ferenczi 1926; Freud 1904; Reich 1949). Psychiatrists in this tradition have looked at both body motion and vocalization, and mostly have used clinical observation, filmed records, microanalysis, and functional behavior classification to assess the diagnostic value of nonverbal behavior for nonverbalized affect. A number of conceptual methodological distinctions were contributed, some of which continue to be used today. Krout (1931) distinguished autistic movements from gestures; Mahl (1968)[9] showed the usefulness of distinguishing movements that are directed at the self and communicative movements; and Ekman and Friesen (1969) and Freedman (1972)[10] both elaborated these distinctions in dealing with hand movements. Ekman (1965) also contrasted the information available from the face and body, as Dittmann (1962)[11] had done, and as many others have done since. Mahl and Schulze (1964)[12] worked with vocalization patterns, such as *ah* and *non-ah*

---

[9] Or see Mahl (1987) for the same article.

[10] See also Freedman (1977).

[11] See also Dittman (1987).

[12] Others include Blass & Siegman (1975); Boomer & Dittman (1962, 1964); Ragsdale & Silvia (1982); Ragsdale & Sisterhen (1984); and Siegman & Pope (1965).

speech disturbance types, which has paved the way for more detailed analysis of vocal behavior.

In the area of voice analysis, clinicians have been pragmatically interested in the diagnostic use of vocal characteristics for signs of particular syndromes and for changes over time. Among the methodological contributions that have been made in this area are the identification of categories for the auditory evaluation of voice quality characteristics (e.g. Moses 1954) and the use of acoustic analysis techniques for the assessment of non-linguistic aspects of vocalizations (Ostwald 1963).

Yet another approach linked to the practice of psychiatry and clinical psychology, and centered mainly around the analysis of interview processes, is the *interaction chronography* approach pioneered by Chapple (1948/49) and subsequently utilized by Matarazzo and Wiens and their co-workers (Matarazzo & Wiens 1972) and Jaffe and Feldstein and their collaborators (Feldstein & Welkowitz 1978; Jaffe & Feldstein 1970)[13]. The methodological innovation introduced by this tradition is the objective and sometimes automatic measurement of time-based parameters of conversation sequences (Scherer 1982, Section 4.6)[14].

Although also coming to the field with clinical interests, Paul Ekman, a trained psychologist, turned toward the investigation of some of the more basic issues concerning nonverbal behavior, such as the nature of emotional expression and the semiotic aspects of nonverbal behavior (resurrecting the questions studied by Darwin and Efron, and influenced also by Tomkins and contemporary ethologists). Ekman developed a theoretical classification of five types of nonverbal behavior, based on differences in origins, usage, and coding. In addition, he attempted to make full use of the methodological canon of psychology in the analysis of nonverbal behavior, including the measurement of frequency and rate of behavioral phenomena, systematic sampling procedures, the construction of category and coding systems with known reliability, and the use of statistical analysis. Together with Wallace Friesen, he invested much research effort in the development of measurement systems for body motion (particularly speech illustrator movements and symbolic gestures) and the more recent development of an anatomical system for measuring the face (Ekman 1957; Ekman & Friesen 1969, 1976, 1978). Ekman and Friesen's methods and conceptual framework have been used by many other investigators.

A research tradition with increasing impact on the study of human nonverbal behavior is ethology and, more recently, the special branch of human ethology. Because all animal behavior is nonverbal, animal ethologists have had to develop methods of observation and analysis suitable to uncovering the organization underlying the observable behavior patterns (Eibl–Eibesfeldt 1970; Hinde 1972)[15]. Among the important contributions made within this tradition is the development of sophisticated techniques for the analysis of sequences and clusters of behavior (van Hooff 1982)[16]. This

---

[13] Or see Feldstein & Welkowitz (1987) for the same article.
[14] See also Chapter 3.
[15] See also Eibl–Eibesfeldt (1989).
[16] See also van Hooff (2000).

approach has had a very strong influence on the recent surge of interest in the study of human development and mother–infant interaction, where these techniques are used and further refined (Blurton Jones 1971).

Finally, methodological impulses come from the research tradition of conversational analysis as developed in microsociology and ethnomethodology (Garfinkel 1967; Goffman 1963, 1971; Schegloff 1968; Schegloff & Sacks 1973)[17]. The particular contributions of this tradition are strategies to uncover the rule systems that govern much of our interaction with others and the role that verbal and nonverbal behaviors play in these systems (West & Zimmerman 1982)[18].

After this short review of some of the major historical developments that have influenced the methodology presently available to study nonverbal behavior, we now turn toward a more systematic discussion of the aspects or features that characterize particular approaches or methods and the choices facing a researcher intent on investigating nonverbal behavior empirically.

Basic issues in studying nonverbal behavior

The study of nonverbal behavior is characterized by two major foci of interest: the study of the individual and the study of the interaction. In a very fundamental sense, these different foci also represent major philosophical traditions, as reflected in the different disciplinary affiliations of the researchers and the rather different strategies and methods of research employed. Biological and psychological researchers tend to be most interested in the determinants and processes of nonverbal behavior on the individual level. These researchers often endorse the belief that it is necessary to understand the factors governing the behavior of the individual better before studying the complex patterns of social interaction between individuals. Many sociologists and anthropologists, on the other hand, believe that it is more important to focus attention on the nature of social interaction and the social and cultural factors that determine the complex interrelationships and interaction processes occurring between social actors. In this tradition, it is often held that individual behavior is strongly governed by social forces and the dynamics of the interaction situation; according to this view, then, studies of the behavior of isolated individuals are rather useless.

---

[17] See also Gumperz (1982) and Tannen (1993).

[18] See also Feldstein & Welkowitz (1987). In addition, many of the approaches described in this section were seen as part of an established interdisciplinary field, namely *nonverbal communication*, with its proper journal (*Journal of Nonverbal Behavior*) and its own textbooks (Burgoon *et al.* 1996; Knapp & Hall 2002; Philippot *et al.* 1992; Siegman & Feldstein 1987). In recent years, the cohesiveness of this research area has waned and many of the issues formerly studied under the label of 'nonverbal communication' are now referred to under 'expression of affect'. While this development has strengthened some of this research by bringing it into the mainstream of exploding research on emotion, it sometimes has the undesirable side-effect of downplaying the communicative aspect of emotional expression (as described in this Appendix, pp. 470).

Apart from the different foci of interest and the underlying epistemological traditions, specific research approaches have dominated in each of these research traditions.
Researchers interested in the individual have tended to use experimental methods that
allow quantitative analysis of individual behavior and aggregation over individuals and
situations. Researchers focusing on the interaction, on the other hand, have preferred
the observation of naturally occurring behavior in social interaction, and have often
used qualitative techniques to describe moment-to-moment changes in behavior, and
structural rather than quantitative description for very short segments of an interaction. However, although such a methodological specialization may have developed to
some extent in past research, it is by no means obligatory, nor is it found universally.
There are, for example, quite a few researchers interested in the individual who use
qualitative moment-to-moment description of naturally occurring behavior, and there
are researchers who study interaction processes by way of experimental and quantitative methodology. Just as there is no logical necessity for choosing a particular method
given a particular focus of research interest, there is no logical necessity for keeping
these two foci of research interest apart or, worse, for considering them as antithetical.
Clearly, both are legitimate and important, and it is hardly possible to make a reasonable judgment about the greater urgency or validity of either one of them.

In this section, we attempt to characterize these different research interests in
somewhat more detail, trying to show that they complement rather than contradict
each other. In order to understand human social interaction, the biological and
psychological determinants of behavior, as well as the cultural and situational norms
and rules affecting interaction processes, have to be taken into account. Unfortunately,
the foci of research on the individual or on the interaction have in the past sometimes
been associated with the issue of innate or biologically determined versus learned or
culturally determined behavior. There is no necessary link here: human behavior is
jointly determined by biological and cultural factors, and it is an empirical issue to
determine the nature and strength of the respective influences. The effect of social
factors can be studied with the individual as the focus of study, as in the investigation of
culturally mediated stereotypical inferences from nonverbal cues. Similarly, biological
issues can be studied with the interaction as a major focus, as in the study of mother–
infant bonding.

Let us now turn to a more detailed discussion of the main questions that have been
asked within the focus on the individual and within the focus on interaction, trying to
relate these to the historical research traditions that they grow out of or draw from.

Researchers focusing on the behavior of the individual have generally been interested
in three major issues:

1. externalization or expression of traits and states;
2. inferences from nonverbal cues;
3. intra-individual organization of behavior.

As pointed out previously, the investigation of the externalization or expression of
personality, action tendencies, or emotion was one of the earliest research issues in
studying nonverbal behavior. This issue has been of both theoretical and practical
interest. On the theoretical level, investigations have concerned, in psychology, expres-

sive styles of personality and the expression of emotion and, in ethnology, intention signals. On the practical or applied level, the diagnostic value of nonverbal behavior for personality and affect disturbances has been explored. The research strategy employed in these studies has generally consisted of searching for correlations between states and traits, as induced or assessed by some kind of external criterion, and measuring particular types of nonverbal behavior.

The study of inferences from nonverbal behavior cues (attributing traits, states, and intentions to the actor) belongs squarely in the area of person perception and impression formation in social psychology. Unfortunately, much of the person perception research has moved away from the person. Researchers in this field have been preoccupied for decades with studying verbal labels rather than behavioral cues, generating quite a bit of evidence on semantic processing but almost none on impression formation and cue utilization (Scherer & Scherer 1981). Most of the relevant research has been conducted recently under the heading of nonverbal communication research. Here, the research strategy consists of exposing observers to stimulus persons displaying various kinds of nonverbal behaviors (often posed) and assessing the inferences observers make from these, sometimes checking the accuracy of the inferences against some kind of external criterion. Unfortunately, this research approach has often not taken advantage of the methodological sophistication in such areas as deciding what kinds of scales to use, the problem of artifacts, judgment conditions, and so on that has been attained within the field of person perception (see Rosenthal 1982).

A third approach with the individual as a focus of research and one that has appeared only recently, is the study of the intra-individual organization of action, including nonverbal behavior. Here, an attempt is made to investigate the hierarchical structure in the organization of behavior, including the execution of plans and strategies on different levels and the synchronization of different types of simultaneously occurring motor activities (see von Cranach & Harre, in press).

Studies in which the interaction process is the focus of interest can also be subdivided into three fairly distinct approaches:

1. the nature of the cultural communication code;
2. the coordination of behavior in social interaction;
3. the study of interpersonal relationships.

The first approach, studying the nature of the cultural communication code, is most closely associated with the work of Birdwhistell. As described in the preceding section, Birdwhistell assumed that nonverbal signals are organized in a culturally shared code similar to the language code. This assumption points toward a research strategy making use of techniques developed for linguistic inquiry. The major aspect of such a research strategy is reliance, for investigation, on a few illustrative cases of the nature of the code, the assumption being that the elements of the code and their relationships are discrete and invariant and that the analysis of a few instances of usage of the code will be sufficient to unravel its structure (just as ancient languages have been deciphered from the inscriptions on a single tombstone).

The second approach, strongly based on the work of Birdwhistell, is concerned with the micro examination of the moment-to-moment structure of the process of interaction. Here, researchers study the way in which interaction partners manage to coordinate their behavior in a complex dance-like pattern. Examples of studies using this approach are Duncan's (1972) work on turn-taking, Condon and Ogston's (1967) study of interactional synchrony, and Kendon's study of greetings (1982, see his detailed discussion in Chapter 8)[19].

The third approach is quite different in that it represents the more typically psychological approach to the study of interaction. Studies of this kind, which often proceed by manipulating the behavior of one person in the interaction, look for signs that indicate the nature of the relationship of the interaction partners or their respective status. This approach is concerned with the nonverbal marking of relationships, rather than with the nature of the code or the complex coordination of behavior. Examples of this approach are found in many studies on eye contact (Argyle & Dean 1965; Ellsworth & Ludwig 1972; Exline & Fehr 1982) and in work on posture (Mehrabian 1969, 1972)[20].

To summarize, the distinction between approaches with the individual as focus and those with the interaction as focus is based on differences in scientific interest and perceived research priorities. Some researchers, partly because of their disciplinary origins, are more interested in studying the individual and the factors that determine his or her behavior, and consider it important to start studying social behavior by considering the contributions made by the individuals. Others are more interested in social and cultural phenomena and consider the interaction of individuals a more logical place to start studying human behavior. Only very extreme adherents of either approach, however, would question the validity of the other perspective, although there are of course some differences of opinion concerning the usefulness of certain concepts and research approaches.

Thus, clearly, these two foci of research are complementary rather than contradictory. It is only the complexity of the appropriate research design and the amount of time and expertise needed that deter researchers from studying the individual and the interaction at the same time. It would seem possible, for example, to study how introverts and extroverts coordinate their behavior in different types of social interactions.

Indeed, there have been some attempts to combine the study of the individual and of the interaction in a single research project. Paul Ekman and his collaborators have studied the effect of stress on the communicative behavior of Japanese and American students, both individually and in social interactions, to assess the effect of social rules and situational determinants on communicative behavior (Ekman 1972). Duncan and Fiske (1977) have looked at variables defining the individual in a context of studying turn-taking behavior and the rules that govern this type of interaction regulation. Scherer and his collaborators have looked at individual variables and social situational variables that determine the behavior of public officials in dealing with clients, trying to assess both the effect on individual behavior and the effect on the nature of the interaction as a whole (Scherer & Scherer 1980). Exline and his collaborators have

---

[19] See also Kendon 1973; Kendon & Ferber 1973; and Harrigan 1985.
[20] See also Harrigan *et al.* 1988; Honeycutt 1989; and Sigelman *et al.* 1986.

studied Machiavellianism in its effect on nonverbal behavior in deception (see Exline & Fehr 1982). It is to be expected that future research using either the individual or the interaction as a focus will make increasing use of the findings of the other approach, and it is to be hoped that integrative studies trying to combine the two foci of interest will increase in number[21].

It is particularly important to stress that the choice of a particular research focus does not necessarily determine the methodological approach to be used. Though there has been a tendency for the two approaches to prefer different research techniques, as already noted, this is more a historical accident than a logical necessity. On the whole, it may be very detrimental to equate research interest, conceptual preferences, and choice of particular research methodologies with possibly exclusive types of approaches. Unfortunately, this seems to have been the effect of the widely cited distinction between *structural* and *external variable* studies introduced by Duncan in 1969 in an attempt to review the literature on nonverbal communication at that time.

This distinction reified two types of research which, as we have been trying to show, cannot really be consistently differentiated on any set of dimensions. The distinction between *structural* and *external variable* implies differences in scientific interest, conceptual schemes, disciplinary orientation, fundamental unit of inquiry, preferred methodology, and research priorities. Essentially, a researcher's decisions on any of these dimensions are independent of one another. If, as has been the case, there is a clustering of some of these decisions in particular historical research approaches, this may be of interest for a historian of science, but it should not limit the choice of options for research.

It is the purpose of this chapter to consider these methodological options in somewhat more detail. Clearly, the points that will be made cover only a small part of the large number of issues relevant for empirical research in nonverbal behavior (see Weick 1968). However, many methodological issues are relevant to any kind of empirical study in the social and behavioral sciences and are adequately treated in many existing sources on research methodology in this domain. Here, we are selecting for discussion either those issues concerning which there are chronic deficiencies or no established standards in the nonverbal literature or those which are unique to a particular approach or have more than general importance.

For the selection of the appropriate method to be used and as a safeguard against possible artifacts, the nature of the phenomenon to be studied has to be carefully considered. In many studies on nonverbal behavior, the phenomenon to be studied consists in the relationship of some nonverbal behavior as a sign to an underlying referent or external variable, that is, in the *coding* of nonverbal signs. The first detailed discussion of the issue of coding of nonverbal behavior was provided by Ekman and Friesen (1969).

Because there are important implications for methodological decisions, we will briefly review the nature of nonverbal coding. The nature of coding (i.e. the kind of relationship between sign and referent) can be described by three major dimensions:

---

[21] Other studies examining individual differences are available: Friedman & Riggio 1981; Troisi *et al.* 2000; Vrij *et al.* 1997; for review see Gallaher 1992.

1. discrete versus continuous/graded;
2. probabilistic versus invariant;
3. iconic versus arbitrary (Ekman & Friesen 1969; Giles *et al.* 1979; Scherer 1977).

Verbal signs are generally coded discretely, invariantly, and arbitrarily; that is, a particular word does or does not mean a particular thing, the word always and for everybody means this thing, and the nature of the word does not bear any relationship to the nature of the thing.

Although some nonverbal signs are coded in the same way, others are coded continuously, probabilistically, and iconically. In other words, a nonverbal sign may change with changes in the extent or strength of a referent (e.g. loudness of voice with degree of emphasis); it may mean a particular thing only for certain persons or certain situations (e.g. high voice pitch may indicate stress for some speakers but not for others, and thus there is only a certain probability that it signals stress in any one case); and it is often part of the thing or a homomorphistic representation of the thing it signals (as blushing is part of the arousal state it signifies).

Thus, the coding of nonverbal behaviors varies from, on the one extreme, language-like coding to, on the other, very loose probabilistic associations between behaviors and external referents that semiotic purists would refuse to call coding. For example, gestural emblems—movements with precise meanings (see Ekman 1976; Johnson *et al.* 1975)—are close to language coding in many respects because, although they often are iconically coded, their signification of external referents is invariant and generally discrete. That loudness of the voice is a sign of extroversion only for some speakers in some cultures (see Scherer 1979*a*) indicates, on the other hand, a probabilistic relationship, and voice level may vary continuously with the strength of the extroversion disposition. It is thus debatable whether we can talk of a code at all in this domain (although it can be argued that this vocal behavior might be used, like other elements of communication codes, in self-presentation and interaction regulation; see Scherer 1979*a*, pp. 197–201) or only of a statistical correlation.

We do not, at this point, want to discuss the nature of code systems and the requirements under which behaviors qualify as code elements. The preceding discussion was intended to show that nonverbal behaviors differ in their relationships to external referents of which they might be signs. Depending on the nature of this relationship, different research procedures are required for study of the characteristics of the signs and their usage. Obviously, the extent to which nonverbal behaviors are coded like language determines the extent to which classical linguistic techniques, such as the contrastive analysis of consensually defined discrete units in fairly small samples, can be used in their investigation. For example, the inter-subjective agreement on the denotative meaning of most words is so high (invariant coding or very high probability of consensual use) that significance testing is superfluous. Of course, this does not mean that statistical methods cannot be used in studying messages that are discretely and invariantly coded. Although the coding may be evident, the *use* of the respective signal (i.e. when shown and by whom) needs to be studied empirically, using statistical techniques. However, the more the coding resembles a statistical association, the more indication there is for standard psychological techniques, relying on operationalized measurement procedures with known reliability and statistical analysis of fairly sizable samples.

Unfortunately, we do not yet well understand the coding characteristics for many nonverbal behaviors, and we are thus faced with the dilemma of having to make choices about research procedures without knowing very much about their appropriateness for the research object. All too often, this dilemma is solved by having recourse to one's theoretical predilections. Thus, researchers trained in anthropology or linguistics tend to presuppose that most of the nonverbal behaviors they are dealing with are coded in a language-like manner and that structural linguistic techniques are appropriate. If the assumption is incorrect, the research results may not be valid. For example, if a researcher isolates what seem to be consensually valid units of nonverbal behavior with a particular signification, without checking on the reliability with which such a distinction can be made, the conclusions of the study will be in error if the behavior is in fact probabilistically coded and the signification varies with sign encoders and decoders or the situation or setting in which it occurs.

Psychologically trained researchers, on the other hand, tend to lean toward the assumption that there are probabilistic relationships between behaviors and external referents and attempt to determine the nature of the relationship by statistical analysis of a number of cases, often trying to isolate variables by controlling or manipulating factors in experiments. The danger of an unreflective use of this approach consists in the strong possibility of missing important structural relationships between nonverbal behaviors in relation to external referents, because often only one-to-one correlations are studied and other variables or behaviors are controlled by manipulation or exclusion. However, appropriate research designs using multivariate procedures and configurational analyses may alleviate this danger to some extent.

We do not want to imply, by these two examples, that there is a linguistic and a psychological methodology and that one has to choose between them in studying nonverbal behavior. This is not the case. The options available and the choices to be made are, of course, much more complex. Apart from different assumptions about the nature of the code, and their subsequent effects on choice of research methodology, there are different views in various disciplines of the social and behavioral sciences on the nature of scientific activity and on what constitutes proof for the description and explanation of a phenomenon.

One can distinguish among at least three kinds of research activities: discovery, proof, and illustration. The role of these three is seen very differently in different areas of the social and behavioral sciences. There are those who believe that the work ends with discovery or with illustration. There are others who believe that these are just the first steps and that very different and more demanding activities are required to establish proof. Most researchers subscribing to an empirical, experimental approach believe that discovery is the first step, which has to be followed by proof and, eventually, by illustration for the dissemination of the findings. Another way to view the difference between traditions is that what is considered proof for some is for others considered only the discovery of a hypothesis still needing proof, or the illustration of a claim not proven. And proof, which is seen as the sine qua non by some, is considered pedestrian reiteration of the already obvious by others.

The methodology and techniques that are most appropriate for discovery, illustration, and proof are rather diverse, and it would seem reasonable to make the appropriate choice of methodology on the basis of the purpose of the research approach.

Sampling nonverbal behavior

Scientific research, including the study of nonverbal behavior, always requires sampling of the object to be studied. Only a limited number of people can be studied in a limited number of settings, and we can observe only a small part of their behavior. Thus, the researcher has to make a large number of decisions about the sampling of the behavior that he intends to study, such as:

- *where* to study the behavior (e.g. in the field or the laboratory);
- *which* behavior to study (i.e. natural or arranged behavior);
- *who ought* to be observed (i.e. which persons and how many of them);
- *how* the observation is to be conducted (e.g. direct observation or recording of the behavior);
- for *how long* these persons will be observed;
- *which aspects* of the behavior are to be noted.

In this section, we shall consider some of the issues involved in making these decisions.

Field versus laboratory

The term *field* is used by social scientists to refer to the typical settings of human behavior, such as living rooms, schools, public places, and a myriad of other social settings in which our daily behavior is situated. The field is any setting that is not a laboratory. Although it is possible to simulate some of the major aspects of social settings in the laboratory, these recreations never completely approximate real-life settings. Thus, if there is no need to observe in the laboratory; one should study nonverbal behavior in the field.

In many cases, however, it is necessary to use the laboratory. Whenever the coding characteristics of the nonverbal behavior studies are probabilistic and continuous, and statistical analysis techniques are required, a certain degree of control of the relevant variables and of comparability of the conditions under which the behavior unfolds is desirable. Furthermore, if film or video records are required for microscopic measurement or if very high-quality audio records have to be made for acoustic analysis, the technical facilities available only in laboratories need to be employed (particularly when cameras are to be used, recorders synchronized, separate audio records made, etc.; see Wallbott 1982). Similarly, the laboratory approach has to be used for studies in which instruments for the direct measurement of particular aspects of nonverbal behavior (e.g. transducers, floor switches; see Rosenfeld 1982) are to be used. (Although it is sometimes possible to use sophisticated recording instrumentation in the field, too.)

Whether behavior is to be sampled in the field or the laboratory depends on the issue and the type of nonverbal behavior to be studied, as well as the nature of the data desired. Both offer advantages and disadvantages (see Exline & Fehr 1982, Section 3.2). If little is known about the nonverbal behavior of interest, it is advisable to start a research project with field observations to obtain a feeling for the characteristics of the behavior and the factors that might influence it. After such information has been obtained, it is more easily possible to devise a representative research design for behavior sampling in the laboratory.

Clearly, not all settings, situations, or interaction patterns can be simulated in the laboratory. Political rallies, religious ceremonies, and weddings, among many other cases, have to be observed in the field. Again, the choice between laboratory and field depends on the interest of the researcher and the nature of the question to be asked. Given the constraints of both settings, concessions and compromises have to be made for usefulness and appropriateness.

Naturally occurring versus arranged behavior

Unfortunately, the choice between field and laboratory is often confused with the distinction between natural and artificial behavior. This is misleading. Nobody wishes to study the artificial, and it goes without saying that researchers studying behavior in the laboratory do not agree that their object of study is artificial behavior. Artificiality is always a problem in behavioral research and is just as likely to be found in the field as in the laboratory.

In a laboratory, people do not behave as they would in their living rooms, but then, they do not behave in their living rooms as they would in a bus, a church, or an office. Many behavior patterns and interactions between strangers are as natural in a laboratory as in any other unfamiliar formal setting. The only exception would be a situation in which subjects tend to be suspicious of everything and everyone around them out of fear of deception and non-acceptance of the roles in which others present themselves. This is often the case with psychology students, who have a long history of participation in complicated experiments in which things never were what they seemed. Fortunately, this is not true for all people whose behavior can be studied in a laboratory.

One precondition for the occurrence of 'natural' behavior is that the task characteristics and the situational demands be such that natural behavior, in the sense of being appropriate to these demands, is functional in that context. If a person is required to do things that seem foolish or irrelevant to that person's life, unnatural behavior will result. If the task characteristics and the demands made are highly realistic and involving, as in simulated jury discussions, for example, or if subjects are required to perform an activity that they are engaged in day after day, as in simulating client contacts with civil service officials (Scherer & Scherer 1980), the resulting behavior will be natural both in comparability with real-life behavior patterns and in affective involvement. Thus, the distinction is not between natural and artificial behavior but between naturally occurring and arranged behavior, by which we mean behavior in the occurrence and possibly in the unfolding of which the researcher has had a hand.

One source of artificiality in many studies in which the interaction is arranged is that the situation is totally ahistorical. Typically, there is no shared past experience between the participants in an arranged interaction, and there is little likelihood of any future interaction once the experiment is over. It is possible, however, to arrange an inter-action in a laboratory that eliminates these problems. For example, friends or couples, or even people previously unacquainted (if they can be expected to interact with each other) may be studied. Another source of artificiality in many arranged situations is that they have little relevance to the subject, quite apart from the participants' un-familiarity with one another. Again, a laboratory experiment may be arranged so that it is relevant to the career, values, or goals of the participant.

One of the problems with the sampling of naturally occurring behavior is the difficulty of obtaining repeated instances of the same type of behavior in a comparable context. Another problem is the lack of control over the factors determining the occurrence and specific characteristics of particular behavior, such as aspects of the physical environment, the identity and behavior of significant others, and so on. Unfortunately, both of these aspects of behavior sampling are essential for the system-atic study of particular issues, as, for example, the correspondence between a wide range of parameter values in the behavioral signs and differences in degree or strength of underlying external referents (e.g. emotional states) or the nature of the inference processes based on different types of nonverbal cues. In many such research situations, sampling of arranged behavior has to be used to obtain the appropriate evidence.

The study of behavior that has in some way been arranged by the observer has many advantages. Not only does it allow study of samples of behavior that may only rarely occur naturally, but the researcher can also arrange the behavior repeatedly to obtain replications of the findings. In addition, the observation or recording conditions of the behavior can be better controlled, and the researcher can attempt to guard against observer bias. Furthermore, it is often feasible to manipulate specific aspects of the setting and thus obtain a better idea of how different factors interact with each other in determining the behavior of the persons studied. One must always be careful to avoid artificiality and to question whether the results can be generalized. However, the same cautions often apply equally to those studies of naturally occurring behavior in which the person or persons observed realize that they are being scrutinized. Similarly, it is not usually possible to generalize from one piece of behavior observed under 'natural' conditions to other behaviors of the same person or other persons even in the same situation, unless one has sampled very many such behaviors.

The literature on nonverbal behavior abounds with examples of different techniques for arranging behavior: role playing, the showing of films, the administration of electroshocks, the manipulation of the behavior of interaction partners (confederates), the use of professional or amateur actors, and many others[22].

Behavior patterns can be induced by the researcher through a wide variety of means. He or she can, for example, ask the subject to perform a certain task, such as wrapping a perambulator, solving arithmetic problems, describing a dirty movie, or occupying a table in the library. The behavioral reactions to each of these tasks enjoin a number of nonverbal behaviors, which may include those of interest to the researcher. Further-

---

[22] Other examples include: mock juries, job interviews, mother–infant interactions, and drug studies on depression or anxiety.

more, the researcher can produce, in the subjects, a certain state, such as a particular emotion (e.g. via stimuli, insults) or a particular motivation (e.g. by food deprivation, exposure to a flirtatious member of the other sex), and observe the resulting behavioral reactions. In many cases, these induced behaviors are 'natural'; they are just not 'naturally occurring'. These methods are among the most powerful techniques available for behavior sampling. They allow the researcher control over the persons to be observed, many of the factors that determine the behavior, and often, the context in which the action takes place. As long as the tasks set for the subjects or the methods used to induce states of various sorts are realistic and part of the subjects' repertoire, there is little reason to expect that the behavior will be artificial.

Any kind of observation of behavior will lead to changes in that behavior; in many cases, even the possibility of observation will produce such changes. Even field observation of naturally occurring behavior, with the naked eye or a camera (see Wallbott 1982, Section A.6) can have an intrusive effect on the persons observed and often will change their behavior. There are a number of studies showing that behavior differs if the subject knows that he or she is being observed (see the studies reviewed in Ekman & Oster 1979)[23].

Increased concern about the ethics of observing or recording behavior without the consent of the observed brings with it the risk that only self-conscious behavior will be studied. This is always a problem in arranged behavior sampling, because subjects know that they are in a contrived situation; but asking for consent to record may make it worse. In naturally occurring behavior in familiar surroundings, observation or even recording would be very unusual generally, and asking for consent could be even more intrusive than in a laboratory. In many cases, institutions concerned with the rights of human subjects will accept a procedure in which observation or recording occurs without knowledge of the observed and consent is obtained afterwards (with records destroyed if agreement is denied). At the very least, the recording instruments should be concealed to reduce their salience, even if their presence is revealed to those observed.

There are two major dimensions involved in arranging behavior: the requests made of the person whose behavior is to be studied and the manipulation of the situation by the researcher. The researcher can, in making requests, explicitly specify a role for the person studied. Such a role may be out of his or her role repertoire (e.g. that of a husband or wife) or the researcher may ask the subject to play a role that is not a normal one (e.g. that of a police officer). Alternatively, the researcher can leave the role implicit, assuming that the person studied will adopt a role appropriate to the situation. Secondly, the researcher can explicitly specify a task (e.g. solving a puzzle, playing a game, posing a specific affect) or the task can be left implicit, defined by the situation (e.g. waiting for an experiment to begin or a partner to arrive).

As far as the manipulation of the situation goes, a researcher can administer a specific external stimulus, such as showing a film, administering electroshocks, or manipulating

---

[23]   There are several studies that show minimal effects of being observed: Carpenter & Merkel 1988; Christensen & Hazzard 1983; Frank (Chapter 9 of this book); Jacob et al. 1994; Marshall et al. 2001; Nelson et al. 1978; White 1977; Wiemann 1981; and Zegiob & Forehand 1978.

the temperature in a room. Secondly, the context or setting in which the behavior is to take place can be changed. This often involves the suggestion of a particular definition of the situation. For example, it may be implied that a person is competing with another person or group, that his or her behavior is being monitored by experts, or something similar. Thirdly, in situations involving an interaction, the researcher can manipulate the nature of the subject's behavior by using a stooge or a confederate who has been briefed about the behavior to adopt in the interaction. Situations in which this manipulation is used vary from the use of interviewers with prearranged interview schedules to the use of confederates whose task it is to anger the subject under observation.

We cannot consider all the techniques that have been used to arrange behavior in research on nonverbal behavior. We will concentrate here on some particularly important ones, discussing issues relevant to reducing artificiality.

One of the most frequent techniques of arranging behavior is the use, in an interaction, of a confederate or collaborator of the researcher. This technique has been a frequent one in experimental investigations of nonverbal behavior in which researchers have attempted to induce a certain behavior or to observe the reaction of the subject in response to the preprogrammed behavior of the confederate. In this case, it is not possible to study interactive effects as they might actually occur. Even if one is exclusively interested in the behavior of the subject, one cannot exclude the possibility of artifacts. For example, the subject's behavior may be unusual in part because he is responding to someone who follows a fixed schedule. In looking at standardized interviews with psychiatric patients, one is impressed by how often the patients' reactions are determined by the need to switch topics abruptly, because that is what the schedule calls for. Thus, standardized interviews may distort the picture of psycho-pathological syndromes and not even represent the usual clinical interview.

Although the interaction in this case is not 'natural', in the sense that the behavioral choices of one participant are preplanned and at least partly independent of the actions of his partner, there is no reason to assume that the behavior of the person studied is always 'unnatural', unless one has reason to suspect that that person is aware of the manipulation. In some cases, the subject can even be told that he is dealing with a confederate in a simulation, as long as the task requirements are such that the subject is forced to react in an appropriate, serious manner. For example, Scherer and Scherer (1980) used lay actors as 'standard clients' (allowing the manipulation of social class and aggressive vs. submissive behavior) in interactions with public officials. The behavioral reactions (and the subjective evaluation) of the subjects showed that the demands of the task and the situation generally were such that they had to use their standard behavioral repertoire for that situation in order to appear competent.

Such experimental simulations should not be confused with role playing. In role playing, nothing is at stake and subjects are generally asked just to portray a particular person or role. In experimental simulations, the person plays himself or herself, and if the situation is properly arranged, his competence and his self-esteem are at stake; he cannot afford not to treat this as a real situation and make use of all his/her skills to establish his/her competence as an actor in the interaction. Again, we do not want to claim that such experimental simulations are exactly like naturally occurring behavior in all aspects. There may indeed be differences in the nature or strength of the behavioral reactions but, as noted before, such effects can never be excluded when the person observed is aware of the observation. On the other hand, using confederates in experimental simulations provides the researcher with a very powerful technique for repeatedly producing particular types of behavior in response to situational factors controlled within an experimental design. Many studies on nonverbal communication are almost impossible to conduct without using this technique (see Exline & Fehr 1982, Section 3.3).

Another type of arranged behavior that has been frequently used is posing and play acting. This technique is generally used in studies of inference processes from nonverbal cues, where the researcher needs some control over, and some range of, parameters or cues—a control and range that are impossible to obtain from the recording of naturally occurring behavior. This has been a particular problem in the area of emotional expression. The open expression of emotion is regulated by culturally determined display rules (Ekman 1972) and most societies do not allow the expression of very strong emotions in public (quite apart from the ethical problem involved in recording such expressions)[24]. Therefore, posing by professional or lay actors has often been used in the study of the recognition of emotion from nonverbal cues. For a more detailed discussion of the advantages and disadvantages of this approach, see Ekman et al. (1972, pp. 35–8) and Scherer (1981)[25]. These discussions show that there are research issues that cannot be studied appropriately without the use of posing. However, as with the use of confederates, there are more or less sophisticated ways of using this technique.

In posing, greater artificiality is to be expected if actors are simply asked to 'show fear' than if they are asked to act out a small scenario in which they can identify with particular persons and particular affects. In some cases, depending on the research issue, posers can be given very precise instructions, based on findings from naturally occurring behavior, about the behavioral cues they are supposed to produce. For example, the Facial Action Coding System (see Ekman 1982) can be used to specify the facial actions to be produced for a study of emotion inference from systematically varied facial cues.

Unfortunately, researchers often choose a particular technique without carefully considering its pros and cons. The issues raised here may help to render the basic decisions involved in the choice of a particular technique more salient. In very many procedures, the requests made of the person whose behavior is arranged are left implicit. Though this procedure has the advantage that behavior is less constrained by the investigator's demands, it has the disadvantage that different persons may construct or perceive their roles and tasks very differently. Obviously, this will render a comparison of the behavior observed very difficult. If roles and tasks are left unspe-

---

[24] Using laymen to systematically produce different expressions carries the risk that many individuals will show very little differentiation between different emotions (e.g. Galati et al. 1997).

[25] Banse & Scherer (1996) provide detailed overviews of the advantages and disadvantages of using actors for the portrayal of emotions.

cified, it is necessary to ask the person observed, after the observation, how he or she defined the situation and which reference or standard was used in deciding on a specific role or task perception. Furthermore, it is essential to establish the extent to which explicit roles or tasks specified are comparable and compatible with roles or tasks normally encountered by the person observed. Clearly, it would be very important for the evaluation of the behavior observed if the role that has been requested is one which the confederate has never played before and of which he or she may have had very little experience[26].

Sampling persons

In the best of all possible worlds in which to investigate research questions, one would like to be able to look at as many people as possible in as many settings as possible, to examine as many different aspects of the nonverbal behavior as possible, and to look at as many of these behaviors as occur within the setting. However, practical constraints usually require that we compromise on many aspects of the sampling issue. The nature of the compromise (i.e. the decision about which requirements have to be sacrificed to the limited time and resources available) should depend upon at least two considerations: the question being asked and the generalization being sought. For example, is one trying to answer a question for all persons or just for a particular type of person? Is one trying to answer a question that independent of settings or one that varies with types of settings? Is one trying to answer a question that cuts across several modalities of behavior, concerning, for example, the organization of different nonverbal behaviors, or is the question specific to a particular type of nonverbal behavior?

A further consideration in sampling concerns the purpose of a particular research project. Sampling considerations will be very different if one is concerned with discovery from what they will be if one attempts to provide proof for a phenomenon discovered in just a small sample. If one is interested in discovery, one is often willing to economize on the number of subjects and often even on the number of settings in order to look at as many modalities of behavior as possible and to observe as much behavior as possible within a particular setting or interaction. Thus, the various aspects of sampling are clearly interrelated and dependent upon the purpose of the research project. This interdependence should be kept in mind during our discussion of the

---

[26] Much of this section has been spent arguing that behavior in the laboratory or arranged behavior are not necessarily artificial and may be very well suited to the study of emotional expression and communication. This does not at all mean that one should refrain from studying naturally occurring behavior in the field. In our opinion, researchers are not making sufficient use of the wide range of possibilities in this respect. It is even possible to find quasi-experimental situations in which different participants can be studied in the same setting and structurally equivalent situation. For example, Scherer & Ceschi (2000) videotaped air line passengers in the baggage delivery section of an international airport, both while waiting at the empty-turning belt and in interaction with a lost luggage agent. While their predicament was comparable, the authors could show that differential appraisal patterns predicted differences in the verbal report and the facial expression of emotion.

particular dimensions. We will first deal with the choice of the type of person to be studied.

In some cases, for example, if one is interested in discovering the basic rules of nonverbal communication, one has little basis for specifying which persons ought to be observed. At the opposite extreme, one can have questions so precise that it is quite easy to specify, very narrowly, which persons ought to be observed. For example, if the nonverbal behavior of babies of a particular age is to be studied, the group of persons constituting the population for sampling is quite well defined. Thus, the choice of the persons to be studied is often inherent in the research issue (e.g. studying mother–infant interaction or kindergarten play, the diagnosis of depression). In such cases, the major problem usually is to obtain access to the group of persons one is interested in observing. In some cases, however, problems may occur because the group to be studied is not well defined or is less homogeneous than one thought. For example, much of the research on the nonverbal behavior of schizophrenics suffers from the fact that this diagnosis covers an enormous number of different psychopathological syndromes (as well as etiological factors)—a situation that vitiates any attempt to treat 'schizophrenics' as a homogeneous group and dashes hopes to find consistent nonverbal behavior patterns (Scherer 1979b).[27] Thus, if the research issue demands a particular type of person, one has to be very careful to assure that the group studied does indeed exhibit the characteristics that are theoretically important.

There are two kinds of generalization issues involved here. First, one needs to be reasonable certain that one is in fact looking at the population that is to be studied. In this case, the question is whether one can generalize from the persons sampled to that particular subgroup of persons. Often, this is not automatically the case. Though the example of psychopathological patients is a particularly difficult one, given the many problems in defining diagnostic groups, the issue is equally problematic with other groups of persons that cannot be easily defined on the basis of objective characteristics such as age or sex. It is quite difficult, for example, to generalize from a small sample of persons observed to social class, occupational group, or some other socially defined type.

The second generalization issue concerns generalizing from the sample observed to the population as a whole. Although many researchers acknowledge that they are studying a specific group of persons, they often seem to assume implicitly that generalization to the population, as a whole, is possible. For example, in the history of nonverbal communication research, the clinical interview has played a major role. Often interactions between therapists and psychologically disturbed patients have been studied, with the implication that the findings can be generalized to the general population. It is possible, however, that the clinical interview is a very specific kind of interaction with rules of its own and that it is not possible to generalize from the nonverbal behavior of disturbed persons to the nonverbal behavior of 'normals'. If one

---

[27] For example, Ellgring & Scherer (1996) suggest, on the basis of digital analyses of voice quality changes during the therapy of depressive patients, that the emotional disturbance underlying depression in females seems closer to anxiety compared to an emergent pattern of frustration and resignation in males.

is interested in applying results to the general population, to illustrate basic patterns of nonverbal behavior, it seems to be necessary to sample at least two different subgroups.

If the type of nonverbal behavior under study can be profitably investigated with any kind of person, the issue of easy availability and easy access becomes central. Often, the natural choice for researchers in university settings is college students, particularly if they have to serve as subjects to obtain course credit. Although college students constitute a somewhat limited population, this would not in itself present a problem, were it not for the fact that many students, particularly in psychology, are often experiment-wise and more prone than others to be affected by demand characteristics (Orne 1962) or experimenter expectancy (Rosenthal 1966) in unpredictable ways. Thus, researchers have to be unusually careful to avoid such artifacts when dealing with students, although the wide distribution of popular body language books may present a severe problem for demand characteristics with any type of subject population, if the purpose of the investigation is known.

An investigator who takes advantage of the easy availability of college students should try to study at least one population of non-students, even if it is only a very small subset, to check on the possibility of artifacts and/or sample specificity. The choice of this second sample is determined by many different considerations. Obviously, if one does not want to generalize to the population as a whole, but only to young people, one would be content with a second group of young persons who happen not to be enrolled in a university. However, if one wants to generalize to the population at large, it might be advisable to choose a second sample that is extremely different (e.g. middle-aged convicts).

Obviously, the more one believes that the phenomenon under study is a very basic one that should not be affected by many social and individual factors, the more extreme should be the comparison samples. In some cases, it is necessary to choose a very highly specialized group to make this point. For example, in attempting to show that many of the basic processes in the facial expression of emotion are innate, Ekman and his collaborators had to study isolated New Guineans to make the point (Ekman *et al.* 1969). Thus, the type of phenomenon to be demonstrated and the kind of generalization that the researcher attempts to make have a very strong impact on the decisions concerning sampling. Of course, given the many different types of groups in any society, it is never safe to generalize to the entire population, even if several groups have been observed. However, a sample of two groups is a vast improvement over a sample of one.

Apart from the type of person to be studied, it is important to decide on the number of persons whose behavior is to be observed. Given that the analysis of human behavior is a very time-consuming task, many researchers in the area of nonverbal communication have been content with rather few cases, in some studies with a single case. This is very problematical, however, because, particularly in a single case, there is no way to determine to what extent the behavior patterns found are a function of the characteristics of that particular person. The assumption that behavior patterns that follow well-defined social or cultural rules can be observed even in a single case is valid only if the existence of such strong cultural patterns has been established before. For most phenomena, this is not the case. Consequently, a minimum of two persons should be studied, even if the researcher is convinced that he or she is dealing with very universal phenomena, to check the extent to which the behavior is determined by the individual characteristics of a particular person.

Similarly, if one attempts to determine differences between types of persons observed, such as differences between males and females, one needs at least two cases of each type to see whether there are smaller variations within types than between types. It would be desirable to have many more subjects for statistical analysis, in which the sources of variation could be determined more precisely. This may be impossible in cases where a particular type of interaction or a particular type of individual is difficult to observe in great numbers or in which the analysis is so time-consuming that it cannot be conducted for a large number of persons. But though it is only rarely acceptable to use single-case studies for any kind of generalization, they may be very valuable in initial approaches to particular phenomena and in an attempt to develop hypotheses to be tested later. Furthermore, it is extremely useful to observe a single individual frequently and over a long period of time, to get a more complete sampling of the behavior in context than is normally possible in studies employing a large number of subjects. Yet a single-case study is not sufficient to establish the existence of a particular phenomenon or relationship. Unfortunately, many of the phenomena studied in nonverbal behavior research have shown rather large individual differences; not very many have been robust enough to survive the sampling variation produced by individual differences.

Obviously, the more probabilistic the coding of the nonverbal behavior, the more important it is to observe a fairly large number of encoders. Here, it is advisable to use a group of encoders with fairly homogeneous characteristics, as otherwise it is impossible to determine, in the case of negative results, whether there is no relationship or whether it is dependent on the type of person. Even if the results are positive, they may be dependent on the particular encoder. Just how homogeneous such groups of encoders should be is difficult to say. Often the researcher has to use prior knowledge or intuition about individual differences to make the decision. For example, if there is good evidence for strong sex differences in a particular nonverbal behavior, it is advisable to limit the study to members of one sex or, if feasible, to include several members of each sex. If the researcher is unable to keep a group of subjects nicely balanced in essential characteristics, he or she should at least attempt, through questionnaires, to assess some of the major characteristics (such as age, education, geographical origin, social class, and, possibly, personality) to be able to check, in at least a rudimentary way, whether these factors may have made a difference. At times, the outcome of such checks allows a better understanding of the pattern of findings (or lack thereof) and suggests hypotheses for further study (see Scherer 1972).

Although more difficult, it is not impossible to find fairly homogeneous groups of persons that can be studied outside colleges. Possibilities include the use of church and community groups, participants in adult education centers, and members of organizations and institutions.

The nature of behavior sampling

On the pages to follow, we will deal with a number of decisions concerning particular aspects of sampling behavior and the procedures used in securing such behavior samples out of a stream of behavior, over time, in social contexts.

Sampling the individual versus the interaction

Obviously, if the individual is studied in a situation where he or she is alone, only the behavior of that individual person can be sampled. Similarly, when the purpose of the research is to study patterns of interaction, two or more individuals will have to be sampled. However, if the focus of interest is the individual and the factors that determine his or her behavior in an interaction, it becomes crucial to decide whether the behavior of that individual alone ought to be sampled or whether it is necessary also to sample the behavior of an interaction partner.

Clearly, this problem can be decided only on the basis of the specific question asked. If the effects of factors totally independent of the interaction partner or the interaction situation as a whole are to be assessed (e.g. the effects of drugs on behavior), it would seem to be sufficient to focus just on the behavior of the individual. However, in most cases, it is difficult to exclude the effect of the behavior of the interaction partner or partners when assessing the determinants of an individual's behavior. Consequently, in most cases where interactive behavior is observed, it is necessary to sample the behavior of all the persons interacting, even if the focus of interest is on one individual. If confederates are used, it is advisable to employ more than one, to be certain that the results are not specific to the effect of one particular person. In some cases, the reason for this is simply to check on the success of a particular manipulation in the experiment. For example, often a confederate or interviewer has been programmed by the investigator to behave in a certain way. In these cases, it is necessary to sample the behavior of the confederate to establish whether the instructions are being followed, as well as to check how the behavior of the subject affects the behavior of the confederate.

Technical problems become almost insurmountable if more than two persons are to be observed or recorded simultaneously, if many modalities are to be investigated, or if close-up recordings are required. Most studies in which the behavior of more than one person was sampled have been conducted with dyads. Clearly, in studies in which the interaction is the focus of research, it is essential that all participants of the interaction be included in the behavior sampling. If exact temporal correspondence between the behavior patterns of two or more actors is to be investigated, fairly elaborate precautions have to be taken to make sure that the behavioral records, and possibly the audiovisual recordings, are well synchronized. This question becomes particularly important if audiovisual recording is used to sample behavior (see Wallbott 1982).

Direct observation versus audiovisual recording

This choice is of major importance for research design and procedure, because a decision to record often has many implications for the approach to be taken. As mentioned earlier, the technical requirements for adequate recording (see Wallbott 1982) are fairly obtrusive, and unless at least some aspects of the recording procedure can be hidden from the subject's view, the researcher has to count on some change in the behavior observed, owing to the subject's reaction to being recorded[28]. Further-

---

[28] There are a number of methodological issues to consider in reducing the influence of the observer on the observed; see Hartmann & Wood 1990; Hayes & Horn 1982; Jacob *et al.* 1987; Kazdin 1982; Webb *et al.* 1981.

more, both the physical setting and the temporal structure of an interaction have to be accommodated to the technical constraints of the recording. Last, though not least, high-quality recording is expensive, both in terms of equipment required and tape and/ or film material used[29].

Despite these disadvantages, audiovisual recording of behavior is becoming more and more frequent in the analysis of nonverbal behavior. There are many important advantages: the possibility of replaying and observing a sequence of behavior over and over, of viewing the behavior in slow motion, of doing microscopic frame-by-frame analysis, of using the material for judgment studies, and many others. Another advantage of obtaining a permanent record is that it is possible to measure, through repeated passes, many more aspects of behavior than can possibly be measured in the one real-time pass possible when no record is obtained[30].

Because of these advantages of recording behavior, direct observation is preferable only if recording is too costly, if it would be too obtrusive in a natural setting, or if the features or categories of behavior to be observed are very simple and are unlikely to be changed in the course of the research. There are such situations, and in them researchers should forgo recordings. They should realize, however, that in direct observation, much more stringent checks need to be made on the reliability of coders or observers, because the scores cannot be checked again later.

In this chapter, the issue of direct observation versus audiovisual recording can be discussed only very briefly. Given the importance of the issue, the reader is referred to the literature on observational methods (Sackett 1978; Weick 1968)[31], as well as to the discussion of specific problems in observation and recording (Ekman 1982; Exline & Fehr 1982; Kendon 1982; Rosenfeld 1982; Scherer 1982; Wallbott 1982)[32].

Single versus repeated sampling

In almost all of the existing studies of nonverbal behavior, encoders have been observed on only one occasion and in only one situational context — the assumption being that the use of nonverbal signals will not differ depending on situational characteristics or the identity of the interaction partners. This assumption may be quite wrong, of course. We do know that even speech patterns change rather noticeably depending on situational context (Brown & Fraser 1979), and it would be quite surprising if this were not the case for the much less stringently coded nonverbal signals. It seems reasonable to assume that the more probabilistic the relationship between a nonverbal behavior and an external referent is, the more situation-dependent it might be. In the civil servant study mentioned earlier (Scherer & Scherer 1980), the officials had to deal with two different cases (differing in the amount of power the official could wield) involving two different clients. Results showed different relationships between personality and

---

[29] The availability of digital recording and cheap storage via DVD will reduce the significance of this problem in the future; see Chapter 12, Appendix 2).
[30] These techniques are becoming ever more elegant and accessible with the increasing availability of affordable digital equipment and dedicated software.
[31] See also Denzin & Lincoln 1994.
[32] See also Chapters 4, 10, and 11.

attitudes and nonverbal behavior for each of the cases, indicating that personality dispositions and attitudes may differentially determine the nonverbal behavior patterns shown under different situational constraints[33].

Clearly, it would be most desirable to sample behavior repeatedly from the same person, both in similar situations and in different situations, with the same interaction partners at different times and with different partners. Such behavior sampling procedures are both more complex and more demanding of time and money than the single-case studies that dominate the field. Yet it is difficult to see how one can confidently assume that the coding and usage patterns found in a single behavioral sample are indeed independent of the situation and the interaction partner.

Single-culture studies versus cross-cultural comparison

Most of the studies in the field have been conducted not only on single cases, but also in a single culture. Although most of these studies have been conducted only in the United States, the authors of textbooks and review chapters usually do not bother to note that the results reported may be culture-specific and that the relationships between nonverbal behavior and external referents might be very different in other cultures. If all, or even most nonverbal behavior were to be strongly biologically determined, as the basis for the expression of emotion seems to be (Ekman 1972), this might not be of great consequence. But even in emotional expression, strong cultural differences in display rules have been found (Ekman 1972) which render generalizations of findings across cultures rather dubious[34]. In some of the studies that have included cross-cultural comparison, very different patterns of results have emerged for the cultures investigated (see Key 1977, pp.138–9). A more extensive discussion of this issue cannot be offered at this point. However, we feel strongly that it is necessary to devote more effort to cross-cultural comparison in order to understand better the effect of cultural factors on nonverbal behavior and the significance of such behavior in communication.

---

[33] A number of studies have shown differential patterns of nonverbal behavior based on personality dimensions: dominance (Tiedens & Fragale 2003); dominance and affiliation (Montepare & Dobish 2003); expressiveness, extraversion, and neuroticism (Riggio & Riggio 2002); leadership (Bucy 2000); self-monitoring (Leck & Simpson 1999; Levine & Feldman 2002); trait anxiety (Harrigan *et al.* 2004); and trustworthiness (Boone & Buck 2003).

[34] One would want to examine systematic observations of many different emotional expressions as they are actually occurring in comparable situational contexts in many different cultures. However, apart from the work by Eibl–Eibesfeldt and his collaborators (1970, 1989), who have routinely filmed, in an unobtrusive fashion, sequences of emotional behavior in a number of non-Western societies, there is little evidence available. Ekman and his collaborators have filmed induced facial emotion expressions in an isolated society in New Guinea (Ekman *et al.* 1969). The vast majority of research in this area uses a *decoding* paradigm, investigating whether members of one culture can reliably recognize expressions produced by members of another culture. In general, this research shows that while there is a strong core of universality in the patterns of emotional expression, there is also quite a bit of cultural specificity (see reviews in Mesquita *et al.* 1997; Scherer 1997*a,b*). In the future, more effort should be devoted to cross-cultural comparison in order to understand better the effect of cultural factors on nonverbal behavior and the significance of such behavior in communication.

Whereas the importance of cross-cultural assessment of nonverbal behavior is only rarely alluded to in studies on nonverbal behavior, there is more frequent concern with the importance of ethnic group or race and gender (see Harper *et al.* 1978; Key 1977)[35]. Clearly, there are other intercultural factors that urgently require more systematic study, such as differences between social classes, ages, or occupations. It is to be expected that our knowledge of nonverbal behavior would be greatly advanced if researchers would turn toward a more complete sampling of the social and cultural contexts in which to observe nonverbal behavior. Similarly, anthropological and ethnographical studies should be considered more frequently in planning research on nonverbal behavior. Finally, apart from the comparison of different social and cultural settings for human behavior, a comparative approach studying similarities and differences in the nonverbal behavior patterns in animals and humans may also highlight the functions of nonverbal behavior (Scherer 1981).

Exhaustive versus selective sampling

One can either observe or record an entire interaction or select certain excerpts. Very often this decision depends on the length as well as on the nature of the behavior being sampled. If out of a lengthy behavior sequence, only one particular time frame is important for the analysis (e.g. the verdict in a jury trial), it is obviously sufficient to record just this segment of the interaction. The situations in which the behavior sequences of interest are so clearly identifiable are very rare, however. Often a researcher may be able to decide only after many repeated viewings of the behavior sequence which parts of that sequence are relevant for his or her question.

If it is impossible to record the total interaction or behavior sequence because of practical considerations, selective samples are drawn. The two most frequently used techniques are:

1. the sampling of representative segments of the interaction (e.g. taking five-minute sequences from the beginning, middle, and end);
2. fixed-interval sampling (e.g. observing or recording a minute of behavior at five-minute intervals).

Both the choice of appropriate sampling procedures and the decisions on sampling intervals and observation periods depend on a large number of theoretical and practical issues, such as the frequency of occurrence of the behaviors studied, their duration, and so on (see detailed discussion in Fagen & Young 1978; Sackett 1978)[36]. Such selective samples are often drawn for the analysis, even if the entire interaction has been recorded, because an analysis of very lengthy behavior samples is too costly and time-consuming if elaborate microscopic analysis procedures are used.

One of the basic issues is the decision whether to pick naturally defined units (e.g. openings and closings, greetings, departures, interruptions) or to use arbitrary time samples (e.g. every fifth minute of the interaction). If arbitrary time samples are used,

---

[35] See also Brody & Hall 2004 and Patterson & Edinger 1987.
[36] See also Kendall *et al.* 1999.

there is little or no ambiguity about the selection procedure or the definition of the units, because they are defined by the objective parameter time. With this procedure, however, natural social units of behavior are in danger of being fragmented; the researcher is prevented from following a complete pattern of behavioral events and, hence, from understanding the relationships between different behavior patterns over time. The use of naturally occurring units has the advantage of avoiding such fragmentation but the disadvantage of having to reach agreement on the operation for determining beginning and ending of these natural events, which may be difficult to attain. Furthermore, the length of the samples may differ sizably across interactions.

Both of these procedures have the problem of comparability (i.e. of establishing whether one is looking at the same or at different types of time periods or units across persons and interactions). Great care has to be taken in defining such units to ensure that the behavior patterns under study will reliably occur within sampling units chosen across individuals and across different settings.

Complete versus partial behavior sampling

Sometimes, researchers are interested only in one aspect of the total nonverbal behavior pattern, such as gaze, facial expressions, or vocal behavior. They then have the option of observing or recording only this particular aspect of the nonverbal behavior. In many cases, the decision to restrict sampling to a particular behavior pattern or modality has been simply a matter of convenience, resulting from restrictions of apparatus, technique, or time. The problem of isolating particular aspects of behavior or modalities of behavior out of an integrative whole has only rarely been considered. This is unfortunate, because such isolation precludes an analysis of the relationships between different aspects of nonverbal behavior. On the other hand, if audiovisual recording is used, it is often very difficult to record adequately all the different aspects of nonverbal behavior with as much detail as the analysis requires (e.g. obtaining close-ups of the face, adjusting the camera angle to allow determination of gaze). Yet, it may be desirable to record behavior as completely as possible (within reason), even if it is unclear at the time of the recording whether all aspects sampled can be analyzed later.

If one decides to divide up behavior, either because only some behaviors will be measured or because observers will be used to compare judgments based on different sources, how should one proceed? Usually the choice has fallen on the end organs involved in producing the behavior (e.g. hands, legs, body, face, speech). An alternative would be to focus on the central mechanisms that produce the end-organ behavior or the mechanisms involved in the perceiver. Take two examples — one, judgment; the other, measurement. If one is interested in measuring emphasis movements, why study just the hands? The head, the voice, the facial muscles can all similarly produce emphasis. In all likelihood, the same central neural mechanism sends out emphasis signals to various end organs. If one is interested in studying how observers process verbal and nonverbal behavior, one might divide channels according to whether the right or left hemisphere of the brain handles the information, rather than concentrate on the verbal–face–body interaction, because within both the verbal domain and the face there are probably highly symbolic left-hemisphere-processed items and analogical right-hemisphere-processed items.

Measuring nonverbal behavior

After the researcher has decided how to sample the behavior, he or she has to decide which aspects of the nonverbal behavior are to be measured and which measurement procedures are to be used. In the case of direct observation, observers have to be given checklists that they can use to record the occurrence of specific behavior patterns, or instruments (such as event recorders) to codify the occurrence and duration of various behavior patterns. If nonverbal behavior has been recorded on film or magnetic tape, a larger set of options for measurement procedures is available, because measurements of various types can be performed during repeated passes through the material and because there is the possibility of slow motion and frame-by-frame analysis of visual records and acoustic analysis of auditory records. This section describes some of the basic options for measurement procedures; details and examples are discussed in relevant chapters.

The choice of particular measurement procedures mainly depends on the phenomena to be investigated. In some cases, these may be difficult to observe because they are internal to the organism. Examples are anatomic, chemical, or electrical phenomena (e.g. movement of a muscle). In such cases, measurement procedures must either directly assess these internal phenomena, as through physiological recordings, or utilize outward indicators of them. In most cases, however, researchers are interested in the consequences of such underlying phenomena for the visible or audible behavior of the person. The nature of the measurement systems to be used to isolate and measure the respective variables describing the nonverbal behavior under study are hotly debated in nonverbal behavior research. Some of the options available for study and analysis of nonverbal behavior are discussed here.

The major distinction is between descriptive approaches and inferential approaches (allowing for a mixed category that contains some elements of both). What we mean by descriptive approaches are attempts to capture particular aspects of behavior patterns by using transcription or category systems that describe the spatio-temporal characteristics of particular movements. Inferential approaches, on the other hand, go beyond the description of behavior patterns in time and space by using functional or motivational criteria to provide a categorization or typification of particular behavior patterns. Thus, descriptive approaches attempt to use very objective techniques that do not require an observer's inference about the function and purpose of a particular behavior pattern, in terms either of the actor's intention or of the social function of a behavior (see also Ekman 1982, Section 2.5).

Furthermore, the techniques available for the measurement of nonverbal behavior are differentiated by whether they are:

1. highly microscopic, precise, and highly differentiated (that is, capable of making very fine distinctions between various aspects of the behavior observed and looking at very fine-grained changes in the behavior) *or*

2. more macroscopic or global, identifying only fairly large-scale phenomena.

Clearly, the use of a microscopic differentiated system has the advantage of providing a very fine resolution and allowing an empirical basis for the later procedure of collapsing categories into more integrative ones. It has the disadvantage, however, of being very cumbersome, and it presents the danger of losing particular phenomena because of too atomistic an approach. A more macroscopic system has the advantage of being more economical and providing a better relationship between the signal and the function of a behavior pattern, but it presents the problem that important clues might be missed, and it is virtually impossible (except for a re-analysis at very high cost) to decompose macroscopic categories into more fine-grained items.

Finally, measurement systems can be differentiated according to their comprehensiveness or selectivity. It is claimed that some measurement systems will accommodate any kind of behavior that occurs within the general stream of behavior. In other systems, coverage is restricted to just some items or patterns of behavior, selected out of the stream of behavior for recording. In many cases, it is problematic to postulate that a system is comprehensive unless all anatomic possibilities for motor behavior are taken into account. (see Rosenfeld 1982). Selective systems, on the other hand, have the disadvantage that often the selection may be not a reasoned one but one based on opportunism or convenience. As we go on now to consider the advantages and disadvantages of some particular measurement techniques illustrating these dimensions, it should be kept in mind that machines and observers always operate jointly, because almost all machines still need human operators and observers, at least for interpretation of the data.

Judges and coders versus instruments and apparatus

At present, perceptual units can only be identified and categorized by human judges, because even the most advanced computers still lack the pattern recognition ability required for this task. Physical characteristics, however, can be measured both by machine and by human judges. Obviously, in those cases where machines can be used without recourse to human judges, more objective and reliable data can be expected. For example, although listeners hear fundamental frequency of voice as pitch, their judgment of the physical value is not nearly as good as is electro- acoustic measurement, both because of the nature of the auditory system and because of the listeners' lack of appropriate scaling ability (see Scherer 1982, Section 4.6).

In many cases, however, machine analysis must be supplemented by human observers, generally in order to perform pattern analysis tasks that are beyond the capability of even sophisticated instruments. For example, if spatial coordinates for the movement of the hand are to be entered into a computer to allow objective measurement of speed and acceleration of movement, human observers have to be used to mark a fixed part of the hand (e.g. the middle finger knuckle) with a light pen or another computer-access device (see Rosenfeld 1982, Section 5.5). As the examples in many of the chapters in this volume will show, in general, a combination of human judges or operators and machines has to be used for the analysis of physical characteristics. In some cases, movement patterns are so complex that highly trained coders must be used to identify the physical components of an action, as for example in the Facial Action Coding System developed by Ekman and Friesen (see Ekman 1982).

The use of judges or coders in behavioral research is a highly complex research procedure, the dangers of which are underestimated by many researchers. Many published studies in this area suffer from serious problems concerning judge selection, judgment procedure, and, most often, insufficient checks on the reliability of the judgments. A comprehensive discussion of the issues to be considered in conducting judgment or decoding studies is found in Rosenthal (1982; see also Ekman 1982, Section 2.1).

Persons doing the observation can be naive or trained. Naive observers will usually mix description with inference or evaluation. Trained observers can operate at different levels, varying from the strictly descriptive to the inferential. In descriptive approaches, the observer frequently utilizes iconic or digital transcription systems or classifications. Inferences made by observers can be termed judgments and may refer to intent, motive, affect, conversational function, and so on. In most cases, the inferences do not specify the sign vehicles upon which they are based. Intermediate, but closer to description, are behavioral rating systems, which are usually more gross than transcription or classification systems. Closer to inference, on the other hand, are functionally based ratings or classifications.

The terminology in this area is very confusing. Various terms are used — often interchangeably to describe the persons engaged in ratings or classifications. The most general term seems to be *observer* (i.e. a person who does nonverbal measurement); the specific type of measurement is not specified. *Coder, scorer,* or *transcriber* is used if description but not inference is the major type of measurement to be conducted by the observer. In the case of a *coder,* the major task seems to be the recording of data from machine analyses. The term *scorer* is used in those cases where observers are to classify behaviors into different typologies or classes or categories. A *transcriber* is usually involved in transforming or notating behavior into a behavioral record of some written form. The term *judge,* on the other hand, is used in those cases in which the observers are mainly asked for inference rather than description (i.e. cases where the major interest of the researcher is in assessing the judge's interpretation of the behavior). Finally, the more neutral term *rater* is used for global assessment on adjective or attribute scales in which either inferential or behavioral characteristics are being evaluated.

Some issues in transcription and classification

Transcription by symbolic notation is very much influenced by the phonetic–linguistic tradition, which assumes that every portion of speech consists of a meaningful unit. Adherents of the transcription method for nonverbal behavior assume that the same is true for behavior generally and that it is, therefore, essential to provide an exhaustive transcription of all aspects of behavior. A large number of transcription systems for nonverbal behavior have been developed or adapted from areas such as dance notation (see Birdwhistell 1970; Hutchinson 1970; Kendon 1982; Scherer 1982).

Some of the advantages and disadvantages of using the transcription method are discussed in chapters of this book. In general, however, it seems fair to state that the usefulness of a thorough transcription of nonverbal behavior as a way of providing evidence for any of the major research issues in the field has not yet come forth. Most of these transcription systems are exhausting to use, but there is no evidence that they are exhaustive. In fact, one of their key problems is that usually there is no explicit statement about how the investigator decided what to include, and the user is led to believe that a transcription is complete just because it is long and cumbersome. Furthermore, many of these transcription systems have been developed in a way that makes them difficult to use in statistical analyses, though there is no necessary reason for this to be the case.

As mentioned before, coding or category systems are selective, in that only a certain number of predefined units are analyzed. There seem to be three major types of such coding schemes: natural language labels; categories of physical characteristics; and functional categories. Natural language-label categories make use of the segmentation and categorization potential inherent in culturally shared language labels. Thus, categories such as *smile, laughter, frown, pout, giggle,* and the like are presumed to be used in a comparable fashion by judges and, thus, to be usable as coding schemes (possibly on the basis of a checklist of labels of this sort). The use of such categories is not infrequently reported in the literature, particularly in human ethology, sociolinguistics, and social psychology. Although this procedure is quick, it may also be rather dirty. Unfortunately, researchers using this method often do not bother to establish whether their judges really do all mean the same facial movements by *smile* or all agree on the sound quality of a *giggle*. Because there may be regional and inter-individual differences in language-label use, the comparability of results obtained with different judges cannot be established. Furthermore, many natural language labels contain evaluative connotations. For example, the label *gloomy voice* contains not only a voice quality description but also a characterization of the state of the speaker. Thus, it is difficult to know to what extent judges using natural language labels use their inferences and attributions about psychological states and interpersonal processes in assigning labels to behaviors.

Category systems using physical characteristics as criteria can be more objectively defined. For example, a scorer could categorize as 'right head lean', all head movements where the head is tilted to the right to at least a particular angle (see Rosenfeld 1982). Or the scorer could determine fundamental frequency (pitch) contours and categorize them as going up or down, or up and down (see Scherer 1982, Section 4.6; Stern & Wasserman 1979). As long as coders can be expected to be reasonably precise about the interpretation of physical measurements, a high reliability of such categorizations will result. One possible drawback is the fact that classification on the basis of particular physical features cannot be guaranteed to result in valid or meaningful categories.

The third approach to coding attempts ensures that valid categories do result by basing them on functional considerations (i.e. classifying behaviors on the basis of their role in communication or individual coping). The best example of such functional coding schemes is a number of hand movement coding systems differentiating self-manipulatory movements such as scratching or stroking (with presumed individual adaptation functions) from 'illustrating' or 'object-focused' movements (with an information–transmission or interaction–regulation function) (Ekman & Friesen 1969; Scherer *et al.* 1979; see also Rosenfeld 1982, Section 5.5). Possible problems with this kind of measurement system include the necessity of making a priori judgments about the functions of certain behaviors, the danger that coders will make inferences concerning the intentions of actors in categorizing movements by function, and the difficulty of differentiating movements that have similar functions but that could be profitably distinguished on other grounds.

Some comments on data analysis

The possibilities for the analysis of the data obtained through the measurement procedures just discussed do not differ dramatically from the choices researchers usually face in analyzing their data. Depending on the purpose of the study, different types of analysis techniques can be used: exploration vs. testing hypotheses, quantitative vs. qualitative analysis, statistical vs. illustrative approaches, and so on. Many examples of these different possibilities will be found in the individual chapters in this volume, and comprehensive coverage of the various aspects of these data-analytic procedures can be found in most surveys of data analysis in the social and behavioral sciences.

One serious deficiency of much of the research in nonverbal behavior is that, in general, only central tendencies in the data are reported. Very rarely is each individual or each individual record examined and in detail. If one is trying to characterize general nonverbal behavior for a specific type of person, let alone the species, then one cannot be content with simply describing the mean or reporting a correlation. An attempt must be made to inspect individual records and behavior patterns and to report the number of instances that fit the general trend indicated in the statistical coefficients. One should try to explain the reason why behavior patterns for some individuals do not conform to the central tendencies. In many cases, this is an important possibility for the improvement of a theory or hypothesis.

For example, in a study of stress and deception among nurses (Ekman *et al.* 1976), a number of phenomena were apparent on the group level, such as increase of fundamental frequency from baseline to stress. However, looking at each of the individual subjects made it readily apparent that there were moderator variables, mostly personality characteristics, that could serve to separate the subjects into two groups characterized by very different types of nonverbal reactions (Scherer 1979*b*).

Very frequently, researchers tend to look not at raw data but only at the output generated by statistical analysis packages. This may be quite misleading in cases where the distribution of various behavioral categories is very important for the question being asked. It is thus advisable to look more frequently at the distributions and the scatter plots between variables, and not just at the means and the variances. In many cases, the data should be transformed before statistical analyses are performed, because changes in the mean might be associated with change in the variance.

Among data-analytic methods that are very relevant for nonverbal behavior research, and are not well established in the social and behavioral sciences, are the qualitative analyses of the structure of interactive behavior (see Kendon 1982; West & Zimmerman

1982), as well as the sequence and cluster analysis methods designed to study sequences and changes rather than aggregates (see van Hooff 1982).

Given that most of the research and the analyses on nonverbal behavior are exploratory, the use of statistical procedures without consideration of individual behavior patterns and raw data is not really justified. It is only after a phenomenon and its characteristics have been fairly well established that we can use high-powered data analysis techniques. Also, given our very restricted knowledge about nonverbal behavior, we should not stick to single cases, as pointed out previously. When we are dealing with measurement techniques that are imprecise, in areas which are not yet well explored, and in which we do not have much conceptual guidance, it is all the more problematical to be content with a single case.

Conclusions

This has been an attempt to survey some of the major methodological issues facing students of nonverbal behavior. Although our review has shown that behavior sampling and measurement procedures are closely linked to research issues and theoretical assumptions, there is no inherent dichotomy between qualitative, structural, and interactional approaches, on the one hand, and experimental, quantitative, and psychological studies, on the other. Although this distinction may have some basis in the historical development of the field, and although it was sharpened by early reviews of the literature, it can and it must be overcome if the nature and function of nonverbal behavior are to be studied comprehensively.

Nonverbal behavior expresses both traits and states of individuals and serves as a culturally shared and structured signaling system. What is more, it performs both of these functions at the same time and often through the very same movements. Thus, studies focused on the individual and studies focused on interaction and communication have to complement each other. Researchers leaning toward a particular focus and raised in a particular theoretical tradition need to take cognizance of the wide variety of methodological approaches available for the empirical study of nonverbal behavior, and need to base their choices on appropriateness rather than prejudice. We hope that this handbook will help them to do so.

References

Allport, G.W. (1968). The historical background of modern social psychology. In *The handbook of social psychology, Vol. 1* (2nd edn) (ed. G. Lindzey & E. Aronson). Reading, Mass: Addison–Wesley.

Allport, G.W. & Vernon, P.E. (1933). *Studies in expressive movement.* New York: Macmillan.

Argyle, M. & Dean, J. (1965). Eye-contact, distance and affiliation. *Sociometry,* 28, 289–304.

Aristotle. *Nichomachean ethics.* Translated by Martin Ostwald (1962). Indianapolis: The Library of Liberal Arts.

Banse, R. & Scherer, K.R. (1996). Acoustic profiles in vocal emotion. *Journal of Personality and Social Psychology,* 70, 614–36.

Bateson, G. & Mead, M. (1942). *Balinese character: a photographic analysis, Vol. 2.* NewYork: Special Publications of the New York Academy of Sciences.

Bell, C. (1806). *Essays on the anatomy and philosophy of expression: as connected with the fine arts.* London.

Birdwhistell, R.L. (1952). *Introduction to kinesics.* Washington, DC: Foreign Service Institute, Louisville: University of Louisville Press. Now available in microfilm only from: University Microfilms, Inc., 313 N. First St., Ann Arbor Mich. Partly reprinted as an appendix to *Kinesics and context* (see next reference).

Birdwhistell, R.L. (1970). *Kinesics and context.* Philadelphia: University of PennsylvaniaPress.

Blass, T. & Siegman, A.W. (1975). A psycholinguistic comparison of speech, dictation and writing. *Language and Speech,* **18,** 20–34.

Bloomfield, L. (1933). *Language.* New York: Holt & Co.

Blurton Jones, N.G. (1971). Criteria for use in describing facial expressions. *Human Biology,* **43,** 365–413.

Boomer, D.S. & Dittman, A.T. (1962). Hesitation pauses and juncture pauses in speech. *Language and Speech,* **5,** 215–20.

Boomer, D.S. & Dittman, A.T. (1964). Speech rate, filled pause, and body movement in interviews. *Journal of Nervous and Mental Disorders,* **139,** 324–7. Also in *Explorations in nonverbal and vocal behavior* (ed G.F. Mahl), Hillsdale, NJ: Lawrence Erlbaum.

Boone, R.T. & Buck, R. (2003). Emotional expressivity and trustworthiness: the role of nonverbal behavior in the evolution of cooperation. *Journal of Nonverbal Behavior,* **27,** 163–82.

Brody, L.R. & Hall, J.A. (2004). Gender, emotion, and expression. In *Handbook of emotions* (2nd edn) (ed. M. Lewis & J.M. Haviland–Jones), pp. 338–49. New York: Guilford.

Brown, P. & Fraser, C. (1979). Speech as a marker of situation. In *Social markers in speech* (ed. K. Scherer & H. Giles), pp. 33–62. Cambridge: Cambridge University Press.

Bucy, E.P. (2000). Emotional and evaluative consequences of inappropriate leader displays. *Communication Research,* **27,** 194–226.

Bühler, K. (1934/1965). Sprachtheorie [Theory of Language]. [2nd Ed.]. Stuttgart: G Fisher

Burgoon, J.K., Buller, D.B., & Woodall, W.G. (1996) *Nonverbal communication: the unspoken dialogue.* New York: McGraw–Hill.

Carpenter, L.J. & Merkel, W.T. (1988). The effects of three methods of observation on couples in international research. *American Journal of Family Therapy,* **16,** 144–57.

Chapple, E.D. (1948/49). The interaction chronograph: its evolution and present application. *Personnel,* **25,** 295–307.

Christensen, A. & Hazzard, A. (1983). Reactive effects during naturalistic observation of families. *Behavior & Assessment,* **5,** 349–62.

Condon, W.S. & Ogston, W.D. (1967). A segmentation of behavior. *Journal of Psychiatric Research,* **5,** 221–35.

Darwin, C. (1872/1965). *The expression of emotions in man and animals.* Chicago: University of Chicago Press. (Originally published 1872, London: John Murray.)

Darwin, C. (1872/1998). *The expression of the emotions in man and animals* (3rd edn). With an introduction, afterward, and commentaries by P. Ekman. Oxford: Oxford University Press. (Originally published 1872, London: John Murray.).

Denzin, N.K. & Lincoln, Y.S. (ed.) (1994). *Handbook of qualitative research.* Thousand Oaks, CA: Sage.

Dittman, A.T. (1962). The relationship between body movements and moods in interviews. *Journal of Consulting Psychology,* **26**, 480.

Dittman, A.T. (1987). The role of body movement in communication. In Nonverbal behavior and communication (2nd edn) (ed. A.W. Siegman & S. Feldstein), pp. 37–64. Hillsdale, NJ: Erlbaum.

Duchenne, B. (1862). *Mecanisme de la physionomie humaine; ou, Analyse electrophysiologique de l'expression des passions.* Paris: Bailliere.

Duncan, S.D., Jr. (1969). Nonverbal communication. *Psychological Bulletin, 72,* 118–37

Duncan, S.D., Jr. (1972). Some signals and rules for taking speaking turns in conversations. *Journal of Personality and Social Psychology, 23,* 283–92.

Duncan, S.D., Jr. & Fiske, D.W. (1977). *Face-to-face interaction.* Hillsdale, NJ: Erlbaum.

Efron, D. (1941/1972). *Gesture, race, and culture.* The Hague: Mouton. (Originally published 1941.)

Eibl–Eibesfeldt, I. (1970). *Ethology: the biology of behavior.* New York, NY: Holt, Rinehart & Winston.

Eibl–Eibesfeldt, I. (1989). *Human ethology.* New York, NY: Aldine.

Ekman, P. (1957). A methodological discussion of nonverbal behavior. *Journal of Psychology,* **43**, 141–9.

Ekman, P. (1965). Differential communication of affect by head and body cues. *Journal of Personality and Social Psychology,* **2**, 726–35.

Ekman, P. (1972). Universal and cultural differences in facial expression of emotion. In *Nebraska Symposium on Motivation, Vol. 19* (ed. J.R. Cole), pp. 207–83. Lincoln: University of Nebraska Press.

Ekman, P. (1976). Movements with precise meanings. *Journal of Communication, 26,* 14–26.

Ekman, P. (1977). Nonverbal behavior. In *Communication and social interaction* (ed. P.F. Ostwald), pp.37–46. New York, NY: Grune and Stratton.

Ekman, P. (1979). About brows: emotional and conversational signals. In *Human ethology* (ed. M. von Cranach, K. Foppa, W. Lepenies, & D. Ploog), pp. 169–248. Cambridge: Cambridge University Press.

Ekman, P. (1982). Methods for measuring facial action. In *Handbook of methods in nonverbal behavior research* (ed. K.R. Scherer & P. Ekman), pp. 45–90. Cambridge: Cambridge University Press.

Ekman, P. (1997). Expression and communication about emotion. In *Uniting psychology and biology: integrative perspectives on human development* (ed. N.L. Segal, G.E. Weisfeld, & C.C Weisfeld), pp. 315–38. Washington, DC: American Psychological Association.

Ekman, P. & Friesen, W.V. (1969). The repertoire of nonverbal behavior: categories, origins, usage, and coding. *Semiotica,* 1, 49–98.

Ekman, P. & Friesen, W.V. (1975). *Unmasking the face.* Englewood Cliffs, NJ: Prentice–Hall.

Ekman, P. & Friesen, W.V. (1976). Measuring facial movement. *Environmental Psychology and Nonverbal Behavior,* 1, 56–75.

Ekman, P. & Friesen, W.V. (1978). *Manual for the Facial Action Coding System*. Palo Alto, CA: Consulting Psychologists Press.

Ekman, P. & Oster, H. (1979). Facial expressions of emotion. *Annual Review of Psychology*, **30**, 527–54.

Ekman, P., Friesen, W.V., & Ellsworth, P.C. (1972). *Emotion in the human face: guidelines for research and a review of findings*. New York, NY: Pergamon Press.

Ekman, P., Friesen, W.V., & Scherer, K.R. (1976). Body movement and voice pitch in deceptive interaction. *Semiotica*, **16**, 23–7.

Ekman, P., Sorenson, E.R., & Friesen, W.V. (1969). Pan-cultural elements in facial displays of emotion. *Science*, **164**, 86–8.

Ellgring, H. & Scherer, K.R. (1996).Vocal indicators of mood change in depression. *Journal of Nonverbal Behavior*, **20**, 83–110.

Ellsworth, P.C. & Ludwig, L.M. (1972). Visual behavior in social interaction. *Journal of Communication*, **22**, 375–403.

Exline, R.V. & Fehr, B.J. (1982). The assessment of gaze and mutual gaze. In *Handbook of methods in nonverbal behavior research* (ed. K.R. Scherer & P. Ekman), pp. 91–135. Cambridge: Cambridge University Press.

Fagen, R.M. & Young, D.Y. (1978). Temporal patterns of behavior: durations, intervals, latencies, and sequences. In *Quantitative ethology* (ed. P.W. Colgan). New York, NY: Wiley.

Feldstein, S. & Welkowitz, J. (1978). A chronography of conversation: in defense of an objective approach. In *Nonverbal behavior and communication* (ed. A.W. Siegman & S. Feldstein). Hillsdale, NJ: Erlbaum.

Feldstein, S. & Welkowitz, J. (1987). A chronography of conversation: in defense of an objective approach. In *Nonverbal behavior and communication* (2nd edn) (ed. A.W. Siegman & S. Feldstein), pp. 435–99. Hillsdale, NJ: Erlbaum.

Ferenczi, S. (1926). Embarrassed hands. Thinking and muscle innervation. In *Further contributions to the technique and theory of psychoanalysis* (ed. S. Ferenczi), pp. 315–16. London: Hogarth Press.

Freedman, N. (1972). The analysis of movement behavior during the clinical interview. In *Studies in dyadic communication* (ed. A. Siegman & B. Pope), pp. 153–75. New York, NY: Pergamon Press.

Freedman, N. (1977). Hands, words, and mind: on the structuralization of body movements during discourse and the capacity for verbal representation. In *Communicative structures and psychic structures* (ed. N. Freedman & S. Grand), pp. 109–32. New York, NY: Plenum.

Freud, S. (1904). *Die psychopathologie des alltagslebens*. London: Imago.

Fridlund, A.J. (1994). *Human facial expression: an evolutionary view*. San Diego: Academic Press.

Friedman, H.S. & Riggio, R.E. (1981). The effect of individual differences in nonverbal expressiveness on transmission of emotion. *Journal of Nonverbal Behavior*, **6**, 96–104.

Galati, D., Scherer, K.R., & Ricci–Bitti, P.E. (1997). Voluntary facial expression of emotion: comparing congenitally blind with sighted encoders. *Journal of Personality and Social Psychology*, **73**, 1363–79.

Gallaher, P.E. (1992). Individual differences in nonverbal behavior: dimensions of style. *Journal of Personality and Social Psychology*, **63**, 133–45.

Garfinkel, H. (1967). *Studies in ethnomethodology.* Englewood Cliffs, NJ: Prentice–Hall.

Giles, H., Scherer, K.R., & Taylor, D.M. (1979). Speech markers in social interaction. In *Social markers in speech* (ed. K.R. Scherer & H. Giles), pp. 343–81. Cambridge: Cambridge University Press.

Goffman, E. (1963). *Behavior in public places.* London: Collier–Macmillan.

Goffman, E. (1971). *Relations in public: microstudies of the public order.* New York, NY: Harper & Row, Colophon Books.

Gumperz, J.J. (1982). *Discourse strategies.* Cambridge: Cambridge University Press.

Harper, R.G., Wiens, A.N., & Matarazzo, J.D. (1978). *Nonverbal communication: the state of the art.* New York, NY: Wiley.

Harrigan, J.A. (1985). Listener's body movements and speaking turns. *Communication Research,* 12, 233–50.

Harrigan, J.A., Kues, J.R., Steffen, J.J., & Rosenthal, R. (1988). Self-touching and impressions of others. *Personality and Social Psychology Bulletin,* 13, 497–512.

Harrigan, J.A., Wilson, K., & Rosenthal, R. (2004). Detecting state and trait anxiety from auditory and visual cues: a meta-analysis. *Personality and Social Psychology Bulletin,* 30, 56–66.

Harris, Z.S. (1951). *Methods in structural linguistics.* Chicago: University of Chicago Press.

Hartmann, D.P. & Wood, D.D. (1990). Observational methods. In *International handbook of behavioral modification and therapy* (2nd edn) (ed. A.S. Bellack, M. Hersen, & A.E. Kazdin), pp.109–38. New York, NY: Plenum.

Hayes, S.N. & Horn, W.F. (1982). Reactivity in behavioral observation: a review. *Behavioral Assessment,* 4, 369–82.

Hinde, R.A. (ed.) (1972). *Non-verbal communication.* Cambridge: Cambridge University Press.

Hockett, C.F. (1960). Logical considerations in the study of animal communication. In Animal sounds and communication (ed. W.E. Lanyon & W.N. Tavolga). Washington, DC: American Institute of Biological Sciences.

Honeycutt, J.M. (1989). Effects of preinteraction involvement and behavioral responses in initial interaction. *Journal of Nonverbal Behavior,* 13, 25–36.

Hutchinson, A. (1970). *Labanotation: the system for recording movement* (revised edn). New York, NY: Theatre Art Books.

Jacob, T., Tennenbaum, D., & Krahn, G. (1987). Factors influencing the reliability and valididty of observation data. In *Family interaction and psychopathology: theories, methods, and findings* (ed. T. Jacob), pp.297–328. New York, NY: Plenum.

Jacob, T., Tennenbaum, D., Seilhamer, R.A., Bargiel, K., & Sharon, T. (1994). Reactivity effects during naturalistic observation of distressed and nondistressed families. *Journal of Family Psychology,* 8, 354–63.

Jaffe, J. & Feldstein, S. (1970). *Rhythms of dialogue.* New York, NY: Academic Press.

Johnson, H.G., Ekman, P., & Friesen, W.V. (1975). Communicative body movements: American emblems. *Semiotica,* 15, 335–53.

Kappas, A., Hess, U., & Scherer, K.R. (1991). Voice and emotion. In *Fundamentals of nonverbal behavior* (ed. R.S. Feldman & B. Rimé), pp. 200–38. Cambridge and New York: Cambridge University Press.

Kazdin, A.E. (1982). Observer effects: reactivity of direct observation. *New Directions for Methodology of Social and Behavioral Science*, **14**, 5–19.

Kendall, P.C., Butcher, J.N., & Holmbeck, G.N. (1999). *Handbook of research methods in clinical psychology.* New York: John Wiley.

Kendon, A. (1970). Movement coordination in social interaction: some examples described. *Acta Psychologica*, **32**, 100–25.

Kendon, A. (1973). The role of visible behavior in the organization of social interaction. In *Social communication and movement: studies of interaction and expression in man and chimpanzee* (ed. M. von Cranach & I. Vine), pp. 29–74. London: Academic Press.

Kendon, A. (1982). The organization of behavior in face-to-face interaction: observations on the development of a methodology. In *Handbook of methods in nonverbal behavior research* (ed. K.R. Scherer & P. Ekman), pp. 440–505. Cambridge: Cambridge University Press.

Kendon, A. & Ferber, A. (1973). A description of some human greetings. In *Comparative ecology and behavior of primates* (ed. R.P. Michael & J.H. Crook), pp. 591–668. London: Academic.

Key, M.R. (1977). *Nonverbal communication: a research guide and bibliography.* Metuchen, NJ: Scarecrow Press.

Kleinpaul, R. (1888/1972). *Sprache ohne worte: idee einer allgemeinen wissenschaft der sprache.* The Hague: Mouton. (Originally published 1888, Leipzig: Friedrich.)

Knapp, M.L. & Hall, J.A. (2002). *Nonverbal communication in human interaction* (3rd edn). Fort Worth, TX: Holt Rinehart & Winston.

Krampen, M., Oehler, K., Posner, R., Sebeok, T.A., & Uexkuell, T (ed.) (1987). *Classics of semiotics.* New York, NY: Plenum.

Krout, M.H. (1931). Symbolic gestures in the clinical study of personality. *Transactions of the Minois State Academy of Science*, **24**, 519–23.

Laver, J. (1980). *The phonetic description of voice quality.* Cambridge: Cambridge UniversityPress.

Leck, K. & Simpson, J. (1999). Feigning romantic interest: the role of self-monitoring. *Journal of Research in Personality*, **33**, 69–91.

Levine, S.P. & Feldman, R.S. (2002). Women's and men's nonverbal behavior and self-monitoring in a job interview setting. *Applied Human Resources Management Research*, **7**, 1–14.

Mahl, G.F. (1968). Gestures and body movements in interviews. In *Research in psychotherapy, Vol. 3* (ed. J. Shlien). Washington, DC: American Psychological Association.

Mahl, G.F. (1987). Gestures and body movements in interviews. In *Explorations in nonverbal and vocal behavior* (ed. G.F. Mahl), pp. 7–74. Hillsdale, NJ: Lawrence Erlbaum.

Mahl, G.F. & Schulze, G. (1964). Psychological research in the extralinguistic area. In *Approaches to semiotics* (ed. T. Sebeok, A.S. Hayes, & M.C. Bateson). The Hague: Mouton.

Marshall, R.D., Spitzer, R.L., Vaughan, S.C., Vaughan, R., Mellman, L.A., MacKinnon, R.A., *et al.* (2001). Assessing the subjective experience of being a participant in psychiatric research. *American Journal of Psychiatry*, **158**, 319–21.

Matarazzo, J.D. & Wiens, A.N. (1972). *The interview: research on its anatomy and structure.* Chicago: Aldine–Atherton.

Mehrabian, A. (1969). Significance of posture and position in the communication of attitude and status relationships. *Psychological Bulletin*, **71**, 359–72.

Mehrabian, A. (1972). *Nonverbal communication.* Chicago: Aldine–Atherton.

Mesquita, B., Frijda, N., & Scherer, K.R. (1997). Culture and emotion. In *Handbook of cross-cultural psychology, Vol. 2: Basic processes and human development* (2nd edn) (ed. P.R. Dasen & J.W. Berry), pp. 255–97. Needham, MA: Allyn & Bacon.

Montepare, J.M. & Dobish, H. (2003). The contribution of emotion perceptions and their overgeneralizations to trait impressions. *Journal of Nonverbal Behavior, 27*, 237–54.

Moses, P.J. (1954). *The voice of neurosis.* New York, NY: Grune & Stratton.

Nelson, R.O., Kapust, J.A., & Dorsey, L.L. (1978). Minimal reactivity of overt classroom observations on student and teacher behaviors. *Behavior Therapy, 9*, 695–702.

Orne, M.T. (1962). On the social psychology of the psychological experiment. *American Psychologist, 17*, 776–83.

Ostwald, P.F. (1963). *Soundmaking: the acoustic communication of emotion.* Springfield: Charles C. Thomas.

Patterson, M.L. & Edinger, M.L. (1987). A functional analysis of space in social interaction. In *Nonverbal behavior and communication* (ed. A.W. Siegman & S. Feldstein), pp. 523–62. Hillsdale, NJ: Erlbaum.

Pear, T.H. (1931). *Voice and personality.* London: Chapman & Hall.

Philippot, P., Feldman, R.S., & Coats, E.J. (ed.) (1999). *The social context of nonverbal behavior.* Cambridge: Cambridge University Press.

Piderit, T. (1967). *Mimik und Physiognomik.* Detmold, 1867.

Ragsdale, J.D. & Silvia, C.F. (1982). Distribution of kinesic hesitation phenomena in spontaneous speech. *Language and Speech, 25*, 185–90.

Ragsdale, J.D. & Sisterhen, D.H. (1984). Hesitation phenomena in the spontaneous speech of normal and articulatory-defective children. *Language and Speech, 27*, 235–44.

Reich, W. (1949). *Character-analysis* (3rd edn). New York, NY: Farral, Straus & Giroux.

Riggio, H.R. & Riggio, R.E. (2002). Emotional expressiveness, extraversion, and neuroticism: a meta-analysis. *Journal of Nonverbal Behavior, 26*, 195–218.

Rosenfeld, H.M. (1982). Measurement of body motion and orientation. In Handbook of methods in nonverbal behavior research (ed. K.R. Scherer & P. Ekman), pp. 199–286. Cambridge: Cambridge University Press.

Rosenthal, R. (1966). *Experimenter effects in behavioral research.* New York, NY: Appleton–Century–Crofts.

Rosenthal, R. (1982). Conducting judgment studies. In *Handbook of methods in nonverbal behavior research* (ed. K.R. Scherer & P. Ekman), pp. 287–361. Cambridge: Cambridge University Press.

Sackett, G.P. (ed.) (1978). *Observing behavior, Vols. 1 & 2.* Baltimore: University Park Press.

Scheflen, A.E. (1966). Natural history method in psychotherapy: communicational research. In *Methods of research in psychotherapy* (ed. L.A. Gottschalk & A.H. Auerbach). New York, NY: Appelton–Century–Crofts.

Scheflen, A.E. (1973). *Communicational structure: analysis of a psychotherapy transaction.* Bloomington: Indiana University Press.

Schegloff, E.A. (1968). Sequencing in conversational openings. *American Anthropologist, 70*, 1075–95.

Schegloff, E.A., & Sacks, H. (1973). Opening up closings. *Semiotica, 8*, 289–327.

Scherer, K.R. (1972). Judging personality from voice: a cross-cultural approach to an old issue in interpersonal perception. *Journal of Personality,* **40**, 191–210.

Scherer, K.R. (1977). Affektlaute und vokale Embleme. In *Zeichenprozesse: semiotische forschung in den einzelwissenschaften* (ed. R. Posner & H.P. Reinecke). Wiesbaden: Athenaion.

Scherer, K.R. (1979*a*). Personality markers in speech. In *Social markers in speech* (ed. K. Scherer & H. Giles), pp. 147–209. Cambridge: Cambridge University Press.

Scherer, K.R. (1979*b*). Nonlinguistic vocal indicators of emotion and psychopathology. In Emotions in personality and psychopathology (ed. C.E. Izard). New York: Plenum.

Scherer, K.R. (1981). Speech and emotional states. In *The evaluation of speech in psychiatry* (ed. J. Darby), pp. 189–220. New York: Grune & Stratton.

Scherer, K.R. (1982). Methods of research on vocal communication. In *Handbook of methods in nonverbal behavior research* (ed. K.R. Scherer & P. Ekman), pp. 136–98. Cambridge: Cambridge University Press.

Scherer, K.R. (1988). *Facets of emotion: recent research.* Hillsdale, NJ: Lawrence Erlbaum.

Scherer, K.R. (1997*a*). Profiles of emotion-antecedent appraisal: testing theoretical predictions across cultures. *Cognition and Emotion,* **11**, 113–50.

Scherer, K.R. (1997*b*). The role of culture in emotion-antecedent appraisal. *Journal of Personality and Social Psychology,* **73**, 902–22.

Scherer, K.R. & Ceschi, G. (2000). Criteria for emotion recognition from verbal and nonverbal expression: studying baggage loss in the airport. *Personality and Social Psychology Bulletin,* **26**, 327–39.

Scherer, K.R. & Ekman, P. (1982). *Handbook of methods in nonverbal behavior research.* Cambridge: Cambridge University Press.

Scherer, U. & Scherer, K.R. (1980). Psychological factors in bureaucratic encounters: determinants and effects of interactions between officials and clients. In *The analysis of social skill* (ed. W.T. Singleton, P. Spurgeon, & R.B. Stammers). New York: Plenum.

Scherer, K.R. & Scherer, U. (1981). Nonverbal behavior and impression formation in naturalistic situations. In H. Hiebsch, H. Brandstätter, & H.H. Kelley (Eds.), *Proceedings of the XIIth International Congress of Psychology, Leipzig (GDR) Social Psychology.* Berlin/Amsterdam: VEB Deutscher Verlag der Wissenschaften and North Holland.

Scherer, K.R., Wallbott, H.G., & Scherer, U. (1979). Methoden zur klassifikation von bewegungsverhalten: ein funktionaler ansatz. *Zeitschrift für Semiotik,* **1**, 187–202.

Sigelman, C.K., Adams, R.M., Meeks, S.R., & Purcell, M.A. (1986). *Journal of Nonverbal Behavior,* **10**, 173–86.

Siegman, A.W., & Pope, B. (1965). Effects of question specificity and anxiety-producing messages on verbal fluency in the initial interview. *Journal of Personality and Social Psychology,* **2**, 522–530.

Siegman, A.W. & Feldstein, S. (ed.) (1987). *Nonverbal behaviour and communication.* Hillsdale, NJ: Lawrence Erlbaum.

Stern, D.N. & Wasserman, G.A. (1979). *Intonation contours as units of information in maternal speech to pre-linguistic infants.* Paper presented at the meeting of the Society for Research on Child Development, San Francisco.

Tannen, D. (ed.) (1993). *Gender and conversational interaction.* New York: Oxford.

Tiedens, L.A. & Fragale, A.R. (2003). Power moves: complementarity in dominant and submissive nonverbal behavior. *Journal of Personality and Social Psychology*, **84**, 558–68.

Trager, G.L. (1958). Paralanguage: a first approximation. *Studies in Linguistics*, **13**, 1–12.

Trager, G.L. & Smith, H.L. (1957). *An outline of English structure*. Washington, DC: American Council of Learned Societies.

Troisi, A., Belsanti, S., Bucci, A.R., Mosco, C., Sinti, F., & Verucci, M. (2000). Affect regulation in alexithymia: an ethological study of displacement behavior during psychiatric interviews. *Journal of Nervous and Mental Disease*, **188**, 13–18.

van Hooff, J.A.R.A.M. (1982). Categories and sequences of behavior. In *Handbook of methods in nonverbal behavior research* (ed. K.R. Scherer & P. Ekman), pp. 362–439. Cambridge: Cambridge University Press.

van Hooff, J.A.R.A.M. (ed.) (2000). *Abstracts of the 6th Congress of the German Primate Society, Utrecht, August 18–21, 1999*. Basel: Karger.

von Cranach, M. & Harre, R. (ed.) (1982). *The analysis of action: recent theoretical and empirical advances*. Cambridge: Cambridge University Press.

Vrij, A., Akehurst, L., & Morris, P. (1997). Individual differences: I. Hand movements during deception. *Journal of Nonverbal Behavior*, **21**, 87–102.

Wallbott, H.G. (1982). Technical appendix: audiovisual recording. Procedures, equipment,and troubleshooting. In *Handbook of methods in nonverbal behavior research* (ed. K.R. Scherer & P. Ekman), pp. 542–79. Cambridge: Cambridge University Press.

Webb, E.J., Campbell, D.T., Schwartz, R.D., Sechrest, L., & Grove, J.B. (1981). *Nonreactive measures in the social sciences* (2nd edn). Boston: Houghton, Mifflin.

Weick, K.E. (1968). Systematic observational methods. In *The handbook of social psychology, Vol. 2* (2nd edn) (ed. G. Lindzey & E. Aronson). Reading, Mass: Addison–Wesley.

West, C. & Zimmerman, D.H. (1982). Conversation analysis. In *Handbook of methods in nonverbal behavior research* (ed. K.R. Scherer & P. Ekman), pp. 506–41. Cambridge: Cambridge University Press.

White, G.D. (1977). The effects of observer presence on activity level of families. *Journal of Applied Behavior Analysis*, **10**, 734.

Wiemann, J.M. (1981). Effects of laboratory videotaping procedures on selected conversation behaviors. *Human Communication Research*, **7**, 302–11.

Wolff, W. (1943). *The expression of personality*. New York: Harper.

Wundt, W. (1900–1920). *Völkerpsychologie, Vols. 1–10*. Leipzig: Engelmann.

Zegiob, L.E. & Forehand, R. (1978). Parent–child interactions: observer effects and social class differences. *Behavior Therapy*, **9**, 118–23.

INDEX